CONRAD VON SOEST

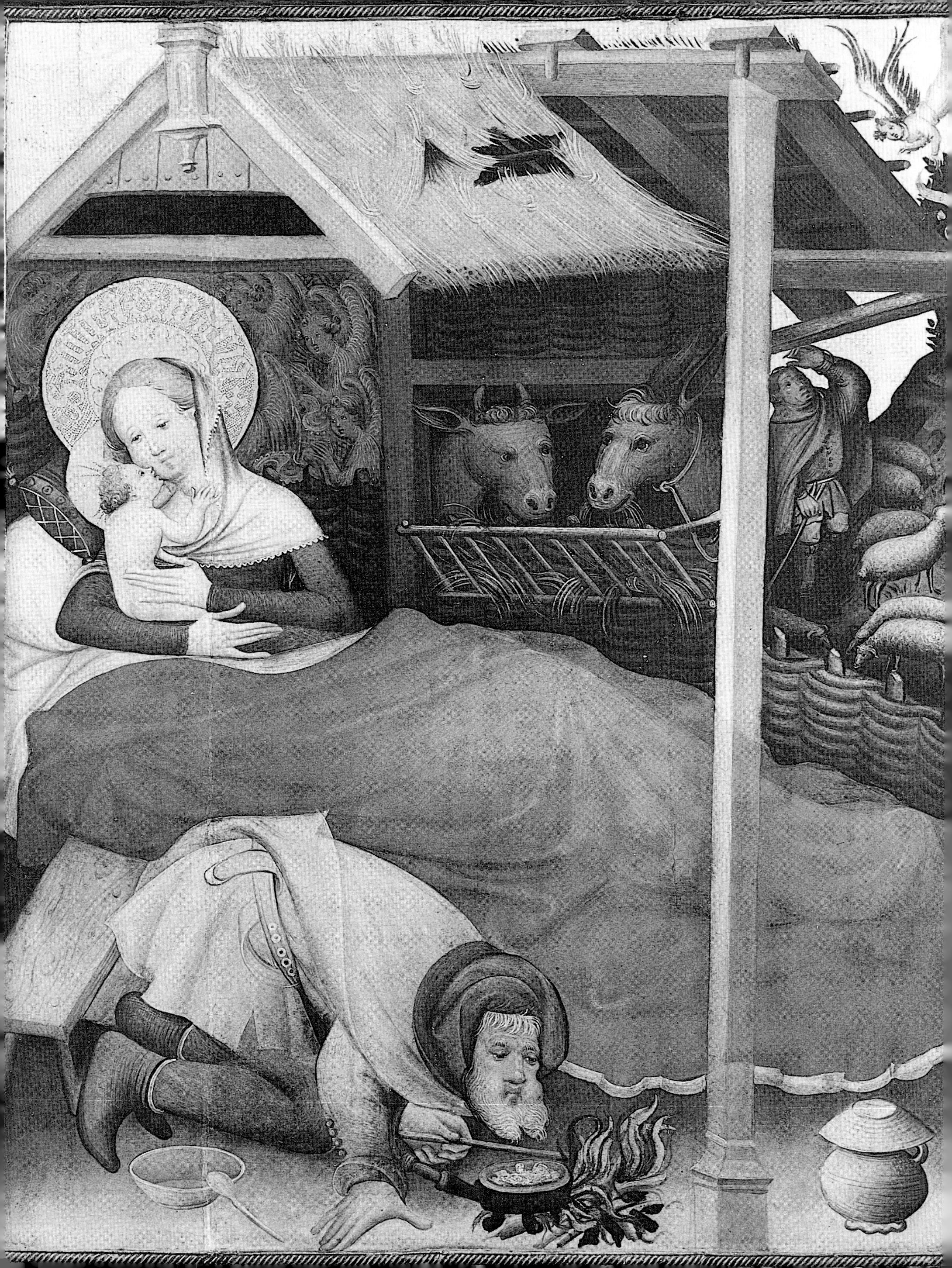

CONRAD VON SOEST

Painter among Merchant Princes

by Brigitte Corley

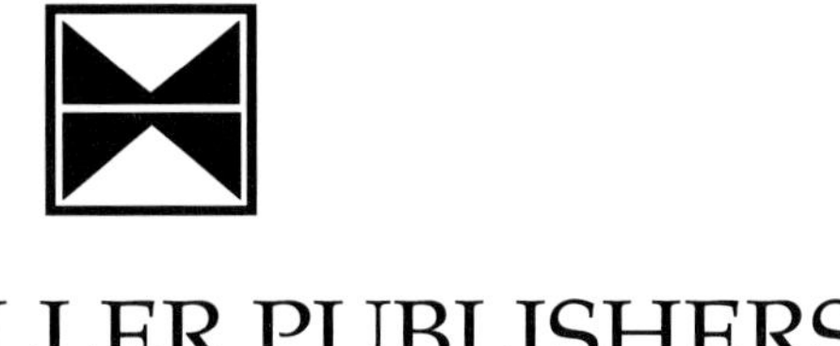

HARVEY MILLER PUBLISHERS

HARVEY MILLER PUBLISHERS
Knightsbridge House, 197 Knightsbridge, 8th Floor, London SW7 1RB

An Imprint of G + B International

British Library Cataloguing in Publication Data
Corley, Brigitte
Conrad von Soest : painter among merchant princes
1. Soest, Conrad von 2. Painters - Germany 3. Painting, German
I. Title II. Soest, Conrad von
759.3
ISBN 1872501583

© 1996 Brigitte Corley

End papers: Map of Northern Germany and surroundings
showing places mentioned in the text
Frontispiece: Conrad von Soest, *Nativity*, Niederwildungen Altarpiece,
Stadtkirche, Bad Wildungen

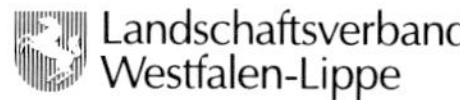

*This publication has been generously assisted by the Cultural department of the
Landschaftsverband Westfalen-Lippe*

Composition by Jessie Lessiep, London
Monochrome origination by Litho Studios, Dublin
Colour and Jacket origination by Gorenjski Tisk, Kranj, Slovenia
Printed and bound by Gorenjski Tisk, Kranj, Slovenia

Contents

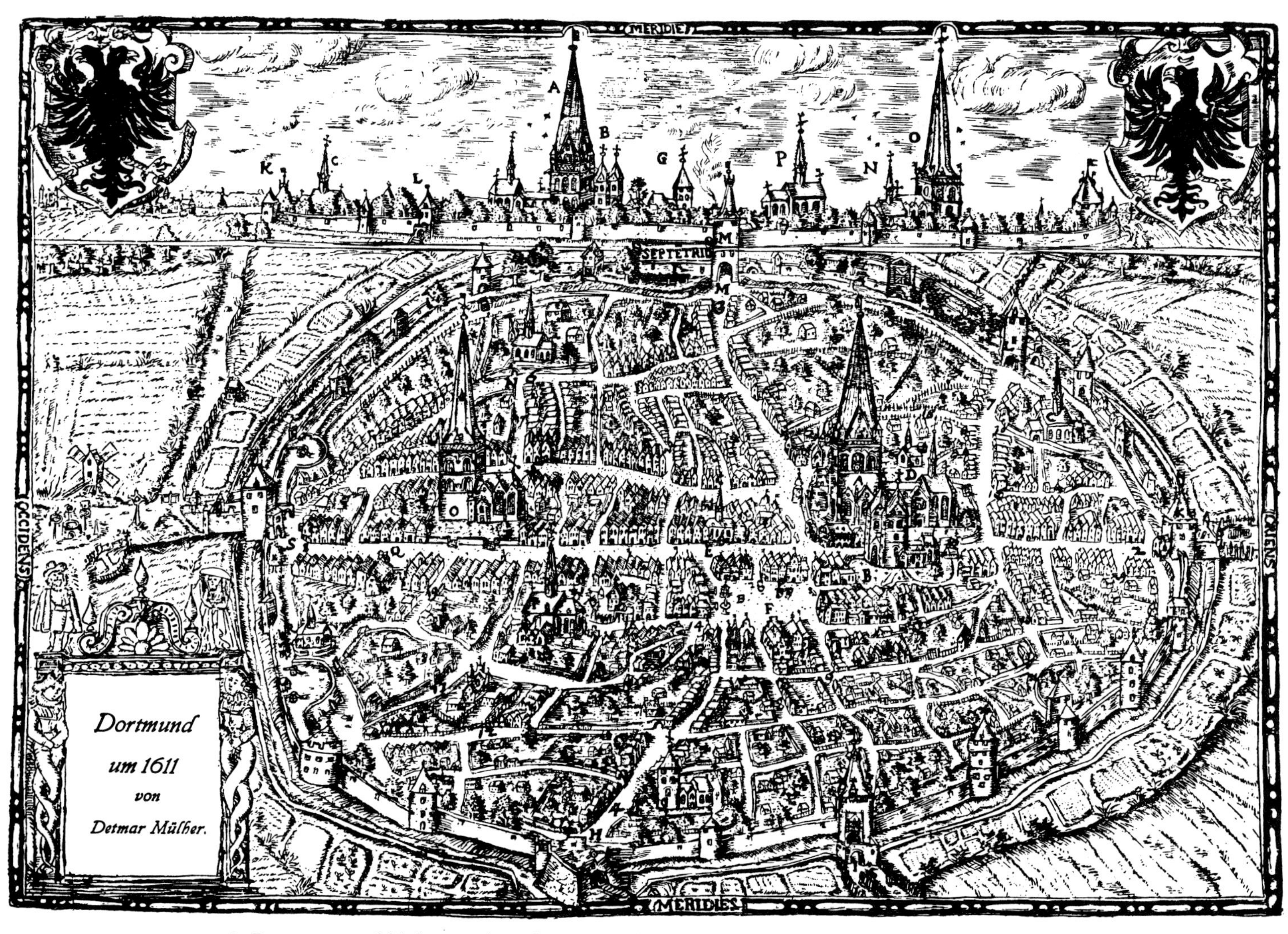

1. *Panorama and birds-eye view of Dortmund around 1611.* Engraving after a drawing by Detmar Mülher. **A**: Reinoldikirche, **B**: Marienkirche, **G**: Nikolaikirche, **S**: Westerntor (Hellweg) and **K**: Ostentor

Preface

CONRAD VON SOEST, master of a very successful workshop in Dortmund in Westphalia, played a pivotal role in the diffusion of the International Courtly Style around the year 1400. He was a consummate craftsman and creative designer who produced his works with remarkable painterly skill. His pictorial sources evolved from the Westphalian tradition with a secondary sphere of influence in Paris. His sojourn as a journeyman in Paris in the 1380s brought him into contact with international stylistic trends which he was to introduce into Germany on his return to Dortmund. Although distinctive, Conrad's works were in tune with contemporary technical and stylistic developments, and in his sophisticated approach to iconography he reflected the religious climate of his time. He was supported by wealthy, well educated and cosmopolitan patrons and, exceptionally for a German painter, was accepted into their privileged social circle. His paintings were clearly judged original by contemporary artists as he attracted a considerable following in Germany and beyond.

A study of the earlier literature on Conrad von Soest shows that, like the work of many other German artists, his altarpieces attracted much, often admiring, comment in local publications which do not appear to have reached the wider public. However, the remote location of Conrad's retables in rather inaccessible churches, the rare and limited publication of photographs of his work, and some adverse comments from those writers who were not always acquainted with the original works, have helped to foster and perpetuate the mistaken notion of an obscure provincial artist.

Even in Germany itself Conrad's reputation fluctuated considerably since connoisseurs in the 1840s first established that art had indeed flourished in medieval Westphalia. The Altarpiece in the Marienkirche in Dortmund was introduced into the literature by Passavant in 1841 as an excellent work by an unknown artist, and was first attributed to Conrad von Soest by Hölker in 1920. The Niederwildungen Altarpiece, in remote Bad Wildungen, was recorded by Curtze in 1850 together with the inscription of the painter's name. Conrad was considered the outstanding master of the 'foremost Westphalian school', that of the town of Soest. Since then, German literature on Conrad von Soest has been largely concerned with the attribution and re-attribution of works displaying a style similar to that of these altarpieces. Considerations both parochial and ethical have had roles to play in such discussions, which have been concerned with stylistic comparisons of a general nature and with such notions as the existence of regional physiognomical and psychological characteristics (Nordhoff, 1879; Pieper, 1964).

In recent surveys of Northern European art in the late Middle Ages, the work of the Westphalian painter Conrad von Soest is usually described in a short paragraph or two. He is generally considered a delightful, rather naive painter, the typical product of provincial training (see, for instance, Cuttler 1968, Musper 1961, and Châtelet and Recht 1988). He is portrayed as a competent yet awkward imitator of the work of greater artists. A journey around or after the year 1400 is thought to have introduced him to the work of court artists in Burgundy, especially that of the Limbourg Brothers, and to have provided him with the models employed in his two signed works, the Niederwildungen Altarpiece and the Dortmund Altarpiece. The dating of the Niederwildungen Altarpiece became a matter of dispute fluctuating between 1404 and 1414. The second retable was plausibly dated to around 1420 on stylistic grounds.

In the only monograph published on the artist, in 1946, Steinbart also commented on the painter's 'childish-naive idealism' and styled him 'an adulator of the Franco-Flemish manner'. This image of a medieval painter, thoroughly trained in his craft and active within the workshop tradition of his master, seemed the more plausible as he is said to have worked for unknown provincial patrons in largely agricultural Westphalia. He could then have added to his inherited repertoire of patterns by travelling as a journeyman and copying from the works of more advanced artists in the Netherlands or in France and still have remained essentially a very competent craftsman, albeit a little 'vulgar' and 'pedantic' in his assembly of images. It has also been suggested that stylistic and iconographic innovations may have come to Conrad's attention through intermediaries whilst he remained in Westphalia, for patterns or works of art could have been carried by other artists, scholars, merchants or even princes whose frequent peregrinations are well documented. The relatively 'low artistic quality' of Conrad's otherwise quite 'charming' works was considered in keeping with the 'extreme provinciality' of German art before Dürer (P. and L. Murray, 1976, pp. 170–72; Cuttler, p. 261).

As we shall see, the problems with this assessment of the painter Conrad von Soest are manifold. The most striking one lies in the dating of the Niederwildungen Altarpiece which is certainly stylistically advanced even for the year 1404 and would still be a 'minor miracle' were it painted in 1414, as proposed by Hölker (1920) and thought plausible by, amongst others, Steinbart (1946) and Panofsky (1971). However, reliable seventeenth and eighteenth century transcriptions of a now rubbed inscription on the frame of the altarpiece confirm that these panels were painted in 1403, which would indicate that Conrad could not have studied the two manuscripts by the Limbourg Brothers, usually cited as the source for Conrad's models, the *Très belles heures* and the *Très riches heures*, which were not finished before around 1408 and 1411–1416 respectively. The only earlier commission from the brothers, a Bible, was apparently their first for the Duke of Burgundy, and that contract was not drawn up until 1402. Nor would a provincial painter have been granted much opportunity to study manuscripts in princely possession or pattern sheets recording their designs. What is more, the underdrawing of Conrad's paintings, revealed by infra-red photography and first published in the magazine *Westfalen* by Fritz in 1953, is of such originality and creative force that it is difficult to reconcile it with the notion of the copying of models.

If we compare Conrad's signed altarpieces with contemporary panels, now in the Louvre, which are thought to have been painted for the Valois princes in France, his elegant forms do not appear at all old-fashioned or inferior in artistic quality and content. We know these princes, King Charles VI and his three uncles, the Dukes of Anjou, Berry and Burgundy, to have been renowned collectors and patrons who were able to attract the best artists from France and its neighbouring countries to their courts; in addition, they had close cultural and personal ties with Italy. Conrad's panels compare very favourably with works by, for instance, Jean de Beaumetz (*Crucifixion, c.* 1389–1395), Jean Malouel (*La grande Pietà ronde, c.* 1400) and Henri Bellechose (*The Martyrdom of St. Denis*, finished in 1416), three contemporary painters who worked successively as official artist to the Duke of Burgundy. Furthermore, it must be remembered that Dortmund, where Conrad had his so-called 'provincial' workshop, was not an small agricultural market town, but a flourishing, chartered imperial city which could expect to receive visits from the Emperor and his courtiers; it is thus unlikely to have been a mere backwater cut off from the currents of fashion and taste.

Over the years, the perception of Conrad's early career was changed considerably by the discoveries of two local historians: Rübel, who reported in 1890 that a marriage contract in the Dortmund archives, dated 1394, bore the name Conrad von Soest; and Winterfeld, who in 1925 was able to establish that Conrad had in fact been a citizen of and active in Dortmund.

Later, the juxtaposition of the Niederwildungen and Dortmund Altarpieces in two exhibitions provided a catalyst for further researchf. Following the first of these exhibitions in Münster in 1930, Stange (see 1934–61, III, p. 29) felt able to reduce the numerous attributions to Conrad von Soest, on stylistic grounds, to nine works. Until now six of these have remained ascribed to Conrad, namely the two above mentioned altarpieces, the St. Nicholas Panel in Soest (cat. no. 7), two panels showing St. Dorothea and St. Odilia in Münster (cat. no. 3) and a panel depicting St. Paul in Munich (cat. no. 4). The other paintings in Stange's list are now universally attributed to other masters. In 1933, Nissen (pp. 107–114) analysed the repeated and varied patterns used for the poses of hands in Conrad's altarpieces. Then, in 1938, Schmidt (pp. 195–206) suggested an Italian provenance for the silk brocade patterns in Conrad's retables. After the second exhibition at Cappenberg in 1950, Fritz made the most significant contribution to our knowledge of Conrad's work when he discovered concealed signatures in the Niederwildungen and in the Dortmund Altarpiece (*Westfalen* 28 1950, pp. 107–122) and noted that geometric principles had been used in the designs of both retables. In 1953, he exposed Conrad's creative underdrawing style (*Westfalen* 31, pp. 10–19). The display of a wing of the Niederwildungen Altarpiece at an international exhibition in Vienna in 1962 proved less productive, although it stimulated considerable acclaim for the artist by way of the small catalogue, which unfortunately contained no photographs of his work.

Until now no coherent study had been undertaken to shed new light on the controversies surrounding the art of Conrad von Soest. Blaschke (1976) and Zehnder (1981) took refuge in 'Zeitgeist' to explain the remarkable stylistic coincidence between the work of Conrad von Soest and that of the Master of the Golden Panel from Lüneburg (cat. no. 13) and the Veronica Master respectively. Pieper (1974) agreed with the principle of fortuitous similarities and relied on a perceived difference in the psychology of artists of Westphalian and Cologne provenance to differentiate their oeuvre. Pieper noted the 'subtle, sensitive delicacy' of artists active in Cologne, whilst Musper (1961) was able to characterize those of Westphalian provenance, including Conrad von Soest, as 'coarse, steadfast and slow of thought'. It would appear that serious research on the oeuvre of Conrad von Soest had stopped around 1950 and most of the important questions about the artist and his work had remained unsolved. Pieper could therefore justifiably lament, in 1986 (p. 39), that no comprehensive monograph had yet been written about Conrad von Soest.

The present systematic study of Conrad's signed altarpieces and other attributed panels is based on recent intensive research. Close examination of the painter's sources, his influence, and the historical setting in which he was active, points to an artist of exceptional skill and quality. It is hoped that this re-assessment will help to establish Conrad von Soest's name securely among the significant and influential artists of the International Courtly Style.

Acknowledgements

The research on which this book is based was guided by three supervisors at London University, and I am grateful for their encouragement and advice. Dr Lorne Campbell, Courtauld Institute, generously invited me to undertake this research and was particularly interested in problems connected with Northern painting. Professor Michael Kauffmann, at that time Director of the Courtauld Institute, took a keen interest in questions concerning iconography. Dr Francis Ames-Lewis, Birkbeck College, discussed historical facts and workshop conditions, and he challenged and guided me during the crucial final stages of writing my Ph.D. thesis.

My work would have been impossible without the help of scholars, librarians and the staff of museums and archives in Britain, Germany, France, Belgium, the Netherlands, Italy the United States and Finland. Notable generosity was shown me at the Bibliothèque Nationale, Paris, the Bibliothèque Royale, Brussels, and the British Library, London, where I was permitted to study original manuscripts. Among the many eminent scholars who have given liberal support, I am especially indebted to Dr Jochen Luckhardt, the late Dr Rolf Fritz, the late Professor Andrew Martindale and Alistair Smith. Many other people have been helpful and stimulating in various ways and I thank, particularly Caroline Villers, the late Professor Theodore Schultheis, Dominique Thiébaut, Carol Plazzetta and Molly Faries. I am also grateful to my husband Roger, and my sons Martin, Kevin and Steffan for their patient support, their assistance with the photography and their readiness to solve my sporadic computer problems.

I have much cause to thank all those who were involved in the production of this book: Elly Miller for her unfailing encouragement and interest, Clare Reynolds for her many sound editorial suggestions, Jean-Claude Peissel for his perceptive design work and Isabel Hariades for patiently compiling the index. I am indebted to the many individuals and institutions, listed elsewhere, who have generously supplied photographs for this book.

I gratefully acknowledge the generous support of the University of Dortmund and financial assistance from the Central Research Fund of the University of London and also wish to thank the Cultural Department of Westphalia-Lippe for their monetary contribution towards this publication.

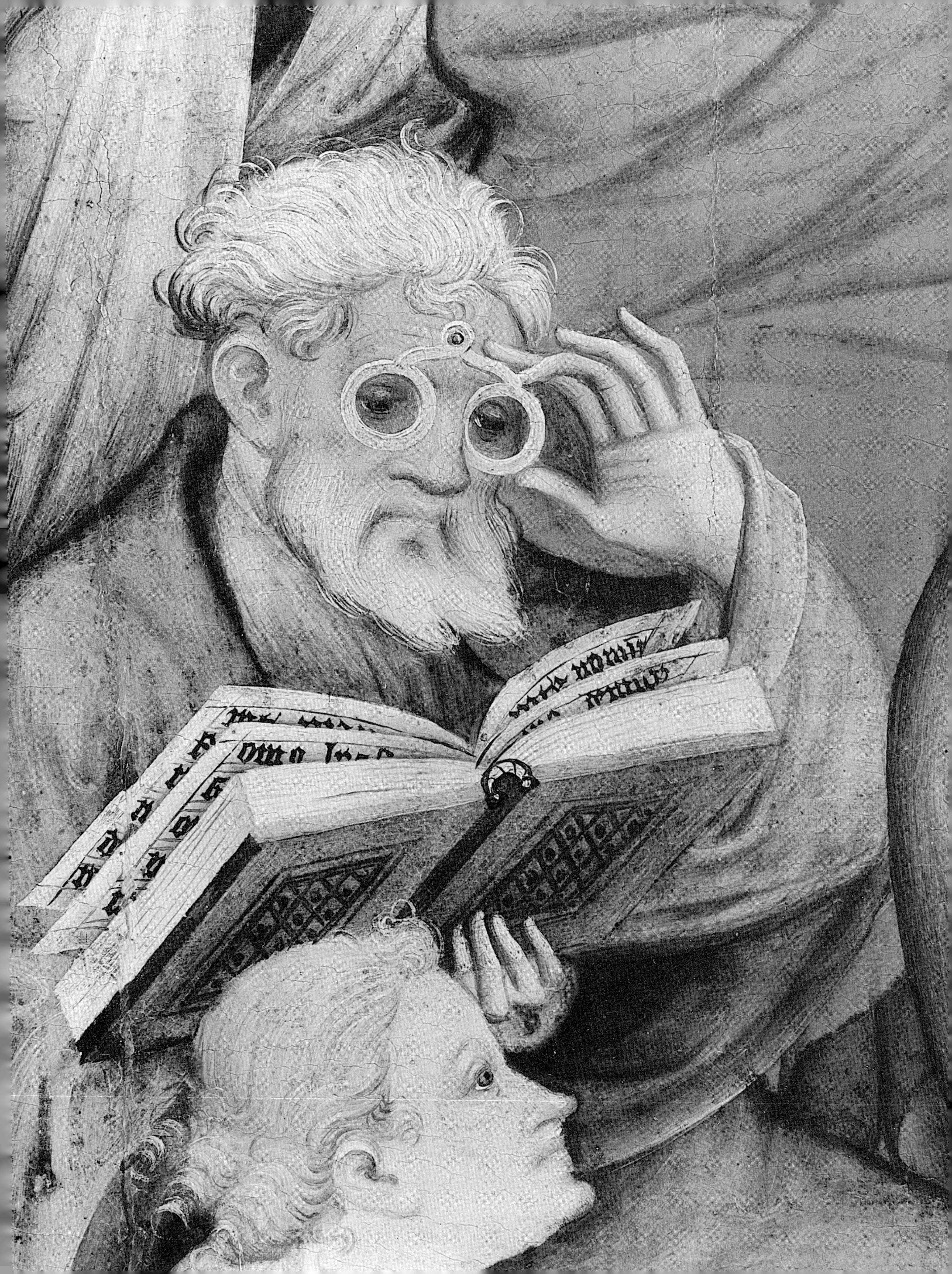

1. Conrad von Soest,
Citizen of Dortmund

C ONRAD VON SOEST was one of the most significant German painters of the late Middle Ages. He was the master of a prospering workshop in the Westphalian town of Dortmund, then a chartered imperial city. Although few relevant documents have survived the ravages of time, a plausible description of Conrad's life can be pieced together from his signatures on two altarpieces, from the documentary and historical evidence, and from stylistic considerations.[1]

The name Conrad von Soest is known through a now damaged inscription on the reverse side of the wing panels of the Niederwildungen Altarpiece (pls. 3 and 4) in the Stadtkirche of Bad Wildungen. According to a manuscript of 1617 by the Wildungen teacher Christianus Dickius, the lines originally read as follows: '*hoc opus est completum per co[nradum pictorem de susato]/ sub anno domini MCCCC [terc]io [i]pso die beati egidii confessoris/ temporibus rectoris divinorum conradi stollen plebani*'.[2] The letters in brackets can no longer be deciphered today. This reading was, however, confirmed by Ludwig Varnhagen, a reliable Waldeckian historian, in his manuscripts of 1778 and 1793 (pl. 5). The name of the artist also appears concealed in the margin of books in the Niederwildungen panels of the *Annunciation* [..nrad] and the *Pentecost* [conradu.] (pls. 6 and 7). Another retable, the Dortmund Altarpiece in the Marienkirche at Dortmund, datable to around 1420 on stylistic grounds, also carries Conrad's signature [con.ad]; here it is placed in the edge of a book in the *Death of the Virgin* (pl. 8). The inscription of signature and date on the frame of the Niederwildungen Altarpiece is consistent with frequent Italian trecento practice, which may also have become popular in Westphalia. The signature in the outer edge of the page of a book, however, appears to be an invention peculiar to Conrad.[3]

The words 'de Susato' (von Soest) in the signature are unlikely to denote the painter's provenance, although Soest is the name of a Westphalian town. They indicate what had become his inherited family name.[4] In Westphalia, surnames which were originally derived from the place of residence were quite common at this time. The stonemason Wilhelm de Hammone (von Hamm), for instance, was the son of a stonemason who lived in Cologne. Wilhelm retained the name 'de Hammone' when he registered in Dortmund in 1349, in Soest in 1350 and on his eventual return to Cologne. A number of patrician names in Dortmund, such as von Herdecke, von Brackel and von Wickede, similarly reflect Westphalian place-names. It was a widespread medieval practice to place the profession after the Christian name and before the surname, as in the inscription 'Conrad pictor de Susato'.

2. Conrad von Soest: *Reading Apostle.* Detail from *Pentecost.* Niederwildungen Altarpiece

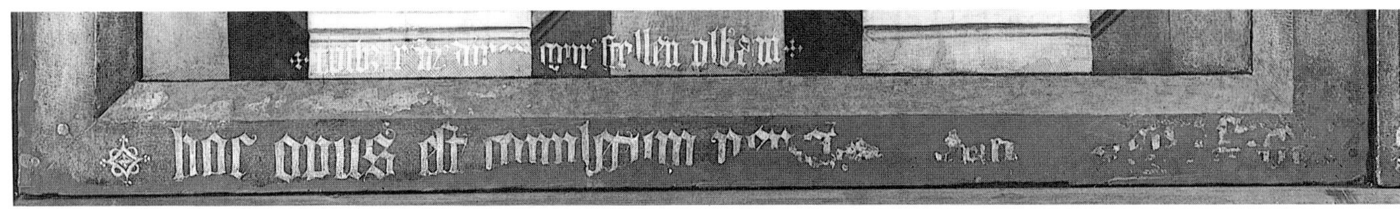

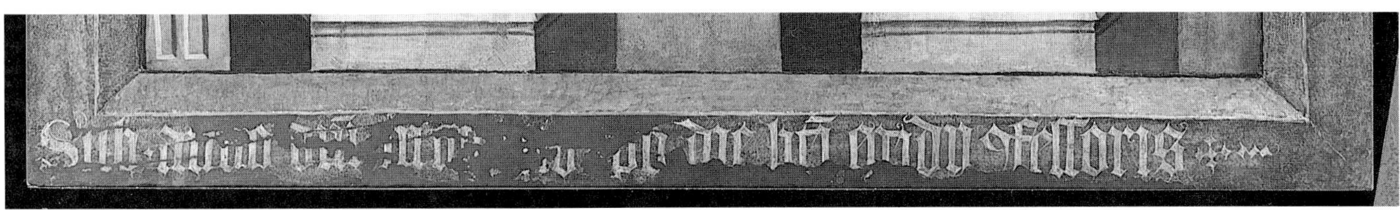

3–4. Inscriptions on the reverse face of the left and the right wings of the Niederwildungen Altarpiece

5. Detail from the Varnhagen manuscript of 1793 with a transcription of the Niederwildungen inscriptions

6–8. Conrad von Soest's signatures. Details from the *Annunciation* and *Pentecost*, Niederwildungen Altarpiece, and from the *Death of the Virgin*, Dortmund Altarpiece

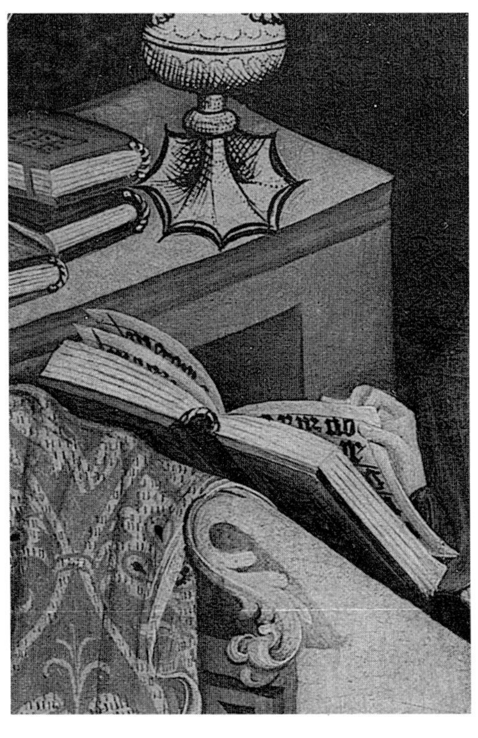

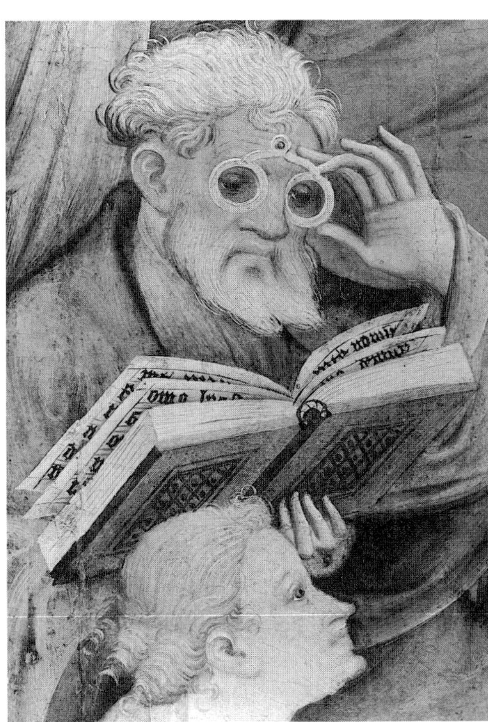

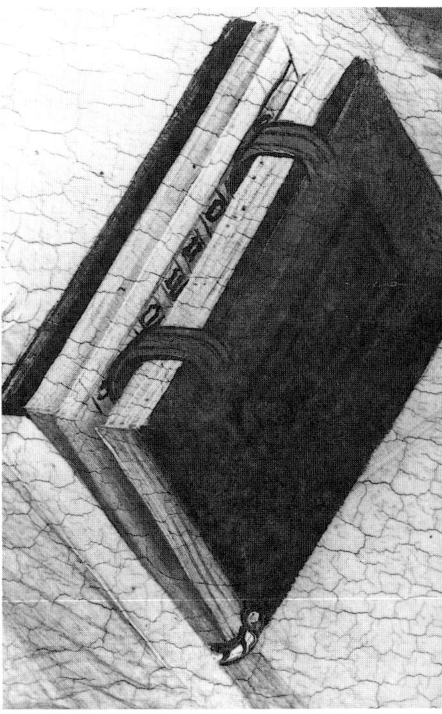

Conrad von Soest may have come from a family of painters. A 'Wernerus pictor de Sosato' is mentioned in the register of new burghers of Dortmund in 1331, and the name was inscribed there again in 1348. It is not possible to say whether the same person enrolled as a burgher a second time, after a spell abroad, or whether a further person arrived who bore the same uncommon name. Wernerus could have been Conrad's grandfather or father. Furthermore, in the register of new burghers of Soest in 1308 a 'Conradus pinctor' is mentioned. It is tempting to conjecture that Wernerus was the Soest painter's son who decided to settle and find work in Dortmund in 1331 and that, having established himself successfully, he called his own son Wernerus to join him there in 1348. Conrad von Soest could then have inherited his Christian name from the 'Conradus pinctor' in Soest with the provenance of this great-grandfather expressed by the family name. Of course there is no evidence that Conrad's family did originate in this way in Soest. However, it is not unreasonable to assume that there was a family connection between the cited Dortmund painters. Not only did they share a name that was uncommon in Dortmund, but they were also members of a profession that tended to run in families in Westphalia. The Koerbecke, Baegert and tom Ring workshops, for instance, can be traced over several generations, and a painter named Johann von Soest was still recorded in nearby Münster in 1487, 1493 and 1502.[5]

The earliest surviving document that can reasonably be connected with the painter confirms that he was a citizen of Dortmund. A marriage contract (Appendix A, pl. 170), dated 11 February 1394 and written according to Dortmund town law, which only applied to Dortmund burghers, bears the names Conrad von Soest and Gertrud von Münster. The marriage contract took the form of a 'Morgensprache', a document that had to be witnessed 'before the married couple left their marriage bed in the morning'. It was customary in Dortmund to invite 'two honest men, which are our burghers, called by both parties' as marriage witnesses. Conrad, however, was in a position to invite six prominent members of important patrician families to sign his marriage contract. At that time, Dortmund patricians elected from amongst their number two burgomasters and two 'sheffers' [sheriffs] each year to preside over the ruling town council. Conrad's witnesses were the two current burgomasters of the town, Lambert Berswordt and Arnd Sudermann, and four members of the council who were frequently elected to high office, Dethmar and Hermann Cleppink, Everd Wystrate and Clawes Swarte.[6]

The financial agreements set out in the marriage contract reveal that Conrad had a substantial fortune at his disposal in 1394. He pledges the sum of 200 Marks, 'in the event that Conrad predecease Gertrud, his wedded wife, without issue living at the date of his death'. Amounts under 20 Marks were more common in Dortmund marriage contracts. Furthermore, 'all his other goods' would remain *wederkar* according to Dortmund law, which means that they were to be returned to his 'next of kin' in the event of a barren end to the marriage, and a further 200 Marks could be granted by the bridegroom 'whether in sickness or in health' (the Dortmund *godegift*). The extent of Conrad's fortune becomes apparent when one considers that the highest paid local government employee, the legally-trained town scribe, earned 20 Marks for the year 1393—and this included extra fees for notarial work and teaching. The bride, the 'daughter of the deceased Lambert von Münster', also had appreciable means, pledging 100 Marks 'if Gertrud predecease her husband Conrad, without living issue at the date of her death' and, apart from the *wederkar* for her next of kin, being 'entitled to grant' a further 100 Marks *godegift* at will.[7]

The attendance of six leading patricians at the marriage of a painter and the considerable sums disposed of in his contract encourage a new interpretation of the status and age of Conrad von Soest at the time of his marriage. For Conrad's wealth and the high standing of his witnesses suggest that Conrad may not have been a young man when he married in 1394. The marriage contract does not mention whether this was a first marriage. However, a first marriage would normally take place at the time the painter was granted his mastership so that he could be in charge of a workshop, as guild regulations prevented an unmarried master from housing apprentices. If therefore the marriage in 1394 was Conrad's first, it would have to be deduced that his labours to that date could not have added much to his own fortune and that his wealth was inherited. It seems difficult, though, to find reasons that could have persuaded the prominent and prosperous patricians to honour a young painter at the very beginning of his career with their presence as witnesses at his marriage, even if he had inherited his father's fortune, especially as Conrad himself was not of patrician status.[8] It therefore seems reasonable to suggest that he was honoured on this occasion by prominent citizens because he was the prosperous master of an already flourishing workshop and that the marriage Conrad von Soest celebrated in 1394 was his second one; if so, it is more likely that his birth date would have been around 1360 rather than in the 1370s, as hitherto presumed. The hypothesis of a birth date around 1360 is supported by stylistic evidence, discussed below, that suggests the painter worked as a journeyman in Paris in the early 1380s.

Conrad's considerable financial and social status can also be deduced from membership records of the Confraternity of the Marienkirche, the Dortmund church which houses Conrad's great altarpiece in its choir. The church, dedicated to the Virgin, was not only the council church but also the parish church for many prominent patrician families. The fragmented membership register, which dates from 1396 to around 1424 in its first surviving section, includes 'meister Conrad meler et uxor', the painter Conrad and his wife.[9] No precise information about the function of this congregation confraternity survives; judging from the lists, however, it appears to have embraced only the privileged worshippers of the church. Significantly, three witnesses to Conrad's marriage contract can still be found listed in the fragments, namely 'Nycolaus [Clawes] Swarte', 'Hermann Cleppink' and 'Lambert Berswort'. In the register, Conrad and his wife are shown as resident in the eastern part of the Hellweg, the fashionable end of the main thoroughfare of the town which passed between the Marienkirche and the Reinoldikirche (pls. 1,9). Surviving documents show that their neighbours in this short stretch of road came from wealthy patrician families such as the Hengstenbergs, Cleppings and Gold-smeds, whilst members of the Berswordt, Sudermann and Swarte families owned houses nearby.[10]

It is surely a measure of Conrad's considerable social standing that, like some members of the distinguished Berswordt and Sudermann families, he was in due course also included in the Confraternity of the nearby church of St Nicholas (demolished in 1812). In the membership lists, covering the years 1413–70, 'mester Conrad meler et uxor' appear between 1413 and 1422. As Conrad is unlikely to have cancelled his membership of the confraternity, he must have died soon after the date of that last entry.[11]

Members of the social circle into which Conrad had been welcomed were part of a privileged group whose influence extended far beyond the town walls of their city. The patricians of Dortmund in the fourteenth century may be compared, in terms of education, trade, wealth, internal power and external influence, to leading citizens of Florence, such as the Bardi and the Medici. For, at that time, the chartered imperial city of Dortmund, with around 10,000 inhabitants, was by no means a provincial backwater. It was the leading member of the thriving Hanseatic League. This great mercantile confederation, which continued into the nineteenth century, provided protection and privileges for its towns and seaports, and largely control-led the economy of Northern Europe in the years 1350 to 1470. Dortmund patricians acquired wealth and influence as international merchants, and also as money-len-ders to powerful foreign princes. Dortmund's influence may be reflected in the fact that the accepted Hansa language was the low German spoken north of Cologne. Fiercely independent, Dortmund considered itself a rival to Cologne in prosperity, power and patronage; it did not yield the leadership of the Hanseatic League to Cologne until 1417.

Dortmund patrician merchants showed great enterprise. Throughout Europe, they traded in copper and silver from the Harz mountains, salt from Lüneburg, metal products from Westphalia, wool from England, cloth from Flanders, bro-cades from Greece, furs from Russia, silks which were imported through Venice, and many other goods. The main road through Dortmund, the Hellweg, had become a significant trade route in the thirteenth century, connecting western towns with emerging eastern trade centres such as Lübeck and Reval [now Tallinn]. The association between Dortmund and Lübeck was particularly close; by 1259, a third of those inhabitants of Lübeck whose provenance has been identified, derived from Westphalia and many of these came from Dortmund. For another century the direct connection with Dortmund continued. Around 1370, for example, Johann and Arnold Wintermast from Dortmund controlled an international group (with other Dortmund partners) which traded between Lübeck, their principal residence, and Bruges. Hildebrand Veckinchusen (d. 1428), a sporadic resident of Lübeck and son-in-law of the marriage witness Clawes Swarte, founded an ambitious Venetian trading company in 1407, whilst his brother Siegfried remained as a prosperous citizen in Lübeck.[12] The presence of Dortmund patricians in Lübeck may well have helped to draw the art of Conrad von Soest to the attention of local artists. Many surviving late medieval panels in Lübeck reflect Conrad's paintings (see pp. 151–152).

During the fourteenth century, England played an important part in the creation of the wealth of Dortmund patricians. From the year 1307, when King Edward I placed Hildebrand Sudermann (d. before 1353) under royal protection, Dortmund merchants enjoyed an exceptionally privileged position and considerable influence in England. They dominated the German wool trade with England, and were at one time given the complete German allocation which amounted to over ten percent of the total English export.[13] Tidemann Lemberg (d. 1386), a Dortmund patrician, even advanced to 'Keeper of the Royal Wool Seal' and was placed in charge of both the royal household of Edward III and that of the Prince of Wales, the Black Prince, until he fell from favour in 1363. At that time, Lemberg owned eight large estates (including castles, villages and churches) in England. Dortmund merchants also helped England to pay for the power struggle with France—the Hundred Years War of 1337–1453—which had to be partially financed by foreign loans. Edward III borrowed half a million gold guldens from Dortmund merchants and raised additional funds by pawning the English state crown [the crown of Edward the Confessor] for 45,000 gold gulden. This crown came into the possession of Dortmund merchants until it was returned by the patrician Conrad Cleppinck at Bruges in 1344. When the Florentine money-lenders Bardi and Peruzzi went bankrupt in 1345, Dortmund merchants welcomed the opportunity to act as principal money-lenders to the English kings. In consequence, Dortmund merchants enjoyed additional royal favours in tax and trade which encouraged both the purchase of property and the constant transport of goods between England and Dortmund. Surviving documents show that 216 men from 68 Dortmund families lived in London between 1271 and 1408. It is feasible that merchants from Dortmund carried small panels or patterns from Conrad's workshop in their luggage (see pp. 160–162).

There is also evidence that Dortmund patrician merchants were frequently resident and held substantial property in other foreign and Hansa cities, notably in Bruges, Antwerp, Cologne, Soest, Thorn, Danzig, Stockholm, Novgorod and Smolensk. In Bruges the presence of Dortmund merchants was once acknowledged by the 'Dortmund Street', whilst property formerly owned by them in Antwerp is still commemorated by 'Sudermann Street'. Between 1376 and 1405, almost without interruption, one Hanseatic alderman in Bruges and two in Novgorod were Dortmund patricians, who also acted in a similar capacity in other towns; until 1473 Dortmund was the only Westphalian town with the right to provide aldermen in London.

Patrician merchants enjoyed considerable social status, which is best described by the Parisian author Christine de Pisan. In *The Treasure of the City of Ladies*, an epistle of 1405 on virtuous conduct, she explains that these patricians are merchants 'who go abroad and have their agents in every country, buy in large quantities and have a big turnover, and then they send their merchandise to every land in great bundles and thus earn enormous wealth. Such ones as these are called noble merchants'. Sumptuary laws did not apply to them and they were allowed to wear princely garments 'because there are not so many distinctions of high rank as in Paris in their towns'.[14] Dortmund patricians thus seem to have worn the elaborate court fashions that are familiar from French manuscripts of the time. They also shared the chivalric ideals of the international aristocracy, for they carried coats-of-arms and, around 1400, they called the house of Egberts von Werle, where they congregated, 'King Arthur's Court'.[15] They lavishly entertained Emperor Charles IV in 1377, his wife Elisabeth of Austria in 1378, and the King and Queen of Denmark in 1385. Less exalted occasions must also have encouraged considerable ostentation in Dortmund, for at least 30 immigrant goldsmiths, 68 shoemakers, 50 furriers and 89 tailors joined the indigenous craftsmen there to produce luxury goods during the fourteenth century.

The affairs of the city were firmly in patrician hands, and they remained so after a revolt in 1400 in which the guilds were able to gain a minor foothold in the council. Even the Count of Dortmund enjoyed no political power or status above patricians who, just like the nobility, continually strove to strengthen their power and social position by intermarriage, in their case within Hanseatic patrician circles. Patrician families were also influential in the universities and in the church. Dortmund patricians are recorded both as students and as professors at many famous German and foreign universities. It was also customary to endow patricians with benefices and prebends which did not demand frequent attendance of the beneficiaries, and were therefore acceptable from disparate provinces and often treated as if they were scholarships or extra income. Five of the eight sons of Johann Sudermann (d. c. 1364), for example, were Canons at Louvain, three at Maastricht, three at Münster, one at Cologne, and most of them held other benefices as well. They may well have owed their good fortune to Dr Heinrich Sudermann (d. 1377), legate at the papal court at Avignon, who had a multitude of important benefices in his gift for all his family, including the five 'nephews' he fathered, and for numerous friends. Many patricians were, of course, deeply committed to serving the church and to spreading the gospel. Such connections with the cosmopolitan intellectual and religious communities influenced the cultural climate in which the Dortmund patricians and Conrad von Soest flourished.

Although an independent city, Dortmund was connected to the rest of Westphalia both through its function as Imperial Court of Appeal [Reichsoberhof] for Westphalian towns, bishoprics and abbeys, and through the Hanseatic League which granted privileges to burgesses of nearly eighty 'urban centres, large and small' in Westphalia.[16] 'Westphalia' was first mentioned in a manuscript of around 775.[17] In 1180, parts of Westphalia came under the jurisdiction of the archbishops of Cologne; in 1372, as the Mainz chronicler reported, the Archbishop Friedrich von Saarwerden was created 'ducatus Westvalie tamquam feudum', Duke of Westphalia, by Emperor Charles IV.[18] However, the archbishop never held any real political power in the province outside the dukedom of Arnsberg, which he purchased in 1368. Supported by the wealth created by the Hanseatic League, by natural resources and by agricultural reforms, towns and feudal lords became increasingly independent and formed their own allegiances. In consequence, the relationship between the archbishopric of Cologne and certain parts of Westphalia remained volatile. Disputes concerning the extent of the duchy caused repeated small acts of aggression, even though a peace treaty had been signed in 1325. Nonetheless, against the background of the intermittent Anglo-French wars, West-

9. Marienkirche, Dortmund

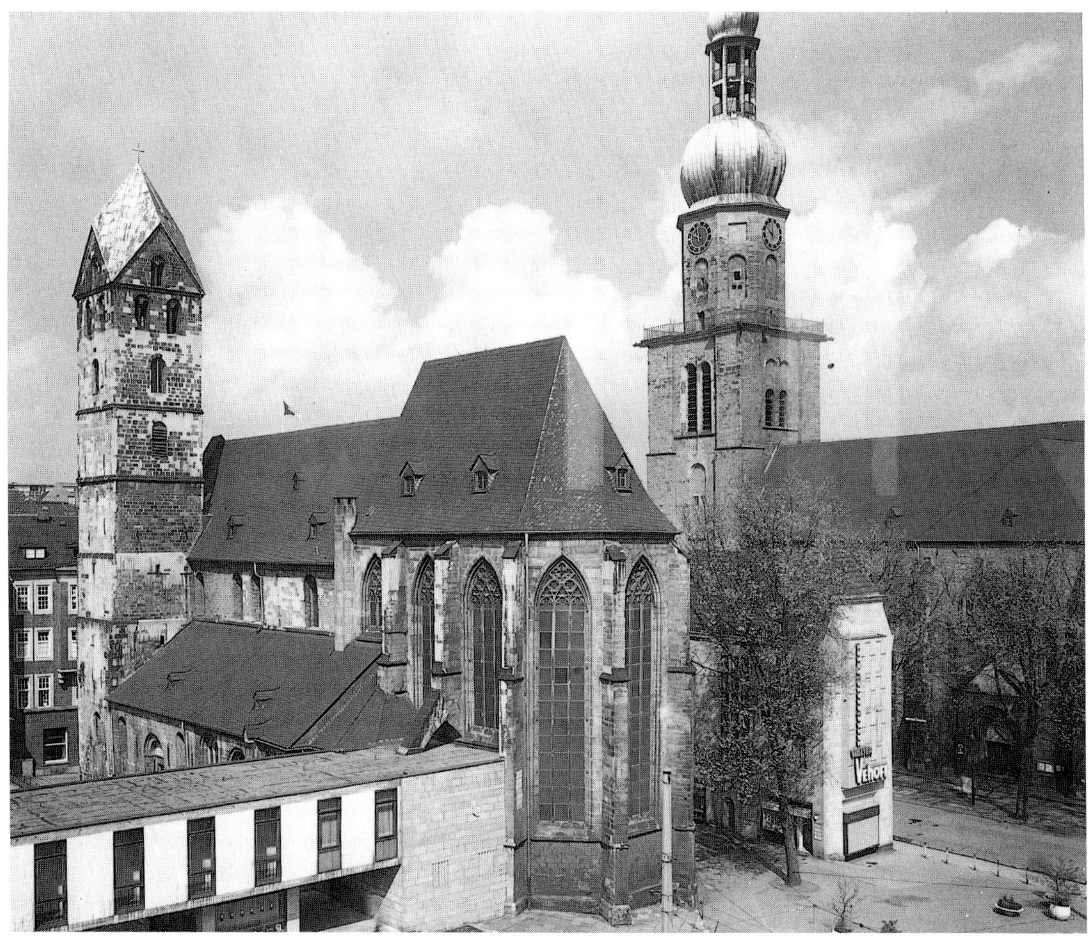

phalia enjoyed a time of comparative peace and great prosperity, which offered ideal conditions for generous patronage. The many great Gothic churches in Westphalia bear witness to the confidence created in this period of economic growth. Four of these, dedicated to the Virgin, St Reinold, St John the Baptist and St Peter, survive today in Dortmund alone.

These years of stability came to an abrupt end for Dortmund when the ambitions of the Archbishop Friedrich could no longer be restrained from attempting to subdue even the imperial free city. Although Emperor Charles IV had initiated a new peace pact in 1371, which was confirmed in 1372 and again in 1385, his incompetent son Wenceslas cancelled the agreement in 1387. This precipitated the damaging Feud of Dortmund of 1388-89, when the joint forces of 45 feudal lords under the command of the Archbishop of Cologne and the Count of Mark laid siege to the city.[19] In 1389, an admonishing letter from Wenceslas finally caused the cessation of hostilities. The archbishop had gained no greater influence, but the cost of resisting the aggression had placed Dortmund under considerable financial strain and the council felt compelled to impose heavy taxes.[20] This led to the internal revolt in 1400, and caused a number of affluent patricians to protect their assets through emigration. Eventually, a new constitution and, in 1417, imperial support from acting Emperor Sigismund, brought about new prosperity for a time.[21] Trade blossomed again, especially with England, Flanders and the Baltic towns. Purchases of land and foreign property, both by the council and the merchants, indicated the renewed wealth within the town, and patrician emigrants began to return to Dortmund with their assets. Hildebrand Sudermann (son of the marriage witness Arnd), for instance, returned from Cologne and contributed to a considerable loan from Dortmund to finance Sigismund's Hussite wars, for which further support was organized by Hildebrand Hengstenberg (one of Conrad's neighbours, d. 1422). The revived prosperity of the town was celebrated in 1421 when Konrad Berswordt laid the foundation stone for the new choir of the patronal Reinoldikirche, about the time that Conrad was completing the large altarpiece for the choir of the Marienkirche.

The renewed fortunes of Dortmund were short-lived, however. Later in the fifteenth century they declined dramatically when the English began to weave and trade their own cloth, and Netherlandish and Baltic merchants began to favour sea routes for their trade.

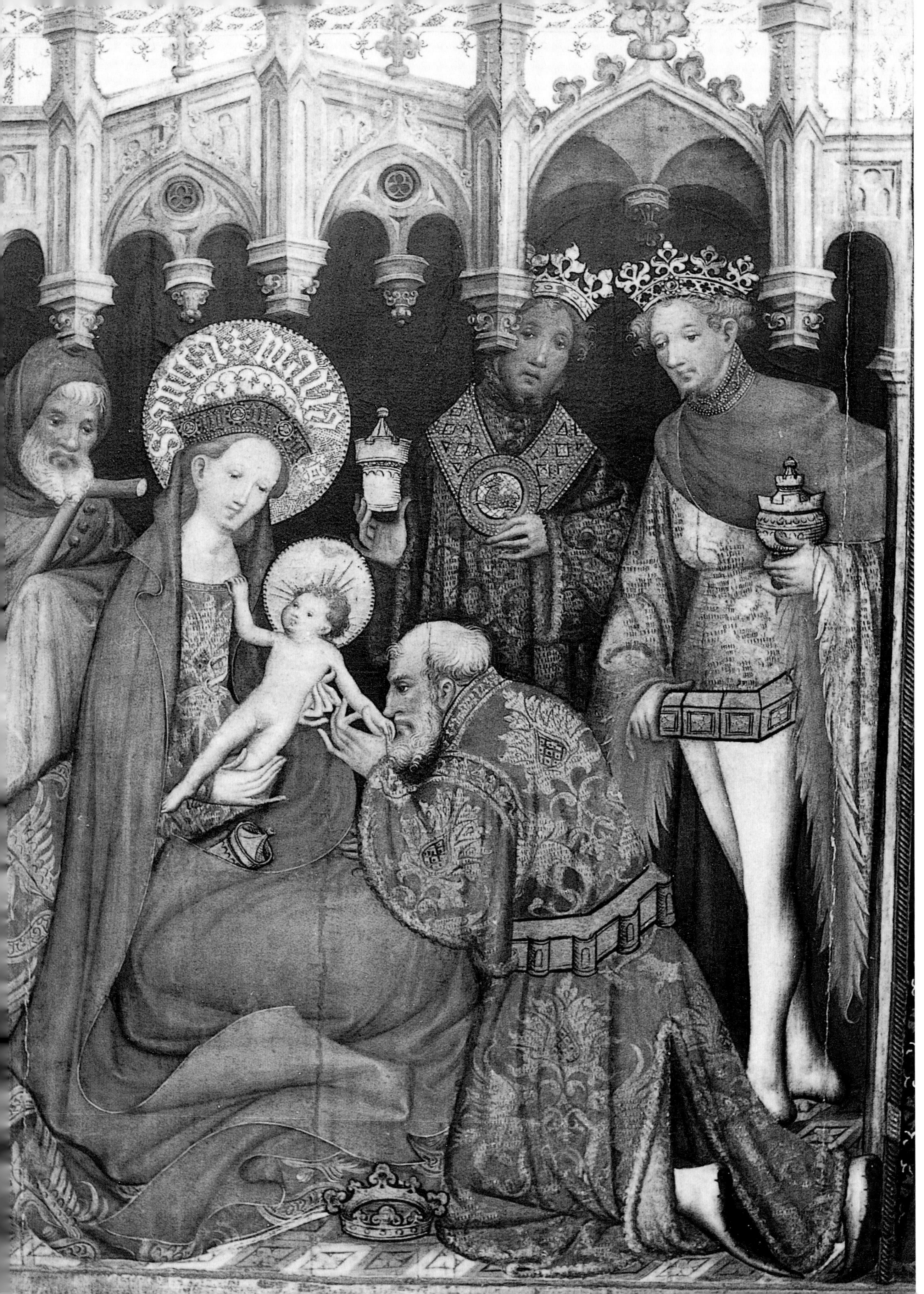

2. The Workshop and the Patron

T HE MEDIEVAL ARTIST, however successful and admired by his contemporaries, remained essentially a craftsman who produced works according to the command of his patrons. His skill lay not so much in the depiction of a subject to satisfy his own creative impulse, as in the imaginative interpretation of his patron's instructions. Detailed contracts stipulated size, content, production method and price according to conventions acceptable to both the purchaser and the master craftsman.[1] Both sides were guided by relevant visual and literary traditions and were restricted by the destined function of the commissioned work. In addition, religious, social and commercial frameworks, which differed considerably from those of our time, influenced their choices. Within these constraints, a painting or sculpture was from its inception the product of co-operation, first between the patron and the artist, and then between the artist and his workshop. The visual and literary traditions will be explored in later chapters. Here we will examine conditions of training and production in the workshop of Conrad von Soest, and the patronage that influenced the form and content of his works.

Conrad's workshop in Dortmund, like those in other European countries, was largely controlled by his local guild. The statutes of the craftsmen's guilds regulated the training and working conditions of their members. By means of restrictions and quality control, they could also have a considerable influence on production methods in the workshops. The guild regulations for the painters of Dortmund have perished, but those surviving in nearby towns may shed some light on workshop practice in Dortmund. Indeed the statutes of the painters' and glaziers' guild in Lüneburg (undated, before 1497) state specifically that they are written to match those of other towns. Detailed guild regulations also survive, for instance, in Münster, a prosperous town near Dortmund.[2] As usual, the Münster statutes are concerned with trading problems, internal politics, questions of quality control, penalties and festivities. However, they permit a reasonable assessment of the training in, and organization of, a painter's workshop in Westphalia.

The Münster rules, like those of Lüneburg, suggest that an apprenticeship generally lasted six years. After this initial training came 'Wanderschaft' [travel as a bachelor journeyman] for which no particular time-limit appears to have been set. When the painter returned to Münster, a minimum of two years' formal indenture as a journeyman was stipulated, although this could be reduced to only one year if the journeyman was willing to marry a master's widow, or to one and a half years if he chose a master's daughter. However, all these time requirements were doubled if the painter had initially learned his trade in another town. Before such a foreign painter could be accepted as a journeyman by a workshop, he had

10. Conrad von Soest: *Adoration of the Kings*. Niederwildungen Altarpiece

to submit to a test of skill, and show proof that he had completed an apprenticeship of at least four years and that he was still a bachelor.[3] Once accepted for indentures, a journeyman was not entitled to produce independent work without special permission, nor to change masters within the town. The problems of life as a journeyman are vividly described in letters, written between 1521 and 1551 by two travelling brothers to their mother; one man had to travel for eleven years, the other settled quickly by marrying a widow with 'house and land and all that belongs to it which cost me not a penny'.[4] There is no reason to think that the life of a journeyman would have been different when Conrad von Soest first travelled.

After completing his indenture, an aspiring master had to produce his masterpiece in his own master's workshop within six months. More than one example of his skills may well have been required.[5] If the applicant was accepted for mastership, a heavy fee (17 gold gulden in Münster) and a moderate feast for guild members was due to the guild. Again, the price was reduced considerably if the painter was willing to find a bride amongst the guild families. In any case, the new master was expected to marry before establishing his own workshop so that he could provide a stable and moral home for his apprentices. His choice of a bride was of crucial importance for the workshop, for the wife of a master had considerable influence in the management of apprentices and journeymen, who were all obliged also to perform menial tasks in the house for her. However, a master painter in Northern Germany was apparently rarely allowed to keep more than two journeymen and two apprentices in his workshop; and in Münster the second apprentice could only enter service during the last year of the first apprenticeship. In a number of recorded cases, only one assistant was employed.[6] Even being a master afforded only limited freedom of choice, as the workshop was always under the supervision of the guild; in Lüneburg, for instance, two elders of the guild could, 'when it suits them, go to the workshop of the master and inspect the work'. Should the elders find the work produced in the workshop unsatisfactory, the master would be forbidden to practise his craft.

Although the guild regulations, as statements of what should have happened, are not necessarily completely accurate records of what did in fact happen, surviving law reports in Dortmund suggest that the guilds were in firm control there. The Dortmund guilds demonstrated their power and efficient organization in detailed inter-guild statutes, issued in 1402, which determined their legal position in relation to the town council and to each other.[7] Such strength suggests that they would have been competent also in controlling their members' workshops. It seems therefore reasonable to deduce from the available evidence that Conrad von Soest was apprenticed to a local workshop, possibly his father's, for around six years. After a thorough technical training he was ceremoniously awarded the freedom of a journeyman. He was then expected to travel for several years. Stylistic evidence, discussed below, indicates that Conrad travelled to Paris. On his return, he worked as a journeyman in Dortmund for at least one year if he had been willing to marry the widow of a Dortmund master, or two if he did not marry into a guild family. He then spent around six months producing his masterpiece. Once accepted, the ceremony accompanying the attainment of mastership would soon have been followed by that of his first marriage. Only then was he entitled to establish his own independent workshop and employ his own apprentices and journeymen. This workshop was subject to the training and quality controls of the guild. Technical evidence, discussed below, suggests that Conrad von Soest led a tightly controlled workshop, in which he employed no more than two apprentices and one or two journeymen, in line with the cited guild regulations. The quality and the expense of the materials of his altarpieces are a clear indication that it was a very successful workshop. As head of a workshop, however prosperous, Conrad would have had to abide by guild rules concerning fair trading, personal integrity and religious observance, and would have been expected to take an active interest both in guild politics and festivities. Eventually, judging by his position in society and his wealth, he is likely to have played a leading part in the political and social life of the guild itself.

Conrad's workshop, placed in a prime position in the town, presumably attracted as potential patrons his neighbours, the affluent, well-travelled and sophisticated patrician merchants of Dortmund. Although no documents survive to reveal the names of Conrad's patrons, records still exist of generous donations by these patricians for churches and monasteries in Dortmund, Cologne, Soest, and a number of other Hansa towns. The patrician family Berswordt, in particular, were liberal patrons closely connected with the Marienkirche, and it has been suggested that Conrad's Dortmund Altarpiece (cat. no. 2) may have been commissioned by them. Their coat-of-arms adorns another work attributed to Conrad von Soest, the surviving wing of a portable altarpiece in Munich (cat. no. 4). But the Berswordt family endowed their own chapel in the Marienkirche with a still extant Crucifixion retable (cat. no. 9). Moreover, commissions for high altars tended to be the preserve of communities rather than individuals.[8] The most obvious candidate for corporate patronage of the Dortmund Altarpiece was the town council itself, for the Marienkirche was the council church. Yet the council already owned the St Anthony altar and retable 'bey der ersten grossen Kirchenthüre' [near the first large church portal] and would be unlikely to commission another.[9] The only other community closely connected with the church, and thereby entitled to place an altarpiece on the high altar, was the church's own congregation confraternity. This group is the most likely patron for the altarpiece: many of the wealthy patrician merchants, identified above as potential donors, and also Conrad von Soest himself were members of the confraternity.

The iconography of the altarpiece certainly supports the hypothesis of confraternity patronage. The patron saint of this church, and therefore of its confraternity, was Mary, so a retable depicting scenes from the life of Mary was appropriate. The main subject of the retable is not Mary in her Glory, but Mary at the moment of her death. This unusual choice of narrative reflects the concerns of the confraternity: lay confraternities, although also functioning as mutual protection societies and social clubs, were mainly concerned with their members' spiritual welfare. During a brother's last hours, fellow members attended to his comfort and care. All members of a confraternity were obliged to be present at a brother's requiem mass and burial.[10] 'At the first mass let each one of the brethren present offer a candle with a piece of money' ordered Raimond du Puy, Grandmaster of the Order of St John (1120–1158/60); this Catholic rite for a burial mass, depicted in the *Death of the Virgin* (pls. 149, XXII), may also have been followed by the confraternity of the church of St Mary in Dortmund.[11] The rules (1316) of the confraternity of St Mary in Soest certainly stipulated that special services, consisting of vigil and morning mass, should be held for the souls of former members on the four main Marian feast days each year.[12] It seems significant that these services were held in St Walpurgis before the Blankenberch Altarpiece (*c.* 1421–43), which is a direct copy of Conrad's Dortmund Altarpiece. The flavour of such services can still be gleaned from the instructions in a verger's rule book (Appendix C). In the Dortmund Altarpiece, the caring functions of confraternity members are also poignantly expressed in the actions of the angels, who minister to the dead Virgin (pl. 81).

It was not unusual for lay confraternities in Hanseatic towns to become patrons of altarpieces. The exclusive confraternity of patricians in Lübeck (the 'Zirkel-brüder', founded 1379), for example, commissioned a retable for the church of St Catherine there.[13] The thesis that the Dortmund Altarpiece by Conrad von Soest was similarly donated by a confraternity, that of the congregation of the Marien-kirche itself, is confirmed by an entry in an inventory of around 1432 of the altars of the Marienkirche, copied more than two centuries later by pastor Brügman, which has hitherto been overlooked. It reads: 'The high altar in the choir belonged and consecrated to the Blessed Virgin Mary and her congregation'.[14]

It is more difficult to identify potential patrons for Conrad's other signed work, the Niederwildungen Altarpiece in the Stadtkirche, Bad Wildungen (cat. no. 1). The wealth of the burghers here was more modest than of those in Dortmund.[15] The medieval Wildungen, situated on the Cologne/Siegerland/Eisenach Hanseatic trade route, was ruled by the counts of Waldeck from 1263 and, for religious fealty, was part of the archbishopric of Mainz from 1247. Under Count Heinrich VI of Waldeck ('der Eiserne', d. 1397) economic development—which included moving from a barter economy to a money trading base—brought wealth to the town.[16] Wool-weaving, dyeing and leather work flourished; a charter to mint coins had been obtained in 1370, and wine, metals, salt and wood also became major sources of income. Wildungen attracted travellers early, both as a spa and as a staging post on the great pilgrimage route to Marburg.[17] The large town church of Niederwil-dungen, mostly built during the fourteenth century, bears witness to the wealth of the town at that time. The affluent burghers valued education, and the names of students from Wildungen can be found in the registers of major European univer-

11. Conrad von Soest: *Presentation in the Temple.* Niederwildungen Altarpiece

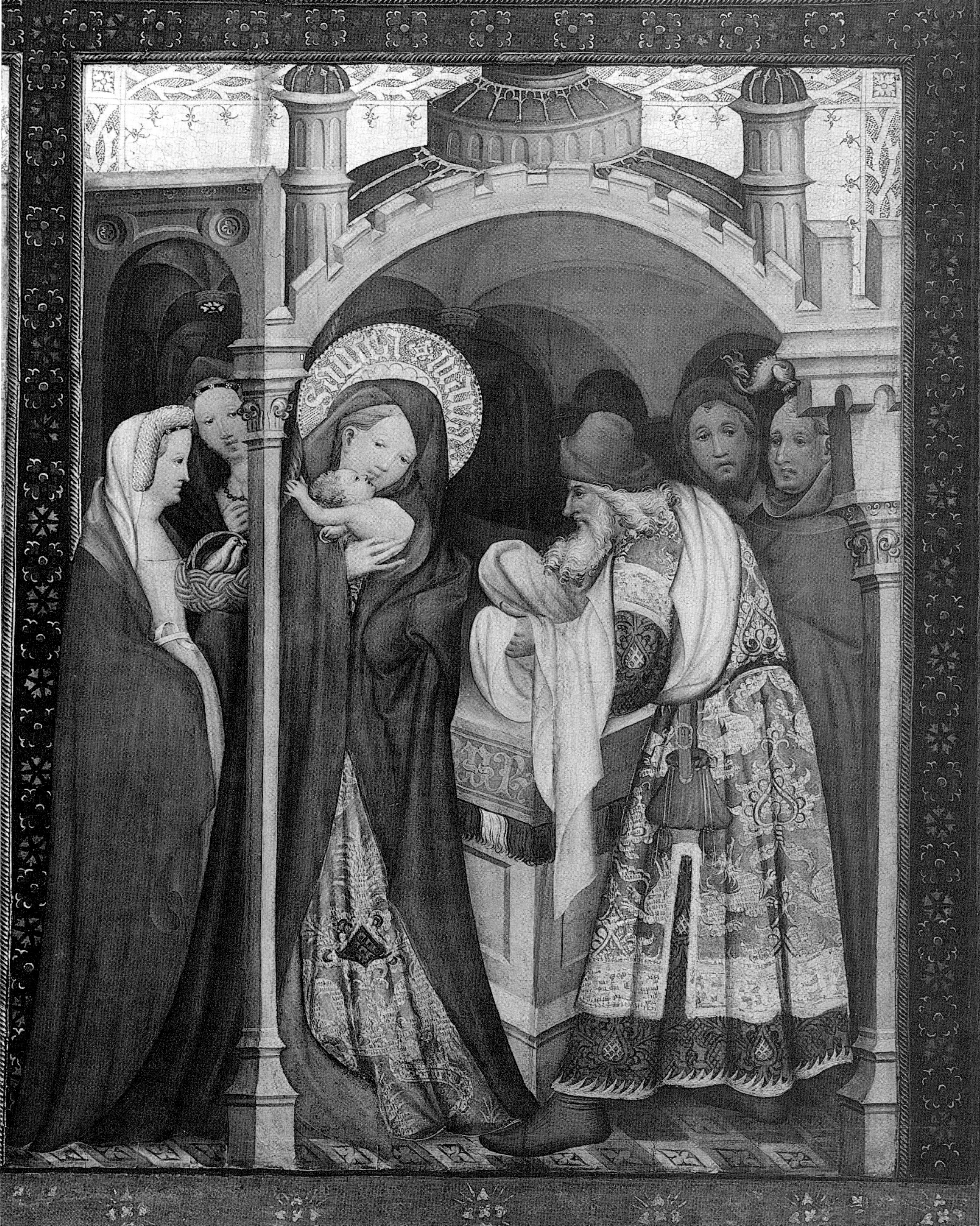

sities. However, whereas general prosperity was apparent in Wildungen, no prominent families or persons have been identified as potential donors. By 1400, the counts of Waldeck themselves were clearly no longer prosperous, being even obliged to sell some land, and were therefore unlikely to have been the main patrons of a costly altarpiece.

It has often been suggested that the priest Stollen, mentioned in the inscription on the wing panel, was the donor of the Niederwildungen Altarpiece. However, the inscription ['...*temporibus rectoris divinorum conradi stollen plebani'*] indicates only that the altarpiece was painted during his time as the priest of the church; it does not identify him as the donor. Stollen himself may have had this part of the inscription added, as it seems to be written by a different hand from that of the signature line on the frame below (pl. 3). His name also appears next to that of Conrad on the outer edge of a page in the book held by the apostle with the spectacles in the *Pentecost* scene (pl. 2); and the painter may well have portrayed Stollen as the cleric in the *Presentation* (pl. 11), which shows a priest present at the event, but not kneeling in the customary donor pose. Furthermore, the altarpiece was intended for the high altar, and therefore, as we have seen, would not have been available for individual patronage. Nor would it have been a corporate commission from the town council as this body had already endowed its own altar *'ante chorum'* in 1336.

However, one other relevant group can be identified as connected with the church in 1403, namely the Order of St John. Curd (Conrad) Stolle(n), priest of the Stadtkirche (where he is first recorded in 1400) was a member of the Order and was a hospitaller at Wildungen. The Order of St John itself, with headquarters at Rhodes, had by then developed into a powerful Order of Knights, a strong sea- and land-force in the service of the Church, with wealthy hinterlands in Italy, France, Spain, Germany and England. The local hospital had been founded in 1358, when Count Otto II von Waldeck had given land in Wildungen to the Order of St John for a hospital.[18] This was built and equipped from the donations of affluent burghers, swelled by the sale of indulgences, and was supervised by the town council. In 1372, Otto's son, Heinrich VI, having returned from a crusade and a pilgrimage to Jerusalem (where he was invested with the knighthood of the Holy Sepulchre in 1356), added a small church to the hospital. Count Heinrich and his wife Elisabeth also confirmed freedom of tenure to the hospitallers, then under the command of Wiesenfeld Priory. Heinrich died of the plague in 1397 and is interred in the family chapel in nearby Netze. He was, presumably, cared for by his hospitallers and this may explain why his heirs, Heinrich VII and Adolf III, invested the Order of St John in Wildungen with feudal tenure of the town church of Niederwildungen in 1402.[19]

In November 1403, Pope Boniface IX not only confirmed the Order's right of tenure of that church but elevated the hospital of St John to a Commandery, in which he included further houses and churches of the Order in the area (Appendix

D).[20] This generous response suggests that something had been drawn to the Pope's attention beyond a mere request for confirmation of tenure; it may have been the gift of the splendid altarpiece to the Stadtkirche by the hospitallers of Wildungen. If this is so, the altarpiece would have been ordered during protracted negotiations concerning the status of the Wildungen Order, with the intention of improving the Stadtkirche in preparation for the expected honour. The altarpiece was ready two months before the papal bull was issued. The town council subsequently donated windows for the church. It is known that Conrad Stollen held the office of local Commander in 1419 but the now incomplete list of Wildungen Commanders does not record whether Stollen also held this office when Wildungen first became a Commandery in 1403.[21]

No documents have been discovered to confirm that the Niederwildungen Altarpiece was commissioned by the Order of St John,[22] but circumstantial evidence is strong. A number of items of evidence can be found in the iconography of the altarpiece. First, the Order itself was founded 'in the name of the Almighty, the Blessed Mary and the Blessed John' and the Order's Wildungen hospital was founded 'in honour of the Virgin Mary and the Martyr St Catherine'.[23] In contrast to other Crucifixion altarpieces, the Niederwildungen Altarpiece accords unusual prominence to both Mary and St John the Evangelist, and St Catherine appears on the reverse side of the wing panel. The other saints depicted there are St John the Baptist, equally revered by the Order, Saint Nicholas, the church's patron saint, and St Elizabeth of Hungary, the pilgrimage Saint who had lived in nearby Marburg, and in whose honour the high altar had been dedicated before 1306 (pls. 134,138). Secondly, in a *Last Judgement* scene the souls of the redeemed are usually received into heaven by St Peter, but here they are welcomed by St John the Evangelist (pl. 12). Thirdly, the trumpets of the angels in the *Last Judgement* bear standards displaying the cross potent of the Order of St John.[24] Fourthly, the crescent-moon and star emblem, a symbol of both the crusaders and the Knights of St John, who often led them in battle, forms a prominent part of the pattern on the frame (pl. 135).[25] Finally, the rules of Roger de Molins, which amended those of Raimond du Puy in 1182, stipulated that members of the Order should be buried in a plain red linen shroud.[26] Although Conrad von Soest, like his contemporaries and followers, favoured coloured linings for robes, and at Niederwildungen used a contrasting lining for Christ's red garment in both the *Last Judgement* and *Last Supper* panels, he depicted Christ in a plain red cloth in the post-burial scenes of *Resurrection* and *Ascension*.

The added inscription suggests that Conrad Stollen was proud of his involvement in the commission of the splendid altarpiece. Stollen was not the donor but must surely have mediated on behalf of the patrons. The inclusion of his name in the signatures suggests that he had taken financial, and probably also iconographic, responsibility for the commission on behalf of the Order. Donations, income from legacies and receipts from the sale of letters of indulgence may have contributed

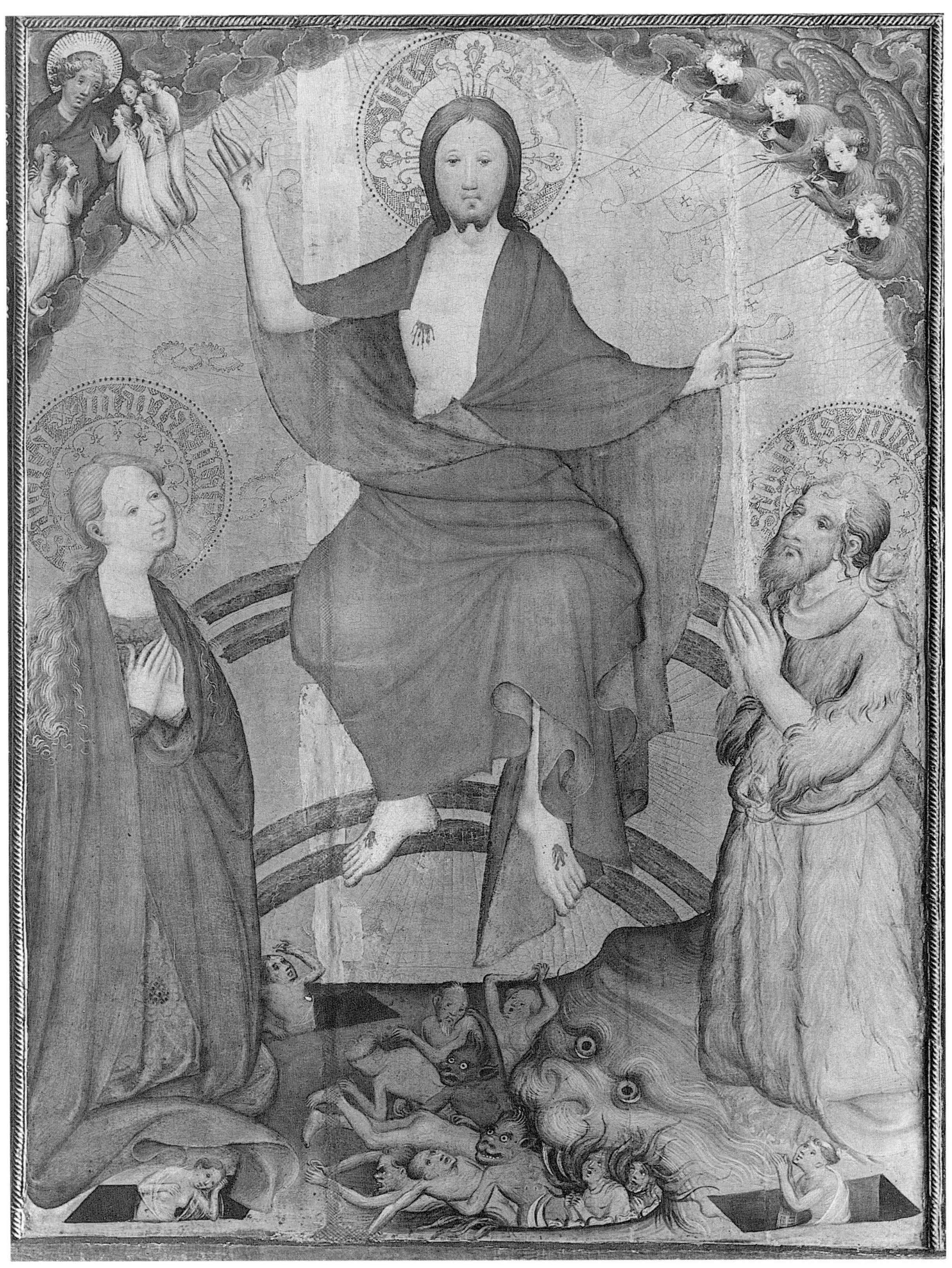

12. Conrad von Soest: *Last Judgement*. Niederwildungen Altarpiece

to the payment for the altarpiece, as they had done for the building and furnishing of the hospital. An agreement of 1491, concerning communal administration of separately owned altarpieces, does confirm that the commandery owned altarpieces both in the town and hospital churches, but does not specify types, numbers or positions.[27] In spite of the lack of direct documentary proof, the circumstantial and iconographic evidence therefore makes it reasonable to assert that the Order of St John was the patron of the Niederwildungen Altarpiece.

Any contract that may have existed between Conrad Stollen, on behalf of the Wildungen Order of St John, and the painter Conrad von Soest has perished. But a later contract for an altarpiece for the high altar at Wiesenfeld, signed by the Commander of the original Motherhouse of the Wildungen hospitallers, survives (Appendix E). This is dated 1520, shortly before the Reformation reached Waldeck, and it may suggest the terms of the missing contract. The contract, with a Franciscan workshop, is for an elaborate, mainly carved, altarpiece and stipulates the overall size of the retable and the number of its pictorial divisions and demands high quality workmanship, 'the finest and most beautiful according to the proportion of the panels, and skill'. For each section, the subjects of narrative scenes are prescribed and they are to be designed with 'all else that belongs to this'. The painted wings were to be divided into four scenes each, starting like the Niederwildungen Altarpiece with the *Annunciation*, *Presentation* and *Adoration* and also ending with the *Last Judgement* (pls. IV, VI, VII, XVIII; 135, 136). The predella was to illustrate two named subjects. The artists were to supply good gold and good colours at their own expense. The contract includes detailed instructions concerning dates for delivery of the various parts and for the instalments of the agreed payment, and makes arrangements for the work to be appraised by 'pious and knowledgeable people', elected by both parties of the agreement. If these judges were to find the work 'costlier to produce or better' than the agreed price would suggest, the Commander promised to pay a named amount more 'without argument or cunning'. Two identical copies were signed and sealed.[28]

The reasons for the commission of the Niederwildungen Altarpiece from a Dortmund painter, however famous, rather than a more local one must remain open to conjecture. However, Dortmund connections with the Order of St John can be found, with the earliest known dating from 1353 when Christian Hengstenberg was recorded as a Knight of the Order. In 1413, Johann Sudermann, son of the marriage witness Arnd, made a considerable gift to the Commandery of St John in Cologne. This is particularly interesting because, when living in Cologne, Johann had married a Sophie Stolle. In his will, Sophie's father had asked Johann Stolle, Canon of Mariengraden, to protect his daughter's interest against other relatives. [The archdeaconry of Dortmund was under the jurisdiction and guidance of Mariengraden at this time]. The importance of Canon Stolle is indicated by the fact that he was granted the rare papal privilege of owning a portable altar in 1402.[29] Furthermore, a Heinrich Stolle is named in the chronicle report of the defence of

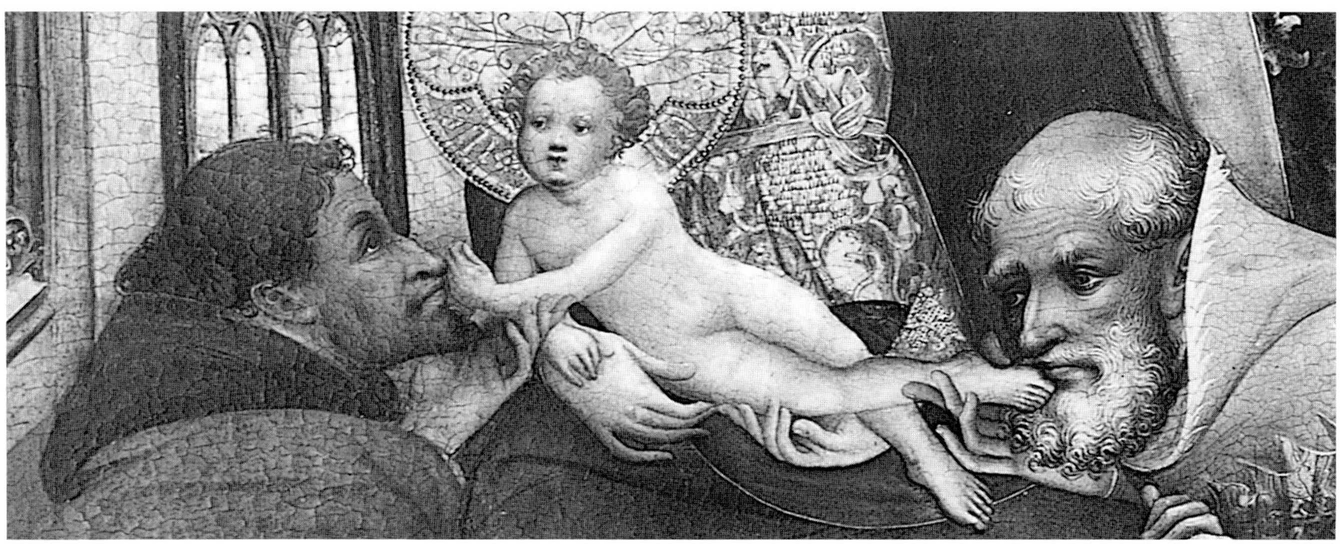

13. *Heads of Kings*. Detail from the *Adoration of the Kings*, Dortmund Altarpiece

Dortmund in 1388. Whilst there is no documentary proof that the Curd (Conrad) Stolle(n) in Wildungen was related to any of these patricians, it can be presumed that he himself was of patrician birth, as this was generally required for the priests of high altars. In view of the fact that benefices and prebends were frequently in the gift of prominent patricians, a connection is at least possible, and would help to explain the choice of the Dortmund artist Conrad von Soest as the painter of the Niederwildungen Altarpiece.

There is just one intriguing feature within the altarpieces themselves to support such a connection. The striking realism of the kings' heads in the *Adoration of the Kings* (pls. 10, 13) of both the Niederwildungen and Dortmund Altarpieces suggests portraiture. No portraits or documents survive to confirm that the individualism of the faces is more than an expression of a new realism. However, the presentation of gifts offers an ideal opportunity for 'hidden' portraiture in paintings of the *Adoration of the Kings*. In the *Adoration* of the Morgan Diptych (*c.* 1355; Metropolitan Museum, New York), for example, one king is identified as Emperor Charles IV by the imperial eagle pattern in his brocade robe. Moreover, it is feasible that prominent patrician confraternity members offered myrrh, frankincense and gold as kings in Epiphany processions in Dortmund, just as the King of France did in Paris and the Medici did in Florence.[30] In Dortmund, the Marienkirche was the main processional church and Conrad may well have recorded two confraternity 'kings', kneeling in the customary donor pose, in his painting for the confraternity of that church.[31] Donor portraits were certainly known in Westphalia, as the Fröndenberg Altarpiece (cat. no. 5), for instance, contains the kneeling donor figure of the Abbess Segele von Hamme.

It may be significant that one king from Niederwildungen (pls. 10, VII) recurs in Dortmund as the (then rather older) foot-kissing king (pls. 13, IX). In view of the possible connection between the Dortmund Sudermann family and the priest Stollen in Wildungen, it seems reasonable to infer that some of the donors, especially members of the Sudermann family, may have bought indulgences in favour of both altarpieces.[32] This is particularly plausible as donations were not politic in Dortmund during the initial period of hardship after the Feud there; but donations were made at this time by Dortmund patricians in other towns, particularly Cologne and Soest. This repetition of realistic facial features in a potential donor figure in both altarpieces provides evidence not only of portraiture but also of a connection between the artist's circle in Dortmund and the town of Wildungen. The suggestion that the altarpieces include portraits is strengthened by the presence of the strong, ugly head of the other kneeling king in Dortmund (pl. 13), with facial features that have nothing in common with Conrad's usual style of face.

If these are portraits, the sitters cannot be identified by the elaborate designs in the royal brocades that they are wearing, as these have no known heraldic significance. The coats-of-arms of Westphalian and Dortmund nobles and patricians are well recorded and none bear any resemblance to the patterns in Conrad's panels. However, motifs in two pieces of late fourteenth-century Italian silk lampas in the Victoria and Albert Museum, London, resemble Conrad's brocade patterns closely.[33] Such costly materials were imported by Dortmund merchants and exported to many Hanseatic towns and foreign countries and could therefore have been available for study by the painter. He may even have admired these brocades in the splendid gowns worn by his contemporary patricians, each no doubt displaying a different material. The very pattern of their festive robes may therefore have been part of the 'hidden' portrait of a donor. In a corporate commission, such portraits may well have identified prominent contributors to the cost, no less so at the time than the several coats-of-arms displayed in the wings of the altarpiece of the confraternity of the 'Zirkelbrüder' in Lübeck, cited above.

The successful workshop of Conrad von Soest would have had many clients, and at times his journeymen may have produced simple images of the Virgin without specific commissions and for passing trade. However, the main works painted by Conrad himself in a workshop with few assistants would have been rather expensive, both in time and in precious materials used, and could therefore only be produced under contract, and thus in accordance with the instructions of a patron. During a career of more than three decades as a master, Conrad must have painted many other panels which have now perished. Sadly, we have no further information about any of Conrad's individual or corporate patrons for extant or lost autograph works.

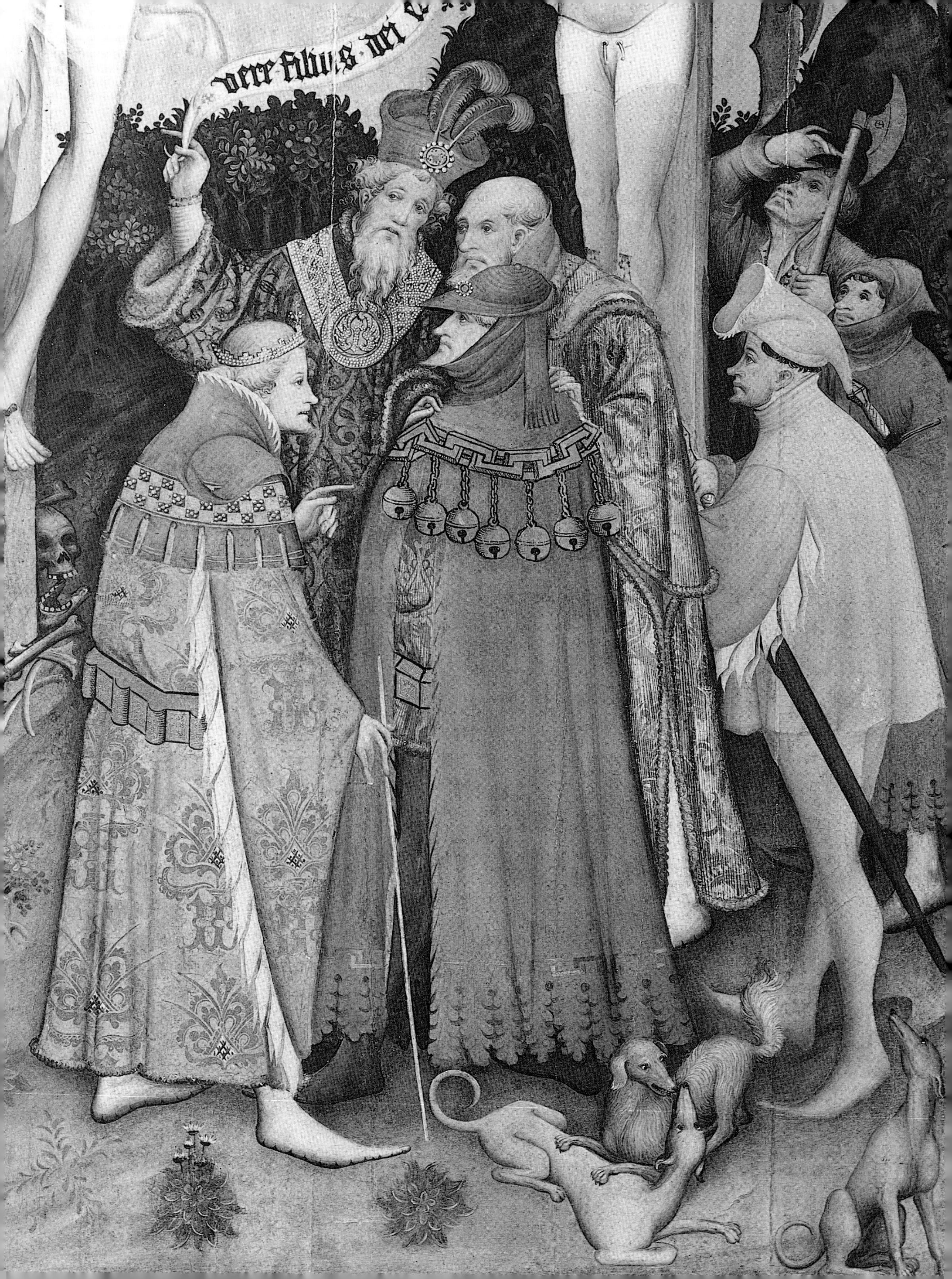
vere filius dei e

3. Production Methods
in Conrad's Workshop

T HE PRODUCTION METHODS in Conrad's workshop coincided with those recommended to aspiring painters by Cennini (in his handbook, probably written around 1390): '…drawing and painting…call for a knowledge of the following: how to work up or grind, how to apply size, to put on cloth, to gesso, to scrape the gessos and smooth them down, to model with gesso, to lay bole, to gild, to burnish; to temper, to lay in; to pounce, to scrape through, to stamp or punch; to mark out, to paint, to embellish, and to varnish, on panel…'[1] Conrad thus followed Italian practice more often than that outlined in surviving Southern German manuals of the later fifteenth-century, such as the Strasbourg and Tegernsee manuscripts.[2] This may not so much reflect the slightly later date of the German manuscripts as Conrad's familiarity with Italian procedures; the possible sources of an Italian influence will be traced in a later chapter (pp. 144–145). The excellent state of preservation of the two large altarpieces signed by Conrad von Soest certainly suggests that he had been well trained himself, and accordingly supervised thorough and skilful preparation of panels in his workshop. The visible parts of the work, such as the delicate punchwork and gesso ornamentation, and the subtle application of colours, confirm exceptionally high standards of craftsmanship throughout. From the consistent quality of the two signed altarpieces, produced at an interval of almost twenty years, it can be deduced that Conrad ran a tightly controlled workshop with few assistants, and this would also be in accordance with guild regulations.

No technical examination of the altarpieces by Conrad von Soest has been published. I have gleaned some information about his working methods from private records and restoration reports.[3] In addition, valuable data has been obtained by means of infra-red photography and optical mineralogy and by an examination of damaged areas in each of the altarpieces. From these sources the following production characteristics have been identified. The oak-wood planks of the altarpieces are braced at the back with crossbars. The panels were glued together and, in the case of the Dortmund Altarpiece, held together by internal iron dowels.[4] The prepared panels were scored deeply and lined with linen cloth, presumably over the whole panel. A damaged patch in the frame of the right wing of the Niederwildungen Altarpiece shows that the linen was extended over the frame. Layers of ivory-coloured gesso (or chalk) were then applied and polished.[5] Next, in areas that were to be gilded, the polished ground was overlaid with what appears to be a reddish bole. This is significant, as whitish bole was apparently the

14. *Courtiers.* Detail from the *Crucifixion.* Niederwildungen Altarpiece

usual priming agent for gilding for Northern German panels. Cennini, however, recommended 'Armenian bole' which Thompson identifies as red clay, and this appears to have been used also by certain artists employed by the Valois princes of France, for instance by Melchior Broederlam for his panels in Dijon (1394–99, Museé des Beaux-Arts, pls. 92, 93).[6] Conrad's use of reddish bole therefore suggests that he may have adopted certain technical practices learnt during his travels abroad. In view of the hypothesis, proposed in a later chapter, that the Veronica Master worked as a journeyman in Conrad's workshop, it is interesting to note that red bole was first used in Cologne at the beginning of the fifteenth century (that is, after the Veronica Master's arrival there).

In Conrad's autograph works, the design was drawn directly onto the prepared panel. In the underdrawing made by the master in bone-black pigment, which can be seen in some areas through the worn paint, some incision is evident. Around the drawn shapes gold leaf has been laid down, burnished and decorated with elaborate but delicately worked punched designs. Cennini felt that 'some practice' was needed to stamp and embellish with punches. In view of the effect the reflecting gold ground has on the colours, he recommended 'a great deal' of stamping because it 'amounts to making the gold lighter' which 'by itself… is dark wherever it is burnished'. The outstanding and original quality of the tooling and punchwork in Conrad's altarpieces suggests that this work was carried out by a gifted journeyman who may have been specially trained in a goldsmith's work-shop.[7] The poignant crown-of-thorns frame punched into the gold ground of the Niederwildungen Altarpiece is an idiosyncratic feature only seen in Conrad's art (pl. 11). Equally, the cloud motif which decorates the background of all extant autograph works by Conrad clearly originates in his workshop and has no earlier parallels in Italian or Northern panels.[8] Here, however, the Veronica Master and his workshop again followed Conrad, by adopting this cloud punchmark. The delicate framing oak-leaf punchwork, and the graceful angels floating in the gold ground of the *Adoration of the Kings* (pl. 15) may have been inspired by commonly found Italian decorations, but they find a new, ethereal elegance in the Dortmund Altarpiece. It is instructive to compare Conrad's creative and refined punchwork with the schematic and rather basic work in the St Nicholas Panel (pl. 155) at Soest or the mainly simple and repetitive work in the St Clare Polyptych (pl. 120) in Cologne Cathedral. Indeed, the drawn and punched angels in the gold ground of the Dortmund *Death of the Virgin* (pl. 16) may have been intended as a virtuoso display of Conrad's consummate craftsmanship. Cennini clearly valued such punchwork which he calls 'one of our most delightful branches…with imaginative feeling and a delicate touch, you may work out foliage ornaments on a gold ground, and make little angels and other figures so that they show up in the gold'.[9] The extremely intricate punchwork, including the lettering and floral decoration in the haloes, must have greatly added to the alreadyconsiderable expense of Conrad's altarpieces.

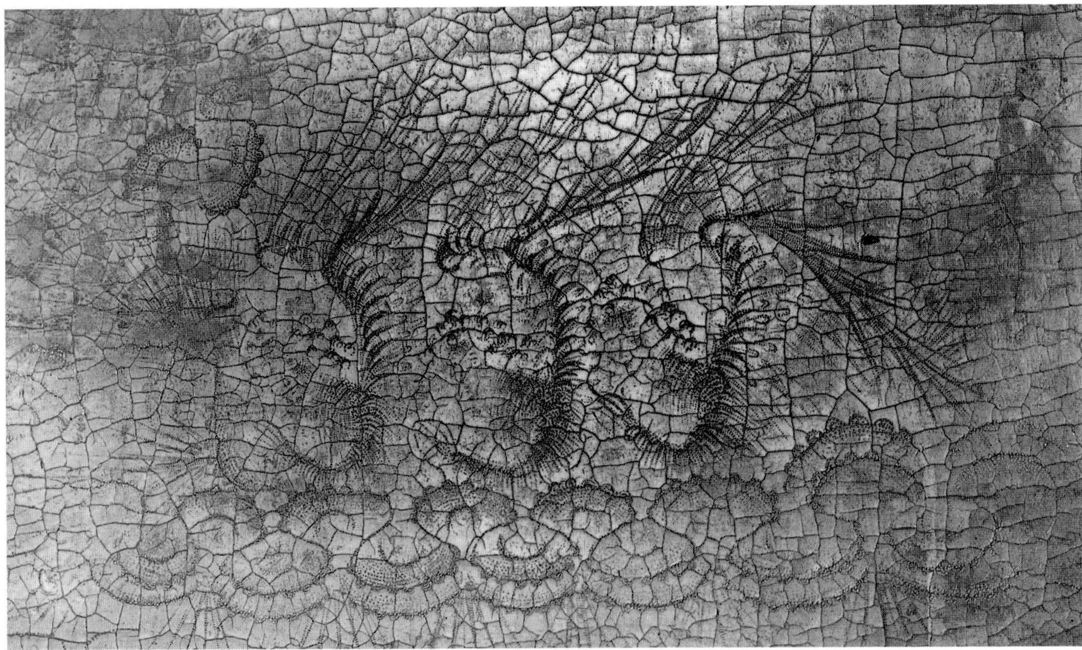

15. Detail of punchwork from the *Adoration of the Kings*. Dortmund Altarpiece

Gold, and probably tin, foils were used for the brocades in the retables and silver foil for armour, swords and knives. In the Niederwildungen Altarpiece the brocades are scored with parallel hatching to imitate the texture of gold thread, a method already visible in the Grabow Altarpiece (1379; Kunsthalle Hamburg) by Master Bertram. This hatching is all but abandoned in the Dortmund example. It only occurs there in the snowflake pattern on the bed cover in the *Death of the Virgin* and in a small area of the Virgin's dress in the *Adoration of the Kings*, not in the royal robes (pls. XXIV, XXV). The brocades are excellently preserved throughout both altarpieces, with the exception only of the brocade of the second king's robe in the *Adoration of the Kings* at Dortmund, where the green pigment has turned black. In the similar green brocade of Longinus's robe in the *Crucifixion* of the Niederwildungen Altarpiece, no change of colour is apparent. In both retables small gesso pearls delicately decorate crowns and other jewels, as well as 'embroidered' areas of garments(pl. 19). Such gesso decorations were quite common at this time, though normally of a much heavier kind than Conrad's elegant ornaments. A restorer's heavy black brush lines around some gold or silver ornaments now distort the original effect of Conrad' subtle outlines.

The vigorous and creative nature of Conrad von Soest's underdrawing style, consistent in both altarpieces, has been exposed through infra-red photography and will be discussed in detail in the chapter that examines the underdrawing of attributed panels. The photographs reveal that Conrad was a skilled draughtsman who designed his forms in a rapid, imaginative manner incompatible with the careful copying implied by authors who have judged him an imitative artist.[10] However, on his peregrinations Conrad, like other travelling journeymen, is likely to have recorded motifs found in the work of excellent masters. For, as the German preacher Johann Taulers (d. 1361) explained, 'a keen painter, who wishes to paint an attractive picture for himself, studies first another well painted painting carefully and copies all its points and lines onto his slate, and then he paints his picture accordingly as best he can'.[11] On his return to Dortmund, Conrad would presumably have bound this 'collection of random motifs' into a pattern book for future reference. The fact that the designs of hands are repeated in his work shows that Conrad had also made the usual model book of highly finished drawings that were 'intended primarily as a stock of motifs to be used in a painter's workshop for direct copying into a painting…', both by the master himself and by his assistants. They were also 'used for apprenticeship exercises in the handling of the silverpoint'.[12] Model books were handed down through the generations of a workshop. Seldom did they, like the model book from the late fourteenth century in the Pierpont Morgan Library in New York (M. 346), contain both fully worked model drawings and pattern sketches.

It seems reasonable to presume that an assistant using a model book would aim to recreate his master's style and design as faithfully as possible to preserve workshop unity. His work could therefore give rise to mistaken attribution at times. It will be argued below that the Fröndenberg Altarpiece (pl. 154) may demonstrate such workshop dependence on Conrad's model book. However, a travelling journeyman would usually be more interested in ideas, motifs and unusual designs than in making a faithful copy of another artist's style. He would therefore not have disguised his own style in his record sheets.[13] A painting that draws on a painter's own pattern book records may therefore reflect the style of another master, but would rarely give rise to an incorrect attribution if studied with sufficient care. The Jacobi Altarpiece (pl. 61) by an unknown master may be cited as an example of dependence on pattern sheets reflecting the designs in Conrad's Dortmund Altarpiece. In contrast, Conrad's own lively underdrawing style, with its searching for form in rapid parallel hatching strokes, indicates a creative quality that is alien to the careful transfer of workshop models onto the prepared panel. Patterns, recording his earlier visual experiences would have served only as a springboard for his own designs. Possible sources for certain motifs in Conrad's altarpieces will be discussed in a later chapter; Conrad von Soest's forceful and inventive underdrawing style suggests that it would be fruitless to search for complete designs borrowed from other masters in the manner of the painter of the Jacobi Altarpiece.

Both altarpieces by Conrad von Soest are striking in the brilliance of their colours. They glow like stained glass windows suffused with light. One should

16. *Angels.* Detail from the *Death of the Virgin.* Dortmund Altarpiece

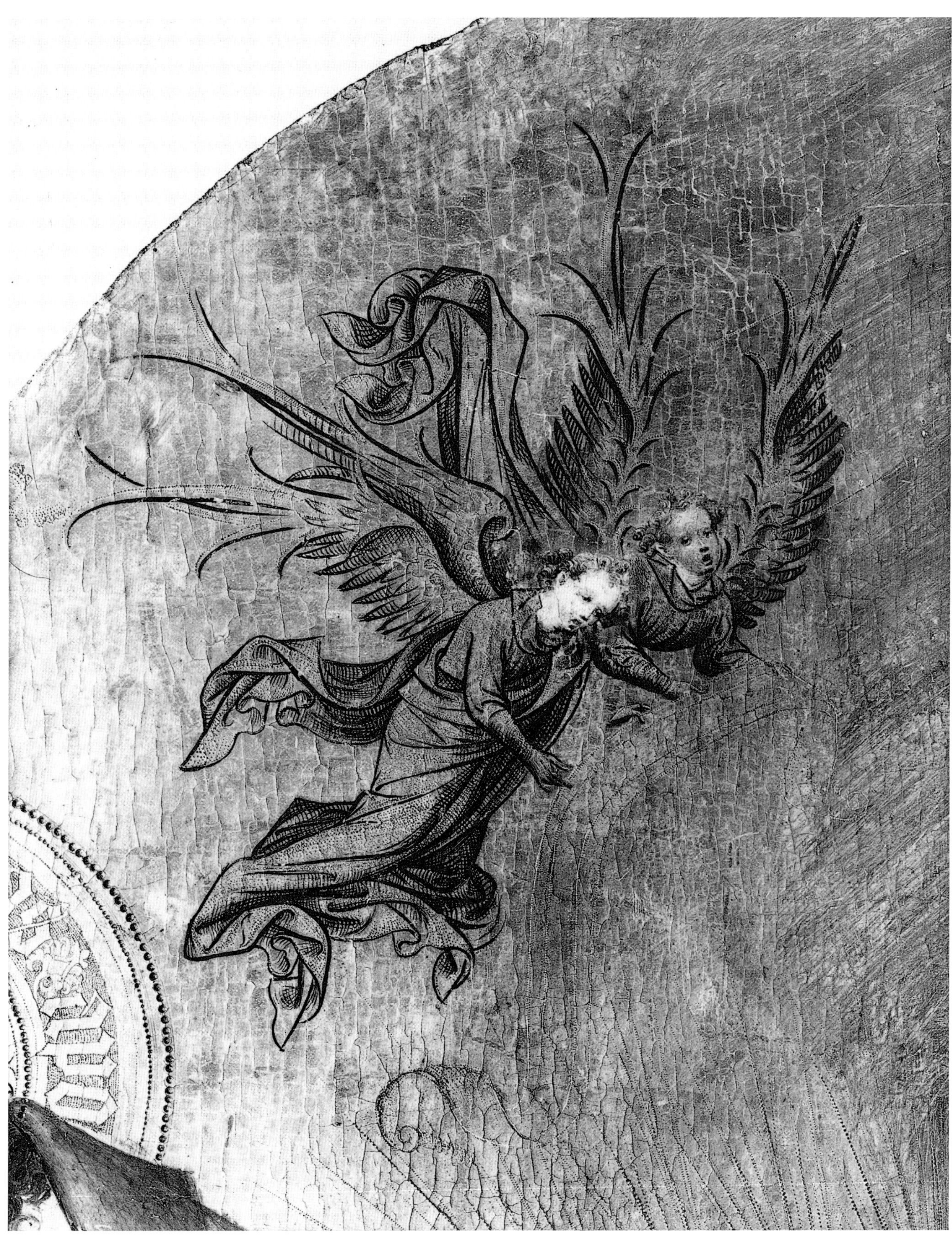

remember, however, that this brilliance of colour would originally have been tempered by light filtering through stained glass windows and, often, by the ethereal effects of candle-light.[14] Examination of the painted surfaces revealed a rapid application technique of thin layers of translucent paint. Conrad's brush appears to have been frequently loaded with two or more colours.[15] Brushstrokes are almost invisible, except in the highlights which are executed with a fine brush in rapid strokes, looped at the end. The lively brushstrokes that create the silken curls under St Mary Magdalene's transparent veil in the Niederwildungen *Crucifixion* attest to Conrad's easy mastery. Examination with an eye-glass suggests a consistency of brushwork that points to a single painter for the whole work, at least in all the surface layers, which is again in keeping with our perception that Conrad's workshop was small.

The extraordinary tonal variety of Conrad's colours becomes apparent on closer inspection. For the colour red alone, thirteen distinct shades have been detected in the Niederwildungen Altarpiece, without counting paler varieties of the shades or tonal nuances within the red areas themselves.[16] The Master of the Golden Panel from Lüneburg (cat. no. 13) in Hanover, who has been shown to be closest to Conrad in terms of colour range, used only seven or eight shades of red, whilst the Master of the Netze Altarpiece (*c.* 1390; pls. 69, 78) registered five. The limited range of thirteen different colours in the Netze Master's palette may be contrasted with thirty-one colours (not including tonal nuances or brocades) at Niederwildungen and twenty-three at Hanover. In Conrad's work the tonal variety within large areas of a colour and the juxtaposition of hues are of remarkable subtlety and beauty. The garments of the group of courtiers beneath the cross in the Niederwildungen *Crucifixion*, for instance, provide a harmonious and subtle range of reds and pinks set against the blue and green robes of the facing attendants(pl. XIV). St John's mantle, on the opposite side, is red in the shaded areas with orange highlights on the folds. Where light touches it strongly, the colour of this garment is transformed through light red to ever paler lemon yellows and finally to a pink-lemon-white at the centre of illumination. These colours are contrasted with a green robe. In the shade this is of a dark, warm tonality which turns pale and cool in the highlights on the raised arms.[17]

Following the common practice, Conrad built up colour from dark to light and applied it in thin glazes. In the colour schemes of Northern late Gothic panels, a predominance of red and green has been noticed, for example in Master Bertram's Grabow Altarpiece (1379) and the Netze Altarpiece.[18] In Conrad's retables, however, the most prominent colours are red and blue. A similar preference for blue pigments can be observed in certain panels in the Louvre, Paris, which were probably painted for Valois princes, such as the *Crucifixion* (*c.* 1389–1395) (pl. 80), by Jean de Beaumetz, the *Entombment* (*c.* 1400) by an unknown Parisian or Burgundian artist, and the *Martyrdom of St Denis* (before 1416) by Henri Bellechose. The illuminations by the Parement Master, notably the *Presentation* (pl. 87), the *Arrest*, the scenes before Pilate and Caiaphas (pl. 84), and the *Crucifixion* of the *Très belles heures de Notre-Dame* (before 1384), are also dominated by blue pigments, which are frequently balanced by areas of what appears to be lead-tin yellow. The brilliant blue pigment in the illuminations by the Parement Master may well be ultramarine. Though the colour yellow was generally unpopular, lead-tin yellow was used by Conrad von Soest as a prominent colour balancing ultramarine; it was also adopted in the workshop of the Veronica Master.[19] The presence of these unusual pigments seems significant in view of the links discussed below between the Parement Master and Conrad von Soest (see pp. 133–141), and later between Conrad von Soest and the Veronica Master (pp. 162–180).

The visual effect of Conrad von Soest's brilliant colours has been widely appreciated. It has now been possible to analyse the blue pigment which, after the reds, is the most prominent colour in Conrad's altarpieces.[20] A paint sample, taken from existing damage in Mary's cloak in the *Coronation of the Virgin* of the Dortmund Altarpiece, was examined by optical mineralogy. It showed small traces of azurite with a much larger quantity of high quality coarse-grained ultramarine. The high quality of the colour is suggested both by the large particle sizes in the sample and by the excellent transparency of blue areas in infra-red photography.[21] Such use of expensive ultramarine for the outside of an altarpiece is unusual. Natural ultramarine, made from the semi-precious lapis lazuli stone, was so costly that, if used at all, it was generally only applied to the Virgin's cloak on the feast-day side of the altarpiece. In view of my proposed connection between the art of Conrad von Soest and that of the Veronica Master (see pp. 162–280), it is interesting to note that, amongst the panels tested in Cologne, there is only one example from before the arrival there of the Veronica Master which shows any trace of ultramarine.[22] In the later panels, only the Veronica Master, the Master of St Lawrence (trained in the Veronica Master's workshop), and the master of the Wasservass Calvary (WRM 65, *c*. 1420) used small quantities of ultramarine. A trace of ultramarine was also found in the Westphalian *Calvary* from St Andreas (WRM 353, *c*. 1420), now in the Cologne Museum. Other Westphalian painters seem to have used azurite exclusively—with the exception only of Conrad's imitator, the Master of the Blankenberch Altarpiece, who apparently applied a surface glaze of ultramarine over azurite.[23]

The transparency in infra-red photography suggests that for all blue areas in both the Niederwildungen and Dortmund Altarpieces high quality ultramarine was used. Investigation with a magnifying glass confirms consistently large particle sizes and indicates that the most expensive of ultramarines has been applied throughout, even on the obverse sides of the panels.[24] This means that, against the convention of his time and at great cost to the patrons, Conrad von Soest used large quantities of high quality ultramarine pigment in his altarpieces, as well as gold and silver. The liberal use of precious pigments and highest quality workmanship makes the retables by Conrad von Soest exceptional among surviving Northern European panels of his time.

Technical analysis also suggests that Conrad used green underpaint or *terra verde*, as recommended by Cennini, for the flesh tones of his major protagonist; this green is not transparent in infra-red photography. There is, however, no indication in the German manual, the Strasbourg manuscript, that green was used under flesh colours in that workshop. In the early 12th century, Theophilus had already recommended instead that lead white, boiled until it turns 'a yellowish tan colour' and mixed with a little cinnabar should be used.[25] Green underpainting was not the practice in other Westphalian workshops either, although it was not unknown in Northern Europe: Broederlam applied it to faces in the painted wings at Dijon, and it is evident that the Parement Master even experimented with *terra verde* underpainting in manuscripts when illuminating the *Très belles heures*.[26] In the Niederwildungen Altarpiece, Conrad also apparently used the pigments red lead, cinnabar, red lake, root madder, yellow ochre, malachite, copper resinate, lead white and 'fatty' charcoal black, and he employed cherry gum as the binding medium and in his varnishes.[27] The technique of the Dortmund Altarpiece has been described as tempera in a resinous oil medium.[28] The use of oil or resinous binding medium resulted in transparent pigments that were usually applied over an opaque layer to create an illusion of optical depth. Missing surface layers have now partially diminished that effect. Conrad creates great luminosity through his lively application of layers of translucent glazes, which frequently ignore incised and drawn outlines.

It has been suggested that Gothic artists adopted a hierarchy of colours. According to this theory, inanimate objects such as buildings and landscapes were subdued with opaque glazes because they were seen as inferior in the eyes of God.[29] The universality of this attitude in artists' workshops is difficult to accept: the observation of nature's colouring may be an equally important factor. It can certainly be shown that Conrad von Soest did not adhere to the theory of the hierarchy of colours, for the loggia in the Niederwildungen *Christ Mocked before Herod* (pl. XIII) is painted a brilliant orange red on the outside wall, toned down slightly in shaded areas of the stone-coloured entrance arch of the building. Its ultramarine roof is accentuated by white highlights and is itself contrasted by a green ceiling inside. Only this green colour of the barrel vault is truly tempered by light and shade. In the *Presentation* (pl. VI), the vaulting of the temple is painted in the most brilliant red.

Conrad's interest in geometry is revealed by infra-red photography, which shows the design drawings of furniture pieces. The radius of the halo of the Virgin (12.8 cm) in the Niederwildungen *Nativity* scene is the design module on which all Conrad's measurements in this altarpiece are based. Repeated marks across the panels betray the use of a compass in his compositions. But the importance of geometry is also apparent in the construction of the altarpieces themselves,[30] where Conrad relied on the visual harmony of the proportions of the golden section (ratio of width to height 1.618 : 1; often interpreted in whole numbers as 13 : 8). The

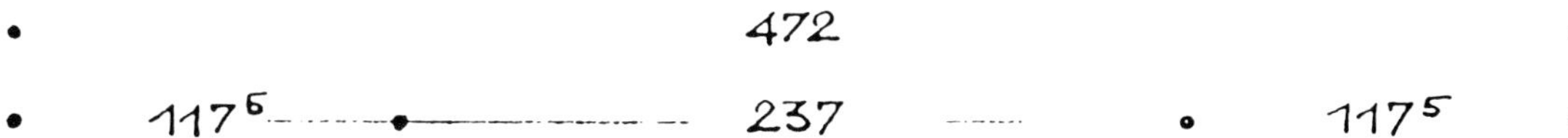

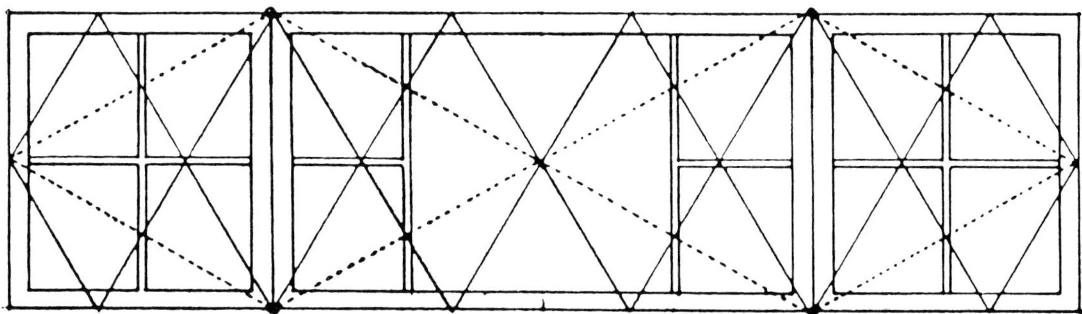

17. Drawing by Erwin Rohrberg of the geometric structure of the Netze Altarpiece

geometric structure of the Niederwildungen Altarpiece thus differs from that of earlier Westphalian works, such as the Netze Altarpiece where the typical Gothic equilateral triangle organization is used (pl. 17). Conrad draws attention to his use of the golden section on the frame of the Niederwildungen Altarpiece: it is decorated with 13 evenly spaced crescent-moon motifs at the top and base and 8 at the sides (pls. 131, 132; I–III). As discussed below (cat. no. 2), for the more complex design of the Dortmund Altarpiece the golden section also applied. The golden section was known in the antique world; it was only sporadically applied in later centuries, until it was rediscovered by Renaissance artists. Its occurrence in Conrad's workshop points to the sophistication of its master, possibly guided by his patrician friends.

The subtlety of colouring in the Niederwildungen Altarpiece, coupled with designs based on sound geometric construction and a lively and confident free-hand underdrawing style, demonstrates that Conrad was an accomplished artist by 1403. This contradicts the suggestion by certain authors (see p. 131), that Conrad was still travelling, presumably as a journeyman, in Burgundy around or after 1400. Even by *c.* 1420, when the Dortmund Altarpiece was created, Conrad's stylistic advances did not call for any moderation of his production methods. Our examination of the signed altarpieces of Conrad von Soest reveals a highly skilled master with a workshop in which consummate craftsmanship was combined with creative draughtsmanship and sensitive and imaginative handling of pigments. Combined with such technical achievements, the elegance of his courtly figures contribute to the harmony of form and content which distinguishes Conrad's autograph work.

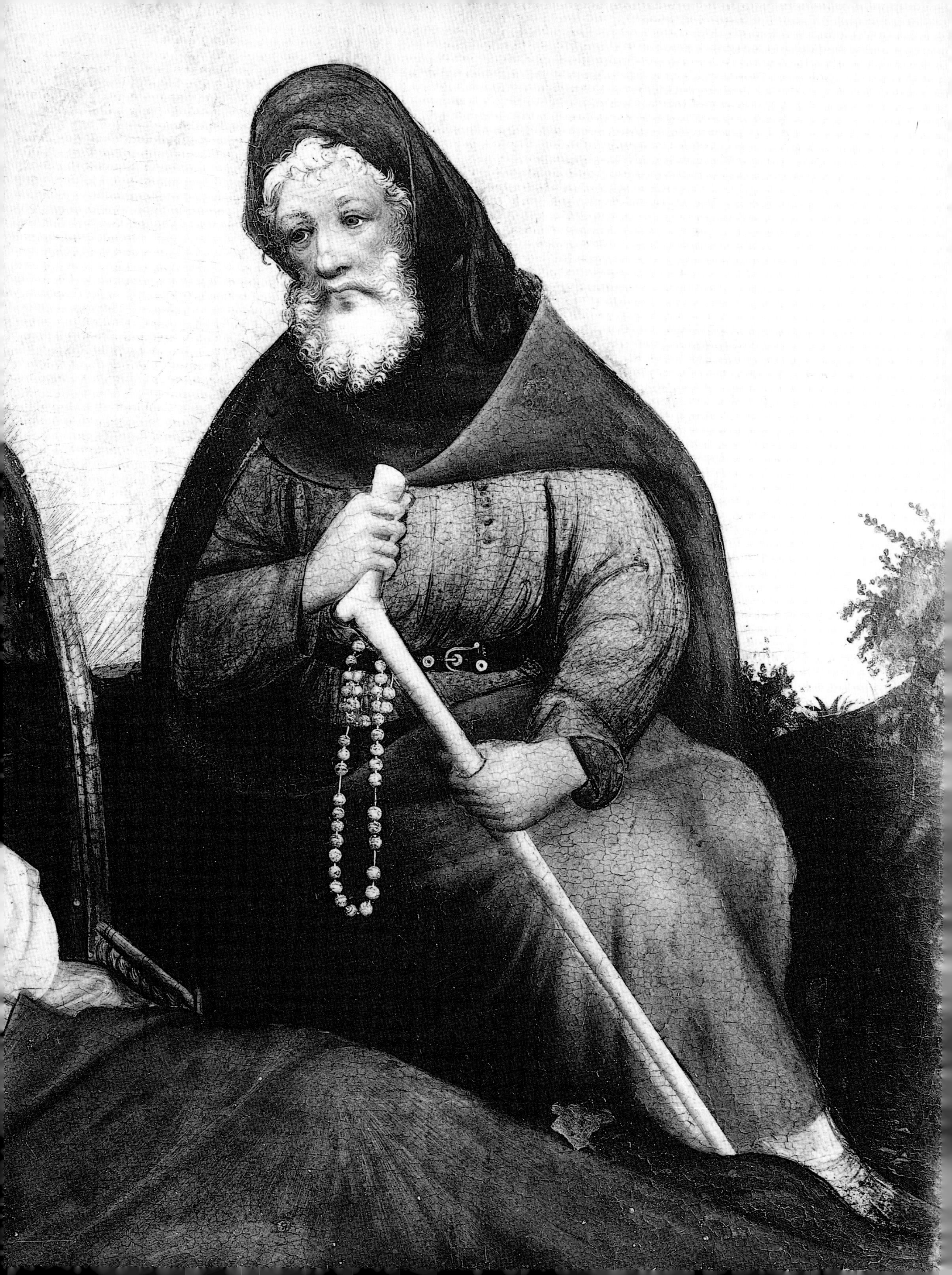

4. Stylistic Considerations

A ROUND 1400, aristocratic and patrician patrons throughout Europe favoured an artistic style that was marked by courtly refinement. In contrast to other international stylistic trends, this particular manifestation achieved a near homogeneous appearance when superseding local traditions. The stylistic cohesion is the more remarkable as it cannot be traced to a single place of origin or to a single precedent.[1] This does not imply that these artistic creations looked identical all over Europe, but rather that they appeared like more or less distinct dialects of a common language. Despite the destruction of a considerable proportion of panels and other works of art from that time, a sufficient number of paintings, manuscripts, sculptures and artefacts survive to convey the flavour of this elegant style and to demonstrate its diffusion. Prominent examples of paintings in this manner include the Wilton Diptych (*c.* 1395–99) in the National Gallery, London; the *Adoration of the Magi* (1423) by Gentile da Fabriano in the Uffizi, Florence; the *Virgin with the Sweet Pea Blossom* (*c.* 1415–20) by the Veronica Master in the Wallraf-Richartz Museum, Cologne; the painted wings of an altarpiece (1394–99) by Melchior Broederlam in the Musée des Beaux-Arts, Dijon; the *Grande Pietà ronde* (*c.* 1400) possibly by Jean Malouel in the Louvre, Paris; and the Retable of St Peter (1411–13) by Louis Borrassá in the church of Sta María, Tarrasa.

The unique proliferation and perceived uniformity of this style caused it to be termed 'International Gothic'.[2] This distinguishes it from other styles which may have prompted international imitation but had been created in a single country. However, the classification 'Gothic' can be misleading. It is difficult to reconcile certain manifestations of art around 1400, for instance the aerial perspective in miniatures by the Limbourg brothers (see pl. 127), with the characteristics of earlier Gothic art. The name might also falsely imply a universal spread of this style beyond the actual limited patronage in mainly aristocratic and patrician circles.[3] Therefore the label 'courtly style' has been suggested to stress the noble grace of art around 1400, but this might also evoke other very different courtly styles, such as sixteenth-century 'maniera'.[4] However, the word 'courtly' does seem appropriate in suggesting that the style was influenced by aristocratic taste rather than practised at a specific court. I therefore propose to use the term 'International Courtly Style', a fusion of these former appellations which may come closer to defining the essential features of the style around 1400.

The International Courtly Style is reflected in a diversity of artistic creations which share an enchanting yearning for exquisite perfection and a sympathy with chivalric ideals. Style, colour, narrative, and costly craftsmanship are all subordi-

18. *Joseph.* Detail from the *Nativity.* Dortmund Altarpiece

nate to the harmony of the whole. In painting, an emphasis on the decorative function of surface pattern results in a rhythm of sinuous lines supported by areas of translucent colour, which are arranged in a melodious balance of intervals. Man, form and nature are all part of this linear rhythm. Light tends to have both a decorative and a narrative function, until it yields to the realism of aerial perspective. Whilst spatial depth is hardly explored in this decorative style, figures overlapping the frame frequently suggest an illusion of frontal space.[5] Elongated, elegant figures dressed in costly materials, extravagantly cut, transform the Gothic sway into a graceful plasticity within their linear patterns. The privilege and breeding of these aristocratic figures is often stressed by the presence of bucolic creatures, kept safely at a distance. Nature frequently enchants by carefully observed realistic details. There is no intention, however, to create a realistic world, but only to enhance the fairy-tale aspects with recognizable anecdote. Costly painting materials and exquisite punchwork can stress the intrinsic value of panels and enhance their aesthetic merit.

The unique stylistic cohesion of this courtly art may be interpreted as a manifestation of an escapist cult, promoted by those most threatened by the realities of the European social and political situation. At a time when Europe was still reeling from the ravages of the 'Black Death', the stability of the old order was further undermined by a number of concurrent events, including the establishment of the rival Avignon papacy (1379), the disarray of imperial political power after the death of Charles IV (1378) and the weakening of manorialism. Italy was troubled by the instability of the city-republics and by the rising power of despotic dynasties. France suffered hostilities with England in the intermittent Hundred Years War of 1337–1453, which brought famine and devastation in its wake.[6]

With town and country dissatisfied and in sporadic revolt, the traditional authority of church and crown undermined and the privileges of the nobility threatened by the emancipation of early capitalist burghers, princes seemed to respond by retreating further into an élitist world. Fenced off from reality by rigid etiquette, the aristocracy of Europe, united both by ties of blood (intermarriage was frequent between dynasties) and in their resistance to these social and political problems, escaped into a make-believe world of chivalry and exquisite beauty. This nobility, affectedly refined in its attitudes, stressed its privilege by adopting elaborate, extravagant and impractical fashions. Princely magnificence achieved new extremes as display of fortune and power proved politically expedient. Patricians, like princes, strove to separate themselves from the upwardly-mobile 'third estate'. They tried to consolidate their positions—threatened when craftsmen's guilds increasingly forced them into concessions and power sharing—by aping the nobility in manner and fashion, and by adopting coats-of-arms. The courtly style and conspicuous expense of Conrad von Soest's altarpieces indicate that his patrons, the patrician merchants of Dortmund who faced a revolt of the guilds in 1400, shared in this ethos of ostentation.

46

The roots of the courtly style around 1400 were as international as its expression. As accidents of inheritance, marriage, politics, and wars seemed to keep nations and provinces in a state of constant flux, artistic ideas touched and fused to grow into a harmonious whole. The evolution of this growth cannot be demonstrated in separate grafts, although diverse roots can be clearly discerned. These roots can be found in the linear refinement and slender late Gothic sway of the style at the court in Paris; in the expressive lyricism of Sienese compositions that had reached the papal court at Avignon with Simone Martini; in the Slavonic-Italian fusion with French elements at the imperial court in Prague; and in Netherlandish influences at the courts of Paris and Burgundy. The well-documented peregrinations of princes and artists may account for the rapid diffusion of these stylistic trends. Scholars and merchants, on their frequent journeys, may have carried patterns and works of art as well. After the decline of the imperial court, French royalty, in particular, was able to tempt some of the most gifted artists from France, Italy, Germany and the Netherlands into their service. The new style therefore thrived on French soil.

In France, the Valois family tradition of quality and taste in the arts, especially at the court of Charles V (1338–80), had established Paris as an important cosmopolitan artistic centre. Surviving inventories testify to the continued patronage of the arts not only at the Paris court of Charles VI (1368–1422), but increasingly at the town and country residences of his regent uncles Louis I, Duke of Anjou (1339–84), John, Duke of Berry (1340–1416) and Philip the Bold, Duke of Burgundy (1342–1404), and also of the king's brother Louis, Duke of Orléans (1372–1407).[7] After 1380, at the time Conrad von Soest is likely to have travelled as a journeyman, the dukes of Berry and Burgundy in particular, aided by a lull in the Hundred Years War, rivalled each other as perceptive collectors and conspicuous spenders. Their lavish expenditure on the building and decoration of houses and castles and on their collections which included tapestries, manuscripts, jewels, medals, sculpture, ivories, enamels, embroideries and costly robes, was partially supported by the imposition of heavy taxes and fines. By 1392, the intermittent madness of King Charles VI and the ensuing power struggle, together with renewed war efforts, were straining the princely purses—although nothing could fully subdue the collecting instinct of the Valois.

The flowering of the arts at the royal court in Paris came to a halt in the years after the defeat of the French at Agincourt in 1415. The Duke of Berry died in 1416, leaving as many fabulous possessions as debts. The court of Burgundy removed itself to prospering Flanders, the Dauphin retreated to Bourges and Chinon. The disarray of royal power and social cohesion in France prompted the decentralization of artistic patronage and a scattering of the artists. However, the Regent of France, the Duke of Bedford, decided to employ illuminators who worked in the Courtly Style, the Bedford workshop (see, for example, the *Bedford Hours*, after 1424). A sporadic late flowering of the International Courtly Style can also be

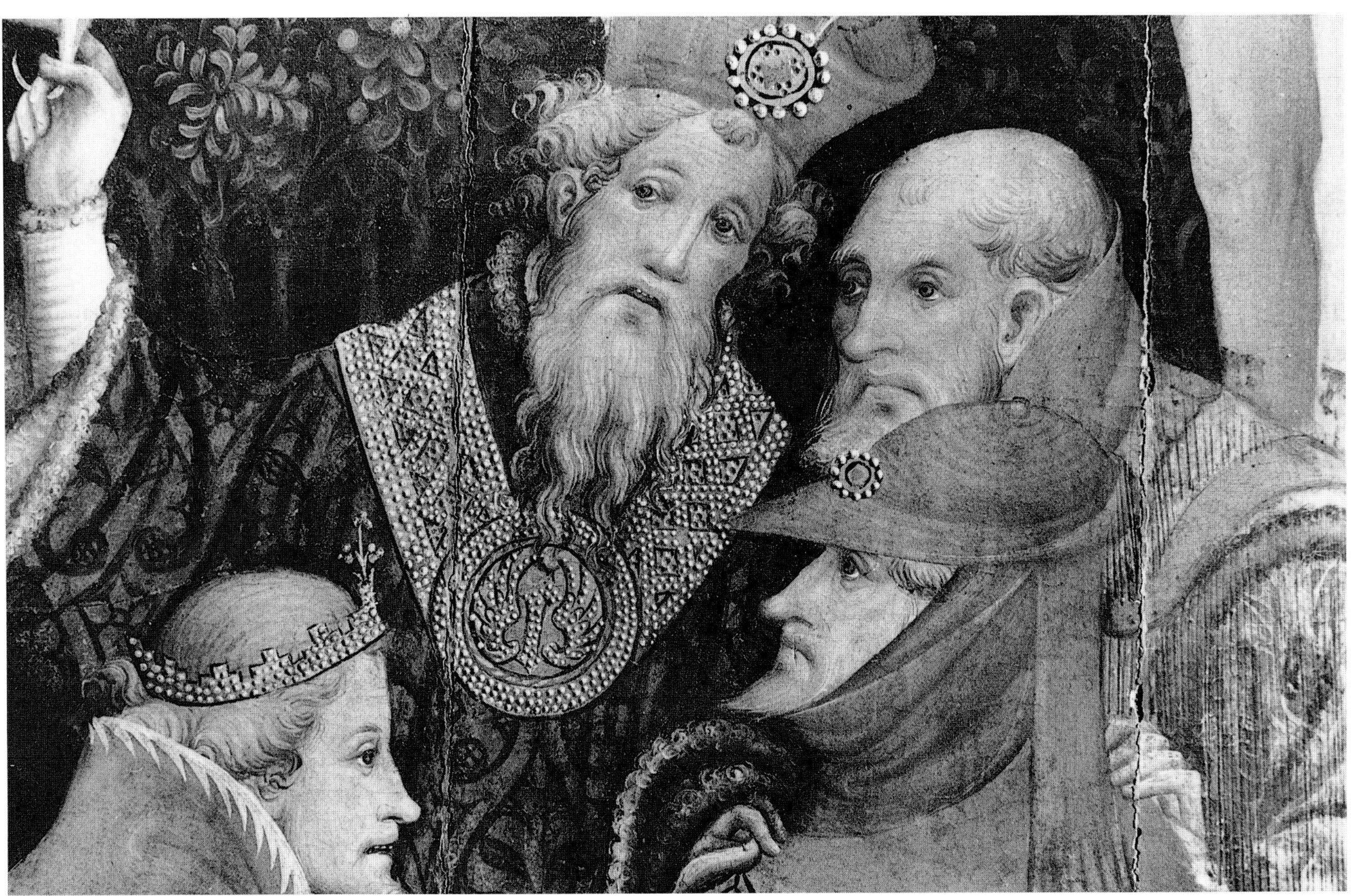

observed after 1420 in other artistic centres. In Italy some fine examples survive, including the *Adoration of the Magi* of 1423 by Gentile Fabriano (Uffizi, Florence) and Pisanello's wall-paintings in St Anastasia at Verona (1436–38) and in the ducal palace at Mantua (*c.* 1446–47). Whilst princes struggled, patrician merchants had weathered the upheavals in cities that flourished as trading centres, especially in the Netherlands and Germany. Not long after the completion of Conrad von Soest's Dortmund Altarpiece, early capitalist burghers began to assert their independence of princes and to express their own values through more sober attire and more realistic art. The new stylistic trends were assisted by the empirical realism of form and space of the Netherlandish panel painters and by the mathematical spatial solutions favoured by the painters of Florence. The historical moment that fostered the International Courtly Style had passed.

The retables signed by Conrad von Soest, the Niederwildungen Altarpiece and the fragments of the Dortmund Altarpiece (cat. nos. 1–2), display the characteristics of the elegant style around 1400 in a harmony of content and form achieved only by the best painters. The easy grace of Conrad's figures is effected through elong-

19. *Heads of Courtiers.*
Detail from the *Crucifixion.*
Niederwildungen Altarpiece

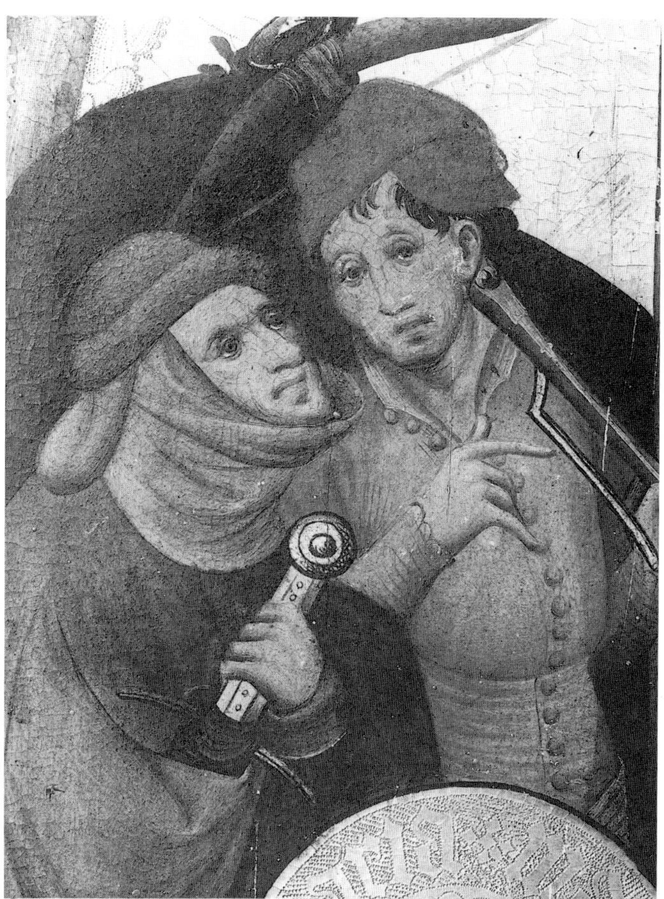

20. *Bucolic Figures.*
Detail from the *Crucifixion.*
Niederwildungen Altarpiece

ation of forms and a method of modelling in light and shade which indicates form but falls short of describing it in a naturalistic manner. His slim, mannered protagonists move with noble poise and carry the narrative by eloquent gestures. Small heads with idealized features, sloping shoulders and stylized hands, posed elegantly and yet capable of being expressive, all contribute to the aristocratic refinement of the figure style(pl. 21). The timeless robes of the Virgin and the apostles are contrasted by the extravagant court dress of certain protagonists. However, this noble sophistication is balanced by a delight in observed detail. The elegance of the main characters is emphasized by the naturalistic description of bucolic creatures, such as the bystanders in the Niederwildungen *Crucifixion* (pl. 20).[8]

Conrad's figures are imbued with a personal style that is most apparent in facial features. Male faces are more individually characterized than those of female protagonists, but a tendency to high foreheads, straight noses, heavy eyelids and small mouths with prominent upper lips may be seen as a typical design feature of autograph work. The sloping eyes in Christ's gentle suffering face and the distinctive features of the Virgin were to become much imitated motifs. Conrad's

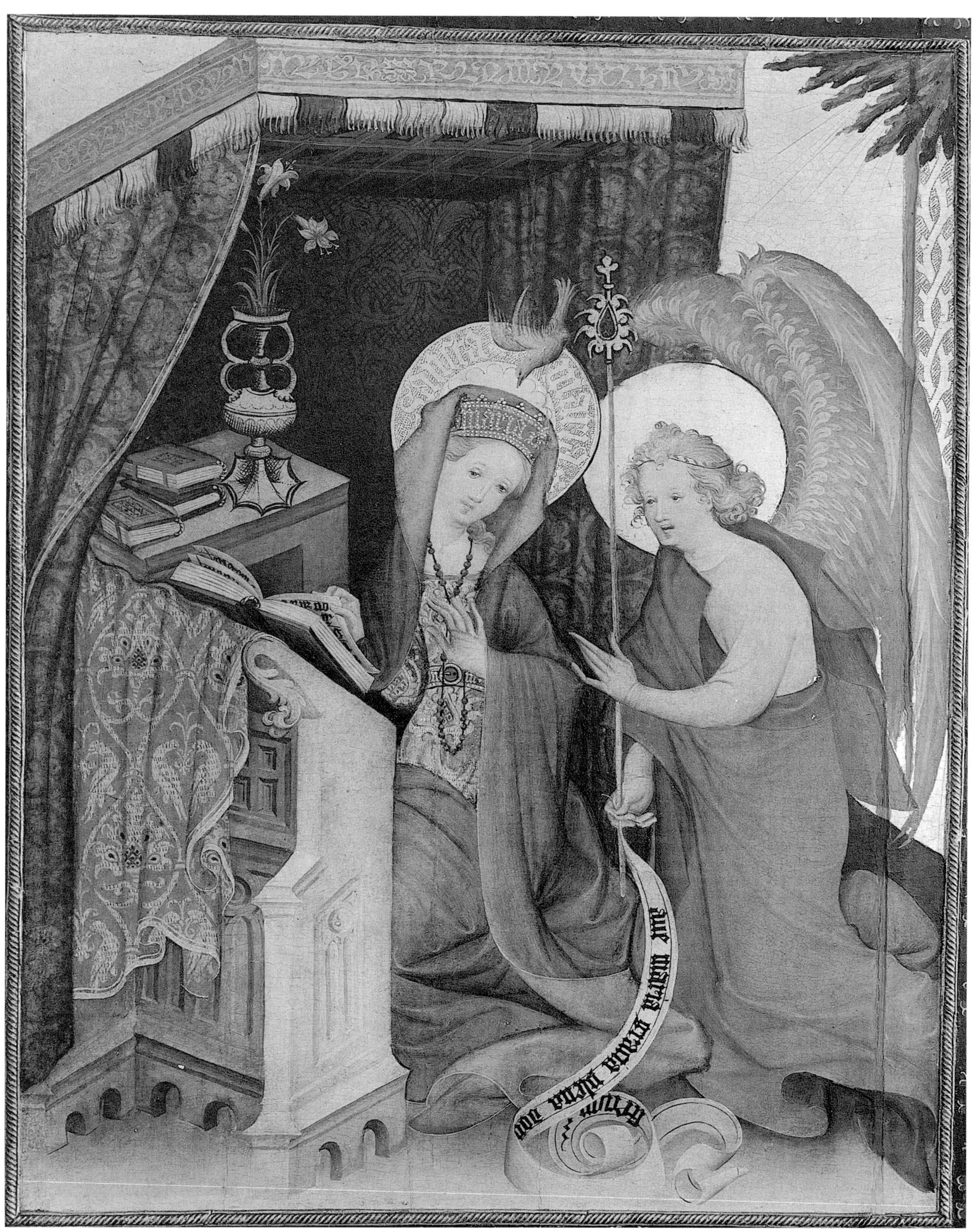

21. Conrad von Soest: *Annunciation*. Niederwildungen Altarpiece

figure style differs considerably from that of earlier Westphalian designs (see pp. 122–129).

A particular characteristic of Conrad's expressive figures consists in their domination of the pictorial space (pl. 11, 12). Space is implied, not by means of a centralized perspective system but by overlapping structures, the placement of figures and objects behind each other, the non-systematic diminution of figures and the use of oblique settings. Conrad's methods, like those of Giotto, were 'empirical, based upon inherited skills, on personal observation, and upon the craftsman's sense of what would give the best results in practice'.[9] But unlike Giotto, Conrad did not use colour to emphasize the weight and volume of the human figure. Through a stress on surface pattern, he denied his figures their full plastic volume to exploit their decorative potential. This effect is enhanced by a harmonious distribution of areas of colour across all the panels so that the sense of interval creates a pattern in itself. The hierarchical scale of Christ in the *Crucifixion* at Niederwildungen is allowed to undermine the space-creating effect of diminution of other figures (pl. XIV).[10] A strong linear surface pattern is contrasted with the firmly foreshortened thieves whose crosses are set obliquely in space. The tension created by the idealized elongated design of Christ and the realism of the stocky bodies of the thieves is underlined by the contrasting positions of their respective crosses in space. This space-creating device appears to have been introduced into Westphalia by Conrad von Soest; it can be found earlier in the Parisian workshops of the Parement Master and Jacquemart de Hesdin (pl. 85).[11]

Conrad's subtle way of denoting space is in harmony with the flat surface and gold ground. The foreshortened frontal arrangement of the architectural settings in the Niederwildungen Altarpiece, occasionally softened oblique, stress their decorative role.[12] Whilst earlier Westphalian spatial construction, for example in the Netze Altarpiece (*c.* 1390) at Netze, may be characterized as shallow stage sets with architectural backdrops, Conrad's interior spaces tightly frame the dominant figures, leaving very little headroom, with apparent disregard for realism. This tension between figures and architectural settings is a feature also of designs by the Parement Master.

In the Niederwildungen Altarpiece, tiles are shown as receding in parallel orthogonals in the adjacent *Adoration of the Kings* and *Presentation*, but they are arranged to converge in the separating border between the two scenes (pl. 22). The outer limits of buildings and some figures are allowed to overlap the borders, thus creating the illusion that they project from the picture plane.[13] This is denied by the main patterned frame, which wholly contains the designs. In a related spatial game in the landscape setting of the *Crucifixion*, the rainbow that spans the scene overlaps the inner frame but disappears behind the outer frame. An illusion of spatial depth is thus created, enhanced in the spandrels of the rainbow by the prophets' scrolls which seem to occupy this space; the space also shelters Christ's cross.

A disregard for perspective construction in favour of decorative harmony can be demonstrated by the architecture of the *Nativity* scene in the Niederwildungen Altarpiece (Frontispiece). Here a pillar, which rests on a base placed at the picture plane, is positioned to cover the intersection line between the rear of the stable and the landscape. To stress the ambiguous spatial construction, a roof sheltering the shepherd behind the stable appears to be supported by this pillar which is based in front of the main protagonists before the stable. This design appears to have been an afterthought: paint loss now reveals the original red paint of the blanket beneath the pillar. The decorative advantage of adding the pillar, which visually balances the temple architecture in the scene below, clearly took precedence over any perspective realism.

Conrad's interest in geometry, discussed in the previous chapter, provides a secure base for the centralized design of the *Crucifixion* at Niederwildungen which is constructed in a pyramid with crossing diagonals. The orthogonals created by the obliquely placed crosses of the thieves meet at the central point of the shafts of Christ's cross, which coincides with the vertical bisection of the composition (pls. 132, 137). The diagonals from the thieves' forward arms converge at the base of the cross. The multitude of onlookers is divided into narrative groups that form coherent areas of colour, symmetrically balancing each other on either side of the cross. The wealth of realistic detail (flowers, dogs, tools etc.) is subordinate to the strong figure grouping. This tight organization avoids the confusion of the crowded Calvaries that follow Conrad's in Westphalia. The *Adoration of the Kings* in the Dortmund Altarpiece is built on the same centralized principle.

22. Conrad von Soest: *Adoration* and *Presentation*. Niederwildungen Altarpiece

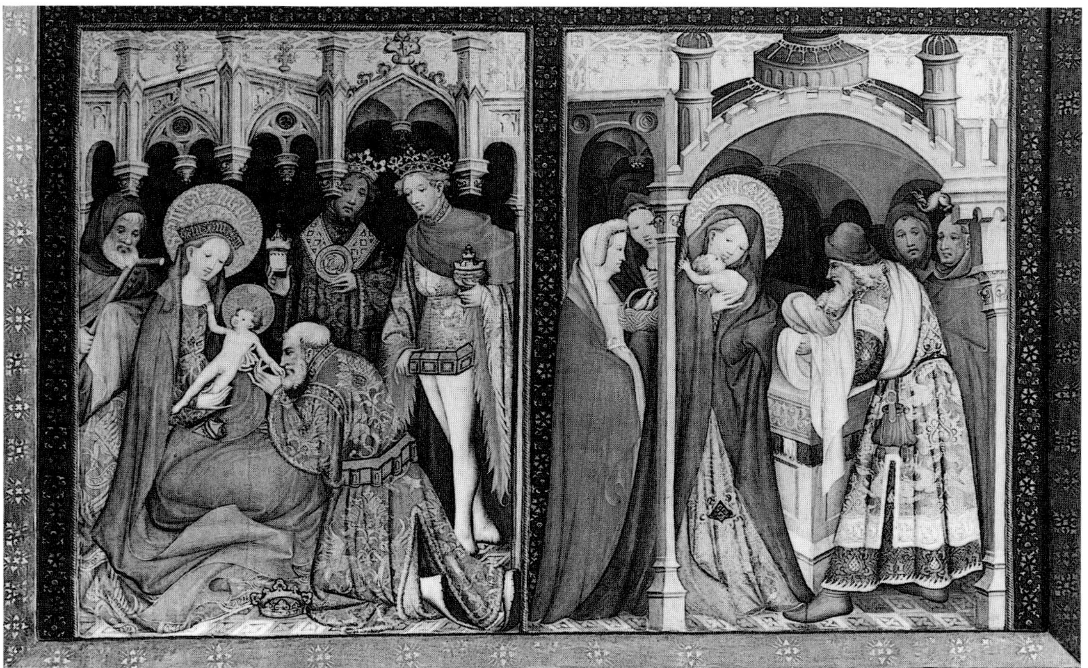

In Conrad's work, light has a narrative and a decorative purpose but it does not derive logically from a consistent light source, nor does it register reflection from nearby objects. In architectural settings, especially in the *Adoration of the Kings*, *Presentation* and *Christ mocked before Herod* at Niederwildungen and in the *Annunciation* at Dortmund, the illusion of a unified space is partially achieved through a deep, atmospheric shadow in the recess of the room (pls. VII, VI, XIII, XXVII). This enveloping shade affects the colouring of figures and garments according to their position within this space. In the Niederwildungen *Adoration of the Kings*, for instance, the diagonal position of the young king causes the right sleeve of his otherwise light blue tunic to take shade from the room. The king in the background is enveloped by the room shade, and his dark green robe and browned face confirm his position in the pictorial space. This 'perspective' of light and shade appears to derive from Italian prototypes. It was known in the Parement and Hesdin workshops but not in Westphalia.[14] Colour is also used by Conrad von Soest to indicate recession in more open settings, using a painterly perspective of dulling colours for which the opaque red of Joseph's cloak behind the bright red bedspread in the Dortmund *Nativity* is an obvious example (pl. XXI). In the *Crucifixion* (pl. XIV), the onlooker shading his eye is placed nearest the edge of a dark wood. His garment, deep pink on the shoulder facing forwards, becomes quite grey in the deepest recession. In contrast to Conrad's methods, certain Parisian workshops began early experiments with aerial perspective. However, aerial perspective around 1400 did not convey the sense of realism achieved by the later Netherlandish panel painters. Although Jacquemart de Hesdin, for instance, introduced a blue sky behind an extended landscape (*Flight into Egypt*, Brussels, Bibl. Royale, MS 11060–61, p. 106, *c.* 1385–90? before 1402), the sky had no luminosity. Even in landscapes by the Boucicaut Master (*Adoration of the Magi*, Paris, Musée Jacquemart-André, MS 2, fol. 83v, *c.* 1399–1411), the impact of aerial perspective, created through radiant atmospheric haze, is reduced by a surface pattern of metallic gold stars.[15] If Conrad von Soest knew about aerial perspective it does not show in his work, for his interest in the decorative effect of colour and line on the picture's surface predominated.

On the other hand, Conrad von Soest used colour and light for narrative purposes to great effect. In the *Crucifixion* of the Niederwildungen Altarpiece, the light which so strongly illuminates St John's mantle as he is seated under the cross emanates from Christ, thereby strengthening the link created by the apostle's upward gesture and gaze.[16] The large pool of lemon yellow draws the eye of the beholder to this central event: the love of Christ for this apostle and thereby for mankind, the very reason for this crucifixion (John 3:16). Again, in the *Last Judgement*, the warm red of Christ's red cloak is echoed in the collar, right sleeve and patch of lining of the Baptist's mauve and yellow garment; it is also echoed in the small areas visible of the Virgin's red dress (pl. XVIII). This triangular emotional link, expressed in colour, is pictorially stabilized by patches of the red colour in the heavenly corners occupied by the Evangelist and the angels. A similar triangle of red colour links the Virgin and two kneeling kings in the Dortmund *Adoration of the Kings* in an emotionally charged relationship, stressed by the near horizontal pose of the child that is tenderly touched by all three protagonists (pl. XXV).

The source of light is not always supernatural, as in the Niederwildungen *Crucifixion* scene; it can be natural. In the *Death of the Virgin* of the Dortmund Altarpiece, the flame of the candle illuminates St John's blond curls (pl. XXII). This candlelight has a further, narrative role as it gently touches the Virgin's forehead also and thus poignantly stresses the emotional link between the two protagonists. Conrad von Soest is a lively and impressive storyteller, employing motifs like the exhausted sleeping Peter in the *Gethsemane* scene; the apostle peering shortsight-edly through his glasses in the *Pentecost* panel [here Conrad takes note of the impurity of the glass which causes him to darken the area around the apostle's eyes beneath the spectacles]; and the apostle opposite him so absorbed in reading that he is tugging at his beard (pls. XI, XVII, XIX). One may also notice the intimate and troubled conversation between the two soldiers in the scene before Pilate in the Niederwildungen Altarpiece, or the impatient young king tapping the Virgin's shoulder in the *Adoration of the Kings* in Dortmund (pl. XXV). The tender descrip-tion of the angels ministering to the dead Virgin in the *Death of the Virgin* at Dortmund epitomizes the painter's sensitive narrative skill (pl. XXII).

The two altarpieces signed by Conrad von Soest were painted with an interval of around twenty years, yet they display remarkable stylistic consistency. The most striking difference between the Niederwildungen and Dortmund Altarpieces is the increased monumentality of the figure style at Dortmund. A smaller number of figures dominate the single scenes of each panel. The figures at Dortmund are nearly double the size of those in Niederwildungen. However, actual size is not the only reason for the appearance of greater monumentality. The figures, although in type and style reminiscent of those at Niederwildungen, are now depicted with proportionately larger heads, with more rounded shoulders and with more plastic modelling. Their almost sculptural quality is softened by painterly hues. A more sensitive awareness of the effect of light and shade assists in a subtle modelling of forms.

It is instructive to compare the image of the Virgin depicted in a frontal pose both in the Niederwildungen *Pentecost* (pl. XVII) and the Dortmund *Adoration of the Kings* (pl. XXV). In each case the Virgin is shown seated, wrapped in a blue mantle that shows a green lining. The Virgin is definitely the same creature, but in Dortmund she seems to have filled out and matured. The elongated form is accentuated at Niederwildungen by the vertical folds of her mantle over the sloping shoulders. These vertical lines are interrupted by horizontal folds in her lap, but then allowed to continue (softened) from her knees. The noble fragility of the Virgin is underlined by the even light on her stylized hands and gentle face. The green lining of her hood frames the upright head evenly and emphasizes her quiet grace. At Dortmund the more rounded features of the Virgin are gently moulded in light

54

and shade. Her inclined head breaks the strict frontality of the pose, and the green hood is allowed to frame the head more naturally. The elongation of her figure persists, but it is balanced by exposing her rounded neck and shoulder. The vertical line created by the edge of her mantle in the upper part of her body is contrasted by a natural fall of decorative folds which softly spread from her knee. The elongation of the graceful form is mitigated by the effect of a patch of green lining turned up over her foot and visually balancing her hood. The very material of the Virgin's cloak appears to have gained considerably in weight in Dortmund and therefore enhances the effect of monumentality. Yet Conrad maintains a surface pattern of echoing and contrasting drapery lines across the panel.

In Dortmund, the use of colour to define the position of forms in space also persists, but as the plasticity of forms is increased, the architectural settings are abandoned altogether (the sole exception is the *Annunciation* on the outside of the wings, which is set in a more complex interior). A single item of furniture suffices in each Dortmund panel to set the stage, and narrative detail is pared down to essential items. The figures alone now carry the story with greater conviction, unaided by the wealth of potentially distracting realistic detail which fills the panels of the Niederwildungen Altarpiece. Decorative surface patterns created by sinuous line and colour persist, as does the gold ground. The tension between surface-stressing lines and colour and the increased realism and monumentality of the figures, serves to illuminate the narrative content with clarity and intensity.

Conrad's altarpieces are in tune with the technical and stylistic developments of major international workshops of his time, but they remain distinctive. The courtly elegance of his principal figures combined with selective naturalistic descriptions, the sensitive use of colour and light, the perceptive narrative and the conspicuous expenditure would have amply satisfied the expectations of Conrad's sophisticated patrons.

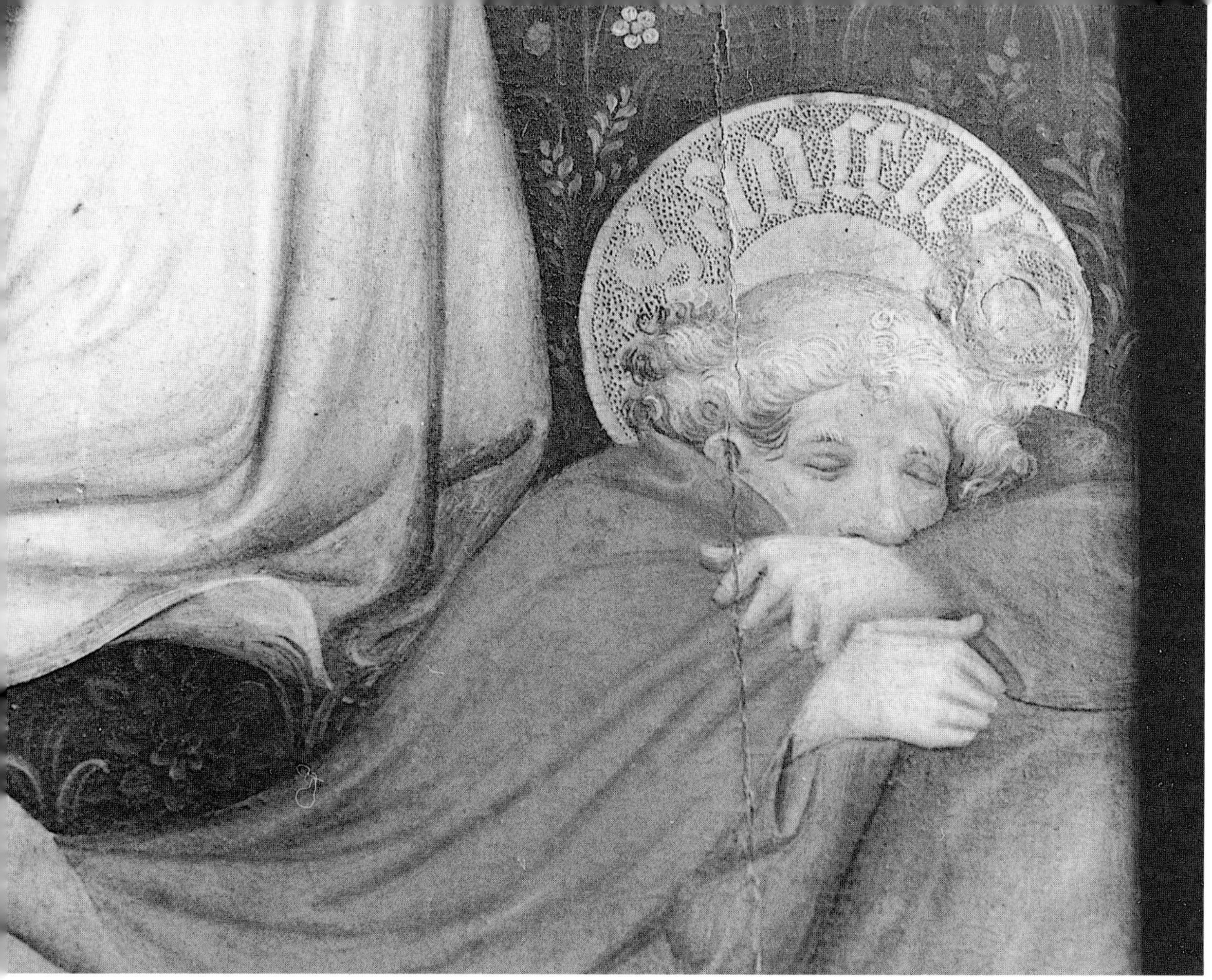

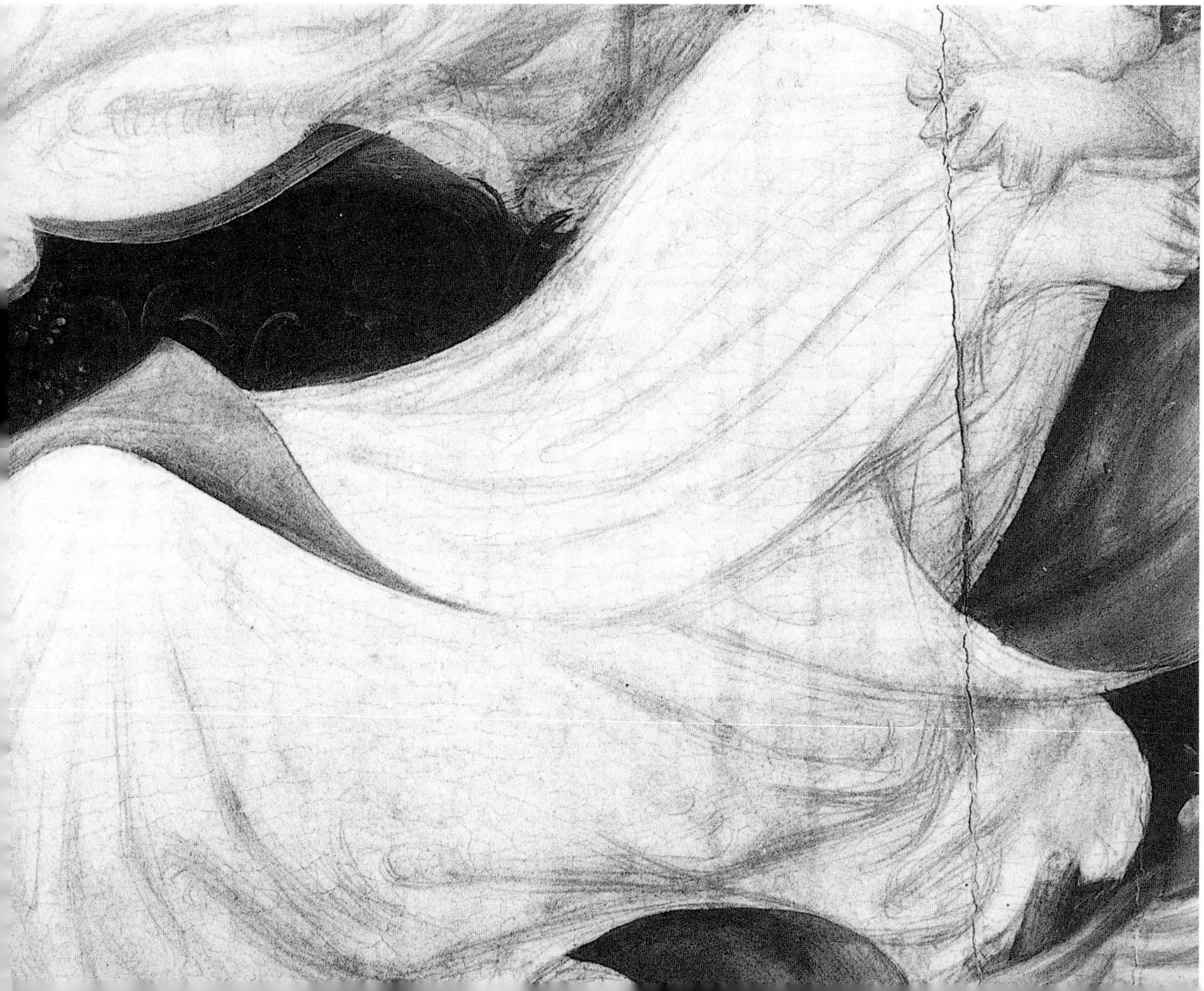

5. Autograph Works
and Workshop Connections

MANY SURVIVING fifteenth-century panels in Westphalia have been empirically attributed to Conrad von Soest or to his direct influence.[1] The attribution and re-attribution of works to Conrad or his followers has been the primary focus of scholars in this field. Considerations, both parochial and ethical, have had roles to play in such disputes, which have been concerned with stylistic comparisons of a general nature and with such notions as the existence of regional physiognomical and psychological characteristics.[2] However, no systematic study of Conrad's work has yet been undertaken, and technical characteristics of the paintings have rarely been taken into account. On stylistic grounds, the many direct attributions to the artist have eventually been reduced to eight works, namely the *Niederwildungen Altarpiece* (cat. no. 1), the *Dortmund Altarpiece* (cat. no. 2), the *St Nicholas Panel* in Soest (cat. no. 7), two panels in Münster, showing *St Dorothea* and *St Odilia* (cat. no. 3), the panel in Munich, depicting *St Paul* (cat. no. 4), the *Trinity* panel in Cologne (Wallraf-Richartz Museum— WRM Depos. 363 pl. 109), and the panel in the Kisters Collection, Kreuzlingen, showing the *Arrest* and *Christ before Pilate* (p. 25).[3] The Kisters panel has now been plausibly attributed to another workshop[4] When discussing the influence of Conrad's style, it has lately become fashionable to deny him any notable followers. Remarkable stylistic and technical coincidences between the work of Conrad von Soest and that of his followers have simply been declared a manifestation of *Zeitgeist*.[5]

Technical developments have now provided scholars with more scientific methods of evaluating the authorship of paintings. Examination by infra-red photography or reflectography permits the study of underdrawings and thus reveals the hand of the designer.[6] A systematic comparison of style, surface characteristics and underdrawing method results in a more plausible attribution of panels. This method is particularly suitable for fifteenth and sixteenth-century Northern panel paintings, as underdrawing is a consistent feature in their production. Underdrawing can be detected with infra-red photography or reflectography as long as it has been executed with a substance containing black pigment (that is bone black or carbon black). Infra-red photography and reflectography are alternative methods. If present, underdrawing can be detected by infra-red photography beneath red, white, yellow, brown (when not mixed with carbon or bone black pigments), and ultramarine or indigo blue areas, provided the thickness of paint layers does not obscure the drawing or affect its legibility. Blue azurite and green malachite look quite black in infra-red photographs, whilst gold and silver

23–24. *St Peter sleeping*. Detail from *Gethsemane* and infra-red photograph. Niederwildungen Altarpiece

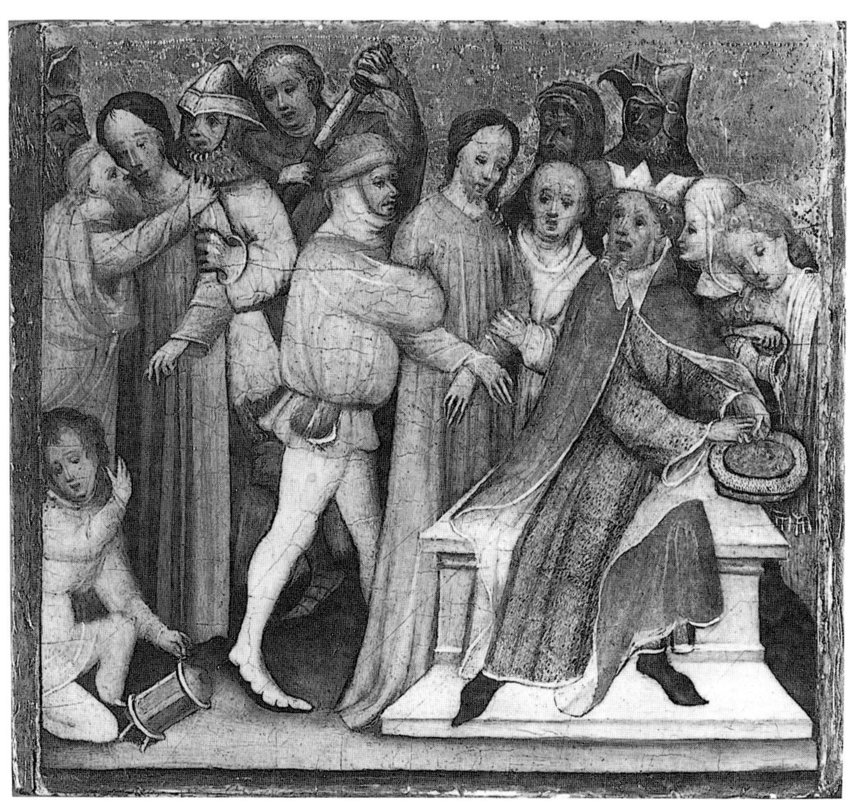

25. *The Arrest of Christ
and Christ before Pilate.*
Sammlung Heinz Kisters

leaf are opaque to infra-red radiation and cannot be penetrated. A more detailed image can be produced by reflectography, which allows the detection of underdrawing in most cases also beneath azurite and malachite and achieves better elimination of overlying paint layers than infra-red photography.[7] For work outside a studio, in churches and museums, only infra-red photography was practicable for my examination of works attributed to Conrad von Soest.[8]

Some problems arise in the interpretation of infra-red photographs. It can be difficult to distinguish between a dark line on the surface or within the paint layers and one in the underdrawing. Furthermore, the thickness of a line cannot always be determined, as overlaying layers of paint can affect its visibility and the strength of tone of the drawing, and thickness of paint can modify legibility or obscure the drawing altogether. However, apparent absence of drawing is not conclusive, as certain pigments used for drawing designs do not contain black and, as mentioned, some colours can conceal the underdrawing. Despite these difficulties, an examination of Netherlandish panel paintings by van Asperen de Boer and his team, who pioneered this use of infra-red photography and reflectography, confirmed that 'major differences in underdrawing style can be observed between one painter and another'.

Infra-red photography has proved a very useful tool in attempting to understand the work of a particular artist. This has recently been demonstrated in a study of certain panels and drawings by Gerard David.[9] Although the work of this late fifteenth-century Netherlandish painter (born in Bruges 1484, died 1523) differs in

58

style and technique from Conrad's early fifteenth-century painting, the method employed in the study is of interest. Having established the autograph style of Gerard David's underdrawing in a representative, if not comprehensive, number of the undisputed works by the artist, more doubtful attributions were examined. Two paintings in the National Gallery in London, the *Adoration of the Kings* and the *Lamentation*, were chosen as they have been considered by certain authors to be part of a single altarpiece by David. However, there is a difference in that the *Lamentation* has a relatively wooden surface appearance. This has caused some authors to contest the attribution, while others have blamed the differing state of preservation for this discrepancy. In the event, the examination of the underdrawing provided 'compelling evidence' that the *Lamentation* is a workshop production, whilst the *Adoration of the Kings* clearly shows the master's hand. In the *Adoration of the Kings*, the rough preliminary sketch in black chalk with detailed rendering in brush of the draperies, and the undermodelling of shadow areas with brushwork is consistent with David's proven method. In contrast to this, the tentative and weak brush underdrawing in the *Lamentation* barely describes the forms. The schematic rendering suggests a 'summary and lifeless recording by a workshop assistant' who copied an established model onto the panel. Having ascertained differing authorship for the two London panels, the validity of this method of examination was studied by investigating a third, substantially restored panel with frequently contested attribution to David, the *Head of Christ* in the Philadelphia Museum of Art. The underdrawing of the head and hands was seen to be characteristic of David's style as consistently observed in other, uncontested works. Consequently the panel was firmly attributed to Gerard David.[10]

In view of the consistency of Conrad's drawing style in his two signed retables, the Niederwildungen Altarpiece of 1403 and the Dortmund Altarpiece of around 1420, a similar method of investigation can be employed when attempting to identify Conrad's *oeuvre*. Conrad von Soest's work is ideally suited for an examination by infra-red photography as his underdrawing pigment contains black, and his drawings are clearly visible. His tempera technique allows a good 'transparency' of the intervening paint layers. Tonal shading in his colours and little use of black pigments permits a clear distinction between underdrawing and surface paint in most areas. Only gold leaf, foil under brocade patterns, some greens, and black-based browns and greys conceal the underdrawing. Since relatively few of Conrad's figures are dressed in brocades or green garments, most of his design is revealed. All the blue areas show underdrawing clearly, and must therefore be painted with ultramarine or (less likely) indigo pigment. The pigment is in fact ultramarine (see pp. 41). The faces of the major protagonists cannot be penetrated by infra-red photography, and this may suggest that Conrad used certain green pigments for the underpainting of their features. In contrast, the faces of bucolic creatures, including those of the thieves in the Niederwildungen *Crucifixion*, reveal detailed design drawing under brownish pigments.

All the panels of the Niederwildungen Altarpiece are designed in the same vigorous underdrawing style. It is characterized by parallel hatching strokes indicating shape and form (pls. 24, 29–32). Sometimes strokes and curves seem to search for form; once found, the desired line is marked strongly and alterations are rarely needed. These confident and rapid strokes define poses and establish the fall of drapery folds with equal clarity. Narrow, precise lines suggest the use of a pointed instrument for drawing. Outlines are marked strongly in places with a thicker, darker line, and at times by incision. The forceful hatchings of long straight and curved lines show the complete design in every detail. In the *Crucifixion* of the Niederwildungen Altarpiece, for example, even the fall of light and shade on the thief's body is indicated and the marking in the wood of his cross are fully described (pl. 26, 27). Shaded areas are delineated with narrowly spaced hatchings, that almost run into each other in the darkest regions. Cross-hatching is rare, but occurs in the areas of deepest shade, for instance in the mantle of the Virgin in the *Adoration of the Kings* (pl. 28), in the drapery near the foot of St Peter in the *Ascension* (pl. 29), and in the folds of Maria Jacobi's garment in the *Crucifixion* (pl. 31). One or two parallel strokes, crossed by a few curved cross-hatching strokes, suffice to indicate the position of highlights that were to be painted in a different colour. Such markings can be observed, for example, in the drapery of St Paul in the *Ascension* (pl. 29), and of St John in the *Crucifixion* (pl. 32).

26–27. *Thief* and infra-red photograph of the underdrawing. Details from the *Crucifixion*. Niederwildungen Altarpiece

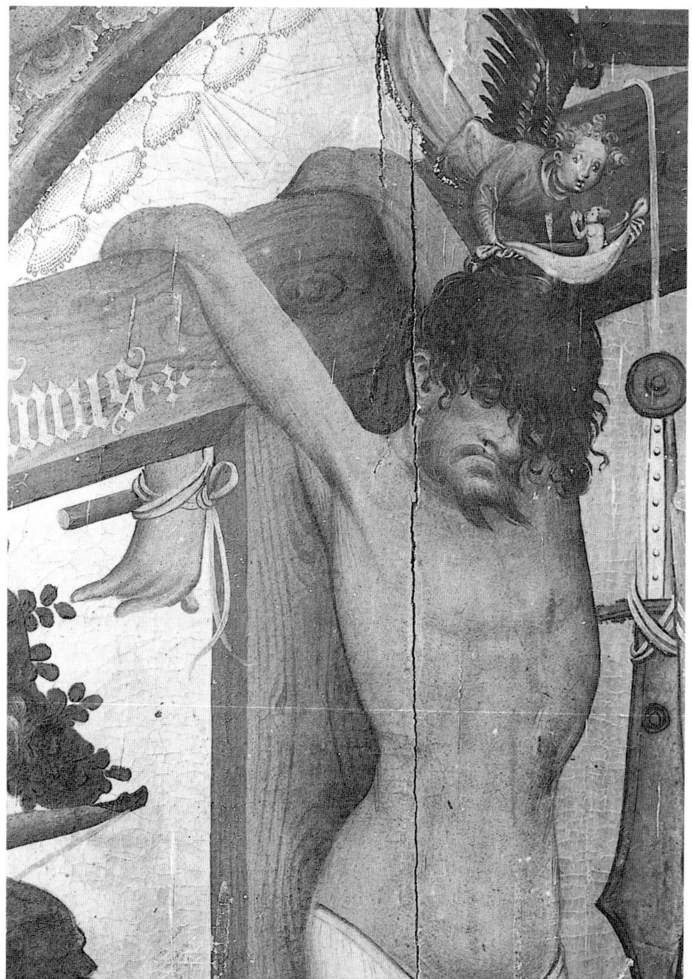
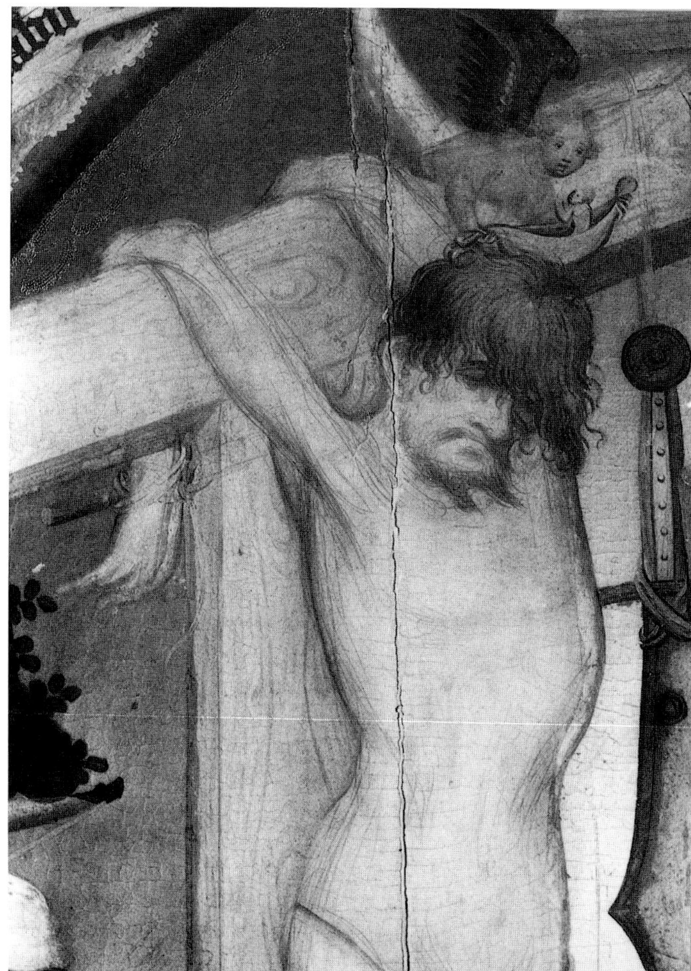

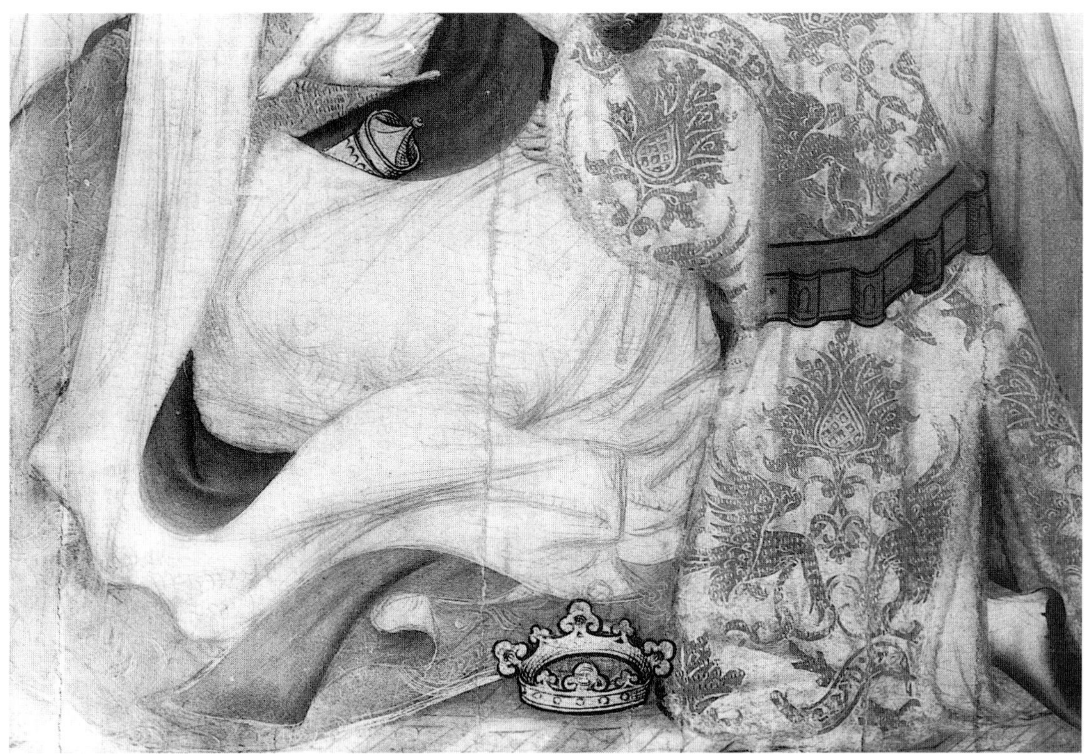

28. *Underdrawing of the cloak of the Virgin*. Infra-red photograph. Detail from the *Adoration of the Kings*. Niederwildungen Altarpiece

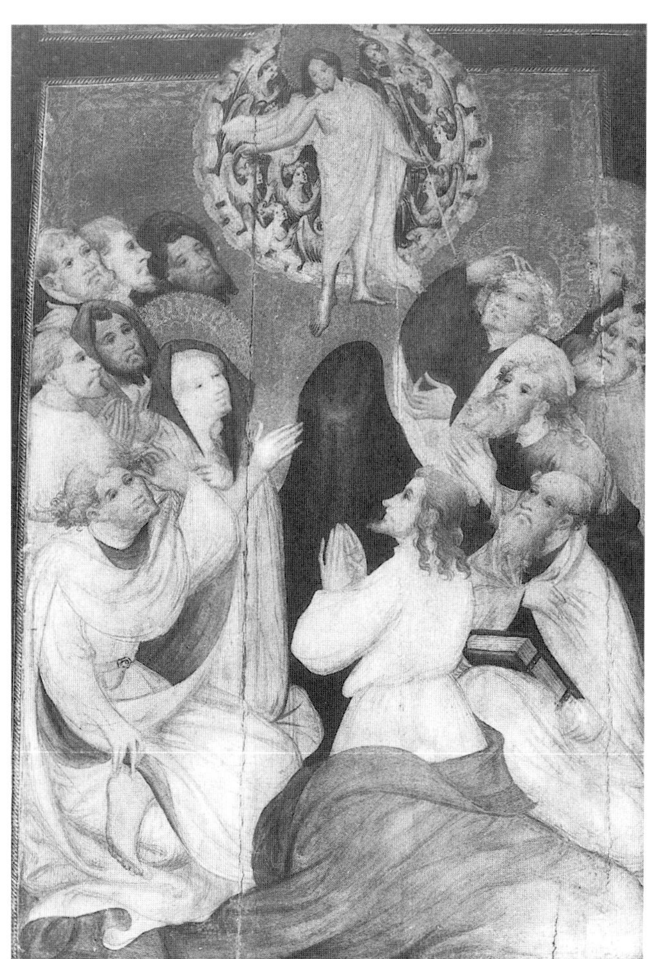

29. *Underdrawing of the Ascension.* Infra-red photograph. Niederwildungen Altarpiece

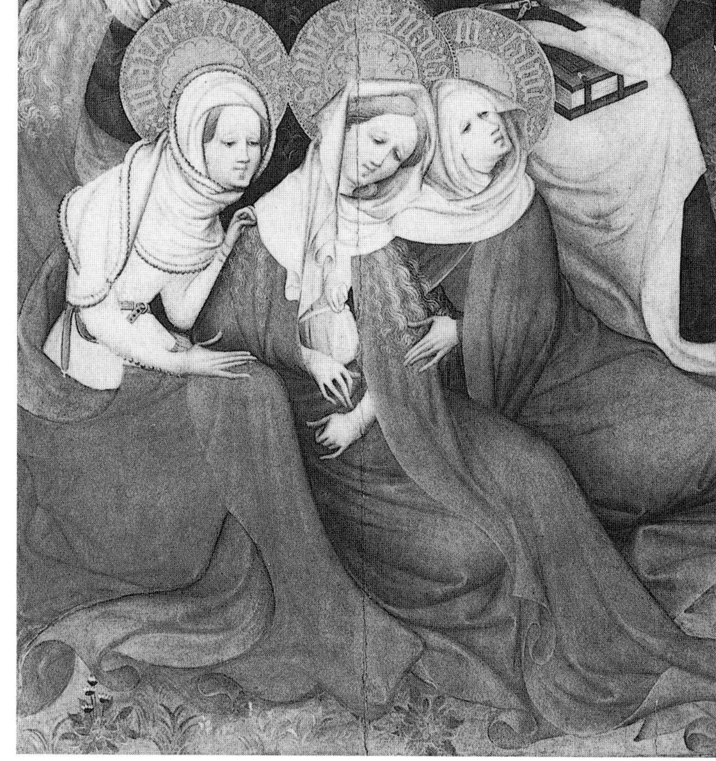

30. *The Women at the Cross*. Detail from the *Crucifixion*.
Niederwildungen Altarpiece

31. *Underdrawing of Maria Jacobi.*
Infra-red photograph. Detail of pl. 30.
Niederwildungen Altarpiece

32. *Underdrawing of the Women at the Cross.*
Infra-red photograph. Detail of pl. 30.
Niederwildungen Altarpiece

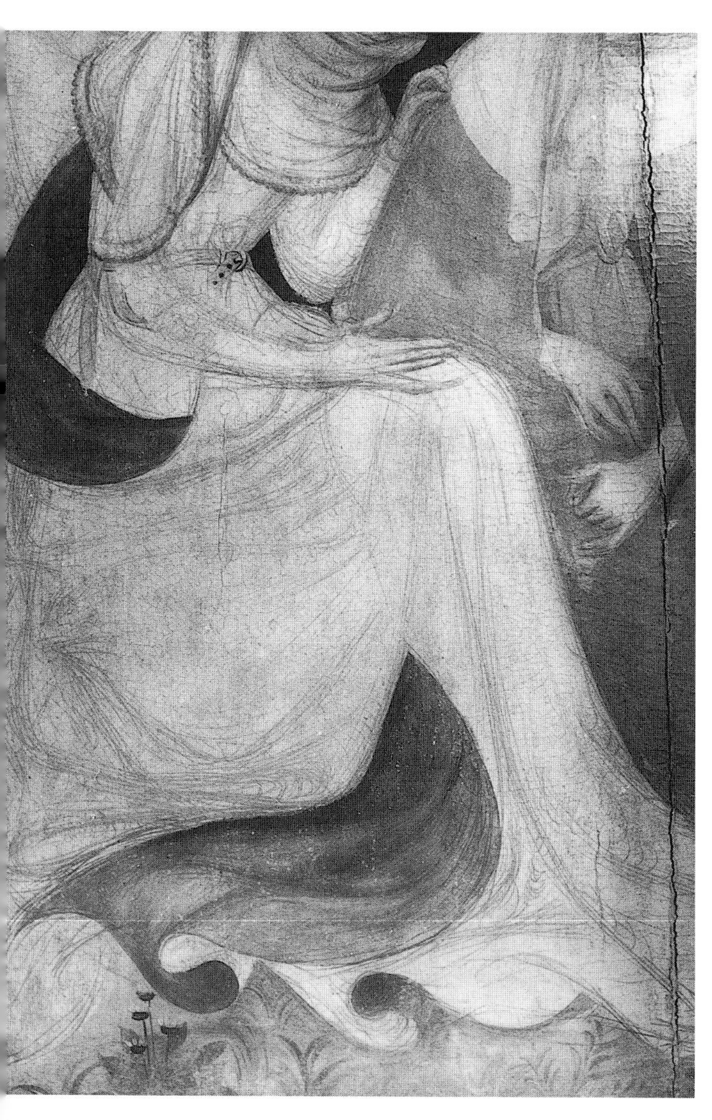

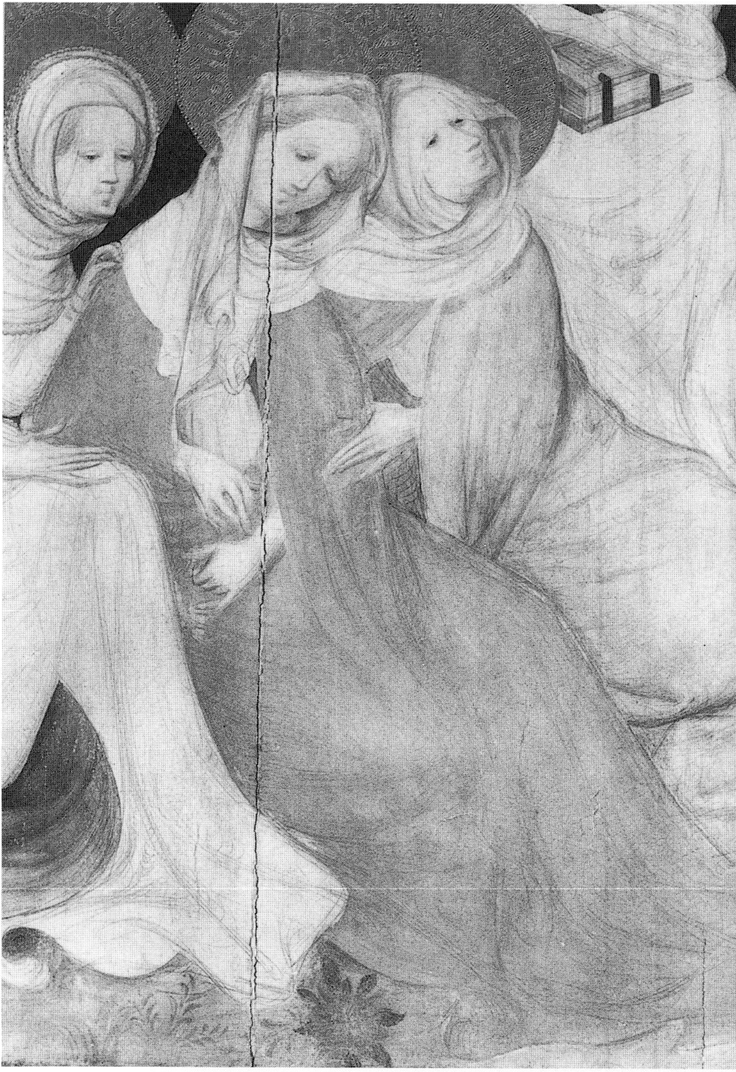

Similar parallel hatching lines and curved cross-hatching for shadowed areas appear in underdrawings from the Campin/Flémalle group, for example in the sleeve of the angel from the Mérode Altarpiece and in the robe of the Frankfurt *Madonna and Child*.[11] Although shorter than the hatching lines detected in Conrad's underdrawing, Campin's drawing lines do not lack vigour.[12] This related designing style is also noticeable in drawings by Rogier van der Weyden, who worked for a time in the Campin workshop, for instance in the sketch of a young man in Berlin (Inv. No. 1372).[13] The drawing shows vigorous parallel strokes in the sleeve with firm cross-hatching for shaded areas of folds, varying in intensity apparently according to the depth of the fold. A fine line with gentle and wider spaced cross-hatching denotes the area which was to be highlighted. In fact, allowing for the differences of personal drawing style and the greater realism of the human form, van der Weyden's drawing method is still close to that employed by Conrad von Soest: parallel hatching strokes are used to indicate shape and form, and outlines are marked strongly in places (here particularly in the curve of the sleeve).

When considering the possible sources of Conrad's underdrawing style, it was unfortunately not possible to photograph the underdrawings of illuminations from the Parement workshop, in which Conrad appears to have worked as a journeyman (see pp. 133–141). However, a study of the underdrawing in the *Heures de Milan* (or *Turin Hours*, Turin, Museo Civico) sheds some light on the Parement Master's underdrawing practice.[14] The *Nativity*, fol. 4v of the manuscript, is thought to belong to the first production campaign under the patronage of the duc de Berry, and is plausibly ascribed to the Parement Master. The authors characterize the Master's underdrawing style as 'energetically curving', with 'parallel hatching lines in the shadows of folds and loops or hooks at the ends of folds'. This underdrawing style was consistent throughout illuminations of the manuscript, attributed to the Parement Master and his workshop. No cross-hatching was observed, and in view of the obvious differences in designing styles it may be deduced that the Parement workshop did not influence Conrad von Soest in respect of his underdrawing method. The altarpieces from Netze (Pfarrkirche) and Osnabrück (Cologne, WRM 350–52), might have yielded some valuable additional information about earlier Westphalian underdrawing practice, but they were not available for infra-red photography. However, their stiff surface forms are unlikely to have been created by vigorous design drawing in the Conradian manner.

Conrad's creative drawing style and his full drapery studies, boldly executed, give the impression that he designed straight onto the prepared panel—a frequent practice among fifteenth-century artists in the Netherlands; such detailed design drawings may have served for the review of patrons.[15] Although *pentimenti* are rare, a small number of modifications appear in the underdrawing. In Niederwildungen, for instance, the Virgin's left hand and Christ's feet in the *Crucifixion*, Joseph's right foot in the *Nativity*, and the feet of the figure on the extreme left in the *Pilate* scene have been modified; and on the reverse side of the panels, the position of St

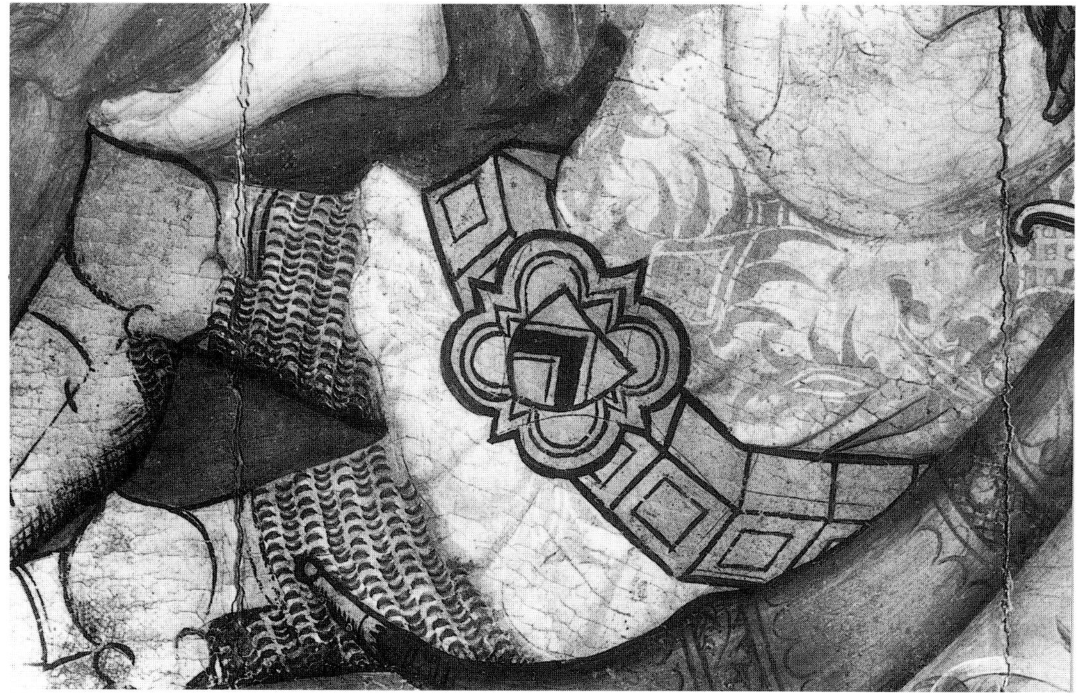

33. *Underdrawing of a Soldier*. Infra-red photograph. Detail from the *Resurrection*. Niederwildungen Altarpiece

Nicholas's right thumb has been reconsidered. The infra-red photographs of the Niederwildungen Altarpiece also confirm overpainting by a later hand in certain areas. In the *Last Supper*, the apostle next to St Paul sports a rather crude beard; close examination reveals that he used to be seen drinking from a glass. The circle of angels in the *Ascension* has cross-hatchings and contours by a different hand. Clumsy black lines have been added in several places over original ones around the edges of gold ornaments. Old and new lines are clearly visible, for example, on the armour and golden belt of the soldier in the *Resurrection* (pl. 33).

Examination of the surface of the Niederwildungen Altarpiece reveals a rapid application technique of thin layers of translucent paint in a great variety of colours; the colouring is characterized by the minute attention to tonal nuances. Conrad's brush appears to have been frequently loaded with two or more colours (see p. 39). Brushstrokes are almost invisible, except in highlights; these are executed with a fine brush in rapid strokes, looped at the end. Examination with an eye-glass suggests a consistency of these brushstrokes that may point to a single painter for the whole altarpiece.

The Dortmund Altarpiece has a greater monumentality and realism, but this did not cause any modification in Conrad's production methods. At Dortmund, lively parallel hatching strokes with occasional cross-hatching still create the design beneath the painterly surface (pl. 35). In the *Death of the Virgin*, for example, the deep fold by the (damaged) right foot of the reading apostle is marked by the

64

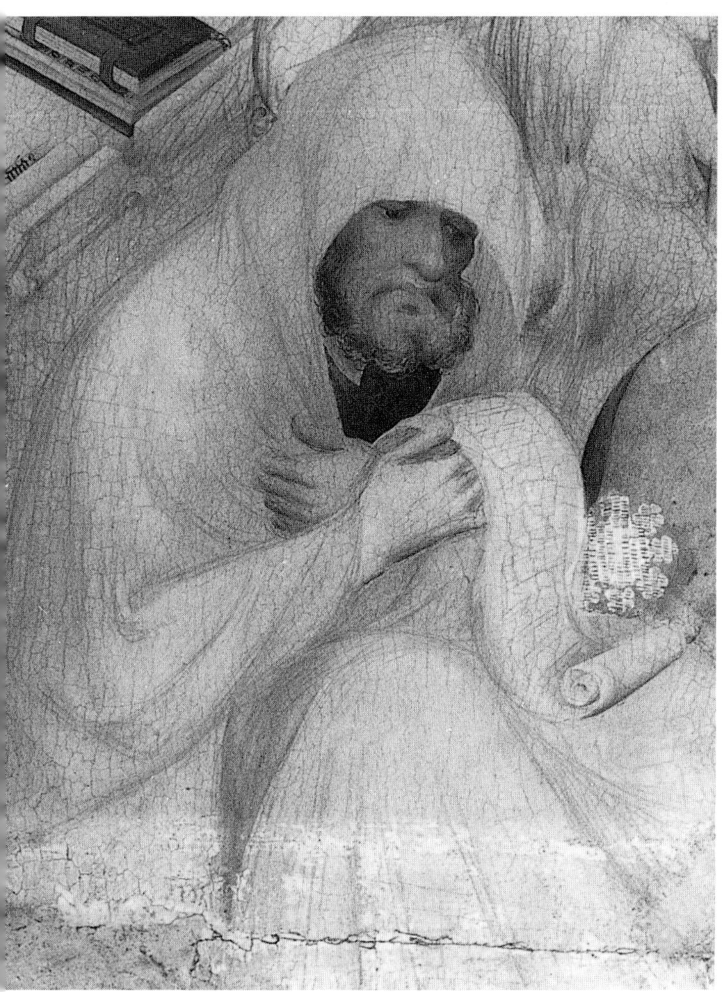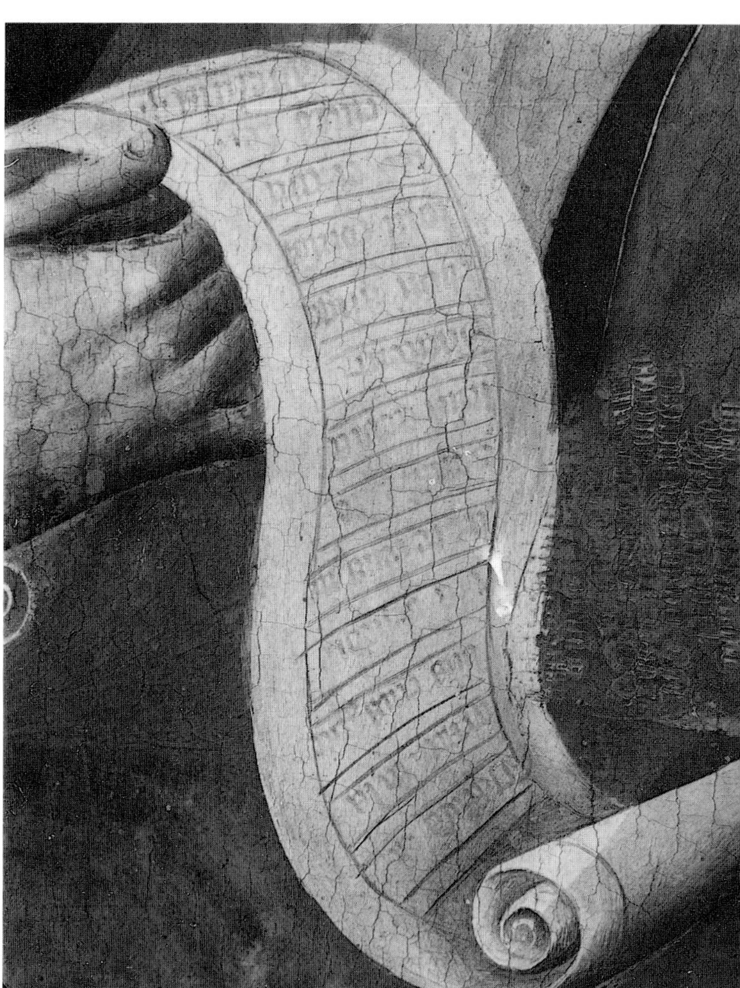

34a, b. *Underdrawing of the Reading Apostle*, and *underdrawing of the scroll*. Infra-red photographs. Details from the *Death of the Virgin*. Dortmund Altarpiece

vigorous cross-hatching noted for shaded areas; and the intended highlight in the red collar of the king kissing the child's hand in the *Adoration of the Kings* is indicated by the single crossed line method. Only two *pentimenti* have been found in the underdrawing of the Dortmund Altarpiece: one in the *Death of the Virgin* (where the position of the left hand of St John has been reconsidered), and one in the *Annunciation* (where the thumb of the angel has been modified). The text on the scroll of the apostle in the *Death of the Virgin*, lost from the surface layers, can be read in the underdrawing (pl. 34).[16] The gold ground, the brocades and the blue, green-lined cloak (overpainted by a later hand) of the Virgin in the *Adoration of the Kings* cannot be penetrated by infra-red photography. Overpainting also obscures the design drawing in the semicircle of angels and in the hood of the hand-kissing king in the *Adoration of the Kings*, in the censer in the *Death of the Virgin*, and in the belt and drapery folds of Joseph in the *Nativity*. Of Joseph's robe, only the sleeves and the lower part show the original tonal shading, and it is in these areas that the underdrawing can be revealed.

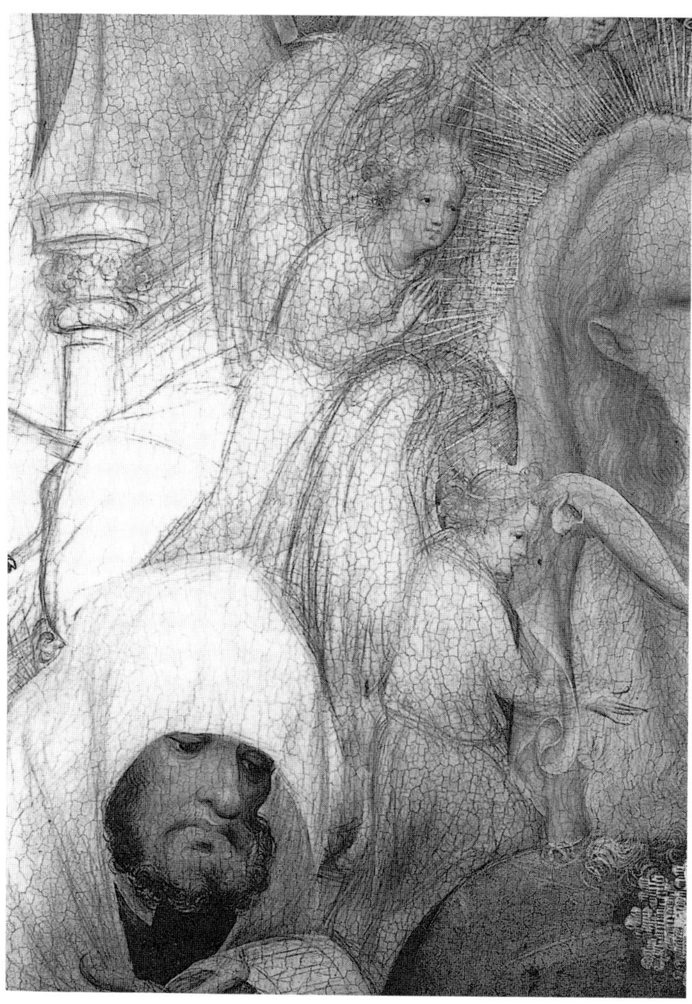

35. *Underdrawing of Angels.*
Infra-red photograph.
Detail from the *Death of the Virgin.*
Dortmund Altarpiece

Despite the numerous attributions of paintings to Conrad von Soest, the characteristics of his drawing and painting styles were only found in one other work: the small tabernacle doors in Münster, depicting St Dorothea and St Odilia (pls. 36, 150, 151, XXIX, XXX; cat. no. 3). In the infra-red photographs, azurite and malachite pigments in the garments and gold leaf underlay in the brocaded robes of the saints obscure parts of the underdrawing. However, the underdrawing for the cloak of St Dorothea can be clearly read. The characteristic application of multiple parallel hatching lines in the search for form, and the closely knit hatching strokes in shaded areas of the cloak here are similar to those noted, for instance, in the garments of the women under the cross in the Niederwildungen *Crucifixion* (pls. 31,32) and in the robe of the reading apostle in the Dortmund *Death of the Virgin.* Cross-hatching can be found in the shadowed area near the left foot of the saint. Three widely spaced cross-hatching strokes indicate the area beneath the loop of azurite cloak-lining, and at the apex of the triangle of brocade, that was to be highlighted. The design is drawn in precise lines with a pointed instrument similar to that employed

66

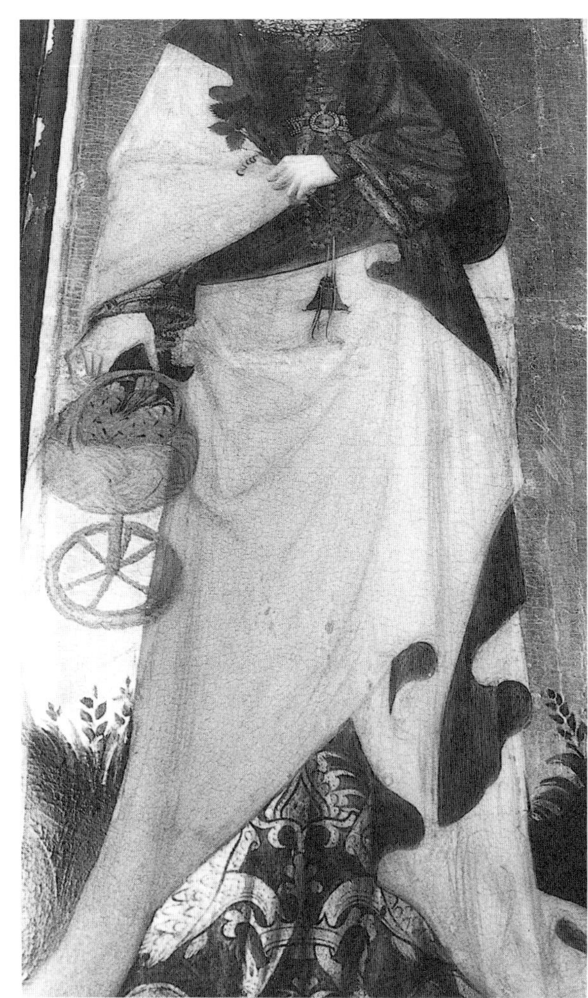

36. *Underdrawing of the robe of St Dorothea.*
Infra-red photograph.
Detail of *St Dorothea*

in Conrad's autograph works. Modifications are not apparent in the revealed parts of the underdrawing.

The surface appearance of the panels also corresponds with that observed in the Niederwildungen and Dortmund altarpieces. The painting technique and style, the translucency and subtlety of colour, the highlight strokes with looped ends, the halo inscriptions and the cloud punchmarks all correspond with those observed in Conrad von Soest's signed altarpieces. It can therefore be concluded that these panels were designed and painted by Conrad himself. On stylistic grounds they should be dated after the Niederwildungen Altarpiece. Although St Dorothea closely reflects the Niederwildungen St Catherine, a tendency towards greater monumentality of the figures, expressed in the Münster panels through the depiction of more voluminous, looser fitting garments and a more prominent position of the figures in space, points towards the achievements of the Dortmund Altarpiece. A date between those of the two signed retables, around 1410, therefore seems plausible.

Infra-red examination of another attributed work, the small damaged panel in Munich, depicting St Paul, with Reinold on the reverse side (pls. 152, 153, XXXI, XXXII; cat no. 4), remained inconclusive, as only a tiny trace of possible underdrawing was revealed near St Paul's sword.[17] Although this apparent lack of underdrawing seems to exclude Conrad as the designer, it is possible that the pigment used for drawing did not contain black, or that a foil underlay or colours conceal the underdrawing. Only the St Paul side could be seen in the museum and even then a close examination of surface characteristics proved difficult. The painting of Reinold had to be studied from colour slides. The problems of assessing attribution to Conrad von Soest posed by areas of apparent overpainting and by paint losses are discussed in the catalogue section. Although the painting style resembles that of Conrad von Soest, the paint does not appear to be applied in translucent glazes. Such glazes are a feature of Conrad's autograph work, even in the small Saints panels in Münster. Any possible connection of the Munich panel to Conrad or his workshop can only be determined when the panel can be studied under more favourable conditions.

In all the other panels ascribed to Conrad von Soest, examination by infra-red photography revealed a variety of underdrawing styles, all clearly different from that of Conrad's autograph works. Of these, the altarpieces closest in surface appearance to those signed by Conrad are the Fröndenberg Altarpiece (pl. 154; cat. no. 5) in the Stiftskirche there and the St Nicholas Panel (pl. 155; cat. no. 7) in Soest. The examination of the Fröndenberg Altarpiece proved more problematic as it was clearly produced by at least two painters in workshop collaboration. Furthermore, the infra-red photographs were difficult to read in parts, due to the considerable use of black-based browns, greens (including facial underpainting), greys and azurite pigments. However, black surface lines on silhouettes and folds showed up in a different density from the underdrawing and could be clearly distinguished; some seem to have been added by restorers to clarify poses where top paint layers or original outlines were missing. Some silhouettes and Mary's drapery in the *Presentation of the Virgin*, the angel in the *Annunciation* and the kings in the *Adoration of the Kings* are particularly affected.

The underdrawing style is inconsistent, which suggests that at least two hands using different methods were involved. The first hand is closest to that of Conrad von Soest in style, but lacks vigour and elaboration. Long, usually single hatching strokes outline the design and indicate form; they rarely run parallel and then do not come close to each other in the most shaded parts. These lines are wider than in Conrad's designs and may indicate the use of a blunter instrument. Thick dark lines, often single, serve to indicate folds, and cross-hatching does not occur. This drawing style can be found in the *Visitation* (pl. 37) and in the *Presentation in the Temple* (pl. 44). It is also revealed in the *Madonna and Child* panel (pls. 38, 39, XXXIII; cat. no. 6) in the Dortmund museum, which has hitherto been considered to be the central part of the Fröndenberg Altarpiece. The underdrawing seems more sketchy

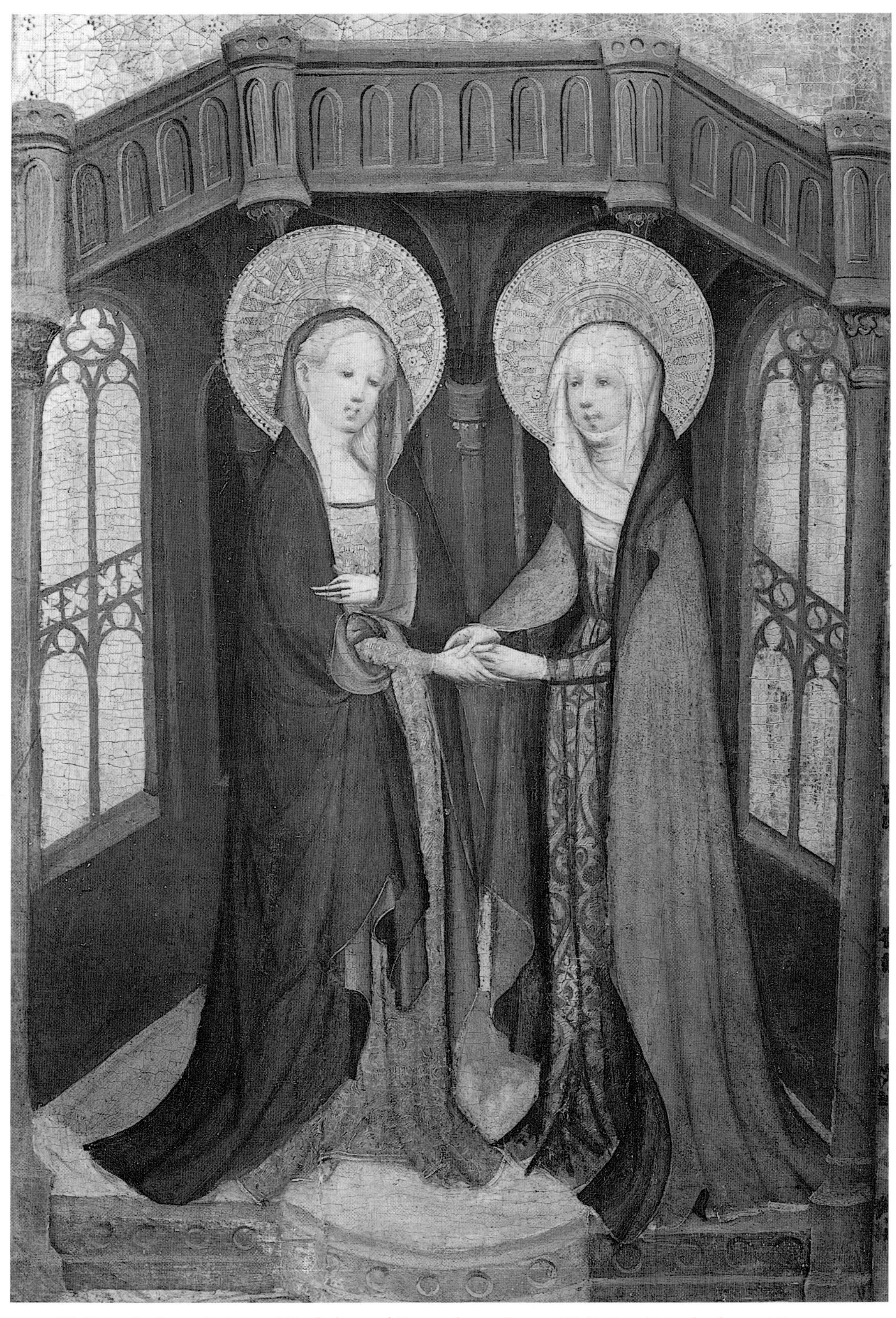

37. Fröndenberg Painter, Workshop of Conrad von Soest: *Visitation*. Fröndenberg Altarpiece, Stiftskirche, Fröndenberg

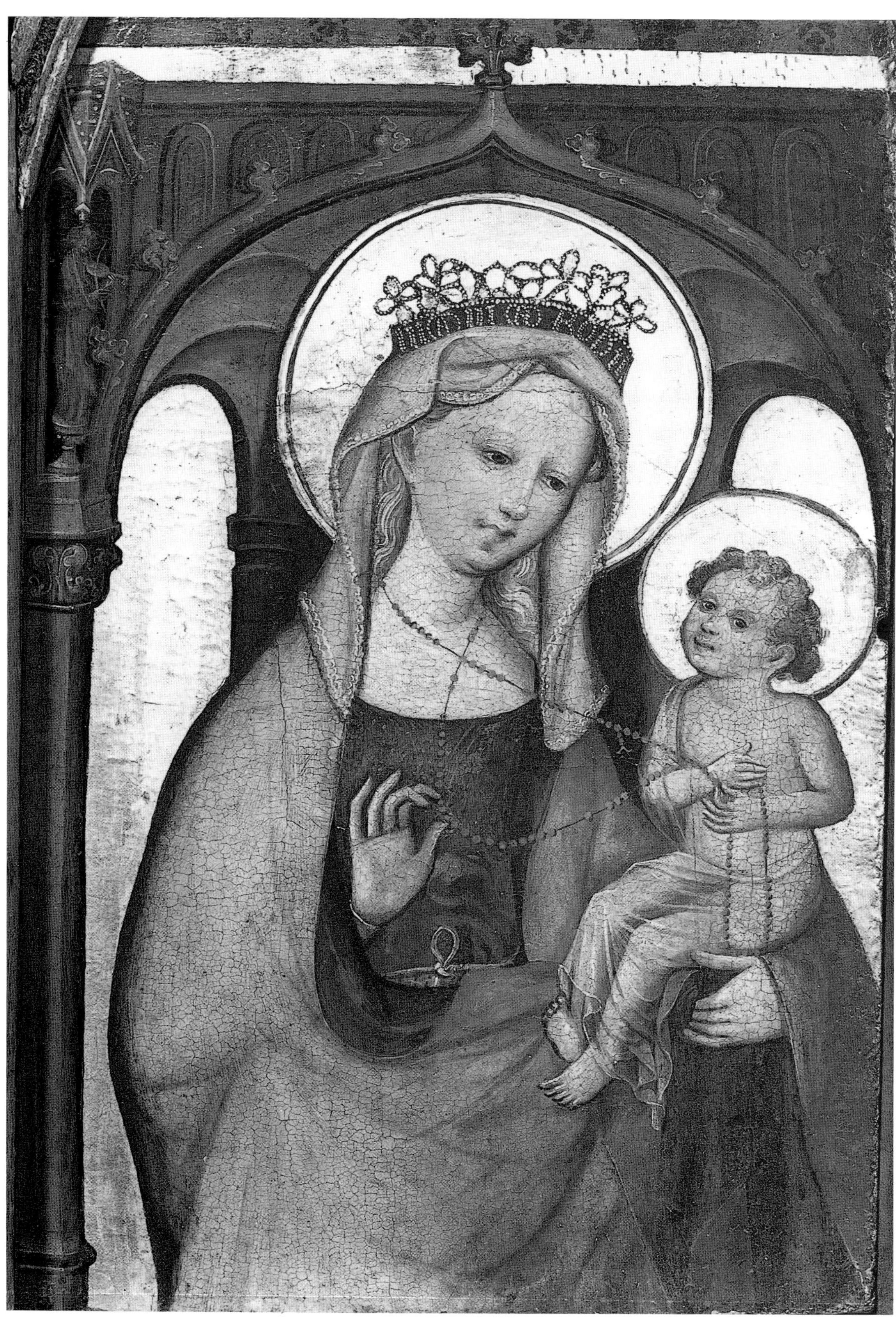

38. Fröndenberg Painter,
Workshop of Conrad von Soest:
Madonna and Child.
Museum für Kunst
und Kulturgeschichte, Dortmund

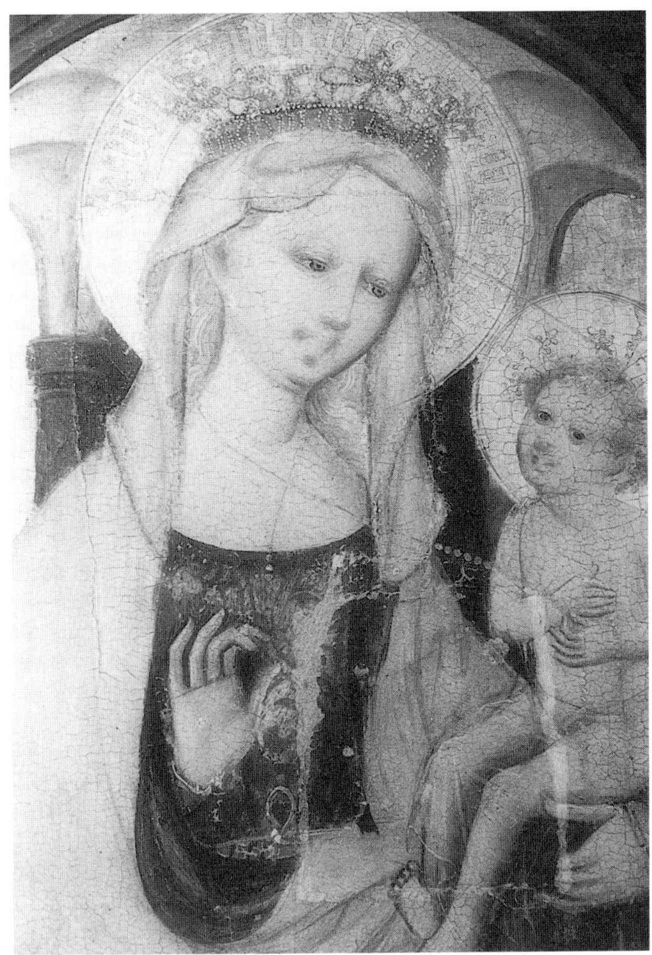

39. *Underdrawing of the Madonna and
Child.* Infra-red photograph.
Museum für Kunst
und Kulturgeschichte, Dortmund

than Conrad's, but confident; its outline style and lack of *pentimenti* suggest reference to detailed workshop models. These models appear to derive from Conrad's workshop. In the *Madonna and Child*, for example, the veil of the Virgin is a reversed close copy of that in the *Nativity* of the Dortmund Altarpiece. However, whereas Conrad's drawing creates form and folds with parallel hatching strokes, this painter carefully traces the outlines of these folds, and thereby loses their natural form. Still, the unusual pattern of the folds showing an escaped piece of veil falling forward over the Virgin's hair only occurs in the Dortmund Altarpiece and in the *Madonna and Child* in Dortmund.[18]

A similar use of detailed models, but following the artist's own design, can be demonstrated in the portrait of *Cardinal Albergati*(?) by Jan van Eyck (1438; Kunsthistorisches Museum, Vienna). A design drawing for the panel survives in the Kupferstichkabinett in Dresden (Inv. C775). The very detailed and lifelike drawing is marked in the margin with references relating to the colours and the system of shading to be employed in the painted portrait. This drawing served as the

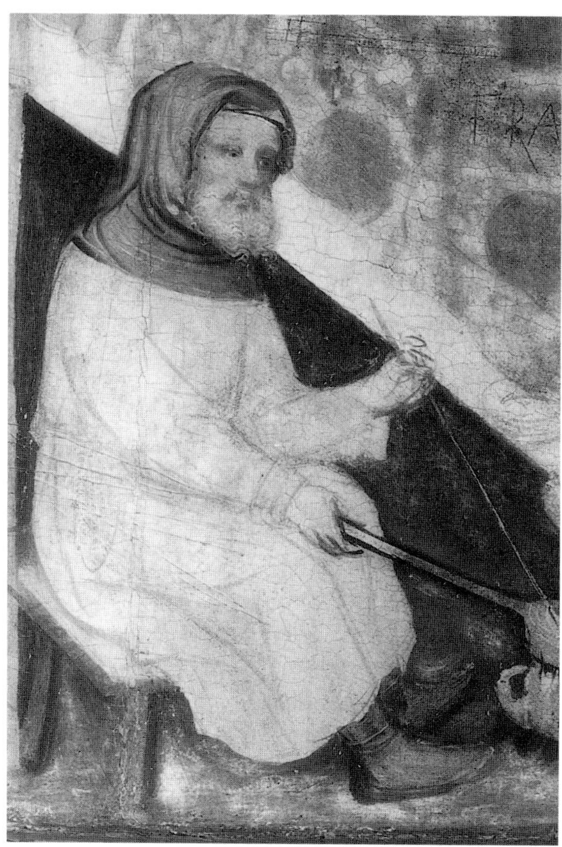

40. *Underdrawing of Joseph*. Infra-red photograph. Detail from the *Nativity*. Fröndenberg Altarpiece

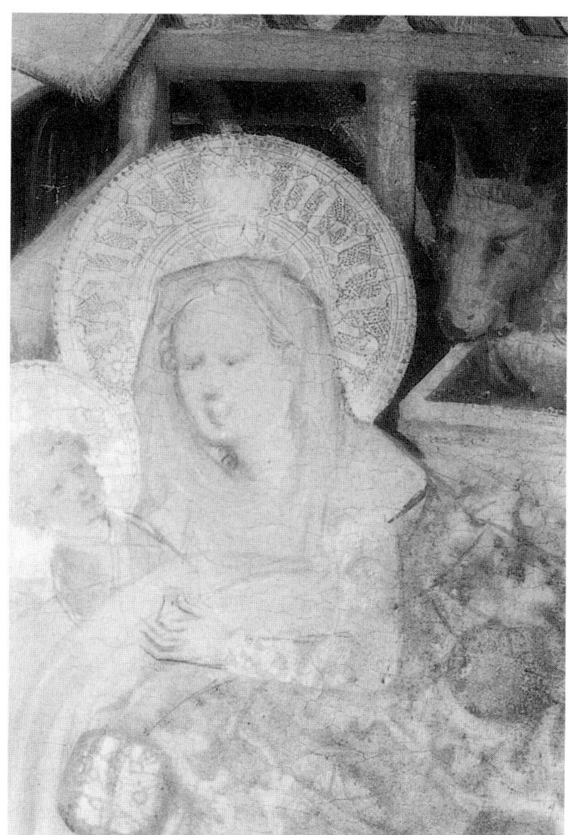

41. *Underdrawing of the Virgin and Child*. Infra-redphotograph. Detail from the *Nativity*. FröndenbergAltarpiece

42. *Virgin and Child*. Detail from the *Flight into Egypt*. Fröndenberg Altarpiece

43. *Virgin and Angel*. Detail from the *Annunciation*. Fröndenberg Altarpiece

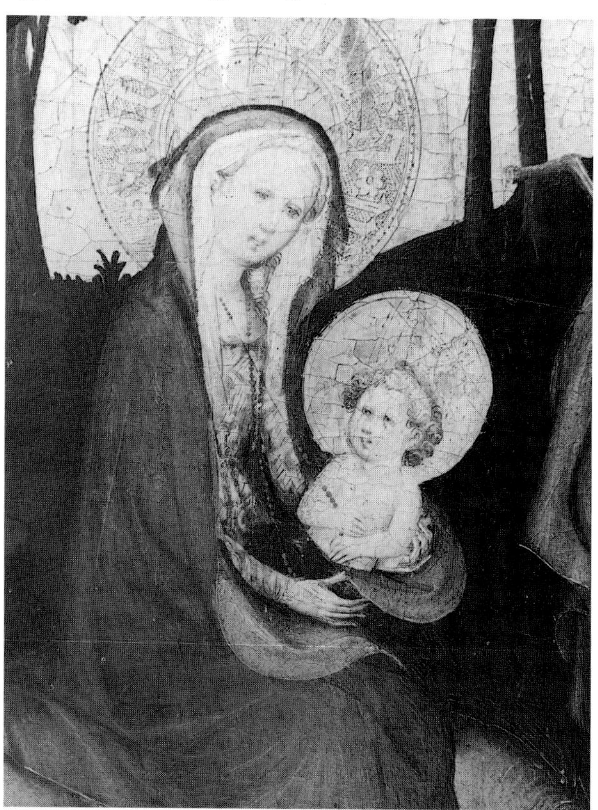

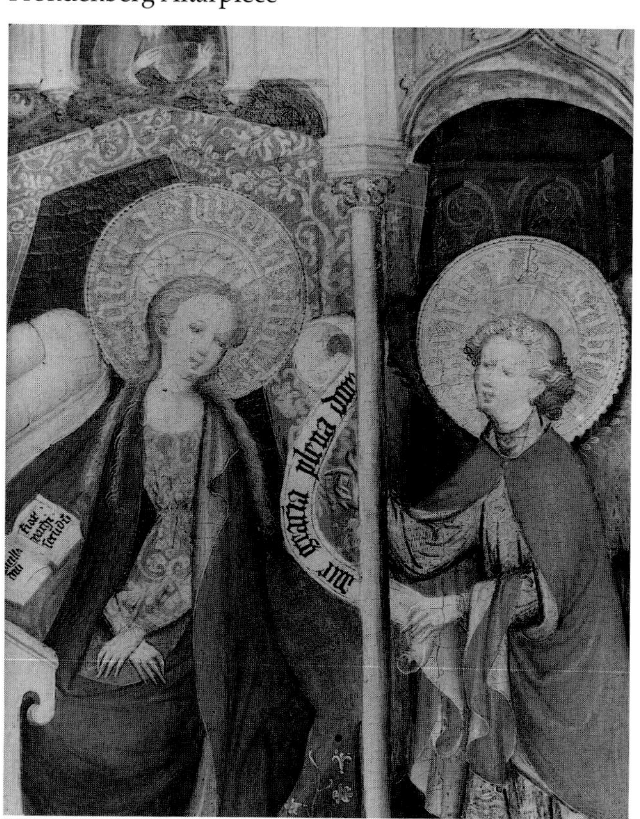

painter's working model as he proceeded with the painting, and therefore on the panel a few contour lines in brush and black pigment sufficed as underdrawing.

At Fröndenberg, the second hand could be described as sketchy and tentative, in need of many corrections and lacking the craftsman's confidence evident in the first hand. These alterations are not, as in Conrad's autograph designs, rapid lines searching for form, but careful corrections of single mistakes, especially in the drawing of hands, for which the Joseph in the *Flight into Egypt* and Mary in the *Adoration of the Kings* provide good examples. *Pentimenti* in the *Nativity* were found in the folds of the bedcloth, in the halo of the Christ child, and in the hands of the Virgin and Joseph. Long, wide and soft drawing lines sometimes supported by a parallel stroke, outline a shape and indicate drapery folds minimally. The hesitant outline drawing is barely descriptive of form; it suggests that the figures, like those in Gerard David's *Lamentation* (see pp. 58–59), may have been transferred onto the panel, tracing a complete workshop design. The work of this second hand is represented in the *Nativity, Adoration of the Kings*, and *Flight into Egypt* panels (pls. 40–42).

It was more difficult to ascribe the remaining panels of the Fröndenberg Altarpiece, as the underdrawings of the *Annunciation* (pl. 43) and the *Presentation of the Virgin* did not show up clearly enough in the infra-red photographs. However, small difference in quality and style between the two painters are sufficient to support identification. For the face of the Virgin, for example, the first painter favoured a narrower and higher forehead; ears have no lobes, but join the chin line, stressing elongated grace. The second painter's work is altogether less elegant, and he seems to have preferred softer, more rounded forms. Judging by this stylistic difference, the *Annunciation* should be ascribed to the first hand and the *Presentation of the Virgin* to the second. Another problematical area is the group at Jesus's feet in the scene of *Christ among the Doctors*. Insufficient underdrawing is revealed to confirm the surface appearance, which suggests a third hand by its much rougher execution, or, judging by the confusion of hands and poses in this area, insensitive overpainting by a restorer. From the dispersed wing panels of the Fröndenberg Altarpiece, a scene depicting *Pentecost* is preserved in the Münster Museum; it is closely related to the same scene in Niederwildungen. On stylistic grounds it should be assigned to the first hand. The outside wing fragment of St Cecilia on its reverse, however, is painted by an inferior hand. It is interesting to note that the *Coronation of the Virgin* in Cleveland, Ohio, forms the lower part of this fragment. On photographic evidence it would appear to be the work of the first hand.

At a first glance, the surface appearance of the panels is close to that in Conrad's signed retables, but they lack the consummate skill that characterizes Conrad's autograph work. Colours lack the subtle tonal nuances, highlight strokes lack the looped ends, other brushstrokes lack consistency, and paint layers seem to be thicker and less fluently applied than Conrad's transparent glazes. Hair, lovingly traced in every curl and delicately placed over the Virgin's shoulder by Conrad, is

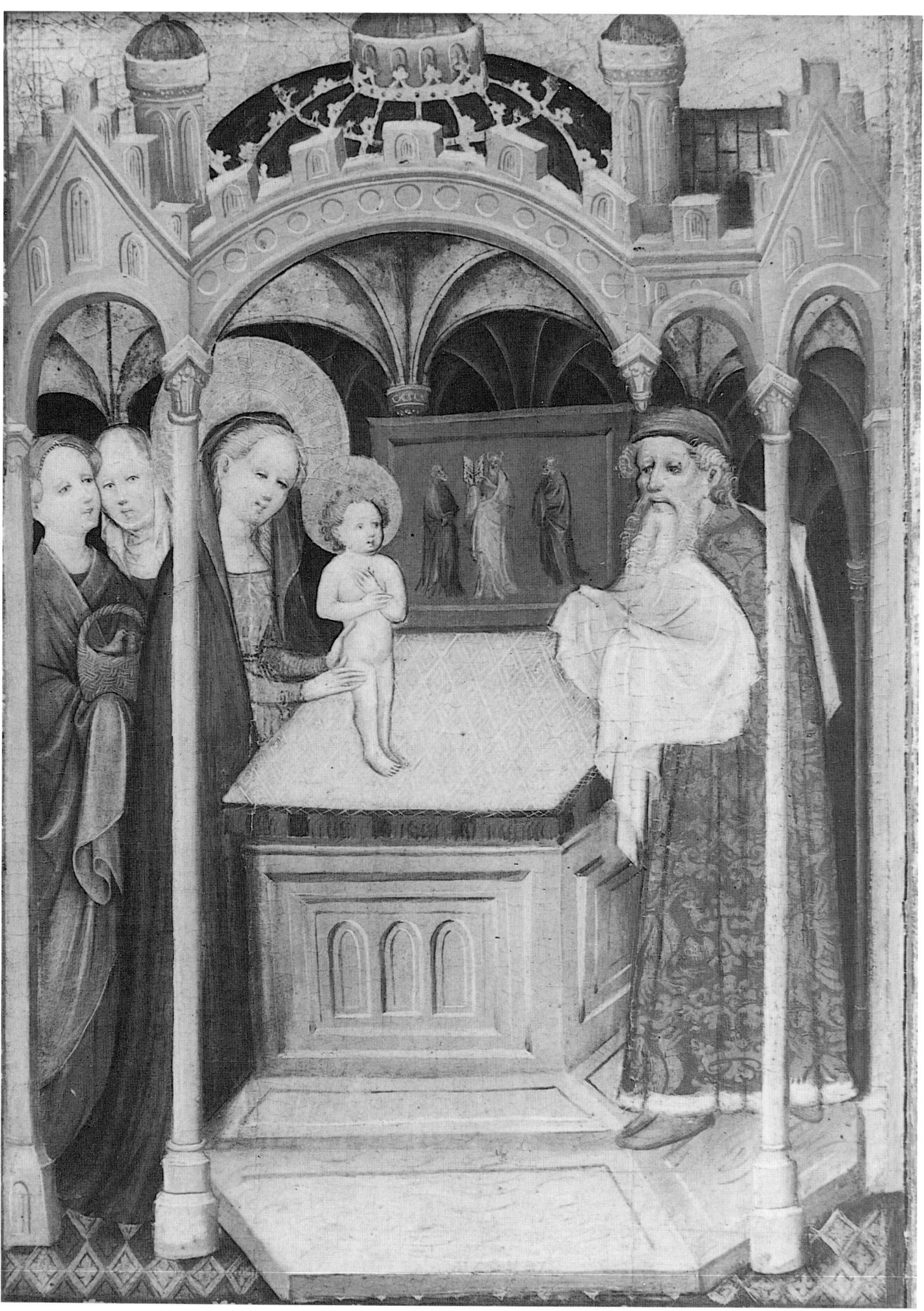

here described in only generalized brushstrokes. It is true that brocades repeat Niederwildungen patterns—the motif of the crown from the *Christ mocked before Herod*, for instance, recurs in the Fröndenberg *Presentation*—but they are sketchily executed and not painted over foil. The modest punchwork, including inscribed haloes, has neither the elegance nor the iconographic significance noted in Conrad's work (pl. 44 and discussed below, pp. 121–122).

As both the underdrawing and production process of the Fröndenberg Altarpiece vary significantly from Conrad's consistent method, the retable was clearly not designed nor painted by him. However, it is tempting to deduce from the close stylistic references, the outline style of underdrawing, and the frequent repetition of designs and motifs found in Conrad's autograph works that the Fröndenberg painters had access to model books belonging to Conrad's workshop. As the Fröndenberg Altarpiece was painted before 1421, and Conrad was still recorded in 1422, it cannot be assumed that the Fröndenberg painters had inherited Conrad's model book. It is, however, possible that in running his small, tightly controlled workshop, Conrad von Soest occupied himself mainly with painting major important commissions and accepted some minor or less elaborate work to be executed independently by his assistants, using designs from the workshop model book. Even if he employed only two experienced journeymen and two apprentices, which surviving guild regulations indicate was the maximum, there would be capacity enough for these lesser works. It would be natural for a journeyman using the workshop model book to aim to recreate his master's style and design as faithfully as possible to preserve workshop unity. Although there is no hard evidence to connect the Fröndenberg Altarpiece with Conrad, an arrangement such as the one described would explain the close stylistic resemblance and the coincidence of motifs that formerly led to its attribution to Conrad himself.

In the case of the St Nicholas Panel (pls. 155, 156; cat. no. 7) in Soest, which has been almost consistently attributed to Conrad von Soest, the reasons for connecting it with Conrad or his workshop are more tenuous than for the Fröndenberg Altarpiece. The claim for Conrad's authorship is based on some obvious similarities between the saints flanking the enthroned St Nicholas in the Soest panel and those on the outside of the Niederwildungen Altarpiece and in the autograph Münster panels. Worrying discrepancies in quality and style are usually excused by dating the retable before the Niederwildungen Altarpiece. This would, however, presume a considerable change in drawing style and painting technique by a master who is known to have been established and affluent by 1394 (the date of the marriage contract), and whose technique did not change in later years.

The St Nicholas Panel has been heavily restored and the use of azurite and green pigment (malachite?) in the original work, as well as colours applied by restorers, prevent transparency in infra-red photography. However, such areas of under-drawing as could be revealed sufficed to establish that the designing style of this painter (pls. 45, 46) differs considerably from Conrad's proven method. Outlines

44. *Presentation*, Fröndenberg Altarpiece

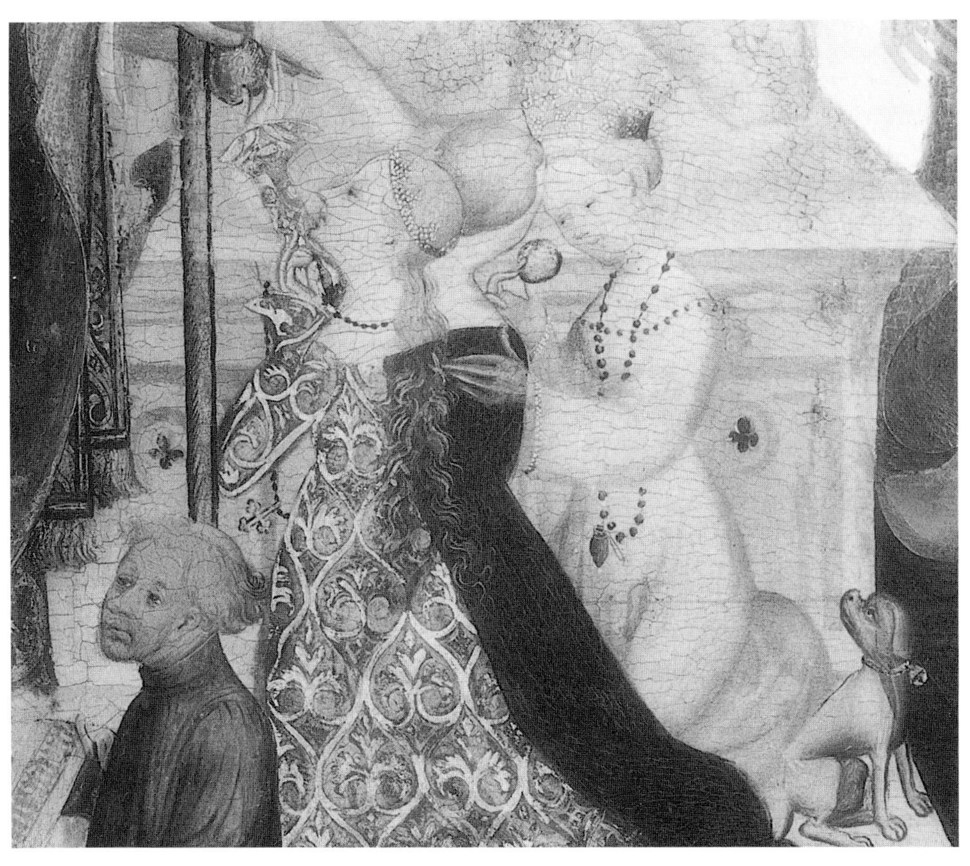

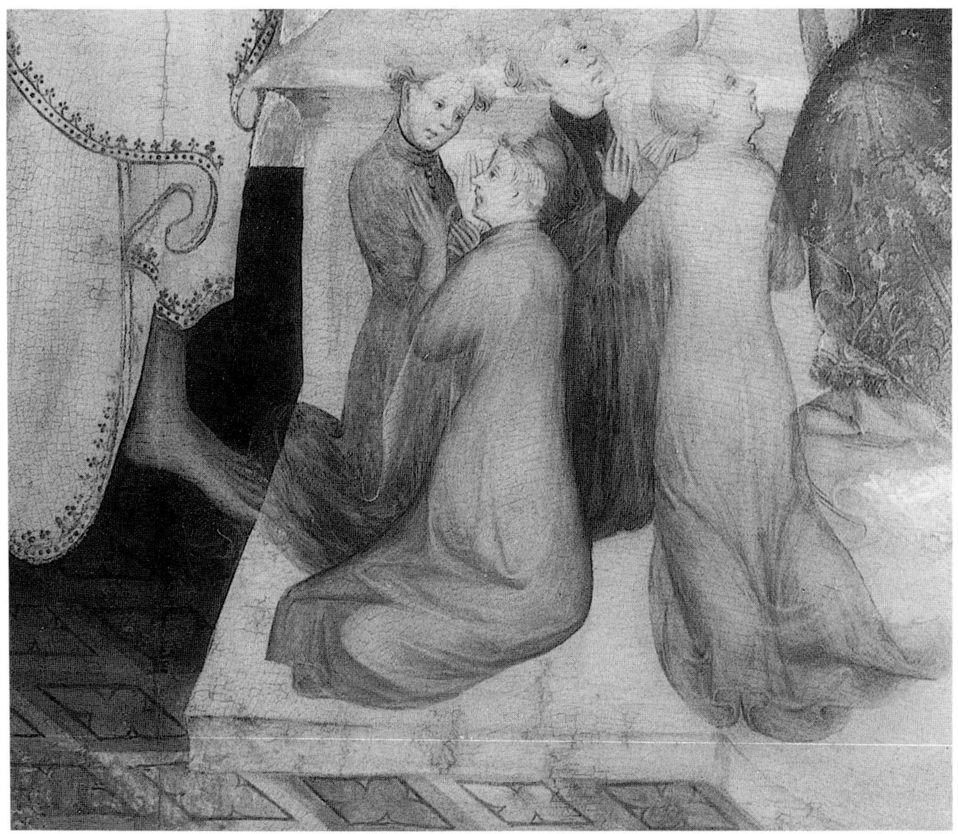

45–46. *Underdrawing of the Donor and Three Virgins* and *underdrawing of the Four Clerics.*
Infra-red photographs.
Details from the St Nicholas Panel.
Chapel of St Nicholas, Soest

only are drawn, with some reinforced contour lines. A long single line marks drapery folds briefly. The lines are broader than in Conrad's design, and suggest the use of a blunter tool or even a brush. Shade seems to be indicated in broad washes, but it is difficult to differentiate between surface and underdrawing washes. In certain parts of the design, additional forms were superimposed onto completed areas. The Baptist's foot, for example, was painted after the podium of the throne was completed and the kneeling cleric was painted over a part of St Nicholas's robe. This production method leads to a degree of confusion in the outlines of the female supplicants, where the front maiden shares half her back with the inward-facing figure behind her. Superimposition of complete forms together with the outline style of drawing suggests a transfer from detailed models, rather than creative design directly onto the panel in the manner of Conrad von Soest. Facial features are not underpainted in green pigment; they are lightly sketched in the drawing. Only the donor figure is described in lively detail. *Pentimenti* in the nose and contour of this figure, and hair curls lost later in the colour painting, hint at original design. The underdrawing of the *Virgin among Virgins* by Gerard David (Musée des Beaux-Arts, Rouen) has been shown to be most detailed in the self-portrait head of the artist (see pp. 58–59). Presumably the need for realistic portrayal prompted the careful and detailed design drawing of features and hair in both panels.

Conrad's creative hatching lines and elaborate definition of folds and shades are alien to the underdrawing technique in the St Nicholas Panel. The painting style also differs from Conrad's subtle method. Broad strokes are applied with a heavily laden brush which leaves visible marks at times. Colours appear opaque; they do not have the variety and translucency of the works signed by Conrad himself. Overpainting by restorers has obscured some of the original brushwork, mainly in the standing saints whose head and shoulder contours have been damaged during earlier regilding. To cover this problem, some thick black surface outlines have been added, which makes determining the original even more difficult. But the punchwork is mechanical and repetitive, with no inscription in the haloes and no reference to Conrad's designs. The large brocade patterns are applied in broad brushwork; they can be considered to be roughly copied from Conrad's elegant designs without access to the same template. Whilst the pomegranate motif of St Barbara's dress is a crude copy of the Münster St Odilia's elegant brocade, the drapery design of the Evangelist's brocade gown traces that of the Münster St Dorothea more carefully, although with some confusion where the clumsy, protruding feet of St John have to be accommodated.

Even though the drapery at Soest imitates basic patterns seen in Niederwildungen and Münster, it is depicted as tightly wrapped around the figures, stressing the Gothic curve of the bodies. Stance and drapery are, in fact, closer in style to Master Bertram's Bohemian-influenced forms than to Conrad's figures with their more natural stance and loosely wrapped garments. Hands do reflect Conrad's patterns, but they lack the grace and expressive force of his design. The broad right hand of St Catherine in Soest, for instance, became sharp, angular and unnatural when the Soest painter copied it from the softly relaxed pose of the small left hand of Conrad's St Odilia (pls. 151, 152). Though they also derive from the Münster prototypes, the faces of St Catherine and St Barbara in Soest differ in that they are hard, elongated, narrow, small-mouthed, and sharp-nosed. The profiles of the maidens kneeling at St Nicholas's feet, and of the angels above the throne, also have a sharpness that never occurs in Conrad's autograph works. It becomes apparent that the eclectic painter of the Soest panel borrowed ideas from diverse artists. The stylized corkscrews of the Baptist's beard, for example, reflect Master Bertram's design rather than the more natural curls of Conrad's protagonist; and the front maiden kneeling before the saint resembles the St Catherine in the Carrand Diptych in the Bargello, Florence.[19] Yet the enthroned St Nicholas, otherwise copying an earlier wall-painting in the same chapel in Soest, is endowed with the features of Conrad's saint. The transcription is not entirely successful, for St Nicholas, looking worried in Niederwildungen, appears frenzied in Soest.

These differences in style and surface characterization, reinforced by the completely distinct underdrawing technique, confirm that the St Nicholas Panel was neither designed nor executed by Conrad von Soest and is unlikely to have come from his workshop. The panel was painted by a master with a different working method and style who borrowed heavily from other artists, including Conrad. This master seems to have collected ideas and motifs, and even copied whole figures, into his pattern sheets which he then worked up into a model book for use in his workshop; he was not an associate who had direct access to Conrad's model book. The surface characteristics and underdrawing style of the St Nicholas Panel link it instead with other Westphalian works which are no longer attributed to Conrad: the Bielefeld and Berswordt altarpieces.

The Bielefeld Altarpiece (pl. 157; cat. no. 8) bears the signs of a workshop collaboration, with the *Sacra Conversazione*, *Resurrection* and *Deposition* (pls. 47, 49, 51) painted by the dominant hand.[20] The underdrawing style of these panels differs considerably from Conrad's proven method, but coincides with that observed in the Soest panel (pls. 48, 50). Again, outlines only are drawn, with a blunt instrument or brush, and occasionally contour lines are reinforced. Shade seems to be indicated in broad washes, but it is difficult to differentiate between the surface and underdrawing washes. A schematic, usually single, line marks some of the drapery folds. Facial features are only lightly sketched. Some surface drawing, especially in the drapery, may well be by a restorer's hand. The parallel hatching on St Catherine's cloak, for example, is surface work of this nature. And, most significantly, the forms are again superimposed. In the *Resurrection*, for instance, the pattern of the sarcophagus is complete under Christ's leg and also under the head, shoulders and foot of the soldier. Superimposition can also be seen where paint is worn in other panels.

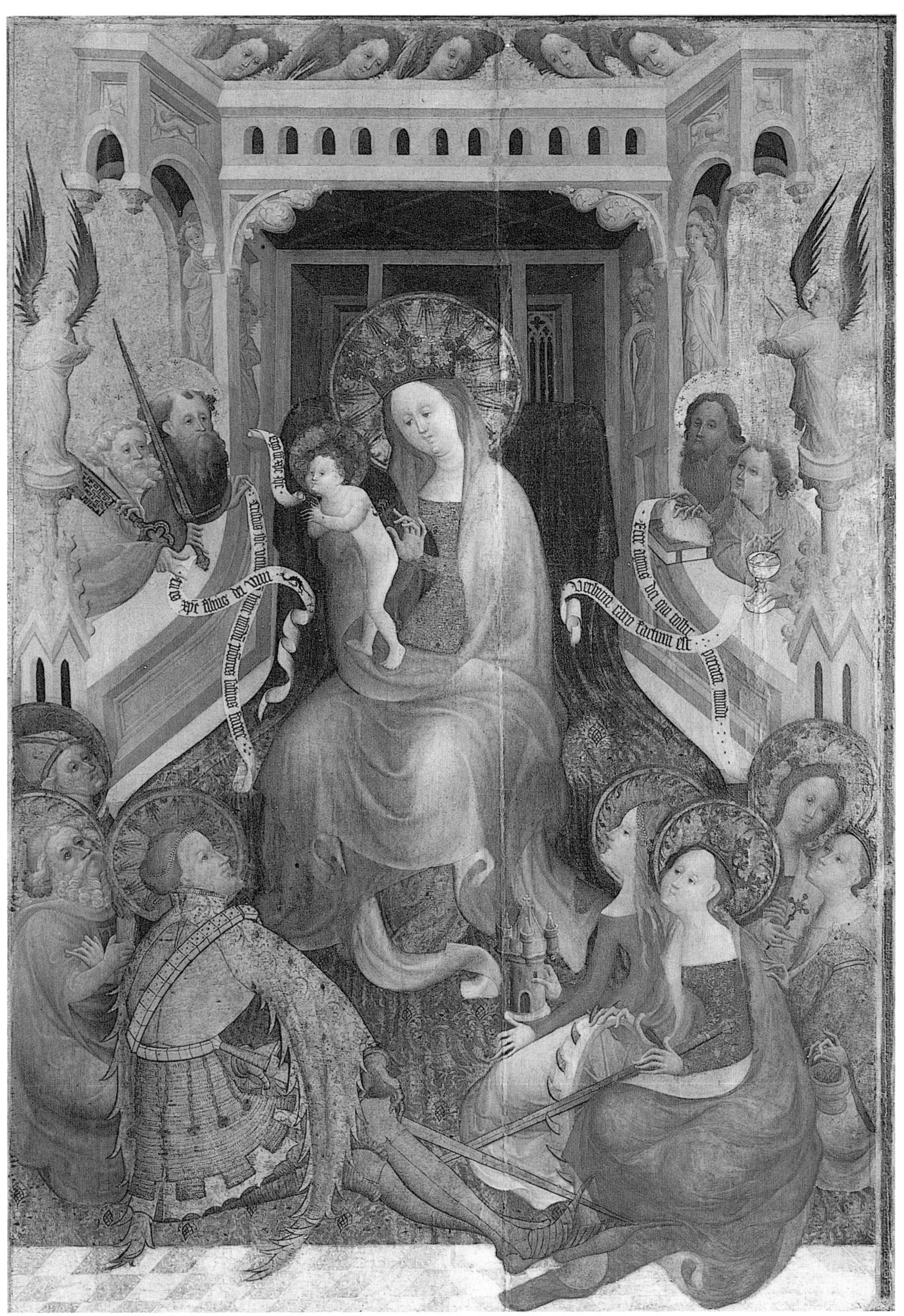

47. Berswordt Master: *Sacra Conversazione*. Bielefeld Altarpiece,
Neustädter Marienkirche, Bielefeld

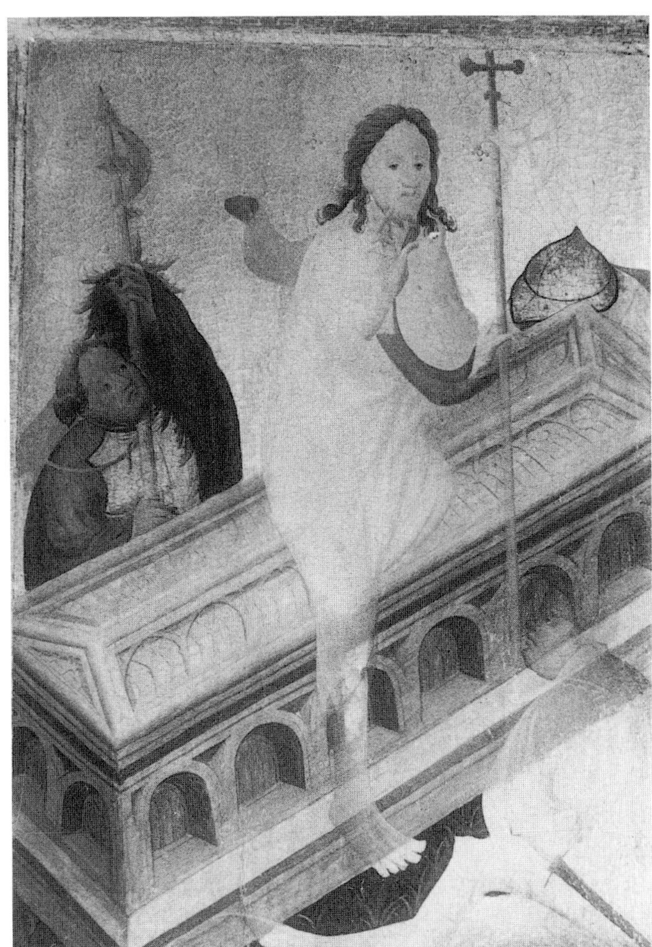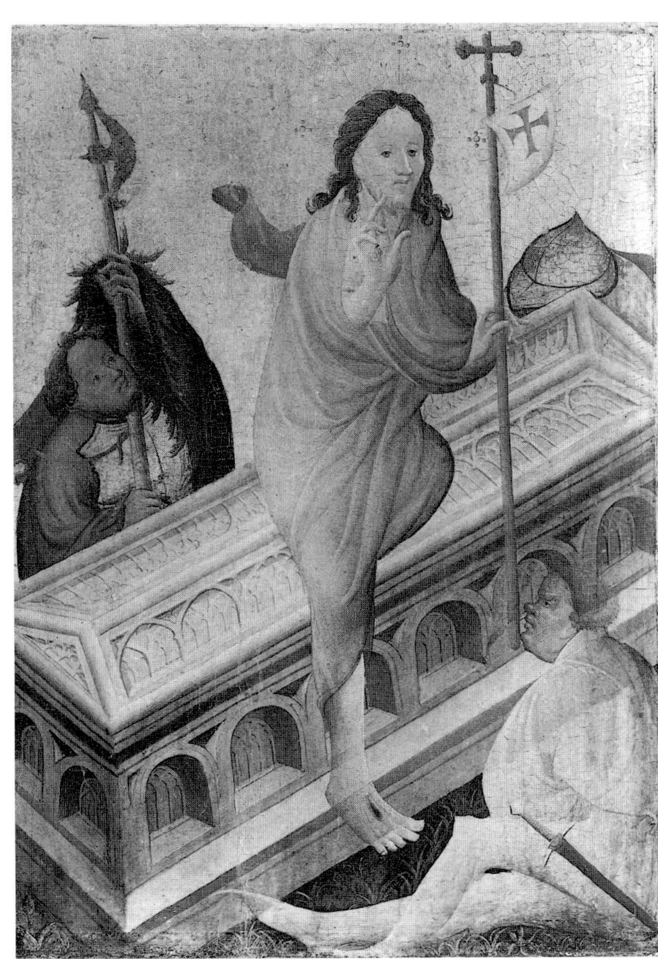

48–49. Berswordt Master: *Resurrection* and *underdrawing*. Bielefeld Altarpiece

In the same way, some small modification of hands, feet and legs can be found in the *Deposition* and *Sacra Conversazione*.

The painting style and production method of the Bielefeld Altarpiece are also similar to those observed in the St Nicholas Panel. Broad, at times long impasto strokes with a heavily loaded brush leave some visible surface marks. Opaque colours show little tonal variety and no translucency. However, missing surface layers and highlights have been restored in some parts of the altarpiece and show different brushwork. Brocades seem to be underlaid with foil only in the *Sacra Conversazione* panel. Simple repetitive punch patterns decorate haloes which bear no inscription, as at Soest. The drapery style of tightly wrapped cloaks also persists. The tubular loops of the Baptist's mantle in Bielefeld follow the same pattern as those of the Evangelist in Soest; and the design of drapery folds over the enthroned Virgin's knees in Bielefeld is a reverse reflection of that of the enthroned St Nicholas in Soest. The broad, angular hands with long fingers and the flat, clumsy feet with overlarge toes noted in Soest also recur in Bielefeld. Like the design in Soest, the

80

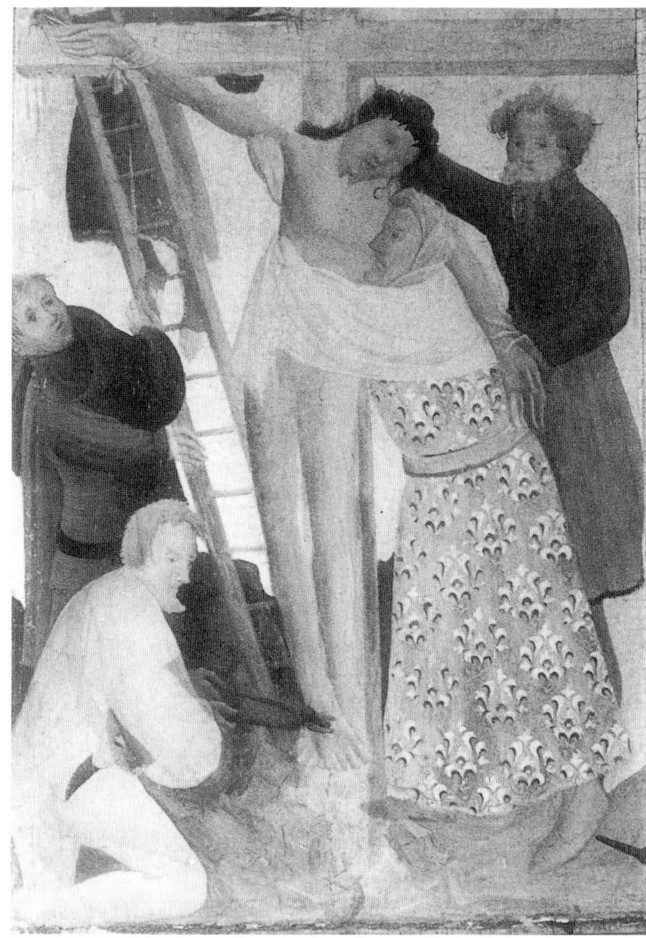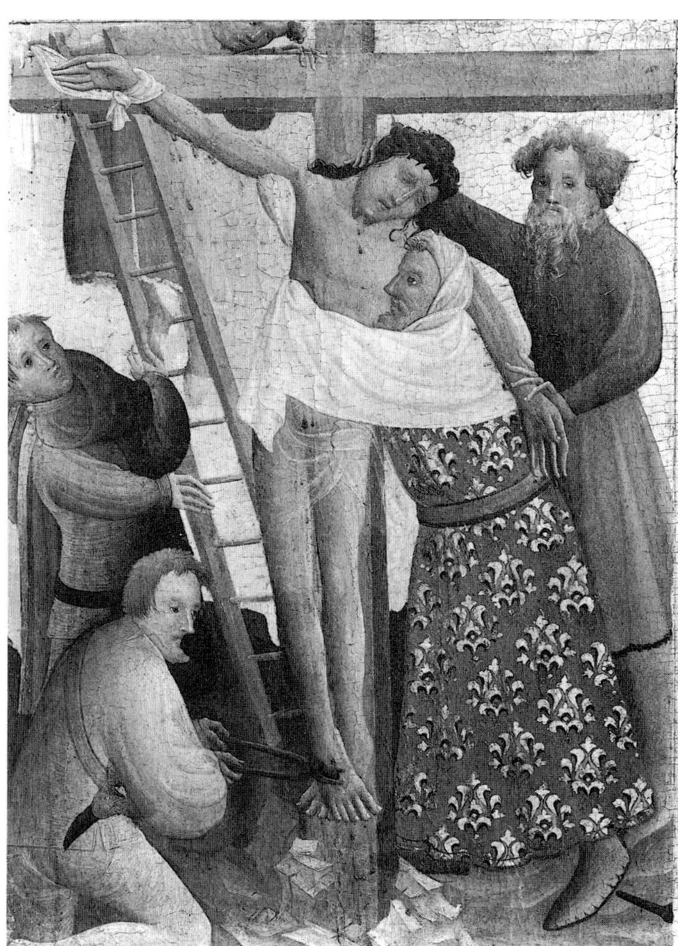

50–51. Berswordt Master: *Depostition* and *underdrawing*. Bielefeld Altarpiece

Sacra Conversazione resembles the Carrand Diptych in Florence. Reliance on the same model sheet leads to considerable confusion in the profiles of the front maiden in Soest and the St Barbara in Bielefeld; a puzzling double contour appears under the chin in the underdrawing to become part of the brocade pattern in Soest and part of the halo in Bielefeld (pls. 45, 47, 156). The male supplicant's features in Soest are closely related to those of the seated saints George and Martin(?) in Bielefeld.[21] Other motifs again derive from the workshop of Master Bertram.[22]

The similarities of underdrawing style and surface characteristics of the St Nicholas Panel and Bielefeld Altarpiece firmly associate the two retables. For the panel in Soest, the workshop reused several models from Bielefeld, and also added patterns recently learned from Conrad von Soest. In both altarpieces a variety of patterns collected from other masters is pressed into service, but not yet fully assimilated into a consistent workshop style.

A third altarpiece can be connected with these panels on stylistic grounds. The Berswordt Triptych (pls. 158–160; cat. no. 9) in the Marienkirche at Dortmund has been attributed to the young Conrad von Soest,[23] but most authors recognize the

81

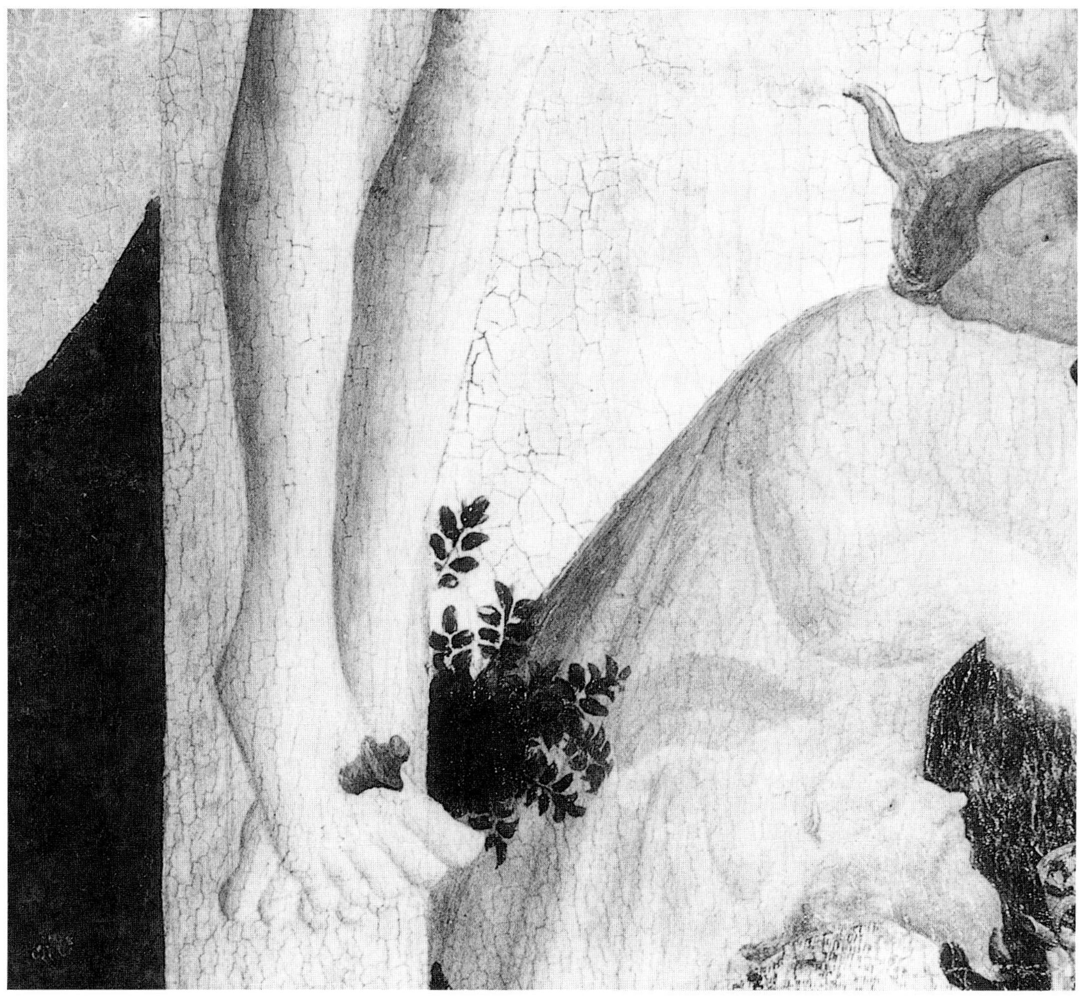

Berswordt Master as a distinct artist. It is not universally accepted that the Berswordt Master also painted the Bielefeld Altarpiece. However, the underdrawing style of the Berswordt Triptych (pls. 52-53) proved to be of the type noted in the Bielefeld Altarpiece and in the St Nicholas Panel. This can best be demonstrated by comparing the underdrawing of the figure behind Pilate(?) in the Berswordt *Crucifixion* (pl. 52) with that of the assistant holding pliers in the Bielefeld *Deposition* (pl. 50), and in turn with that of the kneeling maiden in the Soest panel (pl. 45). It is also instructive to compare the drawing of Christ in these scenes. Essentially the same face and torso are shown with little stylistic advance. But the draughtsman had benefited from thirty years of practice: the straight, tentative lines with modifications in Bielefeld are replaced by more assured undulating contours without alterations in Dortmund.

Despite the greater monumentality of the figures in Dortmund, the small mouthed faces with pointed noses still identify the workshop, as do the broad hands, clumsy feet with overlong toes and the corkscrew beards. Identical designs

52. *Underdrawing of Pilate.*
Infra-red photograph.
Detail from the *Crucifixion.*
Berswordt Altarpiece,
Marienkirche, Dortmund

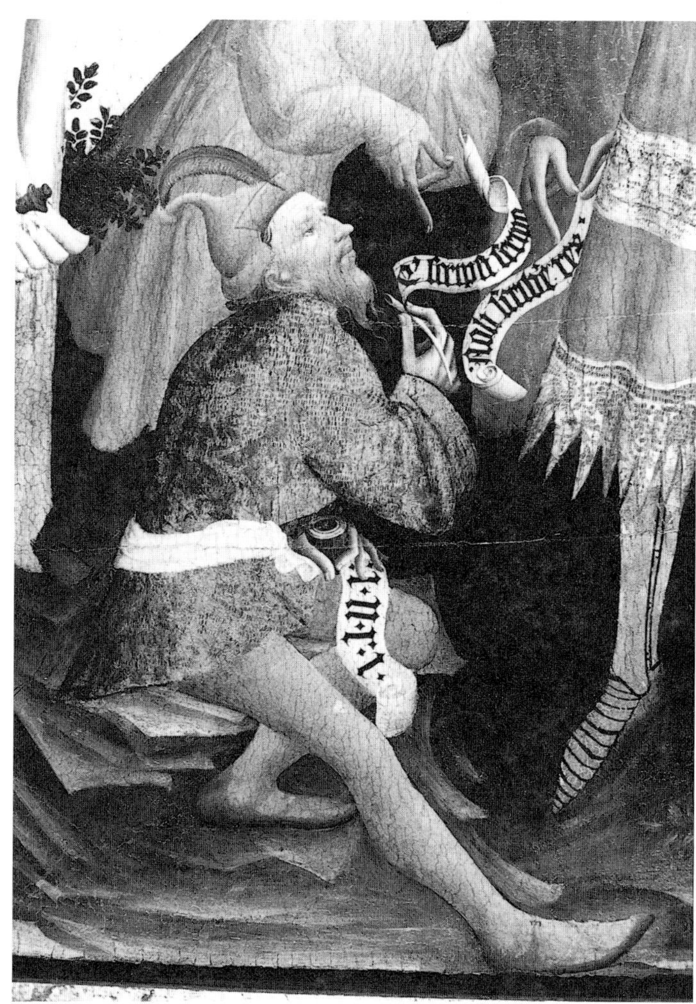

53. Berswordt Master: *Pilate.*
Detail from the *Crucifixion.*
Berswordt Altarpiece

are pressed into service by this workshop for the St Barbara in Soest and the Virgin in Dortmund, for the left supplicant in Soest and the St John in Dortmund. The brushwork denotes similar characteristics to that observed in Bielefeld, especially in respect of the broad strokes. Differing brushwork in the faces of the Longinus and Centurion groups, as well as Christ in the *Deposition*, is the result of considerable restoration work in those areas. There are surface differences, though, in some figures, specifically in the group of the women under the cross at Dortmund, whose drapery is described with greater detail than at Bielefeld. In other protagonists, notably Christ in the *Carrying of the Cross*, a much looser, broader indication of drapery folds is preferred.

The similarities of underdrawing method in the Berswordt and Bielefeld altarpieces confirm the stylistic relationship noted in the painted surface by earlier authors. The close relationship of these retables to the St Nicholas Panel in Soest has hitherto been overlooked, but it is now confirmed by infra-red photography and by detailed stylistic comparison. The Bielefeld Altarpiece is closest to Master

Bertram's work in style and designed by an inexperienced draughtsman; the date of 1400 recorded by Leopold von Ledebur (see cat. no. 8), therefore seems plausible. The St Nicholas Panel includes motifs from the Münster panels by Conrad von Soest and is more assured in handling both of surface layers and underdrawing; a date of around 1410–20 is therefore suggested. The Berswordt Triptych, showing a confident design, and the assimilation of influences from other workshops into a more consistent style, is likely to have been painted nearer the end of the career of the eclectic Berswordt Master. The date of 1431, implied by the document discussed in the catalogue, can therefore also be accepted on stylistic grounds. The Berswordt Master appears to have been Conrad's main competitor; but, although he copied widely and avidly from Conrad's designs he never equalled him in craftsmanship.

A panel still associated with Conrad is the *Trinity* (pl. 109; WRM Depos. 363) in Cologne. Unfortunately no permission could be obtained from the Museum to take or commission infra-red photographs. On stylistic and technical grounds the panel can be confidently attributed to the Veronica Master (see pp. 162–167).

Another workshop is of considerable interest in evaluating the extent of Conrad's originality. The Warendorf, Darup, and Isselhorst altarpieces (pls. 161–163; cat. nos. 10–12), formerly attributed to Conrad von Soest, are now generally ascribed to the workshop of the Warendorf Master. Even then, the panels have been dated before the Niederwildungen Altarpiece.[24] Such a date would imply that the provincial workshop rather than the exceptionally skilled Dortmund master, who was entrusted with costly commissions, acted as stylistic leader. A study of their design method was undertaken to shed some light on this controversy.

The Warendorf, Darup, and Isselhorst altarpieces vary in quality, but underdrawing method and surface characteristics confirm provenance from a common workshop. An underdrawing style with minimal indication of outlines and drapery folds was consistent in all three altarpieces (pls. 55, 56). As noted above, such underdrawing method suggests that designs from the workshop model book were just outlined onto the panel; the artist would refer back to the model for further information as he proceeded with the painting. Only the underdrawing of the *St Lawrence before the Judge* panel (pl. 54) from the Warendorf Altarpiece (Landesmuseum, Münster) reveals a more detailed design of drapery and modification of hand positions. It is possible that no model existed in the workshop for this subject. There is otherwise little evidence of original design in the minimal underdrawing. Its derivative nature, and the imitative style, show that the Warendorf, Darup and Isselhorst Altarpieces were painted in the workshop of a follower of Conrad von Soest. As his production method differs considerably from Conrad's proven method, he is unlikely to have been a pupil.

Motifs in these three altarpieces that appear Conradesque, but cannot actually be found in the Niederwildungen or Dortmund altarpieces, may have been taken from Conrad's lost paintings. Although the notion that lost paintings could account

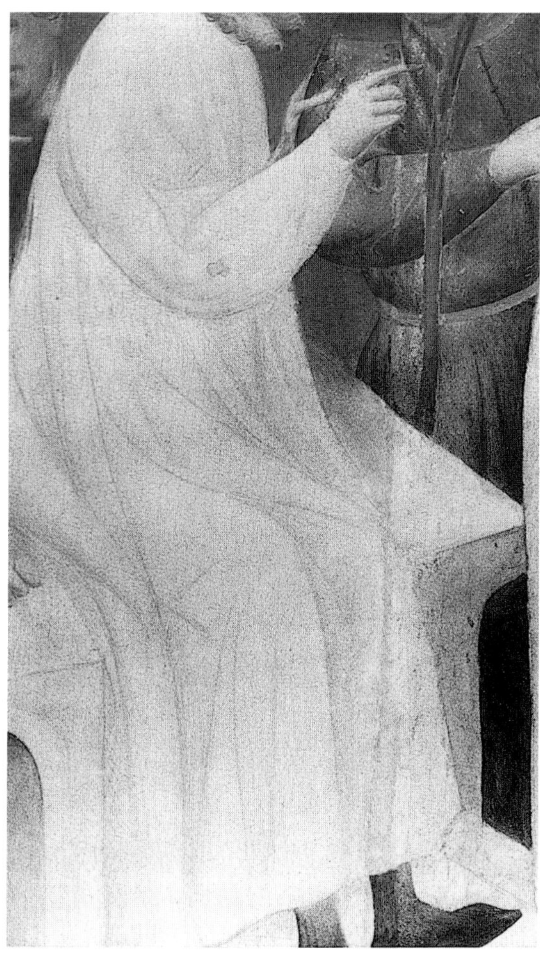

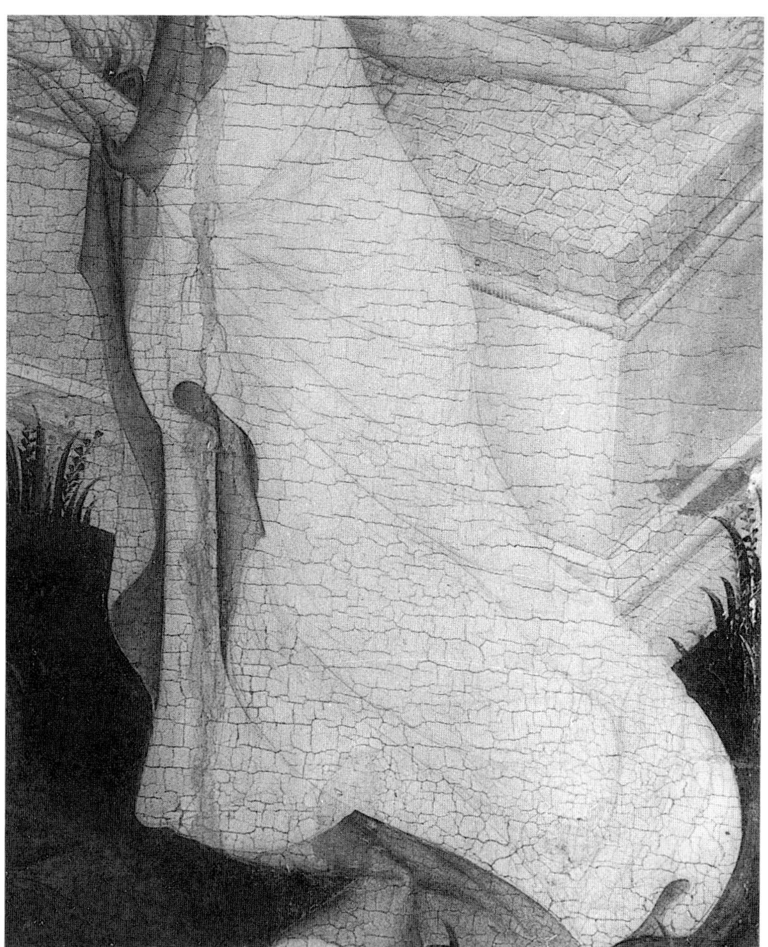

54–55. *Underdrawings of St Lawrence before the Judge*, and from the *Lamentation*. Infra-red photographs. Details from the Warendorf Altarpiece. Landesmuseum für Kunst und Kulturgeschichte, Münster

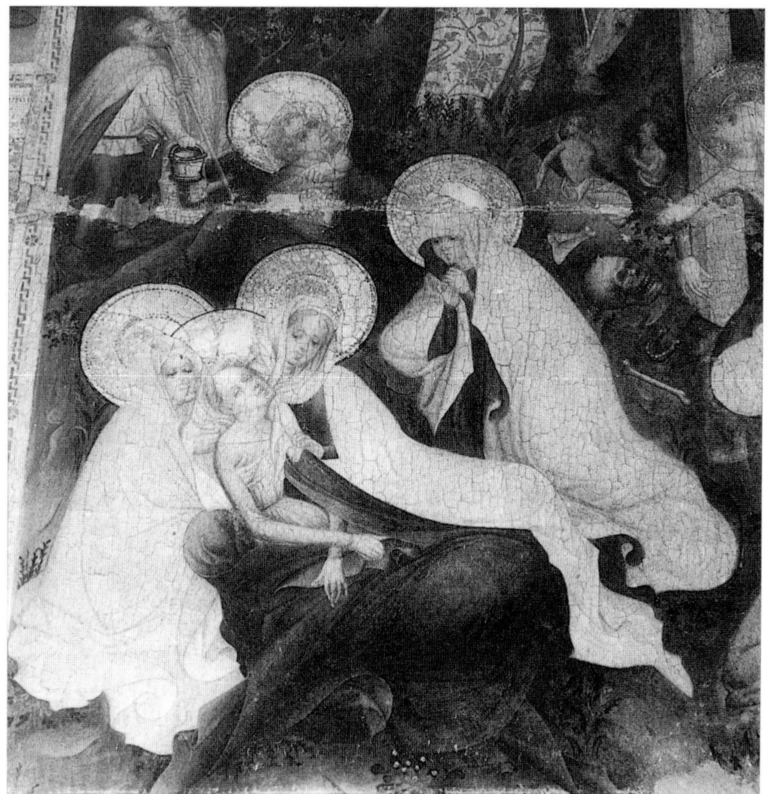

56. *Underdrawing of Women at the Cross.* Infra-red photograph. Detail from the *Crucifixion.* Darup Altarpiece Church of Saints Fabian and Sebastian, Darup

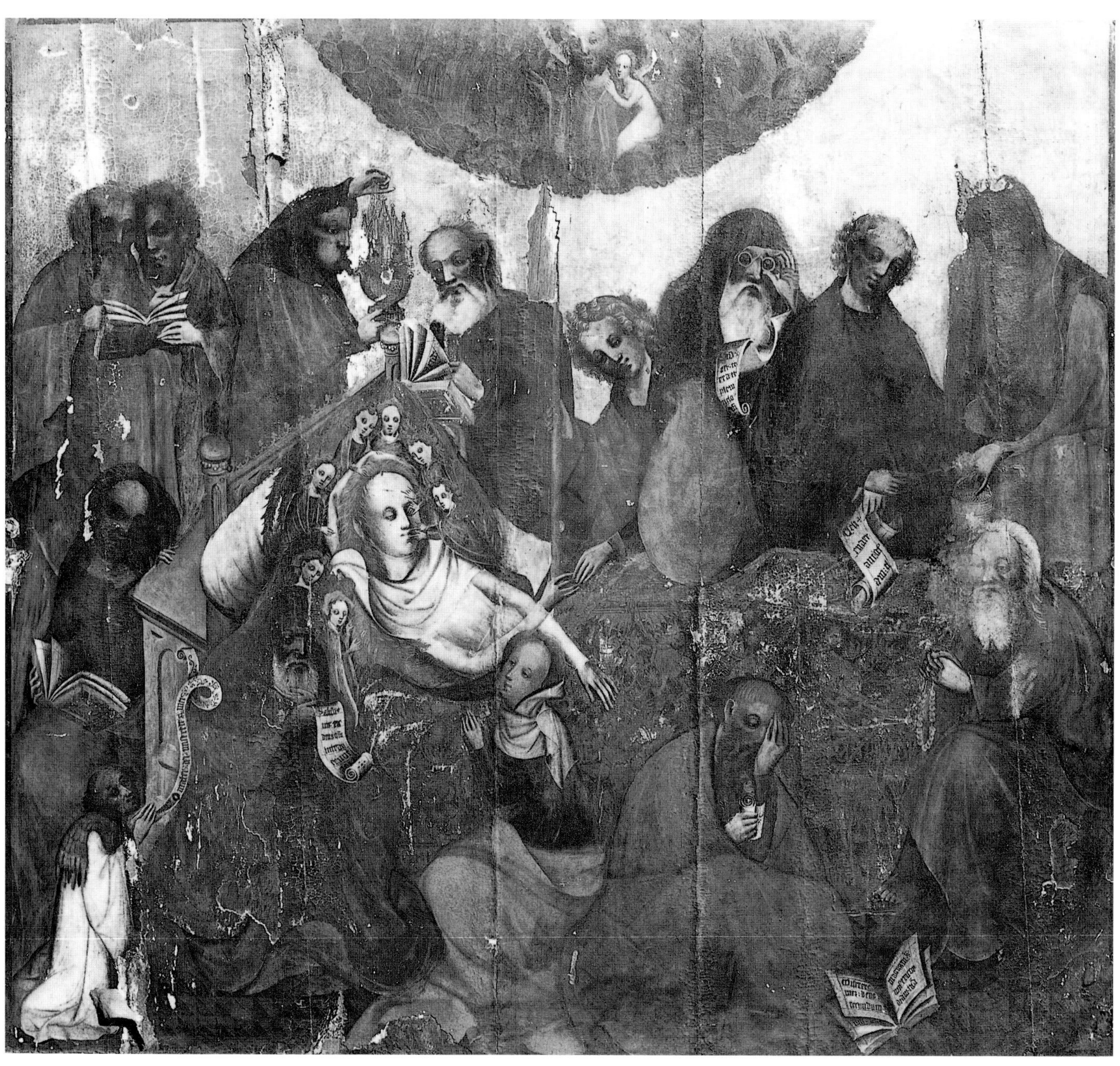

57–59. Master of the Blankenberch Altarpiece: *Death of the Virgin* (before restoration), *Annunciation* (before restoration) and the *Adoration of the Kings*. Blankenberch Altarpiece, Landesmuseum für Kunst und Kulturgeschichte, Münster

60–61. Master of the Jacobi Altarpiece: *Death of the Virgin* and the *Adoration of the Kings*. Jacobi Altarpiece, Wiesenkirche, Soest

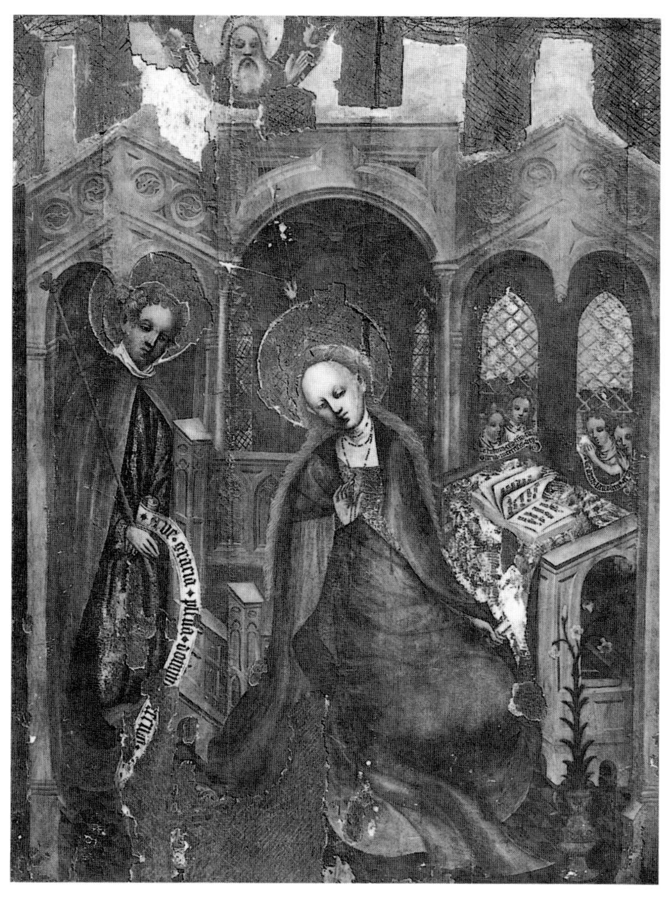

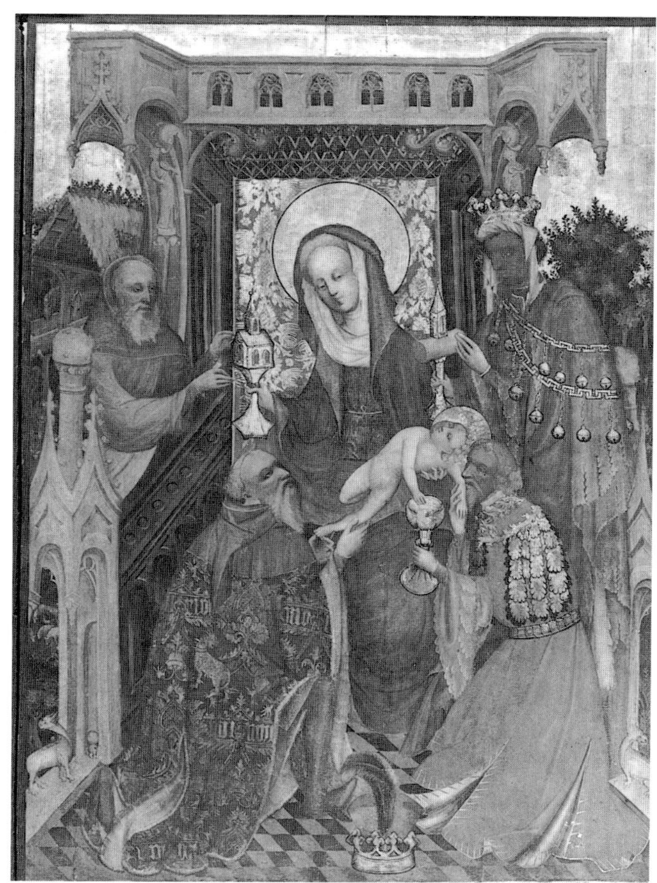

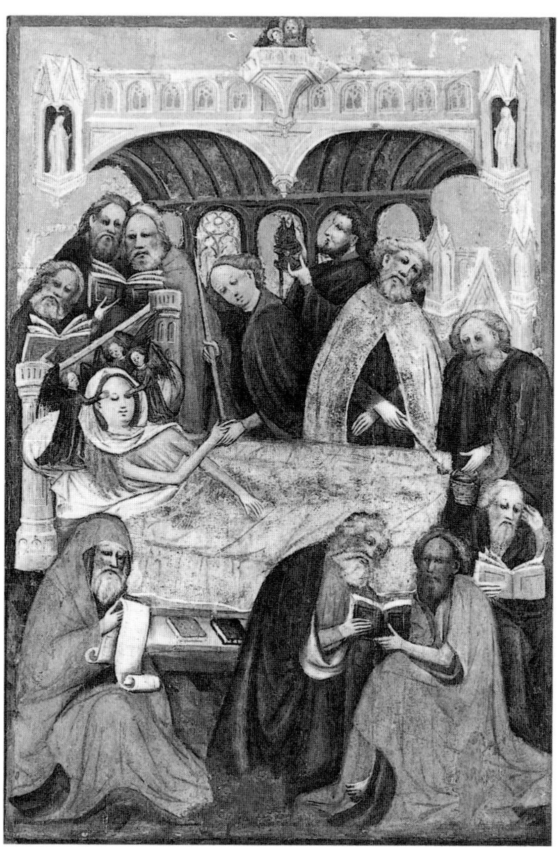

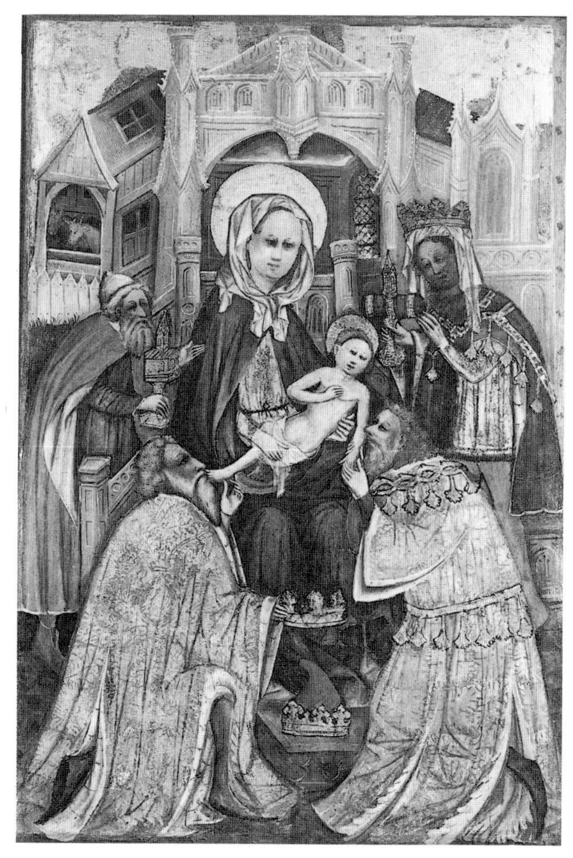

for such motifs in the panels by Conrad's followers has been contested, it is inconceivable that Conrad's workshop only produced two altarpieces and two or three small panels.[25] There is much evidence of iconoclasm in Westphalia.[26] One cannot be certain how closely motifs may reflect Conrad's lost models, but the unusual presence of King Herod under the cross at Niederwildungen, for example, is repeated at Warendorf. In this context, it is interesting to study two copies of the Dortmund *Death of the Virgin*, painted by immediate followers. For the Blankenberch Altarpiece (pls. 57–59) in the Landesmuseum, Münster, a less competent painter copied Conrad's design closely both in terms of style and design; for the Jacobi Altarpiece (pls. 60, 61) in the Wiesenkirche, Soest, a master with a more personal style adapted the scene to a different format. In view of the close stylistic resemblance of the altarpieces from the workshop of the Warendorf Master to Conrad's work and of the outline method of underdrawing, it seems reasonable to suggest that the work of the Warendorf Master provides us with some information about lost designs from the workshop of Conrad von Soest.

An even closer connection links another workshop to that of Conrad von Soest. The Golden Panel from Lüneburg in Hanover, a carved and gilded retable with painted double wings (pls. 164–167; cat. no. 13), was at one time attributed to Conrad. Although striking similarities to Conrad's autograph works are apparent in the design and colouring techniques of the painted wings, close inspection exposes significant differences in style. Recent authors have therefore ascribed the panels to an independent artist.

However, a considerable number of motifs in the painted wings can be traced back to Conrad's autograph works. In the inside *Crucifixion* of the Golden Panel, for instance, the figure of Christ is copied, as faithfully as a different master would manage, from Conrad's Niederwildungen design; the head and the crown-of-thorns, the body and arms, the hands, including the strange position of the thumbs, and the legs, including muscles and veins, are carefully reproduced. Furthermore, the brocaded onlooker is identical with the Niederwildungen pink courtier in everything but the pattern of his gown. In the *Adoration of the Kings*, the symmetrical composition, the motif of a King revealing the royal leg through a long slit in his robe and the unusual pose of the baby lying across his mother's knees, are all derived from Conrad's Dortmund Altarpiece. The borrowing of models can also be demonstrated in the *Last Supper*—not only by the overall composition and by figures like the drinking apostle and Judas, but also by the surely accidental repeat of Christ's image for the apostle on his left. Amongst many further examples, the *Coronation of the Virgin* provides evidence that the Lüneburg master went beyond the usual practice of quoting from other masters, possibly as far as sharing Conrad's workshop model book. The pose of Christ there is identical to that in the Dortmund design. But as Christ in the Golden Panel no longer holds crown and sceptre, the borrowed pose loses all meaning. The kneeling Mary in this scene reflects the Fröndenberg design, and the circle of angels behind the throne may derive from

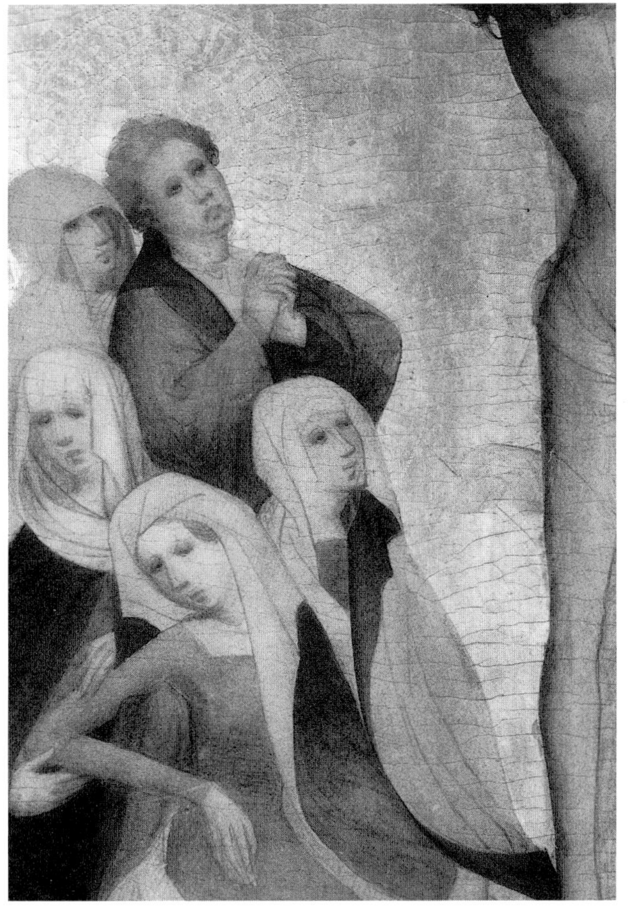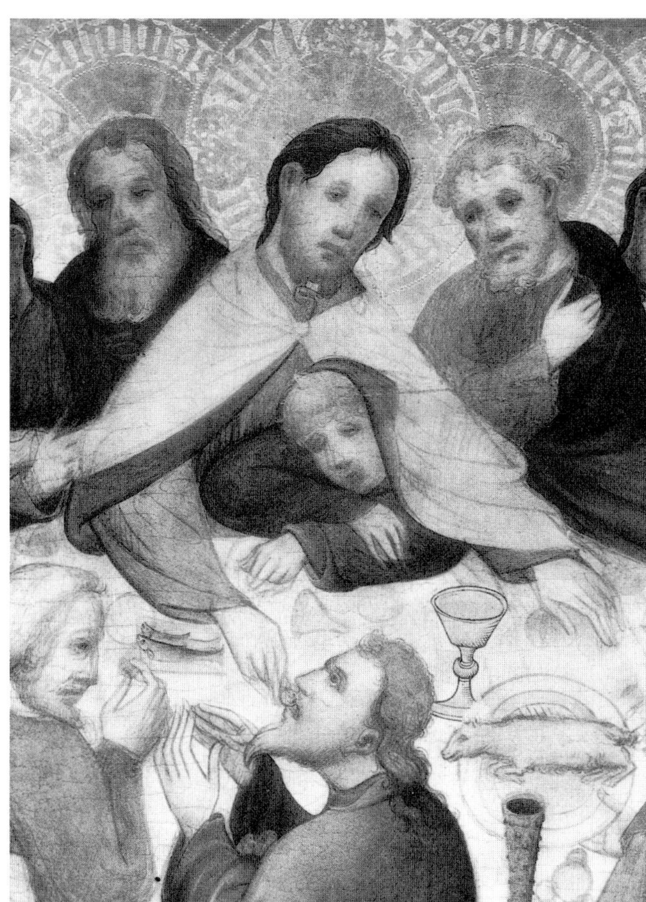

62–63. Master of the Golden Panel: *Underdrawing of the Women at the Cross. Detail from the Crucifixion,* and *underdrawing of the Last Supper.* Infra-red photographs. Golden Panel from Lüneburg, Niedersächsisches Landesmuseum, Hanover

Conrad's *Nativities*. However, the confusion in the figure of the Virgin in the *Annunciation*—whose frontal head is joined to an inward-facing torso—does (like the repeat of the Christ motif) suggest a certain lack of attention in the use of models.

An investigation of the Golden Panel by infra-red monitor (which reveals the underdrawing without providing a permanent record) has led to the suggestion that the original design was modified by a second master.[27] The style of the first master was defined as basic and precise, with heads indicated by barely more than the outline, and with hardly any *pentimenti*. I cannot support this suggestion after my own examination by infra-red photography of three panels attributed to the so-called first master (the inside *Crucifixion*, *Last Supper*, and *Nativity*, pls. 62–65).[28] The photographs revealed detailed, lively drawings in rapid and confident contour lines, frequently corrected or reinforced. All the designs contained multiple modifications. Drapery folds were variously indicated according to their complexity, from a single line to heavy parallel hatching. Areas of shade were marked by

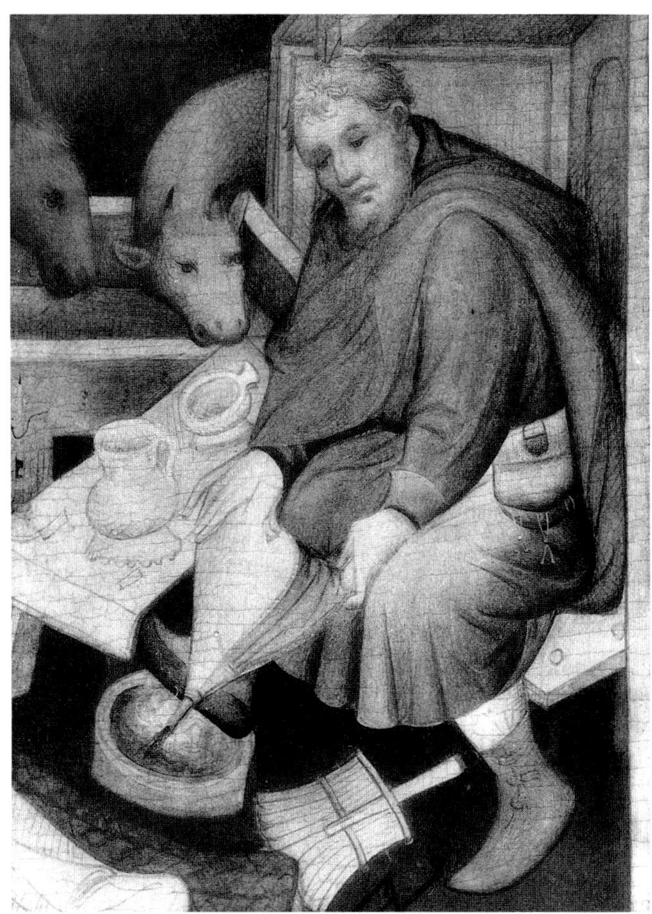 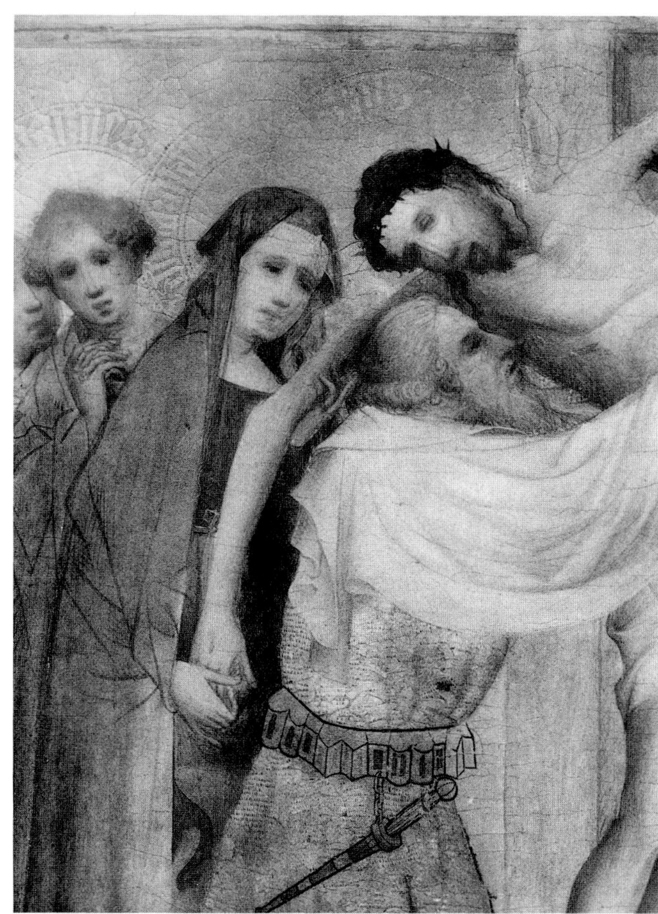

64–65. *Underdrawing of Joseph*. Detail from the *Nativity; underdrawing of Figures*. Detail from the *Deposition*. Golden Panel from Lüneburg

parallel hatching strokes at varying distances and by cross hatching in many places. Faces were not minimally indicated, as claimed, but carefully drawn in every detail with a large number of modifications, particularly in the features of the apostles in the *Last Supper*. Even the idealized faces of the women under the cross were carefully described in the underdrawing. Infra-red photographs of the panels painted by the so-called second master (including the *Annunciation to the Shepherds*, *Deposition*, pl. 65, and *Coronation of the Virgin*) disclosed no perceptible variation in the underdrawing style. It is therefore very difficult to accept the claim that the second master modified the original designs with more elongated forms.

In any case, surface characteristics vary so considerably in the three sides attributed to the second master, that contribution by at least one other painter must be inferred. The low quality of painting in the *Flagellation* is in sharp contrast to the fine execution of the *Miracle of the Wine*. Jesus in *Pilate hands Christ to the People* and *Christ admonishes his Disciples at Gethsemane* differs considerably in proportion and facial features from the Jesus in the *Kiss of Judas, Pilate washing his Hands*, and *Christ before Herod*. Furthermore, the varying colour schemes in these panels testify to the

90

execution by different hands.[29] It can be deduced that the Golden Panel from Lüneburg was painted in workshop collaboration by several painters to the design of one master.

The lively underdrawing style of this master is clearly different from that of Conrad von Soest. But the vigorous design and the surface characteristics, especially the painting method of the main master, have a close affinity to Conrad's signed works. It is possible that the designer of the Golden Panel, painter of the outside and inside of the left outer wing, was trained in Conrad's workshop. His apparent access to Conrad's model book at a date (around 1431–35) after the death of Conrad himself may denote an inherited model book. It is attractive to think that the 'Cord von Soest' recorded in the *Lüneburger Schossrollen* from 1426 to 1451 could have been a son of the Dortmund Conrad von Soest who, having trained according to Westphalian custom in his father's workshop, established himself in Lüneburg after the demise of his father, taking the workshop model book with him. The steadily worsening economic situation in Dortmund, which by then had yielded Hanseatic leadership to Cologne, would explain such a move. However, there is not sufficient evidence to support this hypothesis; it is only safe to say that the designer of the Golden Panel from Lüneburg appears to have had intimate knowledge of Conrad's painting method and possibly access to his model book. He may well have trained in Conrad's workshop.

While bearing in mind the limitations of image in infra-red photography, it seems reasonable, in view of the established differences in underdrawing styles and surface characteristics, to deduce the following workshop connections for altarpieces that have been attributed to Conrad von Soest. In addition to the signed Niederwildungen and Dortmund altarpieces, only the panels in Münster, depicting St Dorothea and St Odilia, can be securely ascribed to the hand of Conrad von Soest. A future examination in more favourable conditions may decide whether the panel in Munich, depicting St Paul, can be connected with Conrad or his workshop. The Fröndenberg Altarpiece, on the other hand, is likely to have been produced in his workshop, but not by Conrad himself.

Other works which have been attributed to Conrad von Soest derived from four distinct workshops. The *Trinity* in Cologne was painted by the Veronica Master in Cologne. The Bielefeld Altarpiece, the St Nicholas Panel in Soest, and the Berswordt Altarpiece in Dortmund were produced in the workshop of the Berswordt Master, who appears to have been Conrad's main competitor. The Warendorf, Darup and Isselhorst altarpieces stem from the workshop of one of Conrad's Westphalian followers whose derivative works give some indication of the likely nature of Conrad's lost paintings. And finally, the wings of the Golden Panel from Lüneburg were painted in a workshop whose master may well have trained with Conrad and may even have inherited his model book.

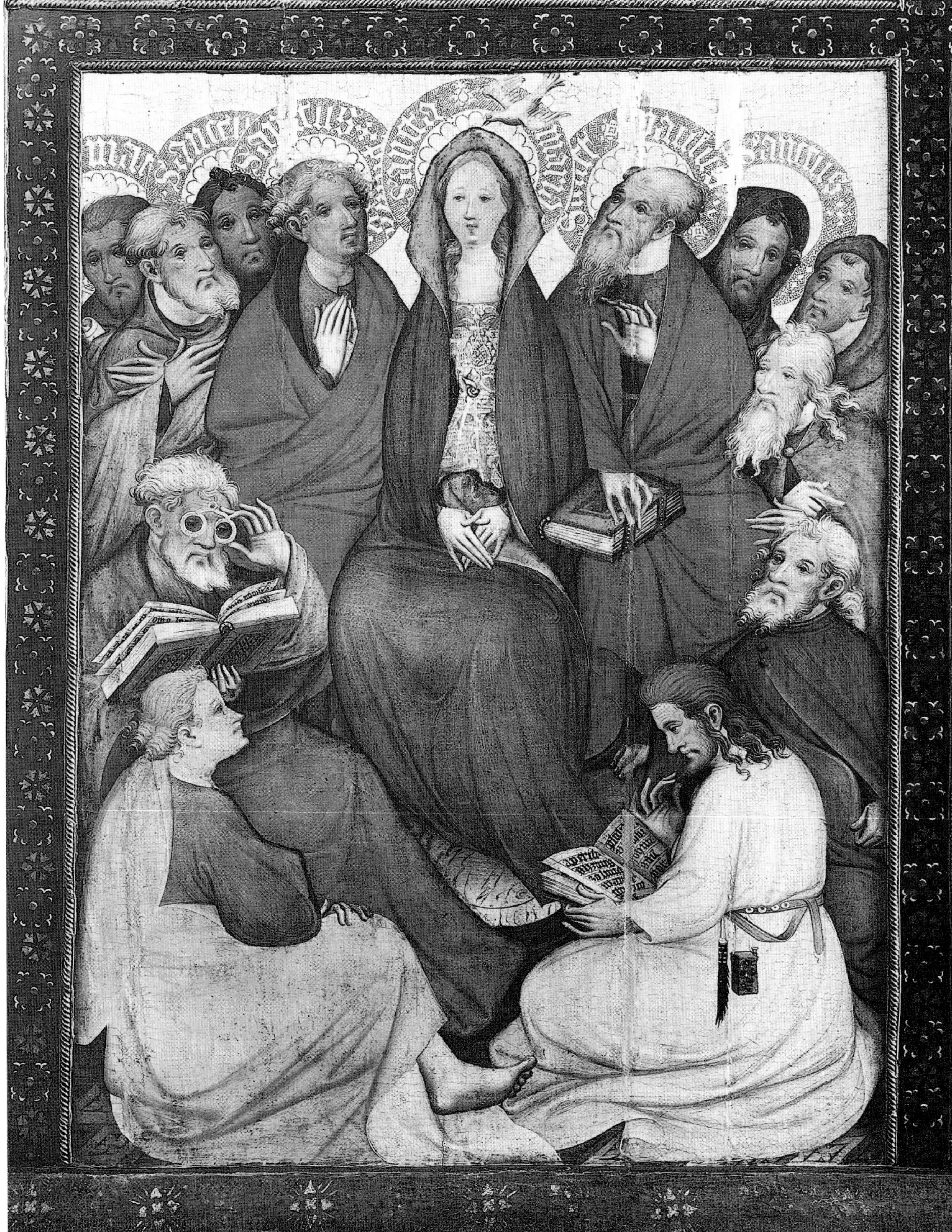

6. The Iconography of Autograph Works

T HE FIRST ISSUE that arises in an iconographic analysis of Conrad von Soest's works is the question of function. To this the priest Eberhard, writing around 1216, provided a partial answer: '…many fair Houses of God have been founded and decorated most beautifully…and richly painted with masterly skill. Lapis lazuli, silver and gold shine in joyous brilliance…Myrrh and incense burn there, and the hearts of men soar aloft to God…There should be reverent attention there to the reading, the singing and the ringing of the bells to the honour of God'.[1] The purpose then of the costly altarpieces and tabernacle doors was, in part, to aid and encourage devotion. For the largely illiterate general congregation, kept at one remove from the actuality of the liturgy by the Latin used for services, pictorial representation acted in some measure as a substitute for what its members could not read in books. This was already perceived by Pope Gregory the Great in the sixth century, when he wrote in defence of pictorial ornamentation of churches: 'What a book presents to the reader, this a picture presents to the illiterate beholder. In the picture even the ignorant see what to follow. In it, the illiterate read'.[2]

While Eberhard's religious experience can, by empathy, be sensed today, when the church is lit only by candlelight during a service, we can no longer 'read' the narrative panels confidently. The medieval congregation could recognize and interpret a symbolic language that is largely lost to us today. The Council of Trent (1545–63), which redefined Church doctrine and stipulated austere adherence to the scriptures in unbending opposition to the Lutherans, marked the end of a universal Gothic iconographic tradition. Only through the study of medieval texts is it possible, any longer, to retrieve some of its flavour and significance. Fourteenth-century vernacular sermons, often delivered by mendicants, that must once have assisted the illiterate congregation in the understanding of religious images, have not been preserved in Westphalia. However, sermons written by two eloquent Westphalian Franciscan preachers from the late fifteenth century, Johannes Brugman (*c.* 1400–73) and Dietrich Kolde (*c.* 1435–1515), active in Northern Germany and the Netherlands, survive to indicate the character of such teaching. Moreover, contemporary documents can shed some light on the Gothic vocabulary utilized by the clergy. A letter of indulgence, dated 1439, refers metaphorically to Mary, Mother of Christ, as 'shining star of the seas, mother of the distressed…path of the strayed…'.[3] Dual levels of interpretation, metaphorical and historical, may have existed for the viewer in the late Middle Ages, depending on his education and experience.

66. Conrad von Soest: *Pentecost*. Niederwildungen Altarpiece

Latin sermons survive from Westphalia, but they were clearly addressed to a different audience for more learned instruction and disputation. The Westphalian preacher and papal inquisitor Jacobus de Sweyve de Sosato (*c.* 1360–*c.* 1440), for example, collected, wrote and delivered undistinguished sermons in Latin which simply present a narrow Dominican interpretation of Bible passages.[4] He was concerned not to explain images, but to dispute ideas. Although he addressed scholars, students, noblemen and patricians, and therefore potential patrons of altarpieces, his particular sermons were hardly sources of innovative narrative imagery for his audience.

An iconographic study of Conrad's works should focus on possible literary sources that may have influenced the patrons' or their advisers' choice of image. They, like the Abbot of Westminster in the eleventh century, appear to have felt that 'pictures exist as representations and symbols of writing'.[5] Although a number of the well-educated Dortmund and Niederwildungen patricians are likely to have studied Latin, vernacular Bible editions, verse adaptations, Books of Hours and passion tracts were available and were chiefly owned by the laity in the fourteenth and fifteenth centuries. The connection of Dortmund and Niederwildungen patricians with Cologne and other universities as well as well-stocked libraries at Fritzlar and at Westphalian monasteries and convents elsewhere, ensured that manuscripts were accessible even to those who did not possess their own copies.[6] Frequent journeys must also have furnished these patrician traders and scholars with fresh ideas of a literary or visual nature.

Iconographic vocabulary for the illumination of such manuscripts and for church decoration was based on biblical exegesis and communal devotion until the thirteenth century. The Dominican Thomas Aquinas (1225–74), who had studied in Cologne in the 1240s, argued for a synthesis between Aristotle's reason and Christian faith. By contrast, the Franciscan Bonaventure (1221–74) defended the traditional Platonist philosophy that eternal ideas of justice and beauty were conceived directly in the soul—as God's gift.[7] Although Christ's humanity and passion had not been stressed in the early years of the church, an embryonic form of passion devotion also existed in the eleventh and twelfth centuries culminating in the heightened intensity of thirteenth-century practices.

It was St Francis of Assisi (*c.* 1181–1226) by dint of his identification with Christ's suffering, through stigmatization in 1224, who initiated an emphasis on personal religious experience through meditation. This method of individual devotion was later encouraged by many Franciscan texts. Pseudo-Bernard, in his *Meditatio in passionem et resurrectionem Domini* urged meditation by exhorting the soul to empathize with the suffering Lord in his passion: 'You gave your body to the strikers and your cheeks to the pluckers; you turned not your face away from them that spat upon you'. Pseudo-Bede abandoned the dialogue form in favour of the narrative tract, the first of its kind, interrupted only by pious interjections, in *De meditatione passionis Christi per septem diei horas libellus*. The most widely read of the

Franciscan aids to meditation was probably Pseudo-Bonaventure's *Meditationes vitae Christi*, written to encourage a Poor Clare in the constant contemplation of Christ's life and suffering: 'We must not be repelled at the thought of those things that our Lord Jesus did not hesitate to bear to redeem us and rescue us from the hands of our old enemy'.[8]

Such meditation became an obsession with mystics like Henry Suso (*c.* 1300–65), who carved Christ's initials on his chest and nailed himself to a cross: 'My beautiful body was torn apart and lacerated painfully by wild flagellation, my gentle head furrowed by thorns and this sweet face soiled with spittle and blood'. For Julian of Norwich (1343–after 1393), meditation upon a crucifix during her serious illness resulted in an ecstatic vision in 1373: 'The precious flow of his blood streamed down into hell, burst its chains and freed all there who belong to the kingdom of heaven'.[9] Bridget of Sweden (1303–73) achieved her *Revelations*, noted down by various confessors, through intense prayer, meditation on Christ's and Mary's sufferings, deprivation and exhaustion: 'occupy incessantly your mind and heart with what I have suffered for you in dying upon the cross, and with the severity of My justice at the day of judgement', demands Christ of her.[10]

These widely read passion tracts fed not only on the Gospels, but also upon poetry, legends, mystery plays (they also inspired new ones) and on apocryphal stories, which had long been tolerated by the church and thereby had assumed the respectability of dogma. Their descriptive detail and anecdotes embroidered the all too succinct Gospel stories, perhaps inspired by the final words of St John's Gospel: 'But there are also many other things which Jesus did; were every one of them to be written, I suppose that the world itself could not contain the books that would be written'. Frederick Pickering has shown that the apocryphal stories are based on metaphorically elaborated imagery of the Old Testament transferred into elaborate New Testament narrative. These apocryphal anecdotes form the core of passion tracts and legends.

Christ's passion was an ideal subject for the stimulation, through empathy, of powerful religious emotions, evoking a broad spectrum of human feelings including compassion, guilt, sorrow, gratitude and adoration. As St Bonaventure (1221–74; Journey 1.8) observed: 'Whoever wishes to ascend to God must first avoid sin…then exercise his natural powers…: by praying, to receive restoring grace, by a good life to receive purifying justice, by meditating, to receive illuminating knowledge, and by contemplating, to receive perfecting wisdom'. Art was inspired by the imagery of such devotion and dwelt on many narrative details. Painting often rivalled in its brutality the pathetic anecdotes of Christ's suffering. The frenzied account of Christ's suffering in *Christi Leiden in einer Vision geschaut* of *c.* 1350 takes a purely voyeuristic approach in its detailed description of the imagined tortures of the passion.[11] It is matched by gruesome scenes in some altarpieces and by the harrowing images of certain carved crosses. The most fervent representations of passion torture date from the second quarter of the fifteenth century and culminate in the powerful expression of Christ's suffering in Grünewald's Isenheim Altarpiece of around 1515 (Unter den Linden Museum, Colmar).

A learned and comprehensive summary of the teachings of the church fathers, Gospels, passion tracts, apocryphal stories and legends was attempted by Ludolph of Saxony, the Carthusian (*c.* 1295–*c.* 1377), in his *Vita Jesu Christi*.[12] In spite of its monumental length, it was designed as an aid to meditation at the canonical hours. Ludolph based his exegesis on accepted theological tradition. His tract was widely read, both in Latin and in vernacular translations, especially in Germany and the Netherlands. Although the story of Christ's passion necessitates some reference to his physical pain, a change in emphasis can be discerned in Ludolph's meditation. It is the intellectual suffering of the human soul of the God made flesh that seems to him the cruellest aspect of Christ's passion: 'And others...struck Him on the Neck...we must not so much fix our minds upon the hurt of the blow as the ignominy and contumely attached to it'. A better understanding of Christ's suffering may guide the sinner to true humility and charity: 'Frequent dwelling on the Passion makes the unlearned learned and causes uninstructed and simple people to become masters—masters I mean not of the "knowledge which puffeth up, but of the charity which edifieth"'. Ludolph stresses that the greatest pain endured by Christ at his Crucifixion was being made a spectacle, exposed naked to humanity, and betrayed by his 'brothers'. 'The mother too...is distressed beyond measure at seeing Him naked. She hastens to approach Him and puts her veil about Him so as to cover Him'.

This tender, compassionate, lyrical account seems closer to the art of Conrad von Soest than the earlier passion tracts. Conrad's still and poetic art, in which even the mocker in the *Christ mocked before Herod* lays an apologetic hand on Christ's arm, avoids reference to physical cruelty wherever possible, and seems to dwell like Ludolph on the suffering of the soul. Compassion is exemplified not only by the fainting Mary and the grieving gesture of St John in the *Crucifixion*, but also by the gentle hand laid on the shoulder of one of Christ's adversaries by a disputing neighbour in the splendidly attired group under the cross (pls. XIII, XIV).

This gentle compassion is also in tune with the quiet yet intensely emotional religiosity of the *devotio moderna*—a religious movement embracing communities of lay brothers and sisters, whose religious life was based on the teachings of Geert Grote from Deventer (1340–84). The communities were represented and guided by the canons of the Augustinian congregation at Windesheim. One reason for the rapid spread of the *devotio moderna* movement was the expansion of lay spirituality through instruction in the vernacular. The emergence of anonymous devotional texts in the vernacular, and translations of religious texts from Latin, enabled a larger section of the public to study religious texts. This seems to have encouraged men and women who could not take monastic vows to live in extra-regular communities. This semi-monastic lifestyle was widely imitated by lay groups and individuals. '*Humilitas*' and '*simplicitas*', practised by community members as a

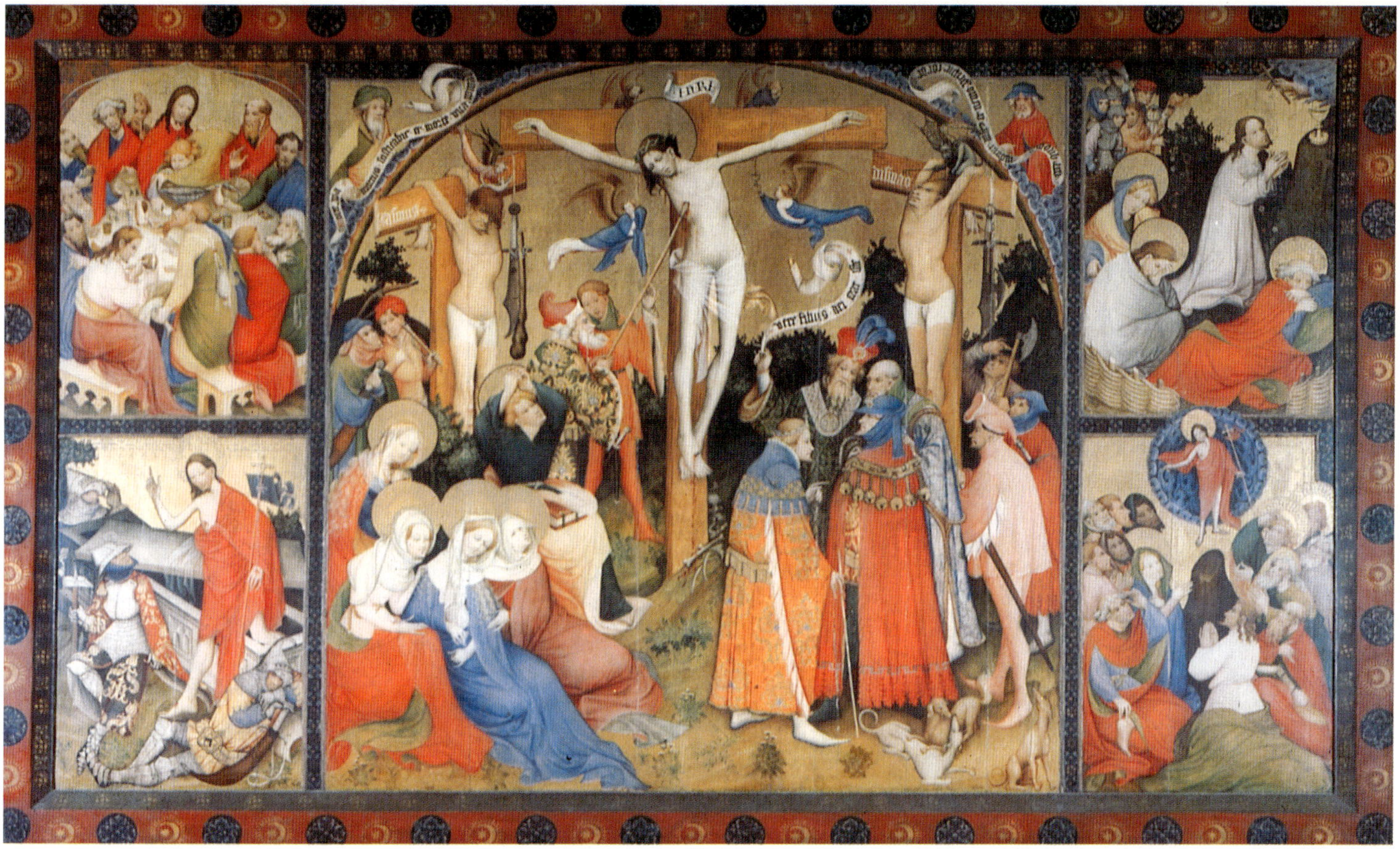

I. Conrad von Soest: *Central panel.* Niederwildungen Altarpiec*e*

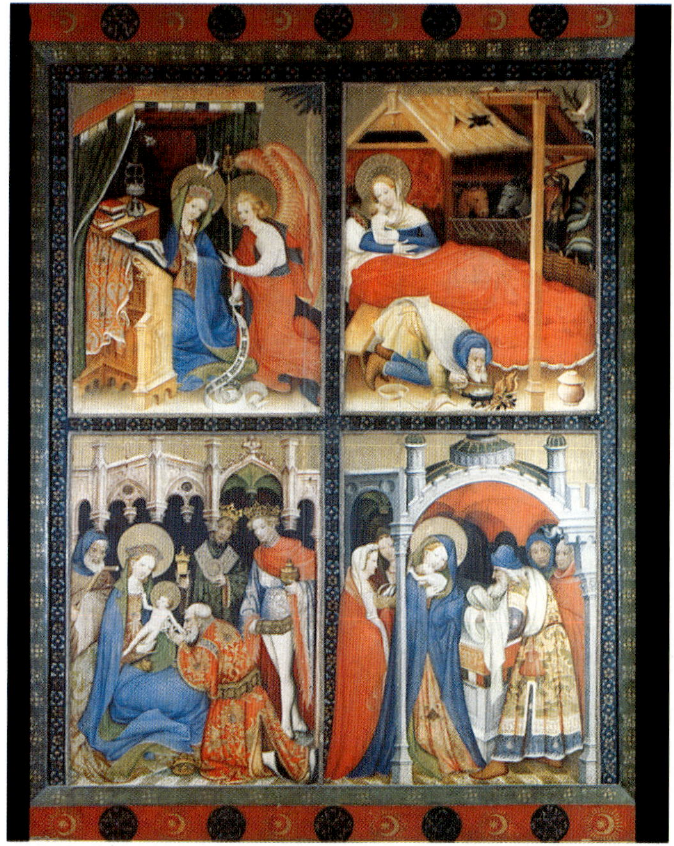

II. Conrad von Soest: *Left wing.*
Niederwildungen Altarpiece

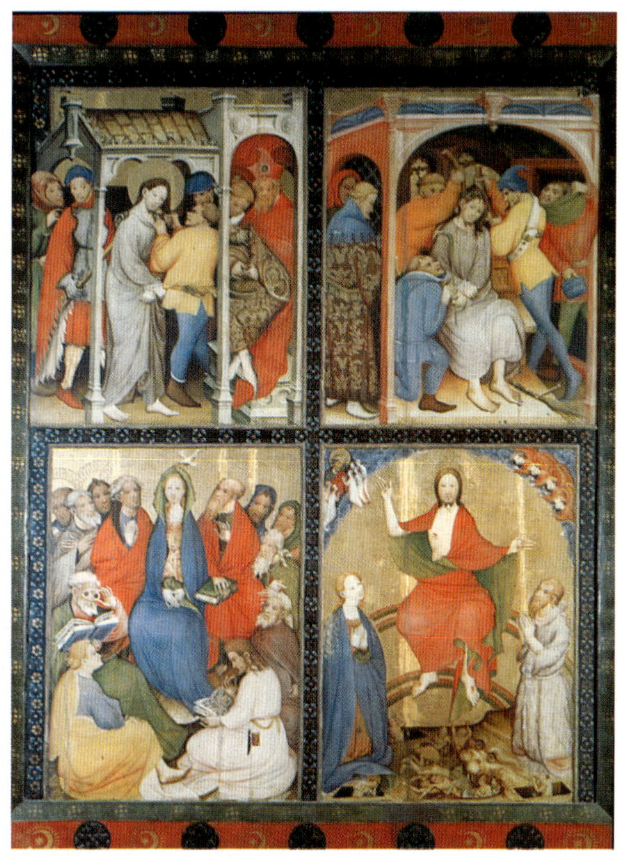

III. Conrad von Soest: *Right wing.*
Niederwildungen Altarpiece

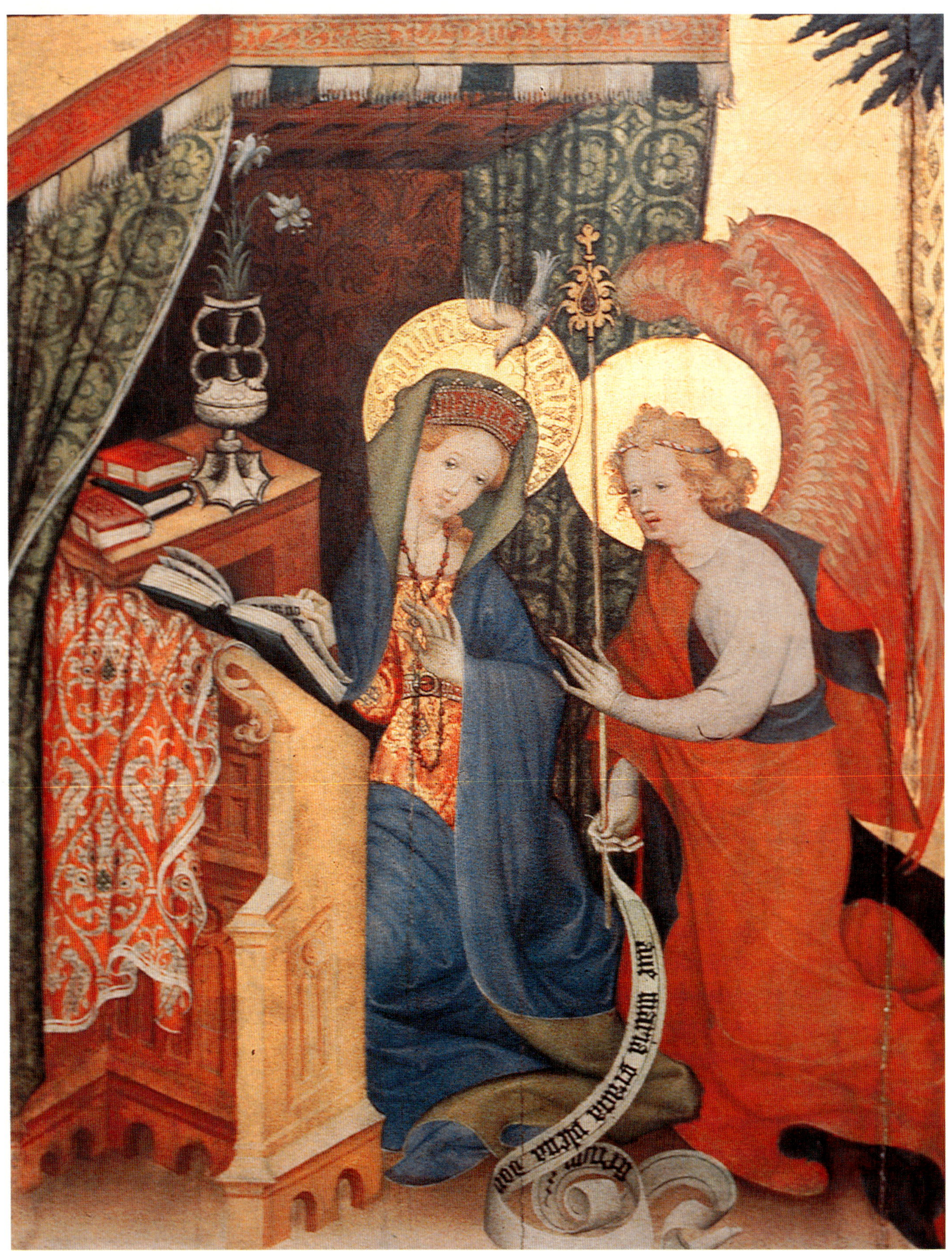

IV. Conrad von Soest: *Annunciation*. Niederwildungen Altarpiece

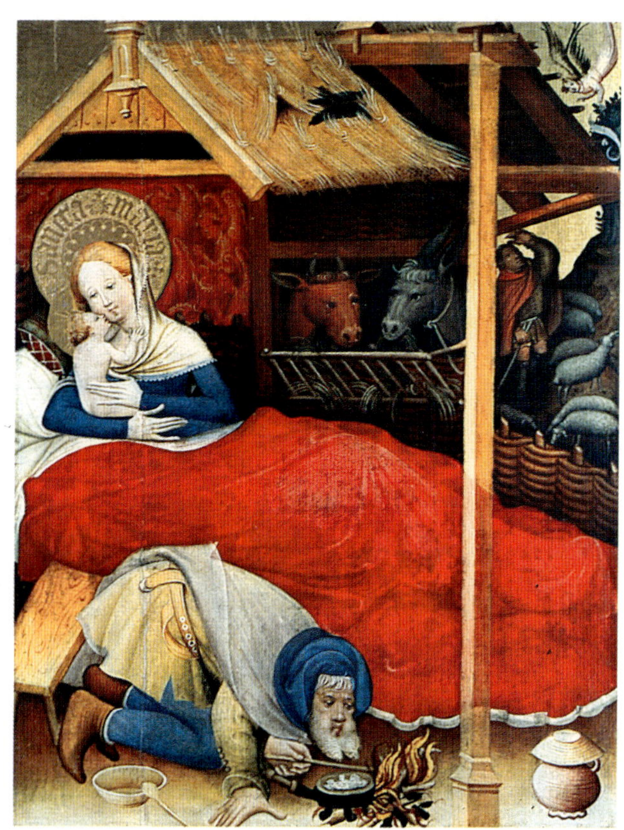

V. Conrad von Soest: *Nativity.*
Niederwildungen Altarpiece

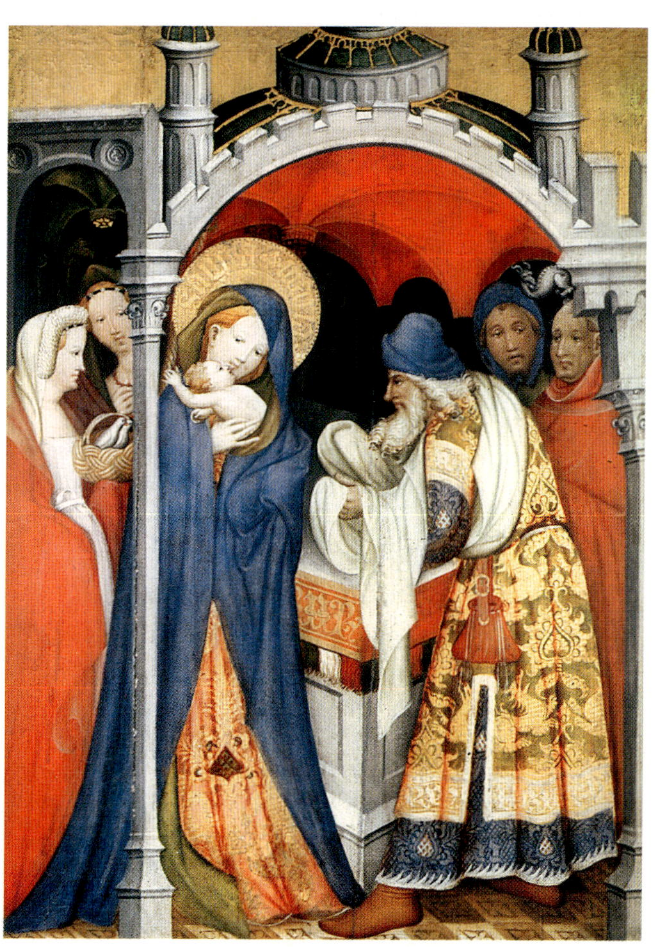

VI. Conrad von Soest: *Presentation.*
Niederwildungen Altarpiece

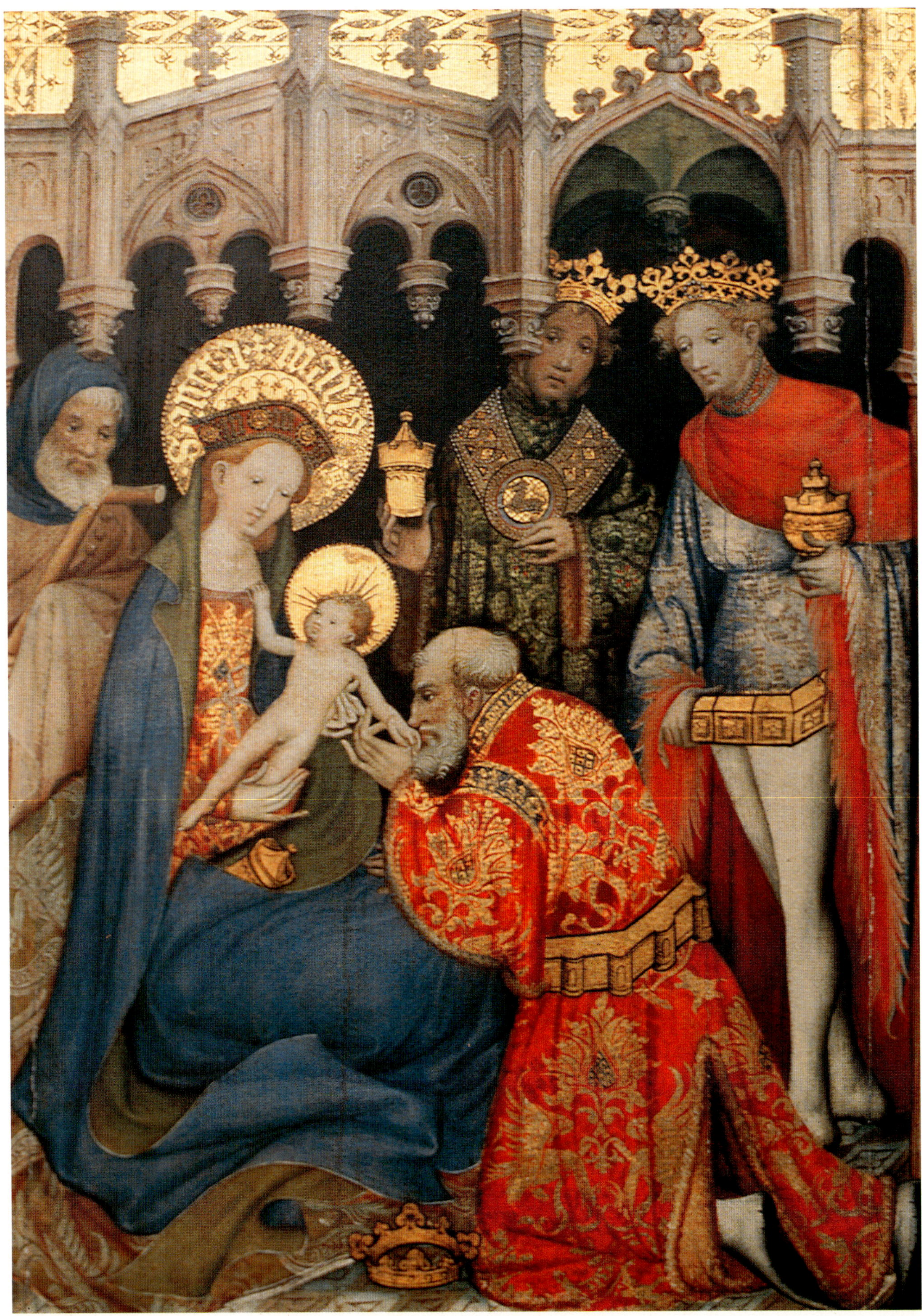
sancta maria

VII. Conrad von Soest: *Adoration of the Kings*.
Niederwildungen Altarpiece

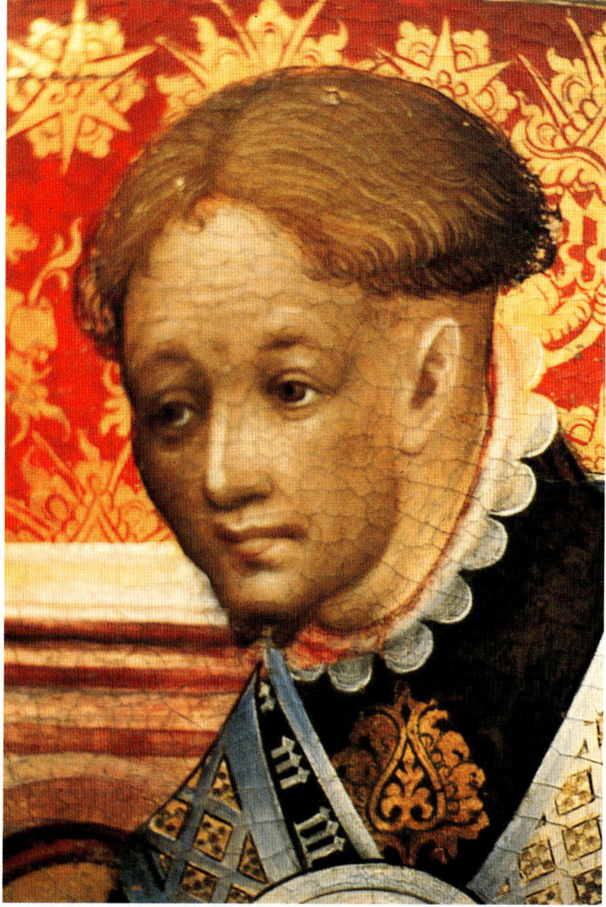

VIII. *Head of Young King*.
Detail from the *Adoration of the Kings*.
Dortmund Altarpiece

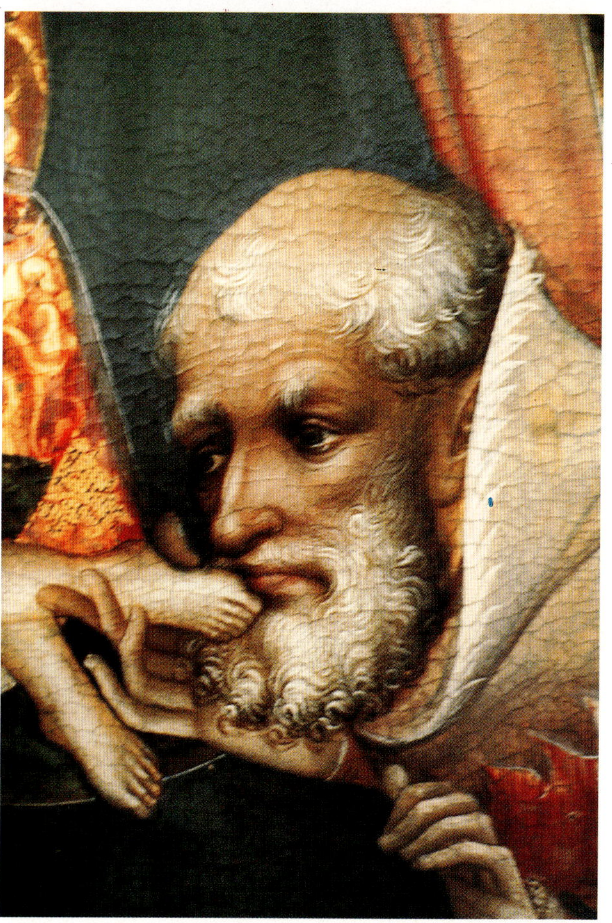

IX. *Head of Old King*.
Detail from the *Adoration of the Kings*.
Dortmund Altarpiece

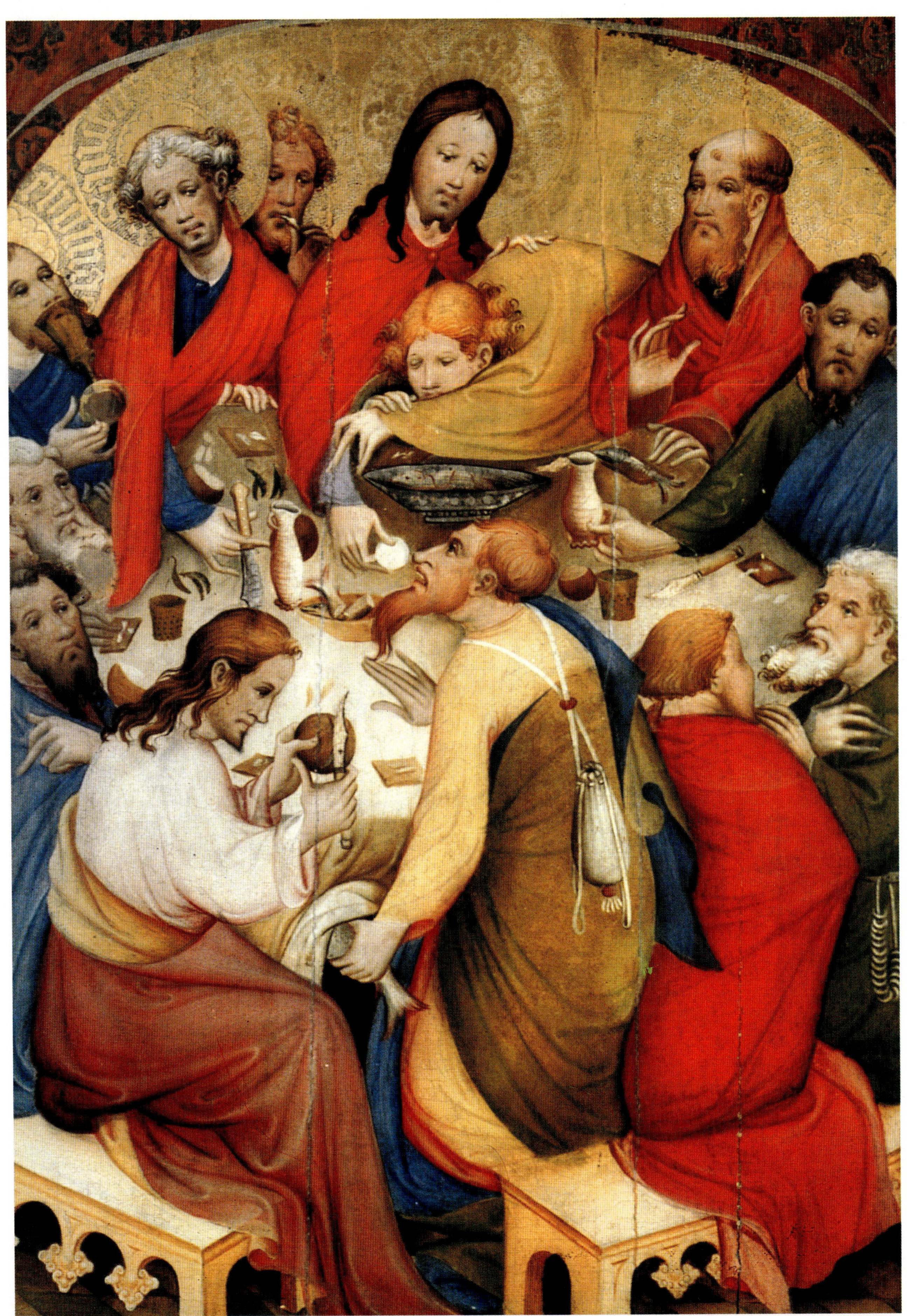

X. Conrad von Soest: *Last Supper*. Niederwildungen Altarpiece

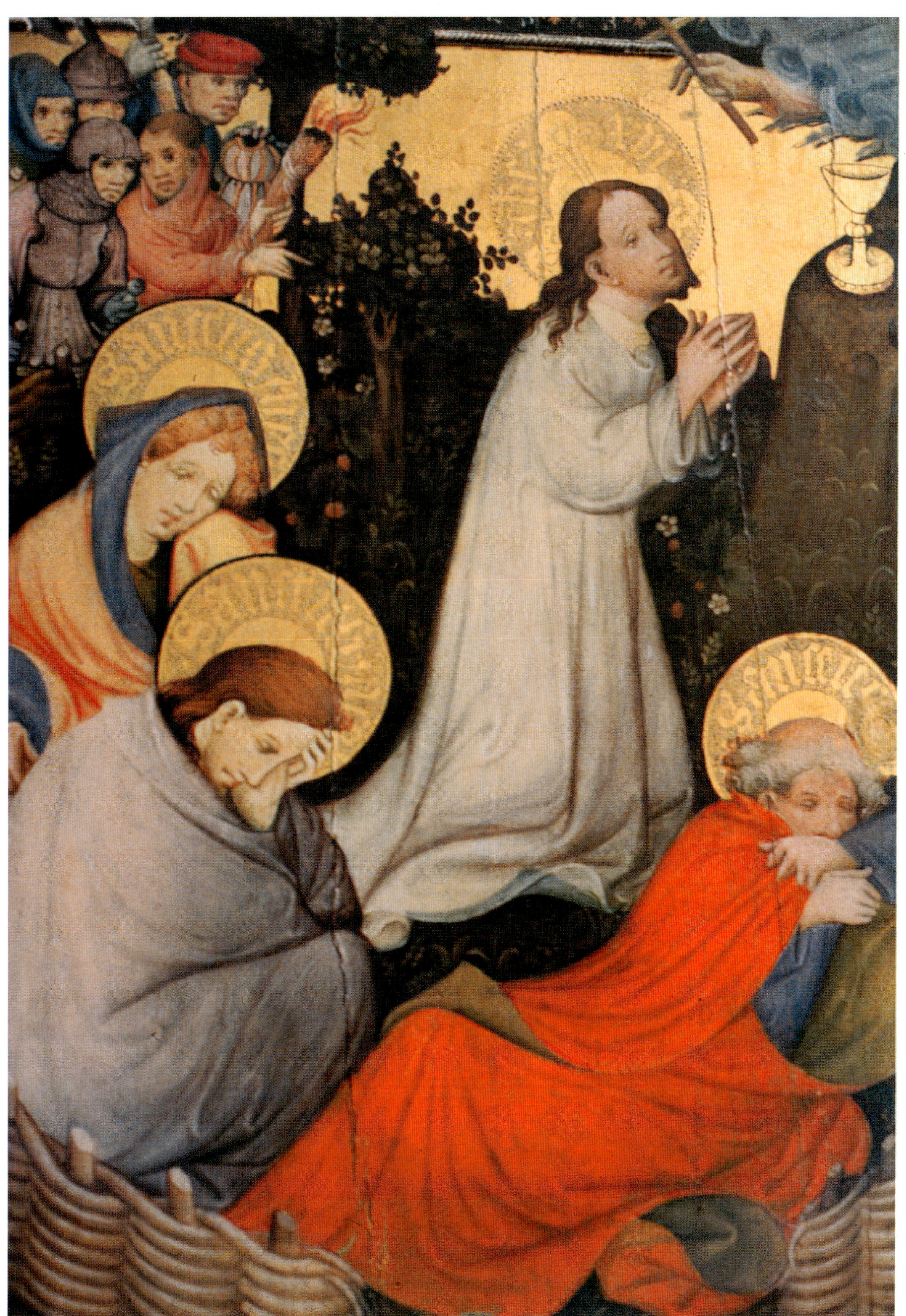

XI. Conrad von Soest: *Gethsemane*. Niederwildungen Altarpiece

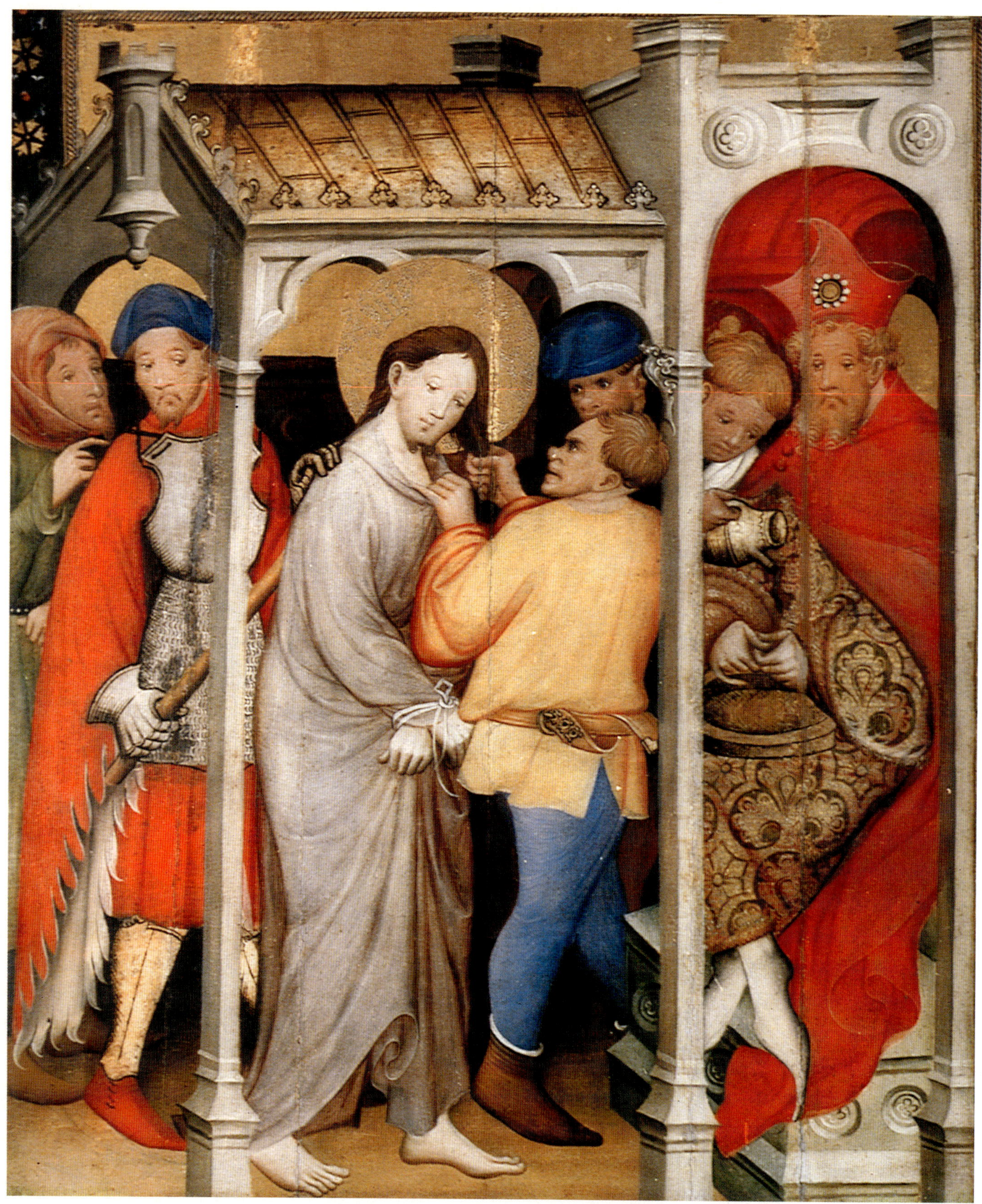

XII. Conrad von Soest: *Christ before Pilate*. Niederwildungen Altarpiece

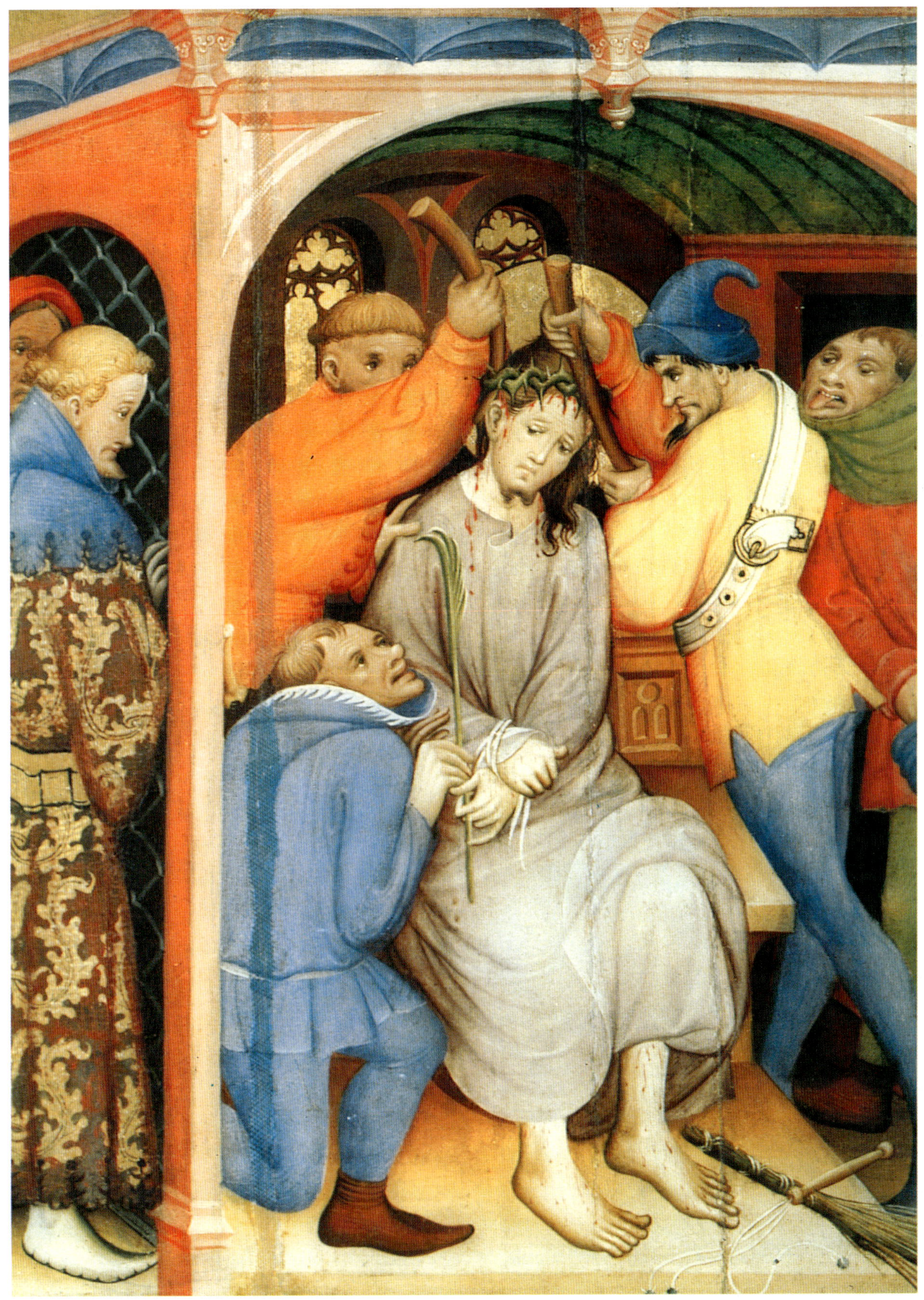

XIII. Conrad von Soest: *Christ mocked before Herod*. Niederwildungen Altarpiece

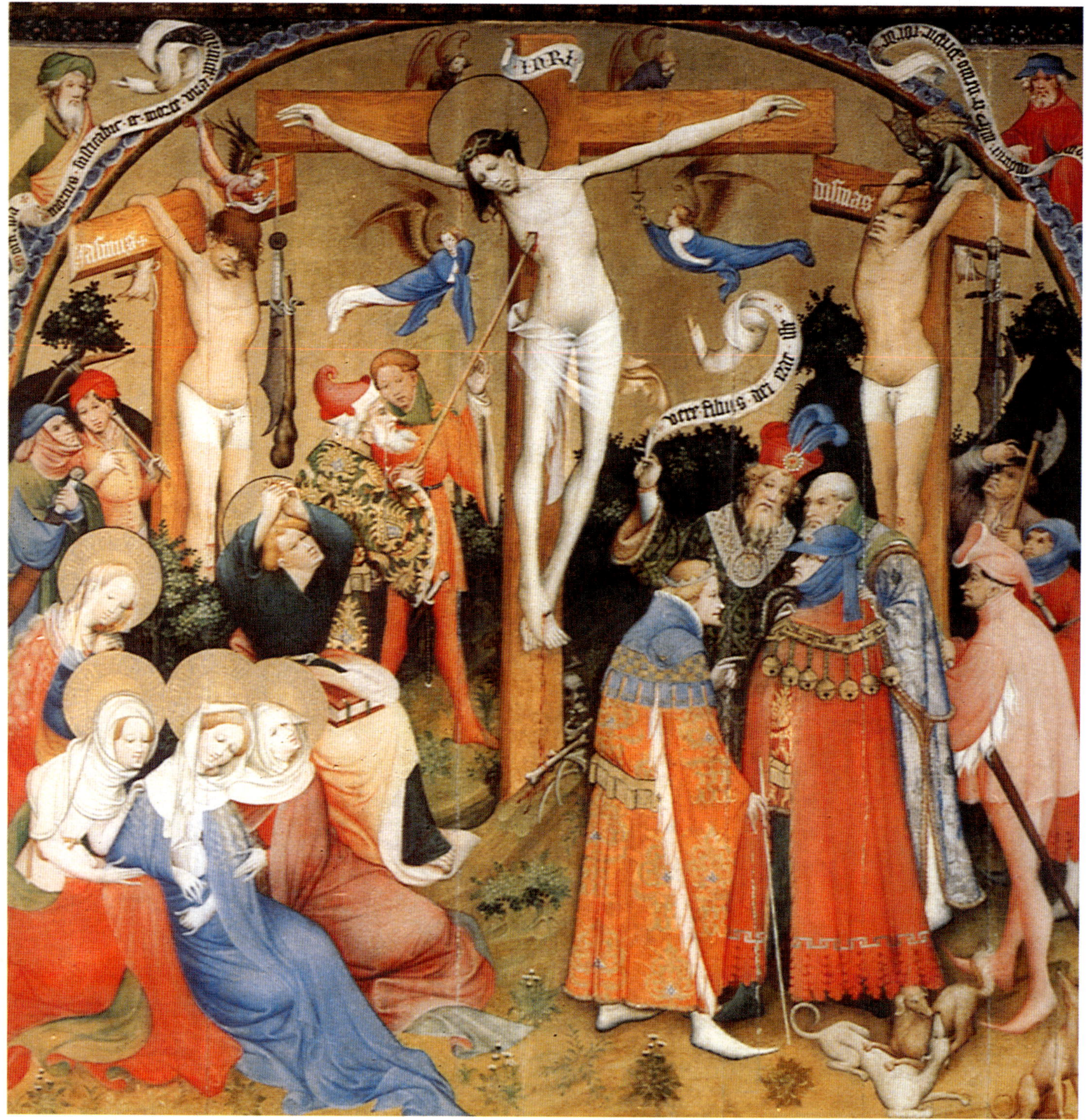

XIV. Conrad von Soest: *Crucifixion*. Niederwildungen Altarpiece

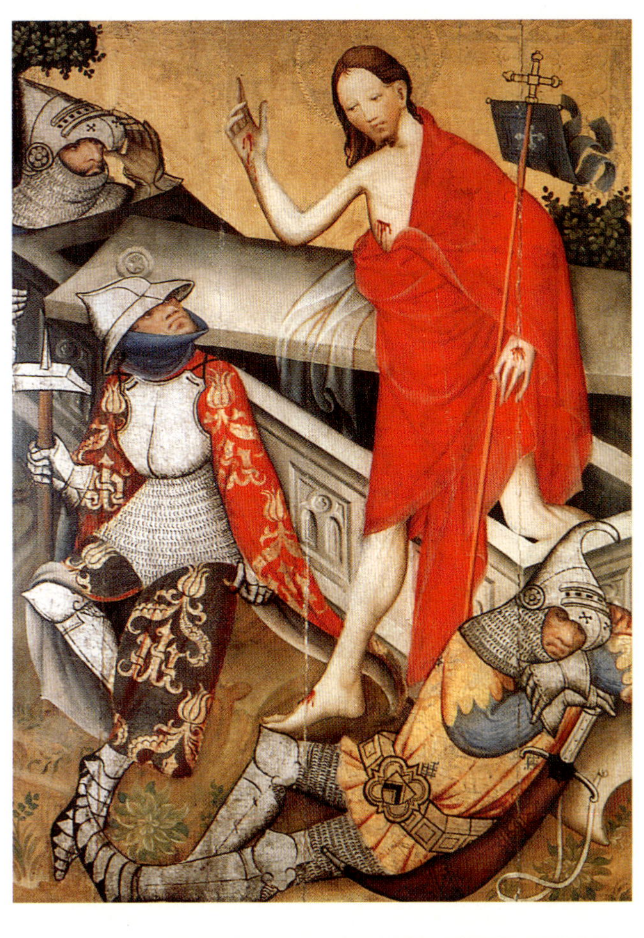

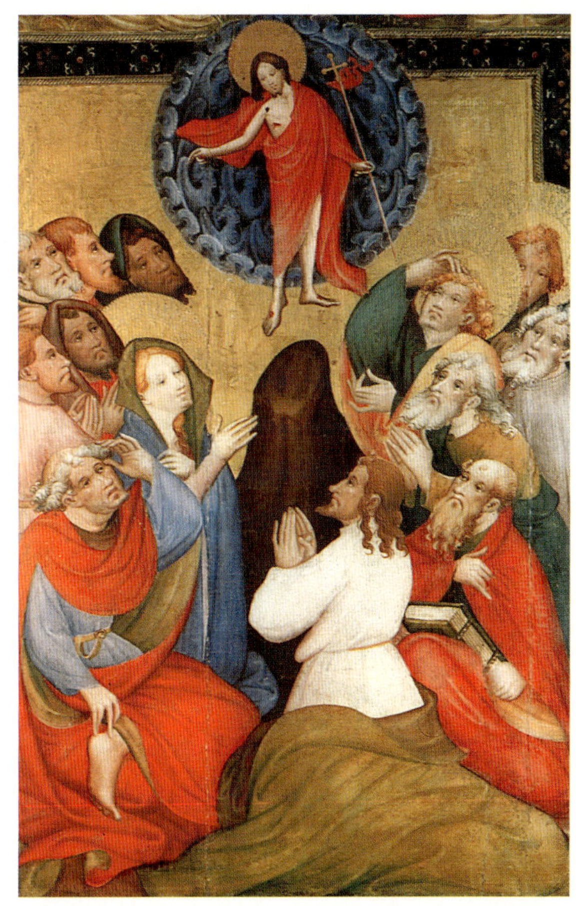

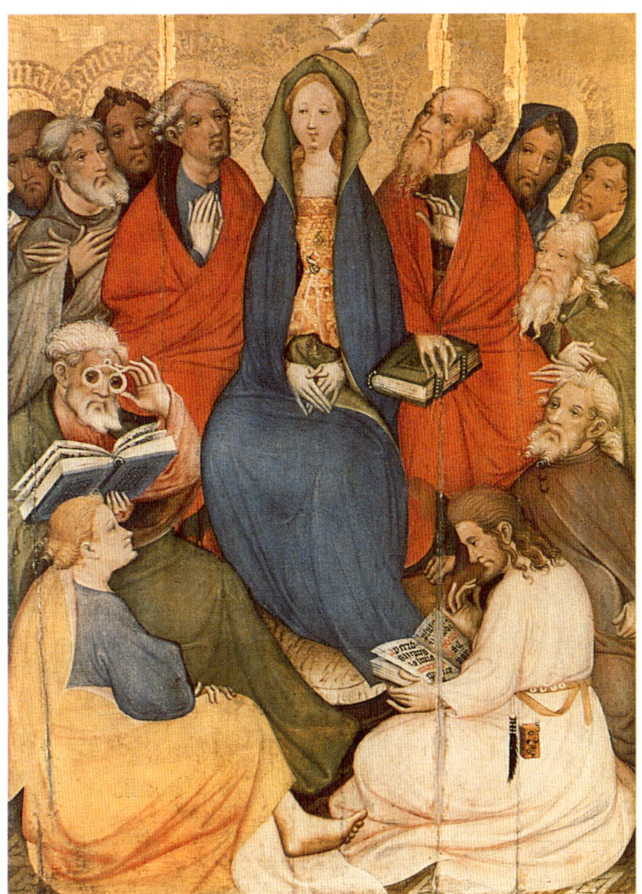

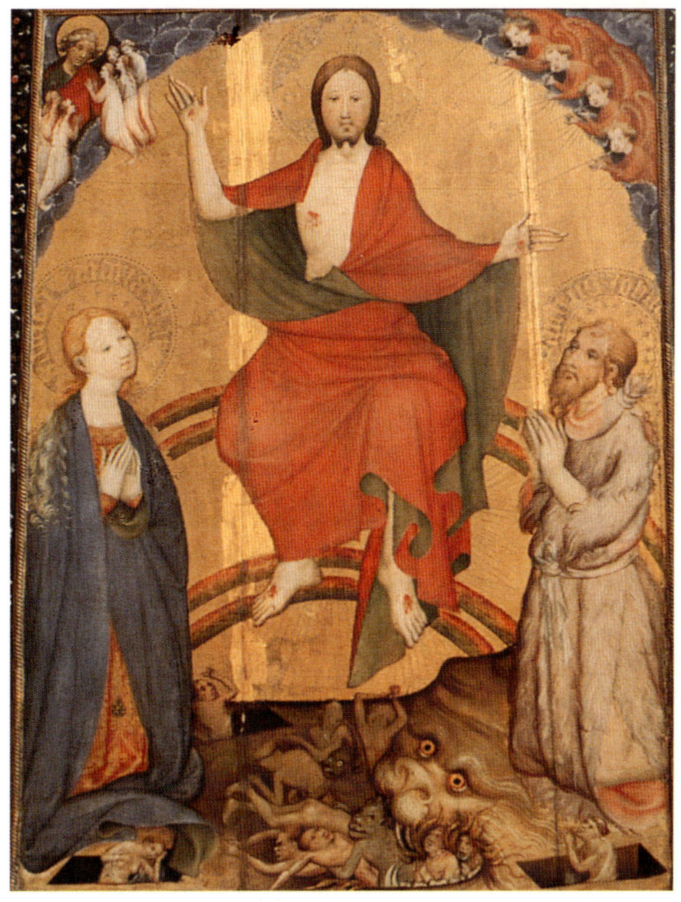

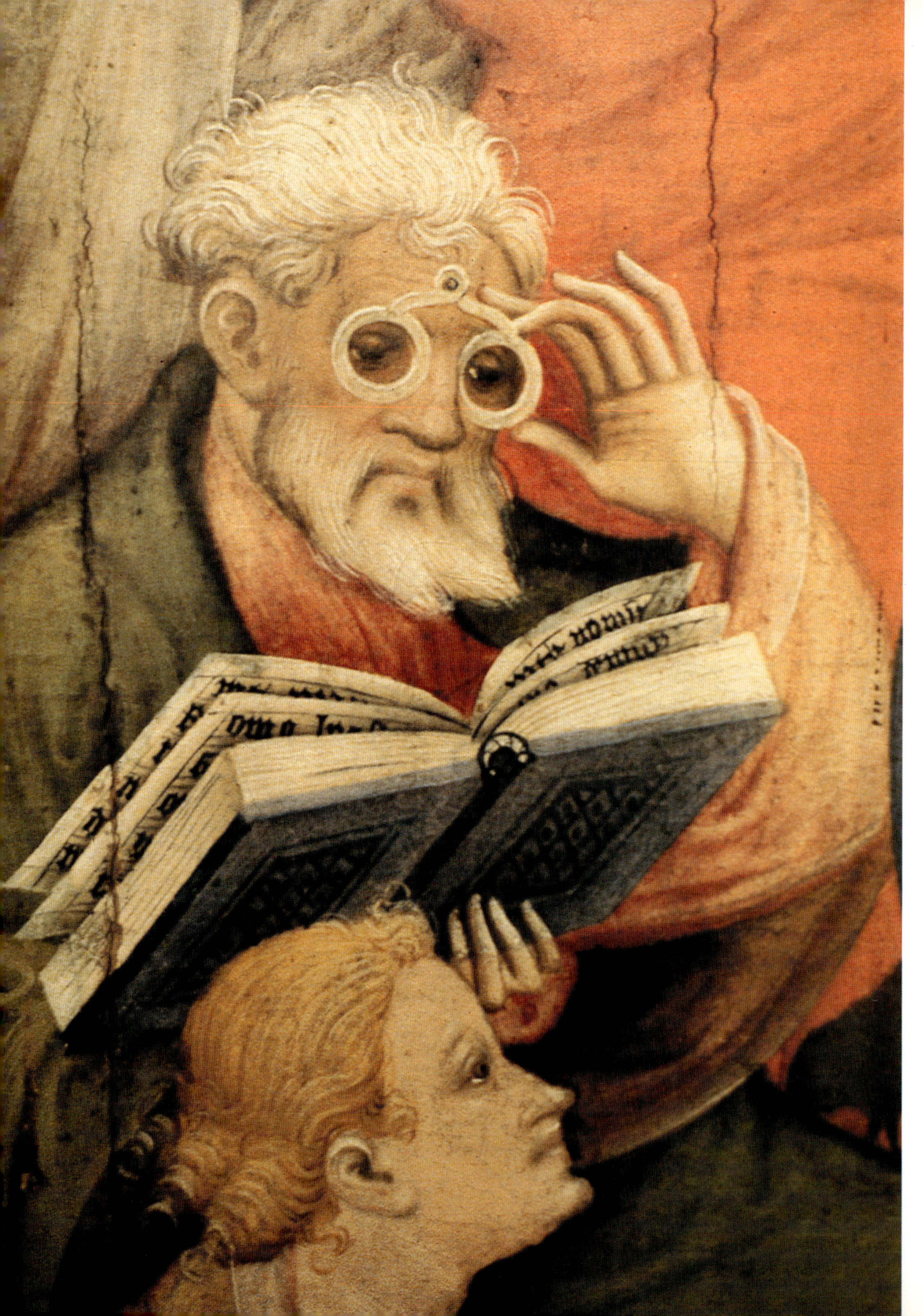

result of meditation on the life and passion of Christ, were complemented by useful employment, mainly spinning and weaving for the lay sisters, and copying and writing of manuscripts for the lay brothers. Their texts belong to the mainstream literature of Christianity. Ludolph of Saxony's monumental guide to meditation was central to the movement's concerns. The *Imitation of Christ*, attributed to Thomas à Kempis (*c.* 1379–1471), a member of the house of the Windesheim congregation at Mount St Agnes near Zwolle, illustrates the spirituality of the *devotio moderna*, urging humility, self-denial and discipline, acceptance of one's lot and trust in the love of God: 'Progress in the spiritual life is made not so much when you have the gracious gift of spiritual comfort, but when you can bear its removal with humility, self-denial and patience...'.[13] True humility should be expressed in quiet contemplation rather than in learned dispute: 'I would rather feel compunction in my heart than be able to define it'. The first Windesheim monastery in Westphalia was founded at Frenswegen in 1394. The *devotio moderna* was firmly established in Westphalia by 1401.

Passion plays were another expression of lay devotion. However, it is difficult to determine the extent to which the texts of such passion plays influenced altarpiece iconography; for the vivid images created by the artists may well in turn have influenced the writers of passion plays. The loss of texts and panels renders it difficult to fix with precision the date at which new images emerged. Passion play scenes certainly formed part of the visual memory of patrons and painters in the late Middle Ages. The imagery may not have been new, but it could have been more widely disseminated by means of passion plays. The texts may reflect some of the language that could have been used in 'reading' and describing the narrative scenes of an altarpiece, and they are therefore of some interest for the purpose of iconographic interpretation. Conrad's narrative style tends towards lyricism as opposed to drama. Yet Joseph, kindling the flames as he kneels to cook in the Niederwildungen *Nativity*—a lively interpretation of the popular 'nutritor domini' image— could well be an example of a scene remembered from a performance of a passion play (Frontispiece, pl. V).[14]

Conrad's altarpieces do not seem to draw their iconography from any particular text, apart from the Gospels. Passion tracts are nevertheless representative of the spiritual climate of the time in which the iconographic programme for the altarpieces was devised. The courtly artist Conrad does not beguile with seductive details of legends, but keeps to the austerity of Gospel narrative and a stress on individual experience. The lavish execution of his art and the beauty of form and detail create a poignant contrast to the simplicity of the narrative.[15] The commandery and confraternity members could indeed be inspired by the 'joyous brilliance' of the decoration, as the priest Eberhard suggested. But they were also encouraged to identify and empathize with the suffering participants in the Salvation story. 'Let us consider the most blessed Passion of Christ, so that our hearts may be melted in it...', counselled Ludolph, who believed that Christ would 'judge the world not

XIX. *Reading Apostle.* Detail from *Pentecost.* Niederwildungen Altarpiece

only as God, but dressed again in his saintly humanity'.[16] The tender humanity of Conrad's interpretation may represent religious feeling as up-to-date as the courtly style of his painting.

The altarpieces by Conrad von Soest differ from earlier Westphalian passion retables not only in the courtly elegance of their style, and the intimate humanity of their actors, but in the close adherence to biblical texts. Scenes depicting the story of Joachim and Anna in the Buxtehude, Bielefeld, Schotten and Isselhorst Altarpieces, for example, are based on apocryphal narrative, elaborated in the *Golden Legend*.[17] In the Buxtehude Altarpiece, Master Bertram also illustrated one of St Bridget's visions in a charming domestic scene showing Mary knitting a seamless garment and the Christ Child reading amongst his toys, which is tragically interrupted by two angels bearing the symbols of the passion (pl. 67). Conrad and his advisers seem to avoid such material. Instead, his altarpieces were functional, interacting with the texts of worship, and therefore some liturgical references feature in the iconographic programmes.

Even though Conrad von Soest introduced a number of extra figures into the Westphalian crucifixion scene, which traditionally only included two groups beneath the cross (the women with St John on the one hand and the soldiers on the other), he again adhered to the Gospel texts in his choice of figures and in their actions. His follower, however, was less faithful to the Gospel narrative; he introduced the Magdalene embracing the cross in the Darup and Warendorf Altarpieces (pls. 161, 162), as well as horses for the soldiers, and saved souls emerging from graves beneath the cross. This dramatic elaboration culminated in Westphalia in a confusion of figures and events in the multiple narrative of the *Crucifixion* (*c.* 1480) by Derick Baegert in the Propsteikirche, Dortmund.

Conrad adhered consistently to the spirit of biblical texts. In Westphalian Annunciations, the passion was traditionally announced by a tiny Christ child carrying the cross. Conrad broke with this established elaboration of the Bible text which is included in the narrative of the Netze (pl. 69), Grabow (pl. 68), Buxtehude, Bielefeld, Schotten and Blankenberch (pl. 58) Altarpieces, as well as the Golden Panel from Lüneburg.[18] He restricted his scene in the Niederwildungen Altarpiece to the essential actors of the Gospel. The tradition was, however, later followed by the Campin/Flémalle workshop in the Netherlands (pl. 104) and revived in Westphalia by Johann Koerbecke. The motif may be based on the Revelations of Sister Mechthild of Magdeburg (*c.* 1212–83), who declared that God the Father asked the Son to take the cross upon himself, before He sent the Angel Gabriel to Mary.[19]

In the *Annunciation* of the Niederwildungen Altarpiece, Conrad's adherence to Gospel narrative is partially confused by the courtly setting (pl. IV). In a further break with tradition Conrad shows the Virgin Annunciate not as a humble maiden but crowned as the Queen of Heaven, kneeling (or sitting—the pose is ambiguous) at a canopied prie-dieu that is sumptuously hung with costly brocades. Although this image accords with St Bridget's vision of the 'Virgin Mary wearing a crown

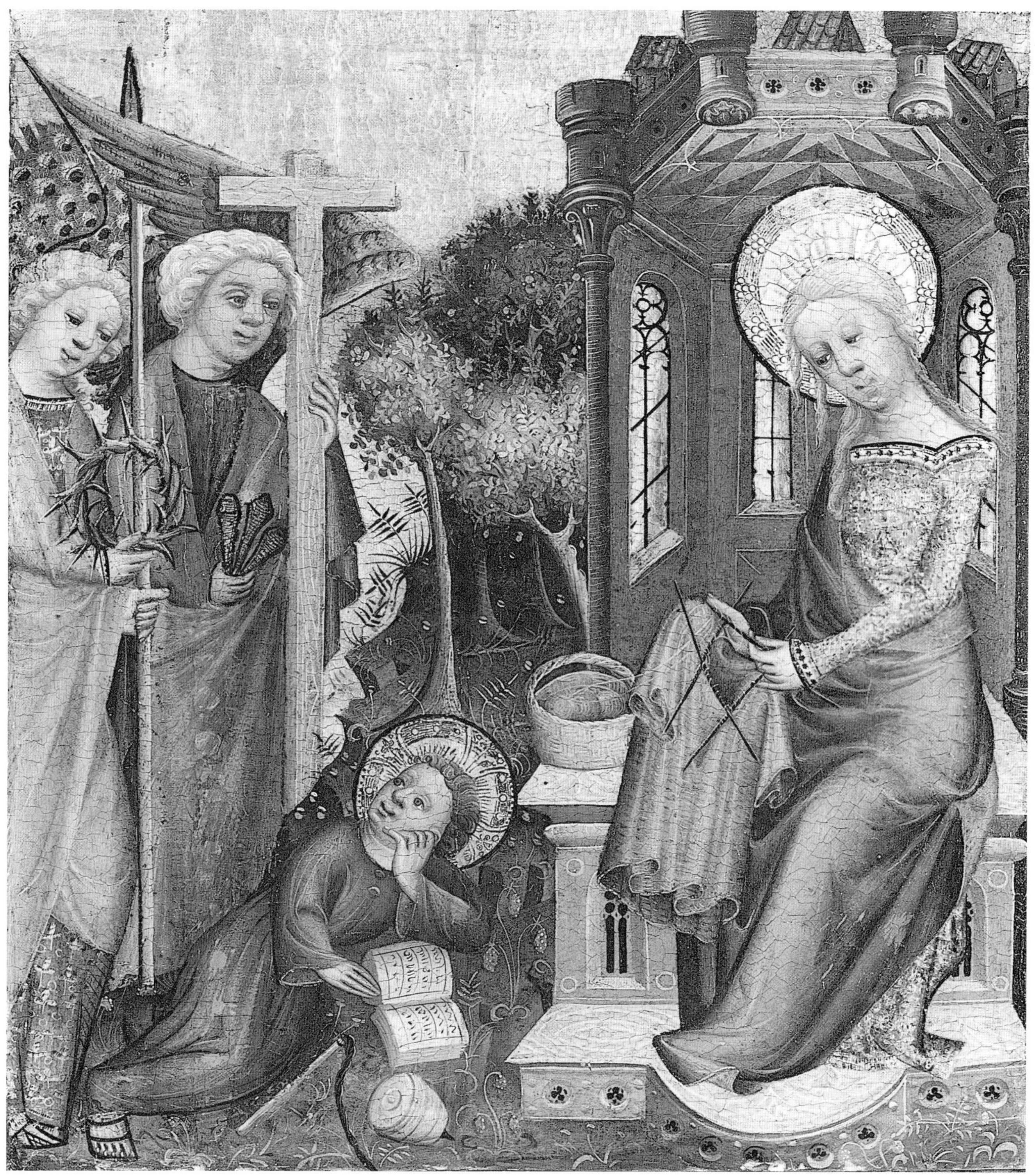

67. Master Bertam and Workshop: *The Angels visit Mary*. Buxtehude Altarpiece,
Hamburger Kunsthalle

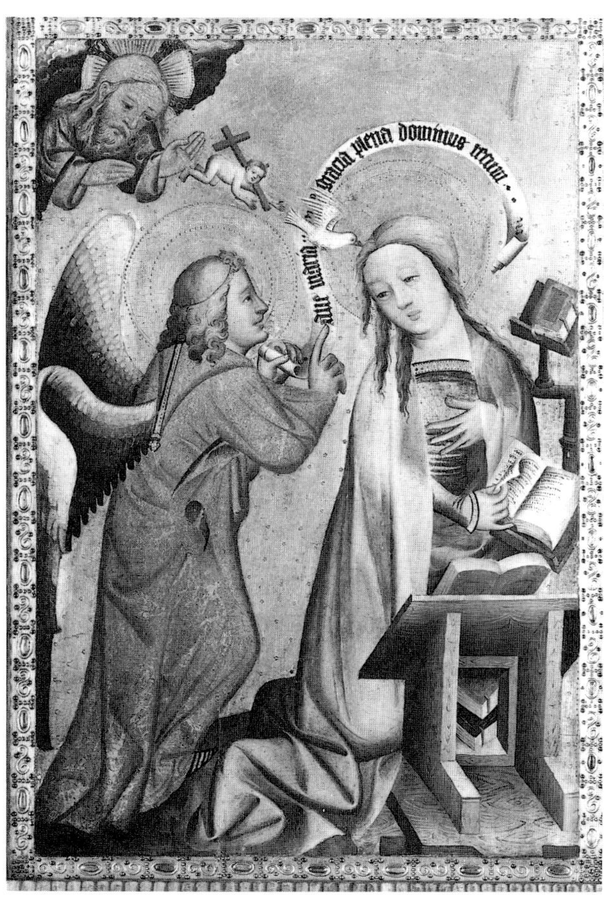
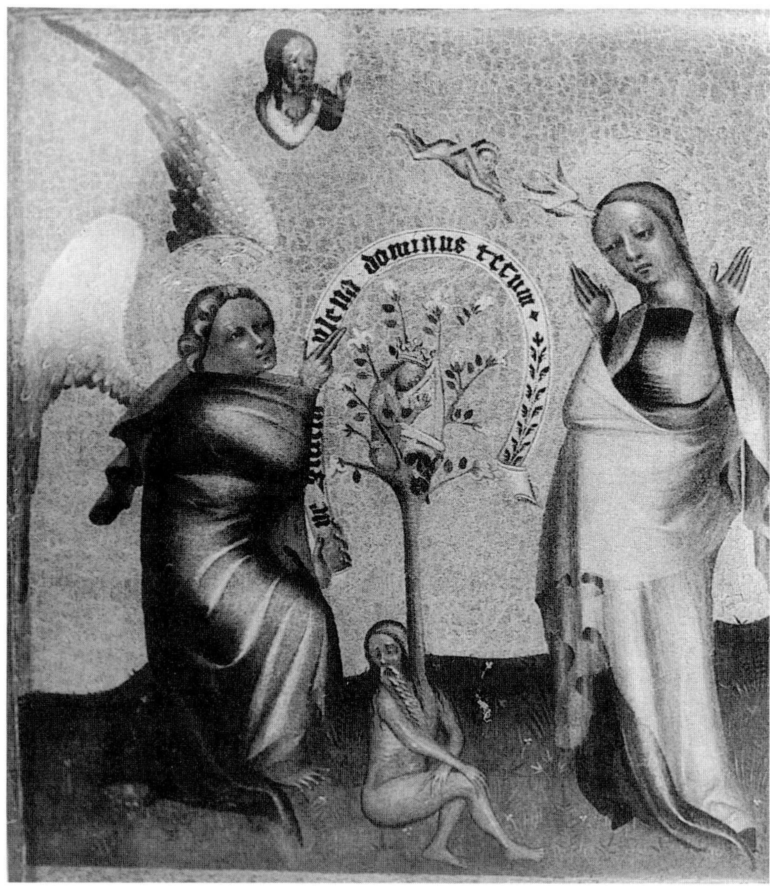

and priceless jewels' (here she is adorned with a rosary around her neck and a jewelled belt at her waist, as well as the crown), St Bridget appears to draw on visual memory herself, perhaps recalling panels seen on her journeys, when she explains that 'the flying hair proves her to be a pure, immaculate virgin, and the blue cloak stresses that all earthly things have died for her' (for blue is the colour of heaven). Conrad's Virgin is therefore unlikely to have been inspired by St Bridget's words; she is rather the 'Queen of Heaven' of hymns and liturgy: '*Salve Regina, mater misericordiae, vita dulcedo, et spes nostra, salve*'.[20] The scene of court ceremonial can be traced back to the *Annunciation* in Sta Maria Maggiore, Rome (*c.* 435).[21]

The regal setting is stressed at Niederwildungen by the curtained canopy sheltering the Virgin, which appears to represent the tent-like constructions in which princes worshipped. A princely room of a comparable nature, sheltering a high-ranking cleric, is depicted in an initial of the Bible of Richard II (*c.* 1385–90; London, BL, Royal I E IX, p. 165). In view of the *ad hoc* nature of the survival of works of art, it remains uncertain whether this design constitutes a progressive conception by Conrad von Soest, namely a fusion of the curtain motif, used for instance by Giotto in the Arena chapel and by Jacquemart de Hesdin (pl. 70), with

100

68. Master Bertram: *Annunciation.*
Grabow Altarpiece, Hamburger Kunsthalle

69. The Netze Master: *Annunciation.*
Netze Altarpiece, Ev. Pfarrkirche, Netze

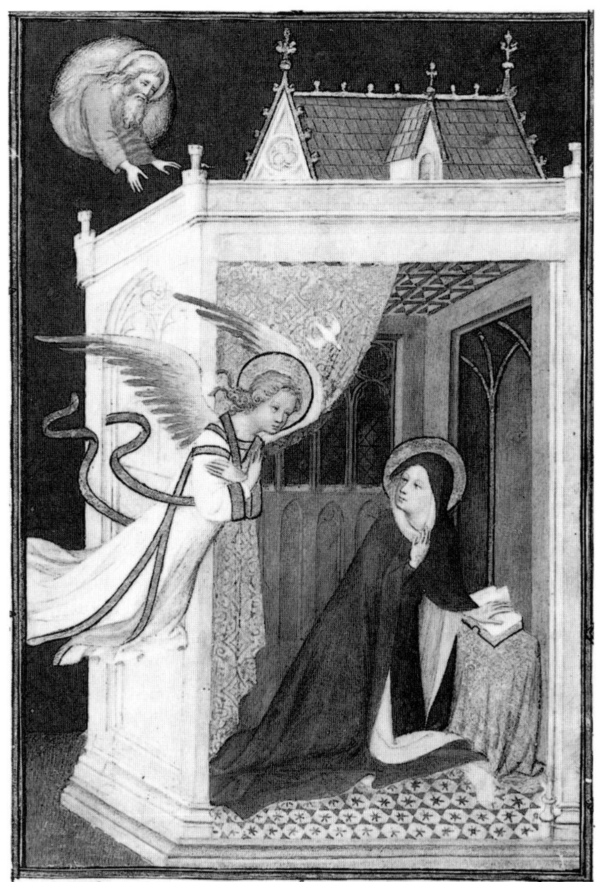

70. Parement Master:
*Annunciation. Très belles heures de
Jean de Berry*, Brussels, Bibl. Royale,
MS 11060–61, p. 18

the regal baldachin that frequently protected the Virgin in earlier narrative scenes.[22] The tester of the curtained construction is decorated with pseudo-Kufic lettering in a manner that became popular in Tuscany from the end of the thirteenth century and flourished in Siena. It also adorns the collar of the kneeling King and the brocade covering of the seat in the Niederwildungen *Adoration*, the altar cloth in the *Presentation* and a soldier's tunic in the *Resurrection*. As such lettering was connected with oriental luxury items (such as ceramics, carpets, goldsmith works and other *objets d'art* which could serve as gifts among princes), the decorative effect of Kufic lettering was exploited by western artists painting in the Courtly Style around 1400.

As the Virgin 'inclines her ear' in the words of the Psalmist (45.11), she turns the pages of her psalter to reveal the painter's name whilst listening, 'troubled', to Gabriel's words, in accordance with the Gospel text (Luke 1.29). Her other hand responds with a gesture of awe. This derives from a prototype which was known at the beginning of the ninth century and was in widespread use by the time the mosaic in the Palatine Chapel in Palermo was created (*c.* 1143). Her features have the timeless beauty, *'ab initio et ante saecula'*, that was praised in her daily office of

101

the church, when the '*Ave Maria*', inscribed on the angel's scroll, was also recited. These liturgical echoes do not deflect from the essential simplicity of the Gospel narrative. The courtly *mise-en-scène* of this *Annunciation* is completed by the herald angel who approaches from the right and kneels ceremoniously to greet the lady. This gesture of homage was probably first introduced by Giotto in his *Annunciation* fresco in the Arena chapel in Padua (*c*. 1304–12). The advance of the angel from the right can be traced back to fourth-century sarcophagus sculpture.[23] Although this placing of the angel became less common in later centuries, it never lost favour altogether and recurred, for instance, in the Cathedral doors at Hildesheim (1015) and in the stone relief at Bamberg Cathedral (*c*. 1230–40). This arrangement also occurs in French manuscripts, most frequently in the Boucicaut workshop, and could conceivably have been known in Westphalia before the first observable instance in the Bielefeld Altarpiece.

Above the angel a leafy branch is painted, in place of the more usual motif of God the Father bestowing the Holy Spirit. It represents 'the branch that shall grow' of the stem of Jesse (Isaiah 11.1).[24] The tree of Jesse, which had already featured in eleventh-century Annunciations in the form of a small shoot, was depicted in the Netze Altarpiece (pl. 69) in the shape of a tree growing from the loin of Jesse and sheltering David. This reference to the prophets illustrates the significance of the Incarnation. 'This is the day on which the Synagogue dies and the Church is born' comments Ludolph. The dove is also present as a symbol of the mystery of the incarnation. It is only present in Annunciations when an allusion to the Eucharistic significance of the Incarnation is desired.[25]

The Eucharistic significance of the Niederwildungen Altarpiece is also stressed by the large central *Crucifixion* (pl. XIV), symbol of reincarnation and salvation. The symbolic significance of Christ's physical death, as proof of His incarnation and therefore the reincarnation in the Eucharist, was argued in defence of images during the time of iconoclasm. The doctrine of transubstantiation had been defined at the Fourth Lateran Council in 1215. As a consequence, a direct connection began to be seen between human sin and Christ's passion and the sacrifice of the Mass.[26] Since the thirteenth century, Crucifixion altarpieces had frequently been placed on the high altar to stress the sacramental character of the sacrificial death of Christ, thus illustrating the real significance of the Mass. This function is confirmed in Conrad's *Crucifixion* by one of the sorrowing angels, who collects the sacred blood in a chalice. 'We dedicate to you the cup of salvation and call upon your name, gracious Lord' (Psalm 116.13), recited the priest and the congregation of hospitallers before they received the blood of the Eucharist contained in the wafer.

The commonly quoted reference to the cup of blood as a symbol of Ecclesia was certainly understood in Westphalia, as the figures of Ecclesia and Synagoga appear in the *Crucifixion* from the Wiesenkirche in Soest of *c*. 1230.[27] As Mary, who often represents Ecclesia, is shown sinking to the ground, she is not intended to symbolize the birth of Ecclesia in this panel. In the Niederwildungen *Crucifixion*,

Longinus (the lance-bearer, see John 19.34) embodies the Jewish people: he is the only figure to wear the Jewish hat, which had been compulsory for Jews since the Fourth Lateran Council.

References to the Old Testament were intended to convey the salvation message; such connection between the Old and New Testaments was perhaps encouraged by the statement in St John's Gospel (19.36), 'those things took place that the scripture might be fulfilled'. Studies of correspondences between the Old and New Testaments had been initiated by the earliest Christian teachers, who perceived countless typological prefigurations. Artistic iconography reflected this interest, as we have seen in Conrad's *Annunciation*. In his *Crucifixion*, the skull and bones at the feet of the cross may not have simply signified the historic place of the Gospel, 'the place of a skull, which is called in Hebrew Golgotha' (John, 19.17). In view of the fact that the altarpiece was paid for by the sale of indulgences, the skull and bones might also have been understood as a reference to Adam, whose original sin was redeemed by the Crucifixion: 'In Adam I fell…in Adam I died…guilty as I was in Adam, now I am justified in Christ', declared Ambrose in the fourth century, and he based his faith on Bible authority: 'For as in Adam all die, so also in Christ shall all be made alive' (I Corinthians, 15.2).[28] This typology of Adam is expressed in a Byzantine Ivory of the tenth century in New York, which depicts Adam lying on the ground with the cross growing from his loin.

Old Testament prophets were frequently represented in art to give authority to the New Testament and thereby to the Church. Their role is aptly expressed in the windows of the south transept of Chartres Cathedral, where four prophets carry the four evangelists on their shoulders. The presence of prophets in Crucifixions is based on Byzantine sources, for which the wall painting in the church of the Virgin at Studenica (1209) is an impressive instance. In Conrad von Soest's *Crucifixion*, two prophets holding scrolls are placed in the spandrels of a rainbow behind the crosses. A row of stylized clouds shows that they speak from heaven. (The rainbow that separates earth from heaven in the *Crucifixion* panel echoes the transverse arch in the church that separates the congregation in the nave from the sacred space of the choir). *'Ecce quo…moritur monstratur (?) et nemo percipit corde'* [the righteous man perishes, and no one lays it to heart], laments Isaiah (57.1), the prophet in the right-hand spandrel. *'Morte propria mortus justificabat et morte vita permanebit'*, rejoices the other prophet. This second prophet could not be identified, as his sentence is not a quotation from the Old Testament. His words may well be a reference to the liturgy, for they were recited during the Easter Vigil. They are still part of modern Cologne liturgy: 'Durch sein Sterben hat er unsern Tod vernichtet und durch seine Auferstehung neues Leben uns erworben' [through his death he conquers our death and by his death life will be eternal]. They seem to have been mistaken for the words of a prophet through the readings of the 'twelve prophecies', mentioned by Ludolph of Saxony, that used to follow the consecration of the Easter candle during this office. However, these prophecies were not all taken from the *Prophets*; rather, they were chosen with the intention of conveying the Easter message.[29]

Another reference to the Old Testament may be intended by the arched body of Conrad's crucified Christ. A slight shift of the outstretched body of Christ towards His left can sometimes be observed in early Gothic art, and had already been introduced into Westphalian art in the Netze Altarpiece.[30] Conrad von Soest, however, painted Christ's body painfully arched, at breaking point, thus creating a large gap between Christ's straight right and bowed left legs. Frederick Pickering cites several literary examples comparing the arched body of the suffering Christ to a taut string pulled on David's harp.[31] Amongst many others, he quotes Cassiodor: 'The harp signifies the glorious passion, that with stretched sinews and counted bones lets its heavy suffering sound like a clerical chant'. He also quotes Bruno Herbipolensis: 'The harp is the human body of Christ in his suffering'. The idea is perhaps most poignantly expressed by Gotfried of Admont: '…this noble bow (*nobilis haec chorda*), His holy body, bent by derision, drawn by insult, was stretched by "affixiones" on the cross for our salvation. That is the same bow that the father promised when he said: I set my bow in the cloud…and it shall be a sign of the covenant between me and the earth' (Gen. 9.13). Pickering could only find literary references to this image but felt it must also have been expressed in art. Conrad von Soest's Niederwildungen *Crucifixion* may be evidence that the image appears also in the visual arts: the rainbow and the arched body of Christ illustrate this very idea. This should not be understood as a specific literary quotation, however, but as a shared understanding of Old Testament symbolism.

A more direct quotation from the Old Testament can be detected in the circle of Christ's adversaries and their dogs under the cross (pl. 14). 'Yea, Dogs are round about me; a company of evildoers encircle me' (Psalm 22.16). The group is dressed in the very latest French court style, and this is usually believed to indicate that Conrad had trained in Burgundy. But Conrad was equally likely to have admired these extravagant court fashions in Dortmund itself. As Christine de Pisan explained in 1405 (see p. 19), patrician merchants were entitled to wear princely garments and were called 'noble merchants'. And if the adversaries in Conrad's panel are therefore dressed in the latest court style, namely as 'noble merchants', this may well represent the splendid donors' humble identification as fellow persecutors through their own sins: '…Christ came into the world to save sinners, of whom I am chief' (I Tim. 1.15) and, as the congregation recited during Mass (Credo): '*crucifixus etiam pro nobis*'.[32] Even if the patron of the altarpiece was the Order of St John, the money was collected from wealthy patricians and landowners.[33] Such contributions towards the cost of altarpieces and other church decorations were made as atonement, in return for the promise of redemption from sin. Furthermore, two of the highly characterized faces, those of the figures identified below as Herod and Caiaphas, appear again as kings bearing gifts, as a type of donor therefore (see pp. 32–33), in the *Adoration of the Kings* (features of other actors are consistent and used for one person only throughout the altarpiece). The group of adversaries is aptly placed under the cross with the centurion who was redeemed from sin (Mark 15.39).

Throughout the altarpiece the holy figures, as opposed to the other characters, are dressed in timeless garments. Only Mary Magdalene and Mary, mother of James, display minute touches of the latest fashion in their veils, transparent material in one and a crinkled edge in the other (pl. 30). It would be consistent with the symbolic language of dress in Conrad's altarpieces to understand this as an allusion to their more worldly natures before they became saintly followers of Christ.[34] Conrad's adherence to Gospel and liturgical texts speaks strongly against any secular intent in his use of fashionable garments here or in the modish group around Herod. It is worth remembering the increased individual religiosity and devotion expressed both in literature and by the formation of the lay confraternities during the lifetime of the painter and his advisers. And there is no other evidence of secularization of art in Northern Germany at this time.

A distinction between the earthly and the divine is made not only in terms of dress, but also by the contrast between the devotional image of a pale, idealized Christ, pinned by three nails to the 'holy' cross, the Roman 'crux immissa', and the historic realism of the sturdy thieves, their arms bent back over the horizontal bars of the T-shaped, or 'commissa' crosses.[35] This type of villain crucifixion had already been explored in Nicola Pisano's pulpit in the Baptistery at Pisa (1259–60), in Pietro Lorenzetti's *Crucifixion* (*c.* 1319–20) in the Lower Church at Assisi and in paintings from the circle of Duccio in Italy, and also in Pucelle's work in France. In Westphalia, however, the thieves' crosses have a second lower horizontal bar to which the hands of the thieves are tied by a rope. It has not been possible to find reliable information about penal methods in medieval Westphalia to research this unusual cross-form. There is also no specific information about medieval drama in Westphalia, but the thieves' weapons, suspended from the crosses, have a theatrical effect: the double cross bars could possibly have been an actor's aid in Westphalian passion play productions. These crosses with two horizontal bars for the thieves, which have hitherto escaped notice, are certainly a persistent Westphalian feature in surviving Crucifixions from the Netze Altarpiece of *c.* 1390 (pl. 78)(which also includes the thieves' weapons), to the retables by Derick Baegert of the 1480s.[36] Outside Westphalia they occur only when a direct influence from Westphalia is likely, most significantly in an early *Crucifixion* by the Veronica Master in Cologne (see pp. 169–176; pl. 108).

A passion-play manuscript from Donaueschingen demonstrates the complex interrelationship of drama and art: it instructs that 'each thief shall have a small picture in his mouth as if it were a soul. Then the angel takes the soul of the good thief and goes to heaven, and the devil the soul of the other and runs with much screaming to hell'.[37] Conrad's actors seem to be a little muddled over their dramatic instructions, for the repenting Dismas has his soul carried away by the devil.[38]

Conrad von Soest's Niederwildungen *Crucifixion*—from the gentle and patient Christ to the quiet suffering of the fainting Virgin, the praying Magdalene and the intense and loving gesture of St John—expresses the shared grieving of the soul that contemplates Christ's sacrificial death by personal devotion, in accordance with Ludolph of Saxony's teaching: 'Grant me the grace…to grieve over thee with tears of repentance and compassion…to bury thee in my heart by undistracted recollection and meditation'.[39] By keeping to Gospel and liturgical texts, Conrad avoids the confusion of crowds and events of some later narrative Calvaries.

There seems even to be a biblical source for the unusual presence in the Niederwildungen *Crucifixion* of the crowned King Herod, seen in dispute with Pilate and (presumably) Caiaphas (pl. 14).[40] It is possible that a lost passion play brought these three adversaries of Christ to the Crucifixion scene to stress their joint responsibility for Christ's death. In view of the lack of literary evidence and Conrad's adherence to Gospel texts, however, the scene may represent a personal interpretation of biblical passages. The Gospel of John (19.19) informs us that 'Pilate also wrote a title, and put it on the cross'. Matthew (27.37) suggests that there was more than one person involved in fixing the inscription to the cross: 'and over his head they put the charge against him'. Luke (23.12) expands: 'And the same day Pilate and Herod were made friends together; for before they were at enmity between themselves'. As Pontius Pilate, the Governor, and Herod Antipas, the Tetrarch of Galilee, together with Caiaphas, the High Priest, caused Christ to be crucified, these new friends may have been seen as jointly responsible for the title on the cross. Luke's assertion (23.35), 'And the rulers also with them derided him', seems then to confirm their presence under the cross. Such personal interpretations of the Bible were common; they were encouraged by the concept of *docta ignorantia*, learned ignorance. The notion that a lay person's understanding was capable, through humble piety and contemplation, of surpassing that of a learned teacher achieved widespread popularity at the time and encouraged variety in Gospel interpretation.[41]

The crowned person under the cross in the Niederwildungen Altarpiece is Herod Antipas, for the same figure appears in the *Christ Mocked before Herod* (pl. XIII). His regal status is confirmed in that scene by the large golden crowns in the brocade pattern of his houppelande.[42] Ever since Duccio illustrated the scene before Herod in the *Maestà* (Siena, Cathedral Museum; 1308–11), it appeared frequently in medieval passion cycles. In the Niederwildungen Altarpiece it is the mocking of Christ rather than his interrogation which is illustrated: 'And Herod with his soldiers treated him with contempt and mocked him' (Luke 23.11). In this iconographic programme, the mocking has been interpreted as the event which took place in the praetorium immediately after the crowning with thorns (and therefore incorporates motifs from that scene) which is described in more detail in the Gospel of Matthew (27.27–30): 'And kneeling before him they mocked him…And they spat upon him and took the reed and struck him on the head'. In this panel, the figure of Herod has consistently been mistaken for that of Pilate, although there is no facial similarity to the Pilate in the adjoining panel of *Christ before Pilate* (pl. XII).[43] Pilate, in any case, was not present in the praetorium; he had only witnessed the flagellation.

Another misunderstanding has arisen in descriptions of the *Last Supper* scene (pl. X). Judas, receiving the morsel of bread, is hiding a fish under the tablecloth. This has been interpreted as 'vulgar theft'.[44] In view of the Eucharistic significance of the *Last Supper* and Conrad's adherence to Gospel texts, it is hardly likely that a mere anecdote of theft is depicted. The fish, indeed, was an accepted symbol for Christ, and Judas's gesture should therefore be understood as the denial of Christ; it marks Judas as 'that man by whom the son of man was betrayed' (Mark 14.21). As in the *Annunciation* and *Crucifixion*, the Eucharistic significance of the *Last Supper* is stressed; here, I would suggest, through the unhistoric presence of St Paul who established the sacrament of the Eucharist (I Corinthians 11.20-26) (pls. IV, XIV). Only a few examples of St Paul's attendance at the *Last Supper* can be traced, for he is more frequently included in the *Communion of the Apostles* and in Eucharistic allegories.[45] His presence may therefore serve as a reminder that the *Last Supper* represents the institution of the sacrament.

An emphasis on the importance of St Paul as teacher and witness to the truth of the New Testament may have been intended by his presence, holding a large book, in the *Ascension* and *Pentecost* scenes.[46] In the *Pentecost* scene, St Paul and St Peter, in whom the church is founded, are seated on either side of Mary, here, as in the *Ascension*, surely the symbol of Ecclesia (pl. XVI, XVII). At St Peter's feet an apostle peers through his spectacles at the book that bears the signatures of Conrad and the priest Stollen in the outer edge of the page. A small realistic item of contemporary fashion, the novel spectacles, act as a foil to the timeless robes of the saints. The spectacles draw our attention to the names in the book. Could these names perhaps, in accordance with our earlier observation regarding Conrad's use of fashion, represent (in the context of the *Pentecost* scene) the artist and adviser citing the liturgical prayer 'Give us thy spirit'?[47] Such an interpretation is also supported by the fact that the actual signatures of both were placed in the main inscriptions of the altarpiece.

The pictorial tradition of biblical narrative cycles may be said to derive from the groups of images depicted in fourth-century catacombs and from sculptural decoration on sarcophagi. By the fifth century, continuous narrative cycles had emerged in visual terms. A fifth-century ivory diptych in Milan already presents some of the features of pictorial organization that can be observed in the Niederwildungen Altarpiece.[48] During the following centuries pictorial schemes became more complex and, gradually, more varied. Scattered examples of the juxtaposition of scenes from Christ's childhood with those from the passion, as in Westphalian altarpieces, can be found in early Byzantine art and on Carolingian and Ottonian antependia.[49] In the bronze doors of Hildesheim Cathedral (1015), and in the painted wooden doors of the church of St Maria in Kapitol in Cologne (*c.* 1050), the pictorial cycles incorporate both childhood and passion scenes. From the thirteenth century onwards altarpieces and antependia frequently stressed the unity of Christ's life and suffering in their design, a synthesis appropriate to altar decorations as the incarnation and the death of Christ both constitute major elements in the celebration of the Mass.

The organization of the pictorial cycle of the Niederwildungen Altarpiece follows the order of the liturgical calendar. Although the Annunciation itself is celebrated on 25 March, the narrative of the *Annunciation* could illustrate the Feast of the Immaculate Conception which was celebrated on 8 December, that is during the second week of the liturgical year.[50] The painted panels might be said to represent most of the feast days on which the wings of the altarpiece were opened. Judging from fifteenth-century instructions for churches in Nuremberg, retables were not opened on ordinary Sundays, but only on main festival days and special feast days relating to the subjects and saints depicted in the altarpiece.[51] An exception to this rule was apparently made only in order to celebrate the visit to a church by a bishop.

All decorative detail is subordinate to the iconographic programme of the altarpiece. The closed pitcher in the *Nativity*, for example, and the unicorn on the king's clasp in the *Adoration of the Kings* are well-known symbols of virginity. The motif of the punched frame representing a crown-of-thorns encompasses all the panels from the *Nativity* to the *Last Judgement* with its message of salvation. The decoration of the inside frame of the retable bears a pattern of crescent moons and eight-pointed stars which, it is contended above, indicates that the altarpiece was owned by the Order of St John. The prominence of Mary and St John, the cross potent decorating the banners of the trumpets carried by angels in the *Last Judgement*, St John receiving the souls into heaven there, and Christ's red burial cloth all refer to the Order of St John (see pp. 28–29).

It was in keeping with the history of this Order to place a Crucifixion altarpiece on the high altar. The crusades of the twelfth century had focused religious thought on the passion of Christ and awakened an interest in the historical events described in the Gospels. This led to pilgrimages, like that of the Count of Waldeck, which recreated the steps of Christ's route of suffering. The footsteps on the Mount of Olives in the *Ascension* panel are explained in a pilgrimage report by the Abbot of Iona: 'In the centre of the Church, where our Lord ascended, can be seen His last footprints, exposed to the sky above (pls. 168, XVI). And although the earth is daily removed by the faithful, it remains undiminished, and still retains these marks resembling footprints'.[52] The knights of the Order of St John had fought in the crusades and protected the pilgrims, the hospitallers of the Order had cared for the sick. The tender humanity in the Niederwildungen Altarpiece and the salvation message of its iconography is in keeping with the caring function of the patrons of the retable, the Commandery of the hospitallers of St John.

The Dortmund Altarpiece celebrates the life and death of Mary, mother of God, the patron saint of the church. The central scene of the *Death of the Virgin* at Dortmund is in keeping with the main function of the confraternity of the church and patrons of this retable, which was to ensure the Christian burial of their dead brethren. Although they also functioned as mutual protection societies and social clubs, confraternities were mainly concerned with their members' spiritual welfare. All members of a confraternity were obliged to be present at a brother's requiem mass and burial. 'All…who have accompanied the sacred body of the Lord and the holy oil to the sick or attended the requiem mass, sermons and other obsequies of the Lord and buried the dead in faith will obtain the mercy of God's pardon'.[53] The caring function of the confraternity is implied by the gentle action of angels in this panel. One angel tenderly closes the dead Virgin's eyes, one carefully lifts her drooping chin, one smooths her hair, and three pray fervently for her soul (pls. XXVIII, 81). Their prayer is answered, for Christ is seen receiving the soul into heaven. 'Blessed art Thou, O my God, who, after the death of the Virgin Mary, Thy Mother, didst receive her soul and her body into heaven, and didst place her above all the angels near to Thy Divinity'.[54] A semicircle of clouds and a multitude of angels define the celestial zone. Two angels float in the golden sky; the message that may have been written on their scroll has long been lost. The words of the scroll of the reading apostle, however, can be retrieved with infra-red photography (pl. 34; cat. no. 2), and they are part of a prayer for the soul of the deceased, the *'commendatio animae'*. Censer and candle refer to the sacrament of Extreme Unction.

St John lovingly places the candle and a martyr's palm into the Virgin's hand. A now rather damaged coin is pressed into this candle. In this Catholic rite the coin should not be interpreted as the obol offered in Greek mythology to the ferryman Charon in order to cross the Styx.[55] In view of Conrad's adherence to Gospel and liturgy, it may instead refer to the atonement and redemption money of the Old Testament (Exodus 30.16; Numbers 3.48–49), used by Catholics to plead the re-mission of sins. Similar candles are still on sale today in the pilgrimage church of Kevelar (Lower Rhine area) and are offered there to the Virgin by penitent pilgrims. The motif of the candle with the coin was adopted by followers of Conrad von Soest in the Blankenberch Altarpiece, in the painted left wing of the Netherlandish carved retable (*c.* 1430–40) in the church of St Reinoldi in Dortmund, and in a panel ascribed to a follower of Campin, now in the National Gallery, London.[56] In a contemporary woodcut, a sick person can be seen receiving the 'Sterbekerze', the candle for the dying, but that candle does not seem to have a coin attached.[57] Whilst the meaning of the coin remains uncertain, the ceremonial use of candle and coin during requiem mass was already prescribed by Raimond du Puy in the twelfth century (see p. 26): 'At first mass [for a deceased brother] let each one of the brethren present offer a candle with a piece of money'.

Ludolph of Saxony prayed to Christ, invoking 'the blessed Virgin Mary, thy mother, the mirror of thy majesty, solace of the angels, image of thy goodness, and source of our salvation'.[58] 'Pray for us in the hour of our death' was added to the prayer *Ave Maria* at this time. The painter Conrad seems to recognize the Virgin's status and to plead for her intercession on his behalf by signing his name in the outer edge of a page of her prayer book. A scroll next to his signature may show the start of his prayer: ['...*noms dns*'] 'in the name of the Lord'. Although the frame has been lost, it is reasonable to assume that Conrad's signature in his capacity as artist would have been inscribed there as proudly as it had been on the frame of the Niederwildungen Altarpiece almost twenty years earlier. As with similar signatures in the earlier retable, the name in the outer edge of the page of the book would be likely to carry a personal message (see p. 107).

The Virgin's death is not reported in the Bible, but it figures in apocryphal sources which are summed up in the moving story recounted in the *Golden Legend*.[59] The apostles, dispersed throughout the world to preach, were miraculously transported to the Virgin's deathbed, so that they 'might prepare seemly obsequies', just as later the confraternity members were obliged to do for each other. The *Death of the Virgin* by Conrad von Soest should not be considered as an illustration of the legend, but rather as a celebration of the Feast of the Dormition, which had been established in the eastern liturgical calendar since the sixth century.[60] The iconographic motifs of this scene, including Christ receiving the Virgin's soul and the apostle with the censer, had been established in western art from Byzantine roots by the tenth century. They feature, for instance, in an ivory relief from the end of the tenth century in Cologne.[61] Western images, however, although they borrowed eastern motifs, rarely represented the eastern legends that had prompted the debate concerning the bodily ascension of the Virgin; instead they stressed the instant reunion of the 'soul without sin' with Christ in Heaven, as it was celebrated in the sermons and liturgy of the Feast of the Dormition (which was first referred to as *Assumptio Beatae Virginis* in the tenth century).[62] From the thirteenth century the subject rarely appeared in manuscript illumination, but had a place in sculpture and window programmes.[63]

The iconography at Dortmund follows that of the earliest extant western narrative of this nature, the *Death of the Virgin* in the *Perikopenbuch Heinrichs II* of 1007 or 1012 in Munich (MS 4452, fol. 161v). It is interesting to note that Conrad's narrative differs from that in the Buxtehude Altarpiece (*c.* 1410) from the Bertram workshop, in that he features another motif from the Byzantine ivory mentioned above, the St John (youthful and beardless according to western tradition) bending over the Virgin. Furthermore, in Conrad's panel Christ does not stand behind the bed; instead, he is seen in a semicircle of clouds that represent heaven, for which the motif in the *Perikopenbuch* of *c.* 1150 in Paris (Cod. lat. 17325, fol. 51v) may be a Westphalian or Lower Rhenish precedent. It is the liturgical and sacramental relevance of the *Death of the Virgin* that must have induced the confraternity of the church of St Mary to take the unusual step of ordering it as the central narrative of their altarpiece.

Whereas the lily in the vase and the snowflakes on the coverlet in the *Death of the Virgin* are understood by us today to be symbols of purity, and whilst we suspect that the three-legged stool in the *Nativity* may refer to the Trinity, we need Ludolph to remind us that the gifts of the three kings in the *Adoration of the Kings* could be 'the myrrh of sincere sorrow, the frankincense of devout prayer, the gold of loyal love' (pl. XXV).[64] The horn, carried by one king at his waist in a manner reminiscent of Giotto's fresco at Padua, reminds us of the unicorn and may therefore be a symbol of virginity. It could, however, refer to Zechariah's words and remind us that the child is 'the horn of salvation' (Luke 1.67–69). In view of the significance of the gifts, it may equally be the horn used for the anointing of kings. The medieval viewer would probably have been better equipped to appreciate the significance of such ornaments.

The colour of angels causes some confusion in the interpretation of Conrad's altarpieces. It has been suggested that seraphim who burned in the love of God are nearest to Him, being the highest order of angels, and are therefore red in colour. Cherubim, filled with the knowledge of God, are blue, the colour of air. This view seems to have been based on the *Heavenly Hierarchy*, attributed to Dionysius the Areopagite, one of Paul's converts in Athens.[65] But the interpretation was not universally accepted. An explanation of the hierarchy of angels has always been needed, as Old Testament sources are ambiguous: Isaiah (6.6) describes a seraph 'having in his hand a burning coal', whilst Ezekiel (10.7) speaks of 'the fire that was between the cherubim'.[66] Conrad von Soest's paintings reflect the general inconsistency: blue angels appear nearest to God in the Niederwildungen *Ascension* and Dortmund *Nativity* (pl. XXI) and *Death of the Virgin*, while red angels accompany Him in the *Last Judgement* (pl. XVIII). Red angels surround mother and child on earth in both Nativities, whereas blue angels minister to the dying Virgin. No iconographic conclusion can be drawn from the colour of angels in Conrad's altarpieces; the choice of colour seems to have simply depended on decorative preferences.

Red angels frame the tender scene in the Nativities of Conrad's altarpieces, as the child presses his cheek against his mother's face, laying his hands softly on her neck. Pisanello has been credited with the invention of this motif.[67] As Pisanello was active between *c.* 1415 and *c.* 1455 and the Niederwildungen Altarpiece is dated 1403, the Italian painter would be more likely to be indebted to Conrad von Soest for this design. The source for the motif may be found in Byzantine Eleousa images like the *Virgin of Vladimir*, and a Westphalian precedent survives in a *Madonna and Child* (*c.* 1260–80) from Soest in the Carrand collection, Florence. It was equally known in the Parement workshop (pl. 87, bas de page) Literary sources seem to confirm a common knowledge of such images. The mother 'laid her cheek on His' and 'the Child…placed His tiny hand on His mother's…face', recalled Pseudo-Bonaventure; and Suso urged Christ to 'remember the beautiful cheeks (of his mother) which were so often pressed full of love against your childish face'.[68]

111

The *Adoration of the Kings* in the Dortmund Altarpiece is also characterized by tender intimacy born of intense personal experience (pl. XXV). Whilst one king kisses the child's hand, another embraces his foot, and the third carries his gift. All three gently touch the Virgin's cloak as if to secure individual attention. I have suggested that the striking realism of the kings' heads may denote portraiture (see pp. 32–33). My tentative evidence for this hypothesis—beyond the donor poses and the characterized features of protagonists—is contained in our earlier understanding of the role of the adversaries in the Niederwildungen *Crucifixion* and their resemblance to the kings in the *Adoration of the Kings* in that altarpiece. The kings represent the three ages of man; they have removed their crowns to pay homage to one greater than kings. The cloth of honour behind the throne stresses the status of the mother and sacred child.

The outside panels of the Dortmund Altarpiece present an interesting narrative contrast: a Madonna of Humility in the *Annunciation* is balanced by a Madonna in Glory in the *Coronation of the Virgin* (pls. XXVI, XXVII). St Bernard cited 'the mother of the Lord' as a model of humility in his instructions towards a saintly life: he explained that Christ 'calls humility "the way" because it leads to the truth. The first is the struggle, while the second is the reward…'. The two panels of the altarpiece therefore held a reminder to the members of the confraternity of St Mary that if they followed their patron's example of a life of humility, they would, like her, be rewarded in heaven. The practice of 'humility' was also of central concern to the members of the *devotio moderna* movement.

The Dortmund *Annunciation* is in some ways more in tune with Westphalian pictorial tradition than the Niederwildungen panel, as the angel approaches from the left and the Virgin is a praying maiden rather than a queen. Her open Book of Hours reveals the prayer *Deus in adiutorium meu[m] in tende domine ad adiuvandum [me festina].*[69] Whereas a domestic interior sheltered the crowned Virgin in Niederwildungen, a version of the Madonna of Humility is placed in a church interior in Dortmund. The image of the Madonna of Humility spread in Italy from Sienese models. It was first combined with an *Annunciation* in the fresco (after 1328) by Taddeo Gaddi in Sta Croce, Florence. The Madonna of Humility combined with an Annunciation is not known so early in French or Franco-Flemish art.[70] Conrad von Soest fused two separate Italian traditions in his Dortmund *Annunciation*: he combined the Madonna of Humility with a realistic interior. Interior settings had only been used in Italy in different narrative contexts; the Annunciation itself was traditionally set in a porch. The porch setting was also popular in northern painting; it can be seen, for example, in Broederlam's painted wing at Dijon (1394–99)(pl. 92). In the Dortmund Altarpiece, the church interior stresses the sacramental significance of the narrative. This sacramental theme is expressed also in the domestic interior of the Mérode Triptych (*c.* 1426)(pl. 104), which is described as a sanctuary by including a candle and a liturgical niche with lavabo and towel. The Virgin of Humility is placed in front of a bench, possibly perched on a footrest, both in the

XX. Mother and Child. Detail from the Nativity. Dortmund Altarpiece

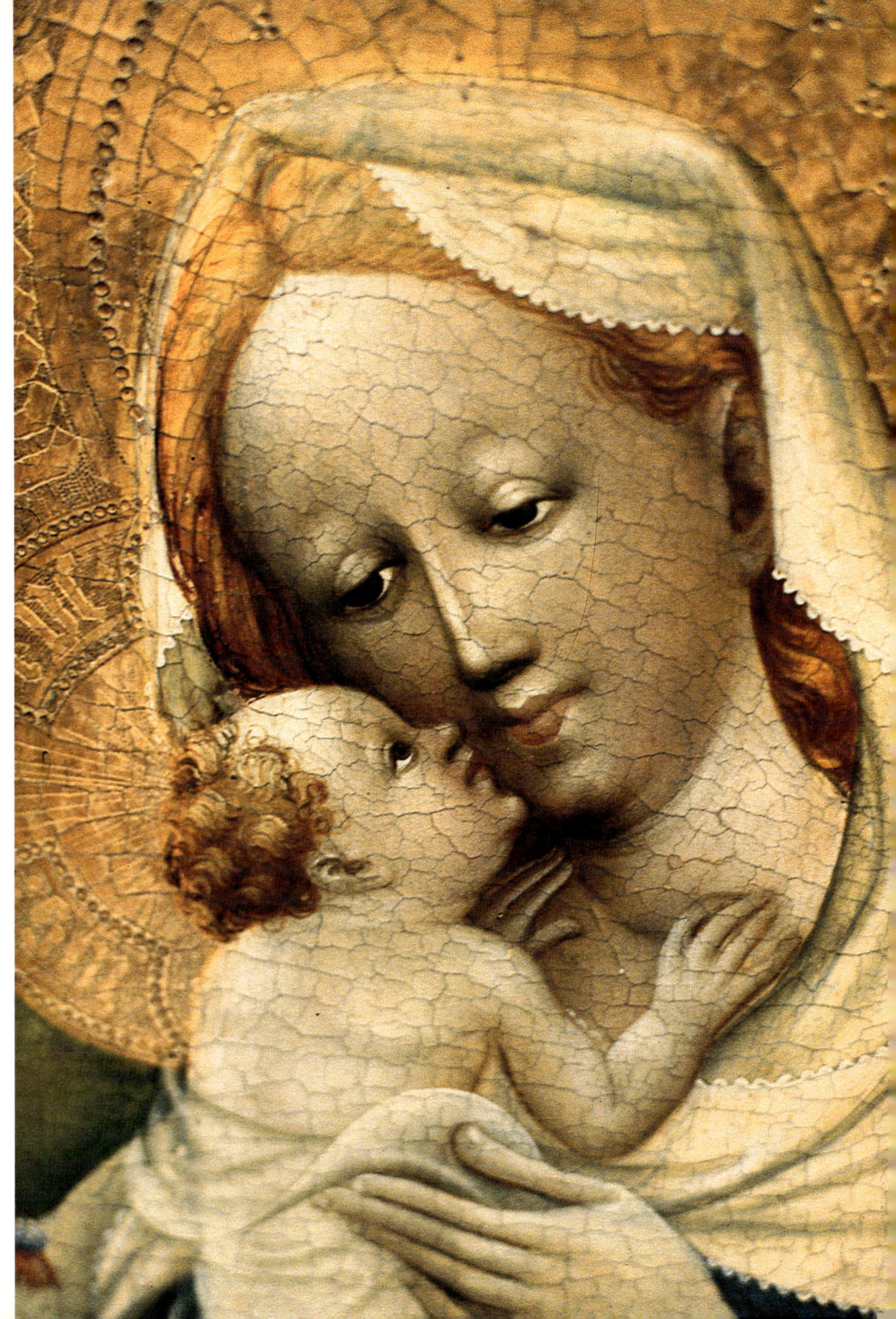

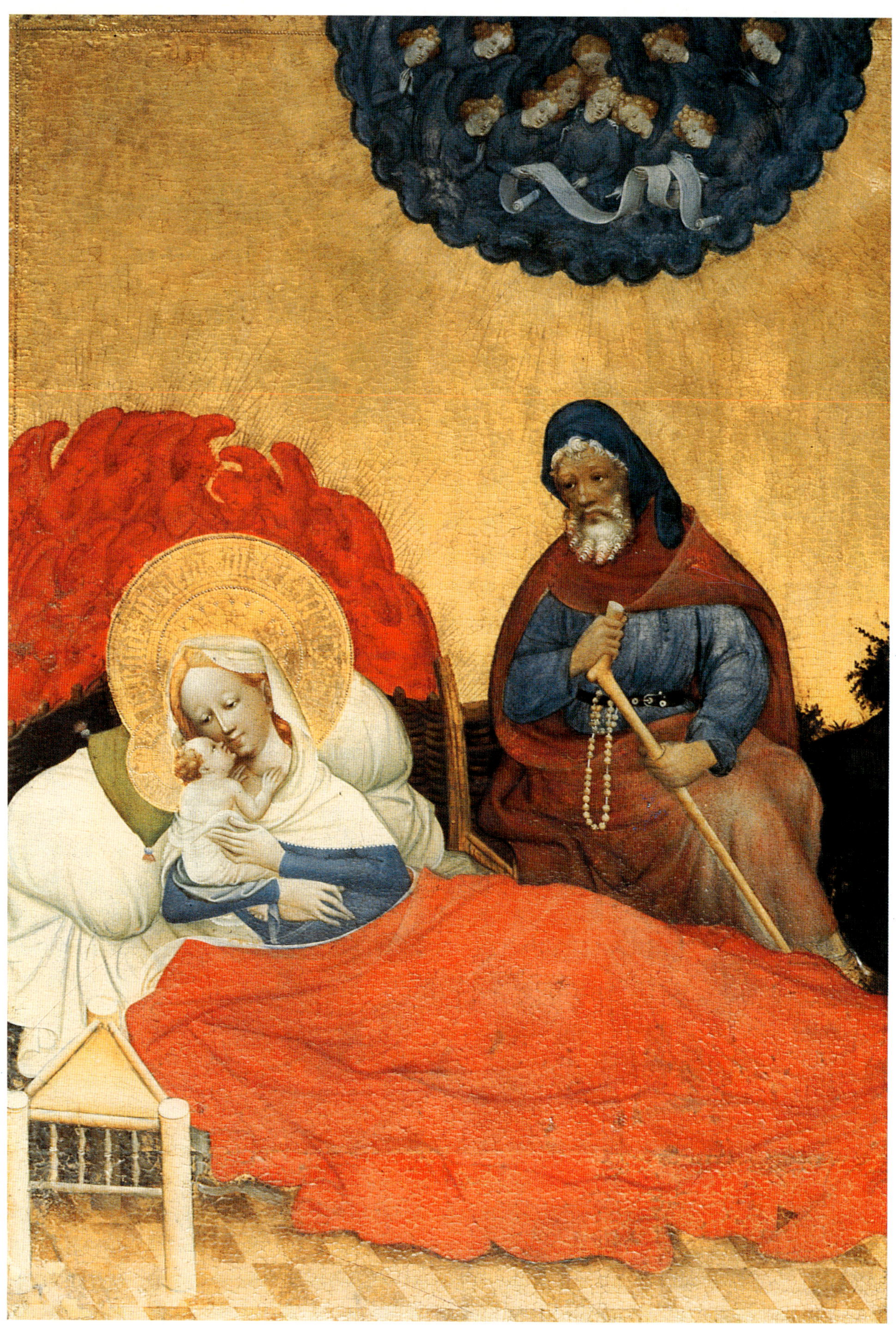

XXI. Conrad von Soest: *Nativity*. Dortmund Altarpiece

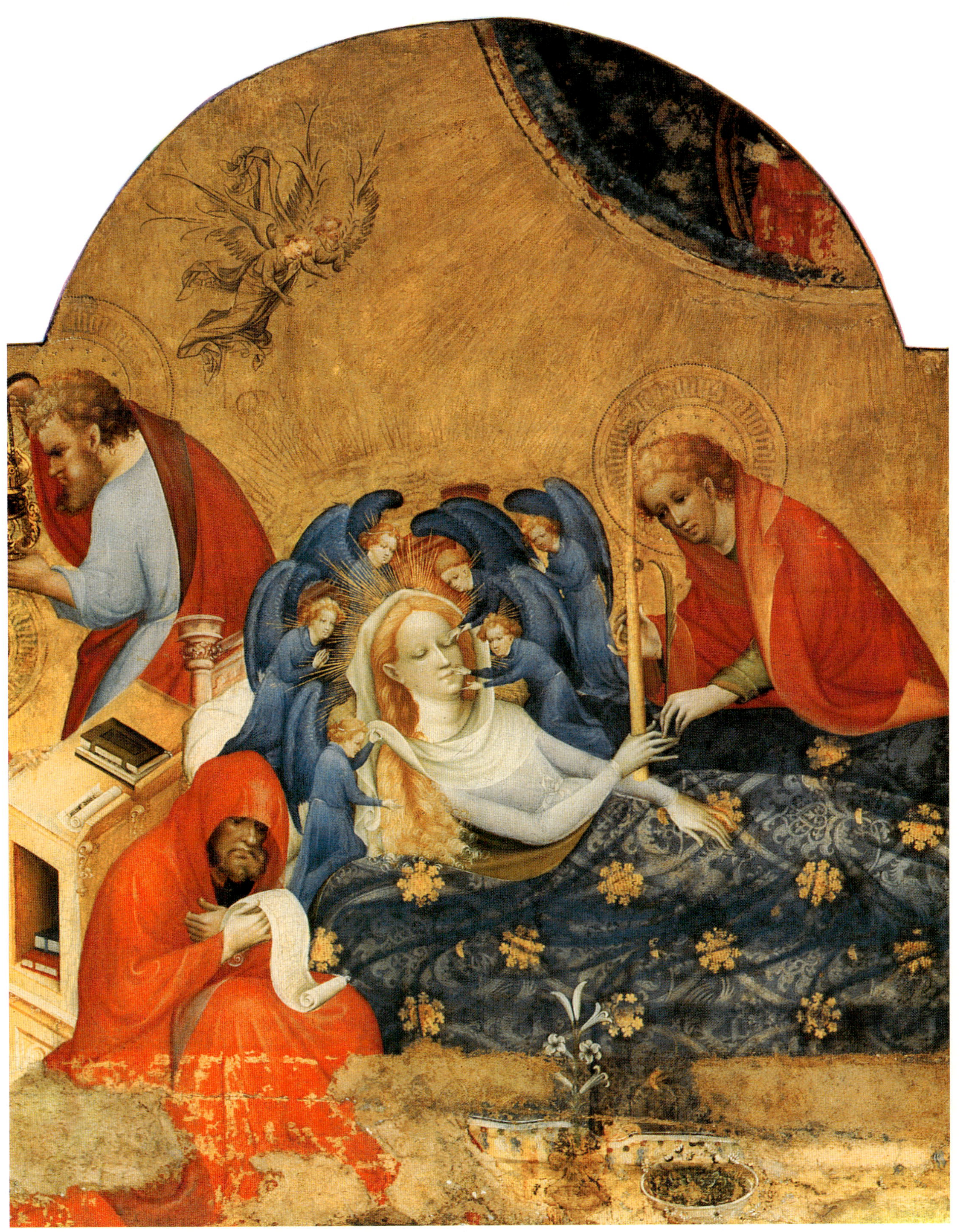

XXII. Conrad von Soest: *Death of the Virgin*. Dortmund Altarpiece

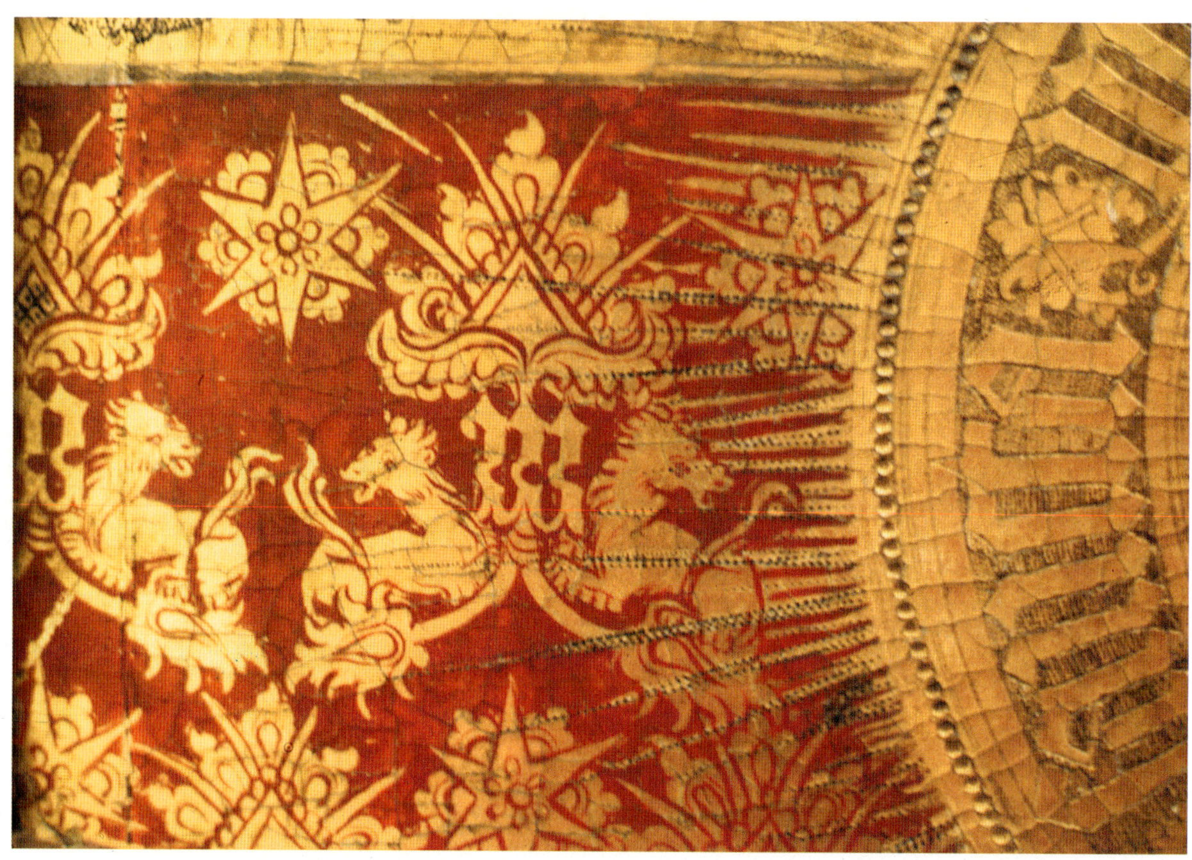

XXIII. *Brocade pattern.* Detail from the *Adoration of the Kings*. Dortmund Altarpiece

XXIV. *Brocade pattern.* Detail from the *Death of the Virgin*. Dortmund Altarpiece

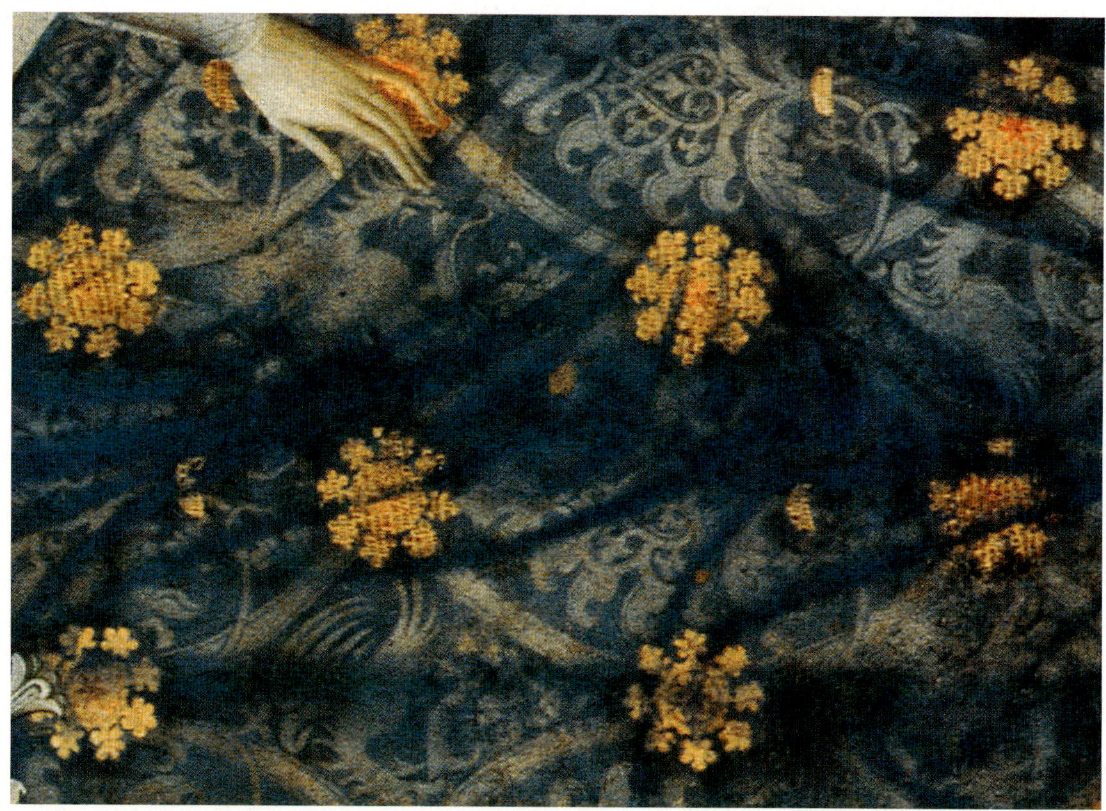

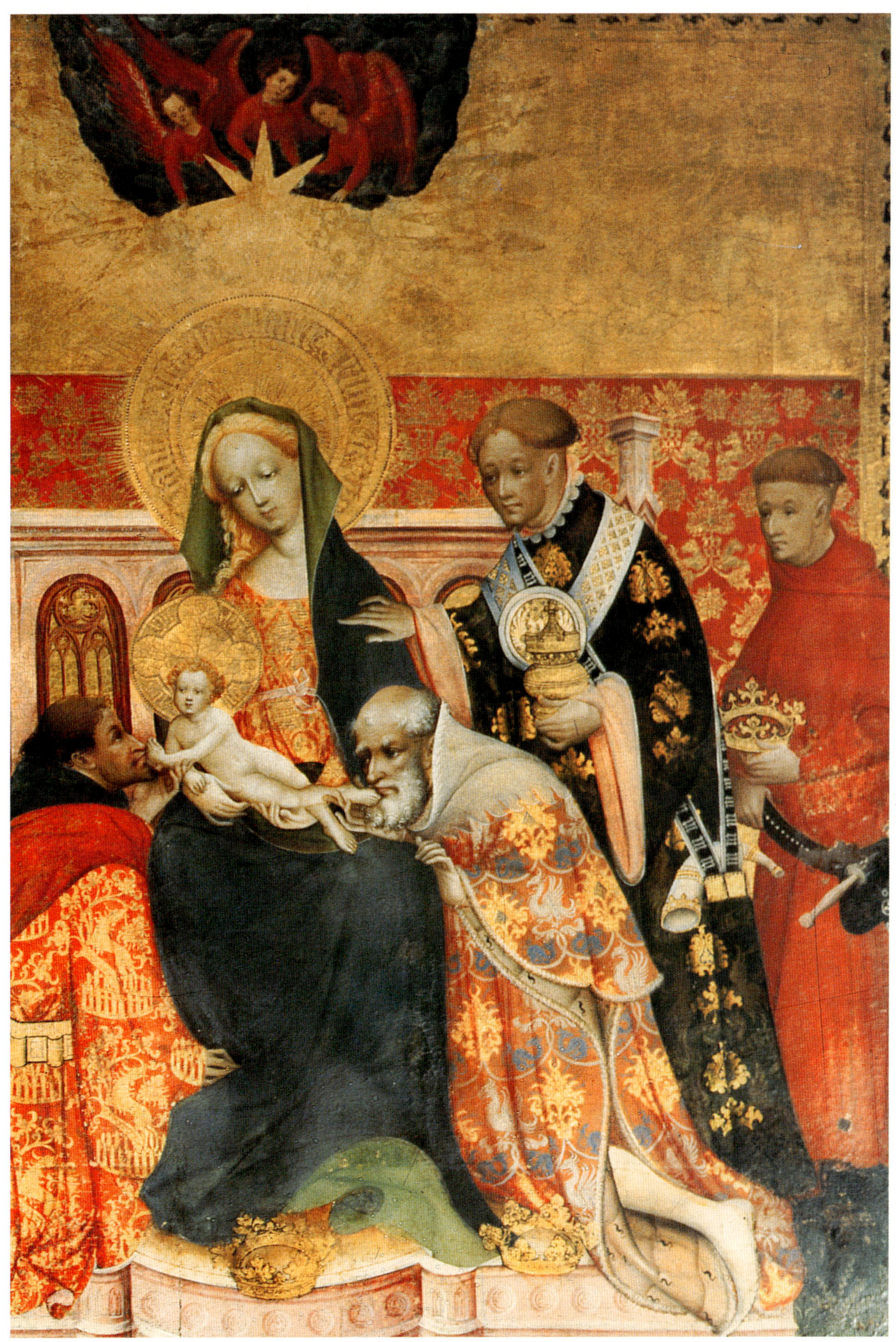

XXV. Conrad von Soest: *Adoration of the Kings*. Dortmund Altarpiece

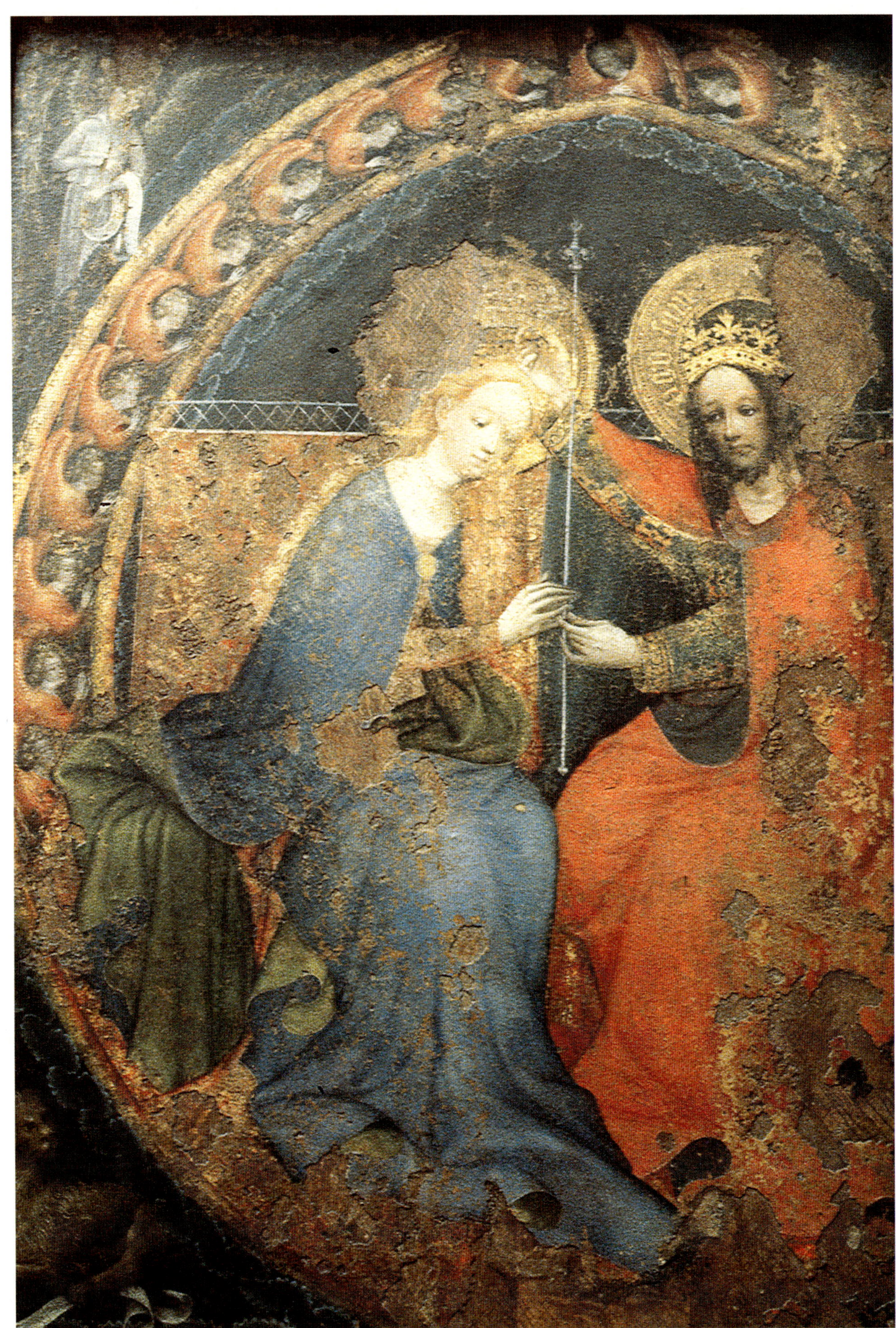

XXVI. Conrad von Soest: *Coronation of the Virgin*. Dortmund Altarpiece

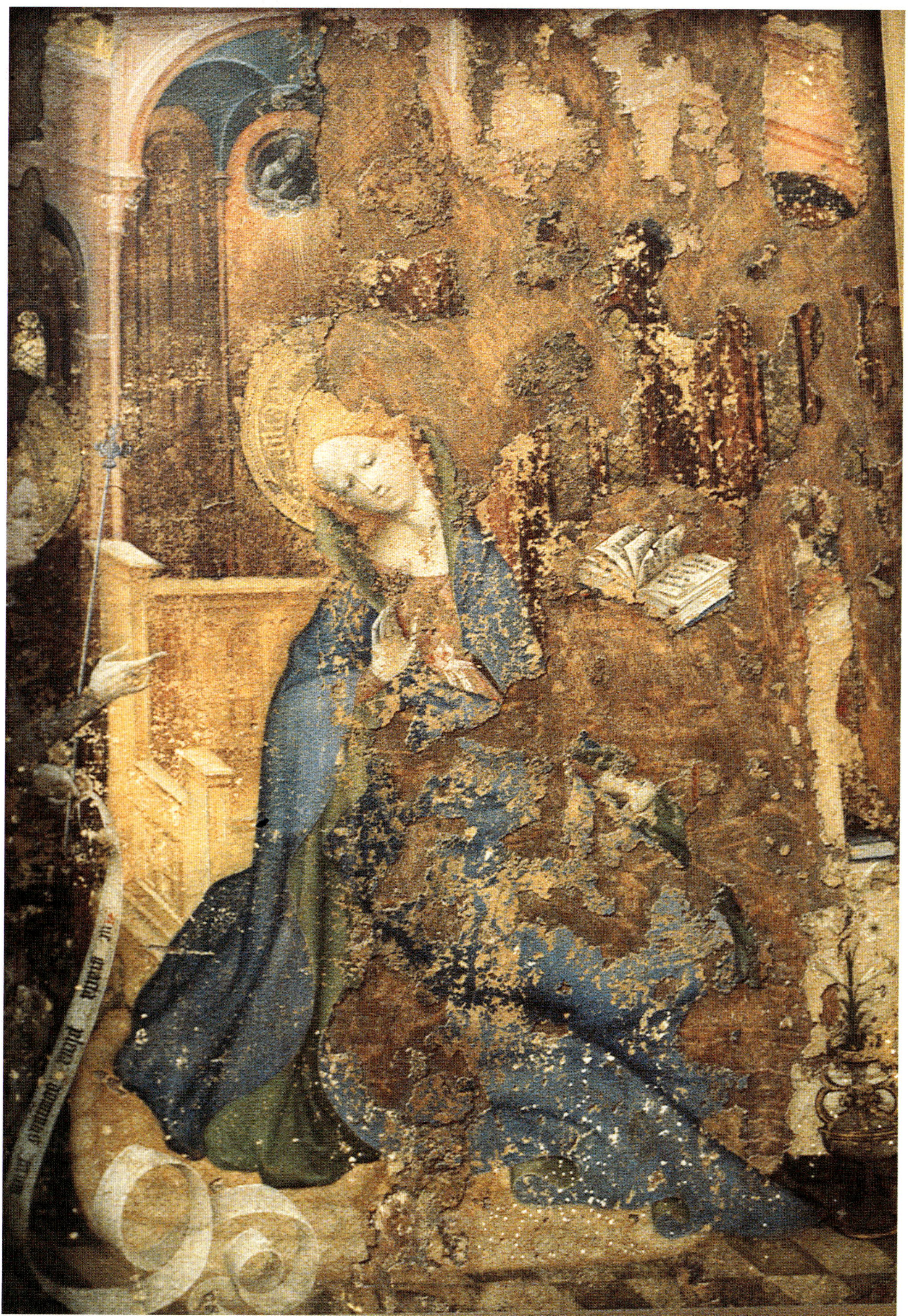

XXVII. Conrad von Soest: *Annunciation*. Dortmund Altarpiece

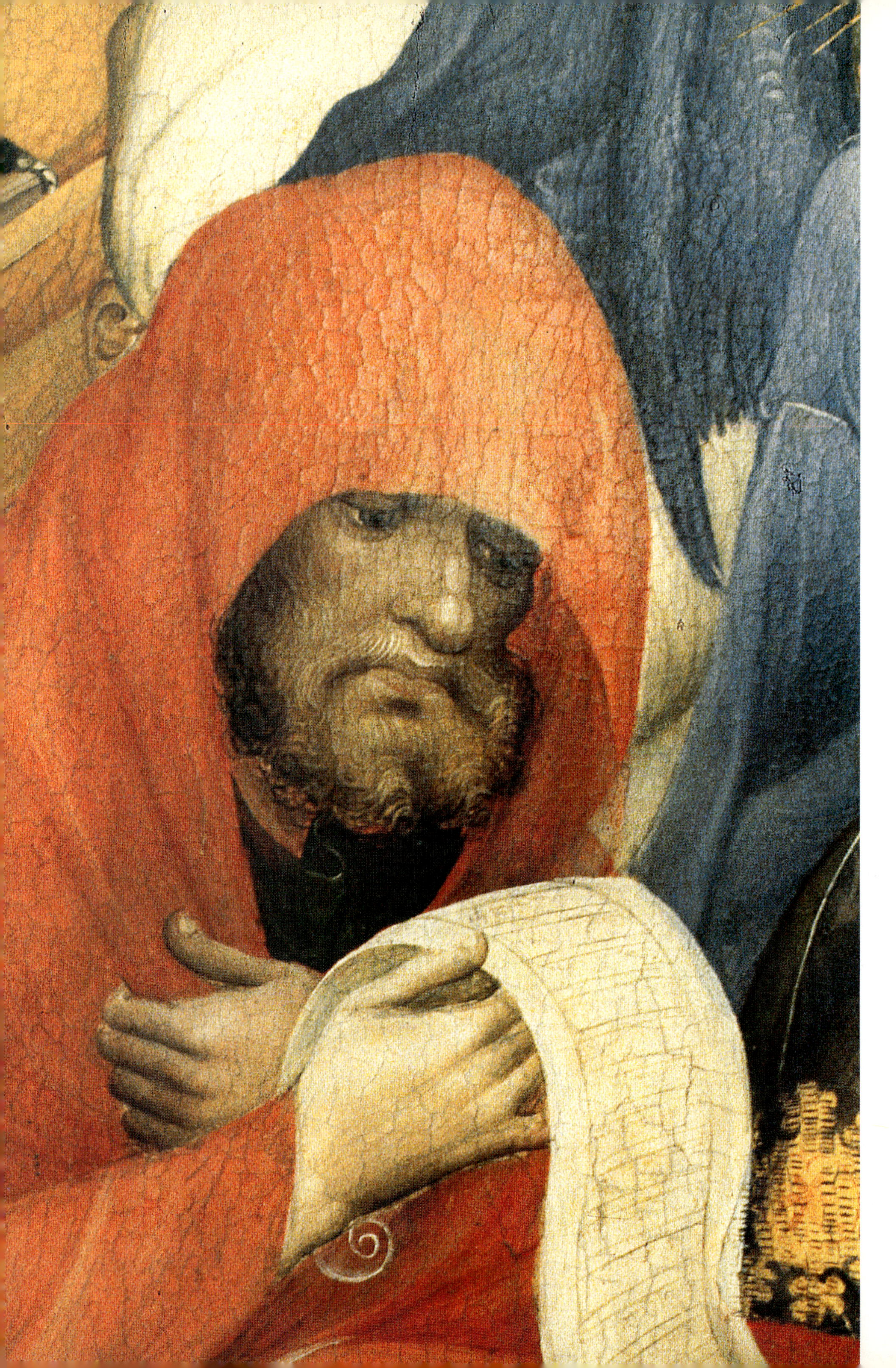

Dortmund and in the Mérode Altarpieces. Conrad may have been the intermediary who introduced this iconographic fusion not only to his Westphalian followers, but possibly also to the Campin workshop, from where it spread to other Netherlandish artists.

The *Coronation of the Virgin* has liturgical sources rooted in the words of the Psalmist.[71] The phrase, 'Your divine throne endures for ever and ever…at your right hand did stand the queen in vesture of gold' (Psalm 45.6–9), passed into the Hours of the Virgin. The Psalmist's words (21.3), 'Thou settest a crown of precious stone on his head', were applied to Mary in the liturgy of the Feast of the Assumption, and the congregation sang *'et altius sedes in superis, O Maria'* [thou art enthroned in Heaven]. But it was not until the twelfth century that the words of the liturgy were given plastic form. Émile Mâle cites the porch of the Cathedral at Senlis as the earliest known example.[72] The Virgin was already crowned at Senlis (*c.* 1170), but at Sens, Auxerre, and Reims, Christ crowned his mother, as he did in the stained-glass oculus window (*c.* 1287–88) of Siena Cathedral and in Jacopo Torriti's apse mosaic (*c.* 1294) in Sta Maria Maggiore in Rome, and also in the Buxtehude Altarpiece (*c.* 1410), from Master Bertram's workshop, in Hamburg. However, George Zarnecki found that the damaged remains of an unfinished carved capital, apparently from Reading Abbey, which he dates to *c.* 1130, contained a *Coronation of the Virgin* in which Christ, seated next to his mother, places a crown upon her head.[73]

The bodily ascension of the Virgin into heaven, based on eastern legends, began to feature in western liturgy in the late Middle Ages.[74] Theological discussion of the notion of bodily assumption, which remained unresolved by dogma until 1950, was frequently based on the perception of parallels between Christ's resurrection and ascension and the death and assumption of his mother Mary. As Christ was believed to be enthroned to the right of the Father after his ascension, so the Virgin was consequently thought to have been crowned Queen of Heaven after her assumption. The imagery of portal sculpture in French Gothic cathedrals frequently reflects this theological concept, for which Senlis, Laon and Chartres provide obvious instances. It is also expressed in the *Coronation* page (p. 78; pl. 71) from the *Très belles heures de Notre-Dame* by the Parement Master and his workshop, which features the *Assumption of the Virgin* in the initial and the *Death of the Virgin* as the *bas-de-page*.

A mandorla of clouds and angels surrounds the enthroned Christ in Conrad von Soest's *Coronation of the Virgin*, in accordance with the prophet: 'God of Israel, who art enthroned above the cherubim' (Isaiah 37.16). He crowns his mother who is seated at his side. An angel is placed in the top left-hand spandrel and a lion in the spandrel below. Each holds a scroll which no longer carries a text. Attempts to reveal the lost texts on the scrolls through infra-red photography proved unsuccessful, as the space behind the altar was too narrow to install the necessary photographic lights. Recovery of the texts could settle the dispute about the iconography of the spandrel figures. It has been argued that the corresponding

XXVIII. *Reading Apostle.* Detail from the *Death of the Virgin*, Dortmund Altarpiece

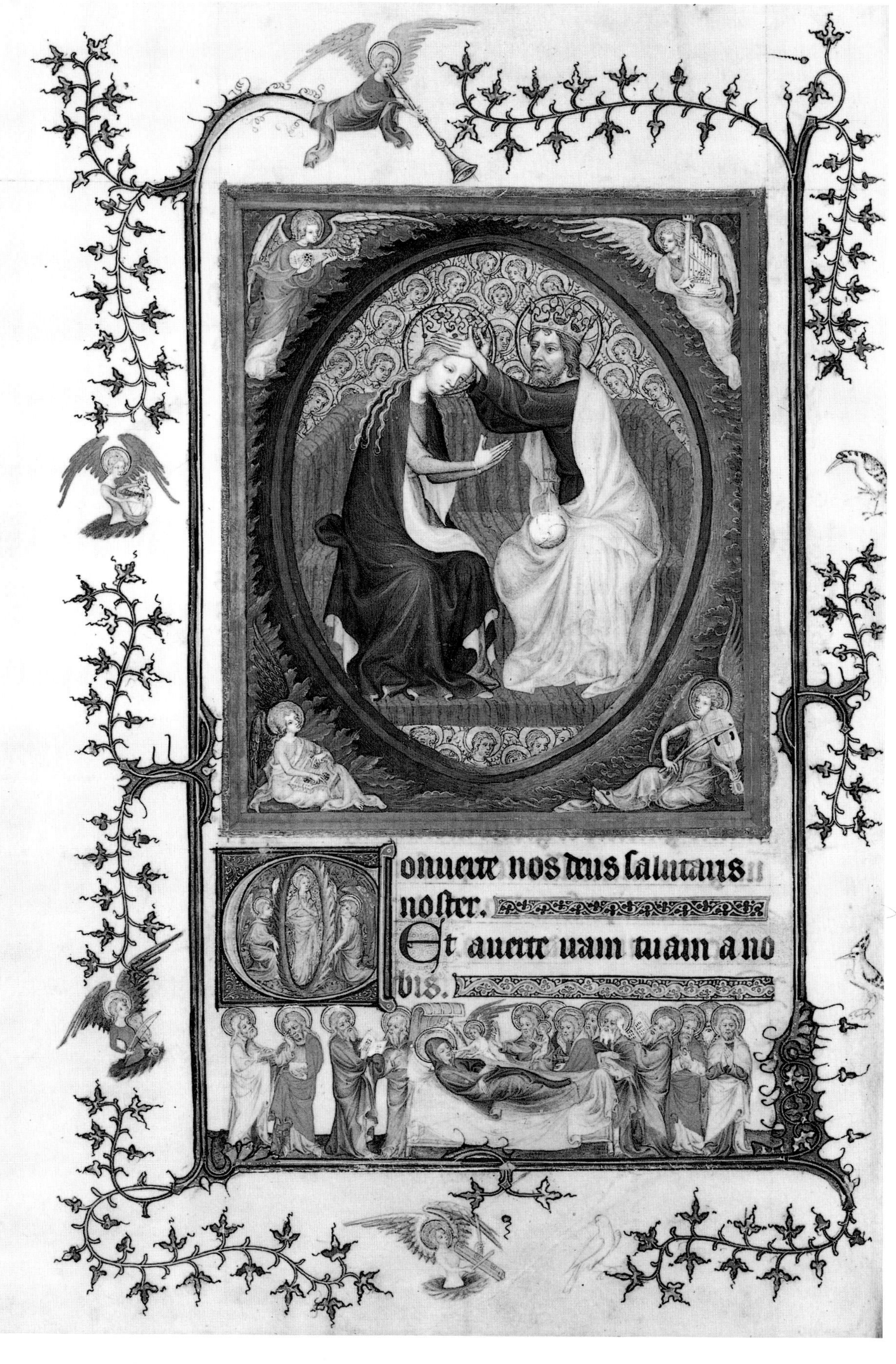

onuerte nos deus salutaris
noster.
Et auerte uam tuam a no
bis.

corners, lost when the panel was cut, could not have contained the symbols of the evangelists, as the series would have started with the eagle in the top left-hand corner.[75] It was therefore concluded that the panel contained a pair of angels in the top corners and a pair of lions from the throne of Solomon at the base, similar to those in the Buxtehude *Coronation of the Virgin* from Master Bertram's workshop. As the composition of that panel is entirely different from Conrad's, and does not contain a mandorla, the argument remains unconvincing. Some manuscripts, including German examples, in any case do show the evangelist symbols starting with an angel in the top left corner in the spandrels of a mandorla.[76] Images of the Coronation of the Virgin can even contain four angels in the spandrels of a mandorla; but the text in Revelation (4.2–8) stating that God sat on the throne with four beasts, a lion, a calf, a man and an eagle by Him, would be more likely to be illustrated by a painter who adhered to biblical texts. Furthermore, the lion and bull are shown without wings in the *Christ in Majesty* in a manuscript from the Hesdin workshop which, it will be argued below, influenced the art of Conrad von Soest (see pp. 140–141). The symbols of the evangelists may well have completed Conrad's panel of the *Coronation of the Virgin*, although we can only be certain if the original texts in the underdrawing are revealed.

Judging from the fifteenth-century instructions for two Nuremberg churches, the Dortmund Altarpiece would have been opened on important Christian festivals, Marian feast days, and during requiem mass for confraternity members.[77]

Conrad's tabernacle doors for the convent church of St Walpurgis near Soest, now at Münster, would have been opened daily during mass.[78] The insides of the doors were decorated with images of standing saints that follow an iconographic convention which is also used in the reverse sides of the wings of the Niederwildungen Altarpiece and can already be noted in the Westphalian Antependium (*c.* 1175) in the Landesmuseum, Münster. St Dorothea, portrayed in the left door, is identified not only by her halo inscription but also by her basket of roses (pls. 150, XXIX). Although she is usually shown wearing a crown of roses, Conrad—possibly following a patron's instructions—here depicted her in a golden jewelled crown. St Dorothea's attributes derive from the legend that whilst being martyred around 303 in Caesarea, she refused to recant her belief and was mocked by a scribe named Theophilus. After her death, Theophilus was converted through the mysterious gift of a basket of roses. St Dorothea is frequently shown in Northern European paintings and was widely venerated as one of the four 'virgines capitales'; her Feast day was celebrated on 6 February.[79]

St Odilia the martyr, portrayed inside the right door, is less commonly depicted (pls. 72, 151, XXX). The better known saint of the same name was Odilia of Hohenburg, the much venerated blind saint who was said to have regained her eyesight through faith, but was not martyred. However, Conrad explicitly inscribed the halo of his saint SANCTA ODILIA VIRGO M(ARTIR) and depicted her holding the martyr's palm. The cult of St Odilia the martyr dates from the thirteenth

71. Parement Master: *Coronation of the Virgin. Très belles heures de Notre-Dame*, Paris, Bibl. Nat. nouv. acq. lat. 3093, p. 78

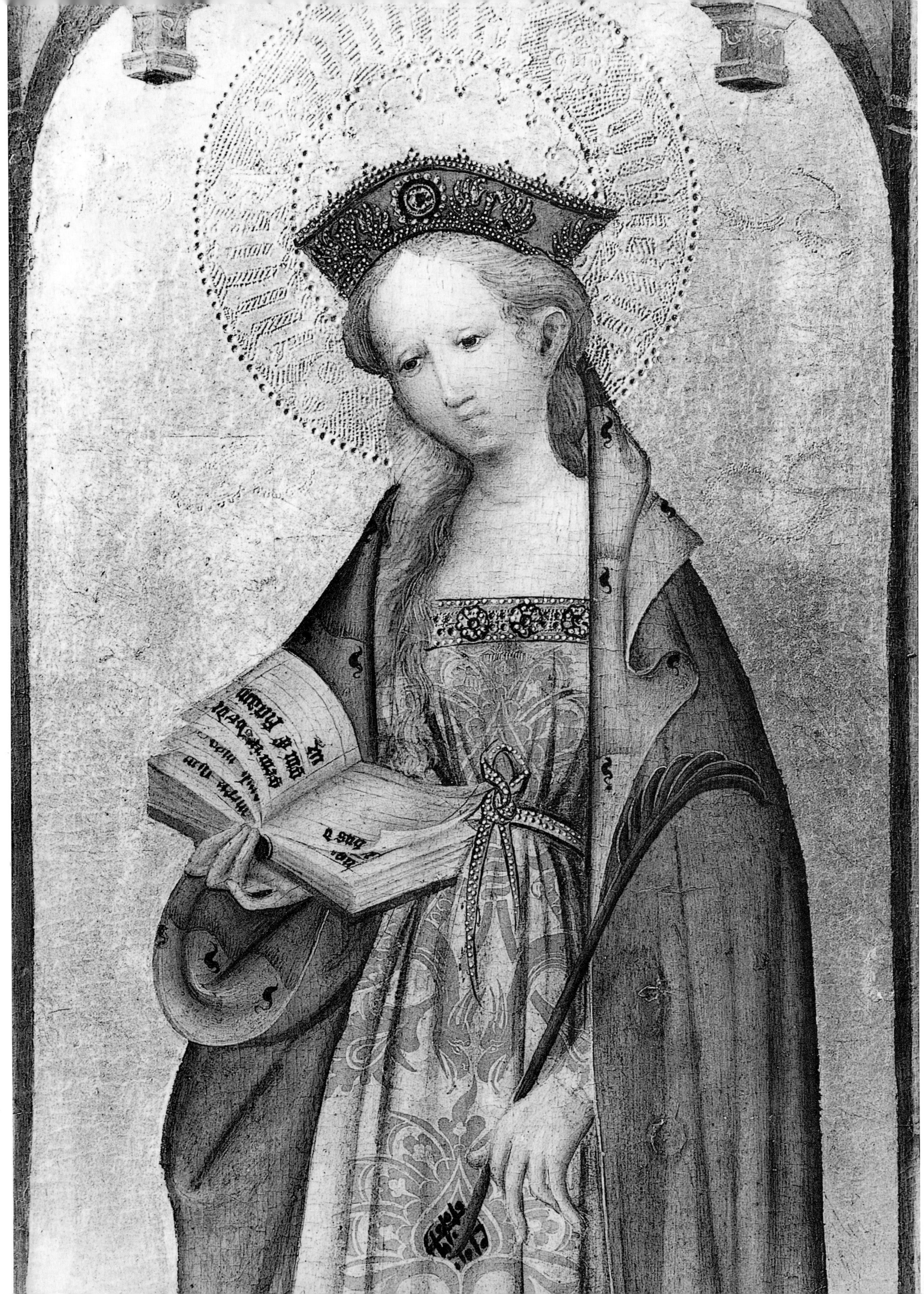

century, when her relics were transported from Cologne to the Augustinian monastery of the Holy Cross at Huy. Legend has it that she, the daughter of a king, had been one of the maidens who accompanied St Ursula to Cologne. Miracles performed by St Odilia are said to have provoked the building of the Cathedral at Huy. The Augustinian monastery at Huy was the Motherhouse of the convent of St Walpurgis at Soest. St Odilia the Martyr must have been venerated there in equal measure for her image to deserve a place in the tabernacle doors.

The liturgical significance of the inscription in St Odilia's book, the words *'genetrix ut digni efficiamur'* from the Laurentan Litany (*'ora pro nobis, sancta Dei Genetrix, ut digni efficiamur promissionibus Christi'* [pray for us, O holy Mother of God, that we may become worthy of the promises of Christ]), is consistent with the adherence to biblical and liturgical texts in the works of Conrad von Soest. It is interesting to note that the inscriptions of the Fröndenberg Altarpiece (cat. no. 5), which appears to have a workshop connection with Conrad, also conform to this pattern. In view of this prayer to the Virgin, it has been suggested that the tabernacle may have housed the carved image of a Virgin: there is evidence in various documents (dating 1304–1624) that a silver statue of the Virgin was venerated at St Walpurgis.[80] However, the Eucharistic subject of the decoration on the reverse side of the doors, the *Mass of St Gregory*, which was painted by a later, less competent hand (around 1460?), strongly suggests that the tabernacle housed a pyx containing the Host. The tabernacle doors are linked to liturgy through their function at mass, and through their prayer inscription. Similarly, the iconography of Conrad von Soest's altarpieces, far from being, as has been suggested, superficial, secular and concerned merely with courtly elegance,[81] is deeply rooted in Gospel and Liturgy. An austere adherence to religious truth, in some measure confirmed by the realism of detail and the perceptive characterization of the protagonists, is contrasted by the grace and beauty of the courtly style. The elegance of the style finds a parallel in the learned subtlety behind the apparent simplicity of Gospel and liturgical interpretation. The consistent approach to iconography in Conrad's work may suggest that the painter himself, accepted into the social circle of his sophisticated cosmopolitan patrons, had considerable freedom in the execution of these contracts and that they express some of his own religious feeling.

Conrad's autograph works were not only precious objects made with consummate skill for demanding patrons; they were an expression of sincere individual devotion and were intended to encourage a meditation totally in keeping with the religious feeling of the painter's time, as expressed by Ludolph of Saxony and the *devotio moderna* movement. The artist's clear manner of representing the Bible passages in his altarpieces and the gentle humanity of his descriptive style would have encouraged the illiterate lay congregation to 'read by looking' and thus be guided to individual devotion, just as their more educated contemporaries would have been by studying Ludolph's written instructions and the 'joyous brilliance' of the painting of Conrad von Soest.[82]

72. Conrad von Soest: Detail of *St Odilia*, from *St Dorothea* and *St Odilia*,
Landesmuseum für Kunst und Kulturgeschichte, Münster

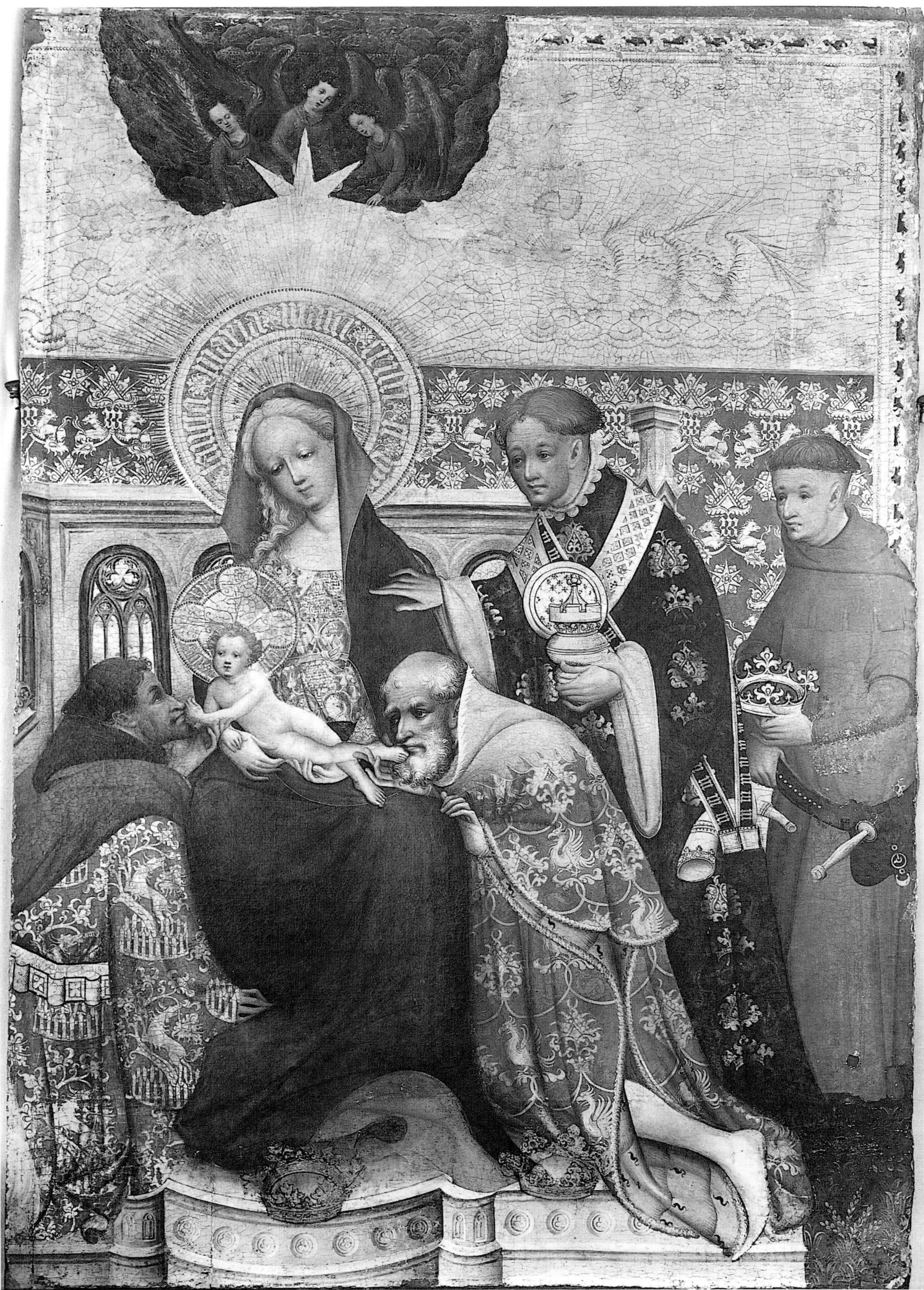

7. The Westphalian Inheritance

P AINTERS OF RELIGIOUS images were recognized as the inheritors of pictorial traditions. When Cennini advised young painters in the late fourteenth century, '…take pains and pleasure in constantly copying the best things which you can find done by the hand of great masters', it is unlikely that he was concerned merely with the acquisition of technical skills.[1] Artists were expected to produce variations of themes known to their audience through other pictures and descriptions, or through meditation texts, which would reflect the visual experience of the author. Where the principal function of religious painting was biblical instruction of the pious illiterate, it may often have been sufficient for the apprentice to learn the pictorial language of his master.[2] Yet, although the essence of pictorial narrative does not appear to have changed markedly, its vocabulary was constantly being expanded. A slow development, guided largely by official theological thinking and the needs of communal worship in the earlier Christian centuries, and interrupted by iconoclasm, was speeded by the proliferation of religious writing in the thirteenth and fourteenth centuries. This literature stimulated individual meditation and presented new problems in pictorial representation. The artist's skill lay in his ability to incorporate such new subject matter into his inherited pictorial tradition.

However, the patron's active piety was balanced by a delight in looking at the painting and the pleasure of possession. As access to education and travel increased for potential donors, their iconographic vocabularies and interpretative skills became more sophisticated, and artists would be required to mirror these new tastes. During his compulsory term abroad, a journeyman artist had the opportunity to study foreign workshop practices and copy 'the best things…by the hand of great masters' into his pattern sheets in accordance with Cennini's advice. In Conrad von Soest's paintings, the style and content are likely to have delighted his patrons, as they demonstrate traditional roots combined with a masterly response to the most recent trends; his consummate craftsmanship will have added in great measure to their pleasure of possession.

In consequence of this perception of the artist as a link in an ever evolving chain, the medieval painter's production method and painting style provide clues about his training and visual experience. In Conrad's case, his advanced technique and linear, elegant style differ markedly from the earlier Westphalian tradition. This discrepancy has given rise to speculation about the sources of his designs, which were usually considered to be copies of Burgundian inventions, although specific examples were rarely cited.[3] Such assessments are based on the notion that a German medieval artist can only be an imitator, for the preconceived idea of the

73. Conrad von Soest: *Adoration of the Kings*. Dortmund Altarpiece

provinciality of German art before Dürer holds fast—even in the face of evidence about Conrad's individual and creative designing style.[4] However, instead of copying the designs of other masters, Conrad von Soest employed for his compositions an idiosyncratic artistic vocabulary which was based on his Westphalian inheritance but widened and modernized by his study abroad.

Any attempt to distinguish Conrad's debt to the Westphalian tradition and to identify the sources of any new elements in his art must take into account the dual effects of selective study and the random survival of works of art. In view of the uncertainties about panel-painting traditions in such important centres as Bruges, Paris, Dijon, London and Milan, much evidence has to be deduced from manuscript illumination, despite the limitations of such a method. However, sufficient panels and other artefacts have survived to demonstrate that it is possible to assess the degree of local tradition reflected in later works. The saints from the Wittingau Altarpiece in Prague (1378? or 1427?), for instance, are painted in the international 'language' of the Courtly Style, but still speak the 'dialect' of the Bohemian figure canon exemplified by the work of Master Theodoric (documented 1359–68).[5] I would suggest that the relatively large number of panels surviving in Westphalia permits a reasonable assessment of pictorial sources there, and that the body of work from major workshops reproduced in classic survey volumes forms a representative sample of European iconographic and stylistic trends.[6]

The long tradition of pictorial representation in Westphalia can be exemplified by four panels of undoubted artistic merit: the Antependium of the twelfth century, now in Münster, two Crucifixion retables from the thirteenth century, now in Berlin, and the retable fragments from the early fourteenth century in the church at Hofgeismar.[7] The first three of these works consist of single panels with tripartite narrative divisions; the fragments in Hofgeismar appear to be the wings of a retable and show narrative scenes divided by arcading on the obverse side, and standing saints on the reverse. By the late fourteenth century, rectangular altarpieces with movable wings and decorated with pictorial cycles containing scenes from the childhood and passion of Christ, seem to have been preferred in Westphalia. In its structure and pictorial organization, the Niederwildungen Altarpiece follows the Westphalian prototype—as do the Netze Altarpiece (Pfarrkirche), *c.* 139;(pl. 78) and the same master's Osnabrück Altarpiece (Wallraf-Richartz Museum, Cologne, *c.* 1385–90)(pl. 77). The Dortmund Altarpiece by Conrad von Soest seems to represent an alternative Westphalian tradition: a rectangular triptych surmounted by a lunette, depicting a single narrative scene in each panel. An altarpiece of 1376 in the Wiesenkirche at Soest, of which only the painted predella and frame survive (pl. 74, 145), appears to have been of this type. In the same church, a small carved altarpiece of around 1370 and Aldegrever's Marienaltar of around 1526 are also surmounted by a lunette. The reduction in narrative scenes in the Dortmund Altarpiece may indicate a shift in the function of certain altarpieces, reflecting an emphasis on individual contemplation rather than religious instruction.

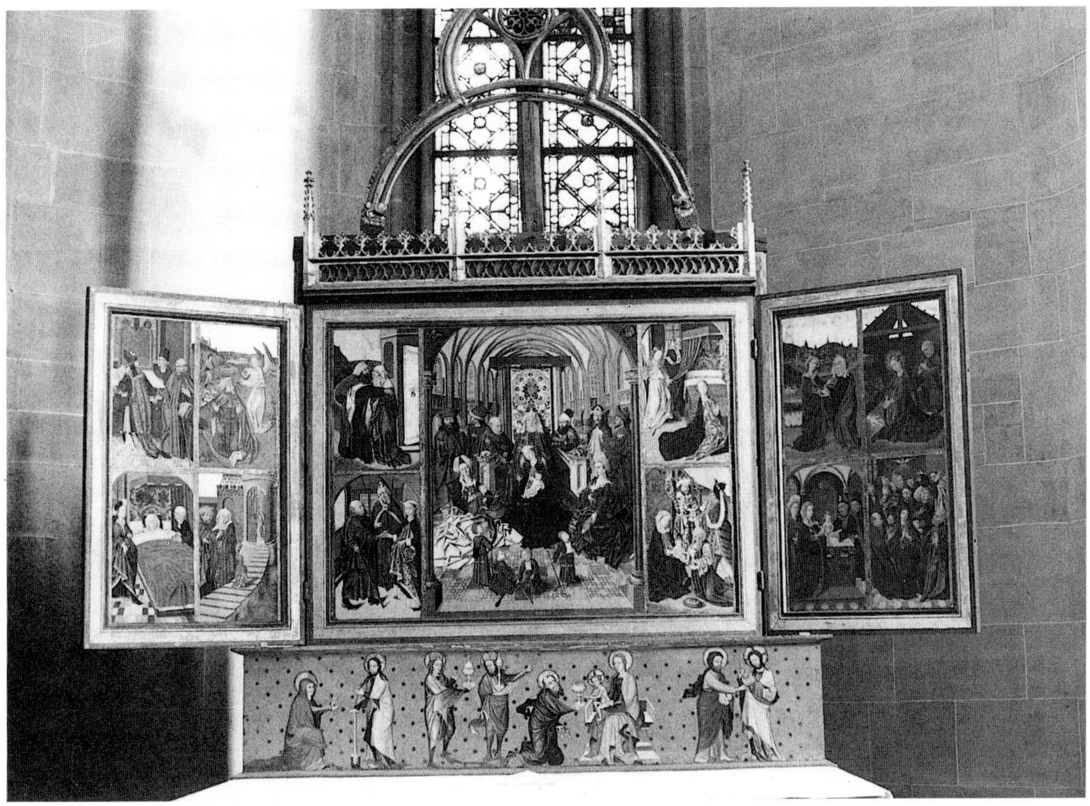

74. Annenaltar, with the predella and frame of an Altarpiece of 1376. Wiesenkirche, Soest

Whilst the narrative content and sequence of pictorial cycles can be presumed to depend largely on patrons' preferences (see the Wiesenfeld contract, Appendix E), Conrad appears to have organized the scenes in the Niederwildungen Altarpiece partially in accordance with Westphalian tradition. The scenes from Christ's childhood in the left wing of the Niederwildungen Altarpiece correspond to those in the Netze and Osnabrück Altarpieces, and all three retables display a central *Crucifixion*. However, the selection and order of the passion scenes differs between the altarpieces. The Saints on the reverse side of the wings at Niederwildungen, and those in the tabernacle doors at Münster, are of a pictorial type that survives in the retable from Soest of *c*. 1345–57 in Berlin (Inv. No. 1519) and at Hofgeismar. Traces of paint on the reverse side of the wings of the Netze Altarpiece suggest that they were also originally decorated with images of saints.[8]

The painted frames and borders of the Niederwildungen Altarpiece depict simple stencilled motifs, in an arrangement similar to that of other Westphalian retables. But the allusion, already discussed, to the patrons of the Niederwildungen Altarpiece, implicit in the crescent-moon and star design, indicates a sophistication beyond Westphalian precedent. It may be more readily compared in its heraldic significance to the painted fleur-de-lis in the frame of the St Louis of Toulouse

121

Altarpiece by Simone Martini, painted *c.* 1317-19 (Naples, Museo Nazionale di Capodimonte), which identifies the Angevin connection. Simone repeated the fleur-de-lis motif in a punched and tooled framing on the gold ground of the main panel which depicts the Saint apparently crowning his brother, King Robert II. A similar reference to the content of his Crucifixion altarpiece is expressed in Conrad von Soest's punched and tooled crown-of-thorns framing on the gold ground.

Conrad's narrative panels reveal an intelligent attitude to his Westphalian inheritance: an appreciation of the sound tradition of his training and a willingness to put it to some new uses. In the Niederwildungen *Annunciation*, for example, Conrad's approach corresponds in many details to Westphalian practice; although as we have seen (p. 98) his adherence to biblical and liturgical texts (whether by personal preference or the intervention of his patrons) caused him to reject a common motif of Westphalian Annunciations—the small child carrying the cross. For liturgical reasons also, he depicted not a humble maiden but the crowned Queen of Heaven. When he placed the Virgin at her desk turning the pages of a book as the angel approaches, Conrad adopted a design which can be seen in Master Bertram's Grabow Altarpiece (1379)(pl. 68) in Hamburg.[9] The motif of desk and book dates back to Carolingian and Ottonian times, when the book superseded the earlier spindle motif which derived from eastern legends.[10] A critical adaptation of earlier sources can be demonstrated in Conrad's modification of the elaborate tree of Jesse from the Annunciation of the Netze Altarpiece (pl. 69; see pp. 102 above). The intrusive imagery at Netze would not have accorded with Conrad's courtly narrative, and his solution to the pictorial problem therefore consists in introducing the discreet device of the leafy branch.

Such a fresh approach to established pictorial tradition can be observed throughout Conrad's altarpieces. The composition of the Niederwildungen *Nativity*, for example, follows a pattern already established in the Netze and Osnabrück Altarpieces. In Conrad's gentle narrative the child rests in the Virgin's arms, as at Osnabrück, but in a charming increase of intimacy the child is depicted pressing his cheek to that of his mother in the manner of the Westphalian *Madonna and Child* (*c.* 1260–80) in the Carrand collection (Bargello), Florence. The host of angels protecting mother and child derive from Parisian precedents (see p. 141). In both altarpieces, Joseph is seen in the role of provider. However, his lively pose at Niederwildungen, where he is portrayed kneeling and bending encouragingly over the flames, constitutes an innovative interpretation of the seated Joseph stirring the soup at Netze. Conrad's theatrical invention recurs in a weak copy at Rauschenberg.[11] At Dortmund, Joseph returns to a more conventional pose; he is shown in a pensive seated position reminiscent of the Osnabrück Nativity.[12]

The *Adoration of the Kings* at Niederwildungen is closely related to Master Bertram's version in the Grabow Altarpiece (pl. 75), notably in the diagonal arrangement of the principal figures and in the outstretched stance of the child.[13] In contrast, the *Adoration of the Kings* at Dortmund is composed in a symmetrical

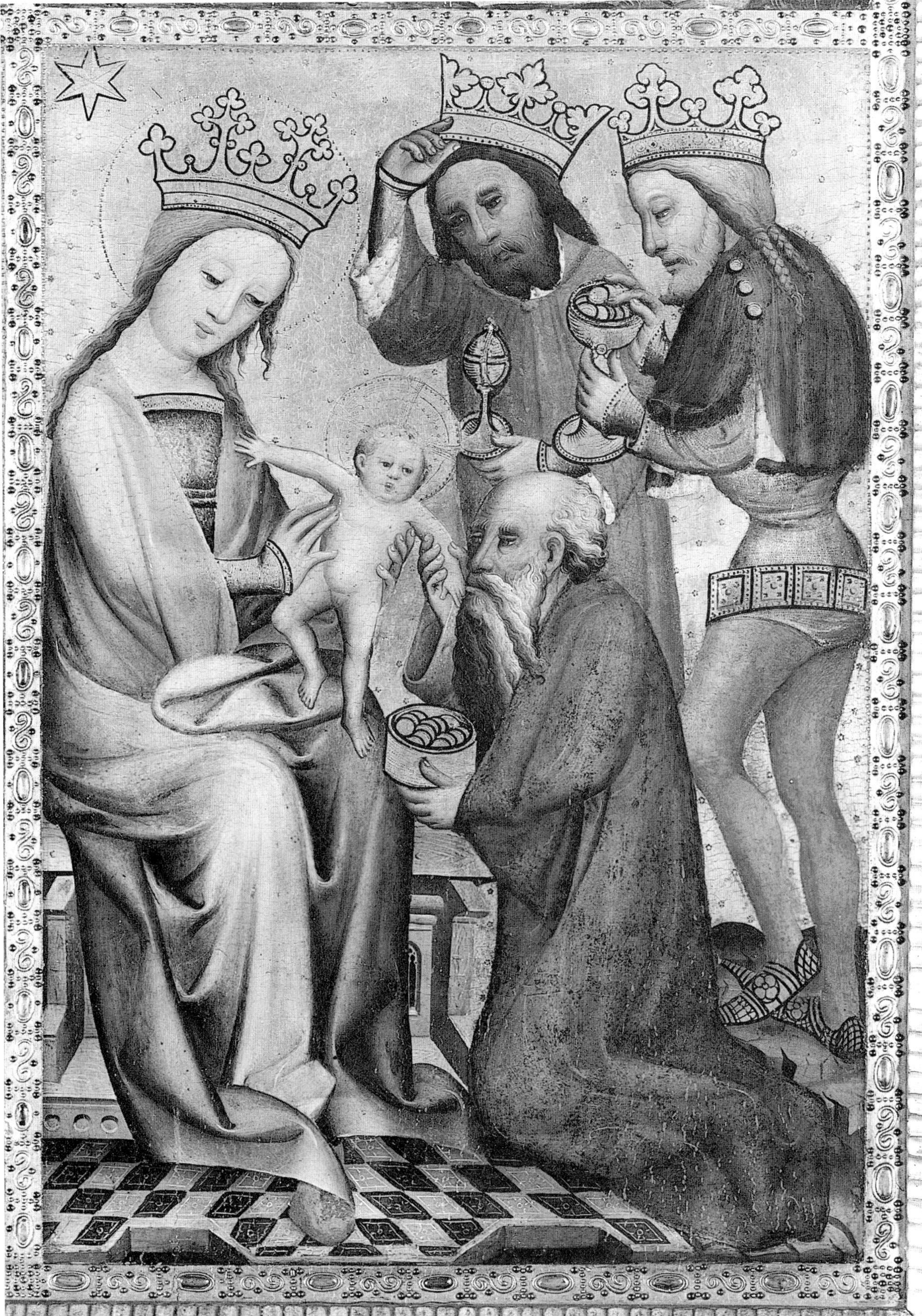

75. Master Bertram: *Adoration of the Kings*. Grabow Altarpiece

design that is appropriate to the hieratic frontal pose of the enthroned Virgin (pl. 73). Symmetrical compositions for the *Adoration of the Kings* occur sporadically in the fourth century, and the development of the design may be traced in the East from the sixth century onwards.[14] The wall-painting (*c.* 1200) in the apse of the church of St Patroklus, Soest, provides a Westphalian precedent. However, Conrad abandoned the usual hieratical pose for the child. In a fusion of the motif of the kissed hand from the Niederwildungen Altarpiece with that of the kissed foot (for which an Italian origin with wide diffusion—including an example by Jacquemart de Hesdin—but no extant Westphalian prototype can be cited), Conrad devised an enchanting pose for the child, who offers His hand for homage to one king and His foot to another. This deviation from pictorial tradition in order to expose the gentle humanity of the child and the poignant veneration of the kings typifies Conrad's attitude to his inheritance; he strove to invest the traditional iconography with new narrative power through stressing the sensitive humanity of his protagonists.

Another instance of emphasis on the humanity of his biblical characters can be detected in the sleeping figure of St Peter in the *Gethsemane* scene of the Niederwildungen Altarpiece (pl. 23). Master Bertram's Passion Altarpiece in Hanover (Landesgalerie; *c.* 1385) contains the same narrative: St Peter appears to be yawning behind the cover of his hand. Yet despite his skill as a lively and inventive story-teller, Master Bertram could not convey the condition of helpless sleepiness overpowering the Saint that Conrad managed to expose in his interpretation.[15] In the Dortmund *Death of the Virgin*, the established narrative scene, which had already appeared in the Osnabrück and Buxtehude Altarpieces, is transformed by adding the tender motif of six caring angels (pl. 81).[16] The iconography of Conrad's Dortmund design differs from these Westphalian precedents in another significant detail. The earlier scenes depict Christ amongst the apostles, attending at the deathbed in accordance with the legend. Conrad, keeping to the liturgical texts, included St John amongst the mourners whilst he showed Christ in a semicircle of clouds that represent heaven. This motif has a Westphalian or Lower Rhenish precedent in the Perikopenbuch of *c.* 1150 in Paris (Bibl. Nat., lat. 17325, fol. 51v). Another lively motif, the apostle strenuously blowing a censer, can already be observed in the *Death of the Virgin* of the Klosterneuburg Altarpiece (1181) by Nicholas of Verdun. For the exceptional feature of the coin in the candle, no precedent can be cited (see pp. 26, 109).

The *Death of the Virgin* is juxtaposed at Dortmund with the *Coronation of the Virgin*. A wall-painting in the church of Maria zur Höhe, Soest (apse of the St Catherine's choir) *c.* 1260 appears to be the earliest extant example of a Westphalian *Coronation of the Virgin*. Diverse renderings of the subject survive from the workshop of Master Bertram; the story is included in the Buxtehude Altarpiece in Hamburg and Apocalypse Altarpiece in London (Victoria & Albert Museum), and in the form of a blessing after the Coronation in the Passion Altarpiece in Hanover. In Conrad von Soest's altarpiece, as in those cited of Master Bertram, Christ is

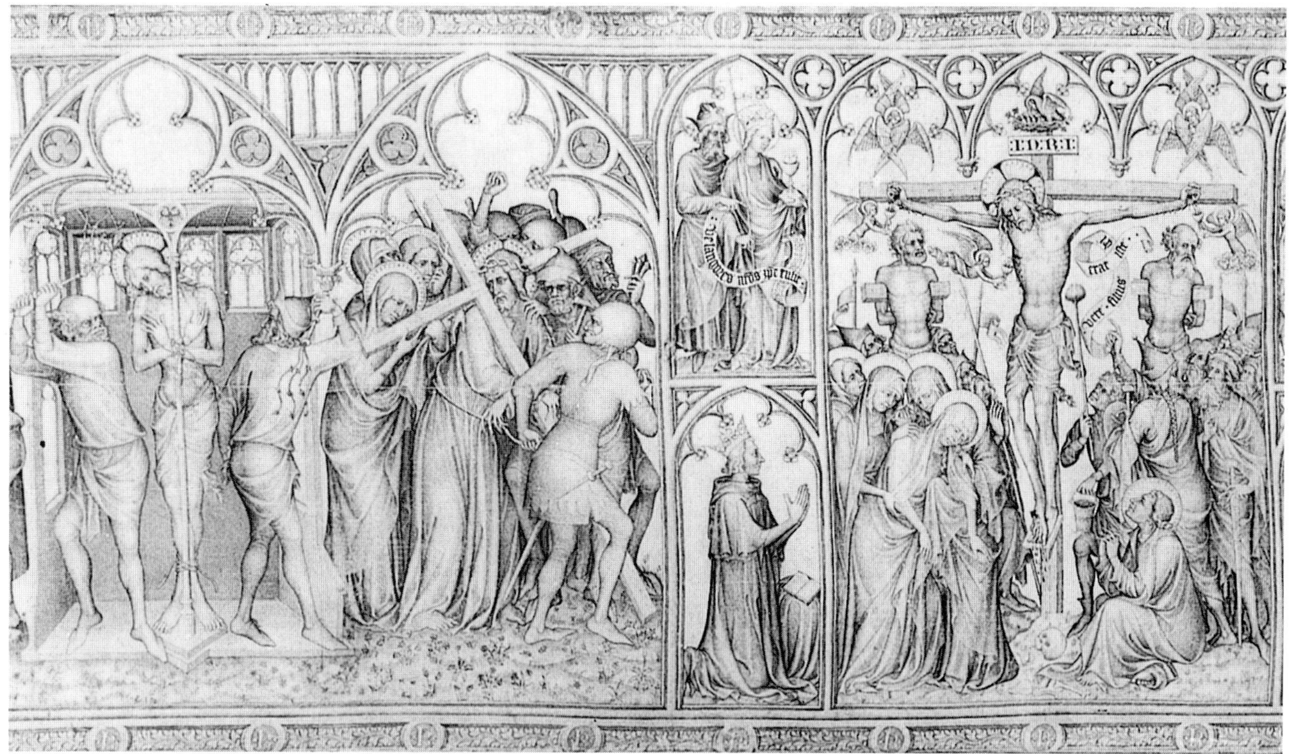

76. Parement Master: *Flagellation, Carrying of the Cross* and *Crucifixion*. Detail from the
Parement de Narbonne. Louvre, Paris

shown crowned as King of Heaven. However, whilst Master Bertram depicted
Christ in Majesty, holding an orb in his left hand and raising the crown towards a
praying Virgin with his right hand, Conrad conceived a more intimate scene in
which Christ gently turns towards the Virgin to place a crown upon her head.

The scene of the *Crucifixion* in Conrad's Niederwildungen Altarpiece appears at
first glance to deviate most from the Westphalian pictorial tradition, as it features
a greater number and variety of figures under the cross. The Wehrden *Crucifixion*
(*c.* 1340) of uncertain provenance, now in the Wallraf-Richartz Museum in Cologne,
was included in the exhibition of early Westphalian altarpieces in Münster in 1964,
and it therefore appeared to constitute a Westphalian precedent for Crucifixions
attended by a crowd. However, it has been convincingly argued that the Wehrden
Crucifixion is a French work, based on Italian prototypes like the *Calvary* of the
Maestà (*c.* 1316) in the Cathedral of Massa Marittima, from the circle of Duccio.[17]
The twelfth-century *Calvary* in the Lower Church of Schwarzrheindorf [near Bonn]
is the earliest known instance of this type of composition which had found wider
diffusion by the fourteenth century.[18] In Paris, the potential of this narrative scene
was exploited in the workshops of the Parement Master and of Jacquemart de
Hesdin (pl. 85). Whilst the compositional scheme of a Crucifixion attended by a

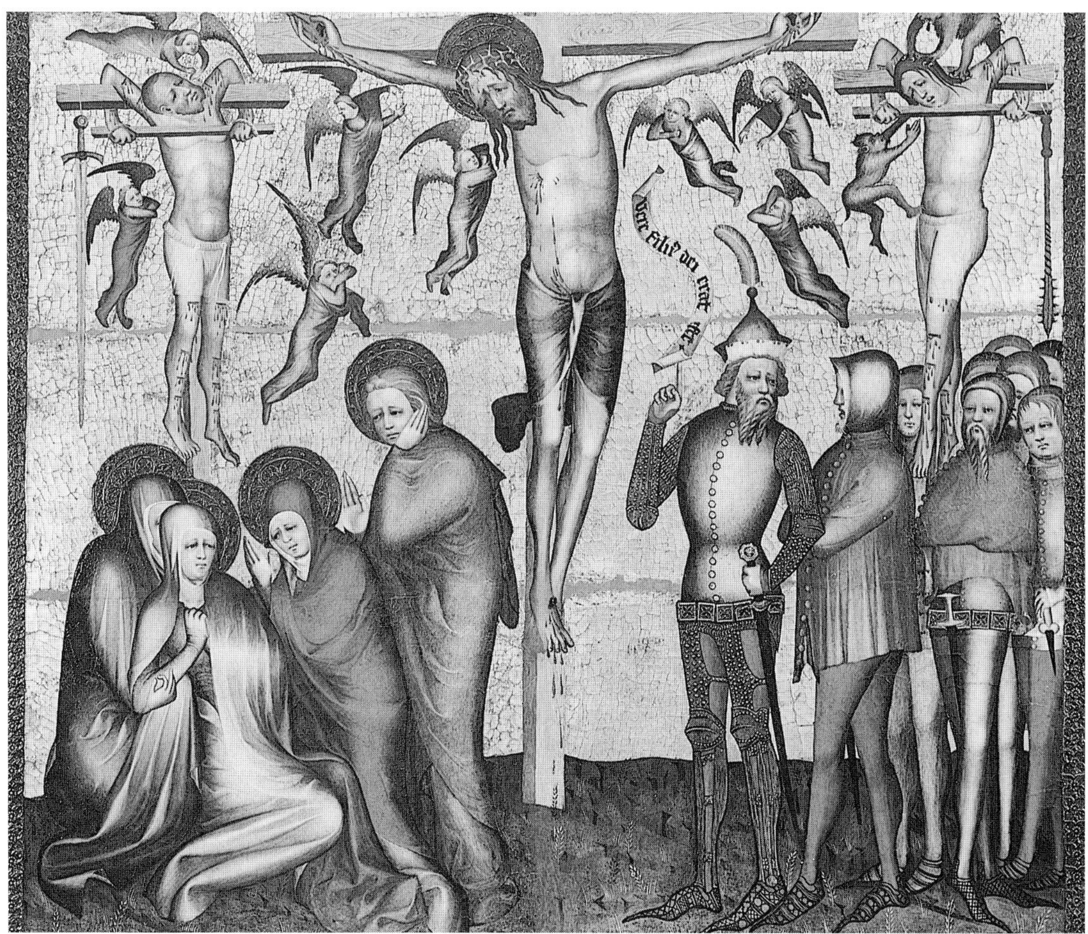

77. The Netze Master: *Crucifixion.* Detail from the Osnabrück Altarpiece.
Wallraf-Richartz-Museum, Cologne

crowd may have been introduced into the Westphalian pictorial tradition by
Conrad von Soest, he in turn appears to have adopted single motifs from works by
the Netze Master for his representation. The painfully arched body of the crucified
Christ in Conrad's scene is likely to be an innovation based on the workshop model
used in the Netze and Osnabrück Altarpieces by the Netze Master, which depict
Christ with His body gently bowed to the right according to Byzantine usage.

The thieves in the Niederwildungen Altarpiece also appear to be progressive
interpretations after the Netze Master's models (pls. 78 and 77). Both masters
portray the thieves hanging—together with their weapons—from crosses made
with two horizontal bars. The arms of these protagonists are twisted over the upper
bar in a pose that can, for example, be observed in Pietro Lorenzetti's *Crucifixion*
(*c.* 1319–20) in the Lower Church at Assisi, and which appears to have been
introduced into French painting by Jean Pucelle.[19] The hands of the thieves are tied
to the lower horizontal bar of the crosses: this has already been shown to be peculiar

126

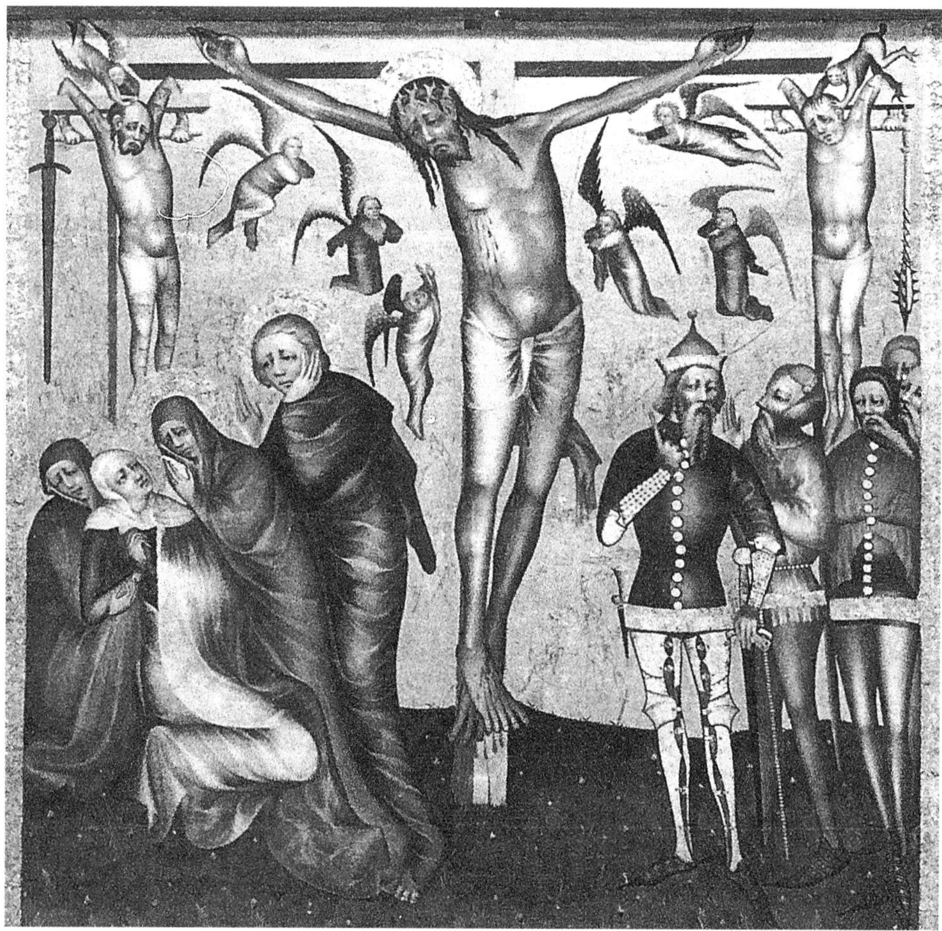

78. The Netze Master: *Crucifixion*. Detail from the Netze Altarpiece

to Westphalian art (see p. 105). Whilst the bar to which the hands are attached is placed across the chest of the thieves in the Osnabrück Altarpiece, it is placed behind the body at Netze and in later Westphalian Crucifixions. It is feasible that the Westphalian motif evolved in this manner from an earlier motif showing the hands fastened with a long string across the chest, for which the French *Crucifixion* from Wehrden is a pertinent example. Conrad diverged from the cited Westphalian models by placing his thieves' crosses diagonally to the picture plane, a space-creating device that appears to have originated in Italy; it occurs in Pietro Lorenzetti's *Crucifixion* at Assisi and was adopted in France in the workshops of the Parement Master and Jacquemart de Hesdin (pls. 76, 85).

In the Crucifixions of both the Niederwildungen and Osnabrück Altarpieces, an angel floats above the good thief to receive his soul, whilst a tormenting devil perches on the cross of the bad thief. The angels attending Christ are familiar from Italian compositions, such as Giotto's *Crucifixion* (*c.* 1304–12) in the Arena Chapel,

Padua. Although the Netze Master only placed the angels below the outstretched arms of Christ, angels mourn above the cross in an earlier Westphalian retable, the panel from Soest of *c.*1230 in Berlin, mentioned above (note 7). Prophets with scrolls are placed in spandrels in that retable as in the Niederwildungen Altarpiece; their presence in Crucifixions is based on Byzantine sources, for which the wall-painting (1209) in the church of the Virgin at Studenica provides an example. In the Niederwildungen and Osnabrück Altarpieces, the centurion displays the scroll declaring his faith in a similar pose. Moreover, the Netze Master depicted the group of women under the cross, attended by the grieving St John, as sinking to their knees. Conrad elaborated the scene by showing the women in their intense sorrow actually sunk to the ground, but allowing St John to wring his hands to his Lord in anguish. John's gesture may be inspired by the *Parement de Narbonne* (Paris, Louvre; pl. 76), although earlier incidents of the saint clasping his hands can be found in both Italy and France.[20] An early Westphalian example of the blind lance-bearer Longinus, piercing Christ's side, can be found in a thirteenth-century fresco of the church Maria zur Höhe in Soest, the *Crucifixion* in the north aisle. The major motifs in Conrad's *Crucifixion* not accounted for by precedent are the bystanders carrying a sword and bow-and-arrow (on the left of the scene) and the unusual presence of Herod and his group standing under the cross, features which he appears to have originated.

This analysis of the motifs which make up the *Crucifixion* scene in the Niederwildungen Altarpiece confirms the impression, gained earlier, that Conrad von Soest could find his principal sources in the Westphalian tradition. The initial impression of pictorial innovation in this *Crucifixion* sprang more from Conrad's compositional scheme and stylistic changes than from innovative iconography. He increased the number of protagonists and (as in the other scenes from the altarpiece), adapted and reinterpreted pictorial motifs in order to accommodate the expanded narrative and harmonize with stylistic requirements. Motifs not represented in extant Westphalian altarpieces can be found, with few exceptions, in works from the workshops of the Parement Master and Jacquemart de Hesdin. Conrad's originality appears to have consisted mainly in his innovative interpretation and deployment of extant motifs, rather than in the invention of new ones. Any Bohemian flavour that may be detected in Conrad von Soest's work can be traced to Westphalian intermediaries. Patterns and works of art carried along the lively trade route between Dortmund and Prague by merchants and scholars may have played their part in spreading knowledge of pictorial innovations.[21] Visits to Dortmund by Emperor Charles IV in 1377 and Empress Elisabeth in 1378 may also have enriched the Bohemian vocabulary of Westphalian artists.

Conrad von Soest was certainly rooted in the Westphalian pictorial tradition which supplied him with the majority of his motifs, and which in turn was in tune with mainstream European usage. Yet he infused this tradition with a fresh approach which suggests a wider visual experience. He met the challenge of new

XXIX. Conrad von Soest: *St Dorothea*

XXX. Conrad von Soest: *St Odilia*

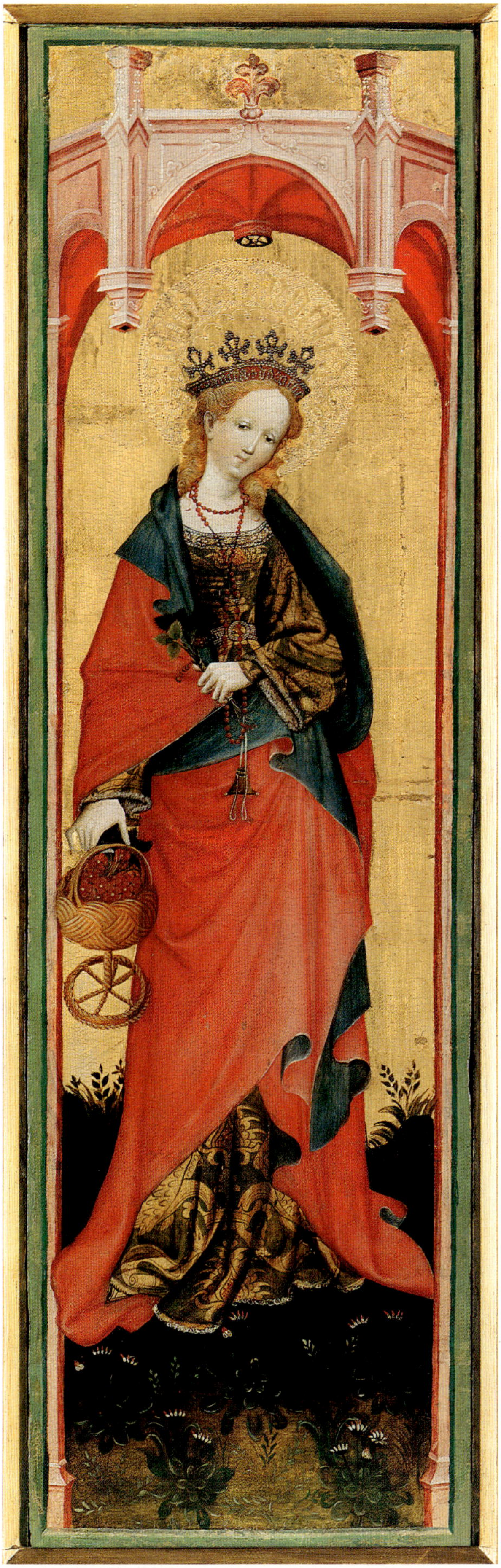

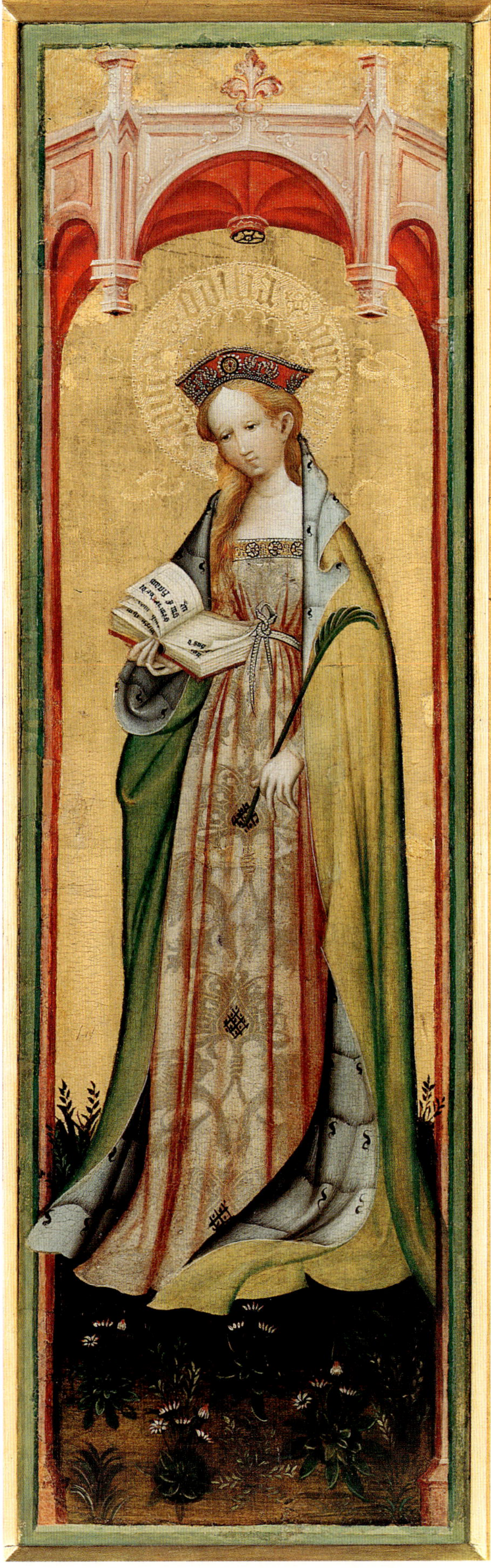

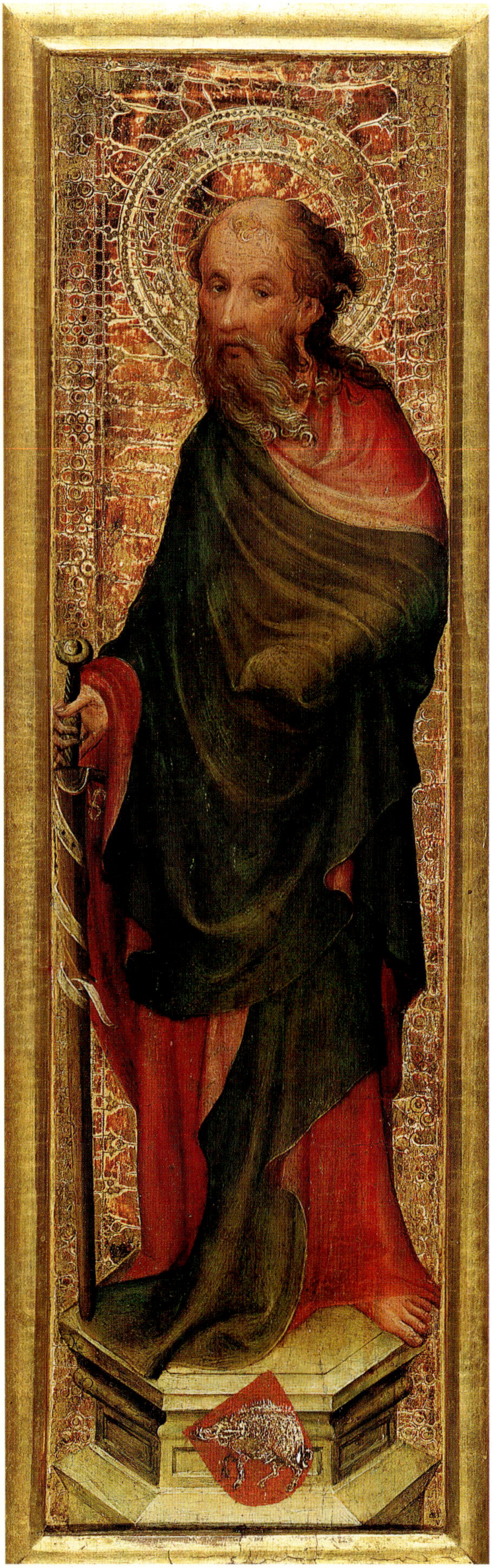

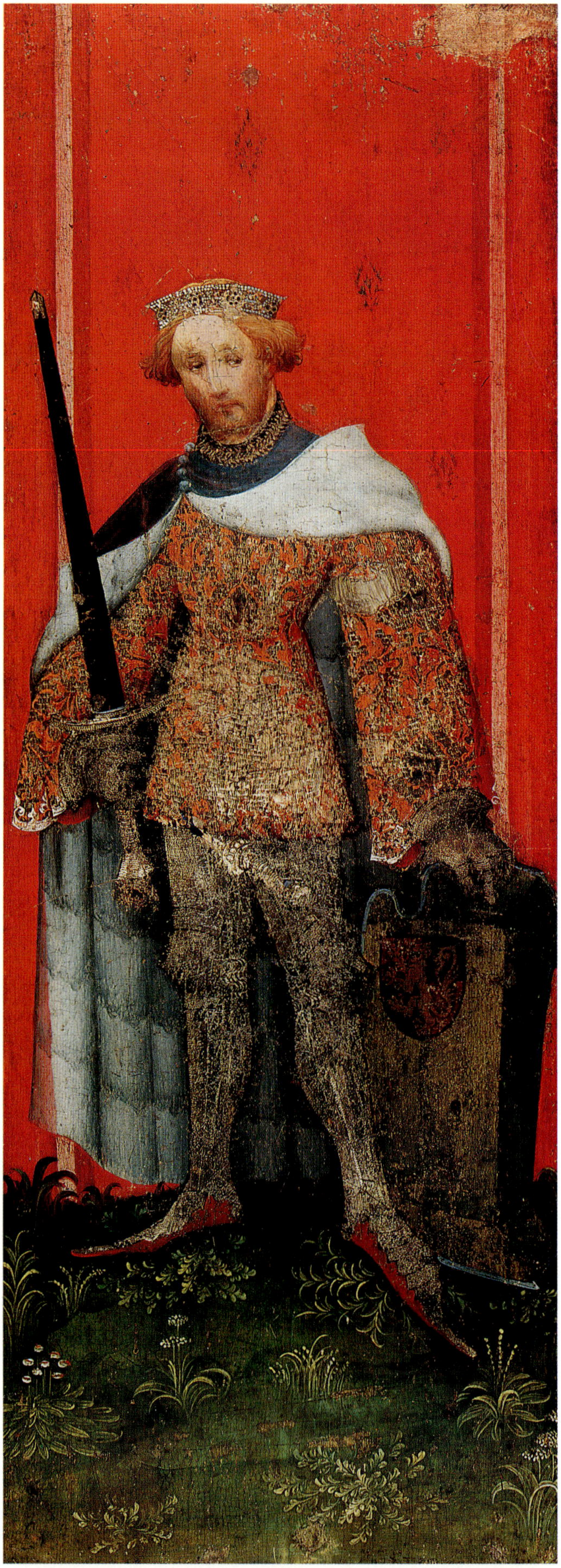

narrative emphases, induced by the shift in religious thinking with faithful adherence to biblical and liturgical sources coupled with a stress on the humanity of his protagonists. He met the pictorial problems consequent on the introduction of the Courtly Style through the selection of suitable iconography. If his contract postulated that he should paint a scene with 'all else that belongs to it' (see Appendix E), he can be said to have produced the traditional Westphalian scene with all pertinent detail, transformed by the courtly style and settings. Motifs that cannot be traced to the Westphalian pictorial tradition appear, like his courtly style, to point to Parisian sources.

XXXI. Conrad von Soest? *St Paul*

XXXII. Conrad von Soest? *Reinhold*

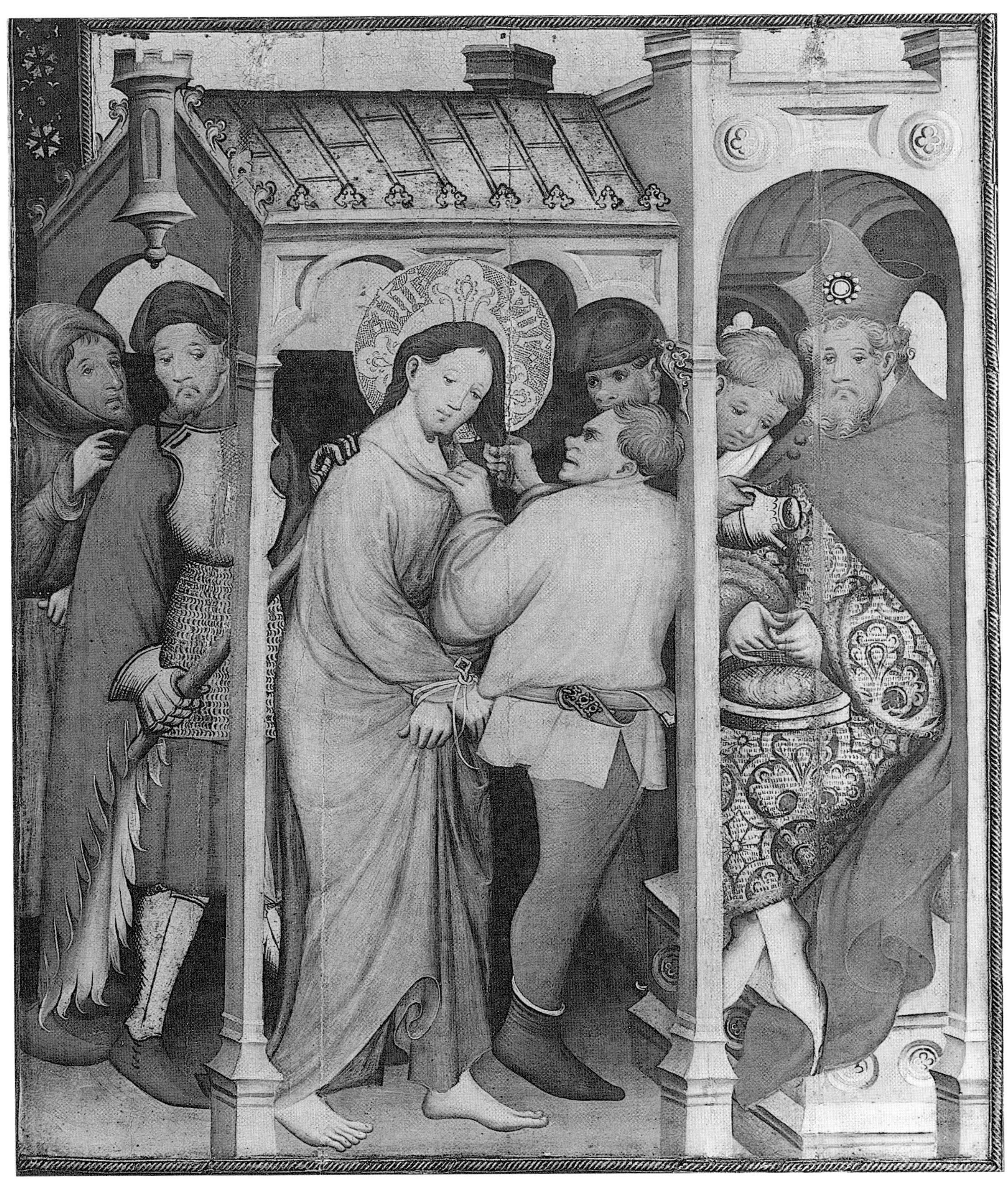

79. Conrad von Soest: *Christ before Herod*. Niederwildungen Altarpiece

8. Foreign Influences

IT IS GENERALLY BELIEVED that Conrad von Soest travelled to Burgundy around or after the year 1400.[1] The *Très riches heures* of the Duke of Berry (1411–16) and the *Livre de chasse* (*c.* 1410) are, for example, frequently cited as his direct sources. If Conrad had studied these manuscripts, his journey could not have taken place until the second decade of the fifteenth century. But it will be remembered that Conrad's two signed extant altarpieces are confidently dated to 1403 and about 1420. It has also been suggested that Conrad visited the Netherlands.[2] However, no document survives to testify that Conrad von Soest travelled as far as France or the Netherlands and we have to rely entirely on stylistic and technical evidence when endeavouring to trace the sources of an apparent foreign influence in Conrad's paintings.

Conrad undoubtedly introduced the International Courtly Style into Westphalia. His elegant creatures with their gentle features, eloquent hands and sensitive faces differ markedly from the sturdy Bohemian-influenced tradition there, best exemplified by the Netze Altarpiece. Whilst it is theoretically possible that Conrad could have learned in Westphalia from models and patterns carried by travelling artists, scholars or merchants, the strong change in his style and technique from Westphalian practices supports the notion of a foreign journey. If the ceremony of 1394 referred to above (see pp. 15–16) was Conrad's second marriage, he would have travelled as a journeyman as early as around 1380. If he travelled to France at that time to acquaint himself with the latest artistic trends and to develop his skills, he would probably have been attracted to the primary artistic centre of Paris rather than to the nascent centre of excellence in Burgundy.[3] Some scholars have argued for two separate journeys abroad: one as a journeyman after 1390 and a second, presumably as an established master, around the turn of the century.[4] However, a second journey can fairly safely be discounted as it is difficult to envisage a reason for an already thriving painter, who was not at the mercy of a prince's whim, to abandon his workshop and search for ideas abroad.

When assessing possible stylistic influences from Paris and other parts of France, the results of any study can be distorted by the accident of survival of works of art. Research on around 300 surviving painted medieval panels of French origin identified few of high quality and few in the International Courtly Style. And a study of surviving Valois inventories indicates that there was a marked preference at the peripatetic courts for small-scale commissions.[5] The relatively few panels in these collections, mostly small in scale, were often placed in private apartments and oratories, and were therefore unlikely to have been available for study by travelling artists. There is also evidence for the existence of altarpieces in French churches; but since many disappeared long ago it is not always clear whether they were painted, carved or made from precious metals.

The courtly style and conservative technique of the Niederwildungen Altarpiece of 1403 can be compared, however, with four surviving panels that may have been Valois commissions and are now in the Louvre, Paris: the *Crucifixion*, c. 1389–1395, by Jean de Beaumetz (pl. 80); *La grande Pietà ronde*, c. 1400, possibly by Jean Malouel; the *Entombment*, c. 1400, by an unknown Parisian or Burgundian painter; and the *Martyrdom of St Denis*, before 1416, by Henri Bellechose. Although it is not possible to be certain that these panels are representative of the traditions in Paris, Bourges or Dijon at that time, surviving evidence is heavily biased towards that assumption. The technical and stylistic affinities between Conrad von Soest's paintings and these French panels contradict the idea that Conrad's art is inferior or provincial in quality.

Some of the wall-paintings and tapestries in royal apartments may have been known to artists and to patrons through design drawings or by repute. The renowned splendour of some courtly commissions, such as the wall-paintings of 1384 in the chapel of the castle at Argilly, with their exceptionally lavish display of gold and ultramarine, may have influenced the patrons of Conrad's altarpieces to attempt similar extravagant standards. This does not imply direct knowledge of such royal commissions; fame by repute may well have sufficed to guide those who aspired to imitate the nobility. Large-scale ephemeral decorations for festivities and tournaments, painted fabrics for processions and churches, tapestries, stained-glass windows, and much large-scale work that is not known to us today may also have inspired a travelling artist in France at the end of the fourteenth century.

Manuscripts survive in abundance and have provoked stylistic comparisons, often without due regard to dating or availability. Precious manuscripts may have been exhibited in churches on occasion, but this would not usually provide an opportunity for the visiting painter to turn their pages. Few artists would have had access to the libraries of princes. This problem was recognized by Vasari when he lamented in 1568 that the works of the illuminator Clovio were 'almost all in the hands of great lords and personages' and commented '…it is certain that the works of men such as Don Giulio are not public, nor in places where they can be seen by everyone, like the pictures, sculptures, and buildings of the other masters of these our arts'.[6] But models, patterns and even copies kept in workshops were likely to have preserved some iconographic ideas and recorded stylistic changes. It has been shown that manuscripts could even serve as models for wall-painting.[7] Verbal descriptions may have been sufficient to spread some knowledge of iconographic or stylistic innovations.

In view of the loss of large-scale works, the use of manuscripts in iconographic and stylistic research seems justified, despite the differences in size, function and method of production between miniature and monumental painting.[8] The pictorial and stylistic history of illumination is an invaluable guide to any study of painting

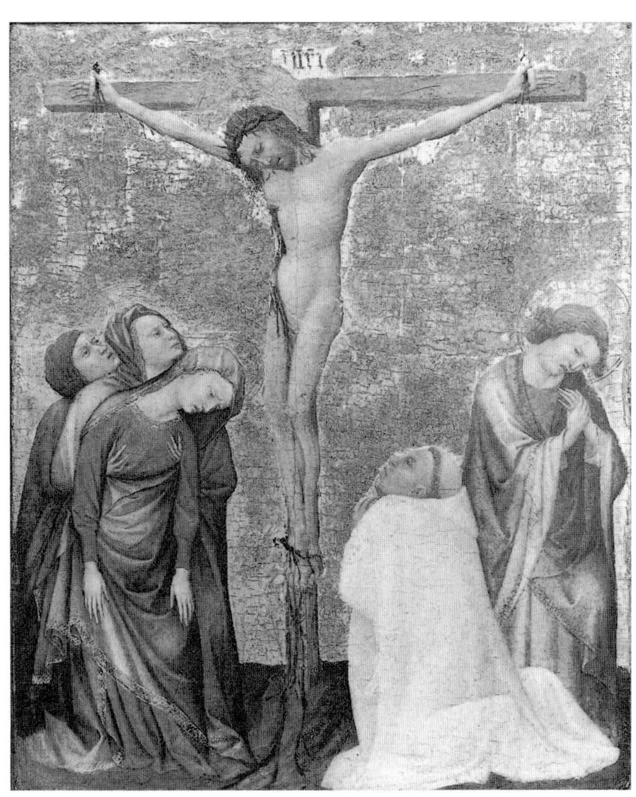

80. Jean de Beaumetz: *Crucifixion.*
Louvre, Paris

in France between 1300 and 1500.[9] Some workshops were equally skilled in illumination and panel-painting techniques: both miniature and large-scale work by the Parement Master, for example, has survived.[10] To examine artistic trends in manuscript painting, a study of the products of the major workshops should provide useful evidence of stylistic development.

The workshop that is most likely to have influenced a change in Conrad von Soest's style away from Westphalian traditions appears to be that of the Parement Master in Paris. With a blend of French, Italian and Netherlandish traditions, the Parement Master had achieved by 1380 a new realism of form and structure.[11] He had introduced into French painting complete interiors, apparently derived from the work of the Lorenzetti. The spatial relationship between Italianate architecture and the figures which dominate the pictorial field in the work of the Parement Master finds a striking echo in the designs in the Niederwildungen Altarpiece. Such interiors did not occur in Westphalian painting at that time.

A number of stylistic and iconographic details suggest that Conrad was thoroughly acquainted with painting in the workshop of the Parement Master. They include (apart from those cited in the previous chapter) the unusual motif of the angel closing the eyes of the dead Virgin in the *bas-de-page* of the *Coronation* page (p. 78)(pls. 71, 82) from the Paris fragment of the *Très belles heures de Notre-Dame* (Bibl. Nat., nouv. acq. lat. 3093; before 1384).[12] Conrad elaborated this motif in his Dortmund *Death of the Virgin*, showing one angel closing the Virgin's eyes, one lifting her chin, one smoothing her hair, and three folding their hands in fervent

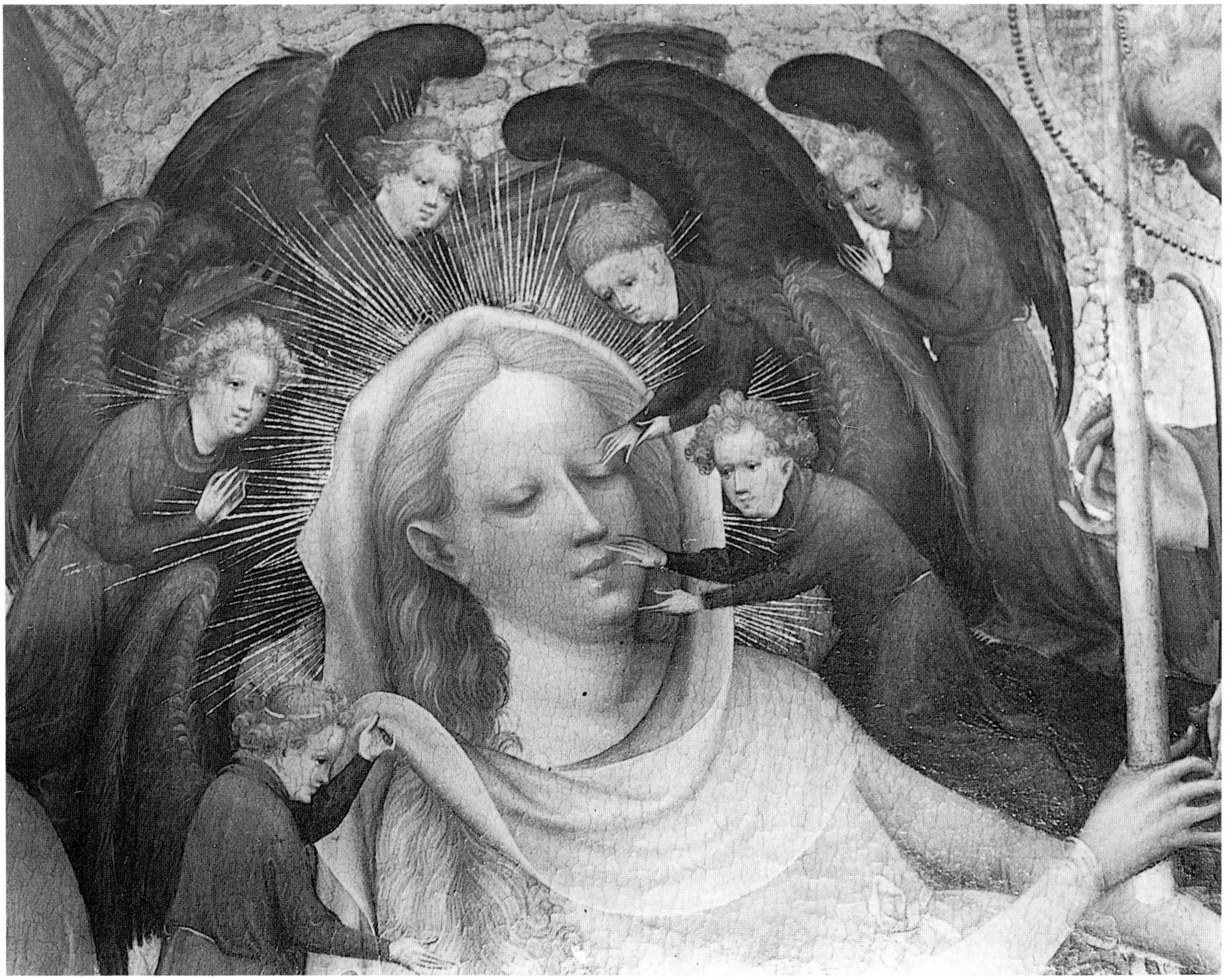

81. Conrad von Soest: *Ministering angels*. Detail from the *Death of the Virgin*.
Dortmund Altarpiece

82. *Death of the Virgin*. Bas-de-page, *Très belles heures de Notre-Dame*,
Paris, Bibl. Nat. nouv. acq. lat. 3093, p. 78

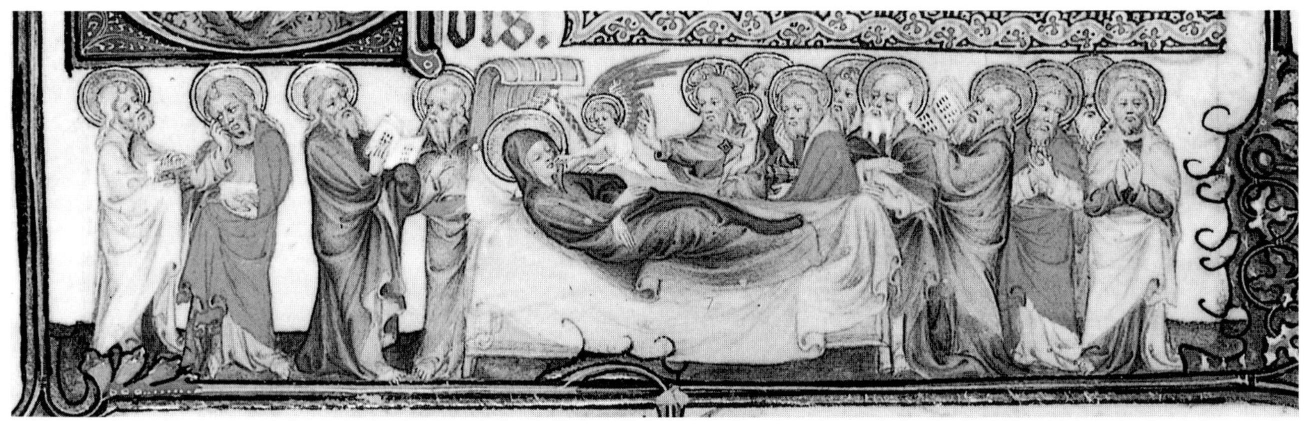

prayer (pl. 81). This page may also have inspired Conrad's intimate narrative of the *Coronation of the Virgin* (pl. XXVI). These scenes in Dortmund and in the manuscript are framed by a mandorla. In both designs, the gentle Christ also turns to a Virgin of similar style and pose. Differences are small, but typical of Conrad's fresh approach to models: Christ crowns the Virgin with both hands in the manuscript of the Parement Master; Christ crowns the Virgin and presents her with a sceptre at Dortmund. Angels decorate the background of the mandorla in the manuscript; they are arranged to form the mandorla at Dortmund. The Evangelist symbols that fill the spandrels of the mandorla in the Dortmund *Coronation of the Virgin* can also be found in the Parement Master's *Trinity* in Turin (*Heures de Milan*, Museo Civico, fol. 87). Close stylistic similarities, discussed below (p. 140), suggest that Conrad's design is directly derived from the patterns in the workshop of the Parement Master.

Conrad's dependence on the style of the Parement Master did not take the form of direct quotations. It consists rather in the assimilation of an apparently well studied visual experience into a personal interpretation. Taking into account the stylistic changes that one might expect by 1403 in the evolving work of a master who was to advance to the monumental figure style of the Dortmund Altarpiece by 1420, the stylistic similarities between Conrad's work and that of the Parement Master seem to confirm the assumption that Conrad is likely to have worked as a journeyman in Paris in the 1380s. In view of the problems of access to princely collections, Conrad's detailed knowledge of the manuscript designs in the Parement workshop can only be explained if he was engaged as a journeyman in that particular workshop. Furthermore, Conrad introduced into Westphalia red bole, *terra verde* facial underpainting, and the predominance of the pigments ultramarine and lead-tin yellow that can all be found in the Parement Master's work (see pp. 40–42).

It is instructive to compare the scene of *Christ before Caiaphas* (p. 189)(pl. 84) from the *Très belles heures de Notre-Dame*, Paris fragment, with that of the *Christ mocked before Herod* (pl. 83) from the Niederwildungen Altarpiece of 1403. Italianate loggias of similar structure, placed parallel to the picture plane, house the scenes in both the manuscript and the altarpiece. In each case, a large open arch reveals the main action around Christ, whilst two approaching figures are framed by a receding side opening. The Parisian work is earlier, and Conrad's stylistic changes are in tune with the demands of the International Courtly Style of around 1400; but the essential relationship of the three-dimensional forms and their dominance of the similar spatial settings remains unchanged. To retain this tension between figures and architecture, Conrad surrounded his slightly more elongated courtly figures with a marginally taller structure. He achieved this by placing the pillars, which support the frontal arch, right up against the picture plane, instead of showing them on the recessed stepped platform as in the illumination. The additional height of the building is stressed by the removal of most of the architectural ornamentation

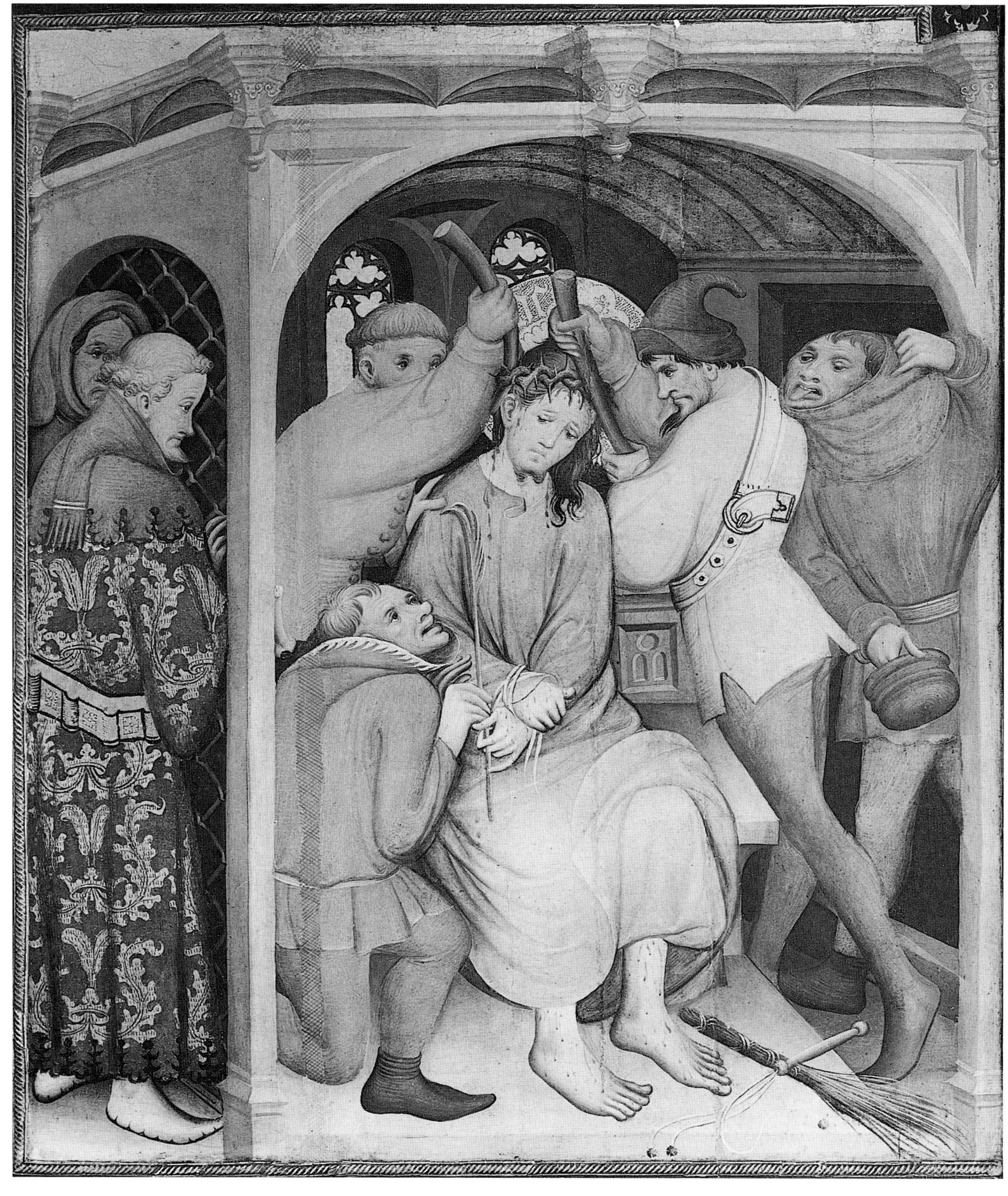

83. Conrad von Soest: *Christ mocked before Pilate*. Niederwildungen Altarpiece

84. Parement Master: *Christ before Caiaphas. Très belles heures de Notre-Dame,* Paris, Bibl. Nat. nouv acq. lat 3093, p. 189

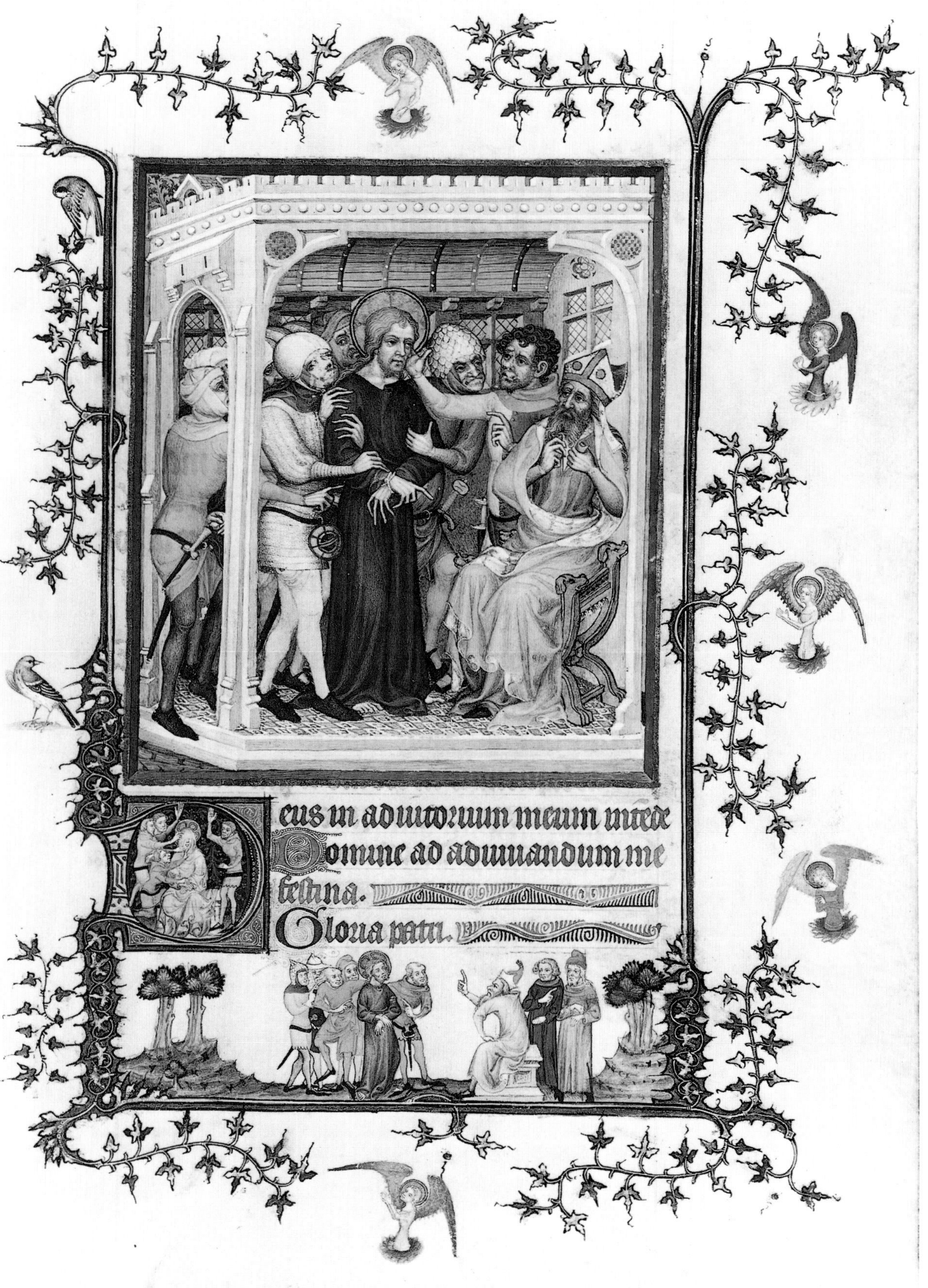
eus in adiutorium meum intede
Domine ad adiuuandum me
festina.
Gloria patri.

of the loggia. The central arch is allowed an uninterrupted span that is echoed by a receding barrel vault; playful suggestions of rib-vaulting replace the severe crenellation of the roof. All this, together with the round-topped windows in the background wall, adds late Gothic elegance, whereas the stress on rectilinear patterns and horizontal lines had suited the Parement Master's thick-set figures. Whilst the Parement Master indicated recession through a vanishing axis style for the orthogonals of a tiled floor, Conrad experimented with light and shade around Christ's platformed seat to create an illusion of spatial depth. The Parement Master's architectural construction is totally contained within the painted frame. Conrad, however, created a teasing illusion of frontal space in the taste of the International Courtly Style: whilst the right-hand pillar of the Niederwildungen loggia appears to press against the picture plane at the base, it is allowed to overlap the frame where it supports the roof. As if to stress this dichotomy, the arm of the mocking onlooker on the right is in turn allowed to project in front of the pillar. Although Conrad's loggia is less crowded with background figures than that of the Parement Master, the spatial relationship between figures and architecture remains the same. Only Conrad von Soest seems to have assimilated the particular tension of figures and space created by the Parement Master, although an imitator perpetuated the style to a degree in the later pages of the manuscript. In manuscripts from other Parisian workshops, like that of Jacquemart de Hesdin, the slighter figures do not dominate architectural space in the manner effected in the Parement workshop, even when their proportions are still too large for the setting.

The increased realism and plasticity of the Parement Master's figures and their dominance of space encourage a concentration on the drama of the event which is supported by the expressive language of their hands. Although the hands painted by Conrad have less spiky fingers and display a new elegance, they seem to repeat gestures created by the Parement Master, and achieve a similar narrative force. In the scenes compared above, the passive acceptance expressed in Christ's crossed and bound hands is contrasted by both masters with the aggressive hand of the tormentor on His shoulder. The kneeling mocker in the Niederwildungen Altarpiece appears in the illuminated capital 'D' below the main scene in the Parisian manuscript. Christ's hair is also being pulled at Niederwildungen, but in a different scene, *Christ before Pilate* (pl. 79). The unprecedented poignancy and eloquence of the hands in the *Christ among the Doctors* (p. 62) of the manuscript is reflected in the Niederwildungen *Ascension* (pl. 168). In this scene, St Peter shades his eyes in a way that may derive from the *Pentecost* illumination by the Parement Master's workshop (p. 166). St Peter, incidentally, exposes the sole of his foot just like the angel of the *Annunciation* (p. 2) in the manuscript (pl. 86).

The articulation of the figures in Conrad's paintings is closer in practice to that of the Parement workshop than to traditions in Westphalia, where Master Bertram had introduced the solid Bohemian canon. A direct descent from the more linear Parement style is clearly demonstrated in the figure of the crucified Christ at

138

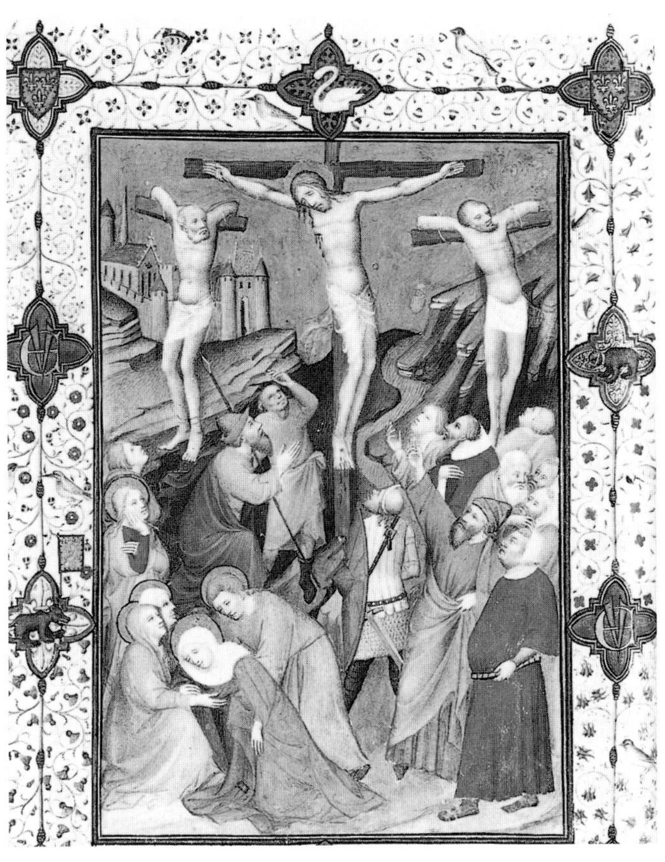

85. Jacquemart de Hesdin:
Crucifixion. Très belles heures de Jean de Berry,
Brussels, Bibl. Royale, MS 1160–61, p. 190

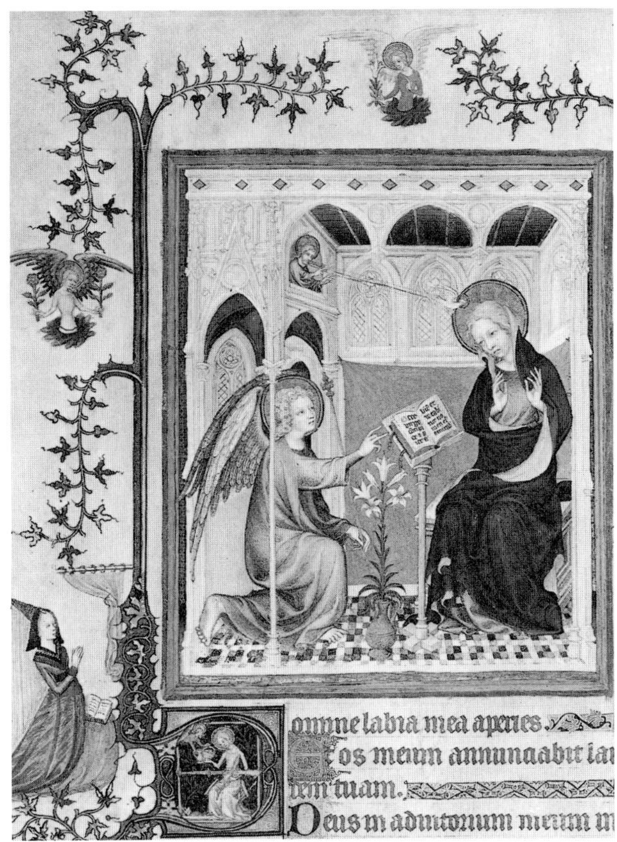

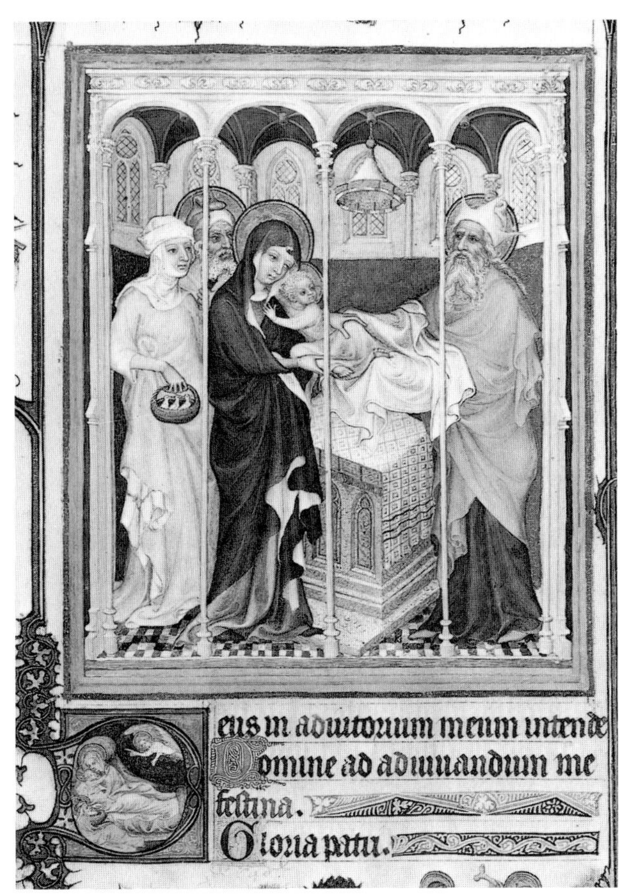

86. Parement Master:
Annunciation. Très belles heures de Notre-Dame,
Paris, Bibl. Nat. nouv. acq, lat. 3093, p. 2

87. Parement Master:
Presentation. Très belles heures de Notre-Dame,
Paris, Bibl. Nat. nouv. acq, lat. 3093, p. 56

Niederwildungen. The careful modelling of limbs, muscles and sinews of His slim body is a transcription of the model from the *Parement de Narbonne* in Paris (Louvre; *c.* 1375) (pl. 76) in a modified pose. The tension of the arms of the Parement Christ is extended to the whole suffering body in the Niederwildungen panel. The head is sunk lower still. The construction of shoulders and arms remains, but culminates here in hands open in resigned acceptance. Whilst Christ's facial features appear to be inspired by Byzantine models, he wears the crown-of-thorns designed in the Parement workshop. The faces of villains in Conrad's work appear to be related to the snub-nosed bucolic creatures from the Parement workshop. One of these, the *contrapposto* figure in the Parement de Narbonne *Way to Calvary* recurs in an updated form in the Niederwildungen *Christ before Pilate*. The elegant figure of Mary in the manuscript *Coronation of the Virgin* (p. 78)(pl. 71) with her sloping shoulders decorated by long tresses of blonde hair, and her high waistline is reflected most closely in the *Last Judgement* of the Niederwildungen Altarpiece; she recurs in the Dortmund *Coronation of the Virgin*. The facial features of the Virgin, however, appear closer to Italian models.

The narrative potential of his carefully modelled figures was exploited by the Parement Master in lively—sometimes almost violent—poses. The agitation of these figures seems to be reflected in the restless fold patterns of their cloaks which are pulled across the figure in a development of Pucelle's style. Conrad's heavier materials display a more natural fall of folds, arranged in the sinuous pattern of lines that is typical of the International Courtly Style. The busy play of vertical and horizontal folds, interrupted by a cascade of loops of Mary's mantle in the manuscript's *Presentation in the Temple* (p. 56)(pl. 87), for example, may be compared in a very similar scene in the Niederwildungen Altarpiece with a still decorative, but more elegant drapery pattern of mainly vertical folds in a heavier cloak. However, the narrative function of the figure within the scene remained unaltered. Conrad consistently favoured a veil that is turned back and reveals the Virgin's hair. This design appears to have been introduced from Italian models into Parisian painting by the Parement Master. It occurs, for example, in the *Annunciation* (p. 2)(pl. 86) and *Nativity* (p. 42) of the manuscript. A veil, falling over the forehead, appears more often in the Parement and other Parisian workshops of the time, and was equally popular in Westphalia. However, the Boucicaut master later made frequent use of the folded veil design.[13]

The drapery patterns adopted by Conrad are indeed much closer in style to those produced by the workshop of Jacquemart de Hesdin (first mentioned in the service of the Duke of Berry in 1384), although no specific design can be shown to derive directly from Jacquemart's models. Jacquemart and his followers abandoned the system of folds pulled across the figures, and developed, possibly through renewed Italian influence, a more vertical fold pattern. It was still decorative, but attempted to follow the structure of the figure in a more realistic way (pl. 89). For example, the kneeling Virgin in the *Crucifixion* from the manuscript (p. 209) by the Parement

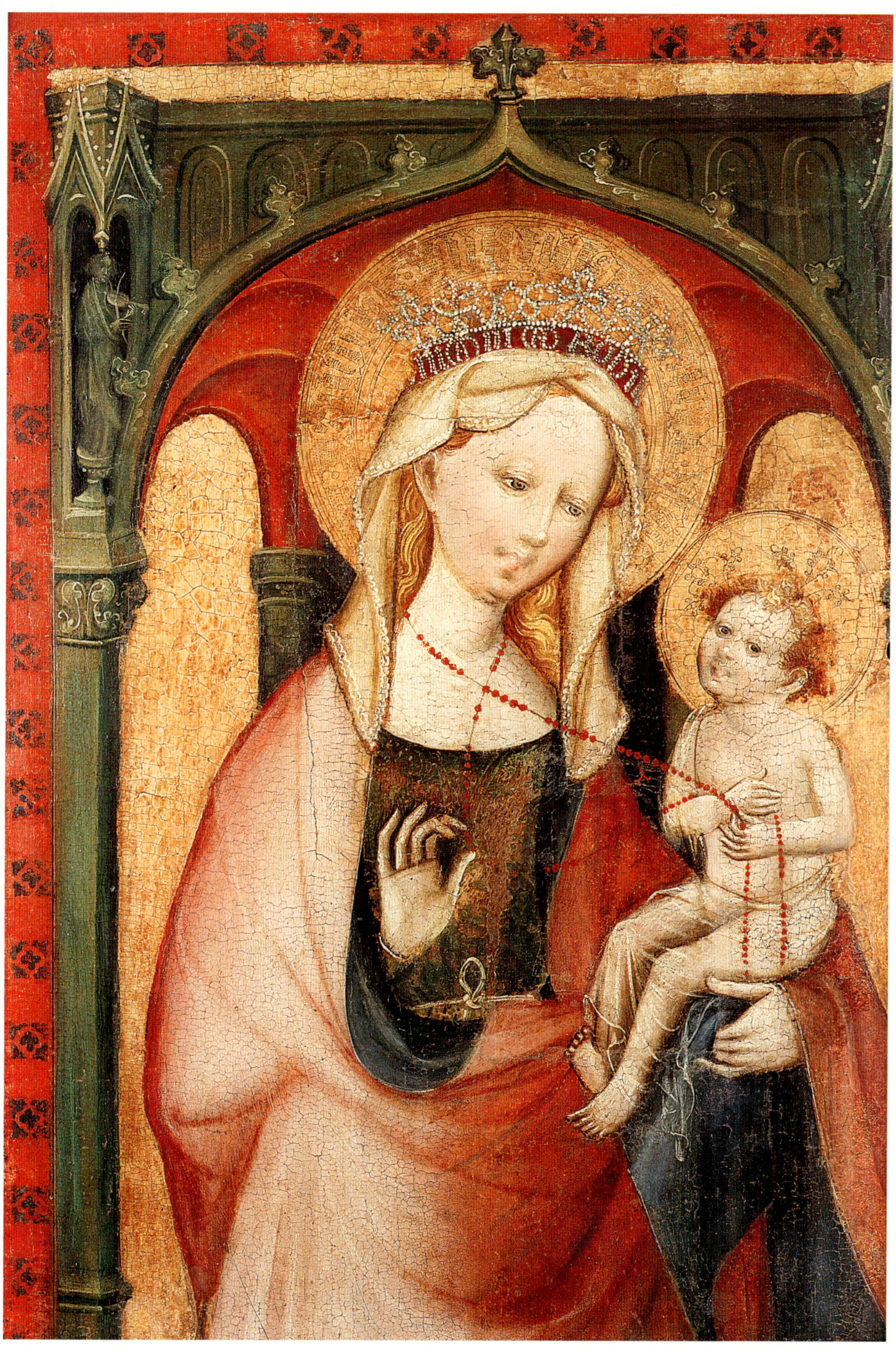

XXXIII. Fröndenberg Painter. Workshop of Conrad von Soest: *Madonna and Child*

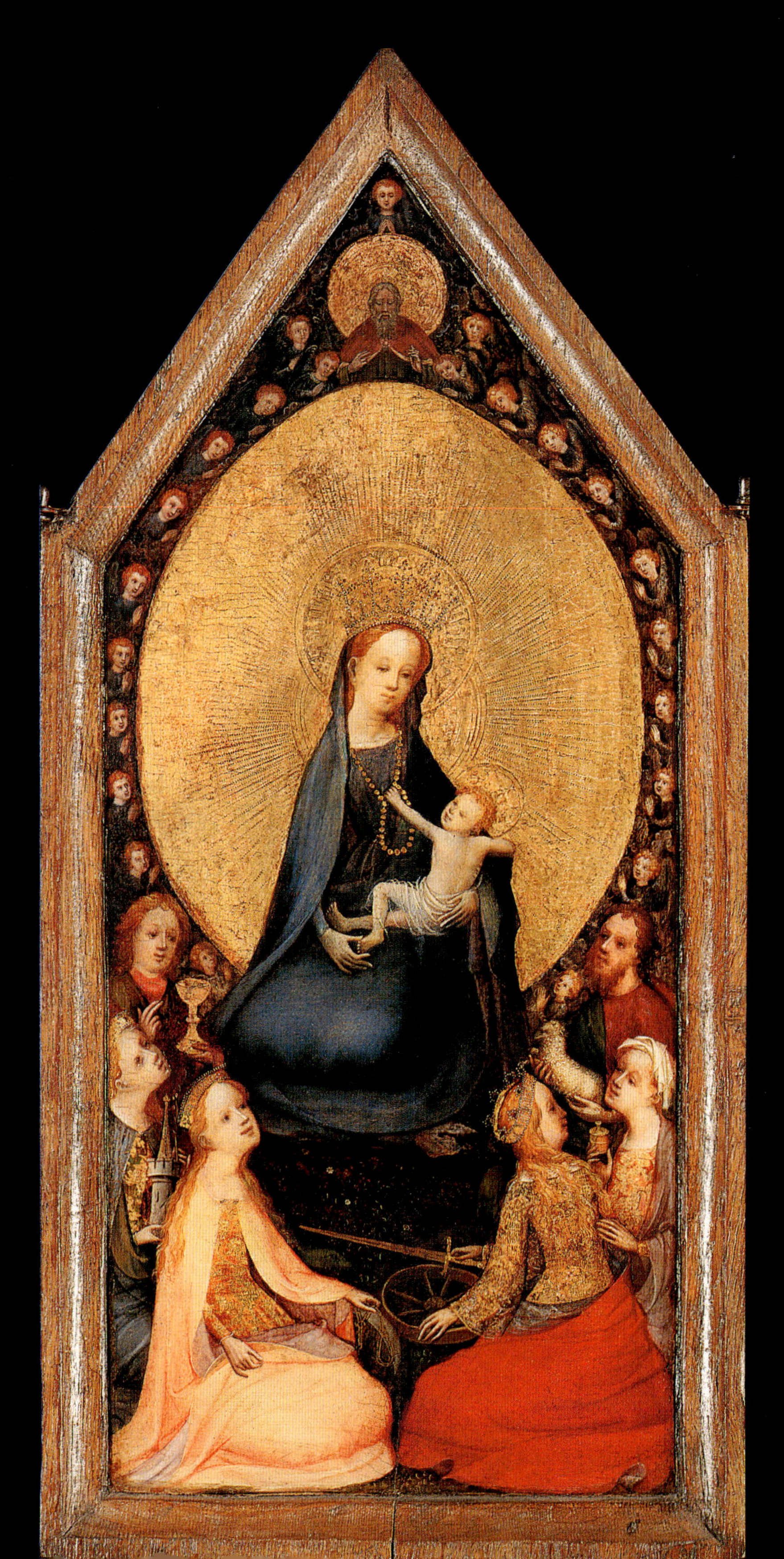

workshop, is wrapped in a cloak which creates a pattern of horizontal folds, balanced by a hectic fall of varied folds and loops over her arm. In contrast to this, the heavy folds in the kneeling Mary's cloak in the *Annunciation* (pl. 70) from the *Très belles heures de Jean de Berry* in Brussels, illuminated by Jacquemart and his workshop, fall vertically from the Virgin's shoulders until they are trapped under her leg (Bibl. Royale, MS 11060–1, p. 18; *c.* 1385–90?, before 1402).[14] The decorative artifice of draping the blue mantle widely around the figure at floor level to reveal yellow patches of lining and gentle patterns of folds is similar in style to that which was later developed in the Niederwildungen Altarpiece. This is exemplified by the *Adoration of the Kings*, where the mantle is folded around the Virgin's knee in a comparable manner (pl. 10). It should be noted that the Virgin in the *Nativity* (pl. 88) in Master Bertram's Grabow Altarpiece (1379) also sits on her cloak in such a way as to reveal the form of her leg under the heavy material. The mantle is not, however, spread out around the figure in the Parisian fashion, and the decorative potential of folds and coloured linings is therefore not fully exploited.[15]

The calmer fold pattern in Jacquemart's work enhances the gentle, lyrical mood of his scenes. This feature is also reflected in Conrad's work, together with the more Italianate style of the faces. The poetic mood in the Niederwildungen *Nativity*, for example, where angels float around the Virgin's head in the bright stable, whilst others bring light to the shepherds in the dark night outside, may be derived from Jacquemart's Brussels pages (pp. 72 and 82)(pl. 89).[16] The plasticity of the Gothic canopy, imitating sculpture, which shades the figure of the third king in the Niederwildungen *Adoration of the Kings* may have its origin in the Jacquemart workshop, where the motif of the foot-kissing king can also be found. The design of the Dortmund *Nativity* and the pattern of the reading apostle in the Dortmund *Death of the Virgin* could also derive from the Hesdin workshop, together with a variety of iconographic detail which seems to have been introduced into Westphalian art by Conrad von Soest (see Chapter 7). Yet Conrad remained indebted to the Parement Master for his diversified cast of characters. An occasional interdependence, which seems to have occurred in the workshops of the Parement Master and of Jacquemart de Hesdin and is noticeable in their manuscripts for the Duke of Berry, has caused their illuminations to be variously attributed.[17] This collaboration may account for Conrad's apparent acquaintance with the work of both workshops. Although more heavily dependent on the style of the Parement Master, Conrad seems to have included those aspects from the work of Jacquemart de Hesdin that were better suited to his own temperament.

Some direct or indirect knowledge of the works of other masters of manuscript illumination in Paris may also be assumed if Conrad stayed for a time as a journeyman in the Parement Master's workshop. But no specific evidence can be found for any stylistic links to other workshops in Paris, Burgundy or Bourges. It has been suggested that Conrad is indebted to the Boucicaut Master for the architecture of the Niederwildungen *Presentation*, but Conrad's simple setting with

XXXIV. Veronica Master: *Sacra Conversazione*

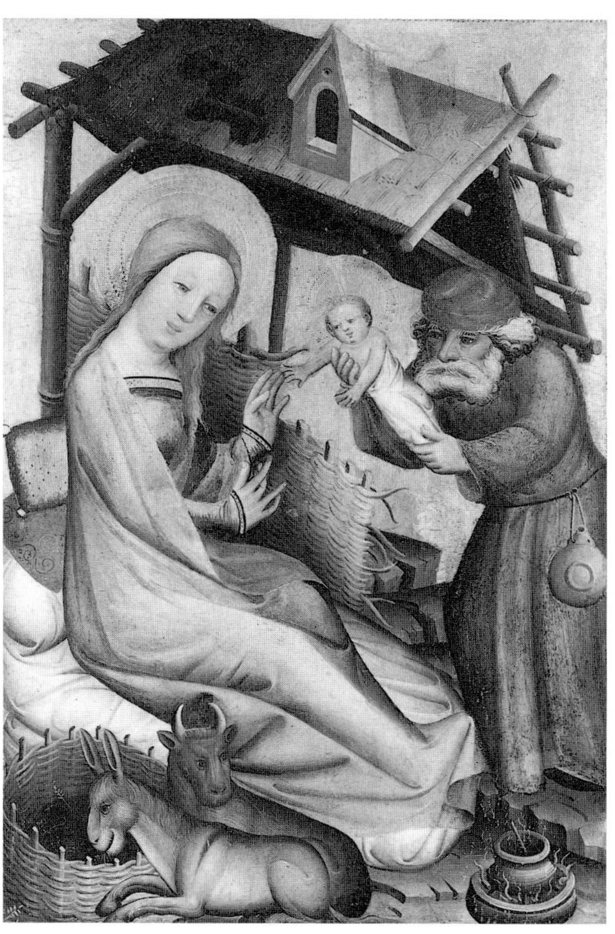 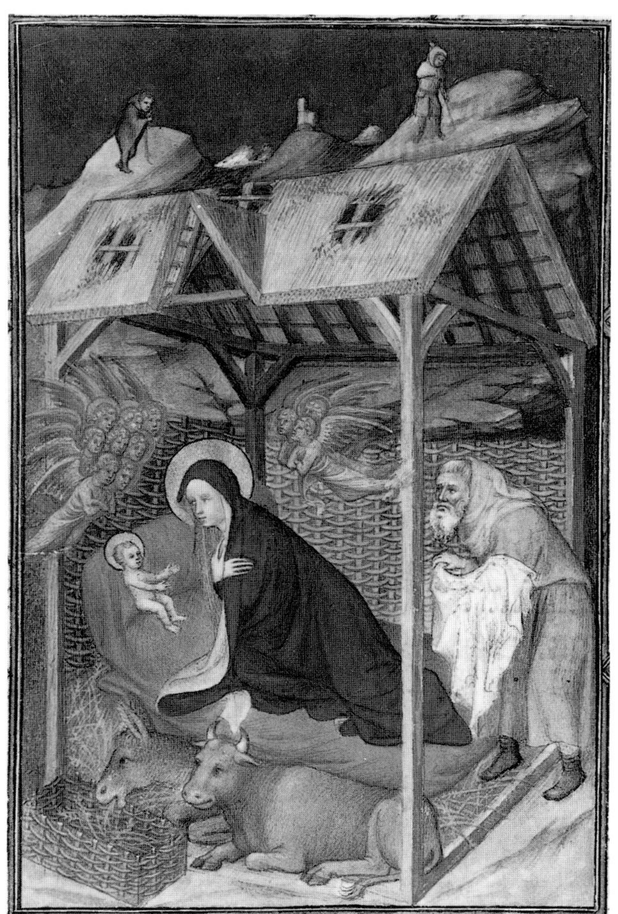

its crenellated arch appears closer in style to designs from the Parement work-shop.[18] Since the relevant *Presentation* (fol. 87v) from the *Hours of Marshal Jean de Boucicaut* (Paris, Musée Jacquemart-André, MS 2, *c.* 1399–1411) is likely to have been painted after Conrad's return to Dortmund and possibly after the Niederwil-dungen Altarpiece, a common source probably inspired the turreted and domed constructions. Conrad is also thought to have worked in André Beauneveu's workshop in Bourges just before 1394.[19] However, the style of the twenty-four prophets and apostles by Beauneveu (*c.* 1380–85) from the Psalter of Jean de Berry (Paris, Bibl. Nat., fr. 13091, fols. 7v–30) bears little resemblance to that of Conrad's figures. The apostles of the window in Bourges Cathedral, probably designed by Beauneveu for the Sainte-Chapelle, are also heavy-limbed and strong-featured with large noses, which contrast with Conrad's small-featured, elegant forms.

Further evidence for Conrad's residence in Paris during the 1380s may lie in the stylistic difference with the work of the Limbourg brothers. Despite suggestions to the contrary,[20] no stylistic or iconographic links can be detected between these artists beyond 'fashion' and 'French spirit'. Like Conrad, the Limbourg brothers were initially influenced by the Parement Master and by Jacquemart de Hesdin, as can be seen in many of the illustrations in the Limbourgs' *Belles heures* (The

88. Master Bertram: *Nativity.*
Grabow Altarpiece

89. Jacquemart de Hesdin:
Nativity.
Très belles heures de Jean de Berry,
Brussels, Bibl. Royale,
MS 11060–61, p. 72

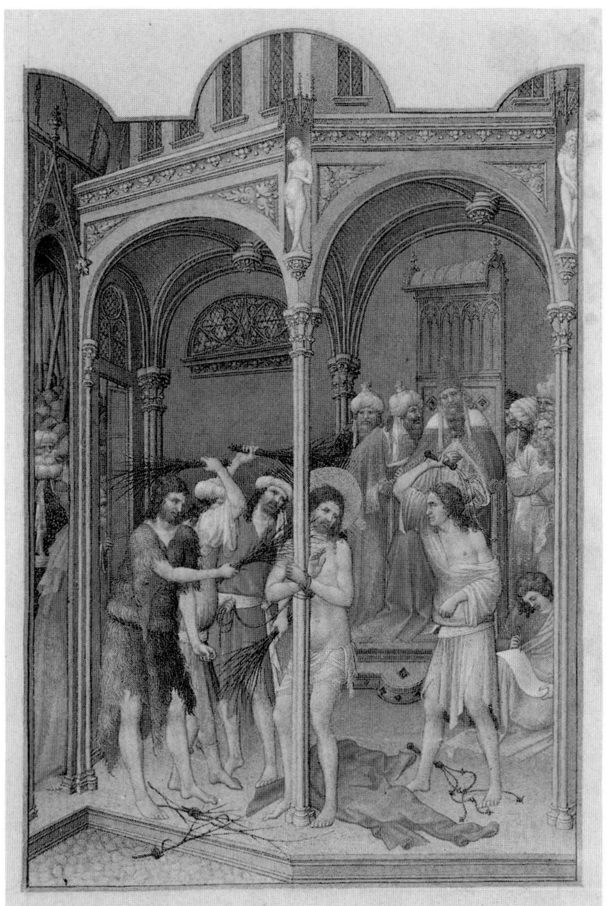

90. Limburg Brothers: *Flagellation.*
Très riches heures, Musée Condé,
Chantilly

Cloisters, New York; *c.* 1404–08). But on other pages of the manuscript (for instance fol. 161), some knowledge of the Boucicaut Master's experiments with aerial perspective is apparent. This perspective system is fully developed in the pages of the *Très riches heures* (Musée Condé, Chantilly, MS 65; *c.* 1411–16), illuminated by the Limbourg brothers. In this manuscript, the Limbourg brothers had perfected a figure canon and style that was alien to Conrad von Soest. It is instructive to compare the relationship between the Limbourgs's figures and architecture in the *Flagellation* (fol. 144)(pl. 90), which is also set in an open loggia, to that in the Niederwildungen *Christ Mocked before Herod* (pl. 83). Whereas Conrad developed the inherent realism and monumentality of the Parement Master's figures even to the exclusion, in his late work in Dortmund, of any setting, the Limbourg brothers advanced the spatial ideas of the Boucicaut Master in extended landscapes that depended on the acute observation of aerial perspective. The designs for *February* (fol. 2v)(pl. 91) and the *Adoration of the Magi* (fol. 52) exemplify the outstanding quality of the Limbourg brothers' landscapes. This stylistic difference supports the contention that Conrad had left Paris before the arrival there of the Boucicaut Master.

Any superficial similarities between illuminations from the Parisian workshops

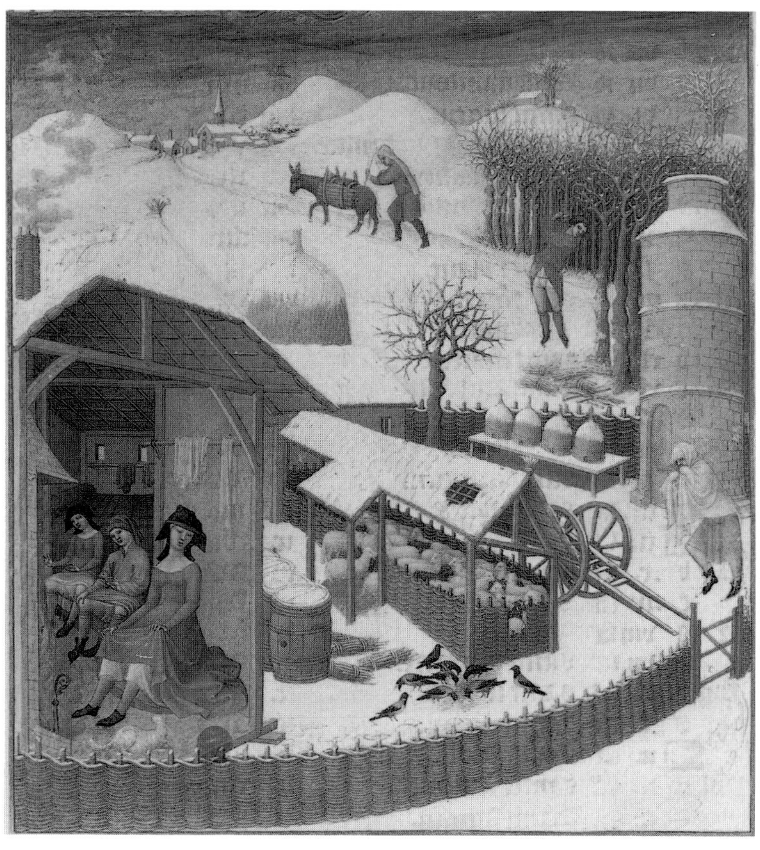

91. Limburg Brothers:
February. Très riches heures,
Musée Condé, Chantilly

92–93. Melchior Broederlam:
Annunciation and Visitation, and
Presentation and Flight into Egypt.
Wings of an altarpiece,
Musée des Beaux-Arts de Dijon

after 1390 and Conrad's designs, even down to the stance of some figures, can be explained by the rapid spread of the International Courtly Style all over Europe and by common stylistic roots in Paris. All the major artists who worked at the courts of Burgundy or Bourges were likely also to have worked in Paris at times and would therefore have shared with Conrad von Soest that rich visual experience that is lost to us today.

The strikingly Italianate features of Conrad's female protagonists are not found in Westphalian nor French sources. The appearance of the Virgin in Conrad's Dortmund *Adoration of the Kings* invites particular comparison with Gentile da Fabriano's *Madonna and Child* in Washington (National Gallery, Samuel H. Kress Collection)(pls. 94, 112). Both were painted around 1420 and suggest Venetian or Lombard sources.[21] In both panels the elegant, elongated head of the Virgin inclines above a heavy neck; the high, narrow forehead is revealed under the decorative fold of a veil; a straight classical nose and slightly protruding, half-closed eyes are balanced by a small mouth; all this, and the elaborately punched nimbus that frames these faces, differs from French usage. Although the facial features of the Virgin, both in Italian and French painting around 1400, ultimately originate from the Byzantine tradition, the Virgin from the Parement Master's workshop has larger features with huge, heavily outlined eyes, broader cheeks and a wider forehead. Presumably due to renewed Italian influence, Jacquemart de Hesdin and

144

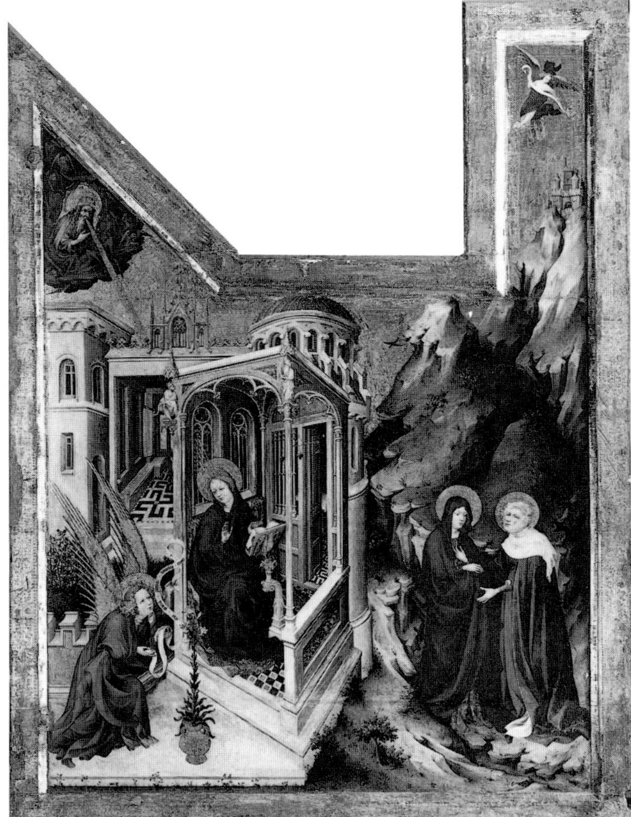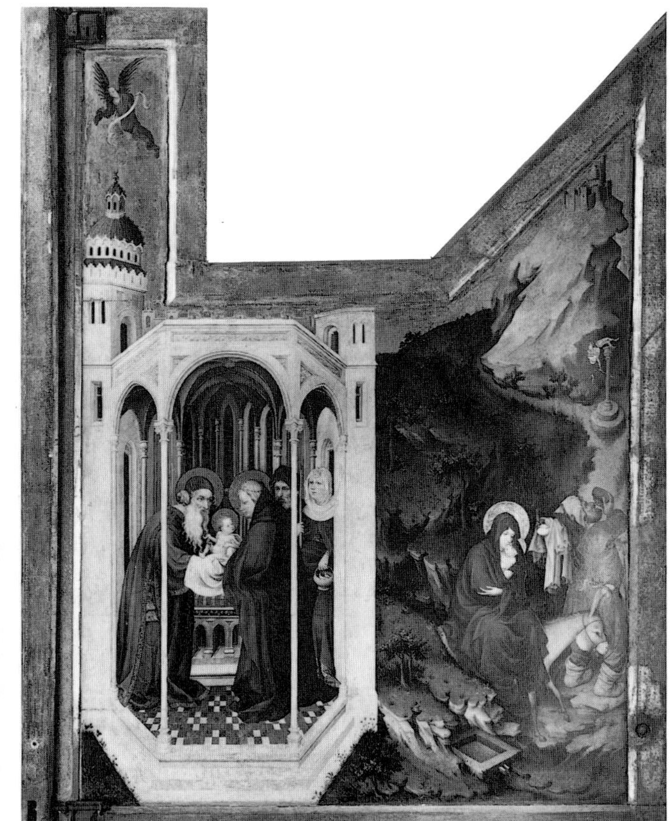

the Boucicaut Master introduced softer features with smaller eyes, a shorter nose, a wider, more rounded, forehead and fleshier cheeks. Broederlam (pls. 92, 93) and the Limbourg brothers seem to have developed individual versions of this less classical, more softly moulded face of the Virgin. The styles of Conrad von Soest and Gentile da Fabriano share an affinity with late fourteenth-century Lombard miniature and panel painting which, although evident, cannot be demonstrated by direct descent. Unless further evidence emerges, it is reasonable to assume that Italian sources, which are no longer extant, came to Conrad's attention through intermediaries.

The realism of selective motifs in Conrad's paintings has provoked comparisons with the Netherlands.[22] The rarity of surviving panels in the Netherlands makes it difficult to judge stylistic development, but the strength of panel painters who worked in the Netherlands appears to have been in expressive realism—as in the suffering Christ, depicted with hair matted and sticky with sweat and blood, in Utrecht Cathedral (Crucifixion fresco, *c.* 1410). Manuscript illumination by Netherlandish artists was also concerned with realism rather than refinement. Although, for example, the considerable production of manuscripts by members of the *devotio moderna* movement helped to spread established iconographic ideas, it did not always encourage high standards of illumination.[23] Any stylistic innovations in Netherlandish art were therefore likely to originate from the major Netherlandish

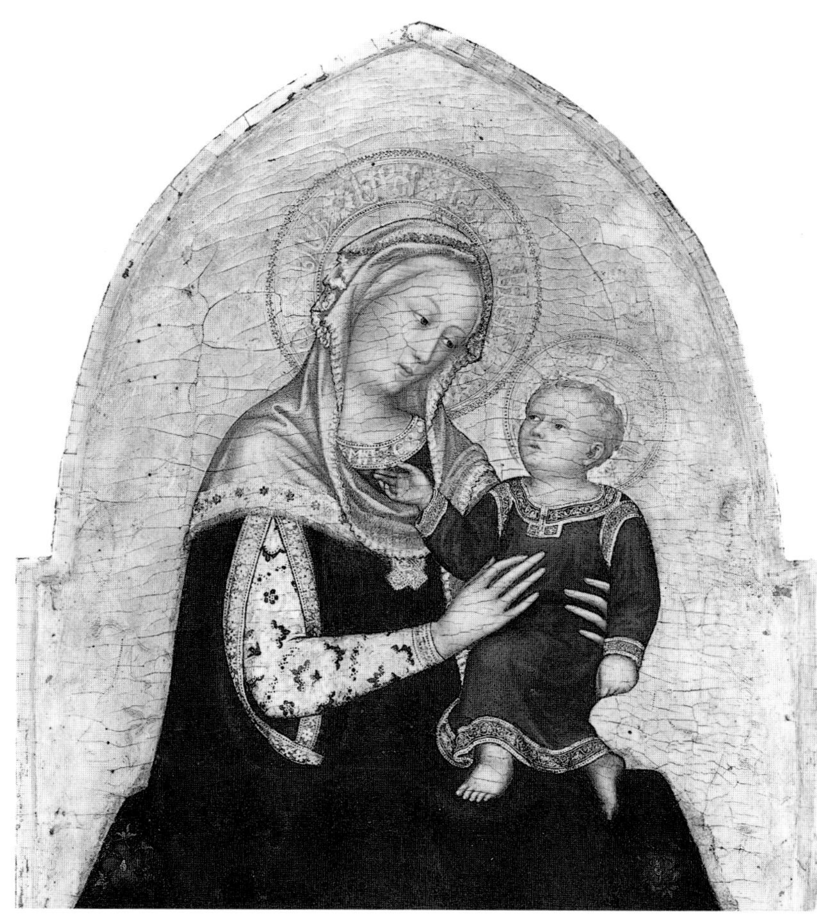

94. Gentile da Fabriano:
Madonna and Child.
National Gallery of Art,
Washington DC,
Samuel H. Kress Collection

masters like Beauneveu, Beaumetz, Bellechose, Malouel, Broederlam and the Limbourg brothers, who had also worked for the Valois princes in Paris, Bourges or Dijon. One need only compare the work of the Netherlandish artists who were stimulated by French and Italian influences whilst working in France with that of those who remained in the Netherlands, to appreciate that the influences most clearly manifest in Conrad von Soest's style are more likely to have been absorbed in Paris.

It may be assumed, however, that Conrad had knowledge of the work of some Netherlandish artists, if only by diffusion, as he assimilated realistic motifs into his compositions. Conrad depicted his flowers in the Niederwildungen *Crucifixion* (pls. 14, XIV) with the same attention to detail which can be observed in Broederlam's retable wings at Dijon (Musée des Beaux-Arts; 1394–99), but his landscape is quite differently conceived from that of the *Flight into Egypt* (pl. 93) in the Dijon wings. It can be seen that such flowers, though of a more stylized variety, also adorn the meadows in Master Bertram's Grabow Altarpiece of 1379. Broederlam and Conrad also share an interest in the faithful reproduction of the texture of brocades, but the heavy robes envelop very differently-shaped figures; the sturdy realism of Mary's form, so convincingly rendered by Broederlam, differs markedly from that of Conrad's elegant, idealized Virgin. The careful description of the latest fashion

146

in the Niederwildungen *Crucifixion* is matched in the Limbourg brothers' *April* (fol. 4v) and *May* (fol. 5v) pages of the *Très riches heures*. But the style and figure canon of the artists, even though the latter varies in monumentality between the brothers, remain quite different. It may therefore be concluded that the altarpieces by Conrad von Soest do not show any direct stylistic dependence on Netherlandish art beyond the general interest in realistic motifs that is typical of the International Courtly Style, other than the influence of the workshop of the Duke of Berry's illuminator Jacquemart de Hesdin. Later Westphalian artists have been shown to be profoundly indebted to Netherlandish panel painters.[24]

No sources for Conrad's art can be detected in the scant survivals of relevant art in England, despite the close relationship between the patrician merchants of Dortmund and the court of England. It is, however, interesting to note that the Wilton Diptych (London, National Gallery; after 1396) displays stylistic characteristics that suggest that the painter, whether he was English or not, had trained like Conrad in the Franco-Flemish circle of Jacquemart de Hesdin. The most notable features include the decorative but convincing fold patterns, the style and narrative power of the hands, some punchwork designs, the small-featured faces and the lyrical mood.[25]

It can be concluded that Conrad von Soest was stylistically at variance with Westphalian precedents, but he largely complied with Westphalian pictorial traditions. He supplemented the Westphalian vocabulary with designs which can be traced to the Parisian workshops of the Parement Master and of Jacquemart de Hesdin in the 1380s. Certain motifs in Conrad's compositions may well have come to his attention by diffusion or directly from works by artists of neither Westphalian nor French origins: a number of his motifs can also be found in Italian, Netherlandish and Bohemian artefacts. However, the close stylistic similarities indicate that the most important influence on Conrad von Soest, after his Westphalian training, was his sojourn in Paris. Conrad's intimate knowledge of models in the workshop of the Parement Master suggests that he may have worked with him as a journeyman in the early 1380s. This would confirm that Conrad was born around 1360 (see p. 16).

Innovative motifs are rare in Conrad von Soest's altarpieces, although they do occur where existing models did not suffice. His originality consists not so much in the invention of new models as in the novel interpretation of existing ones such as the motif of the six angels tending the deceased Virgin in the Dortmund Altarpiece. He tackled compositional problems by arranging traditional models in original schemes, for instance in the Niederwildungen *Crucifixion*. Conrad von Soest's intelligent use of his Westphalian inheritance fused with his wider visual experience furnished him with a sound iconographic vocabulary and impressive interpretative skills. Such achievements were clearly appreciated by his patrons, who entrusted him with important and costly commissions.

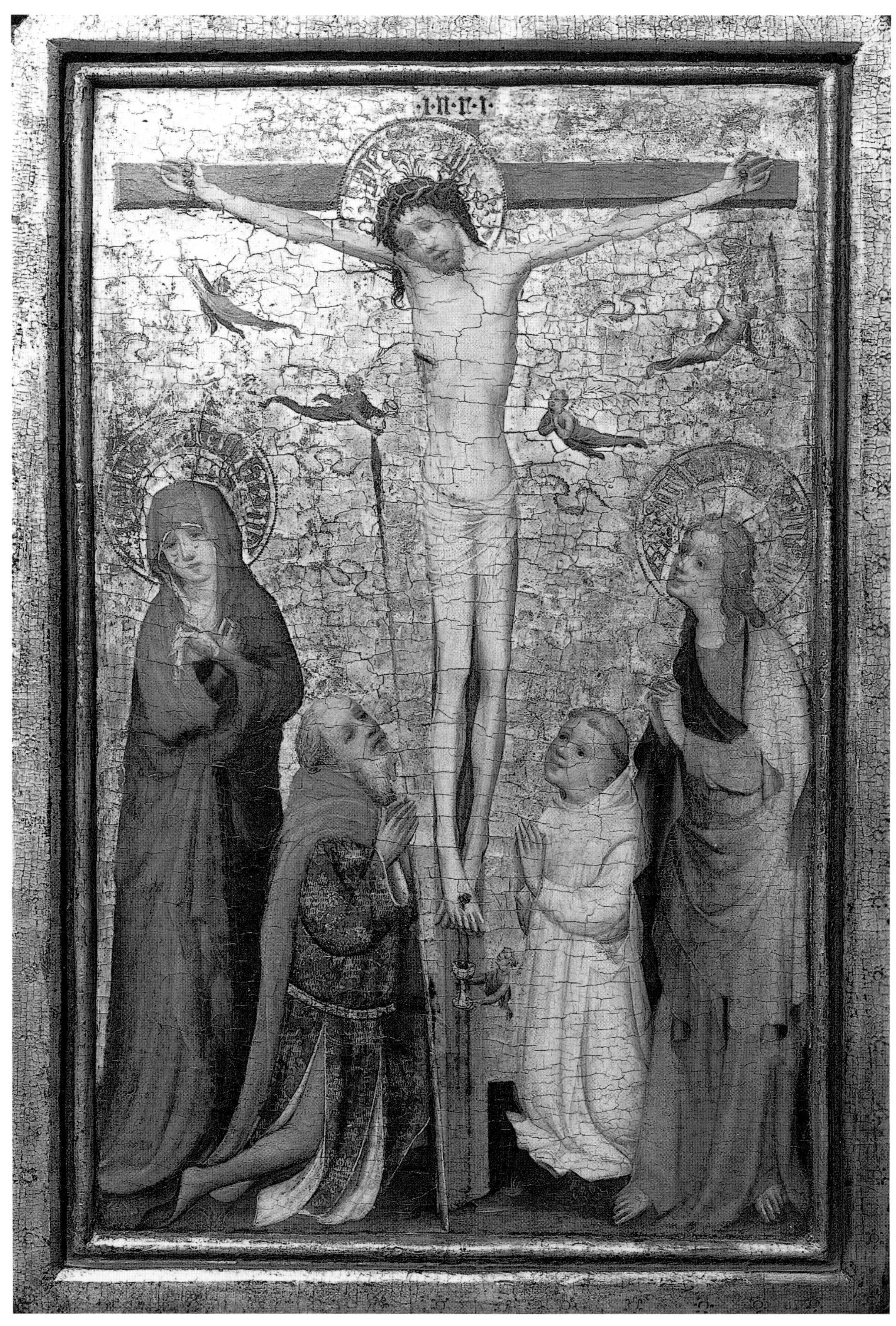

95. Veronica Master: *Crucifixion*. National Gallery of Art, Washington DC,
Samuel H. Kress Collection

9. Conrad's Legacy

A PAINTER'S SIGNIFICANCE is measured not only by his originality and his ability to attract substantial patronage but, most importantly, by the extent of his influence on fellow artists. Bearing in mind the *ad hoc* nature of the survival of works of art, the considerable number of panels that reflect knowledge—whether gained directly or through intermediaries—of Conrad von Soest's paintings testify to his prestige and to his contribution to the developments of art around 1400. Westphalian painters certainly emulated the achievements of their successful contemporary in Dortmund,[1] and the echoes of Conrad's style reached well beyond the borders of his own country.

As we have seen, the relatively large body of panels surviving in Westphalia permits a reasonable assessment of stylistic influences there. In another major German artistic centre, the steadfastly Catholic city of Cologne, artefacts were largely exempt from destruction at the hands of iconoclasts and from plunder by foreign armies.[2] Cologne's financial weakness after the affluent Middle Ages also prevented some of the losses caused when paintings were replaced elsewhere to accommodate changing taste. The surviving panels in Cologne therefore present a reasonably accurate picture of stylistic trends there around 1400. However, the paucity of relevant art surviving in England, the Netherlands, France and Northern Italy demands a cautious approach when evaluating the extent to which Conrad's art may have been known in these countries.

The most significant Westphalian works which have, at times, been attributed to him are described in the catalogue. A variety of surviving paintings in Soest which are directly indebted to Conrad may serve to demonstrate his profound influence in Westphalia: the *Crucifixion* altarpiece (*c.* 1410) in the church of St Paul; the St Nicholas Panel in the chapel of St Nicholas (pl. 155; cat. no. 7); the fresco of the *Crucifixion* (*c.* 1410–20) on the nave pillar of the church of St Peter; the painted *Christ* on the reverse of the carved crucifix (*c.* 1405–10) from a triumphal arch and the pillar fresco of St Patroklus (*c.* 1405–10), both in the church of St Patroklus; and the Jacobi Altarpiece (*c.* 1425–30) in the Wiesenkirche.[3] The *Coronation of the Virgin* (*c.* 1420–30) and the Blankenberch Altarpiece (*c.* 1422–43)(pls. 57–59), both from St Walpurgis in Soest and now in the Landesmuseum at Münster, also derive from Conrad's patterns. Conrad's influence can still be felt in the workshop of the Master of Liesborn in the 1480s.

Conrad's influence on artists further afield owes much to the status of Dortmund in the fourteenth century. Dortmund did not yield leadership of the Hanseatic League to Cologne until 1417. The busy trade routes through the flourishing town of Dortmund facilitated the interchange of artistic ideas, and must have helped to spread the fame of the painter. Knowledge of Conrad's art seems to have travelled principally along the Hanseatic trade routes. Reflections of Conrad's style can still be discerned all over this area, from Frankfurt am Main (altarpiece of *c.* 1420, Peterskirche) to Stockholm (the *Visitation*, *c.* 1415–25, National Museum, Inv. No. 4854), from Darup (high altarpiece, *c.* 1420–40, Pfarrkirche, cat. no. 11) to Göttingen (Barfüsser Altarpiece, 1424, Landesmuseum, Hanover). There can also be little doubt that travelling Northern German artists would have been attracted to Dortmund by the repute of the painter who was entrusted with such large and costly commissions. The relevance of the Hanseatic routes in disseminating Conrad's style can be appreciated by contrast with the few surviving painted panels and manuscripts in Southern Germany. In Nuremberg, for example, the Imhoff Altarpiece in the Lorenzkirche (*c.* 1420) and a Missal in the Germanisches Nationalsmu-

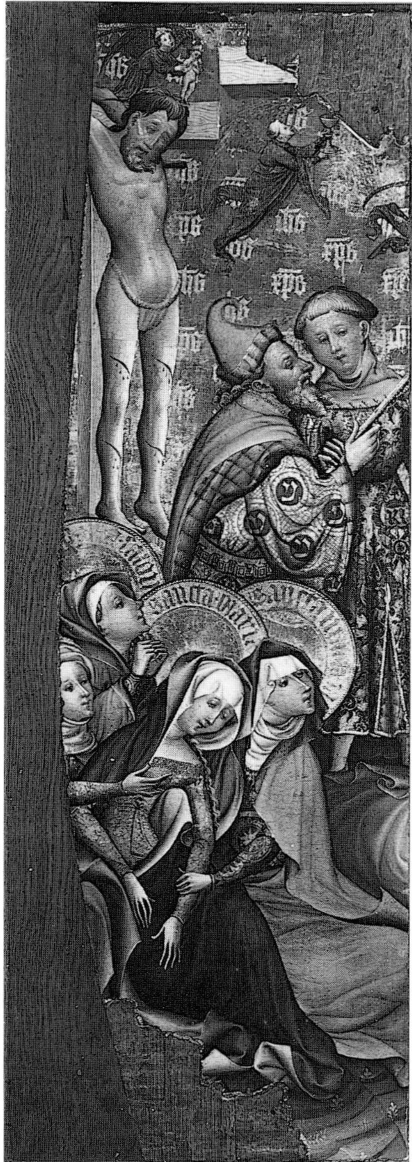
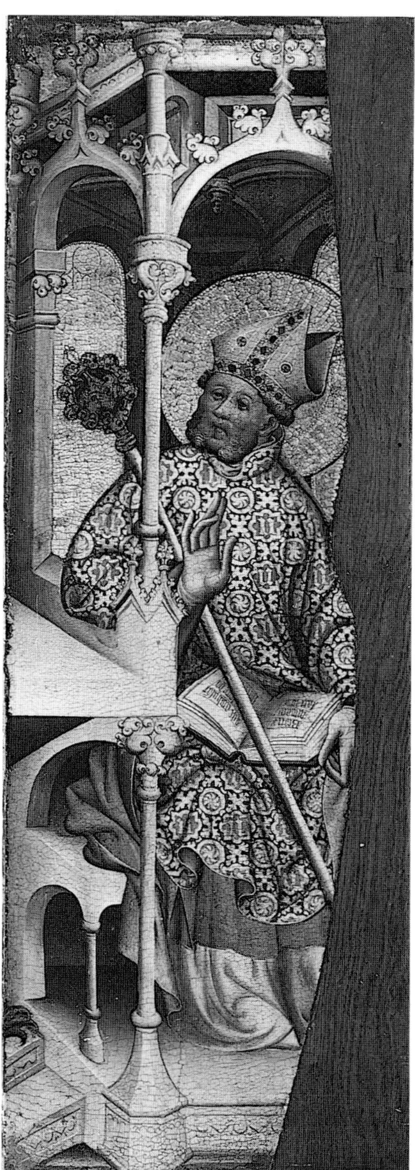

96. Fragment from a *Crucifixion* and fragment showing *St Nicholas*. Museum für Kunst und Kulturgeschichte der Hansestadt Lübeck, St-Annen-Kloster

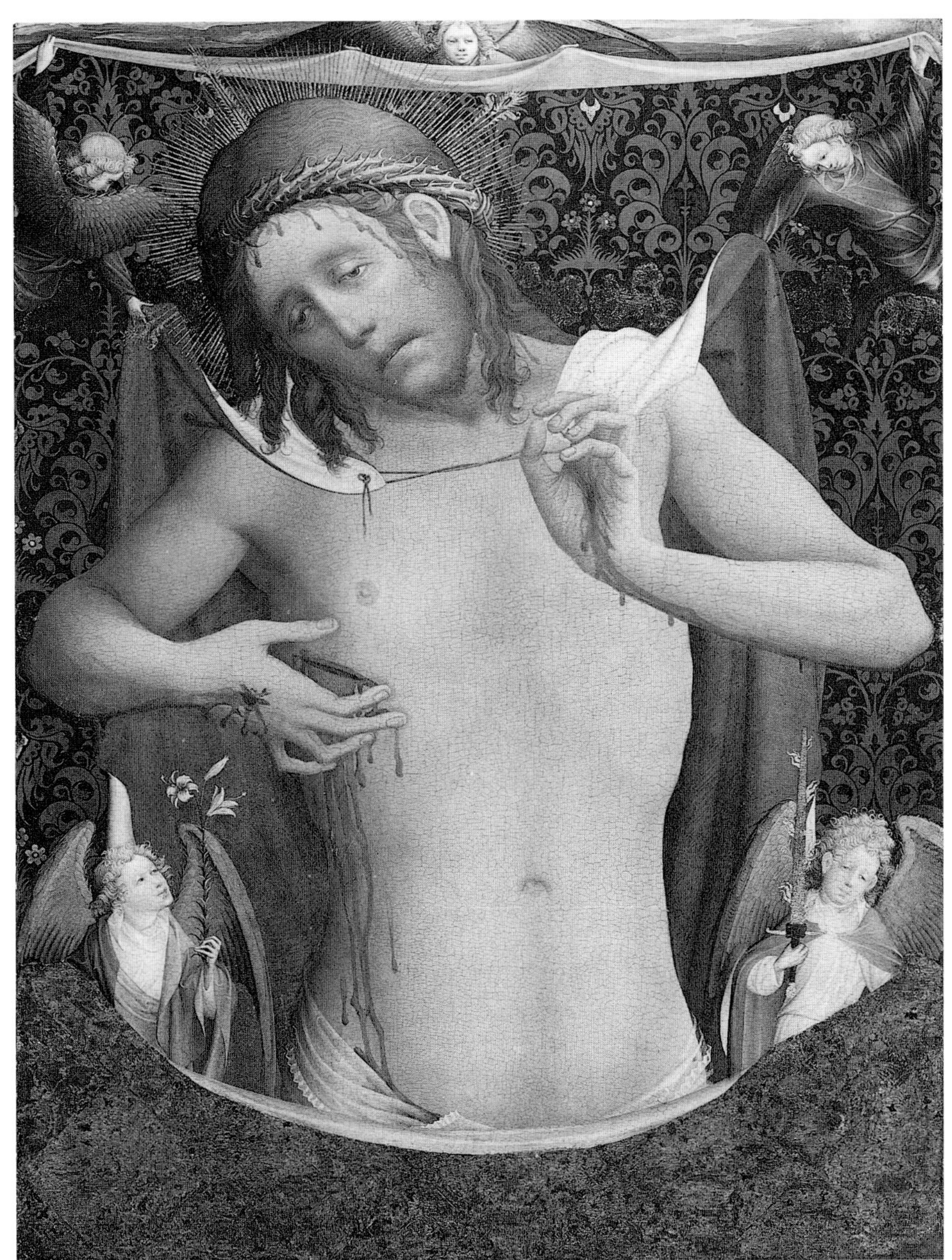

97. Master Francke:
Ecce Homo. Hamburger
Kunsthalle

seum (*c.* 1420; Inv. No. Hs. Merkel 1121) contain elegant figures strongly modelled in dark and light. The influence here is from the Bohemian artists who settled in Nuremberg after fleeing the Hussite insurrection.

Lübeck patrons had particularly strong family and trading connections with Dortmund (see pp. 17–18). They seem to have encouraged local artists to learn from examples by the famous Dortmund painter. One artist from Lübeck modelled his altarpiece for the church of St Mary there on the Niederwildungen Altarpiece. The surviving fragment (*c.* 1410–30)(pl. 96), now in the St Annen-Museum, shows on the obverse side a section copied from Conrad's *Crucifixion*; on the (now separated) reverse side, a seated *St Nicholas* possibly reflects a lost panel by Conrad.[4] This Lübeck master was not a student of Conrad, but merely a faithful copyist who could not imitate Conrad's subtle technique or palette. The powerfully modelled body of Conrad's thief (pl. 26) may be compared with the schematic wooden shape rendered by the Lübeck painter, and we can see the weakness of the imitator's copy. Another follower of Conrad painted the wing fragment of *St Paul and St Thomas*(?) (1425) from the high altar of the same church in Lübeck, now also in the museum. This master depended for his models on Conrad's designs both for the facial type of his saints and for such scenes as the *Nativity* and the *Death of the Virgin* scenes in another of his retables, the Neustädter Altarpiece (*c.* 1430) in Schwerin, which originates from the Jakobikirche in Lübeck.

The flavour of Conrad's art also permeates a variety of other works in Lübeck, for example the painted wings of the retable of the 'Stecknitzfahrer' (1422), and the Altar der kanonischen Tageszeiten (*c.* 1430), both in the Cathedral, and also the painted wings of the altarpiece of the 'Zirkelbrüder' (*c.* 1430) from the confraternity chapel in the church of St Catherine (now in the St Annen-Museum). The design and style of these panels do not imply direct familiarity with Conrad's work, but strongly suggest an awareness of his designs through intermediaries.[5]

Master Francke, a painter active in Hamburg, also seems to have been aware of Conrad's work.[6] A commission, issued in 1424 by the confraternity of 'England-Travellers' in Hamburg for an altarpiece from the hand of a 'mester Franckenn', can be identified as the St Thomas Altarpiece (completed before 1436), fragments of which survive in the Kunsthalle, Hamburg (pls. 98, 99). Other works universally ascribed to the same artist, although not documented, are the St Barbara Altarpiece in Helsinki (after 1420) and the *Ecce Homo* panels in Leipzig (*c.* 1430) and Hamburg (*c.* 1425) (pls. 97, 100, 101).[7]

It appears plausible that Master Francke was the painter monk 'Francone Zutphanico' (from Zutphen, near Deventer, see note 6); his art certainly differs profoundly from that of the principal workshop in Hamburg, run by Master Bertram. In view of Bertram's considerable influence on Northern German art, the different style, figure canon and iconography in Francke's painting indicates that he had not learned his art in Hamburg. Instead, the source of Francke's art has been convincingly traced to the Netherlands, and his wider visual experience has been connected with the Boucicaut and Rohan workshops and Paris in the second decade of the fifteenth century.[8] Francke's sensitivity to the expressive value of line is in tune with that of the Rohan Master and of Rogier van der Weyden. The realism and dramatic force of Francke's male protagonists are strikingly Netherlandish features.

Master Francke painted drama of an intensely emotional nature whilst Conrad von Soest depicted the lyrical poetry of biblical narrative. Yet there are stylistic links between Francke's work and that of Conrad von Soest.[9] The fragment (pl. 99) from the St Thomas Altarpiece, showing the group of the women and St John under

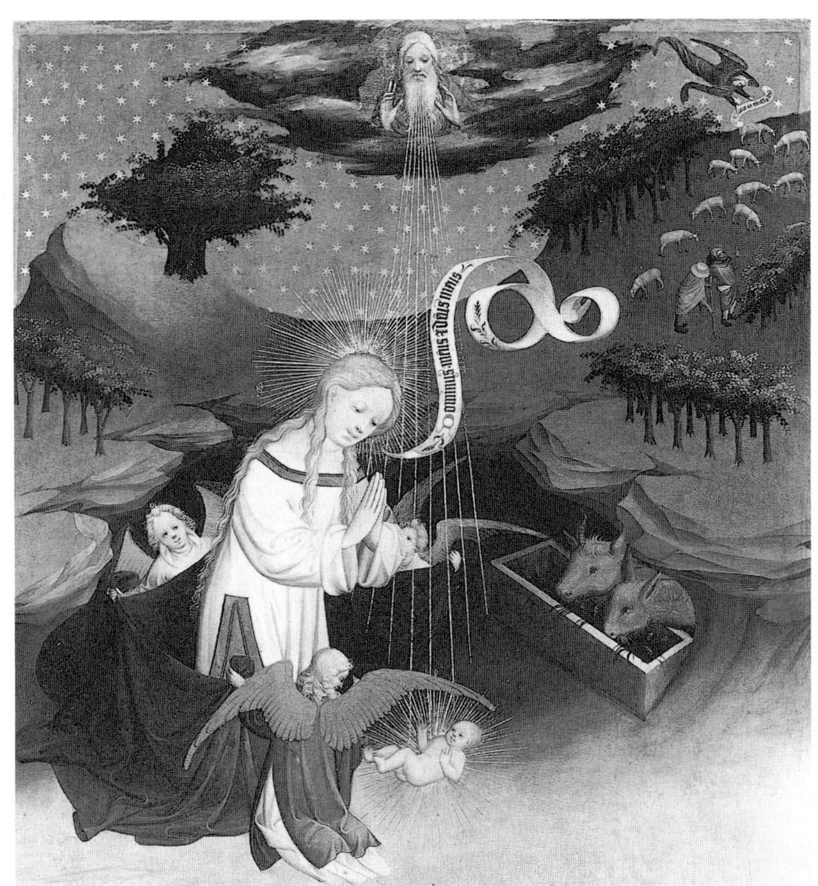

98. Master Francke: *Nativity*.
St Thomas Altarpiece,
Hamburger Kunsthalle

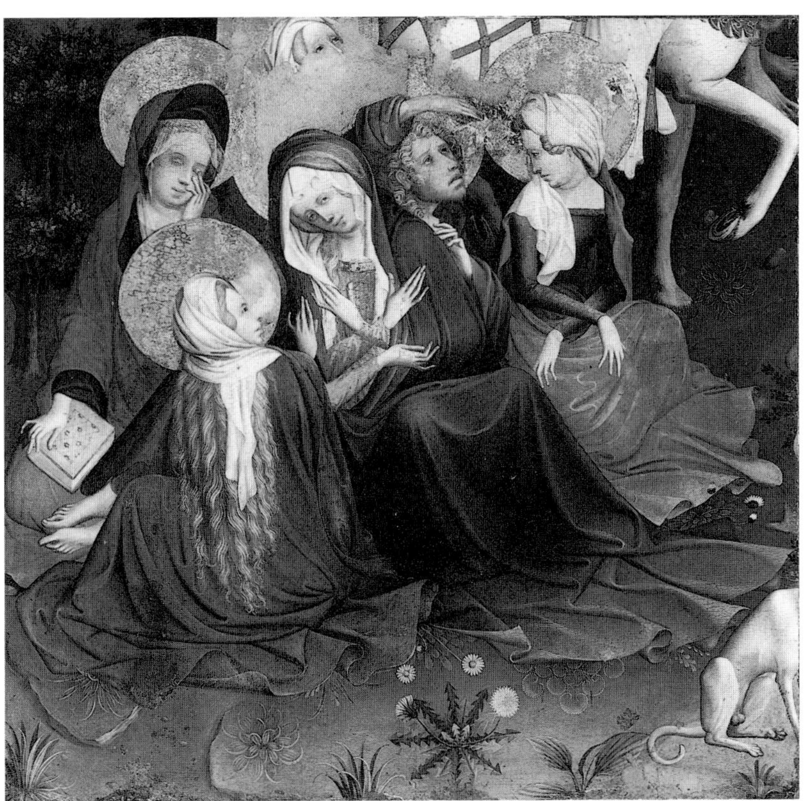

99. Master Francke: Fragment from the
Crucifixion. St Thomas Altarpiece

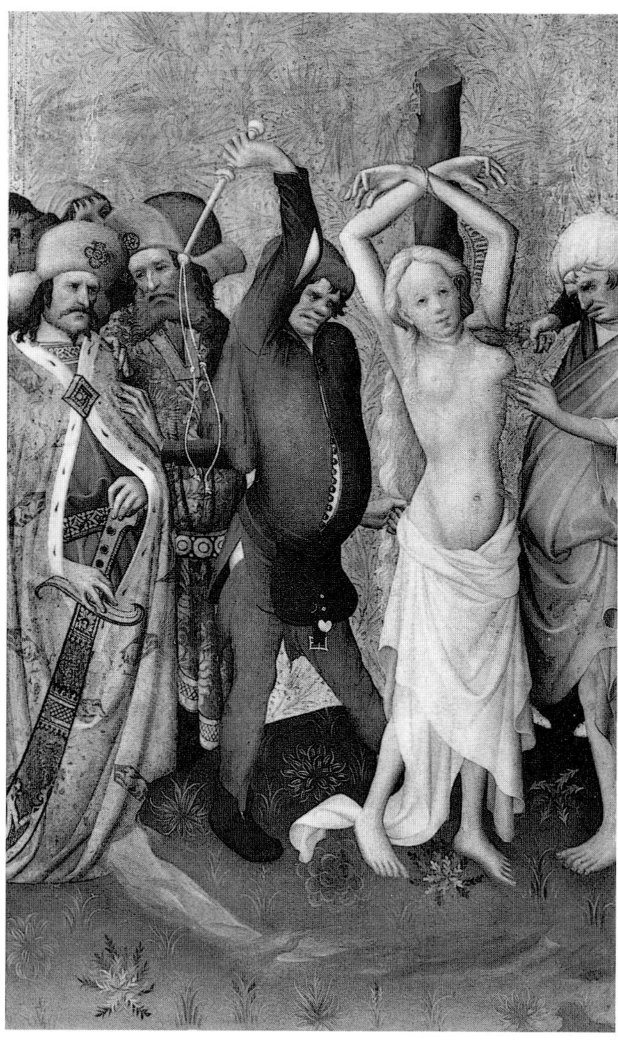

100. Master Francke:
The Flagellation of St Barbara.
St Barbara Altarpiece.
Suomen Kansallismuseo,
Helsinki

the cross, for example, resembles the same motif in the Niederwildungen *Crucifixion*: there are similarities in the curly head of the figure of St John, the facial features of the women, and the folded veils which allow locks of their hair to escape in rich tresses.[10] In the *Entombment* scene from the Francke retable, the female figures, St John and the image of Christ also have affinities with Conrad's style. The Westphalian provenance of these motifs is confirmed in a complete copy of Francke's St Thomas *Crucifixion* from Preetz in Holstein, now in Copenhagen, in which the now lost portion of the original scene is shown to have incorporated the Westphalian cross (with two horizontal bars) for the thieves.

Conrad's influence can also be felt in Francke's *Nativity* scene (pl. 98), where the angel with a triangular shock of curls has apparently descended from the clouds of the Dortmund *Nativity*; he can also be seen supporting Christ in the Leipzig *Ecce Homo* scene, and carrying a flaming sword in the Hamburg version (pl. 97). The Virgin in the Hamburg *Nativity* is essentially the Virgin from Conrad's Dortmund *Coronation of the Virgin*. Only the weight of her blonde curls and the monumentality

154

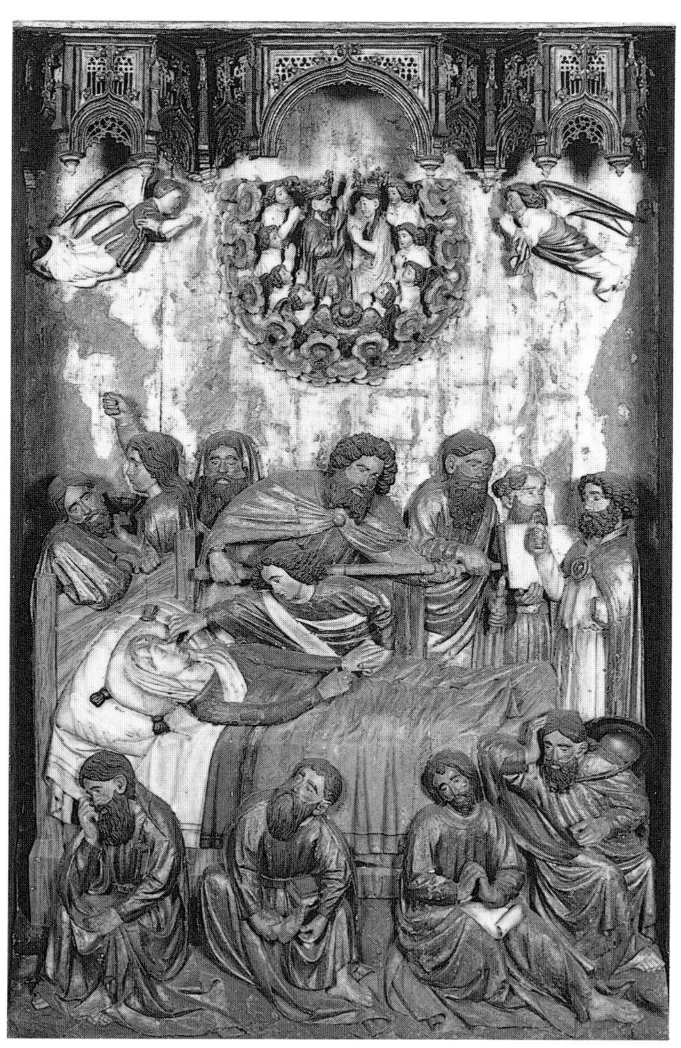

101. *Death of the Virgin.* Relief carved
in oak. St Barbara Altarpiece

of her shoulders indicate the hand of the later artist. However, in the *Adoration of the Kings*, Francke's Virgin shows an advanced naturalism that is closer in design to Campin's *Virgin before a Firescreen* (*c.* 1428; London, National Gallery), and appears to hark back to his Netherlandish inheritance.[11]

The Netherlandish influence is dominant in the earlier St Barbara Altarpiece, and the chosen figure canon, spatial solutions and overall punchwork differ considerably from Conrad's designs, even though the less monumental forms are still close to the International Courtly Style. Only the figure of St Barbara (pl. 100) and the bird pattern in the robe of Dioscurus are reminiscent of Conrad. It is, however, in the carved part of the St Barbara Altarpiece, which was probably executed to Master Francke's own design, that a direct influence from Conrad appears plausible. There, the central *Death of the Virgin* (pl. 101) refers to Conrad's Dortmund narrative with the motifs of St John (instead of an angel) closing the eyes of the Virgin, the apostle with the (now lost) censer behind the bedhead, the seated apostle with the scroll, the central semicircle of clouds sheltering Conradian angels (here surrounding a *Coronation of the Virgin*), and the two angels floating against the gold ground. Francke may well have seen the Dortmund Altarpiece; this would date the carved panels to after *c.* 1420, rather than around 1410–15 as previously believed.[12] If in fact Francke did not return from a journey to France until well after 1415, a date after 1420 is plausible for the St Barbara Altarpiece. After all, the St Thomas Altarpiece, which is more advanced in style, was not commissioned until December 1424; it may not have been finished long before September 1436, the date when the confraternity appears to have placed it in the Chapel of St John.

It seems, therefore, that Master Francke did not serve his apprenticeship in Hamburg, and that his roots were in Netherlandish art; he appears to have travelled to Paris around 1415. Yet he was inspired by some aspects of the stylistic and compositional vocabulary adopted by Conrad von Soest and his circle. In his St Thomas Altarpiece, his closer affinity with Conrad's work would suggest that he may have been in Westphalia before embarking on that commission, a view fortified by reference to panels in Münster Cathedral (see note 6). It is plausible that Francke was the monk mentioned in documents, as he certainly had Netherlandish roots. As a painter monk he may not have worked in a single location; a more peripatetic lifestyle between monasteries might well have taken him to Westphalia at times. The difference in the art of Conrad von Soest and Master Francke is not based on a difference in temperament alone, as hitherto suggested, but emerges from a different spiritual and artistic climate during their working lives. It is now apparent that Conrad visited Paris as much as three decades before Francke. Despite their differences in age and outlook, the younger master was still sufficiently impressed by Conrad's painting to adopt those stylistic elements from it that suited his own artistic purpose.

Conrad von Soest's paintings may also have been known in the Netherlands, either directly or through pattern sheets. The painter of the wings for the Reinoldi Altarpiece in Dortmund (*c.* 1430–40), for example, was clearly aware of Conrad's work, as he seems to have adopted certain motifs and stylistic details that can be found in Conrad's retables. Yet the artist painted in a style that has no relationship to the Westphalian tradition. He may have been resident in the Netherlands, as the *Calvary of the Tanners* in Bruges (*c.* 1415) is attributed to the same hand, and the carved central panel of the Reinoldi altarpiece appears to have been produced in Brussels or Antwerp.[13] Although different in style, the designs in the Reinoldi wings are indebted to Conrad's Dortmund Altarpiece for a number of motifs, including the coin in the candle in the *Death of the Virgin*, the facial types, the frontal figures of the *Ascension*, the kneeling mocking onlooker before Pilate, and in the inward-looking figure in the *Kiss of Judas*. All the scenes in the left wing, and the *Gethsemane* narrative in the right wing are also closely related to Conrad's compositions. The centralized design of the *Adoration of the Kings*, the pose of Christ and that of the Virgin in the *Coronation of the Virgin* bear a strong resemblance to Conrad's Dortmund compositions, whilst the Reinoldi *St Catherine* derives from

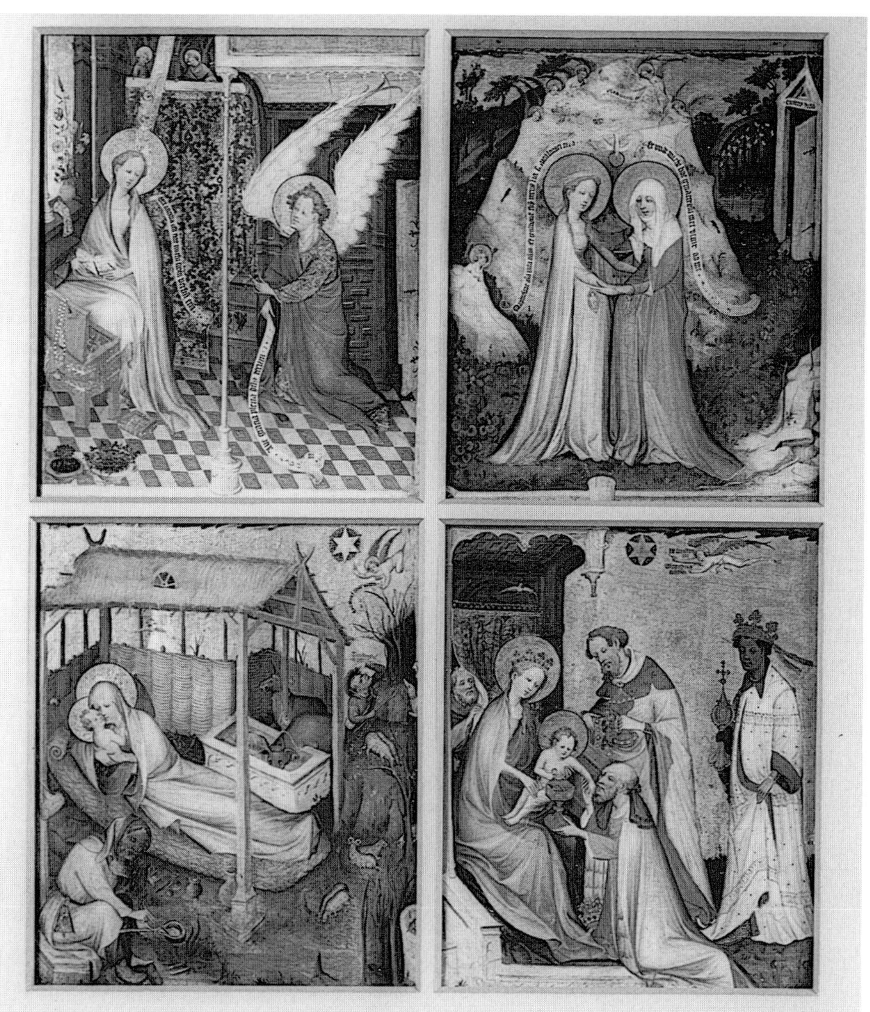

102. Left wing of the Utrecht
Altarpiece, Rijksmueum
Het Catharijneconvent,
Utrecht

Niederwildungen, and the *St Barbara* from the *St Odilia* in Münster. Such a list of similarities cannot be coincidental. It may have been requested by the donors in Dortmund who were familiar with Conrad's work and possibly supplied the painter of the wings of the Reinoldi Altarpiece with patterns recording Conrad's compositions.

Closer in style to Conrad's work and much higher in quality, are parts of the wings of the Utrecht Altarpiece (pl. 102), which are frequently given a Middle Rhenish provenance.[14] A Netherlandish provenance cannot be entirely excluded, because the wings appear to be painted in a workshop collaboration by at least three hands, of which the two lesser show many of the characteristics of Netherlandish artists (a comparison with the *Crucifixion* fresco in Utrecht Cathedral, *c.* 1410 is instructive). The main painter, however, is close in style and execution to Conrad's work. Facial features and the designs on the left wing, in particular, are closely related to Conrad's designs, and details are reminiscent of the Fröndenberg Altarpiece, which was painted either in Conrad's workshop or in close collabora-

157

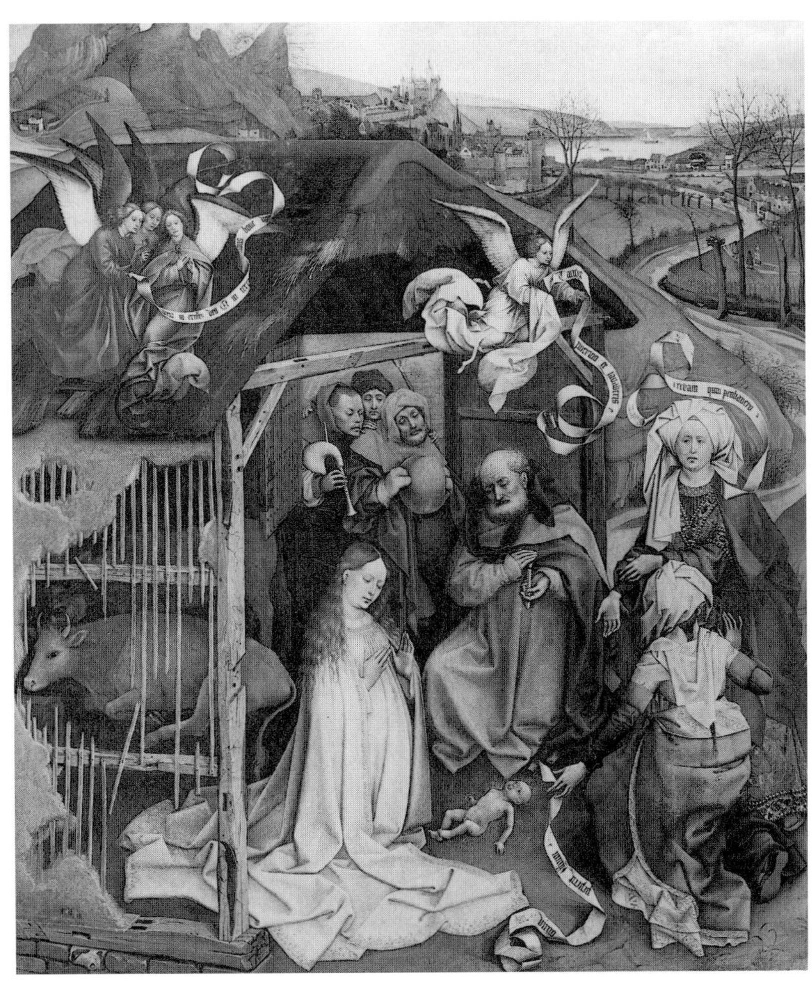

103. Robert Campin/
Master of Flémalle: *Nativity.*
Musée des Beaux-Arts de Dijon

tion with him (pl. 154). The *Annunciation* in the Utrecht wings appears to be an amalgamation of the Niederwildungen and Fröndenberg designs, with poses and drapery following the former whilst facial features and some details of the setting echo the latter. In the *Visitation* at Utrecht the figures appear simply to have swapped their costumes from the Fröndenberg pattern (pl. 37), seemingly wearing each other's dress. The composition of the *Adoration of the Kings* follows that at Fröndenberg, although in the Utrecht painting the third king is black, Joseph is allowed a more dignified pose, and the Virgin is crowned, as at Niederwildungen. The Utrecht *Nativity* scene repeats that of the Niederwildungen Altarpiece in respect of the Virgin and Child and the shepherd, but includes the Fröndenberg Joseph. The scenes in the right wing of the Utrecht Altarpiece are painted by a lesser hand, but the designs of the *Resurrected Christ* and the *Death of the Virgin* are reminiscent of those in Conrad's altarpieces. A third, much cruder hand, painted the obverse sides of the wings, but even there the *Gethsemane* scene is closely related to that at Niederwildungen. These derivations from altarpieces connected with Conrad von Soest suggest that the principal artist of the Utrecht wings, whether Netherlandish or not, had worked for a period in Dortmund. This is the more

158

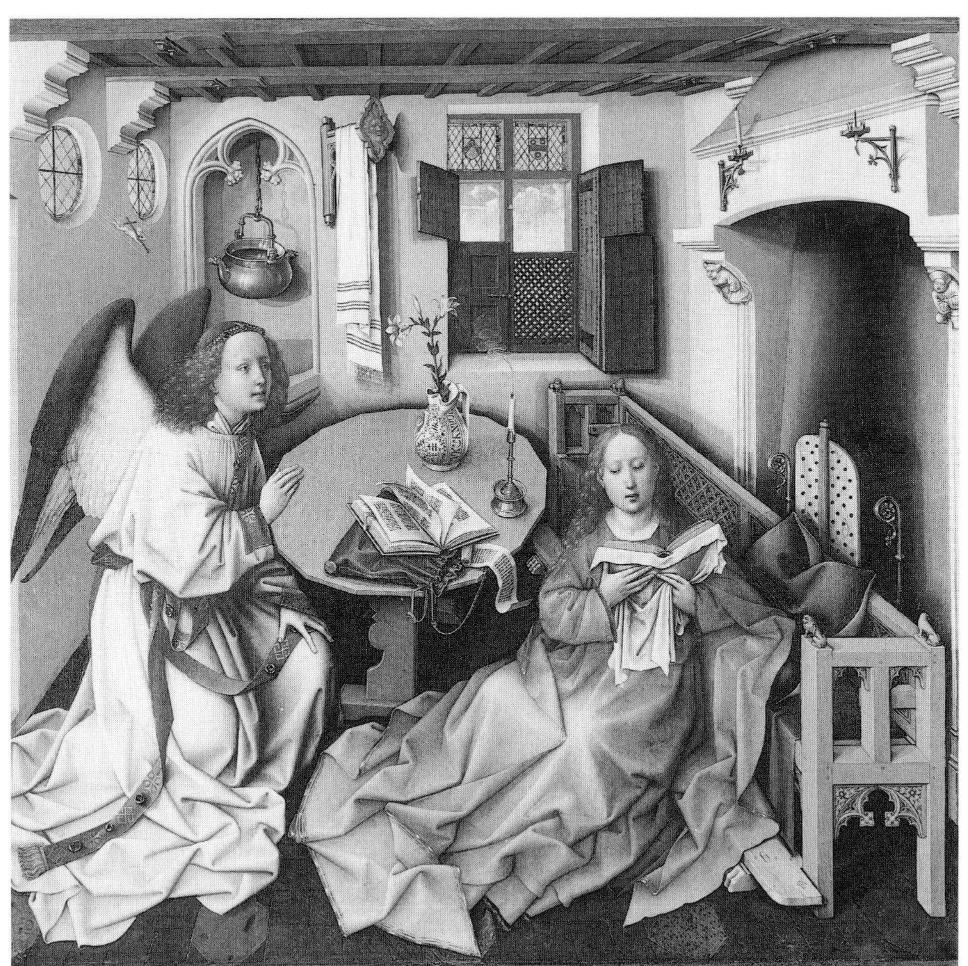

104. Robert Campin/
Master of Flémalle:
Annunciation.
from the Mérode Triptych.
The Metropolitan Museum
of Art, The Cloisters Collection,
New York

plausible as Netherlandish artists around 1400 had developed a different facial type to that painted by Conrad von Soest, whereas the Utrecht panels copy the physiognomic traits of Conrad's figures closely. The suggested Middle Rhenish provenance was (presumably) prompted by some stylistic resemblance to works from the circle of the Veronica Master. The direct quotations from the Niederwildungen, Dortmund and Fröndenberg Altarpieces argue against Cologne being a major influence.

The Conradian facial type can also be noted in panels from the workshop of Robert Campin (1378/8–1444, active in Tournai from 1406). Although the stylistic resemblance is not as close as in the Utrecht wings, the Virgins in the Dijon *Nativity* (Musée des Beaux Arts; *c.* 1420)(pl. 103), the Mérode Triptych (The Cloisters, New York; *c.* 1426)(pl. 104) and the *Madonna in Glory* in Aix-en-Provence (Musée Granet; *c.* 1428–30) appear to follow the Italianate canon adapted by Conrad von Soest. The small-featured elongated face, with a straight nose and slightly protruding half-closed eyes, a high, narrow forehead and blonde wispy hair tucked behind the ear, is inclined above a heavy neck. Whereas a mutual sympathy with Lombard designs cannot be entirely ruled out for this coincidence in facial type, the proximity of

Dortmund to the Netherlands and the important trading connections between the two, together with the undoubted repute of Conrad's costly panels, all favour Conrad's altarpieces as the inspiration for the Campin design. It has been noted above (p. 155) that some other panels by Campin, for example the *Virgin and Child before a Firescreen* (*c.* 1428; London, National Gallery) follow the rounder, more realistic Netherlandish features for the Virgin, also favoured by Broederlam.[15] This need not necessarily imply a separation of hands: the bourgeois setting of the London panel may have encouraged a more realistic characterization of the Virgin. The Conradian facial type was later adapted by other Netherlandish painters, for instance Rogier van der Weyden (1399/1400–64), who had worked in the Campin workshop from 1427 to 1432; it can be noted in his *St Luke painting the Virgin* (*c.* 1435–37; Museum of Fine Arts, Boston), and in the Columba Triptych (*c.* 1460–62) from Cologne, now in the Alte Pinakothek, Munich.

Campin's knowledge of Westphalian art is suggested by another motif in the Mérode Triptych (attributed to Campin)(pl. 104): a tiny Christ Child carrying the cross announces the passion in the *Annunciation* scene. As we have seen, this motif was a feature of Westphalian Annunciations. Furthermore, the Mérode *Annunciation* depicts a 'Madonna of Humility' placed in a domestic setting. The fusion of the seated Virgin and an interior setting as part of the Annunciation scene seems to have been initiated by Conrad von Soest in the Dortmund Altarpiece (see pp. 112–113). The 'Madonna of Humility' at Dortmund is seated on the floor, or possibly on a footrest, in front of a bench, her legs tucked under her, the folds of her garment spread decoratively around her. Whilst Campin's Virgin in New York is placed, with her garments similarly spread, apparently seated on a footrest of the bench to her left, his London Virgin is placed in front of the bench as at Dortmund. In spite of the destruction of altarpieces at the hands of iconoclasts in the Netherlands and the uncertainty about the content of lost altarpieces, the derivation of this motif from Conrad's altarpiece remains a plausible hypothesis. Conrad's *Death of the Virgin* at Dortmund also appears to predate Netherlandish versions. A panel in London (National Gallery; *c.* 1450), usually attributed to a follower of Campin, reflects Conrad's figures of St John, the seated apostle and the apostle blowing the censor. Significantly, the candle with the coin is also adopted.[16] The Germanic features of Campin's underdrawing style, like that of van der Weyden, adds weight to the conjecture that Campin was aware of the work of Conrad von Soest.[17]

There are signs that some of Conrad's paintings may have been known to artists in England. The *Last Supper* scenes in the choir window of Malvern Priory (*c.* 1450)(pls. 105, 106) and in the *Hours of Elizabeth the Queen* (*c.* 1420–30; London, BL, Add. 50001, fol. 7) certainly share iconographic and stylistic details with the same scene in the Niederwildungen Altarpiece.[18] The designer of the priory window not only adopted the same iconography, including the rare motif of Judas hiding the fish and the unusual presence of St Paul, he also followed Conrad closely in terms

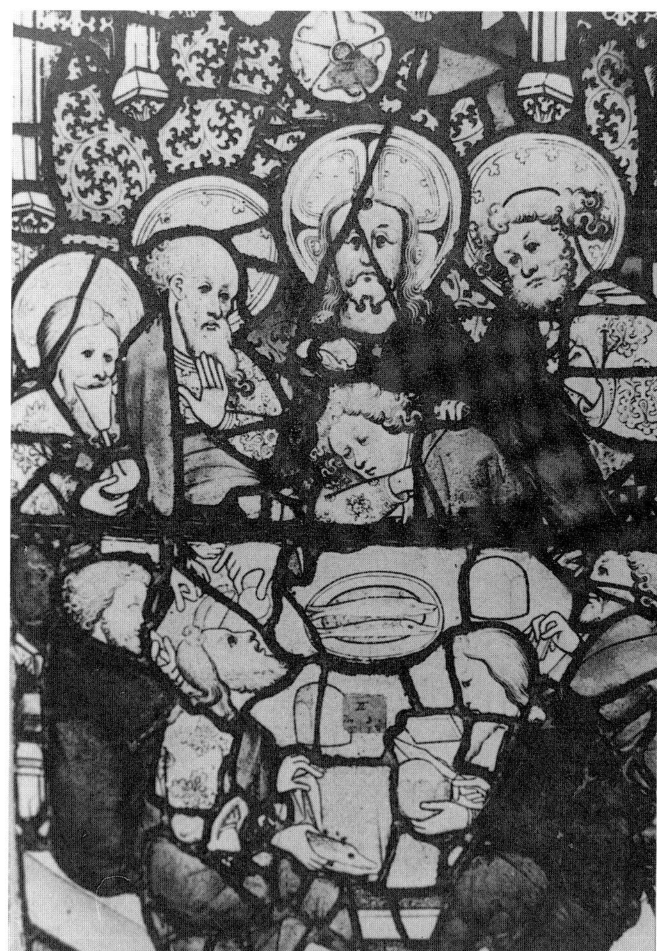

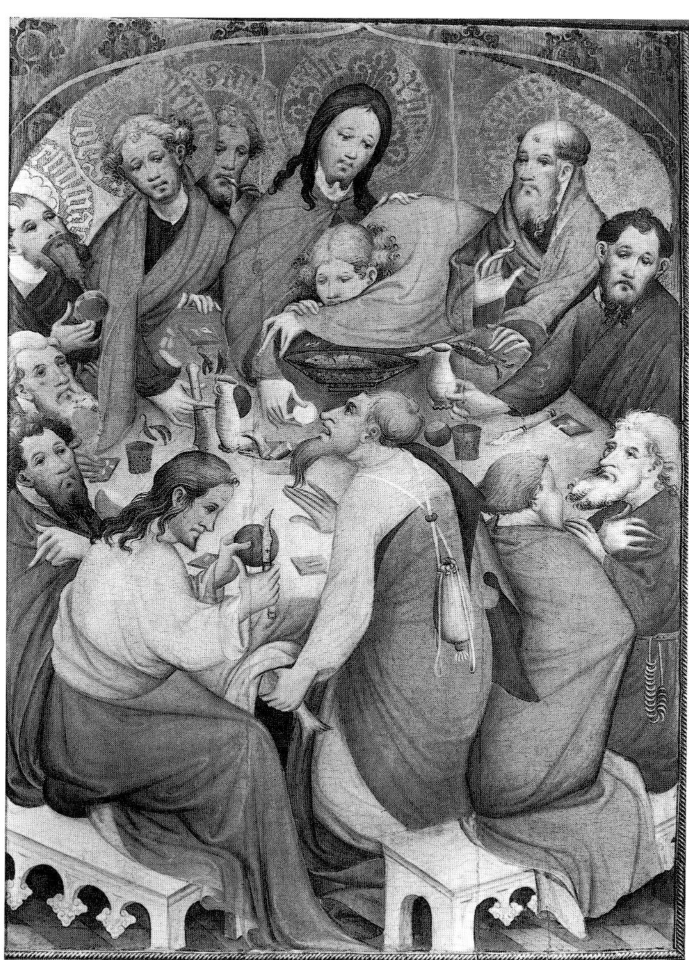

105. *The Last Supper*. East window,
Priory Church, Great Malvern

106. Conrad von Soest: *The Last Supper*.
Niederwildungen Altarpiece

of style. Although the order and number of the seated figures differs in the window design, St Paul's gesture raising his hand, the apostle next to him drinking from the cup, the figure depicted in lost profile, Judas receiving the host and raising his profile head, the apostle cutting into his bread[?] and St Peter inclining his head crowned by jaunty curls—all are closely related to the Niederwildungen example. With the exception of the drinking apostle and the St John, the design at Malvern is reversed from the Niederwildungen pattern.

Master Johannes, who appears to have painted the *Last Supper* scene in the *Hours of Elizabeth the Queen*, also included the hiding of the fish, the figure and pose of St Paul, the cup, the figure depicted in lost profile, the two central profile heads, the diagonal benches, and some draperies reminiscent of Conrad's panel. But although the apostle who had cut the bread in the Niederwildungen Altarpiece holds his hand in the pose apparently devised by Conrad, he does not grasp a knife. All narrative detail is omitted, presumably due to the small scale of the illumination. The differences in certain motifs and in style seem to suggest that this design may have reached the artist through patterns carried by intermediaries.

A Westphalian connection can be firmly established in another manuscript in England. John Siferwas[t] (or Syfewas), the painter of the *Crucifixion* of the Sherborne Missal (*c.* 1400–1407)(pl. 138), reveals his Westphalian sources or provenance in the Westphalian cross of the thieves (with two horizontal bars) and also in the group of women under the cross, which seems to suggest some knowledge of Conrad's design or of Westphalian panels influenced by him.[19] It is interesting to note that in the Easter page of the manuscript (p. 216), the soldier lifting his visor seems to derive from Conrad's *Resurrection*, whilst the Resurrected Christ steps over the rear side of the sarcophagus, in a manner reminiscent of the Darup Altarpiece (by a follower of Conrad) and of Master Francke's Hamburg fragment.

The source of these apparent Conradian influences on English art remains uncertain. It is possible that an English artist travelled to Germany, or, as the name Siferwas may imply, a German painter worked in England. Designs from Conrad's workshop may, on the other hand, have become known in England through pattern sheets carried by intermediaries. Bearing in mind the important trading connections between Conrad's Dortmund patrons and wealthy English traders (see p. 18), it is possible that these Westphalian patrician merchants may have carried evidence of Conrad's achievements to England.

However, stylistic, technical and historical factors combine to indicate that Conrad's influence was profoundly felt in Cologne. Amongst the considerable influx of foreign masters to Cologne appears to have been the painter we call the Veronica Master (the eponymous *St Veronica* panel is now in the Alte Pinakothek in Munich). This artist imported new ideas on style and technique into the indigenous workshops and is now regarded as the founder of the so-called 'school of Cologne'. On stylistic grounds, it is generally assumed that the Veronica Master settled in Cologne around 1400.[20] Attempts to link his work with any painter named in contemporary documents in Cologne have been unsuccessful. His earliest surviving works are the *Trinity* panel in Cologne, the small *Crucifixion* in Washington, and the *Sacra Conversazione* triptych in Kreuzlingen, all apparently painted during the first decade following his arrival in Cologne.[21]

The provenance of the Veronica Master remains the subject of conjecture. Four thirteenth-century works have been cited in a recent attempt to claim him as an indigenous painter of Cologne: a *Crucifixion* in Cologne (WRM 1), a triptych in Hamburg (Kunsthalle, Inv. No. 325), the panels of the St Clare Polyptych (Cologne Cathedral) painted by the older Master, and the Wehrden Crucifixion (WRM 883, which, as discussed earlier, has French roots).[22] On examination, however, these paintings appear alien in style and pictorial content to the work of the Veronica Master. The Veronica Master's style is at variance with local tradition, and this contradicts any notion of an apprenticeship in Cologne. Furthermore, the painters, sculptors, goldsmiths and illuminators working in Cologne were rarely born in that city: extant records show that they came from Flanders, Westphalia, Nuremberg, the Lake Constance area, Vienna, Paris, Dijon, Avignon and Prague.[23]

107. John Siferwas: *Crucifixion. The Sherborne Missal*, British Library, London Loan MS 82, p. 380

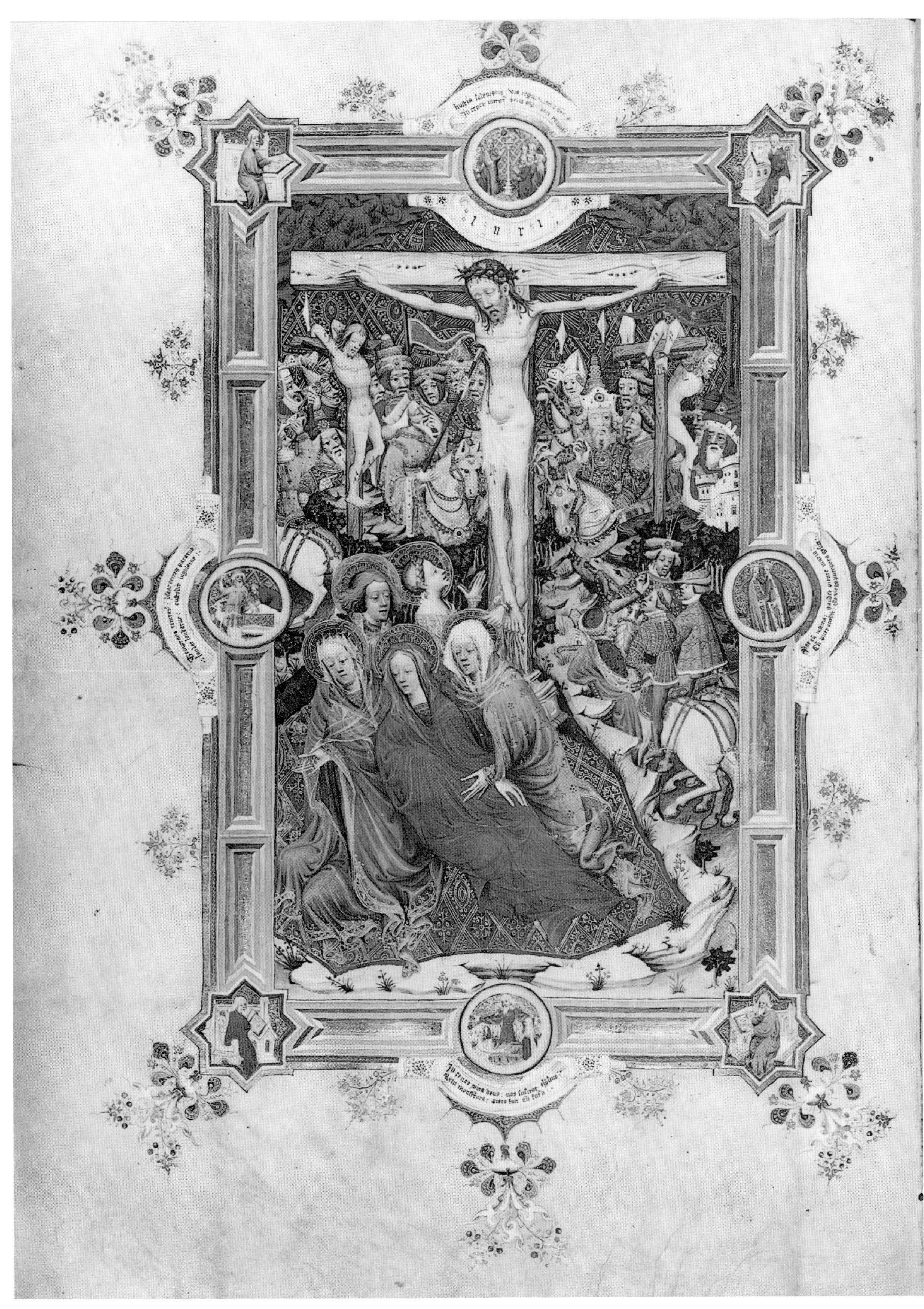

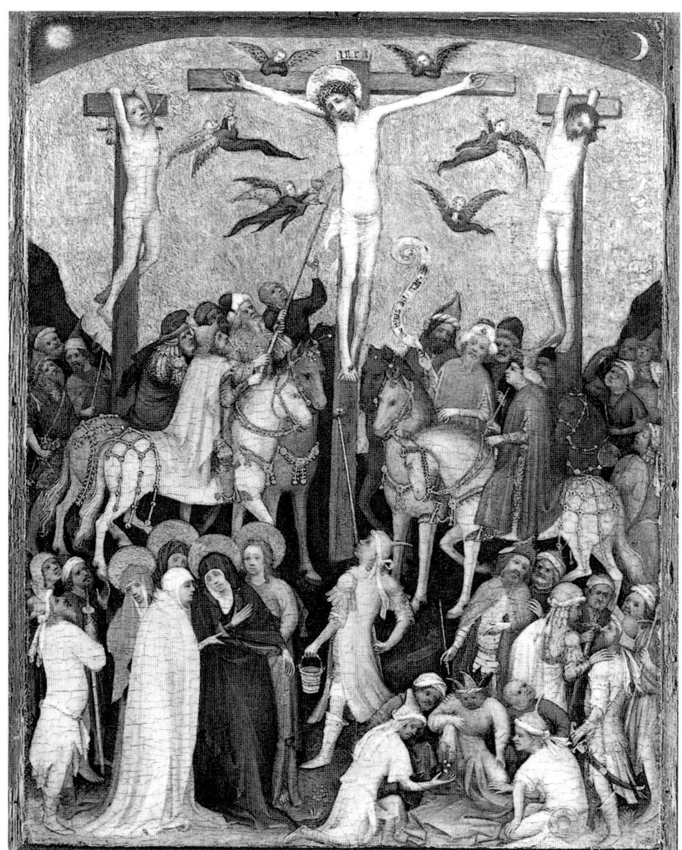

109. Veronica Master: Trinity. Wallraf-Richartz-Museum, Cologne

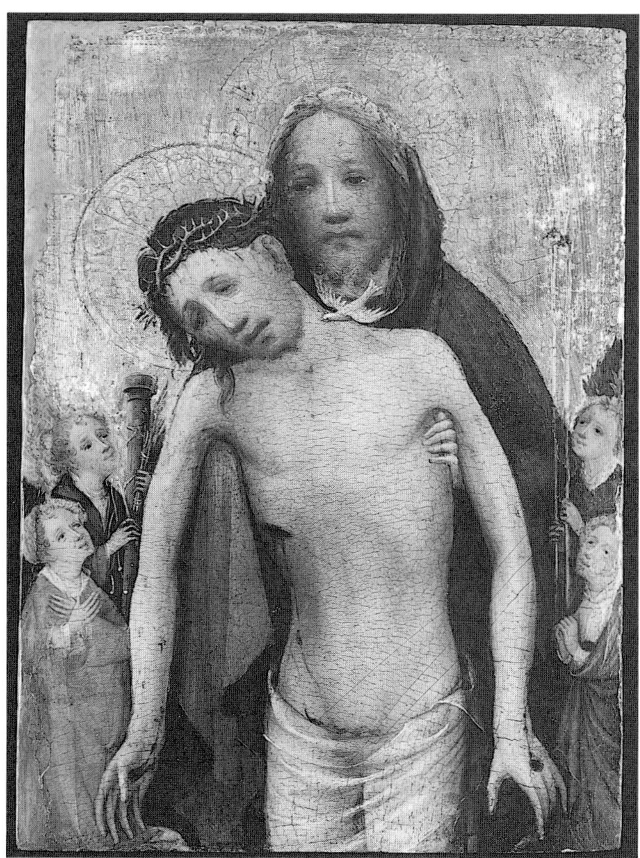

108. Veronica Master: *Small Calvary.* Wallraf-Richartz-Museum, Cologne

When considering the possible provenance of the Veronica Master it is worth noting that the panel depicting the *Trinity* (accompanied by angels carrying the *arma christi*; (*c.* 1405?)(pl. 109), with a *Vera Icon* on the reverse side is so closely related in style to the Niederwildungen Altarpiece that it has been attributed in turn to Conrad von Soest and to the Veronica Master. An initial comparison of individual figures depicted in the panel to those in Conrad's autograph work appears to favour the attribution to Conrad von Soest: the figure of Christ occurs in the Niederwildungen *Crucifixion*, the face of God the Father is adapted from the onlooker in the *Presentation* or from the green-robed king in the *Adoration of the Kings*, and the image of the *Vera Icon* resembles that of Christ in the Niederwildungen *Last Judgement*.[24]

However, attribution of the *Trinity* panel to the Veronica Master has recently prevailed and the panel is now on permanent loan to the Wallraf-Richartz Museum in Cologne. The softer modelling of the forms and the expression of sorrow rather than suffering in Christ's face has been cited in favour of the Veronica Master as the author of the panel.[25] The softer modelling could of course be due to the small size of the panel, and the varying expressions might be explained by the discrepancy in subject matter. But the *Trinity* can be linked to other works attributed to the Veronica Master—such as the small *Crucifixion* (*c.* 1405)(pl. 95) in Washington

164

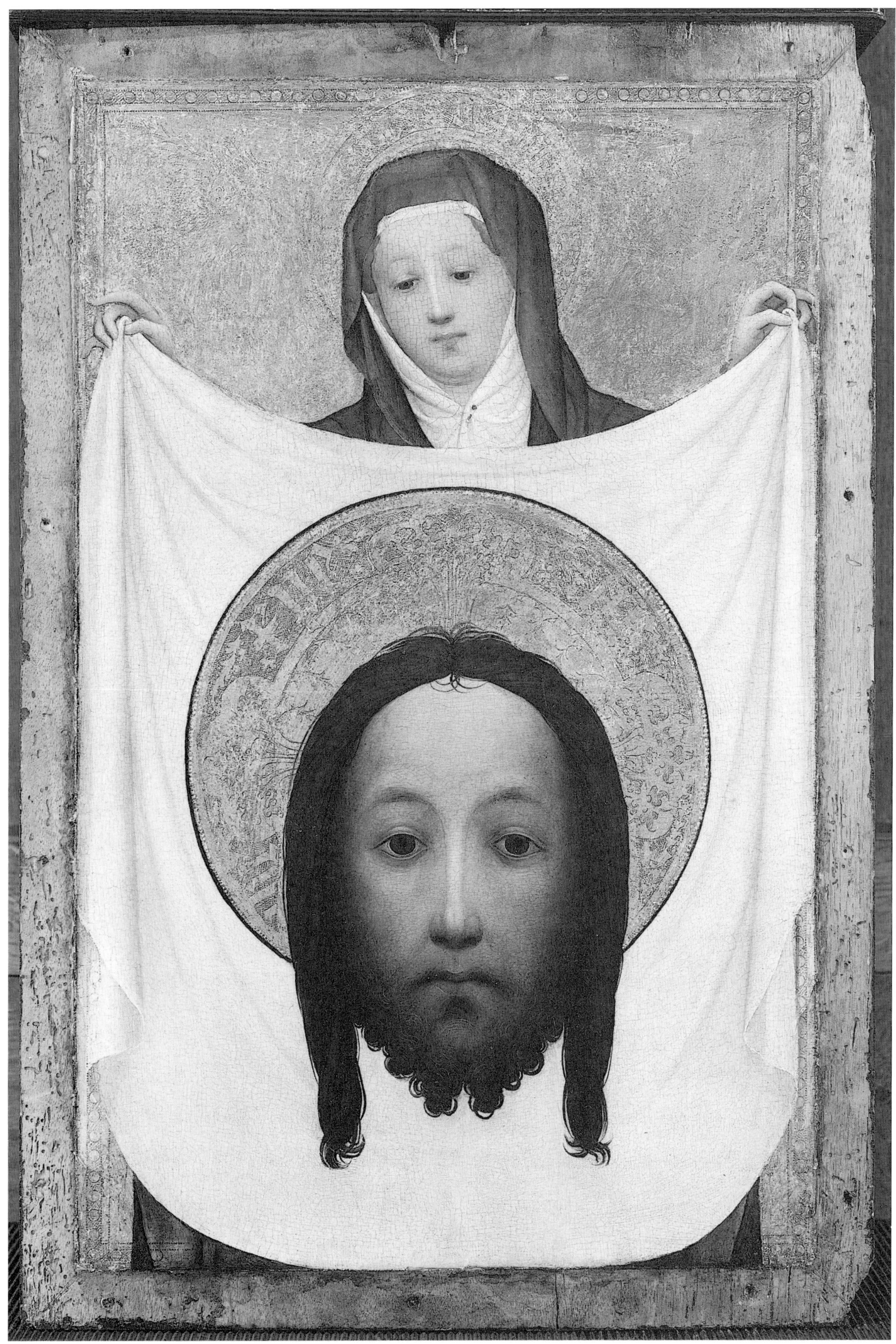

110. Veronica Master: *St Veronica holding the Sudarium*. National Gallery, London

and the small *Calvary* (*c.* 1416)(pl. 108) in Cologne. In these works, the anatomy of Christ's torso is more generalized and the pattern of the crown-of-thorns is more decorative than in the Niederwildungen Altarpiece. Also, the large circles punched into the gold ground framing of the *Trinity* occur in other works by the Veronica Master and his workshop, such as the eponymous panel depicting *St Veronica holding the Sudarium* (*c.* 1415–20; Munich, Alte Pinakothek), a similar panel in London (*c.* 1415, National Gallery)(pl. 110), the *Madonna with the Pea Blossom* (*c.* 1410–15, Nuremberg, Germanisches Nationalmuseum, Inv. No. Gm 4)(pl. 111), and the *Sacra Conversazione* triptych (*c.* 1409, Kreuzlingen, Kisters Collection))(pls. 129, XXXIV). This inner frame of punched circles was a fairly frequent decoration in the Veronica Master's workshop, but it could not be found in panels by other masters in Cologne, nor in Conrad's work. The *Vera Icon* on the reverse of the panel is closely related to the image in the London panel, and the figure of Christ in the *Trinity* is very similar to that in the two Crucifixions mentioned above. In view of these connections with other works by the Veronica Master, the *Trinity* panel may be firmly attributed to him.

This attribution to the Veronica Master has been challenged on the grounds that the soft modelling of the forms would indicate an early date in the *oeuvre*, whilst the statuesque pose of the angels would signify an unacceptably late date. The

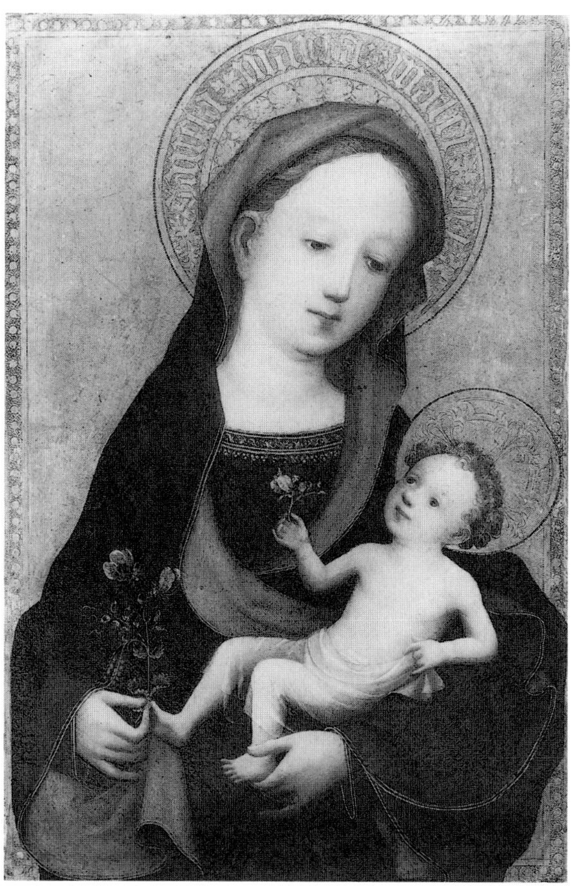

111. Veronica Master:
Madonna with the Pea Blossom.
Germanisches Nationalmuseum, Nuremberg

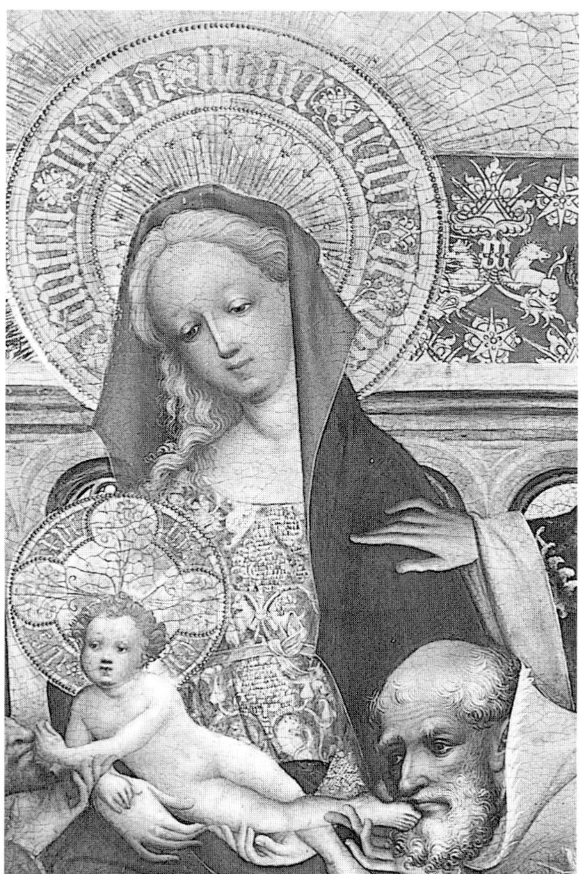

112. Conrad von Soest: *Madonna and Child.*
Detail from the *Adoration of the Kings.*
Dortmund Altarpiece

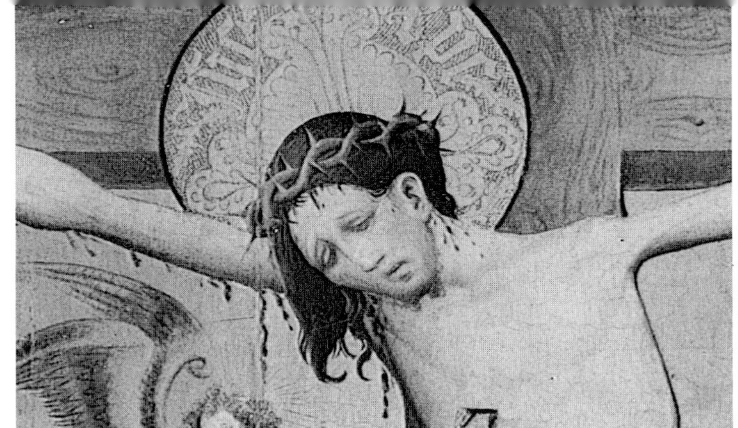
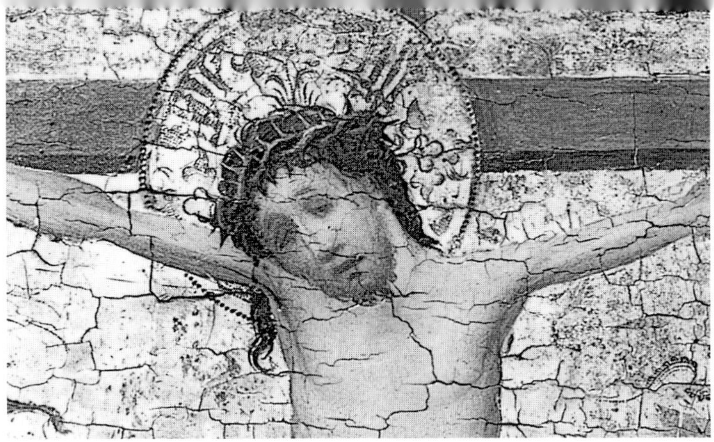

113. Conrad von Soest: *Head of Christ* from the *Crucifixion*. Niederwildungen Altarpiece

114. Veronica Master: *Head of Christ* from the *Crucifixion*, (pl.95)

Lawrence Master has therefore been proposed as author of the *Trinity* panel, probably after he left the workshop of the Veronica Master.[26] The Washington *Crucifixion*, by contrast, has been accepted as an early work by the Veronica Master himself, although it is painted in a similar soft manner, and the pose of St John is almost identical to that of the first angel on the right of the *Trinity*; the pose of the angel on the left also recalls that of the Washington Mary. It might have been possible to shed further light on this controversy by examining the underdrawing of the panel and that of other works by the Veronica Master by means of infra-red photography, but permission for such an examination was not granted by the Wallraf-Richartz Museum.

In spite of the striking similarity of the styles and analogous facial types, a direct connection between the Veronica Master and Conrad von Soest is sometimes dismissed as a mere symptom of the international flavour of the Courtly Style around 1400.[27] The internationalism of the Courtly Style has certainly been responsible for some confusions of attribution between major artistic centres. But it never led to an erosion of individual interpretations by major artists: an accidental emergence of similar images is therefore hardly plausible. Here, a comparison of the features of Christ in Conrad's Niederwildungen *Crucifixion* (pl. 114) and in the Veronica Master's Washington *Crucifixion* (pl. 113) is instructive. I would suggest that the notable correspondence between the styles of Conrad von Soest and the Veronica Master is the result of the Veronica Master's intimate acquaintance with the work of Conrad von Soest.

It could be argued that Conrad von Soest learned his art from the Veronica Master. However, the assertion that Conrad was a provincial artist rests not on his art but in the notion that Westphalia was an agricultural backwater remote from the economic and cultural privileges enjoyed in cosmopolitan Cologne. Instead, the independence of the chartered imperial city of Dortmund and its still significant role in the Hanseatic League at this time should be borne in mind when establishing the relationship between Conrad and the Veronica Master.[28] In any case, Conrad appears to have been the older master. His marriage certificate shows that by 1394 he was the affluent head of a successful workshop in Dortmund. The skill displayed in the large and costly altarpiece he signed and dated in 1403, as well as the impact

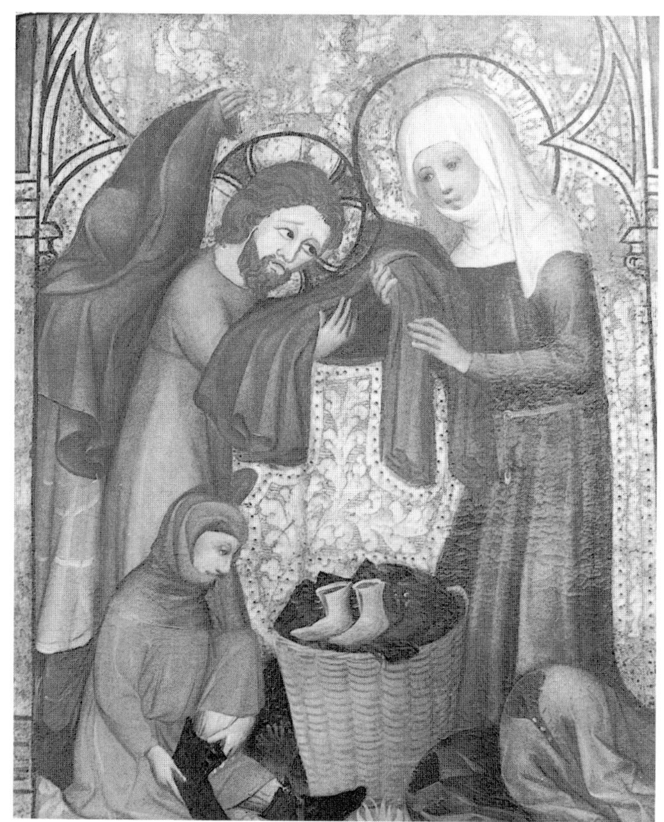
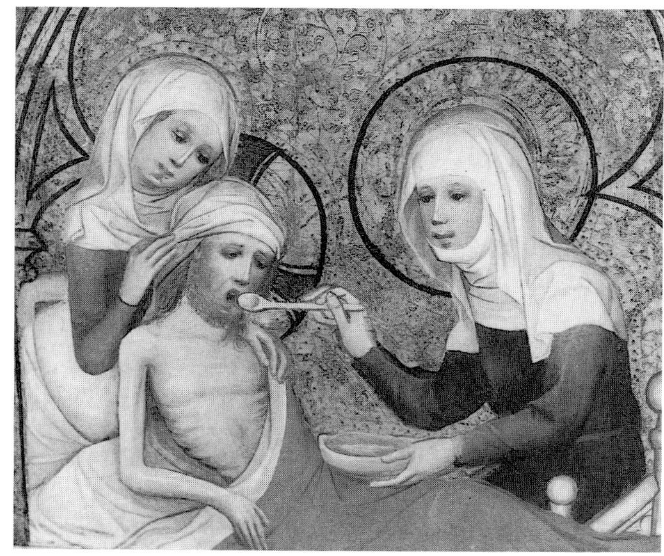

115–116. *St Elizabeth clothing the Poor*, and
St Elizabeth feeding the Sick, St Elizabeth
Altarpiece, Wallraf-Richartz-Museum, Cologne

of his art in other Hanseatic towns, establish both his reputation and his influence on wandering artists in Northern Germany. No signed or dated altarpieces can be connected with the Veronica Master, but as the result of dendrochronological examination a number of his works can be dated with a reasonable degree of assurance. Bearing in mind the accidents of survival, it is still notable that the Veronica Master's panels painted during his first decade in Cologne are very small in scale and do not seem to include strikingly expensive pigments. It has been claimed that the Veronica Master had a preference for the small scale,[29] but one suspects that donor preference had an important role to play in the selection of sizes. The initially small commissions may reflect a certain amount of caution on behalf of his new patrons. Later on in his career they certainly entrusted him with larger commissions, such as the *Crucifixion* of *c.* 1420–25 (pl. 126), as well as the completion of the important St Clare Polyptych (*c.* 1415–20) (pl. 121). The prospering Master Conrad of Dortmund was unlikely in 1403 to be imitating the art of a master who was attempting to establish himself in Cologne at that time.

The Elizabeth Altarpiece (pls. 115, 116) has been cited as proof that the International Courtly Style had been established in Cologne before the arrival there of the Veronica Master. Fragments of this work, which can be dated to after 1370, are now distributed between the Wallraf-Richartz Museum in Cologne (WRM 35–37) and the Wilhelm-Hack Museum in Ludwigshafen (Inv. No. 457/35).[30] Yet close inspection of the panels in Cologne reveals two distinct styles of painting: the poor receiving clothes in the *Distribution* scene (pl. 115), the man pulling the nail out of

168

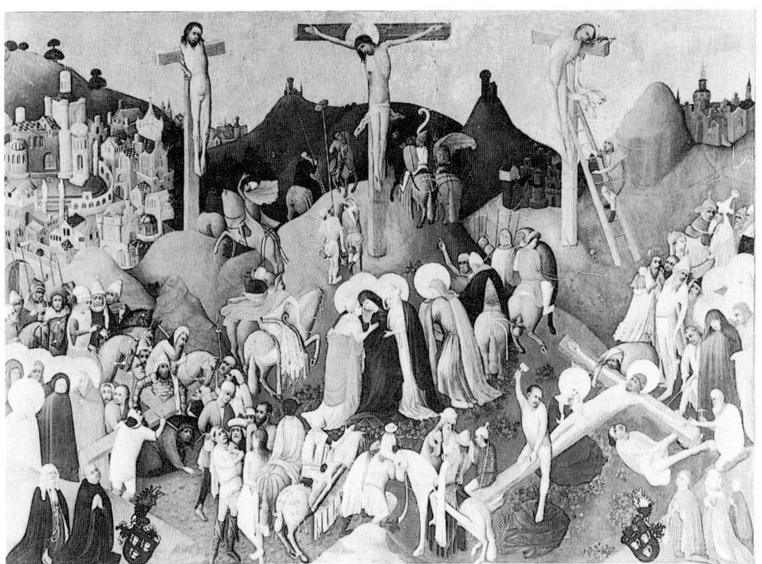

117. *Wasservass Calvary*, Wallraf-Richartz-Museum, Cologne

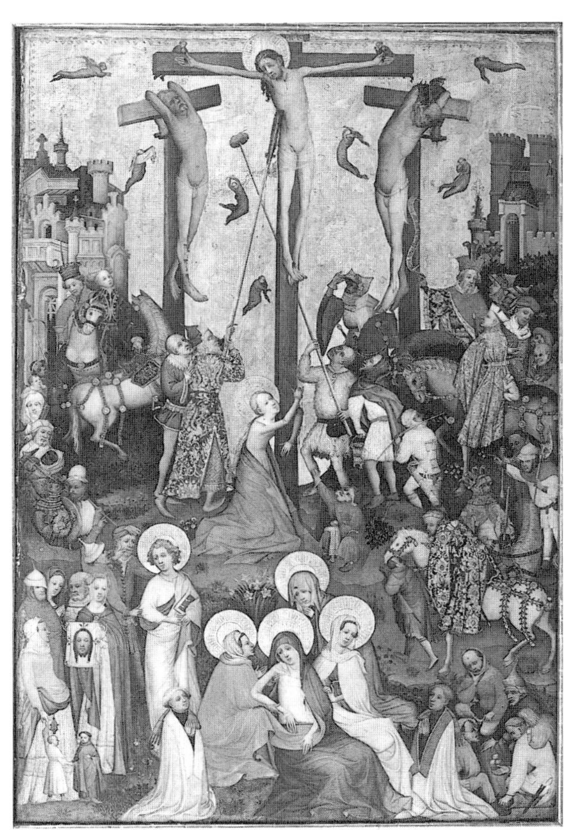

118. *Calvary from St Andreas.* Wallraf-Richartz-Museum, Cologne

Christ's hand in the *Deposition*, and the second blind man in *Elizabeth guiding the Blind*, as well as most of the drapery, are painted in a style that fits with the date of 1370. By contrast, the heads of St Elizabeth and Christ have been modernized by a later hand. Traces of the original incised haloes can be clearly discerned (pl. 116), in spite of visible scraping and rubbing. They indicate that the original heads were larger than the ones softly modelled in the new style; areas between the gold ground and the new painting are bridged by a wide brown outline, and the remaining gaps are shaded in with gold-coloured paint. The proportion of these erased heads had corresponded with those of the figures dating from 1370.[31] The substituted heads were clearly painted much later. There is thus no evidence to support the notion that the style was established in Cologne before the arrival there of the Veronica Master around 1400.

The Veronica Master betrayed his knowledge of Westphalian art not only in his Conradian facial types, but also by using the Westphalian cross with double horizontal bars for the thieves, as in his small *Calvary* in Cologne (pl. 108). This cross-form occurs only in one other panel in Cologne, the Westphalian *Calvary* from St Andreas (WRM 353)(pl. 118) of around 1420. The contemporary Wasservass Calvary in Cologne, for example (WRM 65, *c.* 1420)(pl. 117), depicts the usual single horizontal bar. The Veronica Master's specific knowledge of the work of Conrad von Soest can be demonstrated through his use of Conrad's cloud-shaped punch-mark in his own paintings. Sporadic cloud punchmarks appear in the gold ground of all works by Conrad von Soest: this is an idiosyncratic feature of Conrad's art

169

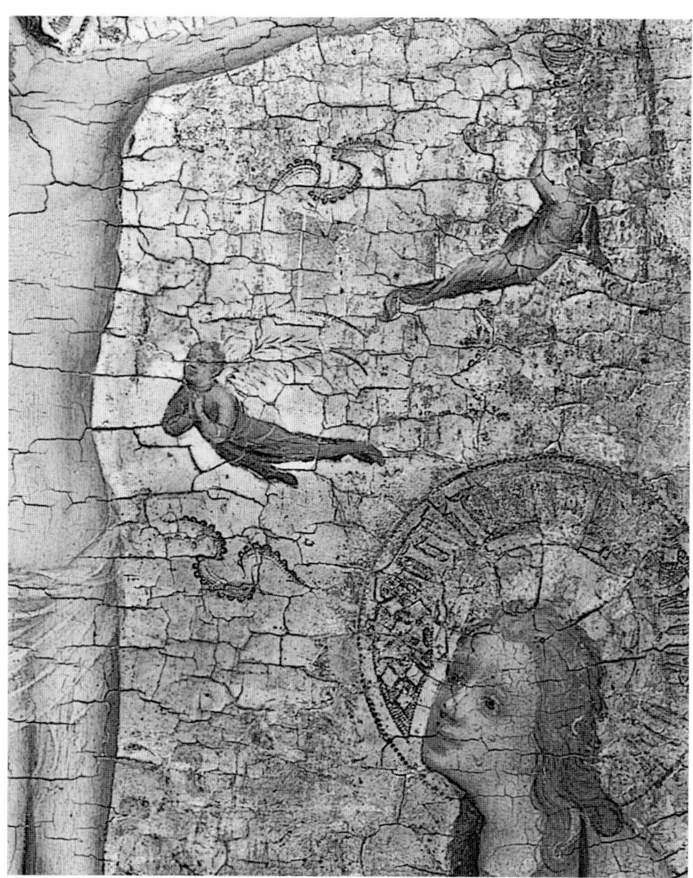

119. Veronica Master:
Detail of cloud from the
Crucifixion (pl. 95)
National Gallery of Art,
Washington DC,
Samuel H Kress Collection

120. *Noli me tangere* and *Ascension.*
St Clare Polyptych,
Cathedral, Cologne

121. Veronica Master and workshop:
Adoration of the Magi.
St Clare Polyptych,
Cathedral, Cologne

(pl. 72). The stylized clouds, decorated with tiny circles on the outer edges and with rows of dots on the inner edges, are copied exactly by the Veronica Master and his workshop. A set of S-shaped, or possibly 'cloud'-shaped, punches seems to have been used to scale, and separate punches for the small circles and dots employed in completion of the patterns. In the Veronica Master's panels, these cloud patterns can be found well preserved in the Washington *Crucifixion* (pl. 119), and in rather rubbed condition in the London *St Veronica* panel, which also bears the remains of punched and tooled angel's wings, strongly reminiscent of those in Conrad's Dortmund *Adoration*. In the Kreuzlingen *Sacra Conversazione*, the cloud punchmarks are joined together to form the border of a *mandorla* with angels similar to those forming the semicircle around the angels in Conrad's Dortmund *Death of the Virgin*. Scratched rays appear in both works. The Veronica Master still used the cloud punchmarks in the gold ground of his late large *Crucifixion* (WRM 14, *c.* 1420–25). Gold grounds in Northern German painting, if decorated at all, were traditionally adorned with an overall floral or geometrical punched design. This can be observed, for instance, in the St Clare Polyptych (pls. 120, 121) in Cologne, (geometrical in some early panels, floral in some later scenes), or in the Westphalian Osnabrück Altarpiece (floral; WRM 350–352, *c.* 1385–90). However, the motif of punched clouds was repeated in the wing of an altarpiece painted by the Lawrence Master (WRM 737, after 1420)(pl. 122), presumably in the Veronica Master's work-

170

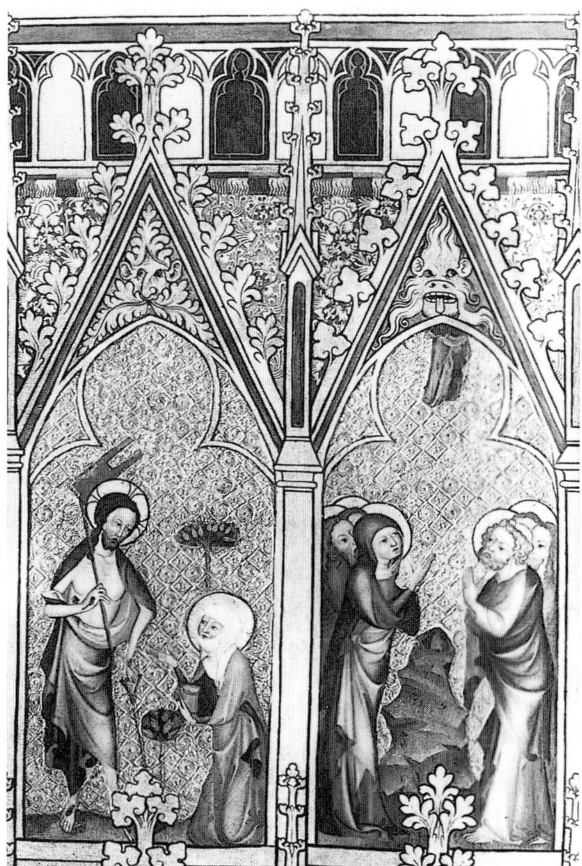 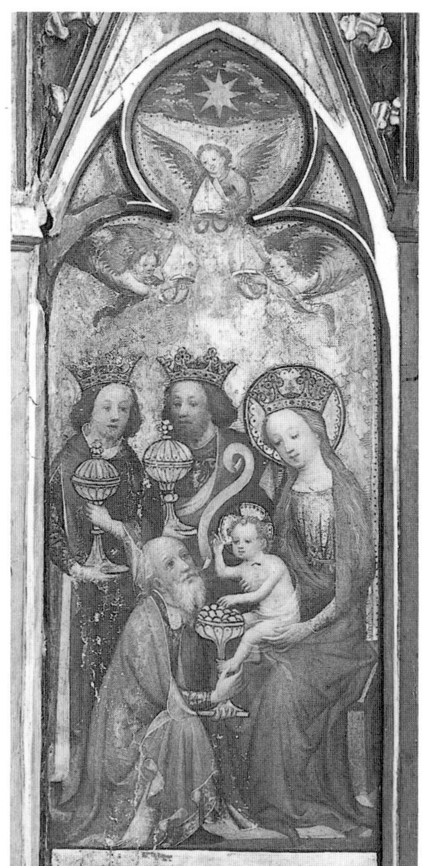

shop, and later adopted by the artist known as Stefan Lochner, for instance in the altarpiece of the Patron Saints of Cologne (or Dombild, *c.* 1440/45; Cologne Cathedral)(pl. 128).[32] These analogous cloudmarks do not seem to have been noted before. Yet the correspondence of the cloud patterns cannot be accidental, and their appearance in early works by the Veronica Master suggests that the Veronica Master was at some time connected with the workshop of Conrad von Soest. If the Veronica Master did not borrow Conrad's set of punches, it would not have been difficult for him to have them copied for his own workshop; the simple shapes needed for making the intricate design are easily copied. However, the method of creating these stamped and punched clouds, exactly following Conrad's design, could only have been learned in the Dortmund workshop.

Further support for the conjecture of a direct link between Conrad von Soest and the Veronica Master is provided by the punched decoration of haloes. In the Veronica Master's *Trinity* in Cologne, *Crucifixion* in Washington, *St Veronica* panels in Munich and London, triptych of the *Madonna with the Sweet Pea Blossom* in Cologne (WRM 10; *c.* 1415–20)(pl. 123), and the panel of the *Madonna with the Pea Blossom* in Nuremberg, the haloes are inscribed in a manner apparently derived from Conrad's workshop. Similar angular lettering, as well as the floral fringe and the diamond ornamentation of five diamond shapes arranged in a cruciform pattern—even the nimbus outlined with punched dots—all feature in the Nieder-

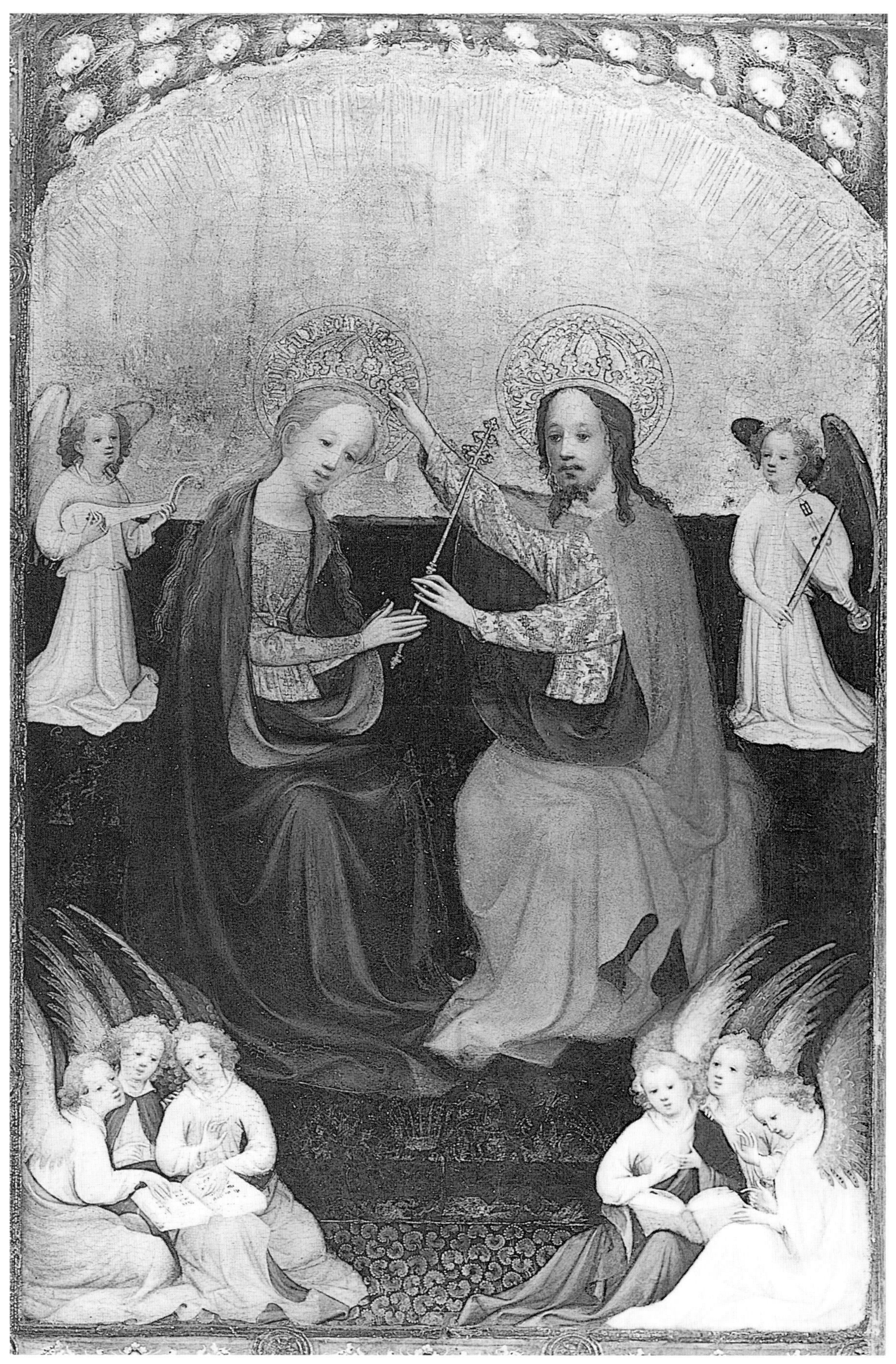

122. Lawrence Master: *Coronation of the Virgin*. Wallraf-Richartz-Museum, Cologne

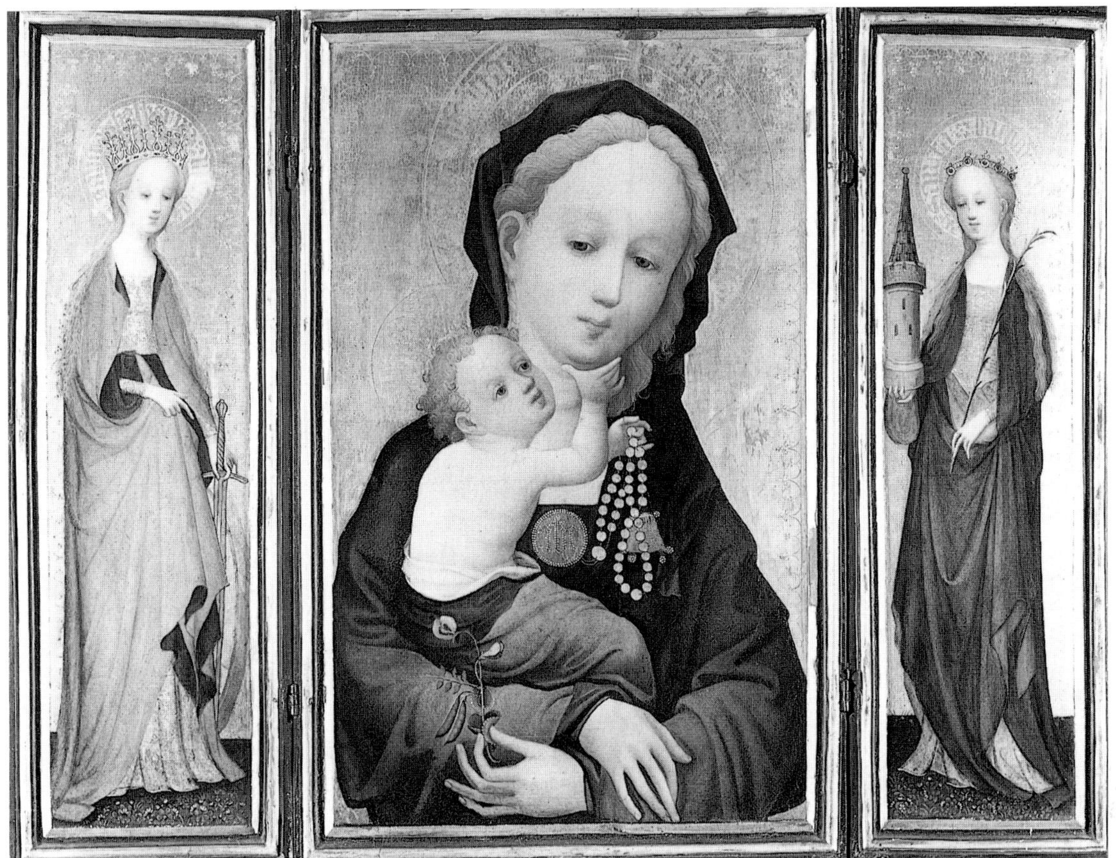

123. Veronica Master: *Madonna with the Sweet-Pea Blossom*. Wallraf-Richartz-Museum, Cologne

wildungen Altarpiece, for instance in the *Adoration of the Kings*. The oak leaf and the blank rings each side of the lettered space in the Veronica Master's halo decoration are evident in the Dortmund Altarpiece. The Veronica Master also adopted the technique, used by Conrad, of imitating the texture of brocade by means of scoring the gold areas, a method used in the robe of the donor in his Washington *Crucifixion*. Furthermore, the Veronica Master appears to have introduced into Cologne certain technical characteristics, observed in Conrad's altarpieces, such as the use of red bole and of the colours ultramarine and lead-tin yellow (see pp. 40–41).

A date around 1390 proposed for the Washington *Crucifixion* has been challenged by dendrochronological examination of the panel; this proposes a felling date between 1394/1398 and 1404+x for the oak-wood and (assuming a ten-year storage for the wood) a date of 1408 or later for the painting.[33] This dating would accord with the thesis of the Veronica Master's dependence on designs from the workshop of Conrad von Soest. A reflectogram of the panel, made at the Washington Gallery, reveals only traces of an outline in the torso of Christ. This may indicate that the outline of the figures only were transferred from a pattern sheet; however, most of the other outlines are now obscured by the overlapping edges of the gold ground. What can be made out of the pattern appears to derive from Conrad's

173

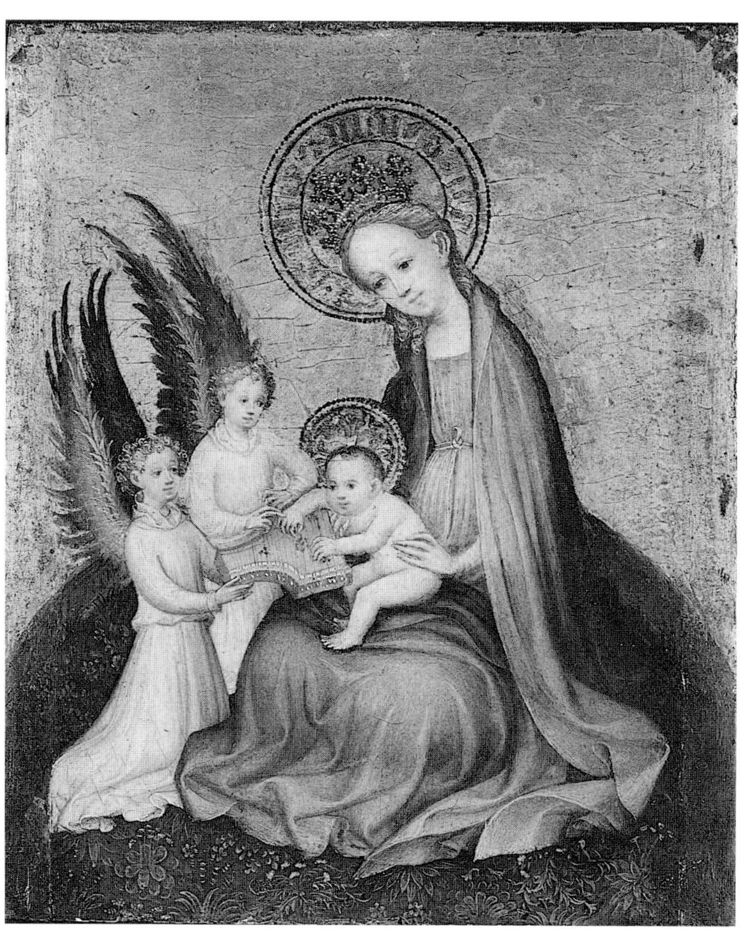

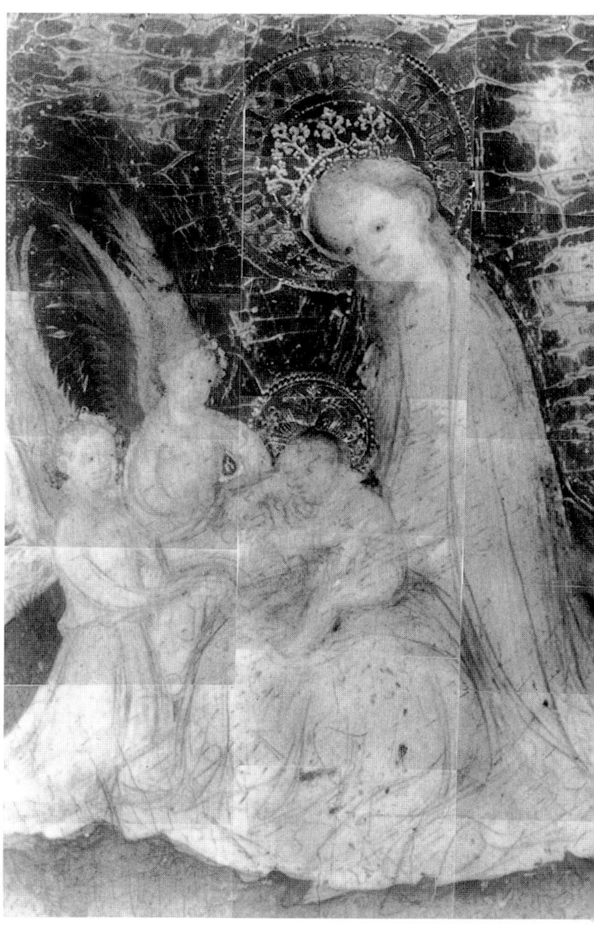

124. Lawrence Master: *Virgin of Humility.*
Wallraf-Richartz-Museum, Cologne

125. *Underdrawing of the Virgin of Humility.*
Infra-red reflectogram by Molly Faries

workshop model. A recent examination of the Veronic Master's small *Calvary* in Cologne has detected a similar lack of underdrawing in all but one small outline area. However, the underdrawing method in a panel by the Lawrence Master, depicting a *Virgin of Humility*, is closely related to that of Conrad von Soest (pls. 124, 125).[34] This is particularly interesting because the Lawrence Master is thought to have worked, at least initially, in the workshop of the Veronica Master. The similarity of his style to that of the Veronica Master may be compared with the stylistic dependence of the Veronica Master on Conrad von Soest.

Motifs and stylistic derivations borrowed from Conrad von Soest's altarpieces by the Veronica Master are not limited to facial features and technical procedures. In the Washington *Crucifixion*, for instance, the folds of Christ's transparent loin cloth and even the half-clotted traces of blood on His forehead and limbs reflect patterns in the Niederwildungen Altarpiece, as do the angels catching the sacred blood in their cups. The donor figure is similar in certain respects to the oldest king in Conrad's *Adoration*, particularly in the way his leg emerges through a slit in his long coat.

174

The small *Calvary* in Cologne (damaged and restored)(pl. 108), dated *c.* 1416,[35] is designed on the same construction principle as the Niederwildungen *Crucifixion*. The three crosses, the thieves' crosses being of the Westphalian type and fore-shortened, are silhouetted against a golden ground which is framed by an arch of blue sky, in accordance with Conrad's design. The area of the separation of gold ground and blue sky suffers from paint loss, but remnants of pigment suggest that a rainbow was originally depicted there, as at Niederwildungen. The body of Christ in the panel is only gently bowed to the right, and all three figures are more softly modelled and weaker in structure than those of Conrad's altarpiece. Yet the resemblance to Conrad's Christ is striking, and the outline of the thieves' bodies seems to follow the Niederwildungen pattern closely. In the Cologne panel, traces of an angel and a devil have been discovered, delivering the souls of the dead men, as at Niederwildungen.[36] The angel to Christ's right, with the end of his cloak slung over his arm, repeats the silhouette and drapery pattern of the equivalent figure in the Niederwildungen Altarpiece. In both paintings, the weeping angel is placed above His left arm and the rustic who is shading his eyes appears behind the thief. The sword-carrying soldier in Cologne is the courtier who is placed in the same corner in Conrad's work, transformed by a change of costume, and the soldier who opens his visor can be found in Conrad's *Resurrection*. In the *Calvary* an additional figure has been included in the group beneath the good thief's cross, but the conversation continues, and the profile head of the Niederwildungen Longinus has been borrowed for the rider on the yellow horse behind Longinus. The other groups do not derive from surviving works by Conrad von Soest, yet they are again arranged in a V-shape formation, so as to reveal the base of Christ's cross. Similarities between these groups and those in the altarpieces from the workshop of the Warendorf Master, a Westphalian follower of Conrad von Soest (cat. nos. 10–12), have frequently been noted. Even without entering into the dispute of the likely nature and appearance of lost altarpieces from Conrad's workshop, there is sufficient evidence in this panel alone to infer some knowledge of Conrad's work on the part of the Veronica Master.

The infant in the painting of the *Madonna with the Pea Blossom* at Nuremberg (pl. 111) and also in the triptych of the *Madonna with the Sweet Pea Blossom* (pl. 123) at Cologne reflect the Conradian child-type, but it could be argued that the Veronica Master had, like Conrad, studied the model in Paris in the Parement Master's workshop. Even if this were the case, it is remarkable that his interpretation of the French prototype resembles so closely that by Conrad. The saints in the wings of the Cologne triptych appear to be more directly descended from the Niederwil-dungen *St Catherine* and the Münster *St Odilia*. The Virgin of this triptych is also reminiscent of the Conradian model. The Nuremberg Virgin derives facial features and pose of the right hand from the Virgin in the Dortmund *Adoration* (pls. 111,112), whilst the fold pattern of her headscarf appears in the Niederwildungen *Crucifixion* and *Adoration*. Nevertheless, the loose brushwork and the frame of punched circles in the gold ground, as well as the more rounded cheeks of the Virgin, indicate that the *Madonna with the Sweet Pea Blossom* was painted by the Veronica Master.

Despite such striking dependence on Conrad's work, the Veronica Master has been considered an independent artist, unaware of Conrad von Soest's altarpieces, whose similar style could easily be accounted for by the influence of *Zeitgeist*.[37] This thesis appears to rest on the contention that a difference can be established in physiognomy and psychology between the inhabitants of Westphalia and Cologne, and that this causes a difference in appearance and temperament of the protagonists in paintings from the two regions which can be used to determine their provenance. The art in Cologne was declared sweet and gentle.[38] However, the Veronica Master was not attuned to the 'Cologne temperament' (for he was an immigrant), nor were his hand and eye originally schooled in that town. Nor can the very realistic narrative of the contemporary Cologne Wasservass Calvary (pl. 117), for example, or of the *Deposition* (WRM 62) from a Passion altarpiece from the workshop of the Older Kinship Master be reconciled with that definition of the Cologne temperament. In considering the proposed sweet and gentle nature of Cologne it may also be remembered that Suso, who described Christ's passion in such horrific detail in his meditations, had studied in Cologne.

When he arrived in Cologne, the Veronica Master introduced there the style formulated by Conrad von Soest in Westphalia from French, Italian and indigenous sources. Judging by the number of paintings that reflect this innovative trend, this style found an enthusiastic response in Cologne. The Veronica Master's workshop itself, notably with the assistance of the Lawrence Master, appears to have been commissioned later to modernize and complete the painting of the Elizabeth Altarpiece and of the St Clare Polyptych. The study, for example, of the *Adoration of the Kings* (pl. 121) from that polyptych reveals a Virgin and Child derived from the same model book as the *Madonna with the Pea Blossom*, a kneeling king closely related to the donor figure in the Washington *Crucifixion*, and a central king whose thoughtful expression is that of God the Father in the *Trinity* panel. A date of around 1415–20 should therefore be considered for this work in the St Clare Polyptych. A *Sacra Conversazione* (no. 742) in Philadelphia, copying the unusual pose of the child from Conrad's Dortmund *Adoration of the Kings* may also belong to the group of works from the circle of the Veronica Master.

Later in his career in Cologne, the Veronica Master appears to have combined the local trend to elongate figures (this elongation may ultimately have derived from the slender French-influenced figures of the early panels of the St Clare Polyptych) with the Conradian courtly style.[39] The *Crucifixion with Mary, St John and Seven Apostles* (Cologne, WRM 14; *c.* 1420–25)(pl. 126) is plausibly attributed to the Veronica Master and his workshop. Stylistic similarities and especially the cloud punchmarks in the gold ground support this attribution, in spite of the much restored state of the panel. The elongation of the figures, as well as the differing punchwork in the haloes, connects this panel with a triptych in Berlin (no. 1627 A).

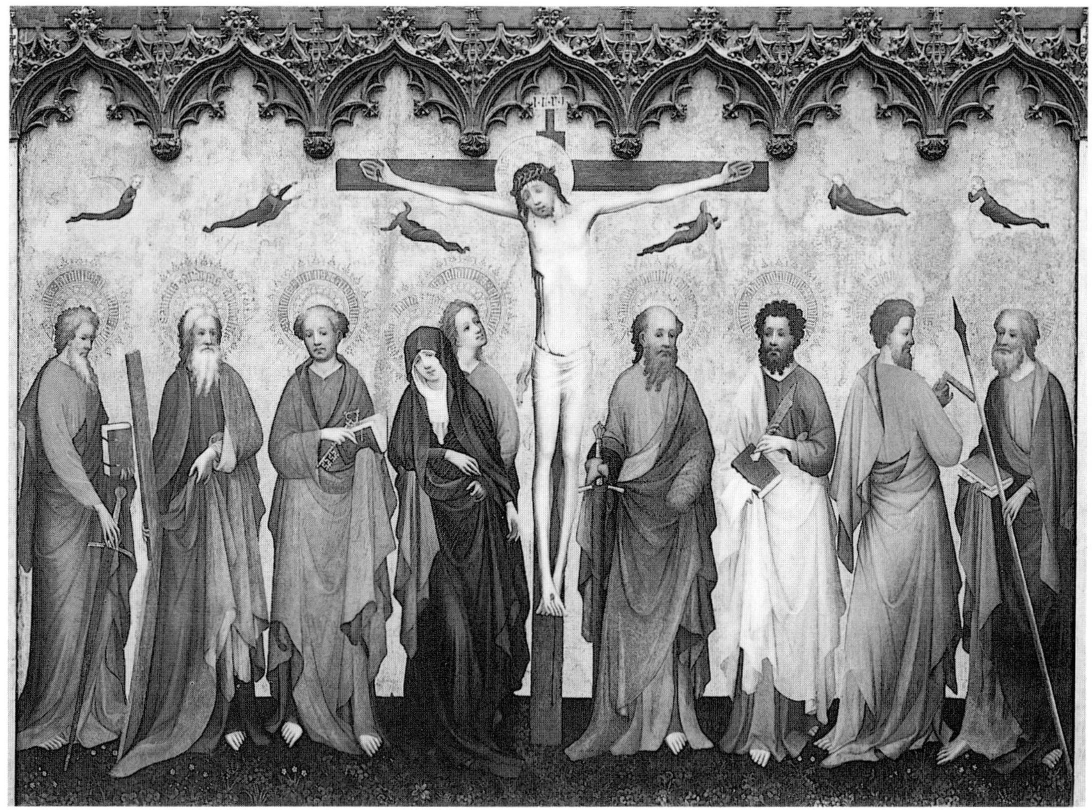

126. Veronica Master and workshop: *Crucifixion with Seven Apostles.*
Wallraf-Richartz-Museum, Cologne

The reverse of the wings of the triptych depict an *Annunciation* with figures and architecture reminiscent of Conrad's style. The angel approaches from the right, as at Niederwildungen, and a tiny Christ child carries the cross in the Westphalian manner. The Veronica Master shared this tendency to elongate figures with, for example, the painter of the *Crucifixion* altarpiece of the Rost von Cassel family (Darmstadt, GK 22; after 1409), the workshop of the Older Kinship Master (probably active into the 1430s), and the painter of the Wasservass Calvary (*c.* 1420) (pl. 117). Elongation can already be observed in the wing figures of the of the *Madonna with the Sweet Pea Blossom* triptych, although they follow Conrad's Münster saints in every other design aspect. The elongated figure style was perpetuated in Cologne into the 1440s by the Master of the Heisterbach Altarpiece.

Echoes of the art of Conrad von Soest persisted in Cologne after the presumed demise of the Veronica Master (after 1425?). The main exponent of the style then appears to have been the Lawrence Master (pl. 124). He reflects the Veronica Master's early style in the wing of an altarpiece (WRM 737; after 1420)(pl. 122) in which the *Coronation of the Virgin*, for instance, appears to be directly derived from Conrad's model. After 1430, the Lawrence Master also adopted the elongated style whilst still reflecting Conradian influence, in his Passion Altarpiece (WRM 20-31) of which only wing fragments survive.[40] An altarpiece of around 1430 from Münstereifel, now in the Pfarrkirche of Kirchsahr (pl. 127), and two Crucifixion triptychs

177

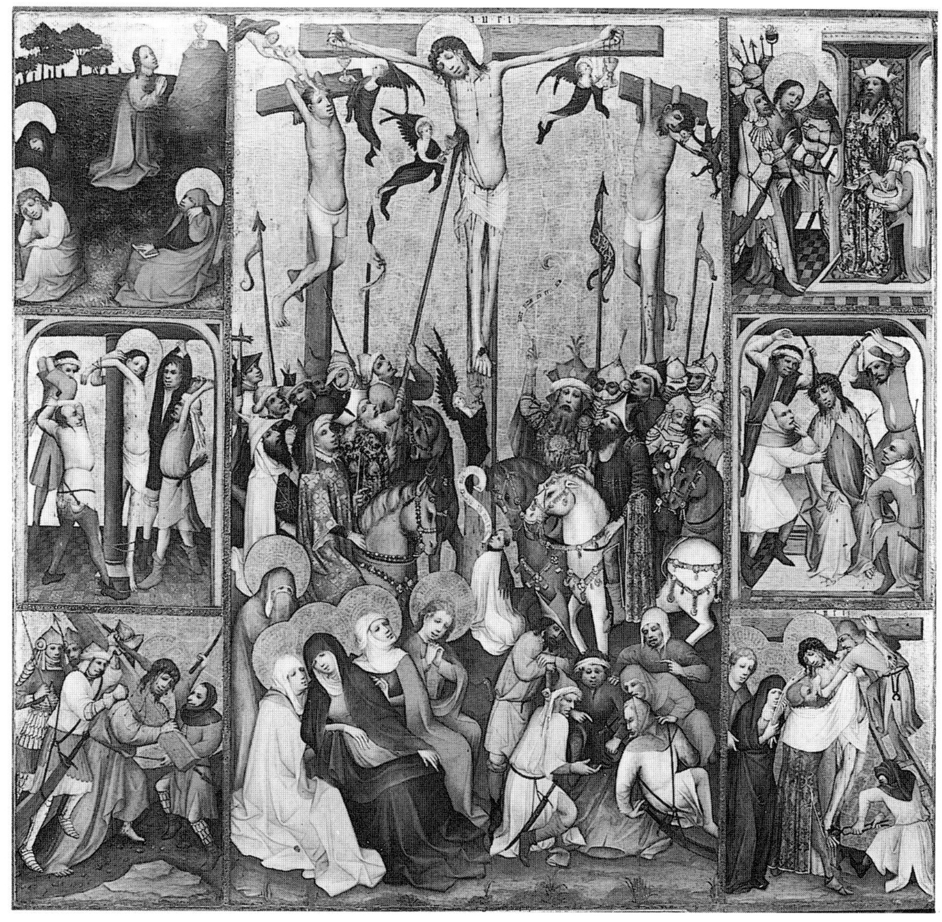

127. Master of the Kirchsahr
Altarpiece: *Central panel*.
Kirchsahr Altarpiece, Pfarrkirche,
Kirchsahr

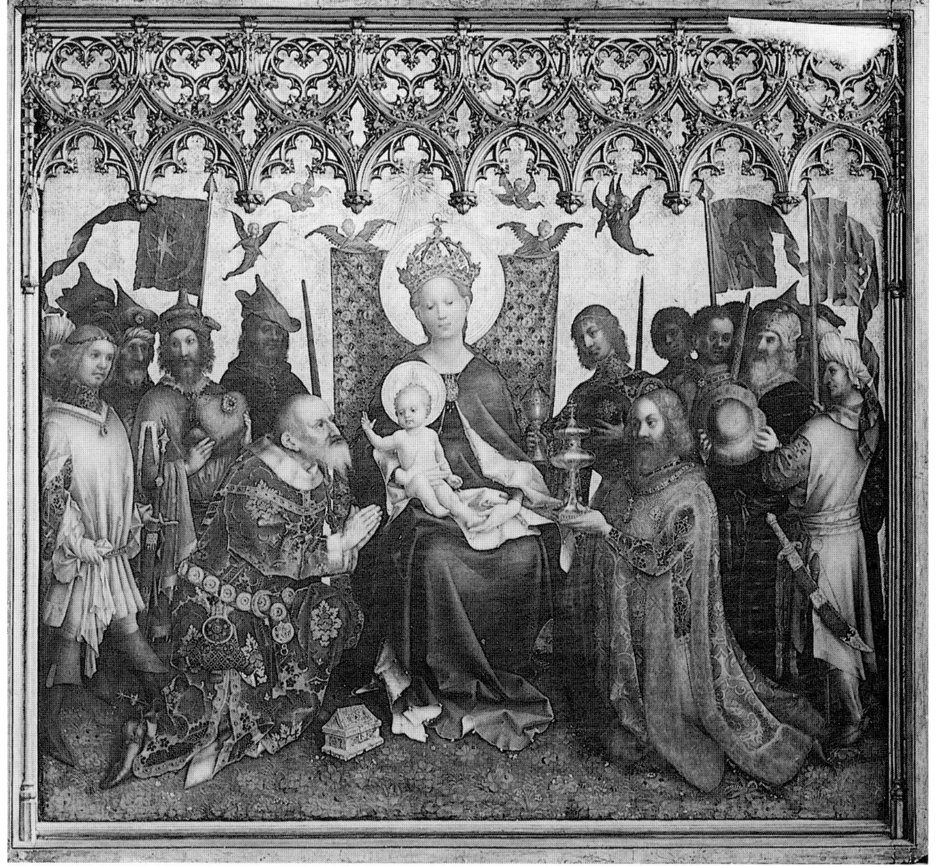

128. 'Stefan Lochner':
Adoration of the Kings. Altarpiece
of the Patron Saints of Cologne.
Cathedral, Cologne

by the Older Kinship Master (WRM 55 and Darmstadt, Landesmuseum, GK 23; both after 1430) provide obvious instances of the continued use of Conradian patterns in Cologne. In the 1440s the artist known as Stefan Lochner introduced new, Netherlandish, stylistic influences into the Cologne tradition. Even in Lochner's work, the continuing influence of Conrad's art is still reflected, for instance in the centralized composition of the *Adoration* in the Dombild (Cologne Cathedral) and in the use of the cloud punchmark in its gold ground (pl. 128).[41]

The soft modelling and different palette of the earlier panels by the Veronica Master make it unlikely that he trained as an apprentice in Conrad's workshop. However, we have seen that he was thoroughly acquainted with Conrad's work and production method, used analogous facial features in his early panels, and borrowed many models from Conrad's workshop. We have noted that he adopted Conrad's cloud punchmark and assimilated the punchwork in the angel's wings as well as the Conradian inscription and decoration of haloes. All this suggests that the Veronica Master entered Conrad von Soest's workshop as a journeyman, later transporting Conrad's style to Cologne.[42]

It may be impossible to provide documentary proof for a sojourn in Dortmund on the part of the Veronica Master, but stylistic and technical evidence point towards such a solution. Historical evidence can lend further support to this hypothesis. As discussed earlier (p. 21), the economic situation in Dortmund in the late 1390s held no promise of prosperity for a talented immigrant painter. The Feud of Dortmund of 1388–89 had drained the city coffers, and internal political unrest further undermined the financial stability of the town. Potential patrons still prospered, but they were unlikely to be indulging in conspicuous expenditure in Dortmund itself. Donations by Dortmund patricians are recorded in other towns at this time. Conrad von Soest himself accepted the commission from remote Wildungen. Members of some of the trading families removed themselves with a part of their assets to other Hanseatic towns for a time, and in the event some settled permanently—as in Cologne where considerable donations are recorded from Dortmund families, including the Lembergs, the Sudermanns, the Berswordts, the Gronpapes and the Trappes.[43] It is possible that one such Dortmund family, newly settled in Cologne, invited this gifted young painter from Conrad's successful workshop to come and work for them.

The Washington *Crucifixion* may provide evidence for this conjecture. The panel is thought to have been painted for the Carthusian monastery of St Barbara in Cologne.[44] Konrad Berswordt, a Dortmund patrician, made considerable donations to this monastery whilst his son Konrad was a monk there for nineteen years. Four brothers of the monk Konrad also became major patrons of the monastery: Johann, professor at Cologne University until his death in 1407, and Rector there in 1390; Nikolaus (d. after 1408); Lambert (witness to the 1394 marriage contract) and Segebodo (d. *c.* 1406), whose generosity prompted the title *magnus amicus et benefactor* in the register of patrons and caused him to be buried before the altar in the chapter house.[45] Since the Berswordt family was among those who moved some of their members and assets to Cologne, the Washington *Crucifixion* could be a Berswordt commission in memory of Konrad, who had died before 1395, or of his son the monk Konrad, who died in August 1396. The younger Konrad may be the Carthusian monk depicted in the panel. Segebodo Berswordt donated silver choir lights in memory of his brother Lambert, who died in 1397 (see cat. no. 4). As a major benefactor of the monastery, he would also wish to commemorate the other brother who predeceased him. For this task Segebodo would employ the young craftsman he had seen earlier in the workshop of his friend Conrad von Soest at Dortmund. This hypothesis of patronage would suggest a date of around 1405 the commission of for the *Crucifixion*, which accords with the felling date for the wood determined by dendrochronological analysis as between 1394/1398 and 1404+x (see note 33). The completion of the commission is then likely to have been supervised by one of Segebodo's surviving brothers or by his nephew Dr. Segebodo (professor at Cologne University until his death in 1455, and rector there in 1415 and 1433/34). The monastery records show that amongst many other gifts, he donated a painting for the chapter house, the burial place of his uncle Segebodo and possibly other members of the family.[46] With this commission, the Veronica Master introduced into Cologne the style of Conrad von Soest which had already found such acclaim in the Berswordts' home town. Because his style was then rapidly adopted in the local workshops, Conrad von Soest should be recognized as the true progenitor of the so-called 'School of Cologne'.

The skill of Conrad von Soest was clearly appreciated not only by his patrons but also by contemporary artists. He was a consummate craftsman and a creative, intelligent painter whose work was sufficiently admired by his cosmopolitan patrician townsmen for him to be entrusted with their most prestigious commissions. He was also—unusually for an artist—invited to join their exclusive social circle. His lyrical, yet sophisticated style came to dominate the art of his Westphalian contemporaries and followers, although none was to equal the quality of his craftsmanship. His influence was most profoundly felt in Cologne, where his style and designs were perpetuated for several decades. His stature was such that his influence spread beyond Northern Germany through the affluent world of Hanseatic trade, and echoes of his art may be found as far afield as England and the Netherlands. Thus Conrad von Soest played a pivotal role in the evolution of Northern European art. In view of the sad destruction of so many artefacts of that period, Conrad's altarpieces and panels represent a precious survival. They were in the mainstream of European stylistic development and their importance as representatives of monumental painting in the International Courtly Style around 1400 should not be underestimated.

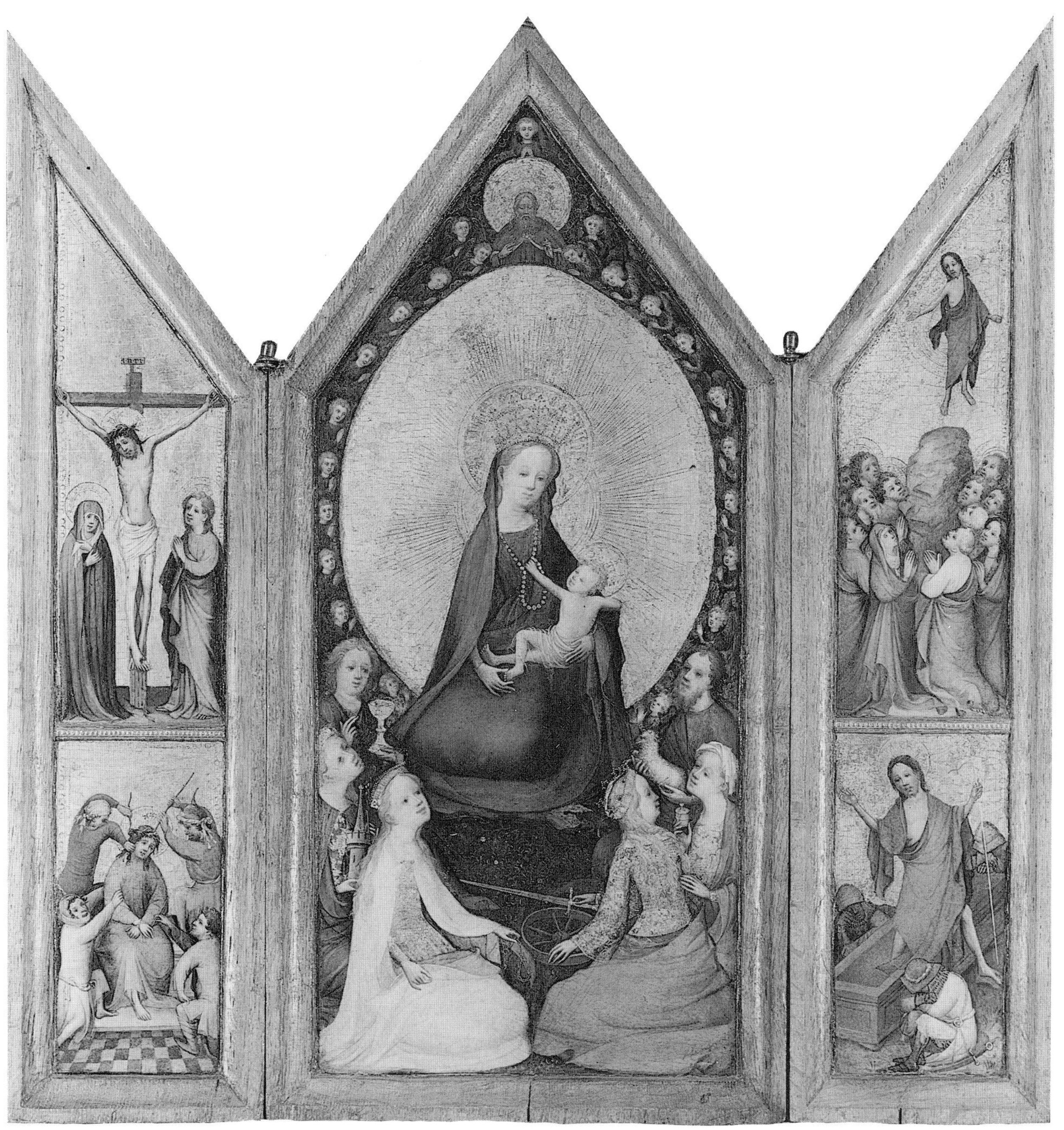

129. Veronica Master: *Sacra Conversazione Altarpiece*. Sammlung Heinz Kisters

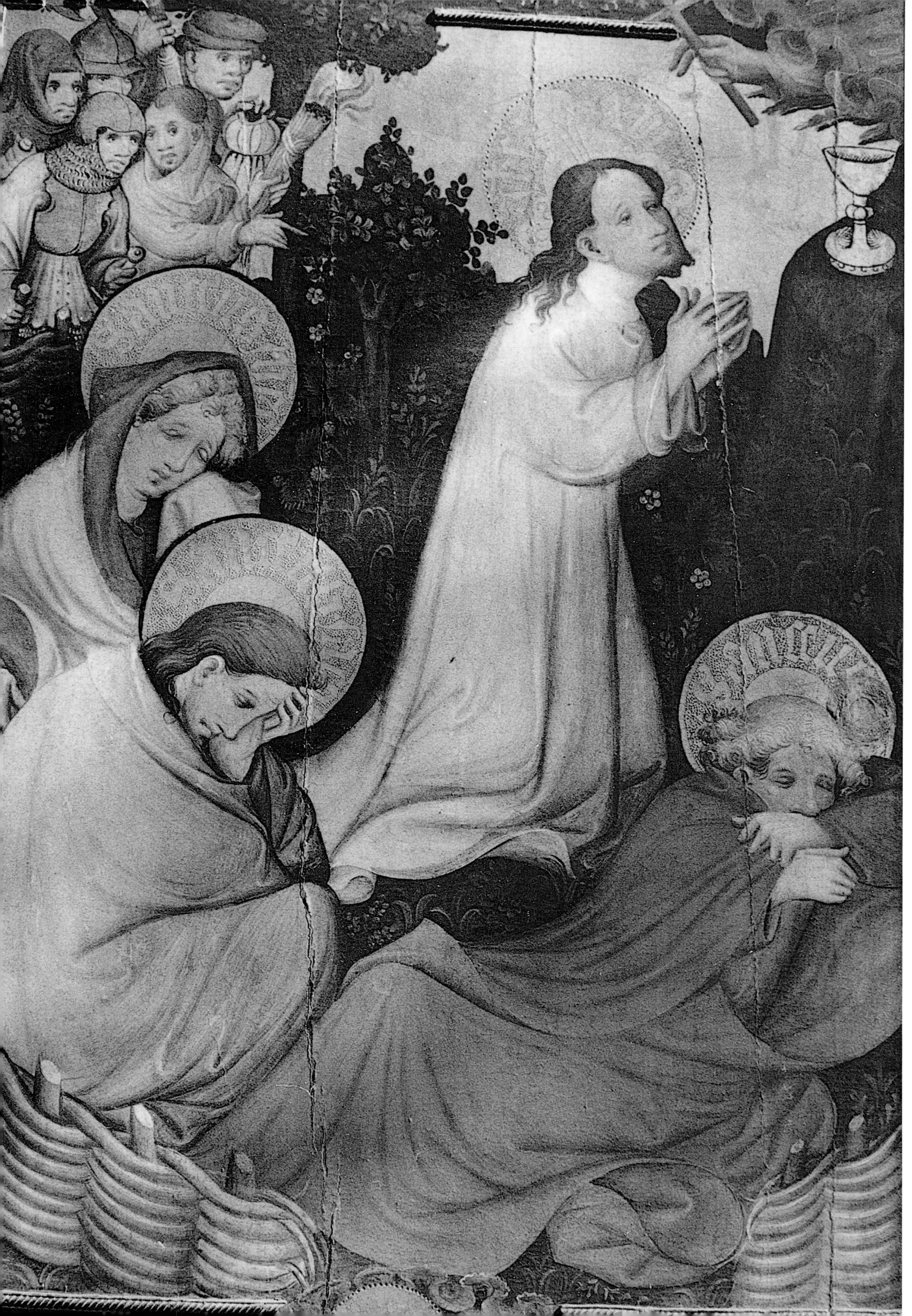

Catalogue

1. The Niederwildungen Altarpiece (pls. 131–138; I–XIX)

Conrad von Soest (signed)

LOCATION
High altar, Stadtkirche, Bad Wildungen.

SUBJECT
The opened altarpiece is decorated on a gold ground with four scenes from the childhood, and nine scenes from the passion of Christ to the Last Judgement(pl. 131). The subject of the left wing is the childhood of Christ, described in four paintings divided by embellished framing strips (pl. 135). The upper row shows the *Annunciation* and *Nativity*, the lower one the *Adoration of the Kings* and *Presentation in the Temple*. The passion of Christ can be read across the main panel and the right wing (pls. 136, 137). In the main panel a large, full-height *Crucifixion* is flanked by four half-height paintings. Events taking place before the Crucifixion are placed in the upper row and show the *Last Supper, Gethsemane* (pl. 130), *Christ before Pilate*, and, an unusual subject, *Christ mocked before Herod*. The lower row is devoted to events that happened after the Crucifixion: the *Resurrection, Ascension, Pentecost* and *Last Judgement*.

The original red frame is decorated with alternating rosettes and crescent-moon and star motifs. The sloping sides of the frame are painted green and are embellished with a stencilled flower design. Black strips, decorated with stylized flowers, frame each panel. These dividers are joined to the panel by a gold rope beading. The figures overlap these borders in some places. The designs on the frames form a strong, simple pattern and do not distract from the many-figured panels.

When closed, the altarpiece shows four saints standing on a podium against a red ground decorated with simple black flowers. *St Catherine* and *St John the Baptist* are shown in the left wing, with *St Elizabeth* and *St Nicholas* in the right wing (pls. 134, 138). The frames on the reverse face of the wings are painted red to match the background of the panels, and have green sides.

ORNAMENTATION
Delicate punched and tooled patterns are worked into the gold ground across all the inside panels of the altarpiece. A subtle inner frame of crown-of-thorns, turning in a rosette pattern at the corners, is softened by a floral 'fringe'. All haloes have elaborate punched decorations, exquisitely worked with inscriptions and floral ornaments. Rays surround painted clouds and angels in the *Crucifixion*, the *Ascension* (pl. 168) and the *Last Judgement*, and can also be found around a leafy branch in the *Annunciation*. A punch of stylized clouds is frequently used, for example in the *Resurrection* (pl. 169) and the *Last Judgement*. The angels in the *Last Judgement* blow punched trumpets decorated with tooled banners displaying the cross potent. Small gesso pearls decorate crowns and other jewels, as well as 'embroidered' areas of some garments.

INSCRIPTIONS
Signatures: inscribed along the base of the outside frame: '*hoc opus est completum per co[nradum pictorem de susato]/ sub anno domini MCCCC [terc]io [i]pso die beati egidii confessoris*' and at the base of the podium in the left wing: '*temporibus rectoris divinorum conradi stollen plebani*'. The letters in brackets can no longer be deciphered today. In addition, the altarpiece has two signatures, written vertically in the outer edge of a page in books in the *Annunciation* (..nrad) and *Pentecost* (conradu.) panels.

Annunciation: '*ave maria gratia plena dom...s tecum*' on the angel's scroll; '*maria*' in the Virgin's crown; and on her belt two letters 'm'.

Adoration of the Kings: three letters 'm' in Mary's crown.

Crucifixion: '*jasmus*' and '*dismas*' on the crosses of the thieves; '*vere filius dei erat iste*' in the scroll, held by the centurion.

130. Conrad von Soest: *Gethsemane*. Niederwildungen Altarpiece

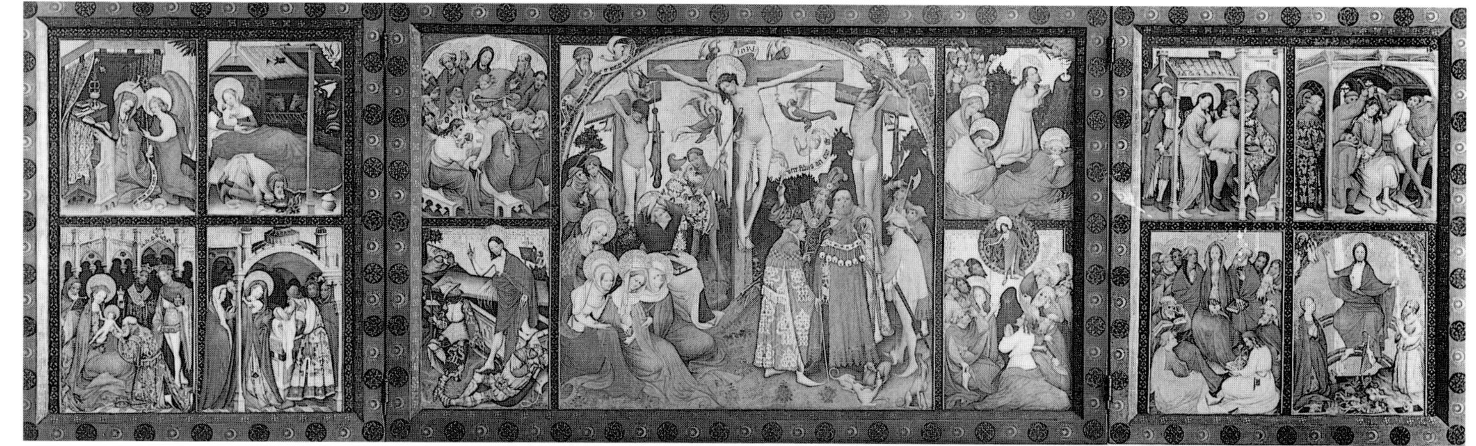

131. Conrad von Soest: *The Niederwildungen Altarpiece*

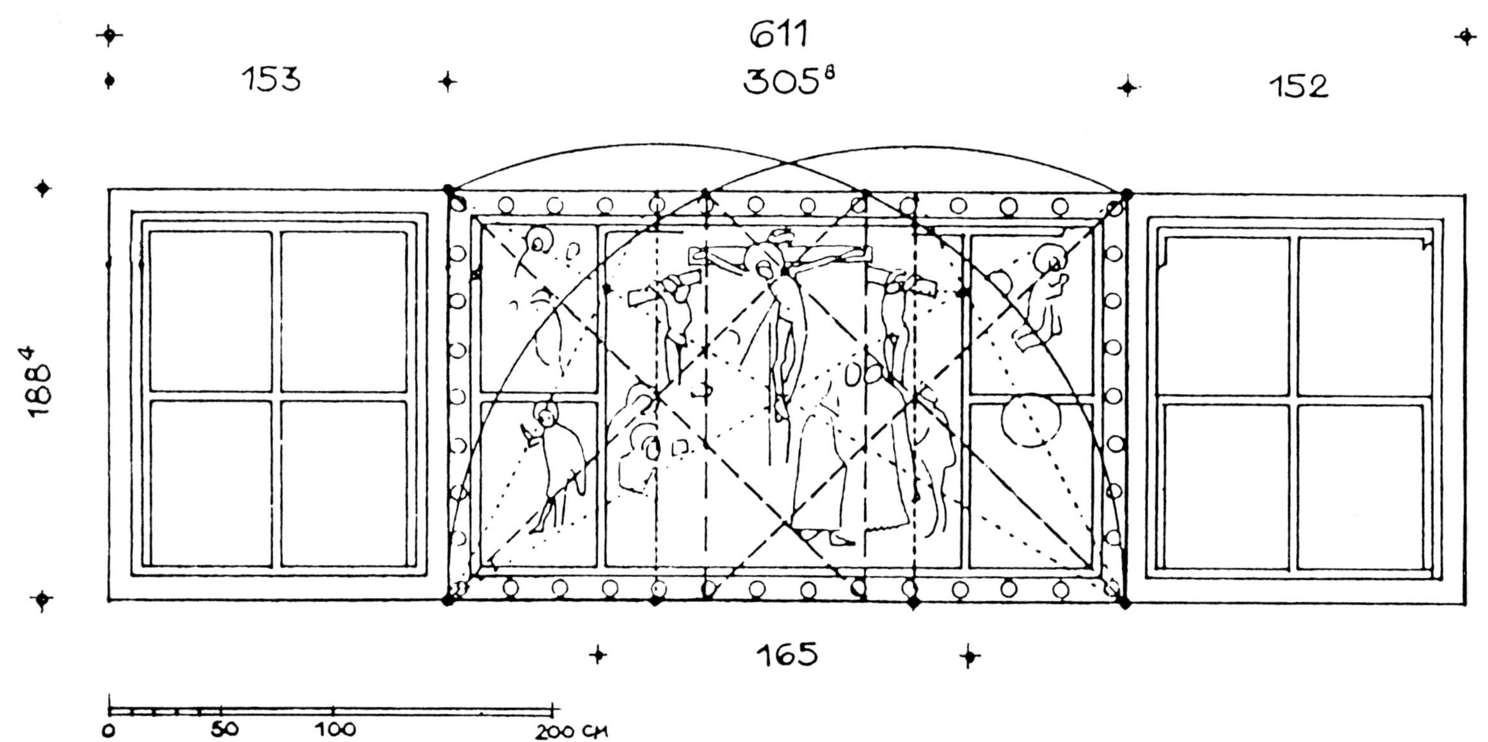

132. Drawing by Erwin Rohrberg of the *Niedrwildungen Altarpiece*

184

In the scrolls held by the prophets: left, *'morte propria mortus justificabat et morte vita permanebit'*, and right, *'ecce quo ... moritur monstratur(?) et nemo percipit corde'*.[1] The centurion's clasp carries the letters 'ESS'.

Pentecost: the text in the book of the apostle begins with the word *'aperit...'* and would therefore appear to recite the event of Pentecost; however, the remaining words are difficult to read owing to considerable restoration work in this area.

Haloes: are inscribed with the saint's name. On the reverse side of the wings, only St Catherine has three letters 's' inscribed in her crown.

Chronicle: The reverse side of the main panel bears scant remains of a local chronicle of the years 1319 to 1420 (pl. 133). The inscription was written in black with red initials on a white ground (Appendix B).[2] The early entries report pestilence and war. In 1378, water was first brought to the town from a spring. The arrival of the pope in 1416 at the Council of Constance is also recorded. The chronicle ends with a report of the Black Death of 1420.

CONSTRUCTION

Painted in tempera; made of oak-wood, with planks about 3 cm thick, of varying widths. The central panel is braced at the back by five cross-bars, the wings are strengthened by two horizontal planks, inset. The heavy wooden frames are part of the original construction.

RECONSTRUCTION

The altarpiece is likely to have had a predella.

SIZE

Opened, including frames:
    height: 188.4 cm, width: 611 cm
    width of central panel: 305.8 cm
    Without frames:
    small panels next to *Crucifixion*: 77 × 54.5 cm
    wing scenes:73.5 × 57 cm
    width of wings: 127 cm
    width of central panel: 276.25 cm
    height of central panel: 160.4 cm
    width of *Crucifixion* segment: 165 cm
    width without framing strips: 158.5 cm

The width of the frame varies between *c.* 12.7 cm in the vertical part of the wings and *c.* 14.5 cm around the central panel. The Golden Section is applied in the altarpiece with a width of 305.8 cm to the height of 188.4 cm (an accurate use of the 13:8 rule would give a height of 188.2 cm, but the difference of 0.2 cm could well be due to the carpenter's lack of precision). Conrad's application of complex geometry is also shown in the measurement of the small paintings on the central panel. Here the height of the rectangle is the length of a diagonal of the square of the base (ratio base to height 1 : 2, that is 54.5 × 77 cm).[3] The painter also considered the relationship between the altarpiece and its surrounding architecture. The choir is formed by five equal sides of an octagon, based on a square of *c.* 7.72 m. Each side of the octagon measures *c.* 3.15 m. Vaulting shafts narrow each actual wall-space to 3.05 m, and this is the size of the closed Niederwildungen Altarpiece. The Gothic window behind the altarpiece measures 165 cm, the size of the *Crucifixion* square.

DATE

The altarpiece was dated 1403 in the damaged inscription on the frame, cited above.

HISTORY

The inscription on the frame of the Niederwildungen Altarpiece records that it was completed on 1 September 1403. It is reasonable to assume that it was placed on the high altar of the Stadtkirche in Niederwildungen near that time.[4]

In 1532, when Count Philipp III of Waldeck ordered the Commander of the Order of St John to remove Catholic ornaments from the church, the retable remained.[5] It appears to have been saved by the interest that the chronicle inscribed on the reverse of the main panel inspired in early visitors to the Spa town.[6] The altarpiece seems to have been placed closed against a side wall in the nave of the church and to have rested there for over 300 years. The Niederwildungen Altarpiece was thus protected from destruction when the choir of the Stadtkirche collapsed in the 1840s. After the rebuilding of the choir, the altarpiece was replaced in its original position on the high altar, and the historian Curtze described

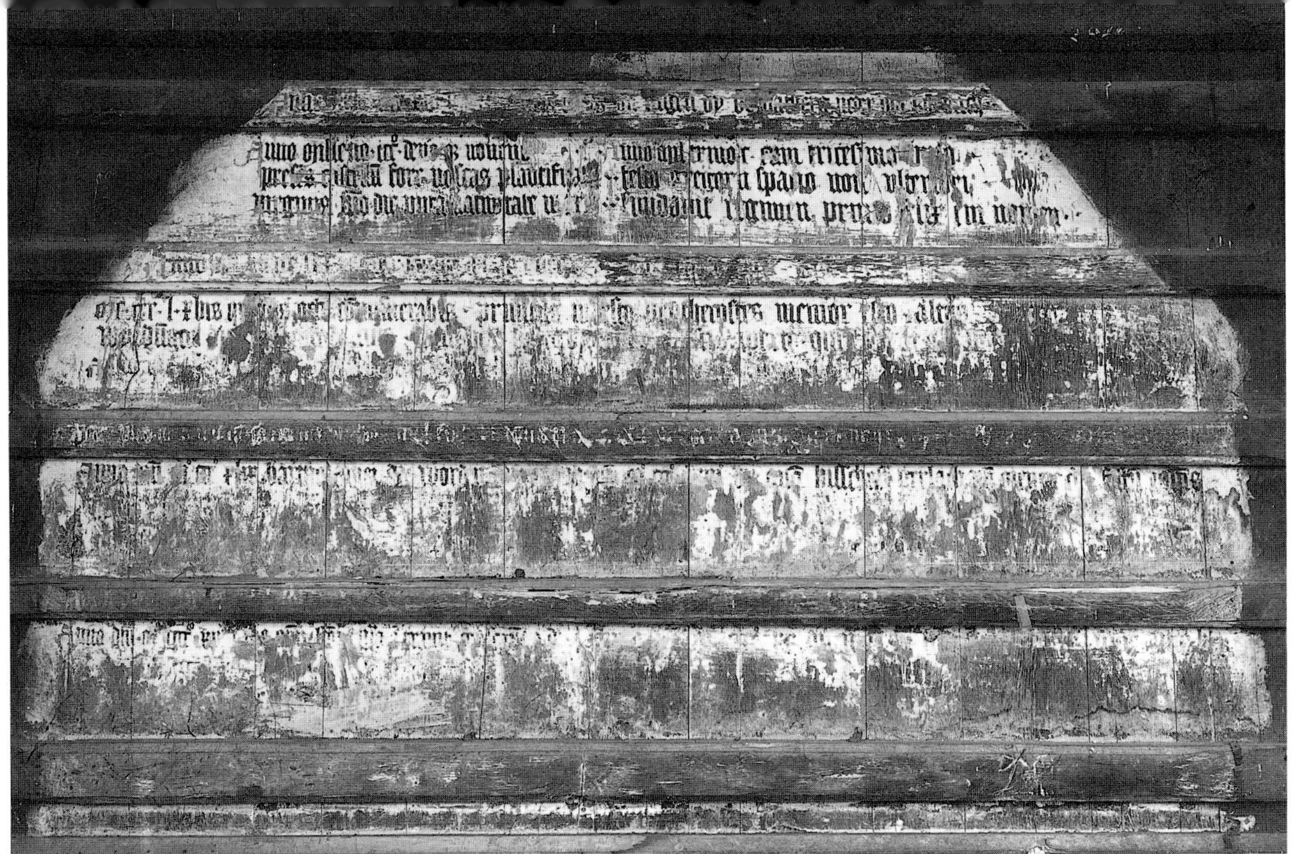

133. *Chronicle*. Inscription on the reverse of the Niederwildungen Altarpiece

it there in 1850.[7] In 1906, Schmitz lamented the fading of colours, the flaking of paint, and the four iron screws defacing the panels; he noted further damage to the panels caused by the use of candles and as a result of droppings from birds and bats. Despite registering his concern over these problems, Schmitz found the condition of the altarpiece unchanged in 1917.[8] During this period, Pfarrer Lau had resisted several offers of a restoration free of charge; he had also refused to sell the altarpiece to the Kaiser Friedrich Museum in Berlin in 1907.[9] By 1924, the use of central heating in the church had caused the first cracks in the wood.

The Landesamt für Denkmalspflege in Hessen has, in their words, 'no records at all of conservation work carried out' and only notes that 'the late Herr Jobst restored this altarpiece [in 1950]'; Alfred Stange only mentions the restoration of 1950.[10] However, the altarpiece was in fact first restored in 1924: the Director of the Gemäldegalerie in Kassel, Georg Gronau, persuaded Pfarrer von Haller to permit the painter Alfred Breuer to conserve the panels.[11] The restoration of the right wing was completed in 1925 and caused a storm of protest. In a local paper August Fink complained of the thoughtless overpainting, which included the completion of the damaged inscription date (to read 1404).[12] An inspection report by Landeskonservator Hiecke (advised by Max Friedländer) criticized the coarse overpainting of this 'valuable work of art' and the damaging experimental crack-filling. It further pointed out that Breuer had only been engaged to remove discoloured glazes and to conserve, not restore the paintings; the removal of all of Breuer's overpainting was therefore recommended, together with his dismissal.[13] As the painting on the obverse side was excellently preserved, it needed only a little cleaning, after removing Breuer's additions as far as possible (with the exception of the frame of the left wing, where small areas of paint had to be stabilized). To prevent further damage it was decided to remove the central heating from the choir area. The altarpiece was exhibited in Münster in 1930 (no. 201) and in Marburg in 1932 (no. 144). During the Second World War it had been stored in a bunker next to the new 'Bürgerhaus' in Bad Wildungen.

186

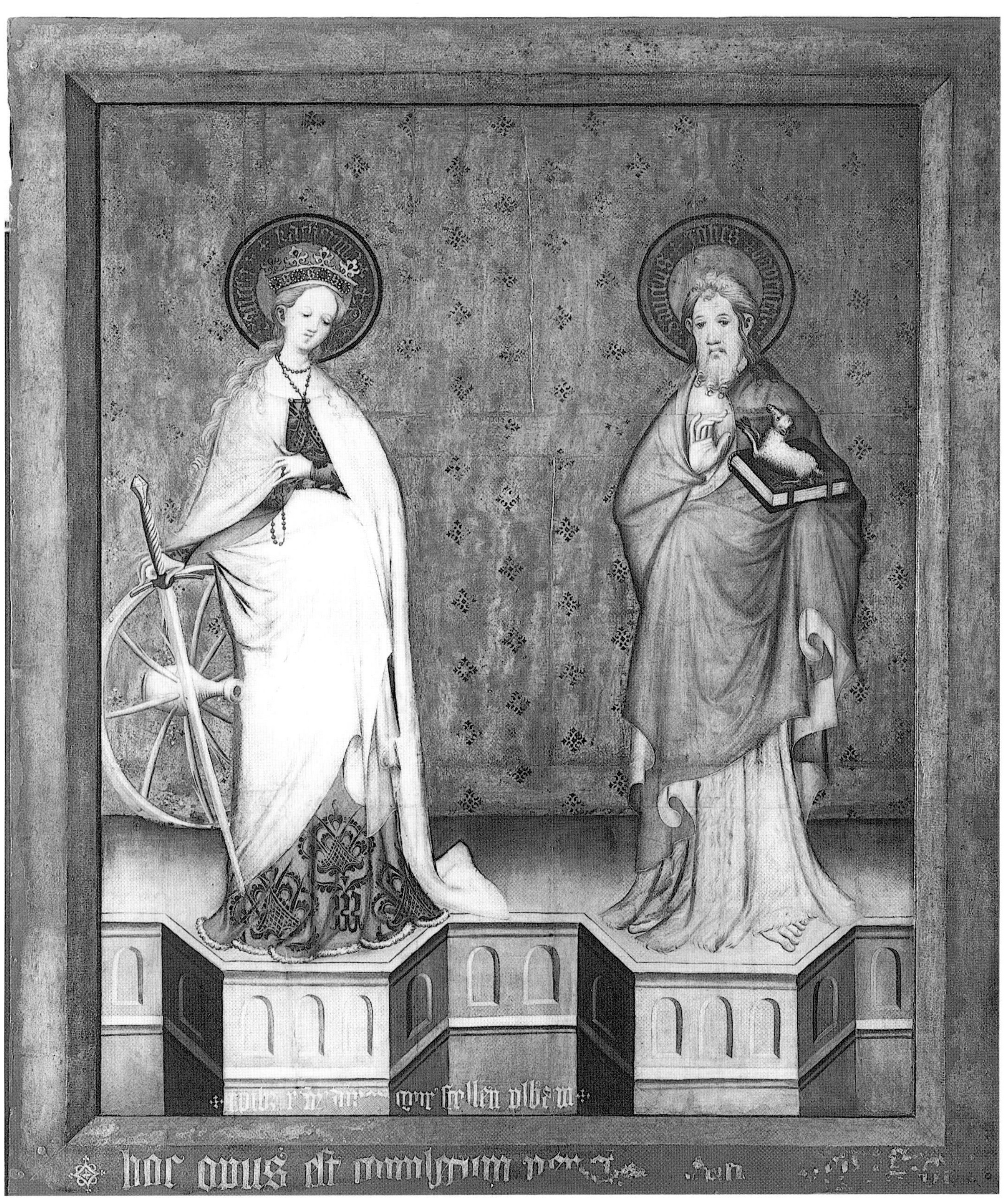

134. Conrad von Soest: *St Catherine and St John the Baptist*. Reverse side of the left wing.
Niederwildungen Altarpiece

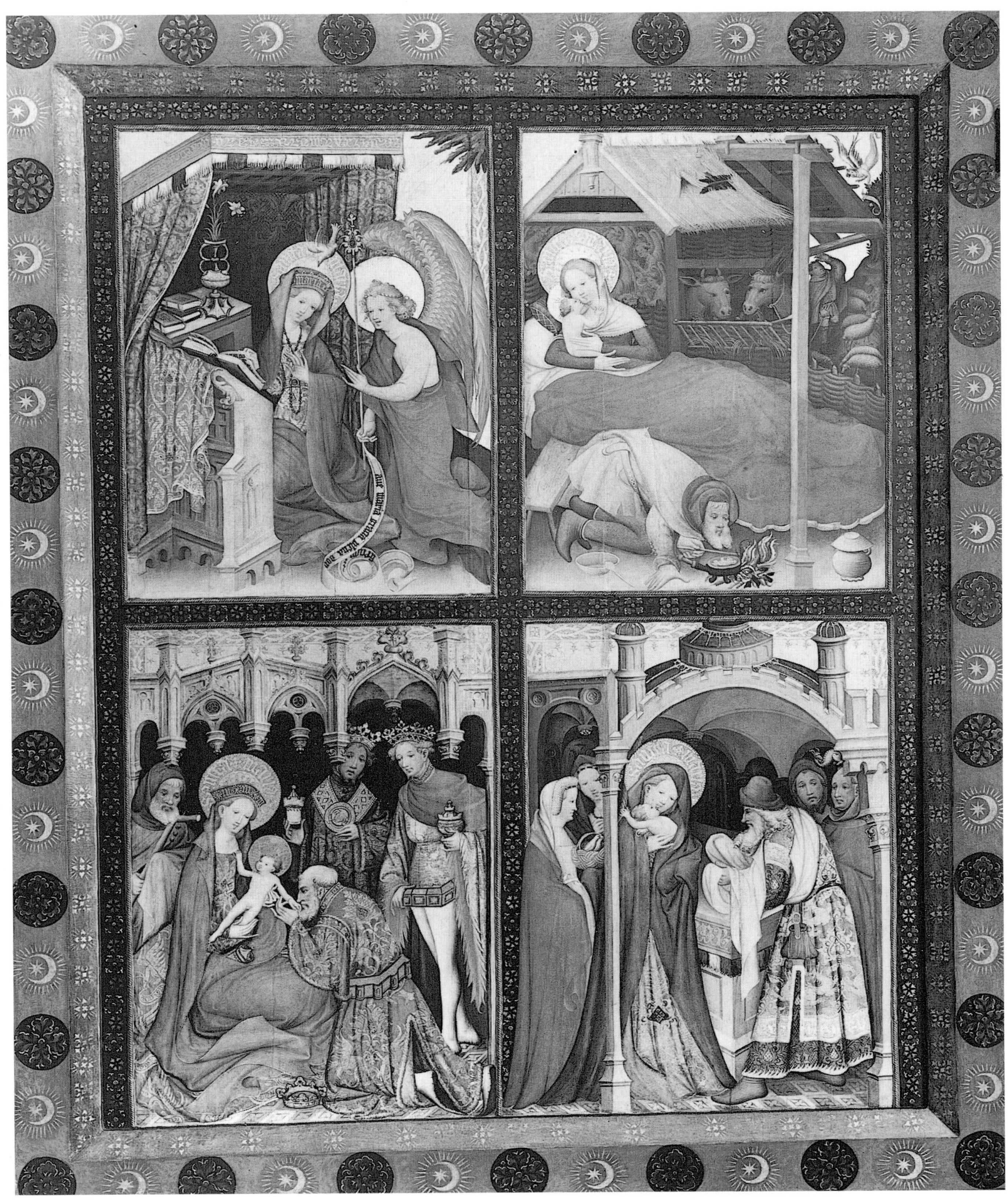

135. Conrad von Soest: *Left Wing.* Niederwildungen Altarpiece

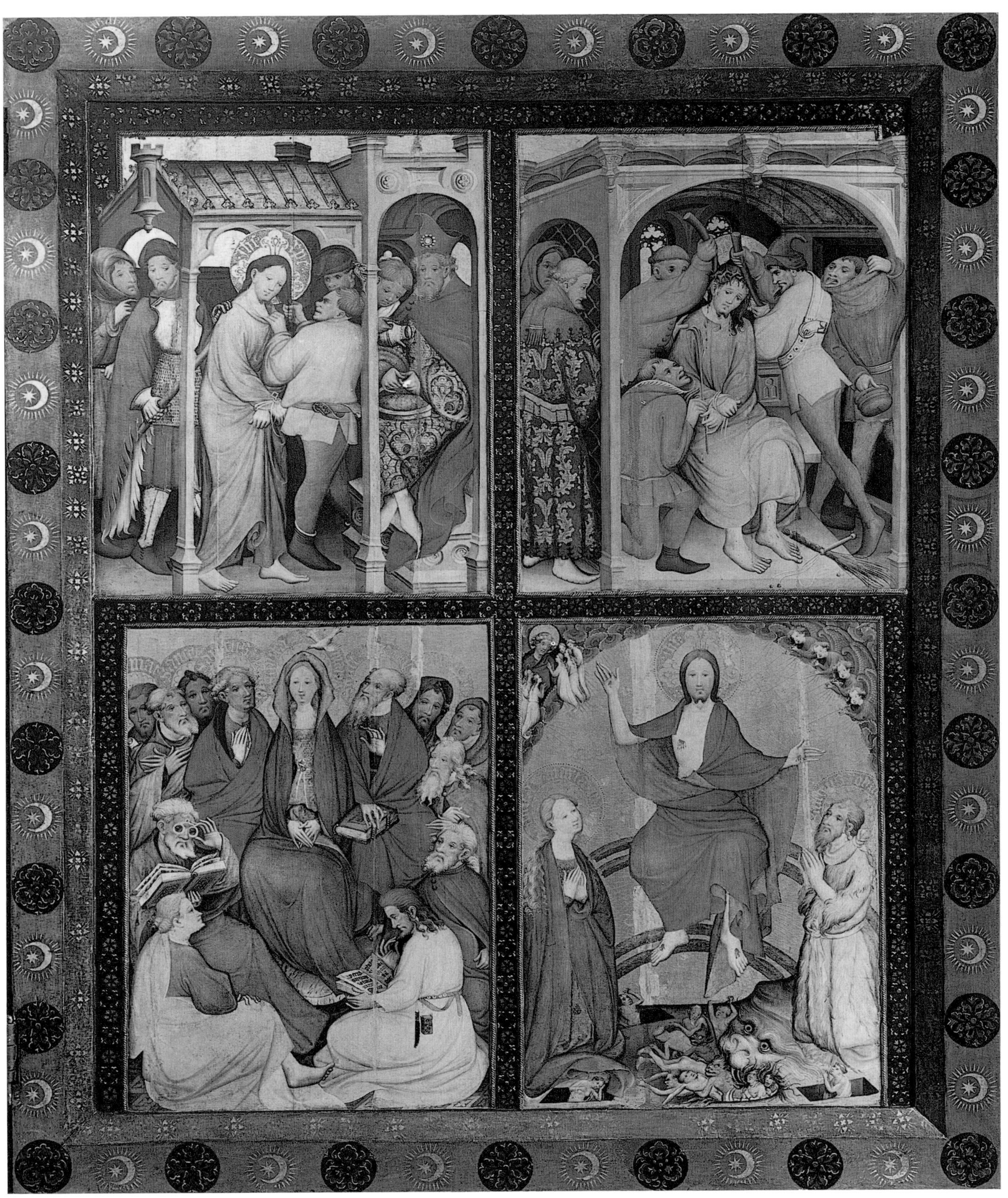

136. Conrad von Soest: *Right Wing*. Niederwildungen Altarpiece

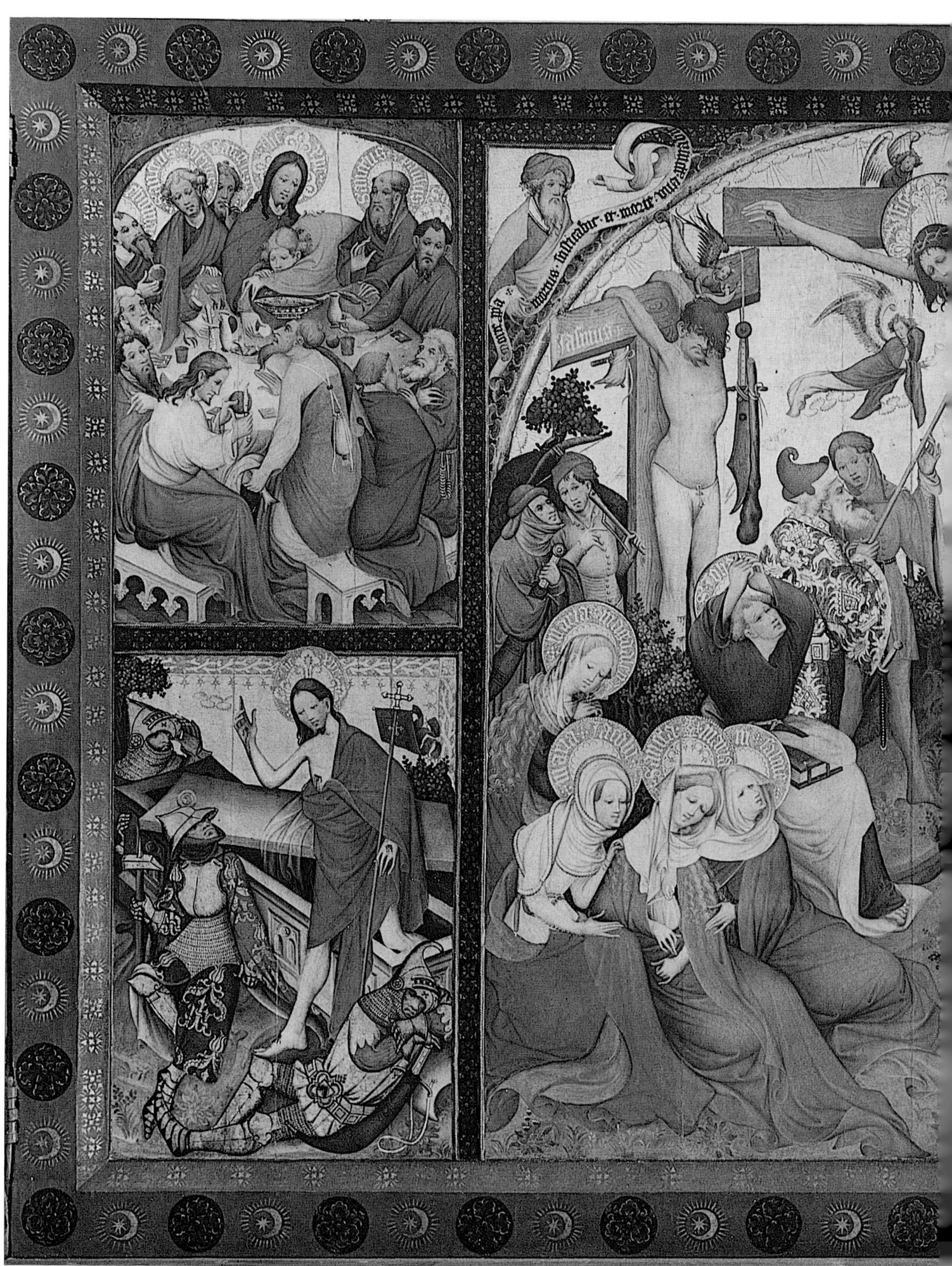

137. Conrad von Soest: *Central Panel*. Niederwildungen Altarpiece

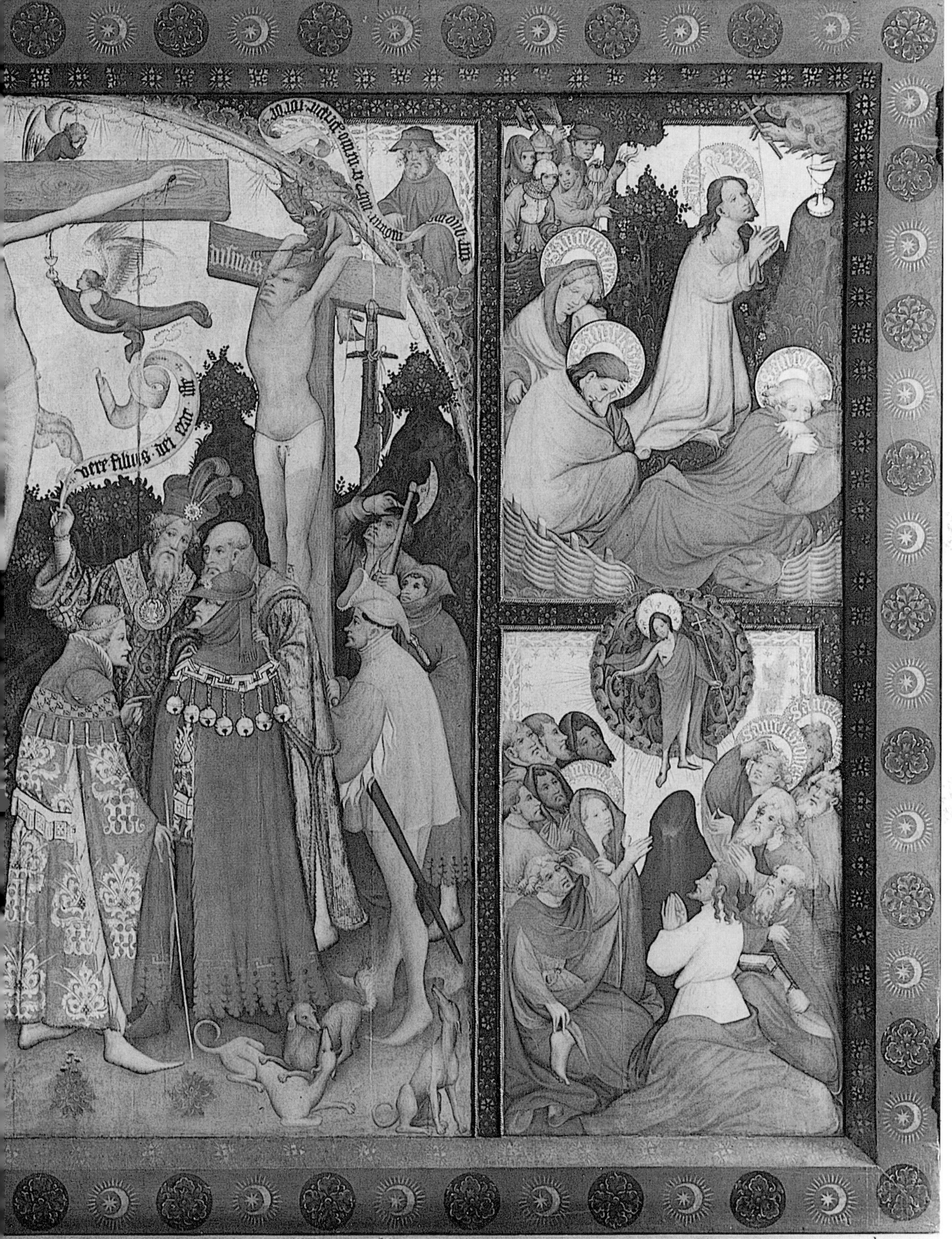

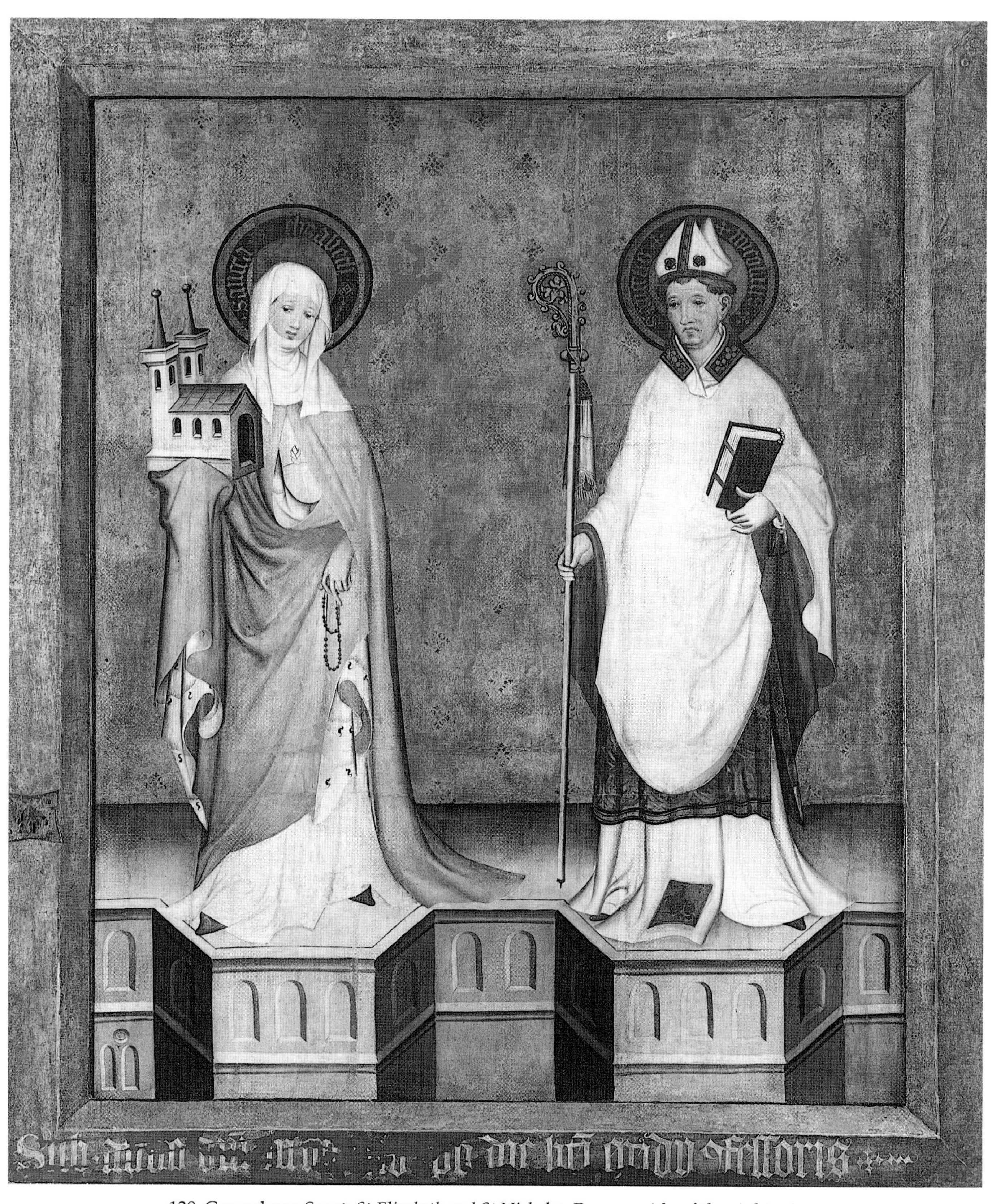

138. Conrad von Soest: *St Elizabeth and St Nicholas*. Reverse side of the right wing.
Niederwildungen Altarpiece

The altarpiece was again cleaned and restored at the time of the exhibition in Cappenberg in 1950 (nos. 38–52), this time by restorer Alfred Jobst under the supervision of the Hessian Landeskonservator Bleibaum. Although Jobst left no record of his work, Wolfgang Medding gave a detailed account of the restoration in a local paper.[14] He recorded that the central heating of the church had caused further large cracks in the wood, and that layers of discoloured varnish had dulled the colours to a 'brown, sometimes black' tonality. He stated that the inside of the altarpiece was only damaged at the base of the panels, possibly owing to amateur cleaning of candle-smoke stains with abrasive materials; the paint of two small flowers in the lower right part of the *Crucifixion* was so damaged underneath the discoloured varnish that it was decided to leave the varnish intact.[15] The reverse sides of the wing panels were seriously damaged and considerable areas of paint were missing.

By the time of the Cappenberg exhibition, only the cleaning of the central panel and the *Annunciation* had been completed. Brilliant colours and beautiful details had been revealed from under the layers of discoloured varnish, although the first coat of varnish had been left intact to preserve the paintwork. Large cracks and the four bolt holes were filled with a flexible material; smaller cracks were just glued together. The colours on the damaged reverse sides of the wings were stabilized, but no overpainting was allowed. Any necessary addition of colour was carefully toned to blend in, but not to deceive. Small areas of the cord-type beading were missing and had to be renewed. The restored panels were finished with two layers of protective varnish and a skim of egg-tempera emulsion. Further areas of overpainting, discovered through examination by infra-red photography, are discussed above (p. 64). The central panel of the Niederwildungen Altarpiece was exhibited after the restoration in Marburg in 1950, and only one wing was shown in Vienna in 1962 (no. 30).[16] It was possible to lend the wing because extensive restoration work in the church had caused the altarpiece to be removed to the Martin-Luther-Haus, where services were being held at that time. The altarpiece was returned to the church in 1966.

In recent years exposure to light through the plain glass windows and through the automatic lighting system, as well as the uneven central heating, have again damaged the altarpiece, causing blistering and reopening of the cracks in the wood. Since September 1993 the Niederwildungen Altarpiece is being restored by the Landesamt für Denkmalspflege Hessen, advised by the art historian Paul Pieper.

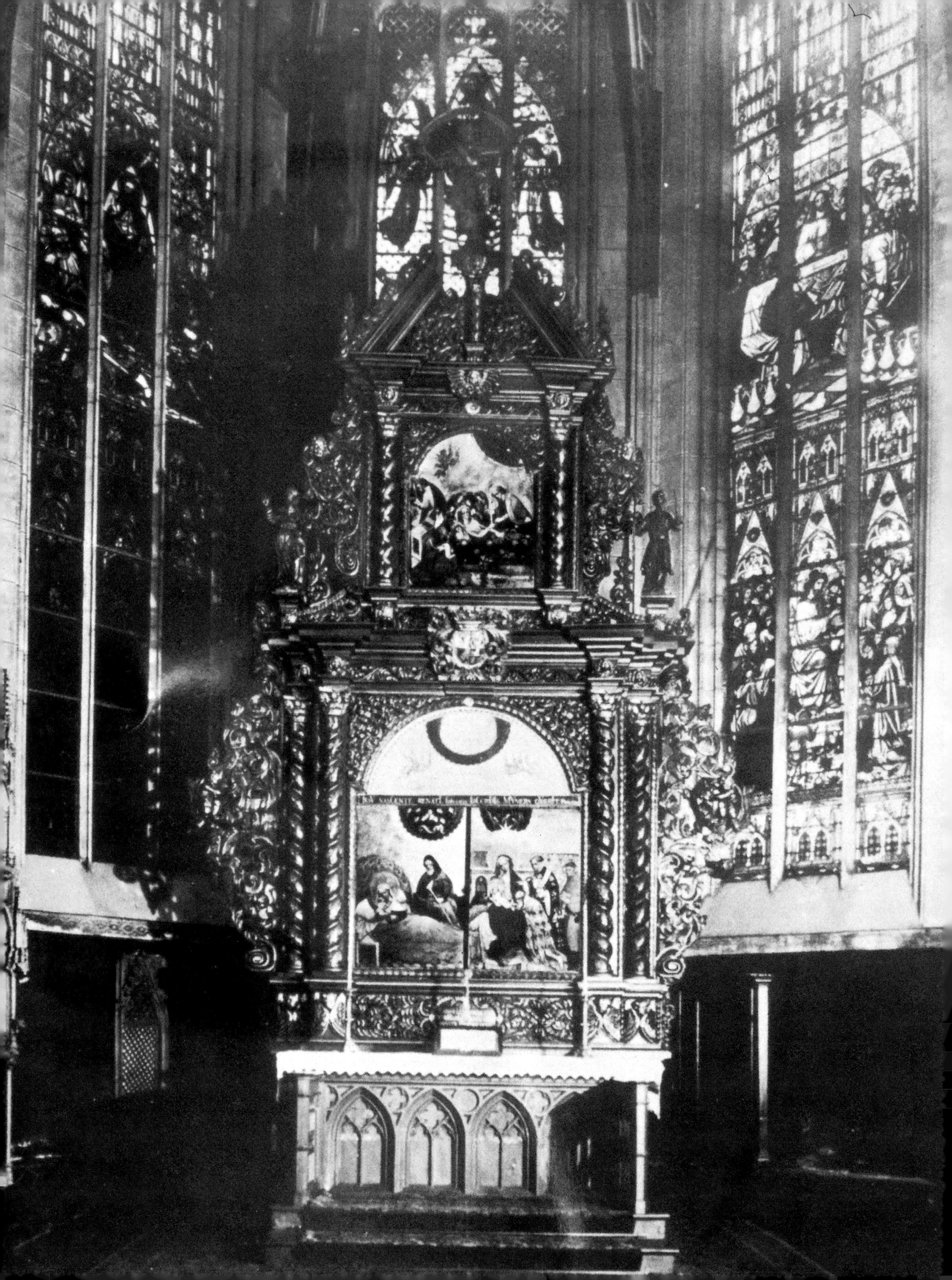

2. The Dortmund Altarpiece (pls. 139–149; XX–XXII, XXV–XXVIII)

Conrad von Soest (signed)

LOCATION
High Altar, Evangelische St Marienkirche, Dortmund.

SUBJECT
The altarpiece is decorated with scenes from the life of the Virgin Mary. The opened altarpiece depicts on a gold ground the *Death of the Virgin*, flanked by the *Nativity* and the *Adoration of the Kings*; the closed retable showed the *Annunciation* and the *Coronation of the Virgin*.

ORNAMENTATION
Delicate punched and tooled patterns are worked into the gold ground: the gilded panels are framed by a band of oak-leaves, with rosettes at the corners, softened by a floral 'fringe'. The punch of stylized clouds, already seen in the Niederwildungen Altarpiece, is used on all three inside panels. All haloes have elaborate punched decorations, intricately worked with inscriptions and floral ornaments. Rays surround painted clouds, angels and Mary's halo. Tooled angels with long, feathery wings float above the cloth of honour on the right side of the *Adoration of the Kings* (pl. 15, 73). The angels drawn on the gold ground above the Virgin in the *Death of the Virgin* pl. 149) are daintily tooled in their wings and robes. They carry a tooled scroll (pl. 16). This tooling gives the angels an unstable, floating, supernatural quality when observed in candle-light. Small gesso pearls decorate crowns and other jewels, as well as 'embroidered' areas of some garments.

INSCRIPTIONS
Signatures: There is a signature of the painter in a book in the *Death of the Virgin* (con.ad), written vertically in the outer edge of a page.

Annunciation: *'ave gratia plena dominus tecum'* on the angel's scroll and in the Virgin's Book of Hours: *Deus in adiutorium meu[m] in tende domine ad adiuvandum [me festina]*.

Death of the Virgin: *'..noms dnos'* on the scroll on the desk; on the scroll of the reading apostle:

*diffusa est/gratia in la/biis tuis prop/terea
benedi/xit te deus...
laus copia/Gaudent/chori ange/loru[m] con-
sor/tiu[m] et ara/cuius Deu[m] /alle-uia*

This scroll inscription, part of a prayer from the *'commendatio animae'*, can now only be read in infra-red photographs (pl. 34).

Adoration of the Kings: 'sancta maria mater christi' in Mary's halo; on the stole of the standing king and on the cloth of honour are several 'm's.

Haloes: all haloes are inscribed with the saint's name.

CONSTRUCTION
Painted in tempera; made of oak-wood, the altarpiece was adapted to fit into a Baroque frame in 1720.[1] Three fragments survive, fitted into an iron framework. They are arranged as a fixed triptych with the reverse sides of the wings protected by sliding doors because of their fragile condition. This framework does not permit examination of the back of the central panel. In a manuscript restoration report, however, Robert Hieronymi states that the retable consists of oak planks, 2.5 cm thick, braced only at the top with a heavy crossbar.[2] He could not measure the width of these planks, as they were concealed behind protective layers of oil paint. Unpublished X-ray photographs taken by Rolf Fritz in 1950 showed that the planks were glued and held by internal iron dowels.[3] Unfortunately, Fritz left the space for the the measurement of the planks blank in his memorandum.

139. Baroque frame of 1720, Dortmund Altarpiece

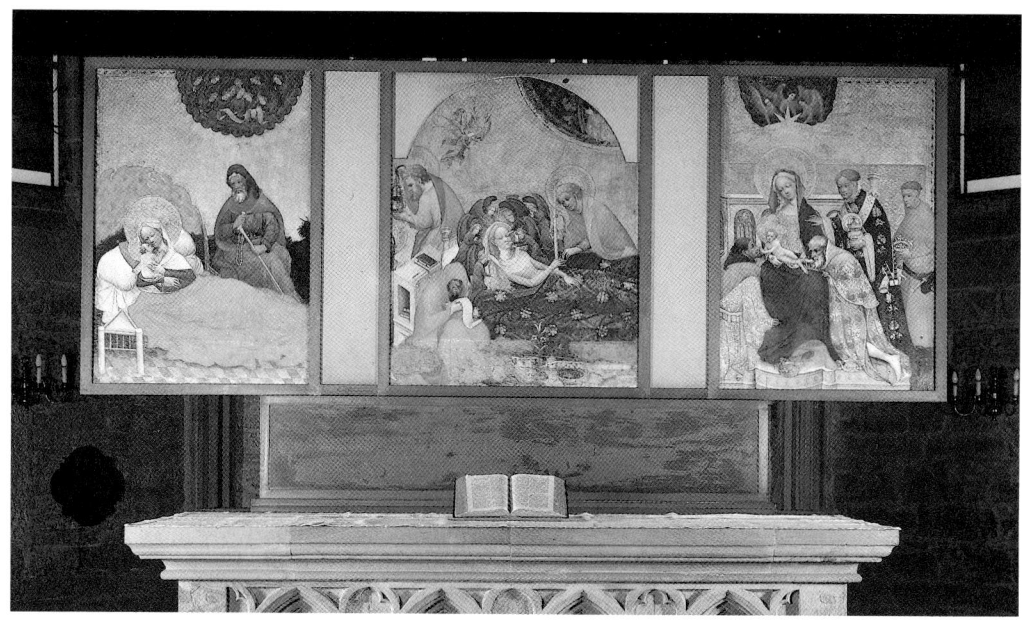

140. Conrad von Soest: *The Dortmund Altarpiece*

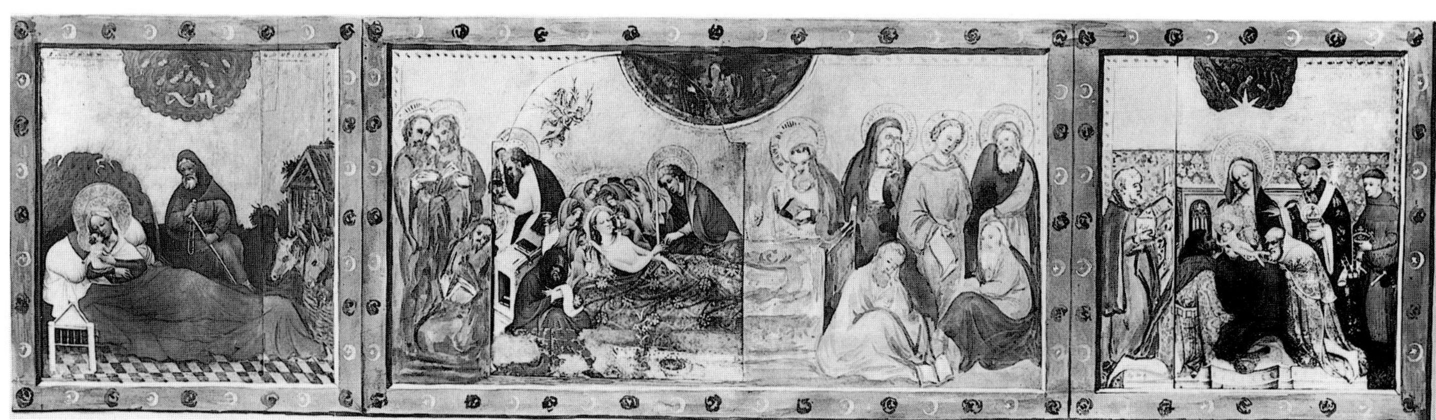

141. Reconstruction by Max Geisberg of the *Dortmund Altarpiece*

142. Reconstruction by Rolf Fritz of the *Dortmund Altarpiece*

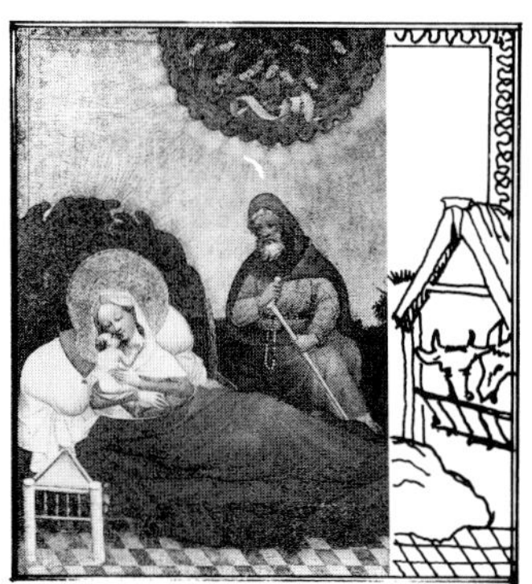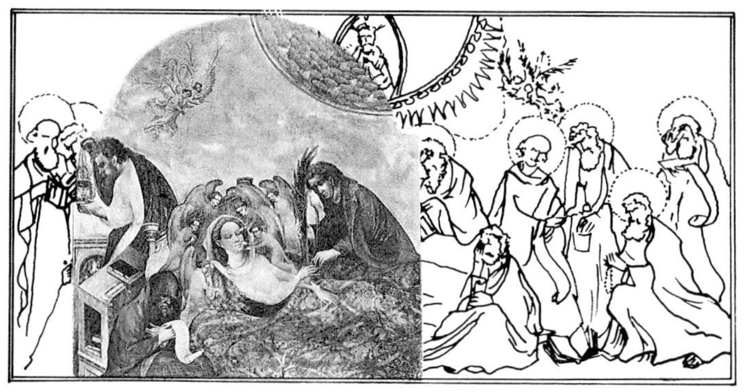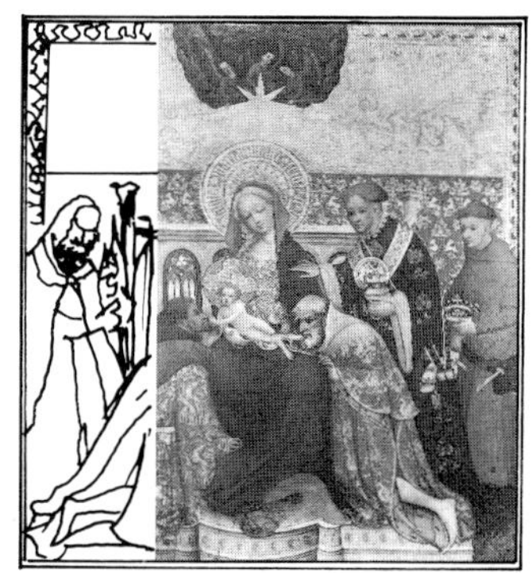

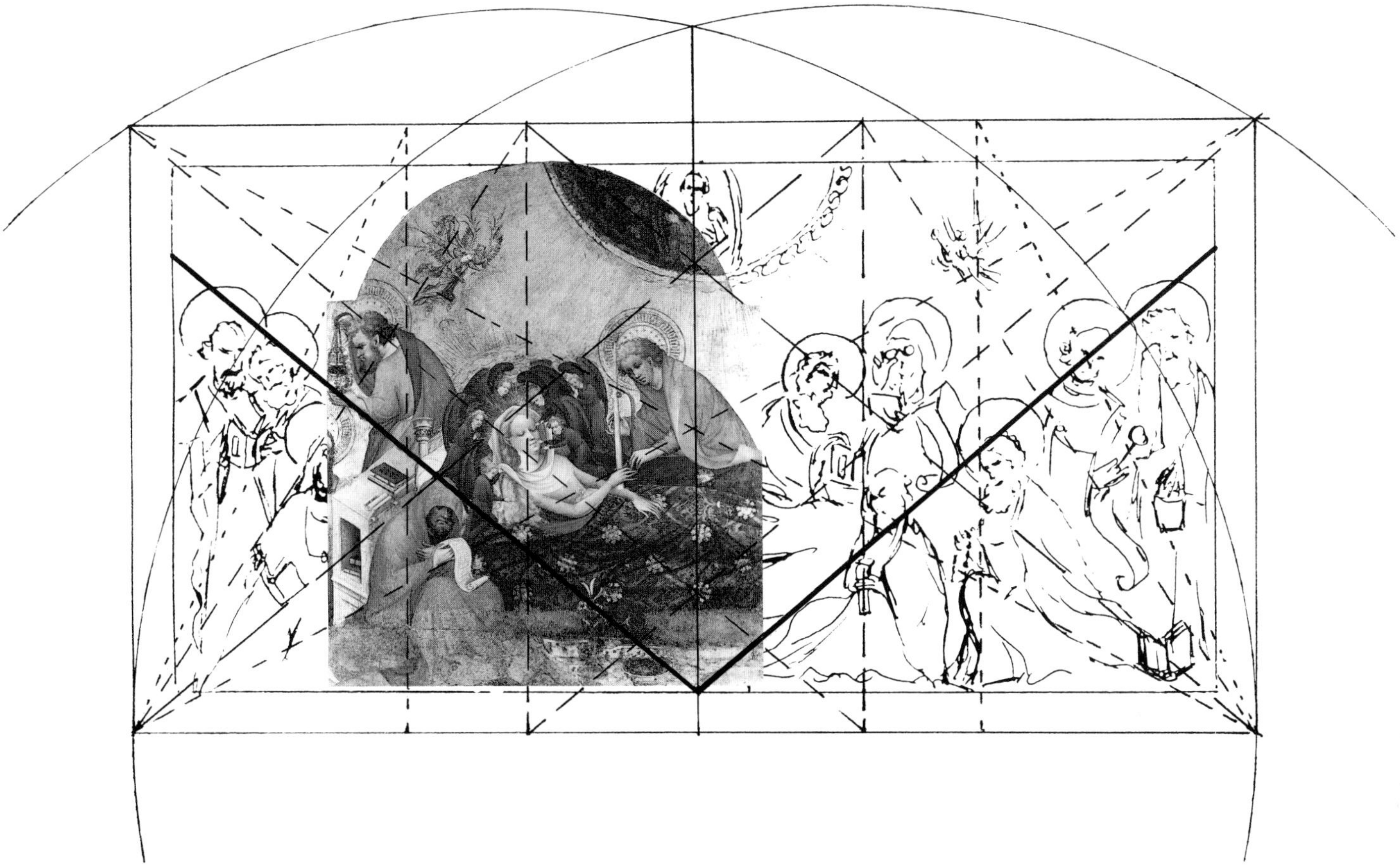

143. Reconstruction by the author of the *Death of the Virgin*, Dortmund Altarpiece

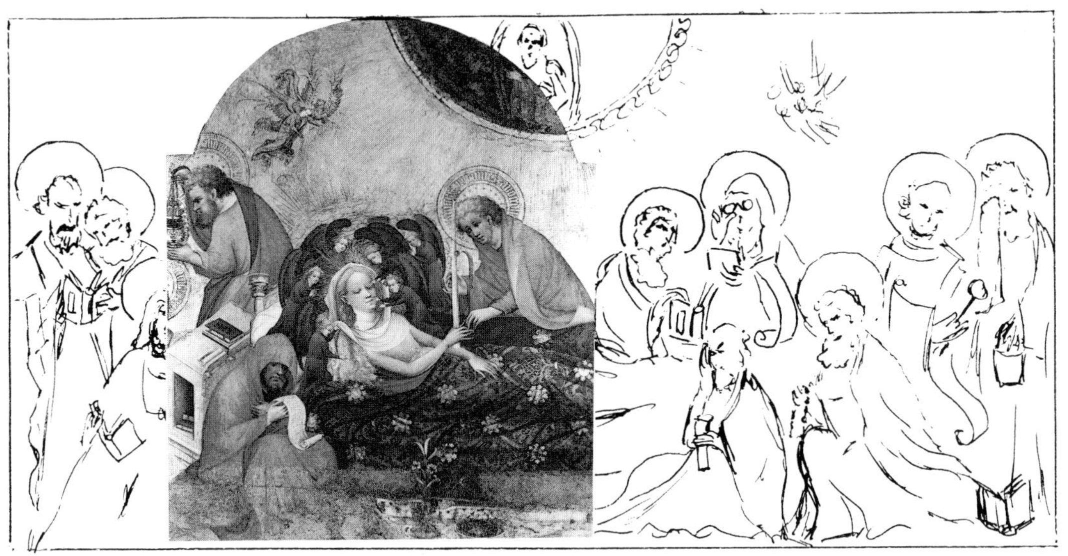

144. Author's suggestion of the original appearance of the *Death of the Virgin*, Dortmund Altarpiece

RECONSTRUCTION

The original size of the altarpiece can be determined as the panels carry symmetrical compositions. The *Nativity* fragment now has a width of 95 cm after being cut at the right edge. The horizontal diameter of the central semicircle of clouds measures at the top of the panel 57 cm, which leaves 35 cm on the uncut left of the panel, and should have left another 35 cm on the cut right. The original width of the wing was therefore 127 cm. Checked against the central point (at 63.5 cm) along the upper edge of the panel, in the mandorla of the *Coronation of the Virgin* (also a symmetrical composition), the measurement would appear to be correct. Interestingly enough, this original width of 127 cm makes the tip of the prominent brocade motif at Mary's chest in the *Adoration of the Kings* coincide with the vertical bisection of that painting, which passes through the central example of the 7 rosettes in the base of the throne. To corroborate this point, the motif also marks the central point of the throne's arcade construction. The centre of the large star, held by angels above the Virgin is, however, part of later overpainting; it misses the vertical bisection line, presumably because the restorer did not understand Conrad's symmetrical design. To complete the floor tile pattern in the *Nativity*, about 1 cm is needed. This suggests an original height of 141 cm.

Having established a width for the wings of 127 cm, which is identical to that of the wings of the Niederwildungen Altarpiece, it seems reasonable to assume that the master who knew and used the 'golden section' there, would not forget it in later years. By adding to the original height frames similar in size to those in the central panel in Niederwildungen, that is twice 14.5 cm, the height of 170 cm for the framed wings was established. Using the rule of the 'golden section' in the nearest whole number equivalent for all calculations (170 × 13 : 8), a width of 276.25 cm was calculated for the original *Death of the Virgin* panel (equivalent to the width of the central panel in Niederwildungen without frames). This width would leave 11.12 cm for the wing frames. Lighter than the wings of the central panel, again as in Niederwildungen, the vertical part of the wing frames would measure 12.8 cm (14.5 + 11.1 : 2). Fritz discovered that the con-

struction module on which all Conrad's measurements were based was expressed in the halo of Mary in the Niederwildungen *Nativity* panel (r = 12.8).[4]

A photograph taken in 1888 (pl. 147) provides evidence that Conrad had applied the Golden Section in the Dortmund Altarpiece measurements.[5] In the Baroque frame of 1720 (pl. 139), the *Nativity* and *Adoration of the Kings* panels were fitted below a gilded lunette. In the 1888 photograph, one can clearly discern in the lunette a frame in the gold ground of punched oak-leaf pattern with a 'floral fringe' and rays, all identical to those in the Dortmund Altarpiece. The lunette was also decorated with a circle of painted clouds, in which traces of a scratched triangle, surrounded by punched rays, could still be seen, as well as a copy of the set of two drawn angels in the *Death of the Virgin*, and a similar, but not identical set of angels in reverse. That this lunette was part of the original altarpiece is established by the intricate matching punchwork and finds confirmation in an article, published by Pfarrer Stein in 1930, before some of the archives were destroyed. He cites a report, dated 12 May 1850, stating that the paintings in the lunette were then 'abgekratzt, neu grundiert, geschliffen und ganz vergoldet'.[6] It was not unusual for an altarpiece in Westphalia to have a lunette above the main panel (pls. 74, 145).

It was possible to work out from the photograph that the original width of the lunette was 172.6 cm. This shows a golden section relationship to the main panel of the altarpiece: 276.25 : 8 × 5 = 172.6 cm, which can hardly be coincidence and therefore supports the argument for my reconstruction. Taking into consideration the slight inexactitude already noticed by Fritz, the module r = 12.8 applies, as 13.5 r = 172.8 for the lunette, and 21.5 r = 275.2, missing only 1 cm from the main panel measurement of 276.25 cm. If the width of the lunette is 172.6 cm, its height would appear to be just under 76 cm in the photograph. However, as the position of the camera, which is unknown, could foreshorten the image, a height of 6 r = 76.8 cm seems plausible.

The measurements suggested for the original Dortmund Altarpiece are therefore:

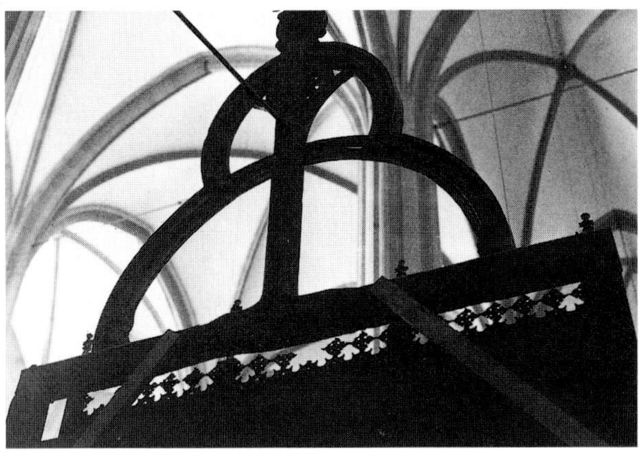

145. Rear view of an altarpiece frame of 1376. Wiesenkirche, Soest

Including frame:
height 170 cm
width central panel 305.25 cm
width wings 152.5 cm
Without frame:
height 141 cm
width central panel 276.25 cm
width wings 127 cm
Lunette:
height (estimated) 76.8 cm
width 172.5 cm
Frames vary in size:
widest point in main panel 14.5 cm
widest point in the wings 12.8 cm[7]

The photograph shows the lunette mounted above the panels, with an inscribed board between them. This seems a reflection of the original design, and it is therefore experimentally proposed here that an inscription or decorative panel (as in the frame of 1376; see p. 120 and pl. 74) may have surmounted the *Death of the Virgin* originally. In order to harmonize the design, this panel would have to measure 18 cm, to give an overall height of 188 cm, as at Niederwildungen. It is not possible to decide whether the wings had similar panels.

It is very likely that the altarpiece also had a predella. It would not only have eased the use of the wings, but would also have balanced the lunette visually. The subject of the predella decoration must remain guesswork. The lunette is likely to have been decorated with an image of God the Father in a ring of clouds and with a dove below him, to form a Trinity with the Son in the *Death of the Virgin* beneath, similar to that in the Limbourg brothers' *Feeding of the Multitude*.[8] The complete original designs of the other panels in the Dortmund Altarpiece are reflected in a copy by a lesser painter, the Blankenberch Altarpiece (*c.* 1421–43)(pls. 57–59), and also in the Jacobi Altarpiece (pls. 60, 61). My reconstruction drawings (pls. 143, 144, 148) for the *Death of the Virgin* differs from those by earlier authors (pls. 141, 142) in that they bear in mind not only these panels by Conrad's followers, but also Conrad's symmetrical compositions, the module applied in his designs of r = 12.8, and the mathematical relationships observed in the Niederwildungen Altarpiece.[9]

Size of the surviving fragments:
Central panel, cut, rounded at the top:138 × 110 cm
Left wing, cut at the right: 140 × 95 cm
Right wing, cut at the left: 140 × 93.5 cm

The spatial relationship between the altarpiece and the architecture of the original choir cannot be examined, as that part of the church was destroyed in 1946 by damage sustained during the war.

DATE
A date of *c.* 1420 is generally accepted for this altarpiece. On stylistic grounds, especially because of the increased monumentality and realism, the retable must be dated well after the Niederwildungen Altarpiece of 1403. The Dortmund *Death of the Virgin* is reflected in the Barfüsser Altarpiece [mendicant Franciscans] in Hanover (Landesgalerie), dated 1424. This indicates a *terminus ante quem* for the Dortmund Altarpiece. Furthermore, Conrad was not mentioned in the membership lists of the confraternity of St Nicolai after 1422 which suggests that he died around 1422. Taking into account the stylistic advance, a date of *c.* 1420 for the altarpiece therefore seems plausible.

HISTORY
The Dortmund Altarpiece is first mentioned in an inventory of 1432, copied by Pfarrer Brügman (pastor 1679–1705), as part of the decoration of the high altar.[10] The congregation of the Marienkirche embraced the Reformation hesitantly and Pfarrer Brügman had inherited a

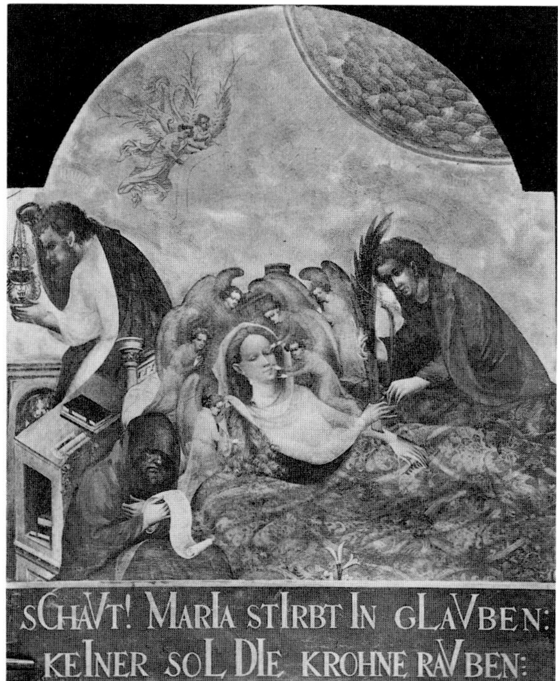

146. Conrad von Soest: *Death of the Virgin*, before restoration. Dortmund Altarpiece

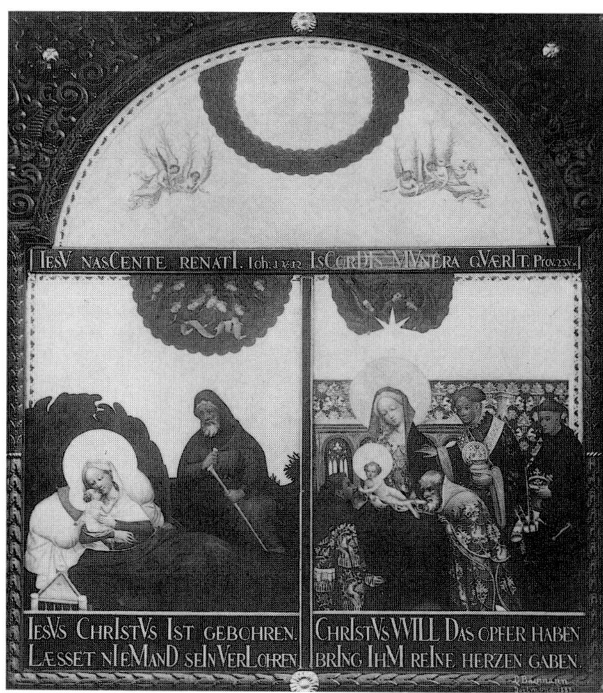

147. Conrad von Soest: *Nativity. Adoration of the Kings* and *lunette*, photograph dated 1888. Dortmund Altarpiece

parish in which both Protestant and Catholic services were held at various family altars.

By 1720 an altarpiece depicting a Catholic sacrament (Extreme Unction) was no longer acceptable. It was, however, decided to adapt rather than replace the beautifully painted panels. Mayor Dethmar Wessel Nies donated a costly, heavily carved Baroque frame (with an inscription of his name) to accommodate the mutilated paintings (pl. 139). The central panel, showing the *Death of the Virgin*, was severely cut on both sides and it was rounded at the top; the offending candle of the last sacrament was hidden beneath a crudely painted palm (pl. 146). The painting was then fitted so high up (12 m) in the Baroque framework that it was hardly visible from below and a black band, 20 cm in width, was painted across the base of the picture and was inscribed: 'SCHAVT MARIA STIRBT IN GLAVBEN : KEINER SOL DIE KRONE RAVBEN' (pl. 146). The obverse scenes of the wing panels appear to have been iconographically more acceptable after painting out St Joseph's rosary, and both were cut to fit together in the lower part of the new frame. The inscription of a plank placed between the paintings and the

lunette read: 'IESV NASCENTE RENATI. Ioh. 1 V 12. ISCORDIS MVNERA QVÆRIT Prov. 23 V 26', and the panels were again disfigured by a black band stating 'IESVS CHRISTVS IST GEBOHREN : LÆSSET NIEMAND SEIN VERLOHREN.' and 'CHRISTVS WILL DAS OPFER HABEN : BRING IHM REINE HER-ZEN GABEN' (see pl. 147).

By 1833, the Marienkirche was no longer in use and the sale of the building was considered. It was saved by the support of the Crown Prince, and funds for restoration were raised by public subscription. In a letter to the local newspaper in 1837, a 'Kunstfreund' demanded that better protection be provided for the precious altarpiece whilst restoration work was causing excessive dust and dirt.[11] It was during the 1840s that the altarpiece first attracted the attentions of Johann David Passavant (1841, p. 414) and of Wilhelm Lübke (1853, p. 340). Lübke approved the restoration of the panels by the painter Welsch in Münster in 1850; Welsch was supervised by the collector and connoisseur zur Mühlen.[12] Although no official record of the restoration exists, a report in the church archives yielded valuable information; it says that the panels were 'thor-

200

oughly cleaned', then considerable overpainting of the *Death of the Virgin* scene was undertaken, which included the semicircles of the angels, most garments, a balustrade to cover St James Minor and careless regilding which encroached on figure contours. The lunette was scraped clean and regilded.[13] Angels, copied from the originals in the *Death of the Virgin*, were painted on top of the new gold, both in their original positions and in the lunette panel. The report does not mention the paintings on the reverse side of the wings of the altarpiece which were, however, described by Lübke as being in poor condition. They were, as a later restoration report was to reveal, concealed by Welsch beneath three layers of *Münster Merkurblätter* (dated 1848) which were covered with several layers of oil paint.[14]

In 1925 the Wallraf-Richartz Museum urged that the obverse and reverse sides of the wing panels be sawn apart. The museum offered free restoration of the altarpiece in exchange for the right to purchase the two paintings from the reverse sides of the wings, the *Annunciation* and *Coronation of the Virgin*, although their condition under the paint and newspaper layers was uncertain.[15] Max Geisberg and Karl Schaefer supported the notion of separating the paintings on the obverse and reverse sides of the wings. However, an appeal caused the presbytery to refuse sale at the last moment; they agreed instead that the parish would pay for restoration of all the panels.[16] Had the wing panels been sawn apart, the paintings would have been splintered: an unpublished X-ray photograph, taken by Fritz in 1950, apparently shows that the panels are connected invisibly by iron dowels.[17]

After exhibition in Cologne in 1925 (nos. 26–27), the two wing panels were restored by Robert Hieronymi in Bonn. Hieronymi reported the restoration of the wings completed in June 1927, and the restored wings were then exhibited in the Wallraf-Richartz Museum in Cologne. Hieronymi's report is preserved in the unsorted archives of the church; it gives a detailed account of his restoration work. Hieronymi carefully freed the paintings of the *Annunciation* and the *Coronation of the Virgin* on the reverse of the wings from the mouldy layers of glued newspaper and discovered the paint and the chalk ground underneath in a powdery

condition. After injecting stabilizers, he removed discoloured varnishes. Hieronymi found large areas of paint missing, but did not replace them; only toning watercolour washes were used on the ivory gesso (or chalk?) ground and in some badly damaged patches the wood stayed bare; then a matt varnish was applied for protection. The obverse sides of the wings were in fairly good condition. After removal of the black paint bands, blisters were settled with a resin adhesive and the paint was stabilized. All fillers and the overpainting, which was especially heavy over Joseph's rosary in the *Nativity* and on the robes and the angel clouds in every panel, were removed. The cleaning of the semicircle of angels in the *Adoration of the Kings*, however, was abandoned, as there appeared to be only a few red and blue areas of pigment left under the oil-based overpaint. Infra-red photography suggests that blue overpainting on the Virgin's cloak and on the King's hood also remained. The heavy gilding of 1850 was removed and haloes and punchmarks became visible once more. Only a few very small areas of paint and gold were toned in by water colours; no missing glazes were replaced, but a coat of matt varnish was again applied.

In January 1930, Hieronymi reported the *Death of the Virgin* panel to be restored. Again, he had first removed the black paint band and all other overpainting and regilding. The candle was uncovered beneath the heavy palm in Mary's hand. Hieronymi stated that the original drawing of the angels in the sky, rediscovered under the 1850 gilding, had only a little damage to the arm of one of the angels. The base of the picture had suffered more, but the vase of lilies and the bowl of flowers and leaves were not quite lost and small parts of a coloured fringe had emerged at the badly damaged lower edge of the bed cover. St James Minor, who had been first covered by a palm, then by a balustrade over new gilding (see pl. 46), could again be seen. Christ appeared once more in the circle of clouds. But the original censer was too damaged, and Hieronymi decided to leave the overpainting, so as not to lose the meaning of St Thomas's gesture.

Although Hieronymi returned the panels with a plea to display them more suitably in the church, the paintings were at first returned to the Baroque frame.[18] But by 1932, after the

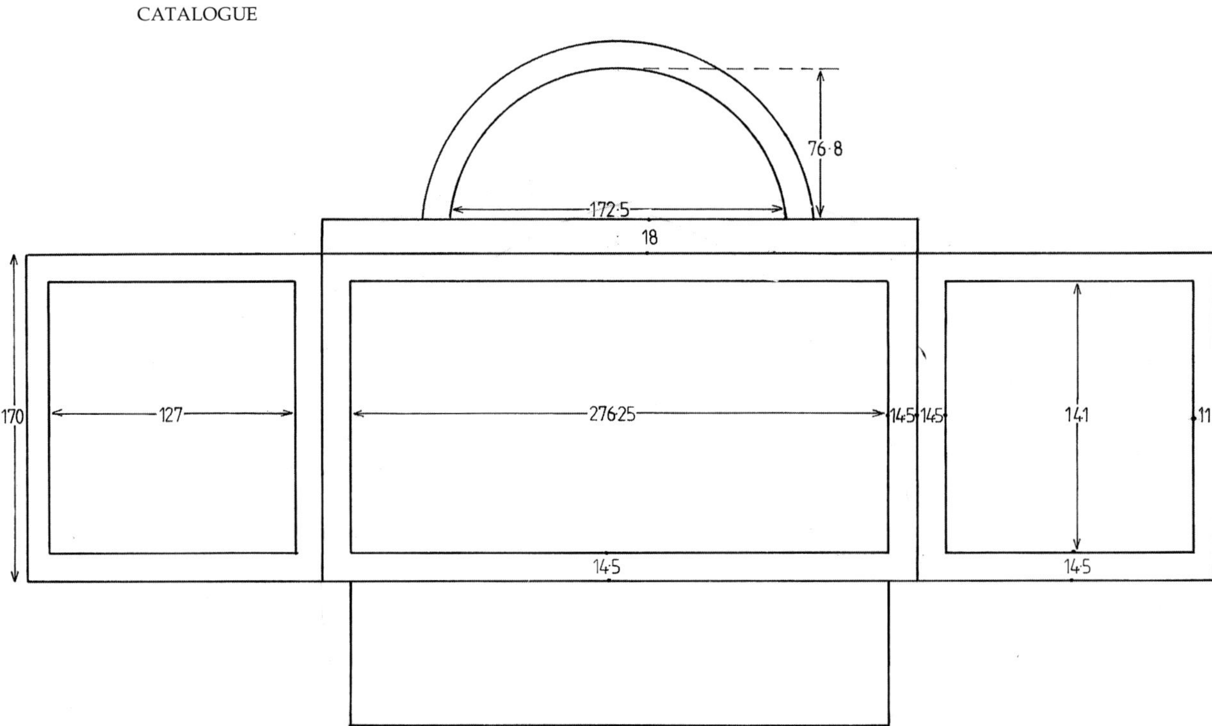

148. Reconstruction of the *Dortmund Altarpiece* by the author

Münster exhibition of 1930 (nos. 201–203), the *Death of the Virgin* was displayed on a pillar in the nave, whilst the wing panels adorned the high altar.[19] An undated photograph, found in the church archives, shows an experimental assembly in a crude frame, apparently fashioned after the frame of the Niederwildungen Altarpiece.

The Second World War caused the removal of the altarpiece, first to the strong room of the Kunstmuseum in Dortmund, where small blisters were treated by the restorer Kohler of Düsseldorf. Schloss Cappenberg was subsequently considered to be a safer storage place, and all the altarpieces from the Marienkirche were given to the protection of Graf Kanitz there. But central heating caused renewed cracks, which were treated by staff from the Wallraf-Richartz Museum, Cologne, before the panels were eventually transported to the Secret Archives of German Museums at Schloss Langenau in Hesse.[20] After the war, the occupation forces stored the panels at Möllenbeck, but permitted their return in 1947 to Schloss Cappenberg (which was no longer heated).[21] The Marienkirche had been severely damaged during the war, but the altarpiece had survived its many journeys in reasonable condition. It was displayed at exhibitions in Cappenberg (1948; nos. 1–5), Amsterdam (1949), Brussels (1949; no. 138), and Paris (1950; no. 2), and then in an exhibition dedicated to the artist, *Conrad von Soest und sein Kreis*, at Schloss Cappenberg in 1950 (nos. 55-59).

On 31 May 1957, the altarpiece was finally returned to its original position on the high altar of the rebuilt church, placed in a specially constructed steel frame. Careful climate control, modern toned glass in the large choir windows, and sliding doors over the damaged reverse sides of the wing panels are all designed to protect the altarpiece from further damage.

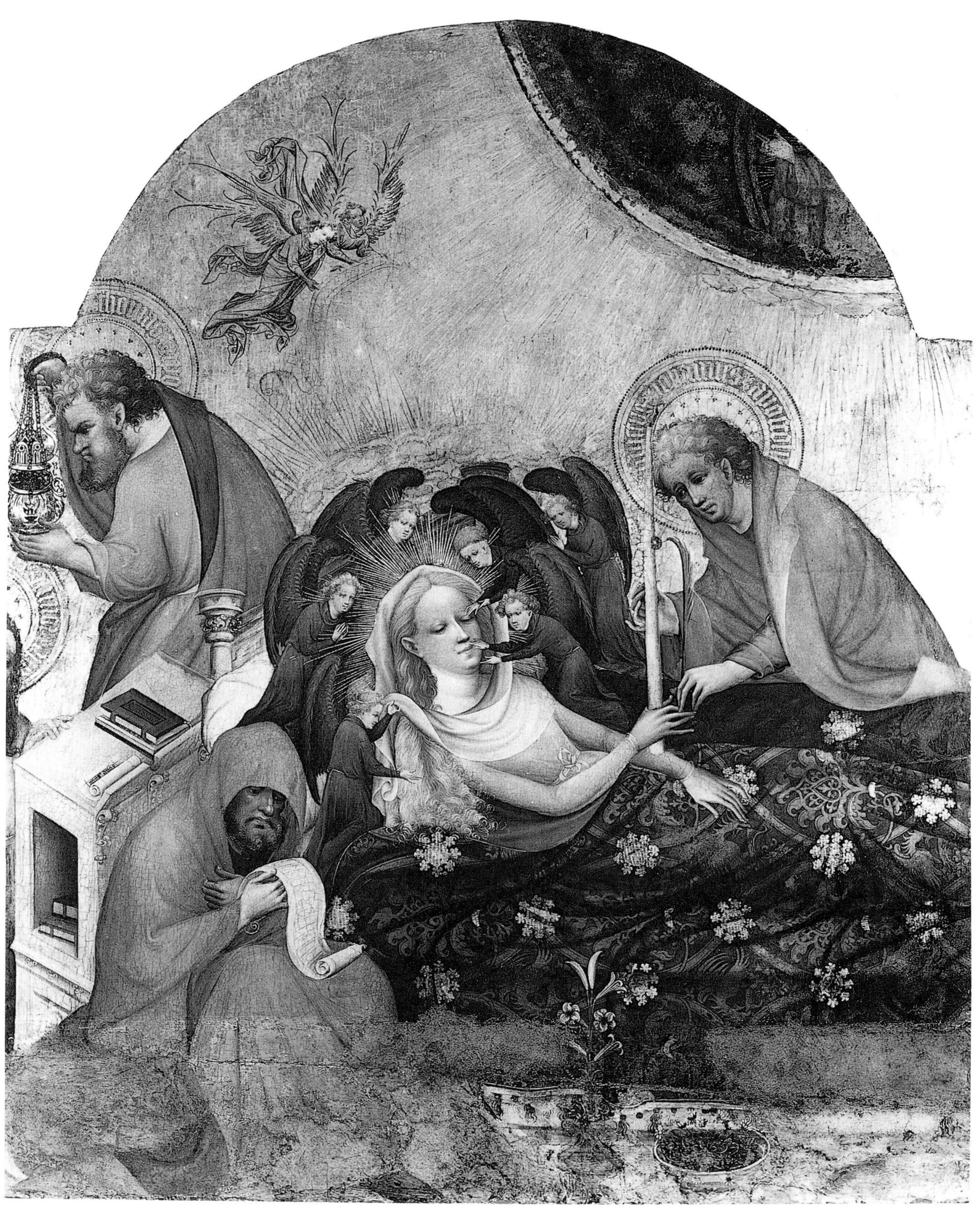

149. Conrad von Soest: *Death of the Virgin*. Dortmund Altarpiece

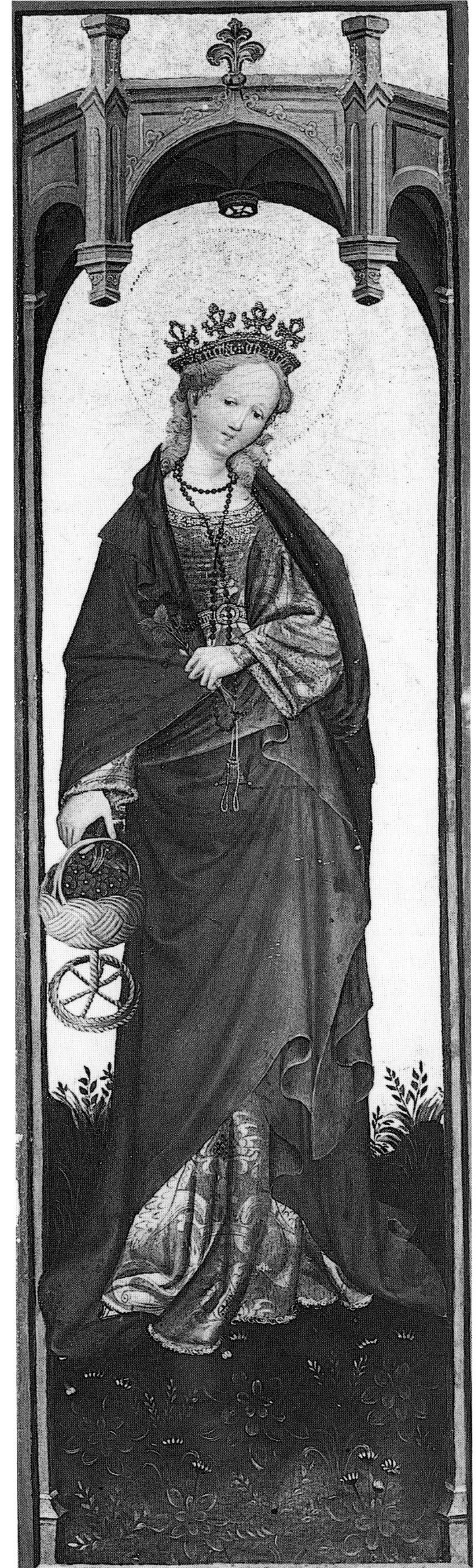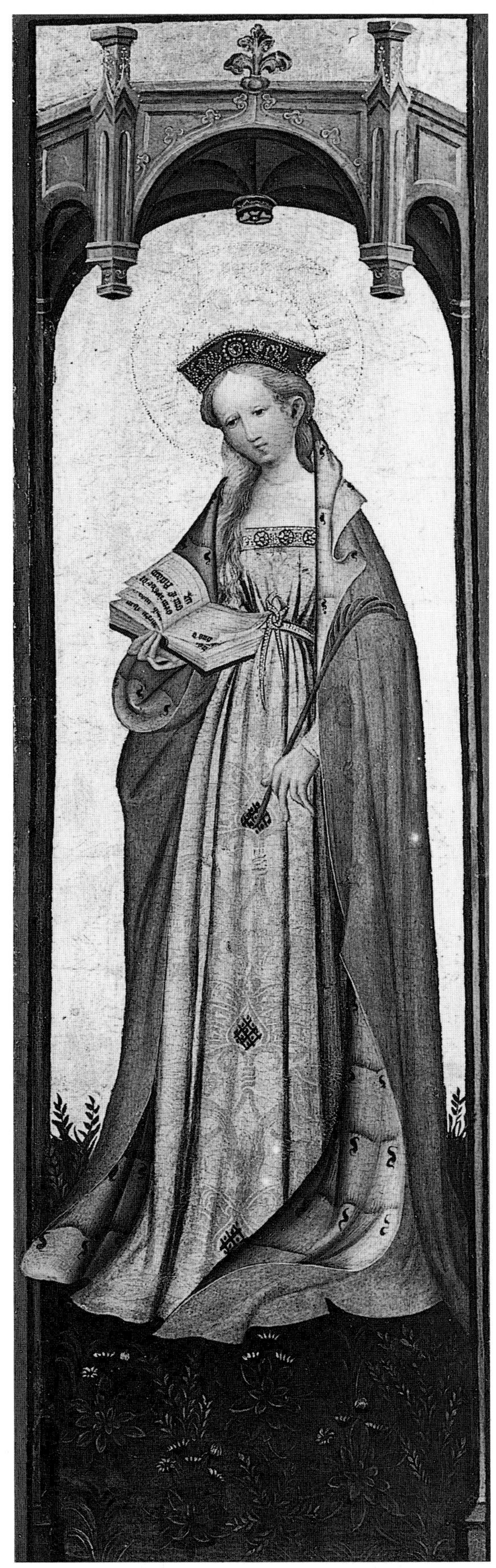

150–151. Conrad von Soest: *St Dorothea* and *St Odilia*. Landesmuseum für Kunst und Kulturgeschichte, Münster

3. St Dorothea and St Odilia (pls. 150, 151; XXIX, XXX)

Conrad von Soest

LOCATION
Làndesmuseum für Kunst und Kulturge-schichte, Münster (Inv. Nos. 2 and 3).

SUBJECT
Two small panels from the Augustinian convent of St Walpurgis, Soest, are decorated on a gold ground with *St Dorothea* (left panel) and *St Odilia*, one of St Ursula's maidens (right panel). The Saints are depicted standing in flowery meadows and framed by architectural baldachins. The panels are edged with a painted green band (1.1 cm); a part of this garment of each Saint is allowed to overlap the painted frame.

The reverse face of the panels is decorated with a *Mass of St Gregory*, painted across both panels by a Westphalian craftsman, probably during the third quarter of the fifteenth century.

ORNAMENTATION
The haloes have elaborate punched decorations, intricately worked with inscriptions and floral ornaments. A punch of stylized clouds, already noted in the Niederwildungen and Dortmund Altarpieces, is used in the backgrounds. Raised gesso pearls decorate the crowns, belts and neckbands.

INSCRIPTIONS
Signature: *St Dorothea*: Fritz (1950a, p. 113, n. 14b) asserted that he could read the letters 'C o n r a d', decoratively fitted into the rounded shape, in the turn-up of the Saint's left sleeve. It seems, however, difficult to accept that the decoration can be interpreted in this manner.

St Dorothea: 'sancta dorothe' in her crown, 'sancta dorothea' in her halo.

St Odilia: the letters 'e' and 'c' in her crown, 'sancta odilia virgo m' in her halo, and '*genetrix ut digni efficiamur*' in the book.

CONSTRUCTION
Painted in tempera; made of single pieces of oak-wood, unframed

SIZE
left panel: 92 × 25 cm
right panel: 92 × 25.8 cm[1]

DATE
On stylistic grounds, the Dorothea being a more monumental interpretation of the Niederwildungen Catherine pattern, the panel should be dated to around 1410.

HISTORY
The panels presumably derive from the original convent of St Walpurgis without the walls of Soest, damaged during the Feud of Soest (1447). The convent moved and is first mentioned within the walls in 1461; a new church for the convent in Soest was largely built by 1485.[2]

After the dissolution of the convent of St Walpurgis in 1812, the panels were moved to the Wiesenkirche in Soest; they were transferred to the Landesmuseum, Münster in 1835.[3] Nordhoff was the first, in 1879 (p. 135), to attribute the paintings to Conrad von Soest. The panels were exhibited in Münster in 1879 (no. 1448), Düsseldorf in 1904 (nos. 106 and 107), Soest in 1907 (nos. 16-17), Münster in 1930 (nos. 198-99), 1946 (nos. 1-2) and 1947 (nos. 9-10), Cappenberg in 1950 (nos. 53-54), Hamburg in 1969 (no. 14), St Dorothea panel only, in Vienna in 1962 (no. 29) and Münster in 1993 (no. B 2.3).

The acquisition report in the museum archives, dated 27 September 1835, described the panels as '*sehr beschädigt*'. This may have been a pessimistic assessment. Pieper recorded that the panels were restored shortly after 1835 by W. Anstatt, Münster, who left them in an unsatisfactory condition: the gold ground had been carelessly renewed and allowed to encroach on the outlines of the figures. In 1951-52 the restorer, Kuchel, Münster, removed the new gold and restored the panels to their original condition; he added a little pigment in the right hand of *St Dorothea* and near the outlines of both cloaks, and he restored the edges of the panels.

COMMENT

It is difficult to accept Pieper's suggestion that the tall and extremely narrow panels could have been the wings of a small altarpiece.[4] Had the panels with a *Mass of St Gregory* been designed for an altarpiece, the painter, to accommodate the frame, would have had to arrange the narrative so as to contain the Saint with his congregation within one wing, and the altar with the vision of Christ in the other wing. At Münster, the narrative scene is painted across both panels, depicting parts of the altar and of St Gregory's garments in each half. However, examples of small altarpieces with a raised frame around the inside panels only (presumably for easier transport of the closed retable) can be cited, for instance cat. no. 4 below, the triptych of the *Madonna with the Sweet Pea Blossom*—with a *Flagellation* painted across its closed wings—(WRM 10), and a small triptych depicting a central *Sacra Conversazione* in the

Kisters collection, Kreuzlingen—with Christ carrying the Cross painted across the closed wings (pl. XXXIV). The painted edging band on the obverse side of the Münster panels is, however, part of the original design and leaves no space for an additional frame. Therefore, it is reasonable to suggest instead that the panels may have been the doors of a tabernacle, similar to those still extant in the choir of the Wiesenkirche in Soest. The subject of the *Mass of St Gregory* would certainly be suitable for the decoration of such doors. It is also interesting to note that Becker, in an essay commemorating the convent of St Walpurgis in 1835, already referred to the panels as *'Türen eines Tabernakels'*; he may still have been aware of their deployment before the dissolution of the convent in 1812. In the four crude hinge-marks defacing the reverse side of the panels, the position of the central hole, out of line with the others, may perhaps mark the place where smaller hinges had earlier been set into the painted frame.

Pieper (1986, p. 43) cited Fritz in suggesting that traces of a sword, detected in St Dorothea's hand, indicate that the figure was originally designed as a St Catherine. However, it is difficult to locate these fragments of pigment, and infra-red photography revealed no trace of a sword in the underdrawing.

4. St Paul with Reinold on the reverse side (pls. 152, 153; XXXI, XXXII)

Possibly connected with Conrad von Soest or his workshop.

LOCATION
Alte Pinakothek, Munich (Inv. No. 459).

SUBJECT
The wing of a portable altarpiece is decorated on a gold ground with *St Paul* standing on a podium, a sword in his right hand, his left hand covered by his cloak. The Berswordt coats-of-arms bearing a boar rampant, similar to that depicted in the Berswordt Altarpiece (cat. no. 9) in Dortmund, are shown attached

to the podium. On the reverse side of the wing *Reinold* is portrayed against a red ground, which is decorated with gold stylized floral patterns and accentuated by two vertical framing lines [the figure is frequently called 'St Reinold' in the literature, but the patron saint of Dortmund was not canonized and is therefore depicted without a halo].[1] The crowned Reinold, nephew of Charlemagne, stands in a meadow; he reflects in pose and attire the wooden statue (1377?) of the patron saint of Dortmund in the Reinoldikirche there. His right hand lifts a sword whilst his left hand appears to shelter a curious monument (?) [he

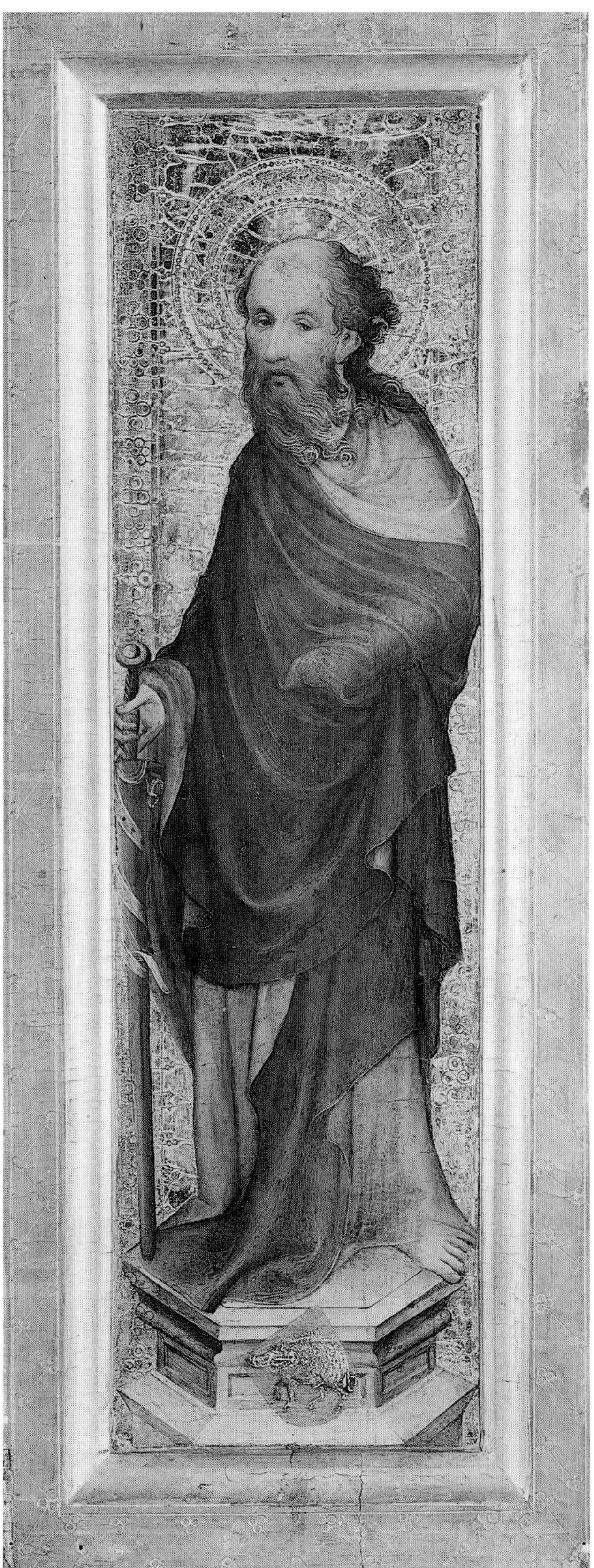

152. Conrad von Soest?: *St Paul.*
Alte Pinakothek, Munich

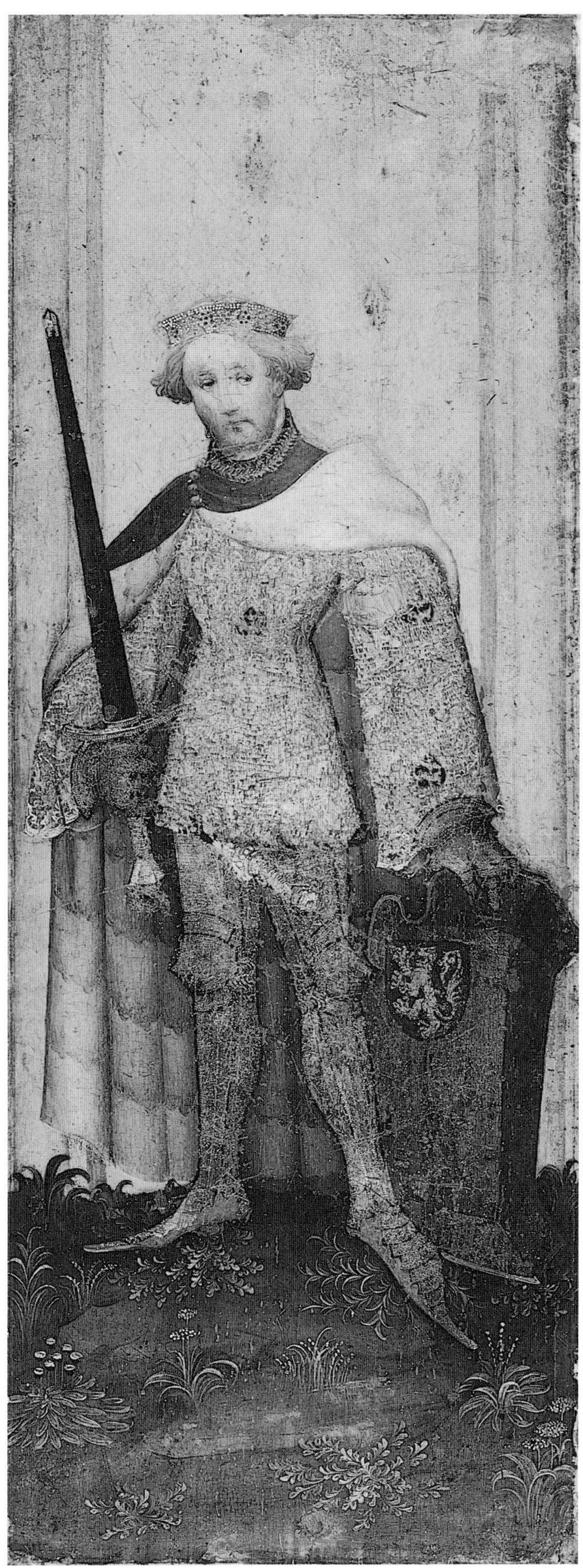

153. Conrad von Soest?: *Reinold.*
reverse of panel pl.152, Alte Pinakothek, Munich

does not carry a shield, as is stated in the literature]. The monument is decorated with coats-of-arms displaying a lion rampant on a field quartered gules and azure. The lion is similar to the device borne in the shield of the Dortmund statue; it remains uncertain whether the colouring of the repainted field there originally corresponded with that in the Munich panel. The coats-of-arms have at times been mistaken for that of the town of Dortmund.[2]

ORNAMENTATION
The halo of *St Paul* is decorated with punched foliage, a floral effect pattern made out of punched and tooled circles provides a frame on the gold ground behind the saint; similar, but not identical [modern?] punchwork is used on the integral gilded picture frame.

CONSTRUCTION
Painted in tempera; made of oak-wood (0.8 cm thick), framed only on the inside.

RECONSTRUCTION
Fritz suggested that the *Madonna with the Sweet Pea Blossom* (Wallraf-Richartz Museum, Cologne, Inv. No. 10, pl. 123), ascribed to the Veronica Master, may reflect the design of the lost central panel of this altarpiece. There is, however, no evidence for this hypothesis, and the decorative programme of the small altarpiece remains open to conjecture.[3]

SIZE
with frame: 53.6 × 19.5 cm
inside panel, without frame: 45.7 × 12.3 cm.

DATE
The figures are close in style to those of the Niederwildungen Altarpiece, and a date around 1404 is therefore plausible.[4]

HISTORY
In 1821, the brothers Boisserée in Cologne received the panel with uncertain provenance from F.F. Wallraf. The Boisserée collection was purchased by King Ludwig I of Bavaria and displayed at Castle Schleissheim from 1827 onwards.[5] The panel was acquired by the Alte Pinakothek, Munich, in 1925 and put on show until it was removed for storage in 1939. After exhibition in Cappenberg in 1950 (nos. 36–37), the panel was shown in the Haus der Kunst, Munich, from 1951 to 1957, when it was returned to the Alte Pinakothek. It was exhibited in Hamburg in 1969 (no. 13). The painting was first ascribed to Conrad von Soest by Stange (pp. 129–130) in 1932. Stange also drew attention to the fact that the Saint depicted was not, as hitherto supposed, St Louis—as he lacked all the relevant attributes (fleur-de-lis etc.)—but the patron saint of Dortmund.

No restorations are recorded, although the panel shows evidence of some renovation. The frame appears to have been regilded and the gold ground stabilized, although it was wisely left in (or returned to?) its rather worn state. Awkward passages in the left hand of *St Paul* suggest confused restoration. Fritz (1948, pp. 106–110) plausibly proposed that the Saint originally carried a Bible in his left, cloaked hand and demonstrated that this was a common iconographical feature around 1400 (he could, in fact, have cited the Niederwildungen *St Elizabeth* who supports a church in her cloaked hand). Goldberg and Scheffler (1972, pp. 185–186), misinterpreted Fritz's perception (understanding him to say that the book projected), and dismissed the idea. Unfortunately, they did not comment on whether any restoration was carried out in this area of the painting. Colour changes in the green pigment certainly appear to support Fritz's hypothesis. The drapery also seems unsatisfactory in the podium area, where the flowing folds come to a sudden, flat end. The poor design in this area is not in tune with Conrad's draughtsmanship. The silver armour and brocade doublet worn by *Reinold* are in a very scratched and worn condition, and this may be responsible for the rather flat appearance of the Saint. One also wonders if the awkward 'monument' may be the result of misunderstood restoration, replacing the shield one might expect in this position. Unfortunately, infra-red photography did not yield any information about the underdrawing.

COMMENT
Although the panel was described by Firmenich-Richartz (1916, p. 487) as the lid of a re-

liquary casket or, alternatively, the door of a tabernacle, the frame on the inside panel suggests that it was rather the wing of a small altarpiece of the type of the *Madonna with the Sweet Pea Blossom*.

The panel was originally attributed to a Cologne artist by Firmenich-Richartz, whose views have found no recent support. Stange's attribution of this panel to Conrad von Soest has not gone unchallenged and Steinbart (1946, p. 9), particularly, expressed 'considerable doubt'. However, most authors have accepted the panel as an early work by Conrad von Soest. The attribution is supported by the undoubted resemblance of the *St Paul* to the same Saint in the Niederwildungen Altarpiece, and of the *Reinold* to the young king in the *Adoration* of the same retable. The designs of the figures do not rely on identical models, however, and competent imitation by a follower cannot be ruled out. Nevertheless, it could be argued that the vigorous handling and design of St Paul's head is in keeping with Conrad's proven ability. A number of problems still appear to militate against an attribution to Conrad von Soest himself: awkward passages in the drapery and the uncertainties of design, discussed above, suggest a lesser master, as does the rather flat appearance of the figure of Reinold, which is hardly in keeping with Conrad's firm draughtsmanship. Unless these problems can be proven to be due to inexpert restoration and paint loss, an attribu-

tion to Conrad's workshop may be more appropriate. The punchwork also differs considerably from Conrad's known patterns. However, in view of the scarcity of comparative material from Conrad's workshop, this evidence alone is not conclusive.

It is tempting to connect the panel with Conrad von Soest, as it displays the coats-of-arms of the Berswordt, a Dortmund patrician family. Lambert Berswordt was one of the witnesses of the 1394 marriage contract, which is thought to refer to the painter. Winterfeld detected a connection between this small altarpiece and the papal privilege granted to Segebodo Berswordt of Dortmund (d. 1406; Lambert's brother) on 1 April 1404, for the use of a private retable.[6] Although the evidence is not conclusive, the argument is persuasive. Winterfeld pointed out that this privilege was only granted to 2 dukes, 11 noblemen, 8 canons, 2 burghers of Cologne and one burgher of Dortmund in Rhineland-Westphalia between 1393 and 1414. (In view of the inscription of the Niederwildungen Altarpiece, it is interesting to note that one of the canons was Johann Stolle of Cologne in 1402). The small size of the panel suggests that it was the wing of such a private altarpiece; a date of around 1404 is plausible. If it can be shown that the apparent problems of draughtsmanship discussed above are mistakes due to inexpert restoration, one might attribute this panel to Conrad von Soest.

5. The Fröndenberg Altarpiece (pls. 37, 42–44, 154)

Possible workshop connection to Conrad von Soest

Central panel: former Cistercian Stiftskirche, Fröndenberg; of the wings, only fragments from the right wing survive: a) Landesmuseum für Kunst und Kulturgeschichte Münster (Inv. No. 692); b) The Cleveland Museum of Art, Cleveland, Ohio (Inv. No. 29.920; cat. no. 10).[1]

The subject of the central panel is the life of Mary, depicted on a gold ground in eight paintings, divided by red framing strips. These frames are decorated with stencilled patterns, alternating black and gold. A now empty niche in the centre of the panel is surrounded by ornate carved framework. Coats-of-arms are displayed in the spandrels of an ogee arch in this framework. The four scenes on the left side of the niche show the *Presenta-*

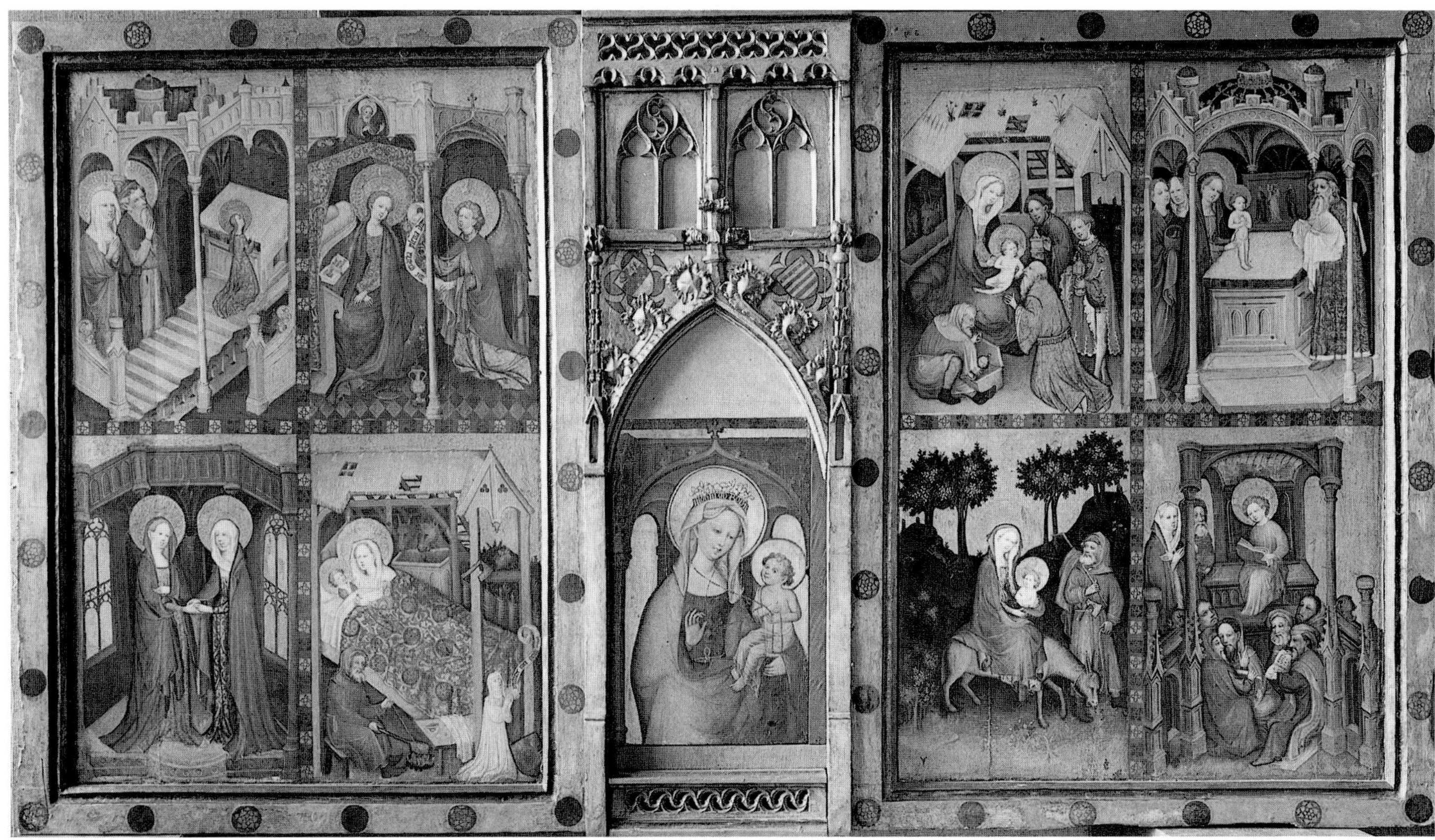

154. Fröndenberg Painter, Workshop of Conrad von Soest: *Fröndenberg Altarpiece.*
Experimental assembly including *Madonna and Child* (cat. no. 6)

tion of the Virgin and *Annunciation*, the *Visitation* and *Nativity with a Donor Figure*. The paintings on the right depict the *Adoration of the Kings* and *Presentation of Christ*, the *Flight into Egypt* and *Christ among the Doctors*. The original gold frame of the retable is embellished with stencilled rosettes, alternating in pattern. The sloping sides of the frame are painted green.

The fragments from the right wing show a) the *Pentecost* and b) the *Coronation of the Virgin*. The *Pentecost* was originally placed above the *Coronation*, for on the reverse faces of these panels together a *St Cecilia* is depicted (on a red ground decorated with small black rosettes). When the wings were closed, the central niche remained exposed.

ORNAMENTATION
A rather basic star-shaped pattern of punched circles, surrounded by scratched diagonal crossing lines, provides an inner frame on the gold ground. The tooled inscriptions of the haloes are punctuated by the simple pattern of a flower.

INSCRIPTIONS
Apart from names in the tooled haloes, the following inscriptions can be read on the inside panels:

Annunciation: in the book *'ecce ancilla dni fiat michi secudu'* and on the scroll *'ave gratia plena dom…'.*

Nativity: on the scroll of the donor figure *'miserere mei Deus'.*

Pentecost: in the book *'domine exaudi'.*

In the halo of St Cecilia on the reverse side of the wing fragments: *'sancta cecilia'.*

CONSTRUCTION
Tempera on oak-wood; the size of the planks could not be ascertained.

210

RECONSTRUCTION

Nordhoff (1880, p. 77) stated that the narrative of the left wing included the *Education of the Virgin* and 'Joachim bei seiner Herde', presumably the *Annunciation to Joachim*. He also noted a *St Mauritius*, first patron saint of the convent, on the closed altarpiece. As the altarpiece depicts the life of Mary, later also adopted as patroness of the convent, the *Birth of the Virgin* would have formed part of the narrative of the left wing, the *Assumption of the Virgin* is likely to have been one of the scenes of the right wing. The subject of the missing scenes remains open to conjecture. Pieper (1986, p. 49) suggested that a *Meeting at the Golden Gate* was shown in the missing panel of the left wing, but other scenes from the life of the Virgin's parents were equally popular in Westphalia.[2] For the right wing, Pieper proposed an *Ascension*, but this would not have made an attractive decorative effect next to an *Assumption*; another of the scenes from Mary's life with Christ, for example, the *Marriage at Cana*, appears more plausible. The altarpiece is likely to have had a predella.

Fritz (1950b, pp. 134–137) proposed that the *Madonna and Child* panel at Dortmund (cat. no. 6, below) originally filled the gap in the centre of this altarpiece. This reconstruction appears to have been generally accepted. However, as the panel is not cut at the top, it could never have fitted into the ogee arch of the carved central frame at Fröndenberg (pl. 154, experimental assembly). It should also be noted that the painted ogee arch in the Dortmund panel does not correspond in shape with the carved ogee arch of the Fröndenberg Altarpiece. The niche is, in any case, too narrow to accommodate the framed complete panel which is now cut down at one side and at the base. Furthermore, the stencilled decoration on the, original, frame of the Dortmund panel differs from that at Fröndenberg. I would suggest, instead, that the niche originally held a carved statue of the *Virgin and Child*, in the manner of the contemporary altarpiece in the Liebfrauenkirche at Schotten.[3] This hypothesis is supported by the fact that the central niche of the Fröndenberg Altarpiece was rather deeper originally.[4] The display of separate coats-of-arms on the carved frame, discussed below, also indicates that a separate item belonged to this patronage, a carved statue rather than one of the painted panels. However, the main painter of the Fröndenberg Altarpiece certainly painted the Dortmund *Madonna and Child*.

SIZE

    height of central panel 168 cm
    width of central panel, framed 299.5 cm
    approx. size of single paintings 72.5 × 48.5 cm
    width of carved portion 55.5 cm
    width of framing strips 5 cm
    width of frame: at top 9 cm
    width of frame, sides 10 cm
    wing:
    size of Münster panel 73.5 × 49 cm
    size of Cleveland panel 67.6 × 51.7 cm.

DATE

The altarpiece depicts a donor figure in the *Nativity* scene, identified by her coats-of-arms as Abbess Segele von Hamme. However, the question of patronage is confused by two further coats-of-arms, displayed in the central carved framework, those of Catharina von der Mark, a nun at the convent from 1383 to 1437. This has encouraged Rensing, for instance, to date the retable before 1400.[5] It should be noted, however, that the abbess is clearly depicted in a donor pose in the painted panels, and the coats-of-arms of the noble nun appear to refer to the carved framework and the lost central statue(?) only. The date of the sculpture(?) must remain conjectural. The date of the retable can be suggested with greater precision. As Segele von Hamme is documented as abbess at Fröndenberg from 1410 to 1421, the altarpiece is likely to have been painted during that time. On stylistic grounds, a date during the second half of her rule appears plausible, and 1415–20 is therefore proposed.

Stange (1967–78, I, no. 461) attributed the altarpiece to a follower of Conrad von Soest and suggested a date between 1420 and 1440. Although single motifs in the Fröndenberg Altarpiece correspond with those in the Dortmund Altarpiece, this does not necessitate a date after 1420, as the same models may have been used in Conrad von Soest's workshop before that date.

HISTORY

After the dissolution of the Fröndenberg convent in 1812, the church became a parish church, and services of different denominations were held there until the end of the nineteenth century. Pieper (1986, p. 49) asserts, without identifying his sources, that the altarpiece had been removed from the high altar in 1776, when it was considered 'alt und vermodert', to be replaced by a classicizing retable. The central panel of the Fröndenberg Altarpiece may have been moved at that time to the altar *'ante chorum'*, its present position. According to Pieper, the wings were at the vicarage in 1878 when they are recorded as having 'met with an accident' after the eviction of the Catholic priest from his residence. The Cleveland and Münster panels were part of the Haindorf collection, Hamm, until 1862, when they were obtained for the Loeb collection, Caldenhof. According to Nissen (1931, p. 62), the Loeb collection was exhibited at the Münster Museum 'für längere Zeit', and the *Coronation of the Virgin* had been 'completed' to resemble the *Pentecost* in size and architectural content. The Cleveland Museum purchased the *Coronation of the Virgin* and the Münster Museum the *Pentecost* panel at auction in 1929 (Lepke, Berlin, cat. 2014, nos. 1–2). The Cleveland panel left Münster in 1930, after the exhibition. The altarpiece was exhibited in Düsseldorf in 1904 (no. 110a), Münster in 1930 (no. 203), Cappenberg in 1950 (nos. 68–79), and in Vienna in 1962. The Cleveland panel only was exhibited in Münster in 1879 (no. 1446) and 1930 (no. 205), in Cleveland (no. 210), New York (no. 38) and Cambridge (Mass., no. 62) in 1936, and in Boston in 1940 (no. 77); the Münster panel was exhibited in Münster in 1930 (no. 203). The altarpiece was introduced into the literature by Lübke (1853, p. 244).

An inscription on the reverse side of the central panel states: 'versetzt und renoviert F.A. Klein, Arnsberg, 1826'. The new gold ground and areas of overpainting were removed in 1950, and missing paint areas were touched up.[6] The reverse face of the Münster panel had suffered considerable paint loss. The retable was also exposed to earlier vandalism: eyes have been poked out, particularly in the lower paintings, and graffiti and scratches have left traces of damage. The panel at Cleveland had been cut at the top. The *Coronation of the Virgin* was freed from the overpainting recorded by Nissen.

COMMENT

Pieper attributes further altarpieces (Inv. Nos. 4 and 6) in the Landesmuseum, Münster, to the Master of the Fröndenberg Altarpiece. However, the *Coronation of the Virgin* (Inv. No. 4) from St Walpurgis, Soest, differs markedly in style and technique from the *Coronation of the Virgin* (from Fröndenberg) at Cleveland and also from the other panels of the Fröndenberg Altarpiece. The retable from St Walpurgis (*c.* 1420–30) should, instead, be attributed to the separate, less accomplished Master of the Blankenberch Altarpiece (Inv. No. 6), which had also been painted for St Walpurgis. Style and technique of the panel warrant this attribution. The *Vera Icon* in the Gemäldegalerie, Berlin (Inv. No. 1217), also seems to share all these characteristics. However, the *St Leonard* in the Koninklijk Museum in Antwerp (Inv. No. 515) and the *St Christopher* in the Statens Museum in Copenhagen (Inv. No. 3789) from the same work (tabernacle doors? or wings of an altarpiece) appear to derive from the main painter of the Fröndenberg Altarpiece.

6. The Fröndenberg Painter's Madonna and Child (pls. 38; XXXIII)

Possible workshop connection to Conrad von Soest

LOCATION
Museum für Kunst and Kulturgeschichte, Dortmund (Inv. No. C 4978).[1]

SUBJECT
The panel depicts the Madonna holding her child; the child fingers the mother's coral rosary. An architectural porch, painted in green and red, separates the figures from the gold ground. Parts of the original red frame, embellished with black stencilled patterns, still survive.

ORNAMENTATION
The tooled inscription of the halo is punctuated by the simple pattern of a flower; Christ's halo is decorated with a cruciform arrangement of floral branches.

INSCRIPTIONS
Apart from the tooled inscription of Mary's halo, the following inscription can be read in her crown: 'M (R) M (R) R O D U'.[2]

CONSTRUCTION
Painted in tempera; made of oak-wood, with an inset of pine or cedar wood beneath the faces of the Virgin and the Child (see Fritz, 1950b, p. 136). The inset consists of two interconnected pieces measuring 22 by 16 cm and 13 by 11 cm.

RECONSTRUCTION
The panel is cut at the base and it remains open to conjecture whether it may have depicted a full-length figure originally.

SIZE
    height (cut at the base) 67 cm
    width (cut at the right side) 45 cm

DATE
The panel appears to be painted by the main painter of the Fröndenberg Altarpiece; it is so close in style to that retable that a similar date, *c.* 1415–20, can be suggested.

HISTORY
The *Madonna and Child* was purchased from the Hainsdorf collection by Loeb, Caldenhof, in 1862 (see Nordhoff, 1880, p. 126). It was obtained by the Dortmund museum from the Loeb collection in 1950. The panel was exhibited in Cappenberg, in 1950 (no. 76) and 1952 (no. 1), and in Vienna in 1962 (no. 48).

In his undated, private notes recording the restoration of the panel (presumably undertaken at the Dortmund museum after the purchase in 1950), Fritz stated that the painting had been inexpertly restored about 150 years earlier, when new gold had been applied, and an oil medium had been used in heavy overpainting, especially around the pine inlays. He commented that the panel had suffered 'barbarian' treatment as the crowbar used had left visible damage on the right edge. However, when the new gold was removed, the old ground was revealed in fair condition. The panel was then freed from all overpainting, repaired and carefully touched up. The fragment of the Gothic architecture on the right edge of the panel was added to match that painted on the left side.

COMMENT
Fritz asserted, with inconclusive evidence, that the pine (or cedar) inlays derived from a cult picture, reputed to have had miraculous powers. That image is thought to have been kept at Fröndenberg until some unknown date. Fritz declared the inlays in the Dortmund panel to be relics from that cult image which may have contained wood from the 'true cross'. More facts would be needed to consolidate such a hypothesis.

7. The St Nicholas Panel (pl. 155, 156)

Berswordt Master, hitherto attributed to Conrad von Soest

LOCATION
Saint Nicholas Ccapel, Soest.

SUBJECT
St Nicholas Enthroned is flanked by four standing saints: to his right St Catherine and St John the Baptist, to his left St John the Evangelist and St Barbara. Four clerics, three virgins and a donor kneel at St Nicholas's feet. The group is depicted against a gold ground; the frame is modern.[1]

ORNAMENTATION
A rather schematic pattern of tooled flowers together with a floral fringe provides an inner frame on the gold ground of the panel. All haloes are decorated with a circle of the flowers. Gesso pearls are used sparingly.

INSCRIPTIONS
The kneeling cleric's scroll: *'infunde ... ionem tuam clemenis* [sic] *nostris censibus'.*

The donor's scroll: *'sancte nicolae ora pro me'.*
On St Barbara's purse: the letter *'e'.*
In St John's book: *'maria b.'.*

In the crown on the virgin nearest St Barbara: the letters *'d e'.*

At the step of the throne: *'S. Nicolaus'*, by a later hand.

Traces of the names of the other saints can still be discerned on the flooring; they were also added at a later date.

CONSTRUCTION
Tempera on oak-wood.

SIZE
height 108 cm.
width 169 cm

DATE
On stylistic grounds a date of *c.* 1410–20 is suggested.

HISTORY
The panel was exhibited in Münster in 1879 (no. 1447), Düsseldorf in 1904 (no. 105), Cappenberg in 1950 (no. 35), Münster in 1952 (no. 22) and 1964 (no. 100), and in Cologne in 1978 (I, no. 248). The St Nicholas Panel was introduced into the literature by Lübke in 1853 (p. 340).

The panel was inexpertly restored in the nineteenth century, when the original gold ground was renewed in a manner that damaged the outlines of the figures. In 1933 the panel was restored by Soetebier, Münster, who repaired the gold ground and redefined the contours of the figures.2

COMMENT
It has been suggested that the confraternity of the 'Schleswigfahrer' which had feudal tenure of the chapel may have been the patron of the panel. However, this hypothesis is difficult to reconcile with the single donor figure, a cleric, depicted in the panel. There is no evidence to suggest that the panel was ever part of a winged altarpiece.

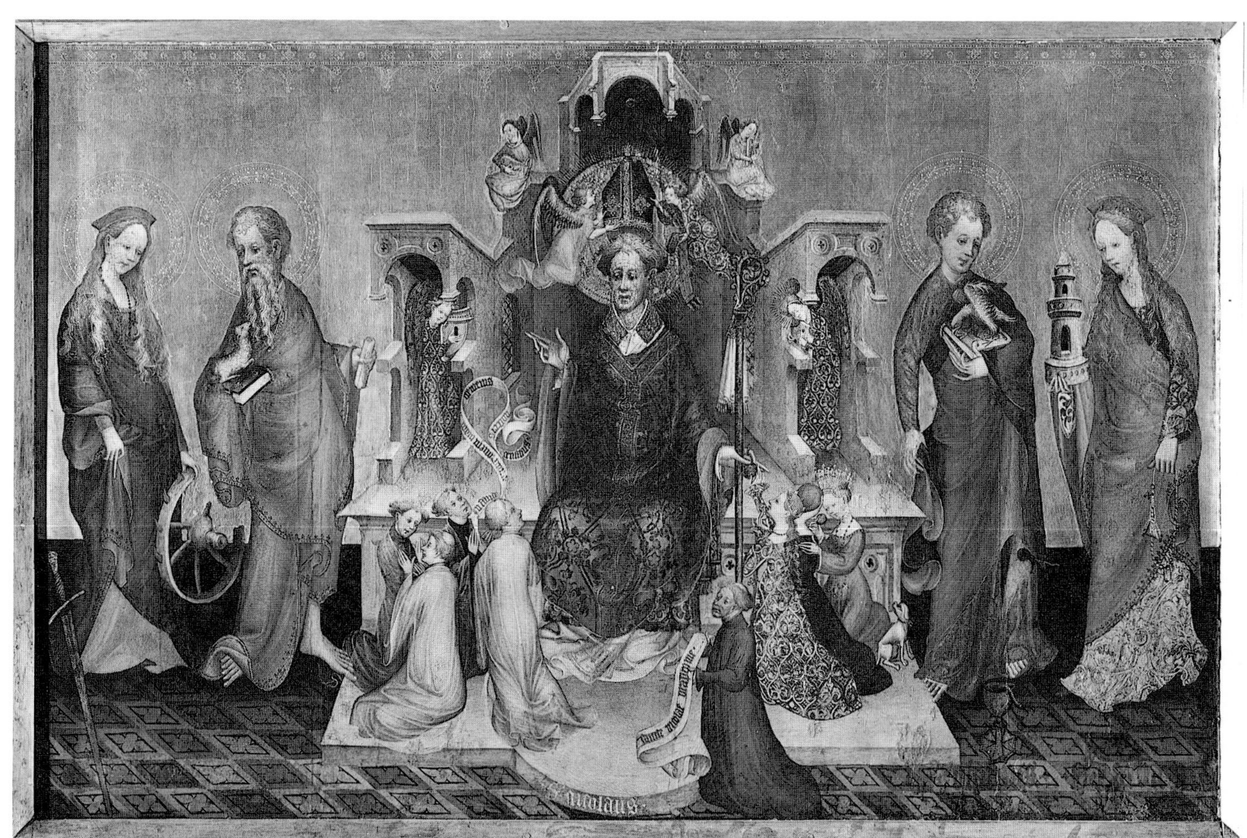

155. Bersword Master: *St Nicholas Panel*.
Chapel of St Nicholas, Soest

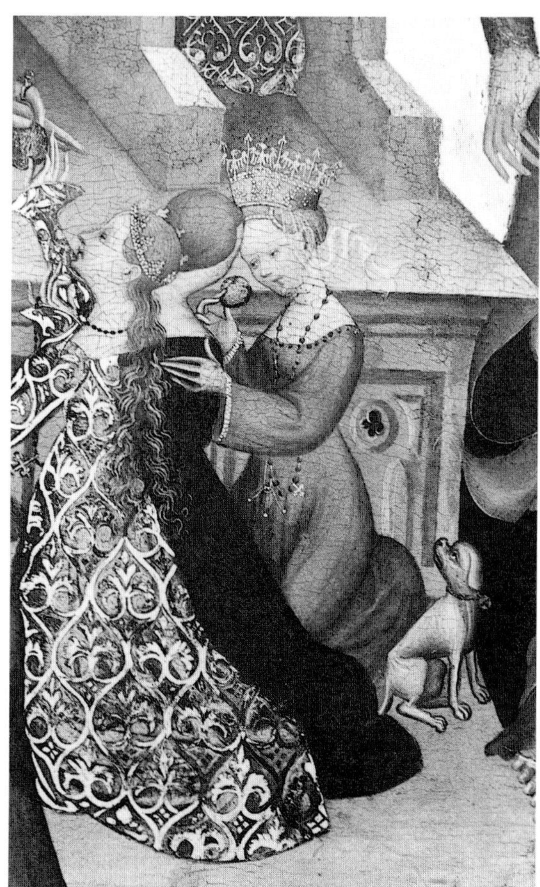

156. Berswordt Master: *Three Virgins*.
Detail from the *St Nicholas Panel*

8. The Bielefeld Altarpiece (pls. 47–51, 157)

Berswordt Master and workshop

LOCATION
Central panel: high altar, Neustädter Marien-kirche, Bielefeld. The present position of the dispersed wing panels will be noted below, against each subject.

SUBJECT
The opened altarpiece was decorated on a gold ground with thirty scenes from the life of Mary and from the passion of Christ, grouped around a full-height *Sacra Conversazione*, and read across the wings in three rows. The paintings are divided by red framing strips, decorated with a meander pattern. The original frame of the altarpiece has been lost. The central panel shows the following twelve scenes, six each side of the *Sacra Conversazione*: in the top row the *Meeting at the Golden Gate*, *Birth of the Virgin*, *Presentation of the Virgin*, *Marriage of the Virgin*; below, the *Baptism of Christ*, *Entry into Jerusalem*, *Last Supper*, *Gethsemane*, and the *Deposition*, *Entombment*, *Descent into Limbo* and *Resurrection*.

The left wing originally contained the following nine scenes: the *Garden of Eden*, *Temptation*, *Expulsion* (all Oetker collection, Bielefeld), the *Adoration of the Kings* (Oetker collection, Bielefeld), *Presentation (Gemälde-galerie Dahlem, Berlin)*, *Flight into Egypt* (Oetker collection, Bielefeld), *Christ before Pilate* (Ashmolean Museum, Oxford), *Carrying of the Cross* (Oetker collection, Bielefeld), and *Crucifixion* (Metropolitan Museum, New York).

The right wing was originally decorated with the following nine scenes: the *Annunciation* (Historical Museum, Bielefeld), *Visitation* (lost), *Nativity* (lost), the *Betrayal* (Oetker collection, Bielefeld), *Crowning with Thorns* (lost), *Flagellation* (Hertha Katz collection, New York), the *Ascension* (lost), *Pentecost* (lost), and *Last Judgement* (lost). The narrative content of the lost panels is known through an inventory of the Krüger collection; the *Nativity*, *Ascension*, *Pentecost* and *Last Judgement* are recorded in nineteenth-century sketches.[1]

ORNAMENTATION
There are only a few traces of simple punchwork on the gold ground. Certain haloes show remains of a repetitive punched and scratched decoration.

INSCRIPTIONS
The following inscriptions can be read on the scrolls:

Sacra Conversazione: the Child *'ego sum christus jhesus'*; St Peter *'tu es christus filius dei vivi'*; St Paul *'cristus jhesus veni(t) in hunc mundum peccatores salvos facere'*; the Evangelist *'verbum caro factum est'*; the Baptist *'ecce agnus dei qui tollit peccata mundi'*.

Last Supper: *'hec est mensa coram domino'*.

Garden of Eden: *'si comederis ex eo morte moriam...'*.

Temptation: the serpent *'nequaquam... moriamini'*; Eve *'ne forte moriamur'*.

Annunciation: the angel *'ave gratia plena dom(inus)...spiritus deus sup...veniet in...'*; Mary *'quodomo fiet istud, esse ancilla domini fiat mihi sec...'*.

CONSTRUCTION
Tempera on oak-wood.

RECONSTRUCTION
The altarpiece is likely to have had a predella. The decoration of the closed altarpiece is not recorded.

SIZE
height of central panel 182 cm
width of central panel 291 cm
size of *Sacra Conversazione* 182 × 113 cm
average height of small panels *c.* 57 cm
average width of small panels *c.* 40 cm
width of framing strips 3 cm
The measurements of the small panels vary; they are recorded individually by Jacobs

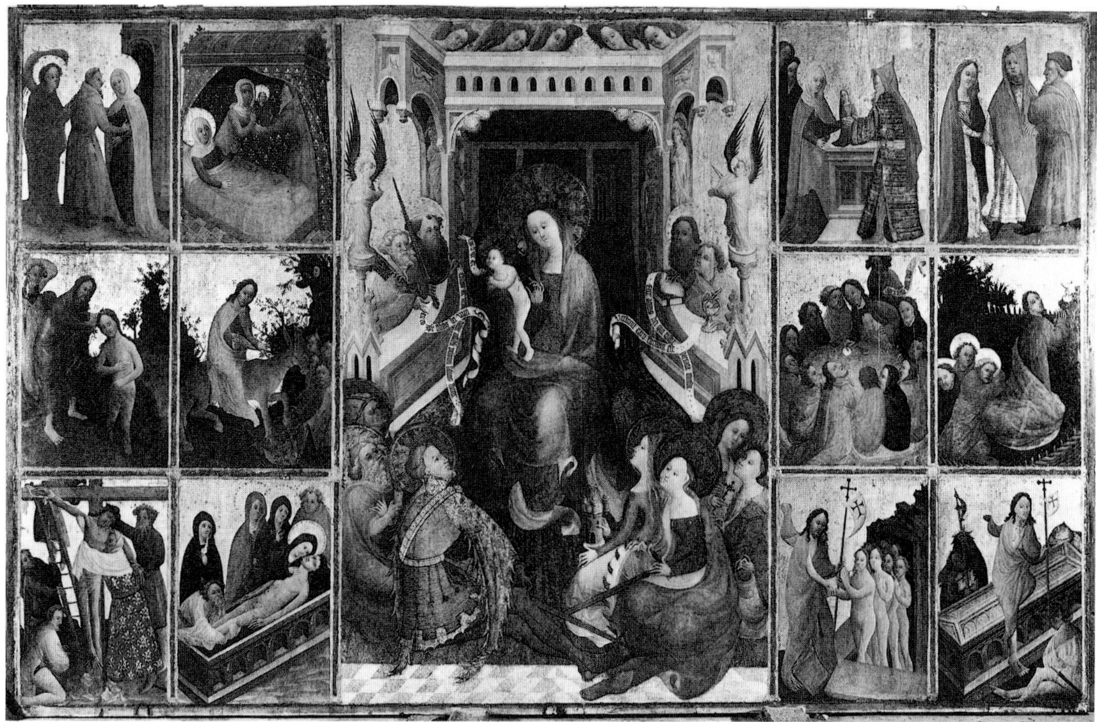

157. Berswordt Master and workshop: *Bielefeld Altarpiece*

(1983, pp. 208–209). Depending on the width of the lost frame, the opened altarpiece would have measured *c*. 630 cm in width and *c*. 200 cm in height.

DATE

Ledebur mentioned in 1825 (or 1828?) that the date of 1400 had been 'an dem Altar', Förster recorded in 1847, that the date had been part of an inscription on the lost frame of the altarpiece.[2]

HISTORY

In 1840 the wings were given to Geheimrat Krüger, Minden; he appears to have sold them to the National Gallery, London in 1854. They were offered for sale at Christie's, London in 1857 (14 February) and were acquired there by a London dealer, Hermann, who separated the panels and offered them for sale. The further provenance for each wing panel is recorded by Jacobs (pp. 212–216). The altarpiece was exhibited in Soest in 1907 (no. 21), Cappenberg in 1948 (nos. 6–10) and 1950 (nos. 3–26), Vienna in 1962 (no. 41), Münster in 1964 (nos. 73–93), and Bielefeld in 1964 (no. 25); the *Fla-gellation* was shown in London in 1923 (no. 54), *Christ before Pilate* was exhibited in Manchester in 1961 (no. 1). The altarpiece was introduced into the literature by Ledebur in 1825 (or 1828?, p. 125).

In 1840 the canvas backing of the central panel was separated from the old wood and not totally successfully transferred to new wood, causing the loss of stucco beading strips and corner rosettes. By 1949 large cracks defaced the panel and it suffered from flaking paint. Considerable restoration work was therefore undertaken by Haustein at Dortmund museum. A meander pattern emerged from under black paint. This restoration, and also those of single panels, are recorded in more detail in Exh. Cat. Münster, 1964 (p. 71).

COMMENT

It is feasible that the lost panels are still preserved in private collections. The altarpiece has been plausibly attributed to the Berswordt Master. However, the quality of the small panels is variable and suggests contributions by workshop assistants (see Eckert, 1956, p. 26).

217

9. **The Berswordt Altarpiece** (pls. 53, 158–160)

Berswordt Master

LOCATION
Evangelische St Marienkirche, Dortmund.

SUBJECT
The triptych depicts, on a gold ground, a central *Crucifixion*, with the *Carrying of the Cross* in the left wing, and the *Deposition* in the right wing. The red frame with gold and green sides is decorated with a simple stencilled design, and with the coats-of-arms of the Berswordt family, a boar rampant, in the corners. The closed altarpiece showed an *Annunciation*.[1]

ORNAMENTATION
The haloes on the obverse side are decorated with a circle of punched dots, representing flowers. On the reverse side of the panels, red haloes are decorated with gold stencilled patterns.

INSCRIPTIONS
The following inscriptions can be read in the scrolls:
    Crucifixion: the centurion *'vere fili' dei erat iste'*; the knight *'si fili' descendat de (cruce)'*; Pilate (?) *'i.n.r.i.'* and *'q' scripsi scripsi'*; and the jew *'noli scribere rex'*.
    Annunciation: *'ave gratia plena dominus tecum benedicta tu'*.

CONSTRUCTION
Painted in tempera; made of oak-wood, *c.* 3 cm thick. The retable is now exhibited in a specially constructed steel frame, the wings permanently opened.

SIZE
    central panel, without frames 95 × 147 cm
    wing panels, without frames 94 × 60 cm.
    frames from *c.* 10.5 to *c.* 11.5 cm
    opened altarpiece 118 × 336 cm.

DATE
Although dating of the Berswordt Altarpiece varies considerably, no detailed stylistic comparison is cited in support of a date before or after the Bielefeld Altarpiece. Jacobs, for example, based his proposed date of 1385 on costume.[2] He quoted the low belt worn by the knight in the Berswordt *Crucifixion* in evidence for a date before 1400, ignoring major works of a later date that show a similar belt.[3] Noting the increased monumentality of the figures, presumably influenced by Conrad von Soest's Dortmund Altarpiece in the same church, Eckert (1956, pp. 79–84) preferred a 'much later date'. The controlled pictorial organization across the altarpiece, consisting of a central V-construction flanked by corresponding diagonals in the wings, is in contrast to the lack of overall design in the Bielefeld Altarpiece. It denotes a more experienced master, and a later date for the altarpiece in Dortmund.

The dates of three documents concerned with the Crucifixion altar in the Marienkirche have been quoted in evidence for various datings of the retable. Examination of their content, however, can only support one date: 1431. In 1385 the altar was clearly still connected with the Lemberg family, but Jacobs (pp. 79–80) chose this date for the Berswordt altarpiece.[4] In 1397, Lambert Berswordt established some joint rights to the altar. However, his untimely death in the same year and the unseemliness of a splendid donation in a town stricken by poverty after a long siege during the Feud of Dortmund, suggest that this was not the date of the donation of the retable.[5] Indeed in 1399, Segebodo Berswordt, brother of the deceased, chose to present in Lambert's memory silver choir lights of great value to the Carthusian monastery of St Barbara in Cologne.[6] Eventually, having given a silver cup with the family coats-of-arms to the Marienkirche in Dortmund in 1430, four Berswordt brothers established the sole right of patron-

158–160. Berswordt Master: *Crucifixion, Carrying of the Cross* and *Deposition* from the Berswordt Altarpiece

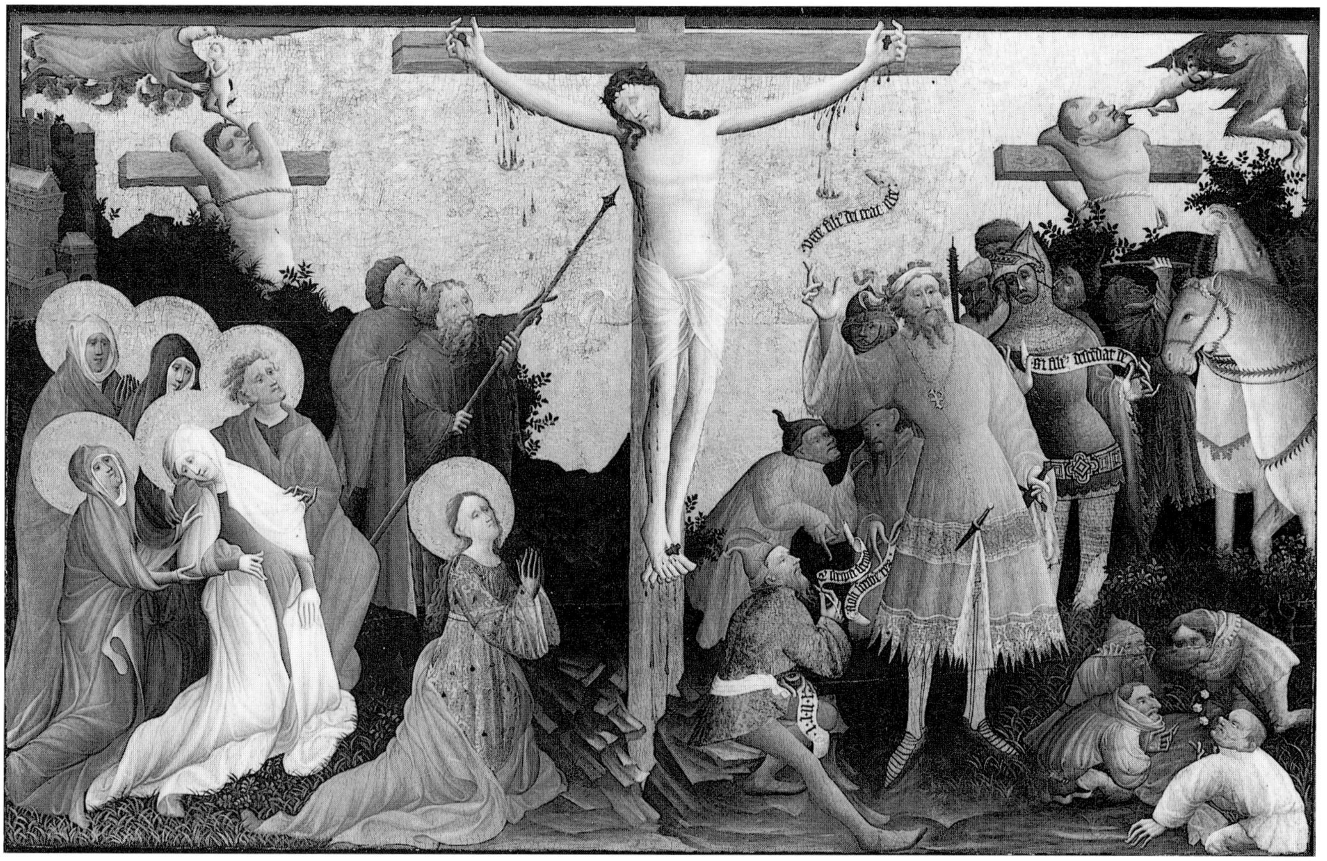

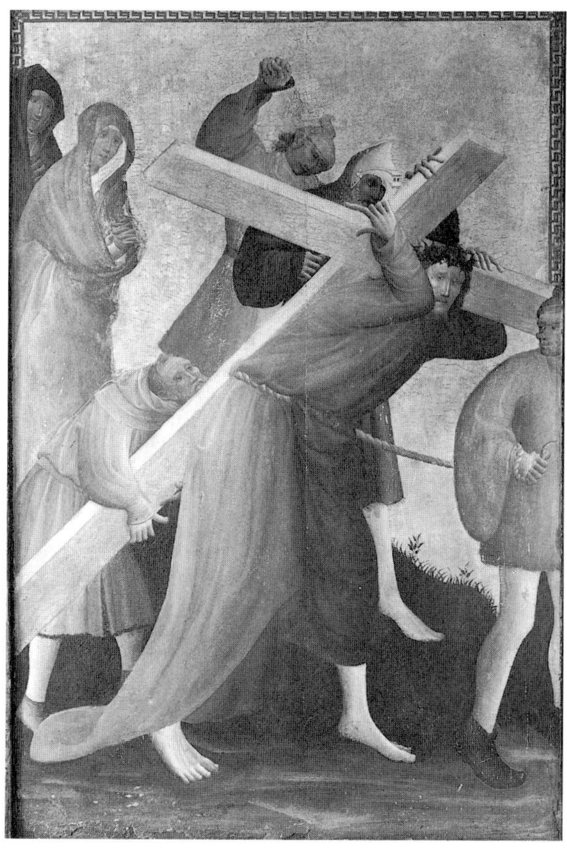

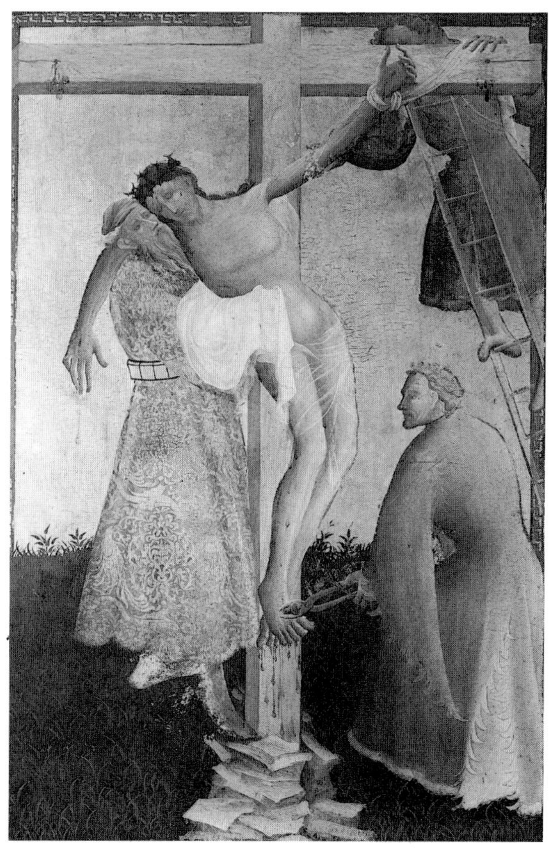

age for the altar in 1431 and honoured the patronage intentions of Lambert Berswordt by generous endowments.[7] This document supports a dating for the altarpiece of 1431. An investiture document of 1 July 1437 (Rothert, 1918, pp. 129–130) concerning the first priest endowed by this patronage confirms this date, as it mentions the *altare sancte Crucis noviter erectum*. The greater assurance in design and execution and the increased monumentality of the forms also indicate that the Berswordt Altarpiece must be painted after the two other retables identified as from the same workshop. The prestigious Berswordt family commission suggests that this may have been the major workshop in Dortmund after the death of Conrad von Soest.

HISTORY

The altarpiece was originally placed in the Berswordt chapel in the Marienkirche; it is now installed on the altar '*ante chorum*'. It was, together with the Dortmund Altarpiece, removed to Cappenberg and Langenau during the Second World War and has thus survived the destruction of the church. The altarpiece was exhibited in Cologne in 1925 (nos. 21–23), Cappenberg in 1948 (nos. 6–10) and 1950 (nos. 27–31), Münster in 1964 (nos. 68–72), and Bielefeld in 1964 (nos. 20–24).

In 1927 Hieronymi restored the retable in Bonn.[8] He discovered the original frame in reasonable condition under heavy Baroque marbled framework. He straightened the warped and cracked wood, removed extensive overpainting and new gold, and repaired damaged silhouettes. He found that the heads of Longinus and the centurion and his neighbours had been deliberately defaced with scratches, and therefore suffered from extensive overpainting. The altarpiece was further restored by Kuchel in Münster in 1963 (see Exh. Cat. Münster, 1964, p. 66), who found the retable disfigured by discoloured glazes, blisters and flaked areas of paint. Kuchel also claimed that inexpert use of glues, insensitive and heavy overpainting and vandalism defacing the figures of Christ, the centurion, and Longinus had to be corrected. The *Annunciation* on the reverse side of the wings is very damaged; the angel is all but lost.

COMMENT

Kuchel appears to have found the retable in a condition that is not consistent with the excellent restoration one can expect of Hieronymi, judging by the Dortmund Altarpiece and the Lochner retable in Cologne Cathedral. It is rather worrying, for instance, that Kuchel removed an edging of meander pattern that Hieronymi must have considered original, and which seems consistent with workshop usage (see Bielefeld Altarpiece).

10. The Warendorf Altarpiece (pl. 161)

Warendorf Master, reflecting lost designs by Conrad von Soest

LOCATION

Central panel: high altar, Pfarrkirche St Laurentius, Warendorf. The present position of the dispersed panels from the wings of the altarpiece will be noted below against each subject.

SUBJECT

The opened altarpiece was decorated on a gold ground with a cycle of thirteen paintings depicting the passion of Christ. In the main panel a large, full-height *Crucifixion* is flanked by four half-height paintings. Four narrative scenes were placed in each wing originally. Events taking place before the Crucifixion were described to the left side of the *Crucifixion*, and showed *Gethsemane* (Landesmuseum

220

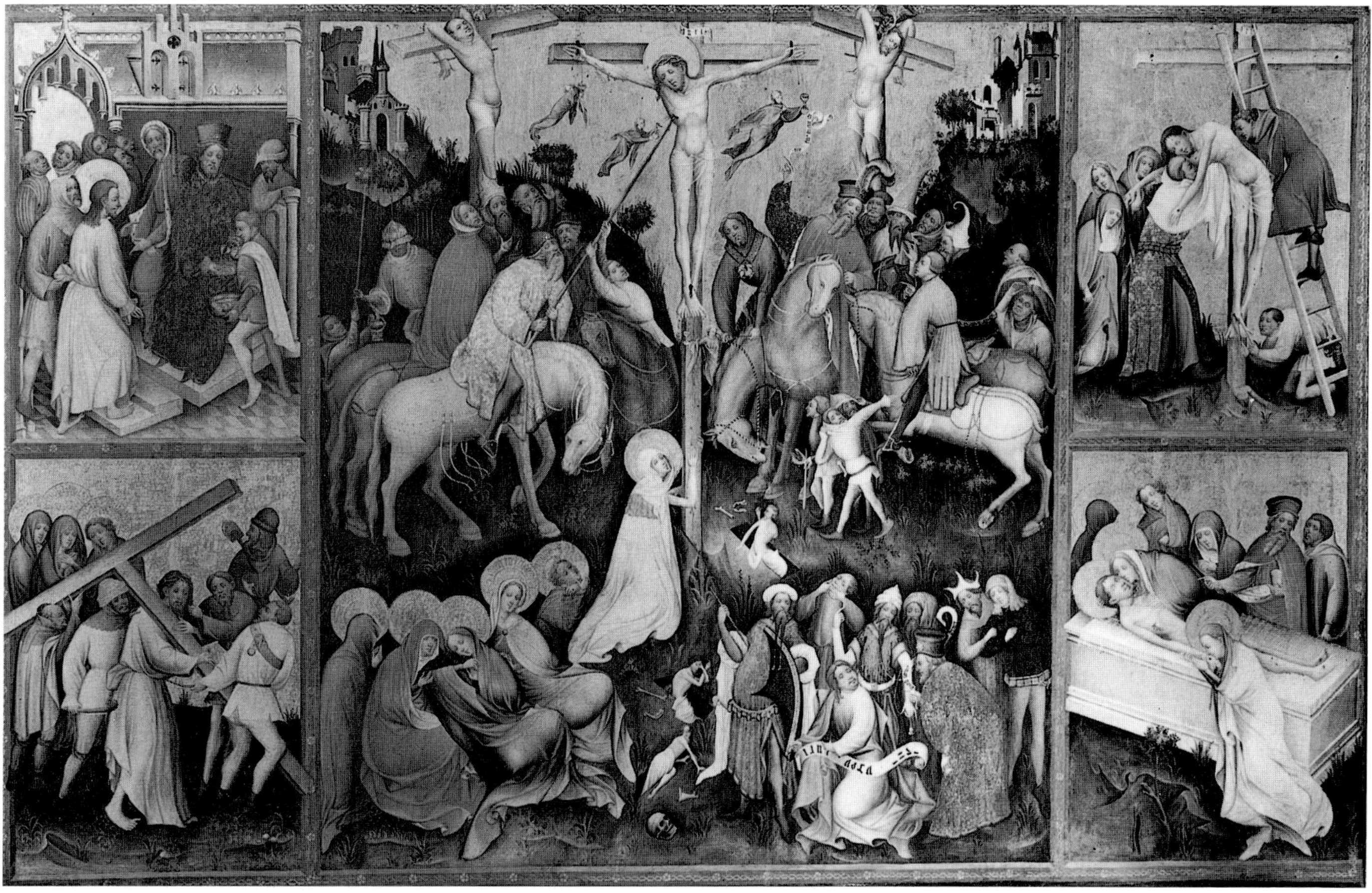

161. Warendorf Master: *Warendorf Altarpiece.* Pfarrkirche St Lawrence, Warendorf

Münster), the *Betrayal* (Pfarrkirche Freckenhorst), and *Pilate washing his hands* (central panel), and in the lower row the *Flagellation* (Pfarrkirche Freckenhorst), and *Carrying of the Cross* (central panel). The fourth panel from this wing is lost. Scenes after the *Crucifixion* commence with the *Deposition* (central panel), the two scenes from the wing are lost, the *Entombment* is depicted in the lower row of the central panel and two further scenes from the right wing are preserved, the *Pentecost* (Pfarrkirche Freckenhorst) and *Last Judgement* (Landesmuseum Münster, on loan from Warendorf parish). Traces of red framing strips, decorated with gold rosettes can be found in some of the panels. The retable is shown in a modern winged frame; the wings contain black and white photographs of some of the dispersed scenes.

Two scenes from the reverse side of the left wing are preserved, the *Annunciation* (Landesmuseum Münster) and the *Death of the Virgin* (Freckenhorst Deanery). Two scenes from the reverse face of the right wing reflect the fact that the church was dedicated to St Lawrence; they show *St Lawrence Condemned* and the *Martyrdom of St Lawrence* (both Landesmuseum Münster). These scenes are depicted against a very dark ground embellished with yellow stars. The narrative content of the missing panels must remain conjectural.

ORNAMENTATION
Traces only of framing punchwork can be discerned, for instance in the *Gethsemane* panel.

INSCRIPTIONS
The following inscriptions can be read on the scrolls:

Crucifixion: scribe *'i.n.r.i.'* in Latin, pseudo-Greek and pseudo-Hebrew letters (according to John 19.20); Pilate *'quod scripsi, scripsi'*; centurion *'vere fili' dei erat iste'*.

221

Annunciation: 'ave gratia plena dns'. Most haloes are inscribed with names; a number of these are lost beneath new gold.

CONSTRUCTION
Tempera on oak-wood.

RECONSTRUCTION
The reconstruction in the church follows Pieper's suggestion (1986, pp. 74–76) and places the *Betrayal* in the lower row of the left wing. This cannot be correct, as it must precede the Pilate scene. The Halderner Altarpiece (*c.* 1440–45) by the Master of Schöppingen in the Landesmuseum, Münster (Inv. No. 1038), may help with a more plausible reconstruction. That retable contains a similar passion cycle in thirteen scenes. The left wing shows *Gethsemane* and the *Betrayal* in the upper row, adjoining the Pilate scene in the main panel, and the *Flagellation* and *Mocking of Christ* before the *Carrying of the Cross* in the lower row. The recurrence of other motifs from the Warendorf workshop in the Halderner Altarpiece (Pieper, p. 107) adds credence to a reconstruction on similar lines. Pieper convincingly suggested that a wing panel in the same museum (Inv. No. 693, *c.* 1489; Pieper, p. 187), depicting four scenes from the life of St Lawrence, may assist in the reconstruction of the St Lawrence cycle at Warendorf. The altarpiece is likely to have had a predella.

SIZE
> height of present retable 171.5 cm
> width of present retable 269.5 cm
> size of *Crucifixion* 160.2 × 141.2 cm
> width of small panels 54.5 cm
> height of upper panels 78.2 cm
> height of lower panels 78.6 cm
> framing strips 3.8 cm

The present sizes of the wing panels are recorded by Pieper (1986, pp. 74–75).

DATE
On stylistic grounds a date around 1420–40 is generally accepted for this follower of Conrad von Soest. Nevertheless, until further evidence emerges, the date cannot be fixed with precision.

HISTORY
The altarpiece was dismantled in 1814, when a new retable was installed. Pfarrdechant Hermann Schulte (1839–59 at Freckenhorst) installed the Freckenhorst panels in the Deanery there. This building was demolished around 1967. The panels, with the exception of the *Death of the Virgin*, which is damaged beyond repair, were then placed in the baptistery of the church at Freckenhorst.[1] The St Lawrence panels are known to have been in the Haindorf collection, Hamm. They were purchased (after temporary loan exhibition at the museum, see cat. no. 5) by the Landesmuseum from the Loeb collection, Caldenhof, at auction in 1929 (Lepke, Berlin, cat. 2014, p. 10). The other two scenes were acquired in 1974 from the zur Mühlen collection, Haus Ruhr. The altarpiece was exhibited in Soest in 1907, Düsseldorf in 1904 (nos. 108–109), Cappenberg in 1950 (nos. 83–96) and—some panels only—in Münster in 1879 (no. 1449) and 1930 (nos. 210–215); the *Flagellation* only was shown in Hamburg in 1969 (no. 17).

A restoration in 1904 included considerable overpainting and regilding; in 1950 discoloured glazes, cracks and blisters were treated at the Dortmund museum and some of the new gold and paint was removed. Large areas with pigment losses were stabilized, but not overpainted.

COMMENT
Meier (1921, p. 29) first experimentally introduced the name 'Master of Münster'. However, the hypothesis, supported by Steinbart (1946, p. 36) and Pieper (1986, p. 70), that this workshop was active in Münster is not based on any evidence. The workshop also produced the retable in Darup, near Coesfeld (cat. no. 11), and there is evidence of seven workshops in Coesfeld between 1367 and 1429 (see $$ *Westfalen*, 27, 1947). It is equally possible that the workshop may have been placed there. As neither is proven, the name 'Warendorf Master' remains more suitable.

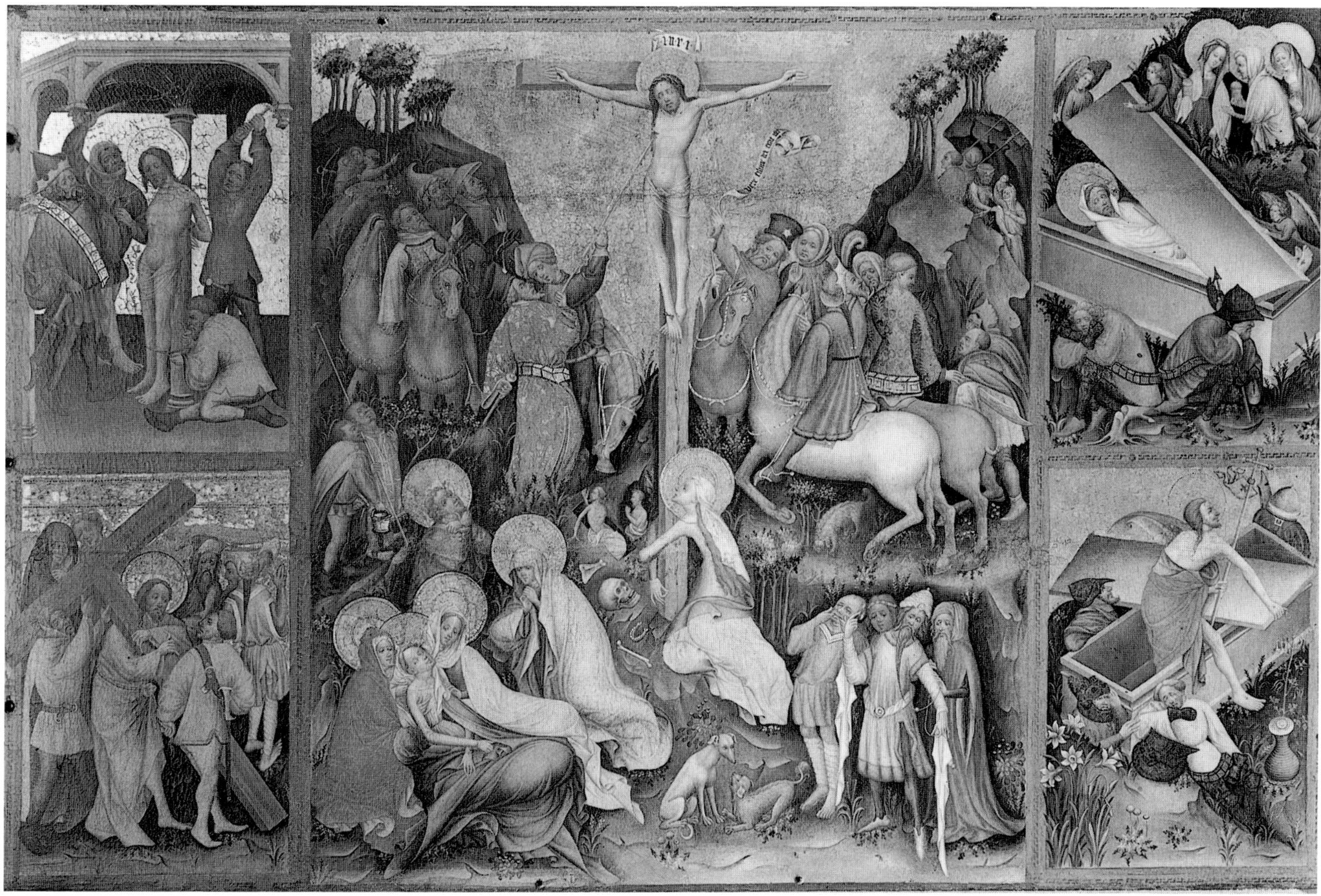

162. Warendorf Master and workshop: *Darup Altarpiece*

11. The Darup Altarpiece (pl. 162)

Warendorf Master and workshop, reflecting lost designs by Conrad von Soest

LOCATION
High altar, Church of St Fabian and St Sebastian, Darup. Only the main panel is preserved.

SUBJECT
The main panel of the retable is decorated on a gold ground with a central, full-height *Crucifixion* flanked by four half-height scenes from the passion of Christ. On the left side, the *Flagellation* and *Carrying of the Cross* are depicted, on the right side the *Three Maries at the Sepulchre* and *Resurrection* are shown. Red framing strips separate the narrative scenes; the frame is modern. The subject of the lost wings must remain conjectural.

ORNAMENTATION
Traces of simple framing punchwork and floral decoration of haloes can be discerned.

INSCRIPTIONS
The scroll of the centurion in the *Crucifixion* reads *'vere filius dei erat iste'*.
    Haloes show traces of inscriptions.

CONSTRUCTION
Tempera on oak-wood. According to Fritz, the planks are held together by iron dowels.[1]

SIZE
    height of the present retable 122 cm
    width of the present retable 188 cm
    size of *Crucifixion* 117.5 × 101 cm
    width of small panels 37 cm

height of upper panels 57.5 cm
height of lower panels 55.5 cm
framing strips 3 cm.

DATE

The altarpiece was clearly painted in the work-shop of the Warendorf Master. There is no stylistic evidence to support Pieper's date (1986, p. 76) of *c.* 1420, 'before the Warendorf Altarpiece', unless one maintains that the lower quality in execution can be equated with lesser experience rather than greater work-shop assistance. However, the firmer and less crowded organization of the pictorial field suggests a date after the Warendorf Altar-piece, between 1420 and 1440.

HISTORY

The retable was exhibited in Münster in 1930 (no. 208), Cappenberg in 1950 (nos. 98–102), and Hamburg in 1969 (no. 16). A short notice in the catalogue of the 1950 exhibition at Cap-penberg remarks that the altarpiece was freed from earlier overpainting and regilding in the Dortmund museum in 1949. Records of this and other restorations at the museum could not be found. Vertical cracks now cause renewed concern.

12. The Isselhorst Altarpiece (pl. 163)

Workshop of the Warendorf Master

LOCATION

Landesmuseum für Kunst und Kulturge-schichte, Münster (Inv. No. 7).

SUBJECT

The altarpiece from the Pfarrkirche in Issel-horst is decorated on a gold ground with five scenes from the passion of Christ in the central panel, and four scenes from the life of Joachim and Anna in the left wing. The right wing, still in Isselhorst, is too damaged for the narrative scenes to be recognized. In the central panel a full-height *Crucifixion* is flanked by two half-height panels each side. On the left, the *Flagel-lation* and *Carrying the Cross* are depicted and on the right are the *Mocking of Christ* and the *Raising of the Cross*. Modern red framing strips separate the narrative scenes and cover traces of gold rosettes discernable in some areas be-fore restoration. The raised cross of the last scene overlaps the framing strip, so that the base of the cross is placed on the same ground as the cross of the *Crucifixion*.

The left wing shows the *Meeting at the Gold-en Gate* and the *Birth of the Virgin*. The subject of the right wing remains conjectural. Only the lower half of the frame is original. It is embel-lished with golden lines on a red ground; the sides are painted yellow. The reverse side of the wing shows crude seventeenth-century paintings.

ORNAMENTATION

There are traces of simple, original punchwork framing the gold ground and decoration ha-loes (now restored).

CONSTRUCTION

Tempera on oak-wood.

SIZE

height of central panel 109.5 cm
width of central panel 146.5 cm
width of wing panels 54 cm
height of upper wing panel 49.7 cm
height of lower wing panel 50.5 cm
size of *Crucifixion* 106 × 41.5 cm
size of *Flagellation* 50 × 47.5 cm
framing strips 3 cm
frames 14 cm.

DATE

In spite of the indifferent quality of this work-shop production, a striving for greater monumentality and simplicity of organization

224

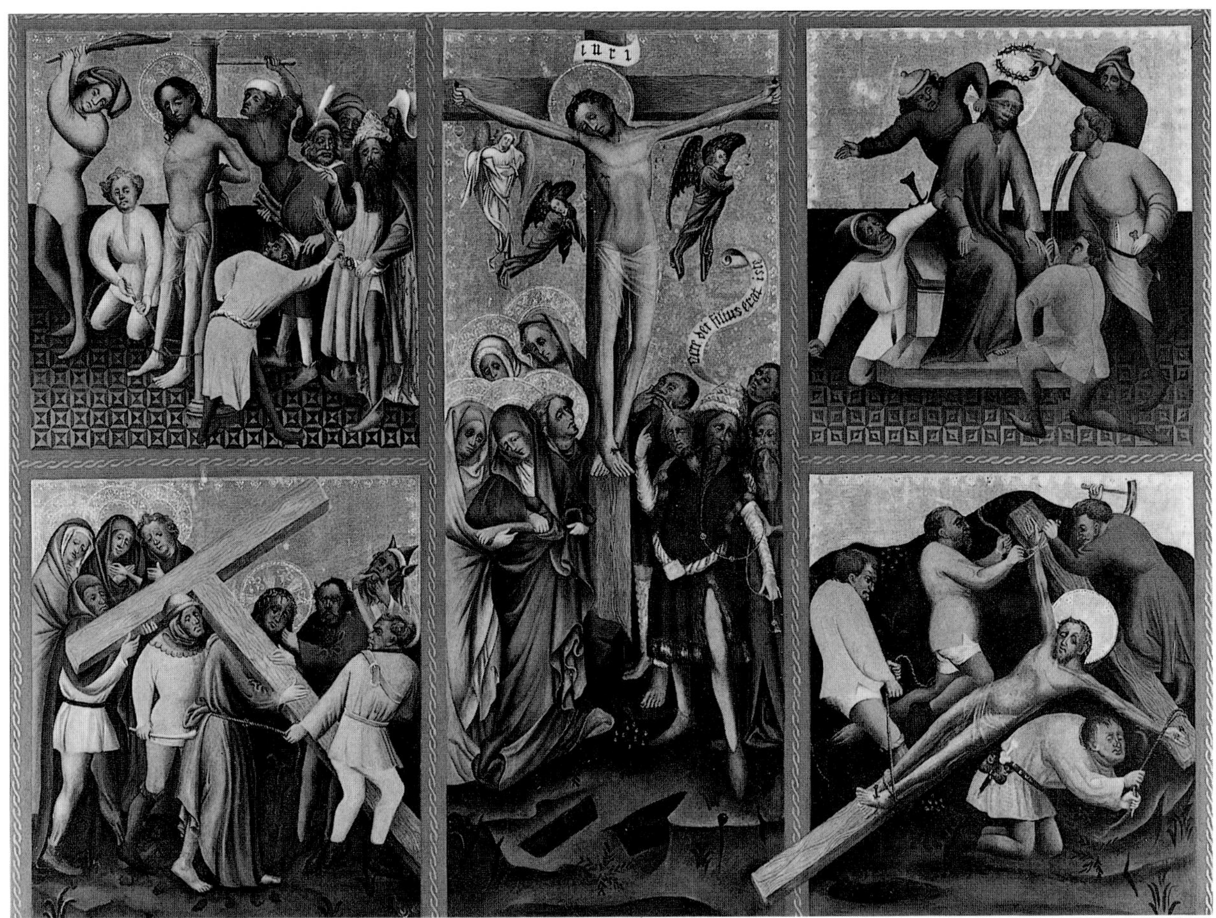

163. Workshop of the Warendorf Master: *Isselhorst Altarpiece*. Landesmuseum für Kunst und Kulturgeschichte, Münster

can be discerned. Pieper (p. 85) disagreed with attempts by other authors to date the retable around 1400 (see, for instance, Blaschke, 1976, p. 63). In view of similar stylistic trends in, for instance, the Berswordt Altarpiece of 1431 (cat. no. 9), a date of around 1430–40, first proposed by Stange (1934–61, 3, p. 40), appears plausible.

HISTORY

The retable was exhibited in Cappenberg in 1950 (nos. 103–110). Schmitz (1908, p. 85) first connected the Isselhorst Altarpiece with the retables in Warendorf and Darup. The altarpiece was acquired from the Pfarrkirche in Isselhorst by the Landesmuseum in 1908. In his purchase report Brüning, the first director of the Landesmuseum (Westfalen, I, 1909, p. 92) recorded that the original work in the altarpiece was completely covered by crude seventeenth-century paintings. The right wing appears to have been returned to Isselhorst when it was decided that no Gothic painting was sufficiently preserved beneath the Baroque work to warrant acquisition of the panel. Recent restoration work has shown this to be correct. Photographs taken of the panels, now in Münster, after the removal of the overpainting (presumably by Soetebier in Münster around 1908) show the panels then in reasonable if rather worn condition. In 1908 missing areas of pigment were touched up. Although the retable was restored again by Kuchel in 1961, Pieper reported in 1986 (pp. 80–83) that some of the oil pigment is already discolouring, further restoration has now been undertaken.

13. The Golden Panel from Lüneburg (pls. 164–167)

Master of the Golden Panel and at least two assistants

LOCATION
Double wings: Niedersächsisches Landesmuseum, Landesgalerie, Hanover (Inv. No. 191).

SUBJECT
The altarpiece from the high altar of the church of the Benedictine monastery of St Michael, Lüneburg, derived its name from the (lost) Romanesque gold antependium for which the double wings in the Hanover museum were originally made. The central panel of the altarpiece consisted of the gold relief, surrounded by relics and treasures from the monastery.[1] The outer wings are painted on both sides, the inner wings are decorated with narrative scenes on the outside and with carved, gilded figures of saints and prophets on the inside. At the first opening, the altarpiece showed, on a gold ground, thirty-six scenes from the life of the Virgin and the passion of Christ. The paintings are arranged in three rows, and the narrative develops across all four wings.

The inside of the left outer wing is decorated with nine stories: the *Annunciation, Visitation* and *Nativity*; the *Raising of Lazarus, Entry into Jerusalem* and *Last Supper*; the *Carrying of the Cross, Fight over Christ's Garment* and *Crucifixion*. The outside of the left inner wing shows the *Annunciation to the Shepherds, Circumcision* and *Adoration of the Kings*; the *Washing of Feet, Gethsemane* and *Christ waking the Sleeping Apostles*; the *Deposition, Entombment* and *Descent into Limbo*. The outside of the right inner wing is embellished with the *Presentation, Massacre of the Innocents* and *Flight into Egypt*; the *Betrayal, Christ before Pilate* and *Christ before Herod*; the *Resurrection, Three Maries at the Sepulchre* and *Ascension*. The inside of the right outer wing features *Christ among the Doctors, Marriage at Cana* and *Baptism of Christ*; the *Flagellation, Ecce Homo* and *Mocking of Christ*; the *Pentecost, Death of the Virgin* and *Coronation of the Virgin*. The panels are divided by dark green framing strips, decorated with golden stencilled motifs. The gold frame is in very rubbed condition and bears no traces of possible earlier decoration.

When the retable was closed, a *Crucifixion* was juxtaposed with its typological parallel, the *Brazen Serpent*.[2] The contemporary dress of the praying figures, kneeling around Moses in this scene, may indicate donor status. The scroll inscription *ora…a nobis serpentes* (see inscriptions, below), certainly appears to support such a hypothesis. Both scenes are shown against a dark red ground decorated with golden stencilled patterns; at the edges, the patterns are arranged to form an inner frame.

ORNAMENTATION
Floral punchwork embellishes some of the inscribed haloes. Small gesso pearls adorn certain jewels and ribbons.

INSCRIPTIONS
Apart from the names in the haloes, the following inscriptions can be read in the scrolls:

Annunciation: 'ave gratia plena dominus tecum' and in the book 'ecce virgo concipiet [et par]iet [filiu]m et vocabitur nom[en] eius emanuel'.

Visitation: Mary 'magnificat anima mea dominum' and Elizabeth 'exultavit infans in utero meo'.

Annunciation to the Shepherds: 'an[n]uncio vobis gaudium magnum'.

Baptism of Christ: 'hic est filius me[us] dil[ec]tus, in q[uo] m[ihi] b[e]n[e com]placui'.

Ecce Homo: 'ecce homo'.

Maries at the Sepulchre: 'non est hic quem queritis, sed cito eu[n]tes nun[c]iate'.

Brazen Serpent: 'Moyses . qui aspexerit serpentem exaltatum salvabitur' and 'peccavimus q[uia] locuti sum[us] contra domin[u]m', 'ora ut tollat a nobis serpentes'.

Both Crucifixions: *'vere filius dei erat iste'.*
Haloes inscribed with names.

CONSTRUCTION
Tempera on oak-wood.

RECONSTRUCTION
A predella, depicting prophets holding scrolls (recorded in a drawing published by Hosmann, 1700), appears to have been lost when the altarpiece was moved to the museum.[3]

226

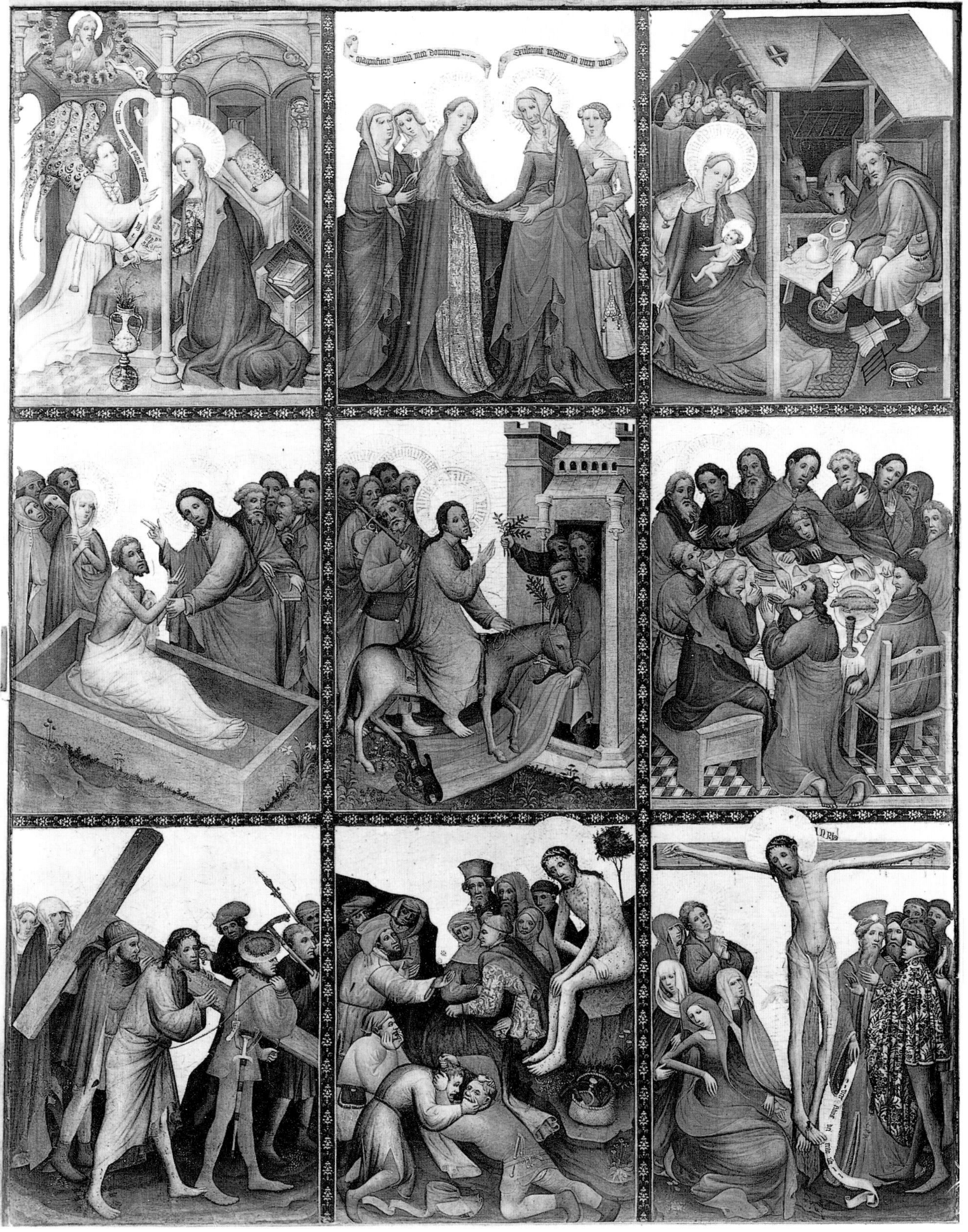

164. Master of the Golden Panel: inside of left outer wing, *Golden Panel from Lüneburg*

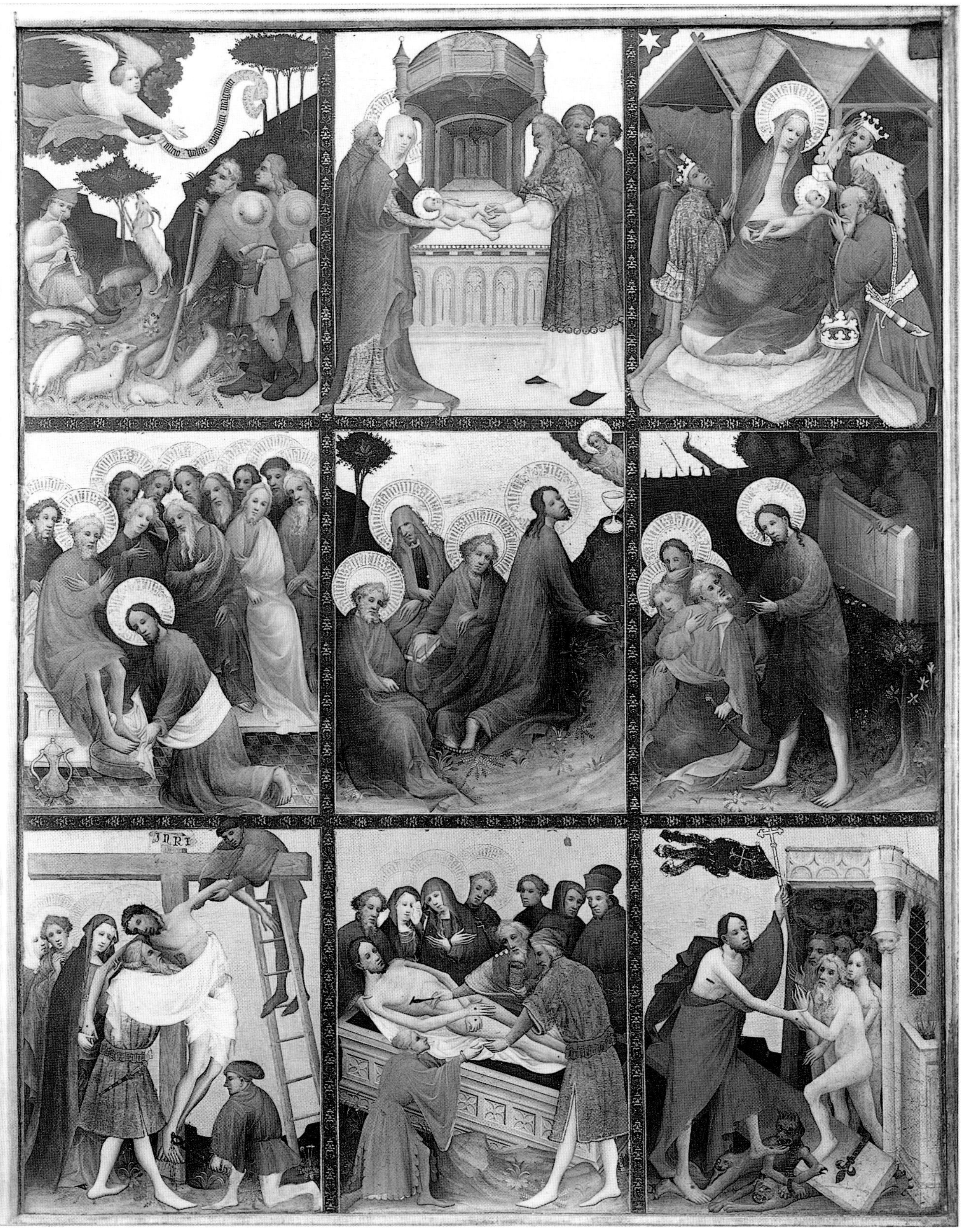

165. Master of the Golden Panel: outside of left inner wing, *Golden Panel from Lüneburg*

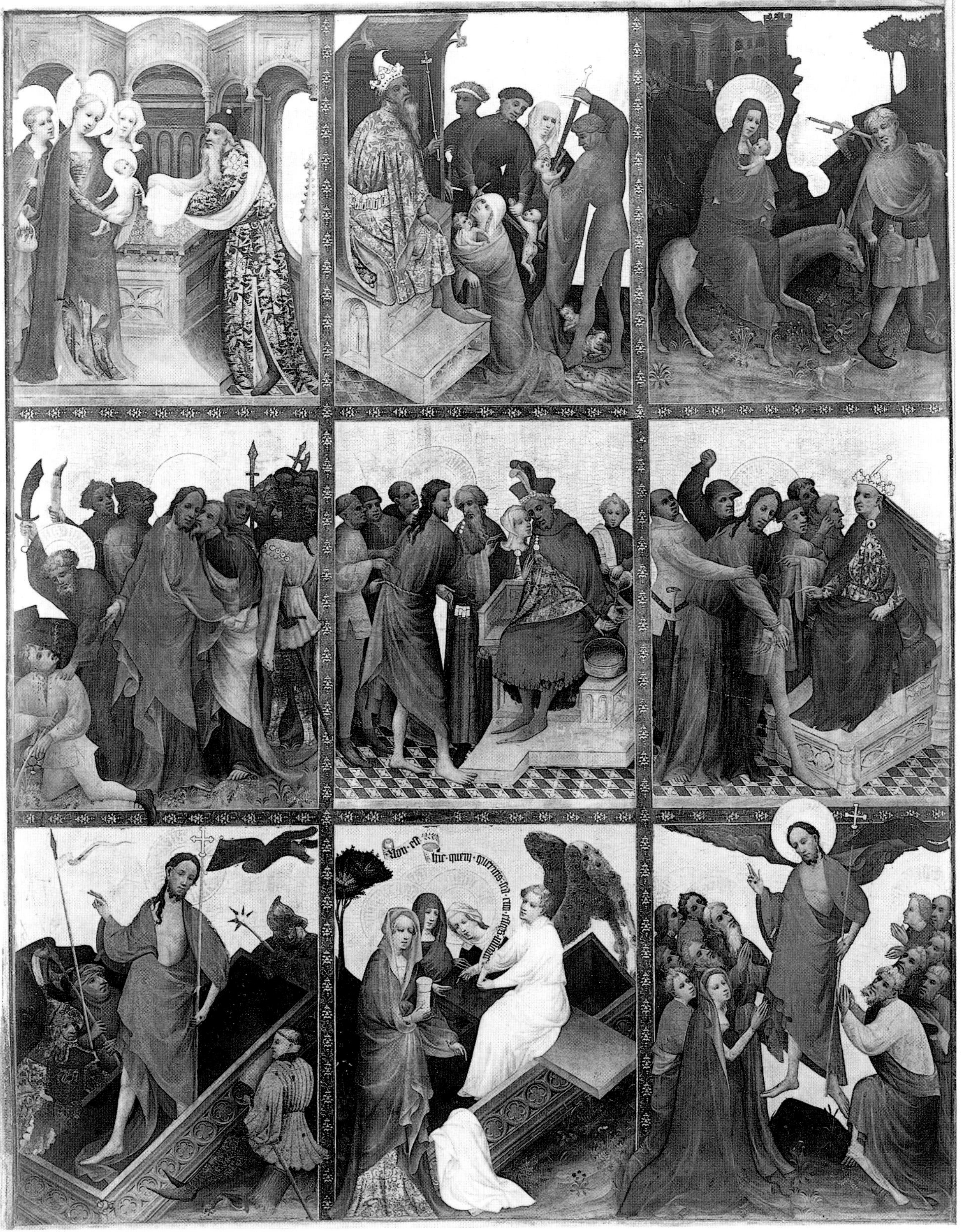

166. Master of the Golden Panel: outside of the right inner wing, *Golden Panel from Lüneburg*

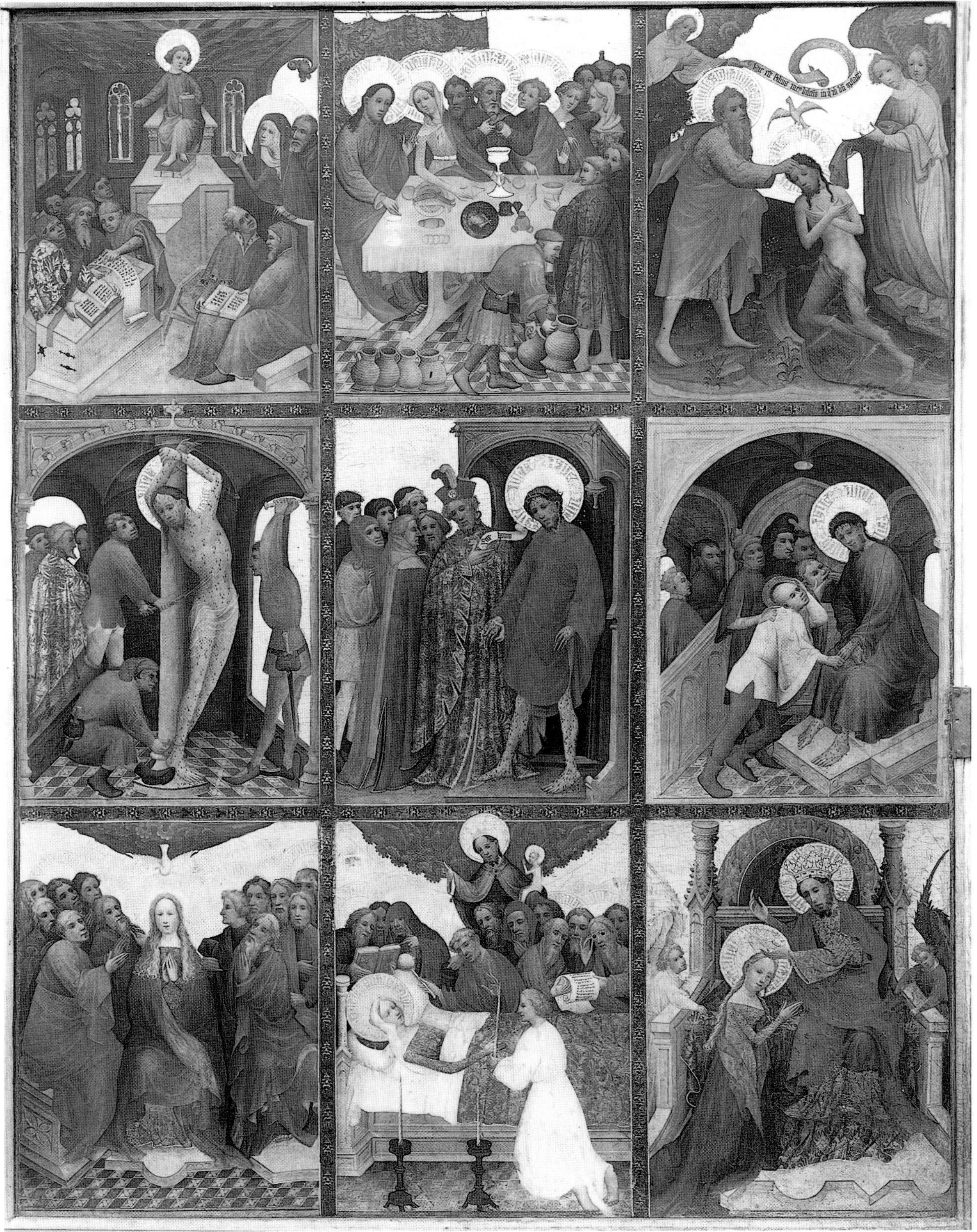

167. Master of the Golden Panel: inside of the right outer wing, *Golden Panel from Lüneburg*

SIZE

Each wing measures
height 231 cm
width 184 cm
individual panels, measured in the bottom row, 51 × 67.8 cm.

DATE

Blaschke (1976, pp. 106–111) stressed the poverty of the town of Lüneburg, devastated by succession feuds, and pointed to the slow progress of rebuilding and the appeals for funds through the sale of indulgences. Nonetheless, he suggested that the major part of the costly wings would have been in progress around 1418, and finished by 1425. Reinecke (1937, p. 54) and Stange (1967–78, I, no. 745), following some earlier authors, cited 1418 as the completion date of the painted wings.[4] They based their assertion on the assumption that the consecration of the hall of the church of St Michael in 1418, rebuilt after destruction in 1371, provides evidence of the existence of the complete altarpiece. However, the antependium had earlier sufficed for the altar. Moreover, the church was not finally completed until 1431. In 1431, however, Duke Bernhard presented the church of St Michael with his valuable collection of 'treasures and relics'. He stipulated that each object should be inscribed *dux behd dedt Ao 1431*. The Duke is unlikely to have been content to have his relics and treasures displayed in a position inferior to that of the abbey collection, housed in the antependium of the high altar. Abbot Boldewin von Wenden (1415–41), councillor to the duke, is also identified by Blaschke as a wealthy and potentially generous man, who had favoured the abbey itself with many gifts; he left Lüneburg to be installed (with great pomp) as Archbishop of Bremen in 1435.[5] I would suggest that a date around 1431–35, after the completion of the church and following the generous presentation by the duke and, if Blaschke's speculates correctly, also gifts from the abbot before his departure (he may, I would therefore suggest, be shown as the cleric in the donor group) appears more plausible for the costly addition of the carved and painted double wings to the

antependium. This date is also supported by the stylistic considerations.

HISTORY

The gold antependium and most of its treasures were stolen from the church of St Michael in 1698. Around 1792–94, the wings were moved by Abbot von Bülow to a 'Ritterakademie' he had founded; from 1861 onwards they were displayed in the Welfenmuseum (now Landesmuseum) in Hanover. The left wing was exhibited in Brussels and in Amsterdam in 1949 (no. 137) and in Paris in 1950 (no. 59). The left outer wing is listed in the catalogue of the *Vor Stefan Lochner* exhibition, Cologne (1974, no. 52), but it was not actually exhibited there. The altarpiece was first praised by the monk Paul Lange in 1515 (see Reuter, 1918, p. 19); it was described by Gebhardi as 'sehr verzeichnet' in 1762 (p. 183); the first art-historical assessment was published by Waagen in 1862 (p. 62).

There is evidence of restorations on the surface of the altarpiece. Blisters and flaking have been treated, and small areas of paint appear to have been touched up, but no record of this work has been kept. However, Reinecke reported in 1937 (p. 54) that the altarpiece had been cleaned.

COMMENT

Blaschke (1976, p. 152, n. 38, and p. 153, n. 47) correctly suggested as *terminus post quem* for the completion of the wings the date of 1412, the last entry in the surviving account book of the monastery. However, his assertion that the lack of any reference to a 'Master of the Golden Panel' in the oldest extant *Lüneburger Schossrollen* of 1426 should be regarded as the *terminus ante quem* is difficult to follow.

Although there is no evidence for this hypothesis, the Cord von Soest mentioned in the *Schossrollen* between 1426 and 1451, could be the son of Conrad von Soest. Painter dynasties were formed in Westphalia, and the painter of the Golden Panel from Lüneburg may have inherited from Conrad von Soest the model book that served as the basis for the design of the altarpiece (see pp. 88–91).

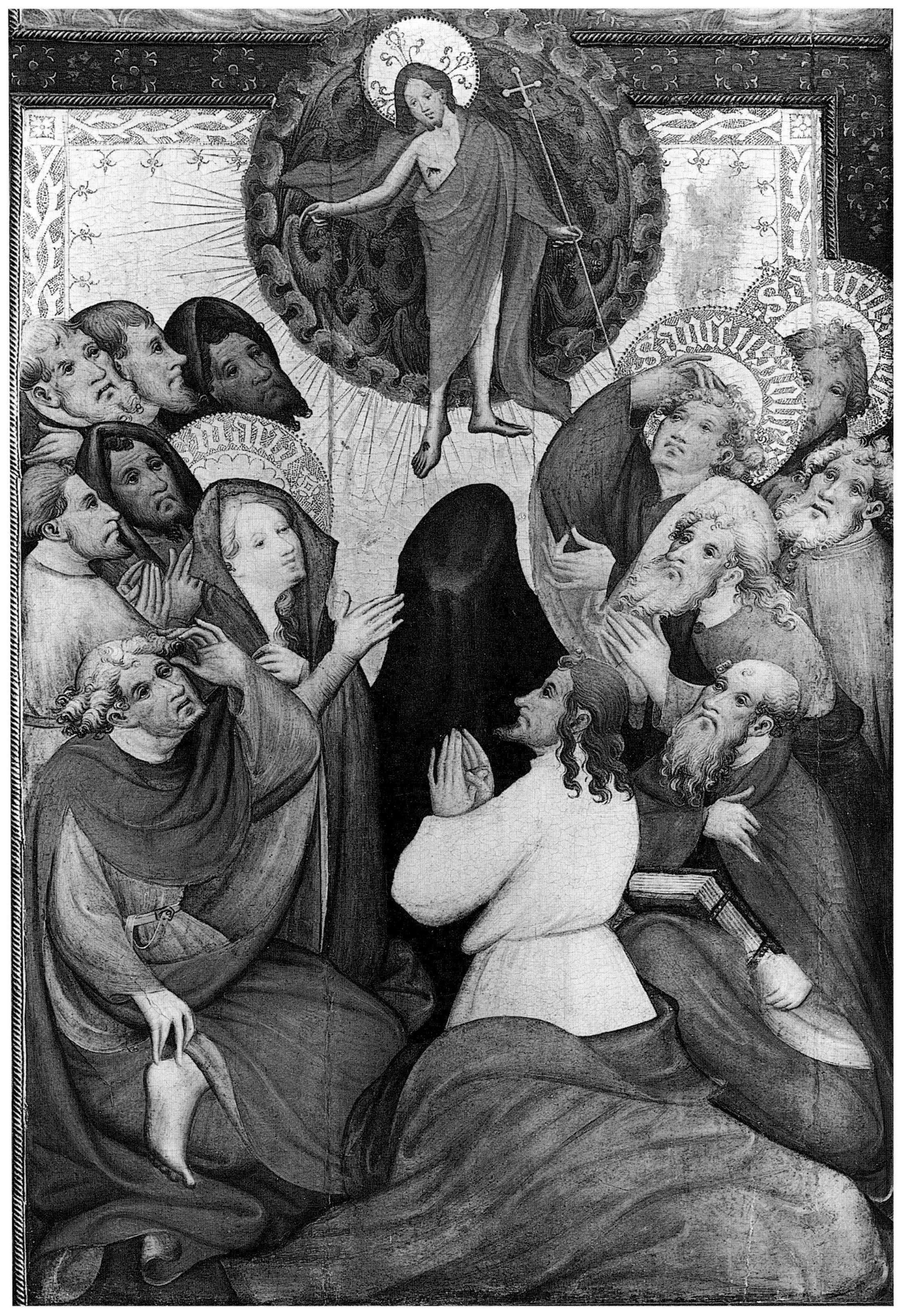

168. Conrad von Soest: *Ascension*. Niederwildungen Altarpiece

Notes

Chapter 1

1. This book is based on my Ph.D. thesis *Conrad von Soest; his Altarpieces, his Workshop and his Place in European Art*, Courtauld Institute and Birkbeck College, University of London, 1991, in which can be found more detailed references and bibliography. A number of documents, cited by historians, have been lost through bomb damage or possibly have been mislaid in certain largely unsorted archives. I am therefore particularly indebted to Herr Hochgrebe, Bad Wildungen, who showed me some earlier manuscript transcriptions by Loewe of documents which are now lost. It was impracticable to undertake an exhaustive study of all extant relevant manuscripts in unsorted archives, and I hope that this initial enquiry may encourage further research.

2. 'This work has been completed by the painter Conrad von Soest in the year of the Lord 1403 on the day of St Giles the Confessor [1 September] in the time of the rector of the Devine Service, the priest, Conrad Stollen'. Because of the damaged surface, infra-red examination yielded no further information. Meyer-Barkhausen, 1931, p. 7, n. 4, seems to suggest that the Dickius manuscript was then in the possession of Prof. A. Eichler. The Varnhagen manuscripts of 1778 and 1793, are in the Archiv des Waldeckischen Geschichtsvereins, Arolsen, ref. 'Varnhagen'; J. A. Th. L. Varnhagen published *Grundlage der waldeckischen Landes- und Regentengeschichte* in 1825 (Göttingen).

3. Whilst no surviving Westphalian panels are signed or dated, the Bielefeld Altarpiece (cat. no. 8) was reported by Ledeburs, 1825/28, to have borne the date 1400 on its frame and the Grabow Altarpiece by Master Bertram was originally dated 1379 (see Platte, 1982). On the signatures, see Fritz, 1950a, pp. 111–113, although it is difficult to accept his suggestion that the word 'tremoniensis' (from Dortmund) is hidden in the remaining letters. De Bruin, 1968, p. 197, interprets other letters as anagrammatical messages, including the use of the 'secret code of Bonifatius'. There seems little justification for such hidden messages, as the same information was clearly written on the frame.

4. The varied latinized spellings of Soest derive from the low German 'Soust'. On the painter Conrad in Soest, see Rothert, 1958, p. 9 (1308: col. 55). The notion that Conrad originated from Soest, and that he had a workshop there, was first suggested by Nordhoff, 1879, pp. 100–137; it is based on the attribution to Conrad von Soest of the St Nicholas Panel (cat. no. 7) in the chapel of St Nicholas at Soest and the panels showing St Odilia and St Dorothea (cat. no. 3) from the convent of St Walpurgis near Soest. However, examination by infrared photography, discussed below, has now revealed that the St Nicholas Panel was not painted by Conrad von Soest or his workshop. The Saints panels (which are by the hand of Conrad) were produced for a convent for patrician daughters which was liberally supported by Dortmund families. Furthermore, no contemporary documentary material exists in Soest which could plausibly be linked with the painter.

5. For the Koerbeckes, see Prinz, 1941, p. 99; for the Koerbeckes and tom Rings, see Kirchhoff, 1977, p. 98; for the Baegerts, see Baxhenrich-Hartmann, 1984, pp. 135–136; see also Geisberg, 1941, p. 147. It is interesting to note that Koerbecke is also a Westphalian place-name. For Johann von Soest, see Kirchhoff, 1977, p. 98.

6. During the 1390s, Dethmar Cleppink acted as a 'sheffer' in 1391, 1395 and 1397, and Hermann as a burgomaster in 1391, 1393, 1395 and 1397, and as a 'sheffer' in 1392; Arnd Sudermann was a burgomaster in 1394, 1396 and 1398, and a 'sheffer' in 1391–93; Everd Wystrate acted as 'sheffer' in 1390, 1396 and 1398; Lambert Berswordt was a burgomaster in 1394, and 1396, and was also active in Bruges where he served as alderman on several occasions; and Clawes Swarte (brother of Albert, burgomaster four times during that decade) was not a burgomaster until 1410; the same names took office also in other years.
The names are listed in the Dortmund Chronicle, the Chronicle of Johann Kerkhoerde, 1405–65 (it includes parts, up to the year 1389, written earlier by Frater Johann Nederhoff). The Kerkhoerde chronicle now only exists in two manuscript copies, one by the historian Detmar Mülher (1567–1633) of about half of its original text. Dietrich Westhoff (d. 1551), in his version, included (in the form of additional sentences in the margin of the text) some parts of the Kerkhoerde manuscript which Mülher ignored. Westhoff also added a mostly invented history which starts in the year

750. The chronicles are published by Lamprecht, 1887.

7. The original has perished, but the contract was copied, apparently as a model for such documents, and the copy was published by Rübel, 1890, II, and by Winterfeld in 1934 (see 1981 edn, following p. 32). However, the copy also perished in 1945, and the translation here (Appendix A) is based on the transcription published by Winterfeld. Conrad von Soest is not named as a painter in this contract, as it was not customary to mention the named party's profession in such documents. The fact that the contract was written according to Dortmund town law, and was also copied as a sample document, demonstrates that Conrad was a burgher of Dortmund. The absence of Conrad's name from the lists of new burghers shows that he had not merely acquired citizenship before his marriage but had been born in Dortmund. The painter Lambert, cited by Winterfeld as possibly the deceased father of the bride, appears in the membership list of the Confraternity of the Marienkirche after 1396. Gertrud's father, however, is cited as 'deceased' in the contract of 1394.
On Dortmund Marriage Contracts, see Rübel, 1900, pp. 1–40.

8. The name von Soest does not appear in the patrician lists for councillors or other documents pertaining to patricians, and Conrad's craft was not normally practised by patricians.

9. Stadtarchiv Dortmund, ref. 'Marienkirche'. The list also records a 'Ghese van Soust, resident in the same part of the Hellweg [in Conrad's house?] and *'Johan van Soust et uxor'* who lived just around the corner. It seems therefore reasonable to assume that the 'painter Conrad' was Conrad von Soest, especially as he painted the high altarpiece for this Confraternity, see below. Another painter, Lambert, is listed for the same part of the road. It is feasible, though not proven, that he worked in Conrad's workshop. A 'Hermann meler', cited by Winterfeld, 1925, who apparently arrived in Dortmund in 1403, is also listed. It is not possible to date this entry.
The fragments (1396–1541) include burial reports until 1424. However, the fact that Conrad is not cited in this fragmentary list does not permit one to conclude that he was still alive in 1424. Nor is it likely that Conrad emigrated to Lüneburg at that time, as has sometimes been suggested because a 'Cord von Soest' appears in the *Schossrollen* there, 1426–51. One cannot really suppose that a successful master would leave a still thriving town when already in his sixties to settle in a less important place. Guild regulations would not have favoured such a move either. If Cord was a painter, it is feasible that he was the Dortmund painter's son who, after an apprenticeship and

travels as a journeyman, was free to settle in a new town. Stylistic similarities between the Golden Panel from Lüneburg and the altarpieces in Niederwildungen and Dortmund which support this hypothesis are discussed below.

10. For references to the Berswordt and Sudermann families, see Knippenberg, 1955, and Meyer, 1930, *passim*; for references to the Hengstenbergs, see Meininghaus, 1930. On the patricians in general, see Winterfeld, 1924–26.

11. Stadtarchiv Dortmund, ref. St Petri-Nicolai.

12. Lindemann, 1978, published the business correspondence of Hildebrand Veckinchusen. These letters show that Veckinchusen also traded in cotton, flax, yarn, gold thread, gum varnish and colours, fish, meat, butter, wine, beer, rice, sugar, raisins, figs, almonds, spices and medicinal plants, wax, copper, lead, cork, corals, amber rosaries, and frankincense from Arabia.

13. 'Germany' is used for the loose confederation of independent German speaking areas at this time.

14. Pisan, 1985 edn, p. 154 and p. 153. Dr Heinrich Sudermann (d. 1377) can be cited as an example to demonstrate the internationality of Dortmund's patricians. He studied in Bologna and was later knighted by King John of Bohemia. After assisting the Archbishop of Cologne at the election of the Emperor, he became *nuntius apostolicae sedis* in turn to Popes Innocent VI, Urban V and Gregory IX at Avignon. See Meyer, 1930, *passim*. See also Chapter 9, note 46.

15. 'Koninck Artus Hof', see Meininghaus, 1930, p. 40. He cites the Dortmund chronicle (XX, p. 43). Patrician confraternities in other towns, such as Thorn and Danzig, also called their house 'Artushof'.

16. On the Hanseatic League, see Dollinger, 1970; on Dortmund and the Hanseatic League, see also Luntowski, 1986. It is difficult to understand therefore that Musper, 1961, p. 203, defined Westphalia as 'a completely agricultural area without the world-wide connections of the Hansa towns'.

17. Since the middle of the 13th century, Westphalia's borders had been the Rhine in the West and the Weser in the East, Oldenburg in the North and Hesse in the South. Waldeck was generally counted as Westphalian by medieval authors; there are uncertainties about the Netherlandish border.

18. On the extent of the dukedom, see Janssen, 1980–81, I, pp. 58–64, 136–142.

19. On the Feud of Dortmund, see Fahne, 1974, and the Dortmund Chronicle, op. cit. (note 6), and Stadtarchiv Dortmund, ref. IV, no. 5: Fehdebuch 1388–89.

20. Between 1389 and 1400 the town borrowed considerable sums from still affluent patricians. For records of these loans, see documents in Stadtarchiv Dortmund, Repositorium, II, nos. 903–911.

21. Wenceslas was deposed in 1400, having acted as uncrowned Emperor from 1378. Sigismund reigned as King of the Romans from 1411; he had the title of Emperor only from 1433. It is interesting to note that the Feud of Soest (1446–1449) further weakened the power of the Archbishop of Cologne. Sigismund reaffirmed Dortmund's status in 1417 by granting a charter to mint coins and by installing the town council as the 'oberste Fehmgericht', the highest law court which judged cases in which a direct appeal had been made to the Emperor. Furthermore, he ordered the Archbishop of Cologne to protect Dortmund, especially against Kleve-Mark.

Chapter 2

1. See, for example, the contract between the Prior of the Spedale degli Innocenti, Florence, and the painter Domenico Ghirlandaio, as cited in Baxandall, 1984, p. 6: '…he is to colour and paint the said panel all with his own hand in the manner shown in a drawing on paper with those figures and in that manner shown in it, in every particular according to what I…think best; and he must colour the panel at his own expense with good colours and with powdered gold…;…and if it does not seem to me worth the stated price, he shall receive as much less as I…think right'.

2. Guild regulations for the various towns are published as follows: for Münster, see Krumbholtz, 1898, pp. 336–346. Although they were written around 1587, the Münster statutes are thought to reflect earlier 15th-century rules, destroyed after the temporary abolition of the guild by the Anabaptists (around 1533) who had destroyed the archives. This assumption is supported by a reference to 'wat for dem jare 1533…hir…' in fol. 9. of the regulations. For Lüneburg (1467–1558, including a copy of regulations of the guild of goldsmiths from c. 1400; separate regulations for painters and glaziers from c. 1497), see Bodemann, 1883, pp. 94–163; for Cologne (1371–96 and 1449, of a mainly political nature), see Loesch, 1984, pp. 134–141; for Soest (law of the ten guilds since c. 1410), see Hauer, typed manuscript, 1931; for Osnabrück (1484), see Philippi, 1890, pp. 64–67; for Brunswick, see Ahrsberg, 1917. More information about painters in Münster can be found in Geisberg, 1941, pp. 147–182. Judging by surviving regulations in Lüneburg of before 1497, 1497, 1523 and 1595, the basic guild rules for painters did not change significantly over the years.

3. See Homann, 1982, p. 9.

4. For the letters of these brothers, see Exh. Cat. Brunswick, 1985, II, p. 724, no. 634. On travelling journeymen, see Reininghaus, 1981, pp. 1–21.

5. In Lüneburg three masterpieces were required, 'so to Lubeke Hamborch unde in anderen steden umme lank her wontlik is'; see Bodemann, 1883, p. 156.

6. See Manske, 1985, II, p. 770 and III, p. 348.

7. See Frensdorff, 1882, *passim*. The 'Sechs-Gilden Recht' (1402) is published in Fahne, 1974, III, pp. 214–225. It gives no information on the rules of single guilds as it was written to consolidate the position of all the guilds. It is not known how many painters were established in Dortmund, apart from those mentioned in the membership list of the confraternity of the Marienkirche and three new masters who became burghers in Dortmund between 1366 and 1424. However, during a conflict in 1395 the town council forbade 'allen Dortmunder Malern und jedem einzelnen', to decorate the Benedictine chapel in the western gate of the town; see Winterfeld, 1981b, p. 82.

8. As Baxandall (1981, p. 63) observes, high altars 'were not usually open to individual patronage' as 'most high altarpiece retables were commissions from communities, in town churches of a parish or town council…and in abbey churches of the house itself…'.

9. Winterfeld, 1981a, p. 34. The Monday evening procession and service at the St Anthony altar was compulsory for councillors. The church was also used for certain meetings of the patrician councillors.

10. On this function of confraternities, see Henderson, 1988, pp. 383–394. The rules of the confraternity of the Marienkirche in Dortmund do not survive, but they may have been similar to those of the Münster painter's guild of c. 1587 (Krumbholtz, 1898, p. 342): 'Tor begrefnissen der gildebroeder, suster and kindere sullen alle gildebroeder bi den brocke 1 Schl. verpflichtet sin, sunder orlof to bidden, dem licham na tom graeve

to volgen...Und dar over jumant sulkes versuimde, so veer he in der stat gewest, als de doede verscheide, sall der gilde geven 4 Schl...'.
The Bielefeld Altarpiece dedicated to the Virgin (cat. no. 8) has a central *Sacra Conversazione*, the Marian Fröndenberg Altarpiece (cat. no. 5) had a painting or sculpture of the *Madonna and Child*. When the *Death of the Virgin* is represented, even in altarpieces that follow Conrad von Soest's design closely (for instance the Jacobi Altarpiece (pl. 60) in Soest and the Barfüsser Altarpiece in Hanover), the scene of Mary's death is shown in the wing panels. The only contemporary retable that does show the *Death of the Virgin* as the central painting is the Blankenberch Altarpiece in the Landesmuseum, Münster (pl. 57) , which is a very close—if not very masterly—copy of the Dortmund Altarpiece. This altarpiece was commissioned by the Prior Johannes Blankenberch (1421–43) of the convent of St Walpurgis near Soest and the subject is as appropriate to the caring function of this convent community at the time of the death of a nun, as to that of the confraternity of St Mary connected with St. Walpurgis.

11. Rules of Raimond du Puy (XIV), see Lagleder, 1983, p. 146; and King, 1931, p. 327; 'in prima missa unusquisque fratrum qui aderit candelam cum nummo offerat'. St John, in the Dortmund *Death of the Virgin* carries such a candle with a coin.

12. I am indebted to Jochen Luckhardt for this information; he will be publishing the document in the near future (see also J Luckhardt, 1996). This confraternity was first mentioned in 1300. The donor of the altarpiece (see note 10), was an ardent supporter of the confraternity.

13. The retable, now in the St Annen-Museum (Inv. No. 1926/312), Lübeck, has painted wings (*c.* 1430) that indicate a strong influence from Conrad's altarpieces. On the 'Zirkelbrüder', see Boockmann, 1986, p. 294.

14. 'Dass hohe Altar auff dem Chor, so der hochgebennedeiten Juffer St. Mariae sampt der gantzen Kirchen weyland zugeeignet und eingeweiht gewesen'. The inventory has been overlooked in the literature on Conrad von Soest, and the problem of patronage has therefore remained unsolved. Pastor J.C. Brügman, priest from 1679–1705 tried to put order into church regulations and family endowments of altars in this Protestant church, where Catholic families still had Mass said at their altars, and where the high altarpiece still showed the Catholic rite of Extreme Unction as its main subject (until 1720). (The Brügman family were pastors of the church from 1622–1775). The Brügman manuscript is now lost, but it was published by Ernste, 1931, pp. 155–184. Brügman quoted an inventory from *c.* 1432 (then in the Dortmund town archives, lost during the Second World War), and thus dated the following altars then still in the church:

> *Beatorum Joh. Baptistae, Catharinae et Barbarae Virginum* (1311)
> *St Annae prope Choru*m (*c.* 1515)
> *St Cruci*s (Berswordt, 1431)
> *St Petri et Paul*i (before 1432)
> *Antonij Confessoris (bey der ersten grossen Kirchenthüre)*, (before 1432; see p. 25 above)
> *Mariae Magdalenae* (and St Fabian, St Sebastian and St Giles, before 1432)
> *Dass hohe Altar auff dem Chor* (before 1432); the Dortmund Altarpiece.

15. Demandt, 1985, p. 623, suggests that an altar, mentioned in his will by Berthold Deines of Wildungen, could show that Deines' father Degenhardt had been the donor of the Niederwildungen Altarpiece. The Deines altar, however, is named as 'St Sebastian and Vallentin' in a document by Berthold's brother in 1416; see Demandt, p. 642. For the same altarpiece, Curtze, 1850, p. 605, suggested that it may have been an atonement gift by Heinrich VII of Waldeck. Heinrich had been involved in the plot to murder Elector Friedrich of Brandenburg on the return from the election of the Emperor in 1400. Although he was clearly one of the ringleaders, Heinrich was never accused of murder, and it is unlikely that he would have demonstrated his guilt by an atonement gift. It is, incidentally, interesting to note the international career of a Wildungen burgher: Berthold Deines, Deyne or Deynhardi was a Doctor of Theology in Bologna; a Procurator at the Councils of Viterbo (1406), Pisa (1408) and Constance (1415); a Canon at Fritzlar (1416). He was an avid collector of prebends which included churches in Utrecht, Mainz and Cologne. He was a professor at the universities of Heidelberg and Pisa.

16. For the history of the town, see Reichardt, 1949. Wildungen was divided into 'Dorfwildungen', a village on the road to Fritzlar, and 'Niederwildungen' [or Alt-Wildungen] a new town, founded in 1242. The much enlarged town is now called Bad Wildungen.
Reichardt, p. 40, suggests that the Count of Waldeck who died in 1397 was Heinrich V; Hochgrebe, p. 11, corrects this to Heinrich VI). Ignoring his will, his sons Heinrich VII (d. 1442) and Adolf (d. 1431) shared the Waldeck lands between them from 1397 to 1421. Heinrich VII held Wildungen. The von Waldeck became 'Reichsgrafen' in 1349.

17. The pumping of water to Niederwildungen is recorded in the altarpiece chronicle (Appendix B). For the veneration of St Elizabeth of Marburg, see Exh. Cat. Marburg, 1983.

236

18. See Varnhagen, 1825, p. 99. Perhaps the hospital was founded in response to the severe plague of 1349/50. On the Order of St John, see Winterfeld, 1859, and also Bradford, 1981. The confraternity of the 'Kalandbrüder' (founded in 1386?) cannot be considered as potential corporate patrons, as they were only granted permission in 1414 to hold mass in the church (by the Commander of the Order of St John).

19. Hessisches Staatsarchiv, Marburg, no. 9908, 17 May 1402. Feudal tenure was granted on the condition that Masses were to be said in the church for the salvation of the departed parents and of their own souls.

20. Bull of Boniface IX, 10 November 1403 (Hessisches Staatsarchiv, Marburg, no. 9910). It should be noted that this document was confirmed to be genuine by Archbishop Johannes of Mainz on 27 October 1405 (Marburg, no. 9913). The term 'commandery' is defined in the Statutes of the Order of St John as follows: 'Sous le nom et le mot "Commanderies" sont compris les Prieurez, la Chatelaine d'Emposte, les Baillages, terres, membres, maisons, possessions et tous autres biens de nostre Ordre, de quelque nature qu'ils soient' (Winterfeld, 1859, p. 42). The name 'Preceptor', although still used in Latin texts, was changed to 'Commander' in the 13th century (King, 1931, p. 79).

21. See Rörig, 1909–14, p. 53. Stollen is also mentioned in documents dated 13 July 1403 and 20 September 1405 (Hessisches Staatsarchiv, Marburg), cited in Loewe, 1928, p. 19. On the names of Commanders, see Eichler, 1930, p. 42, and Hochgrebe, 1986, pp. 30 and 27. Hochgrebe cites Johann Gogrebe as Commander of Wildungen and Wiesenfeld from 1370–81. However, Wildungen only became a commandery in 1403. Curd Stolle is last mentioned in 1428, unless the Curdt Stoll, registered in 1451, is still the same person.

22. The town's *Pfennigrechnungen* (accounts) and records of donations to the Order are preserved in the town archives, Bad Wildungen. The invoices of the Commandery only start in 1532, after the Reformation, but they refer to donations, endowments in connection with all privately or communally owned altars in the Stadtkirche, and to prebends for their chaplains. No donations are recorded in connection with the Niederwildungen Altarpiece, which further suggests that it belonged to the Order itself. Documents show that there were nine altars in the church by 1430:

> 1306 *' in honore glorios. virg. matr. Marie et sancte Elisabeth'*, in the choir. It is not known whether the high altar was adorned with another altarpiece before 1403.

> 1336 *'ante chorum St Crucis, Mariae et St Catherinae'*, endowed by the town council and the burghers which stood in the church (south aisle) until 1930.
> 1371 *'Beate Marie Virgines et triam regum'*.
> 1403 *'St Nikolaus Altar beim Bildnis der Jungfrau Maria'*, south aisle.
> 1405 *'St Andreas'*.
> 1405 *'St Martin'*, south aisle.
> 1425 *of Joh. Geismar*.
> 1425 *'St Johannis et St Jacobi'*, sacristy.
> 1428 *'St Crucis'* (for early masses in the Cross chapel, north).

23. For transcripts of the rules for the Order of St John of Raimond du Puy (1120–1158/60), Gérard Joubert (*c.* 1172–77) and Roger des Molins (1177–87) see Lagleder, 1983, pp. 130–187. There was always confusion as to which St John was venerated by the Order (see Bradford, 1983, p. 21, and Varnhagen, 1825, p. 99).

24. The cross potent was the principal feature of the arms of the Christian Kings of Jerusalem. The Knights of St John displayed it on their standards and shields at times, and it was stitched across their red *'sopraveste'* according to the rules of Raimond du Puy. The eight pointed cross was only displayed 'over the heart' on the black cloak (Winterfeld, 1859, p. 37).

25. The crescent-moon and the star were perhaps adopted, because they are also Marian symbols (Rev. 12.1). As the first hospital in Jerusalem was founded in 1020 by the people of Amalfi, who commemorated their invention of the compass in the 8-pointed star of their coat-of-arms, the star symbol may have further significance (Bradford, 1983, p. 21). The motif of crescent-moon and star was later frequently adopted to indicate the Christian Knight: see, for instance, the Heiligenkreuz Altar by the Master of the Sterzinger Altar (Musper, 1961, pls. 59, 69); the *Adoration of the Kings* (Cologne Cathedral); and the *Epiphany* of *c.* 1445 by Antonio Vivarini (Gemäldegalerie Berlin, Inv. No. 5). According to Nicolai, 1950, the eight-pointed cross, worn on the black cloak of the members of the Order, is a stylized development of the star. The eight-pointed star may also be a reference to the Waldeck star, a 'hidden reference' comparable to the signatures in the edge of the books. The crescent-moon and star were adopted for many coats-of-arms after the Crusades.

26. The rule of Roger des Molins, dated 14 March 1182, commands (chapter VI): *'Postea precepi quod lecti mortuorum fiant ad modum unius archancele, sicut lecti fratrum defunctorum, et cohoperiantur uno cohopertorio rubeo'*.

27. Hessisches Staatsarchiv, Marburg, 14 August 1491, no. 9962, Waldeck, Haus Wildungen. I am indebted to the students at the Staatsarchiv for their help in transcribing this document which I could only partially decipher.

28. In this connection it is interesting to study the contract for the *Coronation of the Virgin* by Enguerrand Quarton (1453) and note the extent to which the artist was given freedom in spite of lengthy iconographic instructions. I am indebted to Jochen Luckhardt for drawing the contract to my attention. It is published in 'Le Couronnement de la Vierge par Enguerrand Quarton', *Études Vauclusiennes*, XXIV–XXV, ed. Y. Grava, Avignon, 1981, pp. 54–55. It is instructive to study the finished panel, now in the Museé de Villeneuve-lès-Avignon, and to note considerable discrepancies between the directions and the execution.

29. Sauerland, 1913, p. 167, VII, 430 (1404, apr. 1). Only 24 persons (13 noblemen, 8 canons and 3 patricians) were awarded this privilege in the Rhinelands between 1393 and 1414.

30. For the King of France see *Grandes Chroniques de France*, ed. M. Paulia, Paris, 1838, 6, p. 382, and Sterling, 1987, p. 230. For the Medici, and Botticelli's De Lama *Adoration of the Magi* (Uffizi, Florence), see Lightbown, 1978, I, pl. 19. Vasari identified the portraits, some wrongly, in 1550.

31. However, the suggestion by Hucker, 1980/81, p. 407, that Emperor Sigismund, King Wenceslas and others are portrayed in the Niederwildungen *Crucifixion* is not supported by any reasoning or evidence, other than (presumably) the beard of the centurion. Great caution should be exercized in hazarding such attempts at detecting crypto-portraiture. The arbitrary identification of such 'portraits' can lead to excesses: Pilate, also bearded, in *Pilate washing his Hands* in the right wing of the Reinoldi Altarpiece has recently also been called 'Emperor Sigismund', ostensibly attended by Joan of Arc and the poet Oswald von Wolkenstein! (W.

Rinke, 'Das Tafelgemälde "Anklage, Verhör und Verurteilung Jesu" in St Reinoldi zu Dortmund', *Jahrbuch der Oswald von Wolkenstein Gesellschaft*, Dortmund, 1987/88). Quite apart from many other objections to such incongruous company, it is hardly likely that a town, indebted to the emperor for renewed prosperity, would show him as Pilate on their main altar. Similarly, suggestions that Conrad von Soest painted his own portrait and that of his wife in the Niederwildungen *Presentation* must be rejected; see Grundmann, 1966, p. 37. The figures cited by Grundmann are frequently found in Presentations and their facial features are of the general Conradian type.

32. On the fact that the features of the king at Niederwildungen also recur for Caiaphas, see Chapter 6 below. The hospitallers of St John were encouraged to lead a modest life of poverty; they are unlikely to have been portrayed in splendid attire. Unpublished documents in the Hessisches Staatsarchiv, Marburg [no. 9881 (1377) and nos. 9904 (1397)–9918 (1414)] record valuable donations to the Order of St John. Most documents mention the hope of salvation of the donor's soul. Letters of indulgence were also sold (for instance, no. 9881). Amongst the donations outside Dortmund is the gift of silver choir lights in 1399 by Segebodo Berswordt in memory of his brother Lambert (d. 1397) to the Carthusian monastery of St Barbara in Cologne. Only in 1430/31 was a donation finally made in the Marienkirche in accordance with Lambert's wishes; see cat. no. 9 below.

33. The silk lampas no. 8263–1863 from the Bock collection resembles the cloth of honour in the Dortmund *Adoration of the Kings*. The silk lampas no. 1304–1864 from the Bock collection resembles the coverlet in *Death of the Virgin*. A similar bird pattern from a 14th-century silk brocade in Berlin is illustrated in Klesse, 1967, pl. 4. See also H. Schmidt, 1938, pp. 195–206, who stressed the eastern derivation of certain Italian brocade motifs.

Chapter 3

1. Cennini (1960 edn, p. 3) promised that training and experience would eventually lead to proficiency in these tasks.

2. For the Strasbourg manuscript, see Borradaile, 1966. The Kloster Tegernsee manuscript is entitled *Liber illuministarius*, and excerpts are cited in Kühn, 1977 and Berger, 1912.

3. Some of this information was found in the unsorted church archives of Bad Wildungen and Dortmund. Of particular interest for the Dort-

mund Altarpiece were restoration reports by Hieronymi (manuscript reports, June 1927 and January 1930, Pfarrarchiv Marienkirche, Dortmund) and for the Niederwildungen Altarpiece a newspaper report by Medding (*Waldecker Landeszeitung*, 8 July 1950). Medding does not mention whether his description of colours is optical or based on examination results obtained by the restorer Jobst. I am also indebted to Rolf Fritz and Mrs M. Junkel for making their private records available to me.

4. See cat. no. 2 below.

5. Kühn, 1977, pp. 179–190, suggests that the ivory colour of gesso may be caused by being infiltrated by the binding medium of the colours, when no priming agent was used. Kühn found evidence (p. 179, note 8) in the Tegernsee *Liber illuministarius* that the application of six layers of gesso, increasingly thick in texture, was recommended.

6. For Thompson, see op. cit. (note 1), p. 79 and p. 73, note 1. See Kühn, 1977, p. 180; for Broederlam, see Kockaert, 1984, p. 7.

7. It may be remembered that the Limbourg brothers Jean and Herman were also apprenticed to a goldsmith in 1399; see Meiss and Beatson, 1974, p. 11. See Cennini, 1960 edn, pp. 85–86.

8. I am grateful to Erling Skaug who confirmed that neither the punchwork depicting a crown-of-thorns nor that of the clouds occurs in Italian panels. Skaug also commented on the excellence of the punchwork in Conrad's panels (verbal communication 5 February 1990). The crown-of-thorns can, however, be seen in the halo of the Christ child of the Wilton Diptych, National Gallery, London, which it will be argued below has some stylistic connection to work by Jacquemart de Hesdin. A mandorla of shapes which may be interpreted as clouds, but are of a very different nature from Conrad's, decorates Master Bertram's *Coronation of the Virgin* in the Buxtehude Altarpiece. As the panel was painted around 1410, the punched design may constitute a free version after Conrad's design.

9. See Cennini, 1960 edn, p. 86.

10. Steinbart, 1946, *passim*; see also Musper, 1961, p. 203: 'without Burgundian, French models one could certainly not imagine Konrad'; see also Châtelet/Recht, 1988, p. 119.

11. Sermon for the fourth Sunday of Advent, *Joh. Tauleri Predigten*, Frankfurt am Main, 1692, p. 35. On Tauler, see Gilson, 1985, pp. 443–444.

12. Ames-Lewis, 1982, pp. 190, 4, 7; this differentiation of terms, although not universally accepted, is adopted here as it is useful later in assessing the various types of relationships to Conrad's works. Ainsworth, 1989, p. 11, demonstrated that a model from the workshop of Dieric Bouts was still in use 'forty or fifty years' after his death.

13. Panofsky, 1971, p. 63, although he used 'model' and 'pattern' as interchangeable terms, noted these differences in drawings: 'When the Master of Klosterneuburg copied the frescos in the Arena Chapel it mattered little whether his model was Sienese or Florentine because he intended to appropriate impressive schemes of composition and not to emulate a style'.

14. Musper's criticism of the colours as 'farbenfroh, beinahe lustig' does not take this fact into account: see Musper, 1961, p. 203. On the effect and significance of candle-light on lustrous surfaces of altarpieces, see Braun, 1932, pp. 492–530.

15. Conrad appears to have dipped his brush, already loaded with other colours, into the lead white. Although certain opaque glazes give a similar impression, it is not possible to be certain that the different touches of colour were not painted into the wet glaze instead.

16. Kempfer, 1973 (pp. 7–49) was attempting to establish workshop connections between certain Northern German altarpieces by analysing their colour-schemes. Measuring against a modern colour-scale, she registered the shades of red in the Niederwildungen Altarpiece as 'cinnabar, saturated cinnabar, brilliant red, saturated brilliant red, carmine, saturated carmine, pale red, pink, white pink, blue red, grey ruby, orange red and saturated orange red'. Although Kempfer studied only the range of colours used in these altarpieces, and was not concerned with the scientific identification of pigments or glazing methods, her careful analysis permits some valuable insight into workshop practices.

17. Kempfer, ibid., listed five greens in this panel, and pointed to many additional subtle tonal varieties.

18. Frodl-Kraft, 1977/78, pp. 89–178.

19. Parement Master: Paris, Bibl. Nat., nouv. acq. lat. 3093, pp. 56, 181, 194, 189 and 209. It is interesting to note that Jacquemart de Hesdin, whose apparent connection with the Parement workshop will be discussed below, also used blue and yellow prominently, for instance in the *Annunciation*, Brussels, Bibl. Royale, MS 11060–1, p. 18.
Frodl-Kraft, op. cit., discusses the unpopularity of yellow as a local colour.

20. Dannenberg (1929, p. 98) and Pilz (1970, p. 42) speak of Conrad's use of 'rare and costly' cobalt blue. That colour, however, was not produced until after 1802, when it was discovered by Thenard. See also Kempfer, 1973, p. 22. These authors give no further information about this pigment. If they refer to the cobalt content of smalt, which Kühn (1977, p. 185) did find as a third layer below both ultramarine and azurite in two altarpieces (WRM 737 and WRM 62) in Cologne, painted between *c.* 1415 and *c.* 1430, it is not explained why

they considered it a 'costly' material. The history of cobalt blue is discussed by Harley, 1982, pp. 56–58.

21. I am most grateful to Gerry Hedley for his analysis of this sample on my behalf, and to Caroline Villers for discussing the result with me. Cennini, 1960 edn, pp. 36–39, describes the laborious production process involved when making ultramarine pigment from lapis lazuli. He comments on the 'heaviness of the blue' and suggests that therefore the blue from the first two washes is the best. He enthuses about the costly colour: 'Ultramarine blue is a colour illustrious, beautiful, and most perfect, beyond all other colours; one could not say anything about it, or do anything with it, that its quality would not still surpass'. The Strasbourg manuscript (see note 2 above) does not even mention ultramarine, and only suggests methods for azurite. Ultramarine is not mentioned by Theophilus either (early 12th century; see 1979 edn).

22. This is WRM 4, a panel painted *c.* 1300. See Kühn, 1977, p. 185 for analysis of panels in Cologne.

23. For the Blankenberch Altarpiece, see Exh. Cat. Münster, 1975, p. 118. The blue areas were, however, not transparent in my infra-red photographs; this seems to indicate significant amounts of azurite beneath any ultramarine.

24. The great transparency of the blues not only confirms ultramarine as the colour, but suggests its high quality. I am indebted to Caroline Villers

for this information. It should be noted that in the *Adoration of the Kings* at Dortmund the Virgins's cloak, the king's hood and the clouds have been restored in a blue colour not based on ultramarine. Cennini, 1960 edn, p. 60: '...your standing will be so good for using good colours...'. Baxandall, 1984, p. 15, explains the importance of 'conspicuous consumption of gold and ultramarine' in Italy in the early 15th century, until such a time when skill came to be valued above 'gilt splendour'. This clearly applies to Westphalia as well.

25. See Theophilus, 1979 edn.

26. For Broederlam, see Kokaert, 1984, p. 8; for the Parement Master, see Meiss 1967–74, I, p. 116. However, the realistic rugged faces of the Niederwildungen thieves, for instance, show detailed underdrawing through the brownish pigments.

27. See also Medding, op. cit. (note 3). Charcoal, however, seems unlikely; it may have been employed for the first sketch, as described by Cennini (p. 17), but would have been brushed off when the underdrawing proper was finished. Bone-black would appear more likely.

28. Hieronymi, op. cit. (note 3), does not name individual pigments in his restoration report.

29. Frodl-Kraft, 1977/78, pp. 89<196178.

30. On Conrad's knowledge of geometry see Fritz, 1950a; for his use of the 'golden section', see Rohrberg, 1968.

Chapter 4

1. See also Pächt, 1962, p. 53. By contrast, the novel structure of Ste-Chapelle in Paris (consecrated in 1248) is a good example of a style, created in one centre, that inspired diverse imitations throughout Western Europe. Its rayonnant splendour was echoed one hundred years later in the large windows of the Marienkirche in Dortmund.

2. The term was coined by Louis Courajod in his lecture of 1889, 'Style international gothique commun à toute l'Europe'; see Courajod, 1901. Whilst Courajod, like Huizinga in his historical perspective *The Waning of the Middle Ages* (London, 1924), tended towards pioneering exaggeration, their work prompted an interest in the style and period that has permitted a more balanced evaluation over time.

3. Alternative terms coined in Germany, 'weicher Stil' and 'schöner Stil', in turn fail to refer to the international flavour of the style and do not relate

to the elegance of its designs. However, these terms seem pertinent to the descriptions of some German sculpture of the time, typified by the 'schöne Madonna'.

4. See Sterling, 1962, pp. 66–78; on Mannerism, see Shearman, 1967.

5. The Boucicaut Master [Jacques Coene?] created deep spatial settings, for example in the *Office of the Dead* of the *Hours of Marshal Jean de Boucicaut* (Paris, Museé Jacquemart-André, MS 2, fol. 142v; *c.* 1399–1411) and in *King Charles VI in conversation with Pierre Salmon* in the *Dialogue of Pierre Salmon* (Geneva, Bibl. Publique et Universitaire, MS fr. 165, fol. 4; *c.* 1412). But in each case the spatial setting is partially denied by large areas of intense surface pattern of a furnishing material that seems to defy the setting. An intentional denial of the depth of a space can be demonstrated in the *Bedford Hours*, London, BL, MS Add. 18850, for in-

stance fols. 32 and 257 (after 1423), where architectural backdrops to several scenes are prevented from having spatial significance by a cloth of honour, stretched across the entire scene, thus creating a shallow stage. For frontal projection see, for example, the *Annunciation* by Jacquemart de Hesdin in *Très belles heures de Jean de Berry*, Brussels, Bibl. Royale, MS 11060–61, p. 18 (*c*. 1385–90? before 1402; pl. 70 below), where the angel is placed in front of the building, which seems to define the picture plane. The master of the *Grandes heures de Rohan*, Paris, Bibl. Nat., lat. 9471, fol. 135 (after 1417), used this device frequently; in the *Lamentation of the Virgin*, for example, Christ's head and foot, and God's halo, overlap the frame.

6. For an historic survey see Waley, 1987. For a contemporary view, see Jean Froissart's chronicle (1337–1410), London, 1906.

7. The published inventories include Guiffrey, 1894–97; Doutepont, 1906; Moranvillé, 1906; and Graves, 1926.

8. On account of the sharply characterized and powerfully modelled thieves depicted there, Panofsky (1971, p. 71) hailed Conrad von Soest as an early naturalist and went on to extol the linear description of his noble protagonists.

9. See White, 1987, p. 60.

10. This archaizing trend may be due to patrons' instructions. It does, however, suit the narrative and decorative intent of the painter.

11. See for example the *Depositions*, Paris, Bibl. Nat., nouv. acq. lat. 3093, p. 216 and Brussels, Bibl. Royale, MS 11060–61, p. 194.

12. Frontal arrangements can be seen in the *Presentation* and the *Adoration of the Kings*; softened oblique settings in the *Christ mocked before Herod* and *Christ before Pilate*, where the lines of the roof run delicately downwards, rather than parallel to the picture plane; oblique arrangements in the *Resurrection* and in the *Annunciation*, where the

obliquely placed prie-dieu and other furniture are contrasted by a softly oblique canopy.

13. This may be observed in the *Christ before Pilate* and *Christ mocked before Herod* scenes, where both architecture and figures overlap. Figures in the *Ascension*, *Gethsemane* and *Presentation* panels also greatly overlap the inner frame. In the *Presentation*, the lady with the basket of doves is shown to stand behind Mary. A pillar in front of Mary positions both figures firmly within the temple. The red mantle of the woman with the dove is, however, allowed to sweep in an elegant curve over the left-hand border, and she therefore appears to be placed in front of the building as well. This ambiguous placing is achieved through the visual trick of painting a floor tile in front of the base of this lateral border to make room for the long mantle. The frame appears therefore to be pushed backwards in the lower left corner, but serves its usual function, marking the picture plane, around the rest of the scene.

14. This 'perspective' of light and shade is not used by Conrad's immediate followers in Westphalia either. Earlier Italian examples include Simone Martini's fresco cycle of the life of St Martin at Assisi. Pucelle employed this method in the *Book of Hours of Jeanne d'Evreux*, for instance in the *Annunciation*, fol. 16 (New York, The Cloisters, Metropolitan Museum of Art). It can then be noted in the workshops of the Parement Master (*Wedding at Cana*, Paris, Bibl. Nat., nouv. acq. lat. 3093, p. 68) and Jacquemart de Hesdin (*Annunciation*, Brussels, Bibl. Royale, MS 11060–61, p. 18).

15. However, the Boucicaut Master used visible brushstrokes on distant objects to indicate forms broken in atmospheric haze.

16. It is further supported by a strong diagonal construction line that moves from St John's clasped hands along the back of Longinus and the drapery of the angel directly to Christ's face. On the use of light in early Italian painting, see Hills, 1990.

Chapter 5

1. As Meiss (1967–74, I, p. VIII) comments: 'In the study of this art as of others the use of the 'eye' alone, while fundamental, is not enough'.

2. For a considerable list of such attributions see, for instance, Nordhoff, 1879, and Meier, 1931; for the argument concerning regional characteristics see Nordhoff, 1879, and Pieper, 1964. The Westphalian characteristics are summarized by Musper, 1961, p. 203 as 'derb, standfest und langsam

im Denken' [coarse, steadfast and slow of thought], and those of Cologne by Pieper, 1974, p. 41 as 'subtile, empfindsame Zartheit' [subtle, sensitive delicacy].

3. See Stange, 1934–61, III, p. 29.

4. See J. Luckhardt, *Das Kunstwerk des Monats*, Westfälisches Landesmuseum Münster, January, 1989; Luckhardt attributes the Kisters panel to the

workshop of the Master of the Calvary of St Andreas (WRM 353)(pl. 118).

5. Blaschke, 1976, pp. 55, 62, for example, resorted to *Zeitgeist* to explain the remarkable stylistic and technical coincidence between the work of Conrad von Soest and that of the Master of the Golden Panel from Lüneburg (cat. no. 13). See also Châtelet/Recht, 1989, pp. 218–222; Snyder, 1985, pp. 82–83; and Zehnder, 1981, *passim.*

6. I am indebted to Caroline Villers for her encouragement and advice. The photography had to be limited to panels that were either reasonably ascribed to Conrad von Soest or had significant implications for our understanding of his work. However, the underdrawing of the *Maria Lactans* in the Kunstmuseum at Dortmund was also studied at the request of the Museum, although the rather wooden surface appearance and the painting technique clearly excluded it from Conrad's *oeuvre*. The hesitant underdrawing (in outline only) confirmed that the panel was not designed by Conrad, and it also showed the derivative nature of the design. Surprisingly, the panel is still exhibited as painted by Conrad von Soest. The *Crucifixion* labelled 'Konrad von Soest' in the Emil G. Bührle collection, Zürich is very different from his autograph work and probably not even Westphalian in origin.

7. Asperen de Boer, 1975, pp. 8–12. Azurite and malachite are copper minerals, so closely related chemically that Cennini believed that malachite was formed from azurite (Cennini, 1960 edn, p. 31). On infra-red photography see also Asperen de Boer, 1970 and 1986; Faries, 1976; Filedt-Kok, 1978; Taubert, 1956, and 1975, pp. 41–73.

8. I am indebted to Peter Oxley of Kodak Technical Services for his advice. Nicolaus, 1976, p. 73, recommends Kodak Wratten filters nos. 87 and 88A. I am grateful to Pfarrer Kurz of Bad Wildungen and Pfarrer Lorenz and Pfarrer Maxeiner of Dortmund, and all those who allowed me to take photographs in their churches and museums and to publish them.

9. Ainsworth, 1989, pp. 5–38.

10. However, a more cautious attribution of just the design might have been preferable, allowing the result of further examination of the damaged surface to determine whether the panel was finished by the designer himself or by another hand in his workshop.

11. On the disputed Campin/Flémalle group see Campbell, 1974, pp. 634–646. The investigation of the Campin/Flémalle group was outlined in *Colloque*, 4, 1983, pp. 98–102, and a short progress report appeared in *Colloque*, 5, 1985, pp. 208–211. See also Dijkstra, *Colloque*, 7, 1989, pp. 37–53, and for the infra-red reflectogram of the Mérode angel, see pl. 9 there. The reflectogram of the Frankfurt *Madonna and Child* is reproduced in *Colloque*, 3, 1981, pls. 30a and b. On the difficulties of interpreting the reflectogram of the *Nativity* at Dijon, see Comblen-Sonkes, 1979, pp. 89–91.

12. Frinta's study (1981, p. 75) of the original reflectograms led her to suggest a possibly Northern German source for Campin's underdrawing style, deducing that 'it may be worthwhile to search for the early instances of the "creative hatching" with strongly graphic overtones which seem to be fundamental in many German drawings'. Conrad's underdrawing style presents an early example of such 'creative hatching'.

13. See Exh. Cat. Brussels, 1979, pls. 21, 24. See also pl. 26 for another example of such cross-hatching.

14. See Butler and Asperen de Boer, 1989, pp. 71–76. On the extent of the Parement Master's contribution to the manuscript, see Smeyers, 1989, pp. 55–57; and Meiss, 1967–74, I, pp. 107–134.

15. See Ainsworth, 1989, pp. 6, 11.

16. See Fritz, 1950a, p. 111. The text of the scroll is recorded in cat. no. 2 below.

17. I am indebted to the Dörner Institute, Munich, for undertaking the study by infra-red reflectography on my behalf and for providing the colour slides.

18. This confirms Stange's impression, gained when studying the surface alone, 1967–78, I, p. 143, that some workshop model book was used for this design.

19. See Rensing, 1950, p. 141; and Steinbart, 1946, p. 23. The date of the diptych is disputed, both works may instead depend on a common, unknown template.

20. The Bielefeld Altarpiece was attributed to Conrad von Soest by Max Friedländer, but this found little support. See M. Salinger, 'A Westphalian Crucifixion', *The Metropolitan Museum of Art Bulletin*, III, 6, New York, 1945, pp. 137–141; see also Eckert, 1956, p. 26. The infra-red photographs were restricted to these higher quality panels as my inquiry was only concerned with the main master.

21. The only attribute of this figure is a mitre; however, St Martin was venerated in this church.

22. See Fritz, 1950c, pp. 193–204.

242

23. Appuhn, Exh. Cat. Cologne, 1978–80, I, p. 224; and 1981, p. 22.

24. Kerber, 1975, pp. 17–23.

25. Blaschke, 1976, pp. 65–66.

26. In the Marienkirche in Dortmund, for instance, only two of the seven altarpieces survive; the one by Conrad von Soest only because it could be pressed into service in a Baroque frame, the other by the Berswordt Master probably because it belonged to a very influential family. In Wildungen only one out of nine altarpieces is still in the church. It survived because it served as a chronicle. The seven altarpieces that were in the Hospital church in Wildungen are all lost. It is interesting to note in this connection that Panofsky (1953, I, p. 175) lists 15 lost works by Campin.

27. Blaschke's thesis (1976, *passim*) is that the painted portions of the altarpiece were designed, and initially painted, by one master who completed the outside decoration and that of the inside of the outer left wing. 'Possibly after the death of the designer', a second master is said to have altered the underdrawing of the remaining panels to suit his own 'advanced, elongated' style and to have painted all the remaining panels.

28. I am grateful to the Niedersächsisches Landesmuseum for taking the photographs on my behalf.

29. Kempfer, 1973, p. 27.

Chapter 6

1. From the *Gandersheim Rhymed Chronicle*, as quoted by Pickering, 1970, p. 138.

2. Letter 11. 13 of Pope Gregory the Great (540–604) to Serenus, Bishop of Marseille; see Migne, 1841–1905, PL 77, cols. 1027–28. See also Tatarkiewicz, 1970, pp. 104–105. For a discussion of this tradition in the Middle Ages and of the hostility towards the religious uses of art, see Jones, 1977, pp. 75–106. The text of the statutes of the Guild of Sienese painters, dated 1355, demonstrates that painters also were conscious of this function of paintings: 'For we are by the Grace of God illustrators for those simple men who cannot read...', see Exh. Cat. London, 1989, p. 6.

3. Letter of Indulgence written by brother Hermann of Arolsen at the request of Count Heinrich of Waldeck and his son Walram in 1439 (Archiv, Bad Wildungen). On the question of the translation of vernacular sermons, see Völker, 1963, pp. 212–227. Margery Kempe (*c.* 1393–after 1433) 'burst out with a great cry, and cried amazingly bitterly' after the sermon on the passion by a friar, a 'good preacher': see Kempe, 1987, p. 188. As Margery could not read, nor speak Latin, certain references to sermons in her book convey the flavour of vernacular sermons, as well as their popularity and their effect on an uneducated audience.

4. For Jacobus de Sosato see Beckmann, 1929; Ruh, 1983, IV, cols. 488–494; and Eckert, 1986, pp. 125–138. Jacobus studied and taught at Prague and Cologne universities.

5. This quote is from Gilbert Crispin, Abbot of Westminster (1085–1117), *Disputatio Judei et Christiani*, as cited in Camille, 1985, p. 32.

6. Schinkel, 1981, I, p. 378, records 267 students from Dortmund at Cologne. Prague, Paris, Orléans, Bologna and Heidelberg also registered students from Dortmund. For the variety of texts available, see Exh. Cat. Cologne, 1987. Niederwildungen was closely connected with the Collegiate of St Peter at Fritzlar. What remains of the Fritzlar library is distributed between the Landesbibliothek der Stadt Kassel, the Dombibliothek in Fritzlar and the Schlossbibliothek in Pommersfelden. The monasteries Corvey, Marienfeld and Warendorf also had large libraries; see H. Schmalor, 1982–83, pp. 499–518.

7. See Thomas Aquinas, *Summa Theologiae* (London, 1963); and Bonaventure, *The Soul's Journey into God* (London, 1978).

8. For Pseudo-Bernard see Migne, PL 184, cols. 741–768; for Pseudo-Bede see Migne, PL 94, cols. 561–568. Pseudo-Bernard and Pseudo-Bede appear to be 13th-century anonymous texts which, like other devotional texts of the time, were attributed to distinguished authors. For Pseudo-Bonaventure, see Ragusa/Green, 1961, LXXIV, p. 320. This text is divided into liturgical times; the manuscript is probably Italian Franciscan of the early 14th century. For a discussion of the author, see Ruh, 1985, VI, cols. 282–290.

9. See Suso, *Büchlein der ewigen Weisheit*, ed. Gabele, 1924, p. 169; it is interesting to note that Suso had studied in Cologne. See also Julian of Norwich, 1987 edn, p. 28.

10. Bridget, 1892, ch. III, pp. 97–98. This small selection from St Bridget's text suffers from severe Protestant editing and alterations; the anonymous editor notes that 'matters are frequently treated of

which at the present day would not excite attention'. A complete edition that includes all writings attributed to her, the rules of her convent, and a history of her children, *Der H. Wittfrawen Birgittae von Schweden Himmlische Offenbarungen*, was edited by P. Andreas Megerle in Rome in 1664. Bridget's Revelations seem to be often based on images that she saw on her pilgrimages to Santiago da Compostela, Naples and the Holy Land. She died in Rome.

11. See Priebsch, 1936. For a discussion of the text see Pickering, 1952; for its influence on art in the Netherlands see Marrow, 1969.

12. See Ludolph of Saxony, *Vita Jesu Christi e quatuor Evangeliis et scriptoribus orthodoxis concinnata*, 1865 and 1870 edns; for a translation into French, see Augustin, 1864. See also Conway, 1976. For a discussion of the text, see Bodenstedt, 1944 and 1973; and also Baier, 1977. On Ludolph, see Ruh, 1985, V, cols. 967–977. For the quotations, see Coleridge 1887, III, p. 117; Coleridge, I, p. 9; Augustin V, 1864, XXXV, pp. 472–477; Coleridge, VI, p. 256.

13. Thomas à Kempis, 1979 edn, 3.7 and 1.1. For details about the organization of the *devotio moderna*, see Exh. Cat. Deventer, 1984; and Iserloh, 1982–83, pp. 191–207; for the Order in Westphalia see Kohl, 1982–83, pp. 203–207. By the 14th century, the Windesheim congregation had appointed a 'librarius teutonicorum librorum'. Grote himself spent the last days of his life translating a breviary. I am grateful to Jochen Luckhardt for informing me of the close connection that is recorded between the commandery of St John at Burgsteinfurt and the *devotio moderna* at Deventer.

14. J'ay apporté du lait aussi, que je vois bouiller sans targer, pour luy faire ung peu à menger, affin que fain ne le soupprende': *Le Mystère de la Passion*, by Arnoul Gréban, written in 1450, 1965 edition, I, p. 72. The 'Nährvater' image has given rise to misinterpretation; an intent to ridicule Joseph was suspected by certain authors. On the theological justification of the image, see Schwartz, 1985, especially p. 151, and n. 21. On passion plays, see Mone, 1846. For the influence of dramatized liturgy on medieval art, see Pächt, 1962.

15. It is instructive to compare Conrad's treatment of the *Adoration* with that by Gentile da Fabriano (1423) in the Uffizi, Florence. It is difficult to determine how closely Conrad's adherence to Gospel narrative reflects the instructions of his patrons. But it seems significant that both altarpieces by Conrad show a similar restraint.

16. Ludolph, I, Coleridge, 1887, p. 26; and XX, Augustin, 1864, V, p. 241.

17. Buxtehude Altarpiece (*c.* 1410) by Master Bertram and workshop, Kunsthalle, Hamburg. Bielefeld Altarpiece (1400; cat. no. 8 below); Schotten Altarpiece (*c.* 1420–40; Liebfrauenkirche, Schotten). Although Master Bertram (*c.* 1340–1414/5) is known to have resided in Hamburg from 1367, his birth in Minden and his considerable artistic influence in Westphalia suggest that he may have trained and worked there before his arrival in Hamburg. He certainly seems to form an important link in the tradition discussed here, and has therefore been included, as he was in the exhibition of Westphalian painting in Münster, 1964. Even the ox and donkey in the *Nativity* have a biblical source, in Isaiah 1.3.

18. Netze Altarpiece (*c.* 1390), Pfarrkirche, Netze. Blankenberch Altarpiece (*c.* 1421–1443), Landesmuseum, Münster. Golden Panel (*c.* 1431–35, cat. no. 13 below). The *Annunciation* of Conrad's Dortmund Altarpiece is too damaged to reveal iconographic details. The tradition of a child approaching Mary to illustrate the Immaculate Conception can be traced in Italy from about 1310. Robb, 1936, pp. 523–526, does not seem to differentiate between this Italian motif of conception and the iconography of announcing the passion, noted in Westphalia. The passion motif became more popular in Italy in the 15th century.

19. As in the Mérode Altarpiece (*c.* 1426; The Cloisters, Metropolitan Museum, New York) and Koerbecke's Marienfeld *Annunciation* (*c.* 1443–57; Art Institute, Chicago). The image of the Christ child with the cross in Annunciations may have been prompted by the fact that the Feast day of the Annunciation and the supposed date of the Crucifixion coincide on 25 March. (Réau, II.2, 1955–59, p. 174, n. 3). Sister Mechthild (Morell, 1869) seems to have based her visions on such texts as *Sermo in Festo Annunciationis* by Bernard of Clairvaux (Migne PL 183, cols. 383–390).

20. This Theotokos image is rare in an Annunciation, but has a precedent in Bamberg Cathedral (formerly St George's choir), *c.* 1230–40. The connection between the iconography of the crowned Virgin Mary and the liturgy is established in an altarpiece in the Landesmuseum, Bonn, (Inv. No. 9), where the image of the crowned Virgin is surrounded by the inscription of a hymn. The choice of the crowned Virgin for the Niederwildungen *Annunciation* and *Adoration of the Kings* may refer to the fact that Mass in the church in Niederwildungen was held 'Godde demme almechtigen unde Marien dere hochgelobthin koninigynen zu lobe'. Staatsarchiv Marburg, no. 9962, 14 August 1491.

21. See Kirschbaum, 1968–72, IV, p. 423.

244

22. The ivory relief plaque (545–53) from the Throne of Archbishop Maximian, Museo Arciviscovile, Ravenna, presents an early example of a baldachined throne. The baldachin is more convincingly constructed in a casket, school of Metz (10th century), in the Louvre, Paris. The curtains in Annunciations by Giotto and Hesdin are cited, although they may in turn be indebted to the motif from eastern legends, because they are used to define an area of private prayer in a manner similar to that used in the Parement Master's workshop for *Jean de Berry at Prayer, Heures de Milan* (*c.* 1385), Turin, Museo Civico, fol. 87.

23. There is some uncertainty whether the angel on a 12th-century pillar in the cloister of Sto Domingo at Silos, cited by Réau (1955–59, II.2, p. 188), forms part of an Annunciation. A number of Annunciations in which the angel approaches from the right are shown in Schiller, 1966–80, I, starting with plate no. 68, the Pignatta Sarcophagus (*c.* 400–10) by craftsmen from the Eastern Roman Empire, Braccioforte Mausoleum, Ravenna.

24. See also Jeremiah 33.15: 'I will cause a righteous Branch to spring forth for David'. Rensing (1950, p. 151) describes the branch as 'quaint branches…that have to be considered inappropriate'. On the tree of Jesse as symbol of the Immaculate Conception, see Mâle, 1986, p. 205.

25. See Réau, 1955–59, II.2, p. 185. Matthew 3.16: '…he saw the spirit of God descending like a dove'; for Ludolph, see 1870, IV, p. 659.

26. See Schröder, 1837. The definition of transubstantiation at the Fourth Lateran Council was provoked by a dispute initiated by the Monophysites, who repudiated the human nature of Christ and therefore his passion and death (Schiller, 1966–80, II, pp. 13 and 21). The dispute lasted for centuries. Anselm of Canterbury (*c.* 1033–1109), for example, joined the debate with *Cur Deus homo?* (Munich, 1956); and Bernard of Clairvaux (1090–1153), defended Christ's human nature in *Tractatus De Corpore Domini* (Migne, PL 182, cols. 1149–50). The introduction of the Feast of Corpus Christi, sporadically since 1264 and compulsorily in 1314, confirmed the teaching of the church (see Gilson/Boehner, 1937, I, p. 22). Nilgen, 1967, pp. 311–316, showed that scenes from Christ's infancy can be used to convey the mystery of the incarnation. The connection between Christ's passion and the Mass is discussed in Schiller, 1966–80, II, pp. 11–13.

27. Gemäldegalerie, Berlin, Inv. No. 1216A; see Kock, 1974. For Ecclesia, see Ludolph, XXXVI, Augustin, 1864, V, p. 504: '…la Mère du Saveur seule resta attachée à ses pas. Un instant, la primitive Église fut tout entière en sa personne. C'est pour

figurer cette circonstance en ce moment que l'Église, à l'office du matin, éteint toutes les lumières, une seule exceptée. C'est par la même raison que l'office nocturne de la passion, pendant lequel s'accomplissent les prophéties au sujet du Christ, se chante à haute voix, tandis que l'office du jour se psalmodie a voix basse'.

28. Ambrose (339–397), *De Excessu fratris sui Satyri*, 1921 edn, 2.6; and Schiller, 1966–80, II, pl. 339.

29. For the Easter Vigil, see *Gebets- und Gesangbuch*, 1949, p. 20, no. 15 and p. 119; also *Missale Romanum*, 1539, pp. 233–248. For Ludolph see note 27 above.

30. Earlier examples include: the *Crucifixion* (*c.* 1240; Huntington Library, San Marino, California), MS HM 26061, fol. 178v, (see Morgan, 1982, I, pl. 250); the *Crucifixion* in the English Amesbury Psalter, *c.* 1250–55, Oxford, All Souls College, MS 6, fol. 189; and the *Crucifixion*, transept fresco, *c.* 1347, Sta Maria Maggiore, Bergamo.

31. See Pickering, 1970, and 1953, p. 29 citing from Migne PL 70, col. 404; PL 36, cols. 671–672; and PL 142, cols. 44–45. For Gotfried of Admont, see Pickering, 1966, p. 191, and Migne PL 174, col. 1150.

32. Musper (1961, p. 203) claims that the group resembles 'a courtly hunting party, chatting as if to inquire about the best place for breakfast'; he sees no further significance in the splendid attire of Christ's enemies and attributes their fashionable dress to a secularization of art. Roth, 1967, p. 89, also believes that the elegant dress is only for decorative effect.

33. Documents in the Marburg Archives, no. 9881 (1377) and nos. 9904 (1397)–9918 (1414), record valuable donations to the Order of St John at this time. Most documents mention the hope of salvation of the donor's soul. Letters of indulgence were also sold; see note 3 above. In a similar fashion, it is thought that Rembrandt, by placing his self-portrait in the centre of the *Raising of the Cross* (*c.* 1633; Alte Pinakothek, Munich), identified himself as one of the sinners for whom Christ died.

34. The women are identified by punched nimbus inscriptions. Mary Magdalene had been shriven of evil spirits; Mary, mother of James, had presumably lived an ordinary 'sinner's' life as a married woman. The women under the cross are those mentioned in the Gospel of St John 19.25–27, and St Mark 15.40.

35. The three-nailed type was the most common from the 13th century onwards. For comments on the theological exegesis of Crucifixion types, see Pickering, 1966, pp. 229–243 and 253–265.

36. Earlier surviving Westphalian Crucifixion panels do not include the thieves. Beginning with the Netze Altarpiece (*c.* 1390, Pfarrkirche, Netze), the two horizontal bars in the crosses of the thieves are a consistent motif in Westphalian Crucifixions. This can be demonstrated by a number of altarpieces in the Landesmuseum, Münster (reproduced in Pieper, 1986): the Lempertz Altarpiece of *c.* 1425 (ibid., p. 435), which appears to be painted by a follower of Conrad von Soest from Lower Saxony; the Warendorf Altarpiece of *c.* 1420–40 (ibid., p. 75 and cat. no. 10 below); the Halderner Altarpiece of *c.* 1450 by the Master of Schöppingen (ibid., pp. 104–105); the Amelsbürener Altarpiece of *c.* 1470 by Johann Koerbecke and his workshop (ibid., p. 191); the Lippborg Altarpiece of *c.* 1475 by the workshop of the Master of Liesborn (ibid., p. 237); and the Crucifixion panel of *c.* 1480 by Derick Baegert (ibid., p. 341). Two other important Westphalian altarpieces, still placed in churches, depict a similar cross form: the High Altarpiece of *c.* 1470–80 by Derick Baegert, in the Propsteikirche, Dortmund (see Baxhenrich-Hartmann, 1984); and the *Calvary* of *c.* 1480 by the Master of Liesborn, in the church Maria zur Höhe, Soest. An interesting exception to this is the Berswordt Altarpiece, where only a single bar is shown (see cat. no. 9 below), presumably because its eclectic painter followed a non-Westphalian pattern (see pp. 75–84).

37. From the Donaueschingen manuscript, as quoted by Binder-Hagelstange, 1937, p. 37.

38. In the apocryphal acts of Pilate, the thieves are given their names. Gestas or sometimes Jasmus or Gesmas (*Golden Legend*) is the name of the bad thief. Dismas or Dysmad is the name given to the penitent thief; it apparently derives from the Greek word for dying, 'dysme'. Dismas is registered as a saint in Farmer, 1987, p. 118, and he is commemorated in the Roman Martyrology on 25 March. Gestas is named in an Icon of *c.* 725–50 in the Convent of St Catherine at Sinai. Conrad and his advisers clearly did not consult the original text. The names of the thieves, like those of the three kings, had become common knowledge.

39. Musper (1961, p. 204) comments that 'there is no evidence of real compassion'; he underestimates the wealth of feeling and thought individually expressed. For Ludolph see Bodenstedt, 1973, p. 160.

40. For Caiaphas, see Matthew 26.57. The blue brocade robe worn by this figure over a white undergarment is certainly reminiscent of a chasuble over a surplice. It is interesting to note that Pilate appears writing the tablet under the cross in the Berswordt Altarpiece (cat. no. 9).

41. For a discussion of the 'docta ignorantia', see Harbison, 1985, p. 88; and Pickering, 1940, pp. 121–137.

42. St Edmund in the Wilton Diptych of *c.* 1396 in the National Gallery, London is similarly identified as a king through a crown pattern in the brocade of his gown. Sluter used a border of harp motifs to identify David in the Dijon *Calvary*. Conrad von Soest used the crown motif again for a king in the Dortmund *Adoration of the Kings*.

43. See for example Meier, 1921, p. 11, and Steinbart, 1946, p. 19.

44. See Fritz, 1954, p. 9. Jacobs (1986, p. 48) commented that 'a traitor will also be a thief'. Schiller, 1966–80, II, p. 46, had argued that as fish are sometimes placed on a plate in Last Supper scenes, they merely represent food. 'Es leuchtet ein, dass man mit dem Diebstahl den Verräter als Dieb brandmarken wollte', concluded Schiller. However, IKHTUS, the Greek word for fish, are the initials for Jesous Khristos Theou Uious Soter (Jesus Christ Son of God the Saviour); on the fish symbol, see Dölger, 1910. Although this fish motif is rare in Last Supper scenes, Judas can already be seen hiding a fish behind his back in the Klosterneuburg Altarpiece (1181), by Nicholas of Verdun.

45. St Paul is depicted in the *Last Supper* (*c.* 1450) of the choir window at Great Malvern Priory and of the *Hours of Elizabeth the Queen* (*c.* 1420–30; London, BL, MS Add. 50001, fol. 7 [both also incorporate the hidden fish motif]); and furthermore in wall-paintings at Savigny, Manche (*c.* 1300), and at The King's Head, Shrewsbury (*c.* 1450–1520). I am grateful to David Park for drawing the wall-paintings to my attention; see his manuscript report of 29 June 1987, Conservation of Wall-paintings Department, Courtauld Institute. The *Communion of the Apostles* is depicted, for example, in the embossed silver paten from Stuma, Syria (565–78), Archaeological Museum, Istanbul. An *Allegory of the Eucharist* is carved on a Romanesque capital at Vézelay, and painted in a fresco at St Kilian church, Mundelsheim. Christ can be seen giving the host to St Paul in an 11th-century fresco of the church in Nekresi, Kaukasus. It is not possible to see which apostle is missing in Conrad's *Last Supper*, as some apostles are shown from the back and few have inscribed halos.

46. 'Lex Moisi celat quae sermo Pauli revelat' proclaims the scroll held by St Paul on the façade of St-Trophîme, Arles. Mâle observes (1972, p. 172, including n. 1) that this 'is a way of saying that the Old Testament if interpreted after the manner of St Paul would wholly resolve itself into the New'.

47. Such a prayer is inscribed above a self-portrait in an altarpiece by the Korbach Master, dated 1519, for which see Witzel, 1988, pl. 6.

48. Ivory relief (*c.* 455–90) from Ravenna or Northern Italy, Cathedral Treasury, Milan. A large panel showing *Christ the Lamb* is surrounded by six small panels with scenes from the childhood of Christ.

49. A pilgrim's reliquary casket (7th or 8th century) from Palestine, Museo Cristiano, Vatican, is painted (inside the cover) with scenes from the birth and passion of Christ. An embossed silver antependium (1143–44), Cathedral Treasury, Città di Castello, and a winged altarpiece of Umbrian origin (*c.* 1270–80), Galleria Nazionale dell'Umbria, Perugia, provide further early examples of the juxtaposition of childhood scenes from the life of Christ with scenes from His passion.

50. See Luckhardt, 1987, p. 23. The canonical hours which form the structure for Ludolph of Saxony's meditation, however, cannot be fitted to the pictorial cycle of the Niederwildungen Altarpiece. That narrative scenes of retables could be arranged in accordance with the canonical hours is exemplified by the Altarpiece of the Canonical Hours in Lübeck Cathedral, which is inscribed with the poem of the hours attributed to Aegidius Colonna (d. 1316).

51. The most likely opening days for the Niederwildungen Altarpiece were: Immaculate Conception (8 December); Christmas (25 December), from the midnight mass for three days, to include the Feast of St John the Evangelist (27 December); First Mass only (1 January); Epiphany (6 January); Candlemas (Presentation, 2 February); Annunciation (25 March); [Monday before Lent, a cloth with passion scenes was placed across the choir in front of the High Altar from Ash Wednesday until Easter night]; Easter, for eight days; Ascension day; St John, *'ante portam latinam'* (6 May); Whitsun, for eight days; Corpus Christi and the eighth day after Corpus Christi; Birth of St John the Baptist (24 June); SS. Peter and Paul (29 June); Visitation *'als si uber das gepirg ging'* (2 July); Octave of the Visitation (9 July); Assumption of the Virgin (15 August), *'alle ding als am ostertag'*, open eight days; Birth of Mary (8 September); St Michael (29 September); All Saints (1 November); St Elisabeth (19 November); St Catherine (25 November); Presentation of the Virgin (21 November); St Nicholas (6 December).
See also Gümbel, 1928, and 1929.

52. Bede, *A History of the English Church and People*, 1976 edn, ch. 17, p. 302. Ludolph, VI, 1864, and XIII, p. 395, also mentions the footsteps. Réau, 1955–59, II.2, p. 584, reports that Henry III offered the footprint stone to the Abbey of Westminster. For the Jerusalem pilgrimage see Browne, 1975.

53. Letter of Indulgence, 1439 (see note 3 above). On this aspect of confraternities see Henderson, 1988, pp. 383–394.

54. St Bridget, 1892 edn, I, ch. VI, p. 42.

55. This is Nissen's suggestion (1936, pp. 68–72). Although Dante (d. 1321) spoke of Charon in *Inferno*, III and Michelangelo may have referred to the coin in his image of Lorenzo de' Medici in the New Sacristy, S. Lorenzo, Florence, mythology does not have a place in Conrad's medieval Christian iconography.

56. On the panel in the National Gallery see J. Dunkerton, 'The Death of the Virgin. A technical approach to an art-historical problem', *National Gallery Technical Bulletin*, 7, 1983, pp. 21–29.

57. Ars bene moriendi, *c.* 1400–20, woodcut 11: see Künstle, 1928, I, pp. 206–207.

58. Ludolph, II.86; Bodenstedt, 1973, p. 180; for the 'Ave Maria' see Mâle, 1925, pp. 380–384.

59. Voragine, 1969 edn, p. 450. Sources included the *Discourses of St John, Pseudo-Melito, Joseph of Arimathea*, and a Syrian *History of the Virgin*.

60. The Feast of the Dormition was reputed to have been introduced by Emperor Maurikios (582–602) (Kirschbaum, 1968–72, IV, p. 334). Pope Sergius I (687–701) certainly ordered a procession for the Feast of the Dormition which was celebrated on 15 August. Kahsnitz, 1987, pp. 91–92, observed that in manuscripts the *Death of the Virgin* appeared only in liturgical texts which are ordered according to the feast day cycle of the church. In the 10th and 11th centuries the western interest can first be demonstrated in scriptoria influenced by Cluny. Images of the *Death of the Virgin* are often inspired by the Song of Songs and therefore stress the mystic reunion (Schiller, 1966–80, IV.2, p. 96). On the *Death of the Virgin* as epitome of Christian death, see Schreiner, 1993, pp. 261–312.

61. See Kirschbaum, op. cit. (note 60). Byzantine ivory relief, end of 10th century, Schnütgen Museum, Cologne (repr. in Schiller, 1966–80, IV.2, pl. 588). The mandorla surrounding Christ is equally based on Byzantine tradition. It features, for instance, in a Russian Icon of the 13th century in Recklinghausen (repr. in Schiller, 1966–80, IV.2, pl. 591).

62. Schiller, 1966–80, IV.2, pp. 89–90.

63. The tympanum of the central doorway, north façade, Chartres, may serve as an example of the *Death of the Virgin* in a sculptural programme; the window at St Quentin may demonstrate its place in window programmes. See Mâle, 1972, p. 250.

64. Ludolph, I.11: Bodenstedt, 1973, p. 12. In the *Golden Legend*, however, the gifts are interpreted as myrrh for the death of the man in Christ, incense for the God in Him, and gold for God the King. A king in the *Adoration* from the Hohenfurth Altarpiece (St George's Abbey, Prague; *c.* 1350) also carries a horn.

65. See H. and M. Schmidt, 1981. Dionysius (Acts 17.34) was probably a Syrian monk, writing *c.* 500. First Latin translation *c.* 850, published by Migne PL 122, cols. 1035–1070.

66. The confusion persists today: in their commentary on the *Belles Heures of Jean, Duke of Berry*, Meiss/Beatson, 1974 describe red 'cherubim' (*The Duchess praying to the Trinity*, fol. 91v); whilst Longnon on *Les très riches heures du duc de Berry*, 1969 speaks of 'flaming seraphim' (*Nativity*, no. 40, fol. 44v). The books are both illuminated mainly by the Limbourg brothers, but whilst the *Belles heures* (*c.* 1404–08) consistently show a semicircle of red angels 'burning' next to God, blue angels nestle closest to God in the *Nativity* of the *Très riches heures* (before 1416), and are surrounded by a crescent of red angels.

67. Rensing (1950, p. 155 and pl. 63) cites in evidence a drawing from the *Codex Vallardi* (Paris, Louvre, MS 2623, fol. 130, *c.* 1420–40) and a panel, *The Madonna appearing to St Anthony and St George* (London, National Gallery). The drawing from the *Codex Vallardi* has not been convincingly attributed to Pisanello. See also Langemeyer, 1983, pl. 168.

68. For Pseudo-Bonaventura see Ragusa/Green, 1961, p. 44: for Suso see Gabele, 1924, p. 223. For the Parement Master, see MS Cal 3093, p.56, initial D.

69. 'Lord, come to my help; Lord make haste to save me', this text is frequently repeated in Books of Hours; it can be found in the *Hours of Mary of Burgundy* (*c.* 1475–1780), for instance in the *Annunciation* fol. 57 and is repeated in fols. 51–54. See Manuscripts in Miniature, *The Hours of Mary of Burgundy* Cod. Vind. 1857, London 1995.

70. Meiss, 1936, pp. 436–437, argued that the image of a Madonna of Humility originates in Simone Martini's workshop.

71. See Panofsky, 1971, I, p. 129. Meiss, 1936, cited the Book of Hours, use of Metz, (*c.* 1360–05), Mor-

gan Library, MS 88, and the Dedication page of the *Rouen Hours* (*c.* 1410), Bibl. Musée de la Ville, Rouen, MS 3024, as the earliest northern examples depicting a Virgin seated on the ground.

72. Mâle, 1972, p. 255.

73. Ibid. Mâle adds: 'the following century proclaimed the royalty of Mary, and inscribed it on front of all the cathedrals'.

74. Zarnecki, 1950, pp. 1–12.

75. See Schiller, 1966–80, IV.2, pp. 90–96.

76. Fritz, 1950a, p. 115. Rolf Fritz based his assertion that the eagle of the Evangelist should be placed in the top lefthand corner on manuscripts showing this arrangement. Fritz argued, in support of his thesis, that the lion of the evangelist would have been winged, whereas the Dortmund lion only carries a scroll. A lost wall painting of *c.* 1400 in the Old Council Chamber opposite the church, however, apparently once showed the evangelist St Mark accompanied by a lion without wings.

77. Examples with the angel placed in the top lefthand corner include: a *Majestas Domini* of *c.* 1130–40 from St Pantaleon, Cologne (see Exh. Cat. Münster and Cologne, 1980–81, II, no. 251); the *Last Judgement*, Helmarshausen Evangeliary of *c.* 1180–90, showing Christ in a mandorla (see Exh. Cat. Münster and Corvey, 1982–83, p. 244, pl. 9). For four angels in the spandrels, see the *Coronation* in the tympanum of the central doorway, north façade, Chartres.

78. The most likely days for opening the altarpiece would be: Immaculate Conception (8 December); Christmas (25 December), from midnight mass for three days; First mass only (1 January); Epiphany (6 January); Candlemas (2 February); Monday before Lent; Annunciation (25 March); Easter for eight days; Whitsun for eight days; Corpus Christi for eight days; SS. Peter and Paul (29 June); Visitation (2 July); Octave of Visitation (9 July); Assumption for eight days (15 August); Birth of Mary (8 September); St Michael (29 September); All Saints (1 November); Presentation of the Virgin (21 November).

79. The convent outside the walls was destroyed by fire (*c.*1447) during the Feud of Soest and was relocated within the town by 1461; the original decoration on the reverse side of the doors may have been ruined by fire. I am indebted to Jochen Luckhardt for all the historic information concerning St Walpurgis.

80. No potential donor with these Christian names could be found in the convent records.

81. Verbal communication from Jochen Luckhardt. The tabernacle could then be closely compared to small altarpieces in Cologne, showing the Virgin, with standing Saints in the wings, for which the *Sweet Pea Blossom* triptych in Cologne by the Veronica Master is a prominent instance.

82. See Musper, 1961, pp. 203–204; Jacobs, 1986, p. 48; Châtelet/Recht, 1989, p. 220.

83. See the quote from Eberhard at the beginning of this chapter.

Chapter 7

1. Cennino Cennini, 1960, p. 15.

2. On the function of altarpieces, see Belting, 1981.

3. Fritz, 1953 was able to expose in infra-red photographs the originality of Conrad's design drawings, but later authors persisted in naming foreign origins for the compositions, often without due regard for the date of the cited material (cf. e.g. H. Schmitz, 1906; Steinbart, pp. 20, 25; Musper, 1961, p. 203).

4. P. and L. Murray, in *The Art of the Renaissance*, London, 1976 (first edition 1963), pp. 170–172, speak of the 'extreme provinciality' of German art before Dürer. Although this book is only intended as a general survey, it is cited here because it aptly expresses the commonly held notion that German art of that period is merely 'a matter of archaeological concern'. Conrad's art is described there as 'low rather than high life in feeling'. See also Cuttler, 1968, p. 261.

5. For Bohemian painting, see Bachmann, 1977; and Pešina, 1989. The Wittingau Altarpiece, St George's Abbey Museum, Prague, was placed upon an altar consecrated in 1378 but a painted seal in the *Resurrection* panel bears the date 1427.

6. The classic surveys of late Medieval/early Renaissance art include: Marle, 1924; Pächt, 1929; Freeman Sandler, 1986; Exh. Cat. London, 1987; Sterling, 1987; Meiss, 1967–74; Panofsky, 1971; Delaisse, 1968; Bachmann, 1977; Stange, I–III, 1934–38; Carli, 1981; Saliger, 1987; Exh. Cat. Cologne, 1978–80.

7. Antependium from Soest or Helmarshausen (*c.* 1175), Landesmuseum, Münster; Crucifixion panels from the Wiesenkirche, Soest, Gemäldegalerie, Berlin, Inv. No. 1216 A (*c.* 1230), and Inv. No. 1216 B (*c.* 1250–60). Fragments of an altarpiece (*c.* 1310), Evangelische Liebfrauenkirche, Hofgeismar. As the scenes in the Hofgeismar fragments describe events before and after the Crucifixion, it seems reasonable to assume that the lost central section of the retable contained a Crucifixion scene. The saints depicted on the reverse of the wings include St Francis and St Clare.

8. The very damaged figures depicted on the reverse of the wings at Netze appear to be those of the 'Quattuor Coronati' and Erasmus. The church at Netze was originally dedicated to these saints and the Virgin. I am indebted to Karl Kann for this information.

9. On the Grabow (Petri) Altarpiece in the Kunsthalle Hamburg, see Portman, 1963; on Master Bertram's Westphalian followers, see Exh. Cats. Münster, 1964 and Cappenberg, 1950.

10. See Schiller I, pls. 66–72.

11. Wing panels only (*c.* 1410), Ev. Pfarrkirche Rauschenberg, Hesse (central part lost).

12. The motif of the seated Joseph holding a walking stick already occurs in the *Nativity* from a German Psalter of *c.* 1250, Nationalmuseum, Stockholm, Inv. No. NMB 1926; it was also known in the workshop of Jacquemart de Hesdin: see *Très belles heures de Notre-Dame* (*c.* 1385–90? before 1402), Brussels Bibl. Royale, MS 11060–1, p. 90.

13. The motif of the Child with outstretched arms was known also in Italy (*Adoration*, Vitale da Bologna(?), *c.* 1350s, National Gallery, Edinburgh), and France (ivory diptych, Paris, *c.* 1270–1290, Inv. Nos. 102c–103c, Bargello, Florence).

14. Schiller, 1966–80, p. 113.

15. This image of the sleeping apostle may ultimately derive from the mosaic in the abbey church at Monreale (before 1183) and may have reached Northern Europe through the sketchbook of Villard de Honnecourt.

16. The Buxtehude Altarpiece (*c.* 1410), Kunsthalle, Hamburg, originates from a convent near Buxtehude which is mentioned in Master Bertram's will of 1410. The design is roughly repeated in a panel of the Apocalypse Altarpiece from the same workshop in the Victoria and Albert Mu-

seum, London. Paint fragments on the reverse side of the wings of the Osnabrück Altarpiece were identified by W. Meyer-Barkhausen, 1929, p. 245, n. 7, as parts of a *Death of the Virgin*. He surmised that the other scene, by 1929 too damaged to be recognizable, may have been a *Coronation of the Virgin*.

17. G. Schmidt, 1977, pp. 10–27.

18. Roth, 1967, p. 36.

19. See *Hours of Jeanne d'Evreux* (*c.* 1325–28), The Cloisters, Metropolitan Museum, New York, fol. 68v.

20. St John clasps his hands in Pietro Lorenzetti's *Crucifixion* (*c.* 1319–20) at Assisi. The motif also occurs in a manuscript by a follower of Pucelle (Bodleian Library, Douce 313, fol. 4). Conrad's group of the women recalls a wall-painting (*c.* 1320), school of Pietro Cavallini, Naples (reproduced in Schiller, 1966–80, II, pl. 319). It is interesting to note that St John also clasps his hands in the scene at Naples.

21. Documentary evidence concerning the sojourn of Westphalian artists at the Bohemian court is scant, but it is recorded that Emperor Charles IV called the goldsmith Master Gert from Dortmund to Prague in 1373.

Chapter 8

1. Musper, 1961, p. 203 went so far as to state: 'Without Burgundian, French models—one thinks of the "Très Riches Heures" of the Duke of Berry at Chantilly or the "Livre de Chasse"...one could certainly not imagine Konrad von Soest'. See also Meier, 1921 and 1931, p. 45; Medding, 1949, p. 27; Geisberg, 1931, p. 8, who included Paris. Musper appears to follow Stange, 1934–61, III, p. 27, in suggesting the *Livre de la Chasse* (Paris, Bibl. Nat., fr. 616). The manuscripts are convincingly dated by Meiss (1967–74, I, p. 218; and IV, p. 308) to 1416 and 'somewhat later' than 1400 respectively.

2. Steinbart (1946, p. 25) proposed Bruges as the most likely town on Conrad's Netherlandish itinerary. He also believed that Conrad visited Paris, Bourges and Dijon during the first decade of the 15th century.

3. Tröscher, 1966, pp. 15–17, confirmed that there is no evidence of significant commissions for panel or wall-painting in Burgundy before the last quarter of the 14th century.

4. See, for instance, Stange 1966, pp. 3–4. Paatz, 1967, pp. 12–13, lists a number of German artists working in France, including Haincelin from Hagenau (1403–15), Herman from Cologne (1401–03), Hans Tiefenthal from Schlettstadt (before 1417), Heinrich Guderolf from Frankfurt (before 1417), and Steffain Unger from Cologne (*valet de chambre* of Philip the Bold, Duke of Burgundy; Unger also worked for King Charles VI, and the dukes of Berry and Orléans, 1384–1417).

5. See Sterling, 1987, pp. 14–18. On panels mentioned in French royal inventories, see Tröscher, 1966, pp. 7–9, 91–110, 147–168 and 397–399. The inventories of Charles V only recorded 18 panels, those of Philip the Bold 5 panels, and those of the Duke of Berry 24 panels (17 probably painted); not

all were painted, however, and some were of Italian, Netherlandish or German origin. This information may be misleading. The Berry inventories, for example, do not seem to refer to any of the 18 panels that were noted in the chapel at Bourges by a group of visitors from Florence in 1461; it is doubtful that many of these would have been donated instead by Charles VII during his exile there. The published inventories include Guiffrey, 1894–97 (this includes gifts to the Sainte-Chapelle in vol. II, pp. 167–186); Doutrepont, 1906; Moranvillé, 1906; and Graves, 1926.

6. Vasari, 1912–15 edn, IX, p. 253; see also Sterling, 1987, p. 16.

7. Tröscher, 1966, p. 29, cites a document from Castle Vaudreuil, dated 29 March 1353: '...historiasque inibi depictas de quodam libro extrahere'.

8. Meiss, 1967–74, I, p. 116, pointed to the cracking and peeling that did arise when (in the Parement workshop) paint was applied in layers, as in panel-painting, on the unstable ground of the illuminator's vellum.

9. Sterling (1987, pp. 16, 18) asserts that it 'is not possible to offer a survey of painting in France during these two centuries [1300–1500] without depending largely on illumination'. Panofsky, 1973 and Meiss, 1967–74 also included manuscript painting in their surveys of pictorial and stylistic developments.

10. Commissions for the court painter Jean de Beaumetz (doc. in 1361–d. 1396) included, for example, production of colourful armour, painting of state coaches, design and painting of large-scale religious canvases and wall-painting. André Beauneveu (*c.* 1330–*c.* 1402) was employed as a painter and sculptor; he was skilled in illumina-

tion and panel-painting techniques. Malouel and Broederlam were paid for tournament decorations in honour of Charles VI in 1390, and a large number of painters gathered to decorate the elaborate wedding tournament of Jean sans Peur in 1406. Rapid wall-painting techniques had to be devised by Jean de Beaumetz in 1387–88, when he was employed with one other master and eight assistants to decorate the interior of the Chartreuse de Champmol in Dijon. The work had to be executed partially by candle-light, and coal fires were used to speed the drying process. By 1399 this hasty work needed repairs.

11. Meiss (1967–74, I, p. 101) describes his achievement as a 'combination of the planar and the tri-dimensional that had been introduced into French painting by Jean Pucelle, drawing from Ducciesque sources'.

12. The attribution to the Parement Master has not gone undisputed since it was proposed by Hulin de Loo in 1911; but it is convincingly accepted by both Meiss, 1967–74, I, p. 113, and Sterling, 1987, p. 229. Sterling, 1987, p. 222, proposed that Jean d'Orléans, whose documented work has not yet been identified, could be the Parement Master. E. König, *Die Très Belles Heures de Notre-Dame des Herzogs von Berry*, Lucerne, 1992, dates the manuscript to after 1404, a date added in the calendar pages, and before 1407, a date he surmises for the death of the main master. This would imply that the style of Parement Master did not change in the 30 years since he painted the *Parement de Narbonne*. The connoisseur Duke of Berry would not have entrusted such an old-fashioned master with an important commission. Moreover, the date of 1404 is not only added to the calendar page, but the page itself may stem from another Book of Hours, as it is written on different parchment. The Book was divided into three parts soon after 1413.

13. The *Thirsting Woman*, by Arnolfo di Cambio (?) (*c.* 1281; Galleria Nazionale dell'Umbria, Perugia), for example, wears this style of veil. In Italian painting, a transparent veil is usually placed over part of the hair, and a braid takes the place of the fold in the veil, as in Ambrogio Lorenzetti's *Annunciation* (1344; Pinacoteca, Siena). Examples from the Boucicaut workshop include the *Visitation*, fol. 65v, the *Nativity*, fol. 73v and the *Adoration*, fol. 83v from the Hours of the Marshal Jean de Boucicaut (*c.* 1399–1411; Paris, Musée Jacquemart-André, MS 2).

14. Sterling, 1987, p. 124, suggested that Hesdin (documented from 1384 to 1413) had mainly worked at Bourges, and that the hand identified by Meiss as Hesdin should therefore only be labelled 'probably Flemish'. However, there seems no compelling reason to accept that the Duke of Berry would not have commissioned his highly esteemed painter Jacquemart de Hesdin with the task of illuminating this manuscript. He is, after all, named as the main illuminator of the *Grandes heures* (1409) in the 1413 inventory ['de la main de Jacquemart de Hesdin et autres ouvriers de Monseigneur']. Stylistic links between the manuscripts, and also with the *Petites heures* (Paris, Bibl. Nat., MS lat. 18014), were convincingly argued by Meiss and Avril (Exh. Cat. Paris, 1981–82, pp. 343–346). Moreover, since the duke, as co-regent, was for the main part resident in Paris before 1388 and after 1392, it cannot be presumed that his painter was mainly kept at Bourges. I have therefore decided to keep the name of Hesdin for the style identified by Meiss and by Avril as this master's work. In view of the close stylistic links between the Parement Master and Jacquemart de Hesdin, I would suggest a date for Jacquemart's contribution of *c.* 1385–90. The manuscript is first recorded in the 1402 inventory.

15. Haussherr, 1979, pp. 63–80, proposed that Master Bertram from Minden (documented in Hamburg between 1367 and 1414, d. by 1415) had travelled to France. Whilst there is certainly evidence in his later work that Master Bertram was aware of the International Courtly Style, the few motifs cited by Haussherr could have reached Master Bertram by diffusion. The receding floor tiles, particularly, may have come to his notice in Italy, if he actually made the journey to Rome mentioned in his will of 1390, or through Italian patterns.

16. The canopy occurs, for example, in the *Annunciation* of the *Petites heures* (Paris, Bibl. Nat., MS lat. 18014, fol. 22; Jean le Noir and Hesdin) and in *David pointing to his Mouth* in a psalter from the workshop of Jacquemart de Hesdin (Paris, Bibl. Nat., MS fr. 13091, fol. 85). For the motif of the king kissing the child's foot, see *Très belles heures*, p. 90. The motif of the reading apostle occurs in the *Petites heures*, fol. 144; and also in a pattern sheet in Paris, Louvre, Cabinet des Dessins (Meiss II, pl. 587).

17. The resemblance of the Parement Master's miniatures to several by Hesdin in the *Grandes heures* (1409; Paris, Bibl. Nat., MS lat. 919) and in the Brussels pages is certainly striking and suggests workshop co-operation. The illuminations showing the *Office of the Dead* by the Parement Master (in the Paris MS, p. 104), and by Hesdin (in the Brussels MS, p. 202), provide an instance of such correspondence. Despite obvious differences in the style of the two masters, Tröscher, 1966, p. 30, suggested that Jacquemart de Hesdin may have been the Parement Master.

18. Rensing, 1950, p. 149.

19. Tröscher, 1966, p. 142 did not specify the perceived influences.

20. Steinbart, 1946, p. 25 cites the *Très riches heures* without any specific evidence.

21. On Gentile da Fabriano, see Christiansen, 1982. The facial features of the Virgin may be developed from Venetian paintings such as the *Marriage of St Catherine* by Lorenzo Veneziano (1359; Accademia, Venice). For Lombard painting, see Exh. Cats. Milan, 1958 and 1988. For this facial type of the Virgin, one could also cite, for instance, the Virgin in Michelino da Besozzo's *Presentation*, on the reverse side of the *Madonna dell'Idea* in Milan Cathedral. For Michelino da Besozzo (active 1388–*c.* 1450), see Matalon, 1966.

22. Steinbart, 1946, p. 25 (see note 2 above).

23. Manuscripts painted by artists remaining in the Netherlands may be exemplified by a Netherlandish Bible, The Hague, Koninklijke Bibliotheek MS 78 D 38, 2 vols. (Utrecht, *c.* 1425) and by De Tafel van den Kersten Ghelove, London, BL, Add. 22288, fols. 82, 128v, 141v, and 160v by Dirc van Delft (*c.* 1400). On the manuscripts of the *devotio moderna* movement, see Knaus, 1973, col. 1081. The standard of certain *devotio moderna* manuscripts may be exemplified by *Die gheestelicke melody*, Universiteitsbibliotheek, Leiden, MS Ltk. 2058, fols. 39v and 26.

24. See Exh. Cat. Münster, 1952.

25. The dating and provenance of the Wilton Diptych is controversial. However, the Franco-Flemish stylistic influence and the iconographic stress on Richard II's kingship (the arms of Edward the Confessor are impaled with the badge of Richard II on the reverse sides of the diptych) suggest a connection with Richard's marriage to Isabel of France in 1396. Richard's collar of broomcods refers to those given him by Isabel and by Charles VI of France.

Chapter 9

1. As Theophilus (1979 edn, p. 12) advised artists in the 12th century: 'Therefore, whoever you are, dearest son, whose heart God has inspired to investigate the vast field of the divers arts and to apply your mind and attention to gather from it whatever pleases you, do not disparage any costly or useful thing just because your native soil has spontaneously and unexpectedly produced it for you'.

2. Budde, 1986, p. 15. Having established the outstanding survival rate of works of art, Budde makes the implausible suggestion that a body of some 17,200 works were painted in Cologne between 1300 and the beginning of the 16th century (taking into account Sundays and feast days, that would approximate one every four days).

3. H. Schwartz, 1948, pp. 23–24, also mentions a *Head of Christ and Donor Figure* in the church of St Thomas and a *Last Supper* and *Gethsemane* under the south choir window in the church of St Peter, both destroyed by bombs in 1945. For a more detailed account of Conrad's influence in Westphalia, see for instance Meyer, 1921 and Hölker, 1920.

4. Inv. No. 1912/2. This panel was found lining a chimney in 1903.

5. In the *Adoration* of the altarpiece of the Stegnitzfahrer, for instance, the kneeling king and the child both reflect the unusual poses of Conrad's Dortmund design; the youngest king appears more indebted to the Niederwildungen Altarpiece. It is significant that the Altar der kanonischen Tageszeiten depicts the crosses of the thieves with the Westphalian design of two horizontal bars. The painted wings of the altarpiece of the Zirkelbrüder were added to the central carved stone retable of *c.* 1420 (?) around 1430. The facial features of the protagonists and other designs, particularly the *Coronation of the Virgin*, also denote knowledge of Conrad's altarpieces.

6. The continuing discussion concerning the relationship between these two artists is partially confused by uncertainties as to whether some documentary references to a painter monk named 'Francke', including one concerning panels in Münster Cathedral which mentions a 'fratre Francone Zutphanico', should be connected with the Hamburg artist. For a discussion of the documents connected with Master Francke, see Grohn, 1969, pp. 17–21. In view of the reference to Zutphen, it is interesting to note that the motif of the inward-facing Christ stepping over the rear of the sarcophagus in the *Resurrection* in Hamburg, occurs also in the Darup Altarpiece (cat. no. 11 below; Darup is not far from Zutphen) and in the *Gebetbuch der Maria von Geldern* of 1415 (Duchess Maria was also a countess of Zutphen), Berlin, Staatsbibl. MS Germ. Quart. 42, fol. 39v. The motif also occurs in the sandstone part of the altarpiece of the Zirkelbrüder; see note 5 above. On Master Francke, see also Martens, 1929 and Exh. Cat. Hamburg, 1969.

7. I am indebted to Kirsti Melanko for her discussion of this altarpiece and for her special permission to take photographs. The provenance of this altarpiece is uncertain. If, as is frequently suggested, the retable was commissioned for the altar dedicated to St Barbara in Turku in 1412 (referred to in a papal letter of Indulgence), a later date for the commission of the altarpiece is still plausible. In the carved scene of *Theophilus before the Virgin*, Theophilus is depicted kneeling in a donor pose. It may be possible eventually to identify the donor Theophilus and thereby to shed some light on the original history of the altarpiece. It is feasible that the altarpiece did not originate in Finland; it may well have been transported there with much similar loot from Germany after the Thirty Years War (1618–1648). Many altarpieces were apparently deposited in Finnish churches by returning soldiers. The *Ecce Homo* in the Museum der bildenden Künste, Leipzig, should be dated to around 1430, as figures of Christ and the angel there show the same stage of stylistic development as those in the *Deposition* of the St Thomas Altarpiece.

8. Martens, 1929, p. 197 cited, for example, *Le livre des merveilles du monde* (*c.* 1411–13), Boucicaut Master and workshop, and Bedford Master, Paris, Bibl. Nat., fr. 2810; and the *Heures de René d'Anjou* (*c.* 1415), mainly workshop of the Rohan Master, Paris, Bibl. Nat., lat. 1156A. In his introduction to the *Rohan Book of Hours*, Meiss (1973, pp. 9, 16) suggested that the Boucicaut Master may have trained in Bruges, but he disputed the Netherlandish provenance of the Rohan Master, tentatively proposing that he trained in Provence and subsequently worked in Troyes. This view has found little support.

9. See Vitzthum, 1930, pp. 247–253.

10. See Pächt, 1969, p. 26. The group of women under the cross differs in iconography from that in the *Crucifixion* of the Hours of the Marshal Jean de Boucicaut (*c.* 1399–1411), Musée Jacquemart-André, Paris, MS 2, fol. 105v, which is cited as its model in the Exh. Cat. Hamburg, 1969. The relationship to Christ of both John and Mary differs considerably (as do the facial types).

11. For clarity of argument the name Campin is used here to represent all the works in the disputed Campin/Flémalle/Mérode group. On the problems of attribution, see Campbell, 1974, pp. 634–646. The systematic investigation by infrared reflectography of underdrawings in the Campin/Flémalle/Weyden group, in progress under the guidance of van Asperen de Boer, may eventually shed some light on the problems of attribution outlined by Campbell.

12. See Pächt, 1969, pp. 25–27.

13. The Reinoldi church, Dortmund. On the provenance of the painter, see also R. Didier and J. Steyvaert, Exh. Cat. Cologne, 1978–80, I, p. 97. Although it remains uncertain whether the *Calvary of the Tanners* has always been in Bruges(Cathedral of Saint-Sauveur), a Netherlandish provenance seems plausible.

14. Rijksmuseum Het Catharijneconvent, Utrecht. The wings are usually dated *c.* 1410–15; in view of the quotation from the Dortmund *Death of the Virgin*, a date of *c.* 1425–30 might be considered. S. Beeh-Lustenberger's suggestion (Exh. Cat. Cologne, 1978–80, I, p. 262) that the turbulence of style in the obverse scenes connects them with the 'Middle Rhenish' altarpiece in the Felsenkirche, Idar-Oberstein a. d. Nahe (also reproduced on p. 262 of the catalogue), is unacceptable because there are no other stylistic similarities. The altarpiece at Oberstein (the proposed date of *c.* 1400 is surely too early) betrays its Westphalian connection in the cross of the thieves with two horizontal bars. Beeh-Lustenberger cites unspecified western influences as mutual sources for Conrad and the main master of the Utrecht wings. Yet both the direct stylistic and iconographic quotations from Conrad's models by the master of the Utrecht panels and Conrad's creative art itself speak strongly against that thesis. When assessing possible Westphalian influences, it should be remembered that the ecclesiastical principality had strong links with Westphalia through its bishops Jan van Arkel (1342–64) and Floris van Wevelinchoven (1379–98), both from Münster. On the other hand the collector who purchased the altarpiece from an unknown church, and insisted on keeping the provenance mysterious, was private chaplain to a family with very strong Westphalian connections.

15. This facial type links the London panel with the Flémalle group in the Städelsches Kunstinstitut, Frankfurt.

16. The motif of the candle with the coin later recurred in a version of this narrative by Petrus Christus (*c.* 1460–65; San Diego, Timken Art Gallery, Putnam Foundation).

17. Frinta, 1981, p. 75. See also Chapter 5, note 12. For Rogier van der Weyden, see Périer-D'Interen, 1985, pp. 26–28.

18. Hamand, 1957, p. 51, noted the foreign character of costume and armour in the priory window scene. The *Hours of Elizabeth the Queen* (London, BL, Add. 50001, *c.* 1420–30) are named after the signature of a later owner, Elizabeth, wife of Henry VII, on fol. 22: 'Elysabeth ye quene'. Although the possible Italian prototype of the *Last Supper*, by a follower of Pietro Lorenzetti (1330s)

in the lower church at Assisi includes profiles and lost profile, it is very different both in style and iconography.

19. The Sherborne Missal, London, BL, loan MS 82, p. 380. The manuscript was commissioned by Richard Mitford, Bishop of Salisbury (1396–1407) and Robert Bruyning, Abbot of Sherborne in Dorset (1385–1415). Thomas, 1979, p. 113, notes Rhenish and Bohemian influences, and cites Millar, who suggested the Rhineland region (with certain Netherlandish influences) as the most likely source. The motif of the women under the cross (here Magdalene is shown in the pose of the Niederwildungen St John) may have been in Conrad's workshop before 1403. The repeat of motifs in Conrad's workshop can be noted in the two altarpieces, for instance in the pose of the Virgin and Child of the Nativities.

20. The guild regulations for the painters of Cologne of 1371–96 would suggest that the town welcomed well-qualified painters. See Loesch, 1984, I, p. 136: 'He who wants to be admitted to the guild, shall appear before the senior masters appointed by the Council and prove to them whether he knows his craft. If he knows it, he may settle in Cologne… When he has proven his craftsmanship and wants to settle, he shall pay 4 Gulden'.

21. The *Trinity*, WRM Depos. 363 from the Landesmuseum Münster; the *Crucifixion* is in the National Gallery, Washington, Samuel H. Kress Collection Inv. No. 1390; the *Sacra Conversazione* triptych is in the Kisters Collection at Kreuzlingen. Budde, 1986, also includes the *Ecce Homo* (between Mary and St Catherine) at Antwerp (Koninklijk Museum voor Schone Kunsten, Inv. No. 5070) in the early works of the Veronica Master. The elongated forms and the weak modelling, however, suggest a later date and workshop execution.

22. See Zehnder, 1990, pp. 316–325; however, he has reservations about the Wehrden Crucifixion.

23. Zehnder, attempting to claim the Veronica Master as a native of Cologne ignores the historical fact, stressed by Budde (1986, p. 15), that Cologne masters tended to be immigrants.

24. See Stange, 1967–78, I, p. 142; and 1934–61, III, p. 31.

25. See Pieper, 1950a. Pieper's attribution of the *Trinity* panel to the Veronica master has been much disputed, but it is convincing. Pieper also suggested that wing panels in Dessau formed part of the *Trinity*. However, they are of such inferior quality that they cannot have been painted by the Veronica Master. It is doubtful whether a second master would have been employed for such a

small altarpiece. The difference in punchwork between the panel in Cologne and the wings in Dessau also suggests a different workshop.

26. See Zehnder, 1990, pp. 493–494; he did not note the correspondence of punch patterns in the *Trinity* panel and other works by the Veronica Master and his workshop.

27. Zehnder, 1974, p 38; Zehnder, 1981, *passim*, e.g. pp. 57, 62, 64.

28. See Musper, 1961, p.203: 'a completely agricultural area without the worldwide connections of the Hansa towns'. Cuttler (1968, pp. 56–58) mistakenly assumed a commercial and political supremacy of Cologne over Dortmund in the Hanseatic League around 1400 and misjudged the milieu in which the Veronica Master worked. As a consequence, he considered Conrad's art provincial and 'less luminous in its expression'.

29. See Zehnder, 1990, p. 316.

30. In his 1990 catalogue, Zehnder accepted that two campaigns of painting were involved in the altarpiece. However, he dated the second campaign to around 1400, and persisted in his opinion that works by this master must be regarded as the earliest examples of the new style in Cologne. In spite of recognizing similarities in the application of pigments and in style (p. 123), he felt the technique of the painter of the St Elizabeth Altarpiece predated the 'zarte Malweise' (soft modelling) of the Veronica Master.

31. It is interesting to note that Budde (1986, p. 37) mentioned a technical examination of the St Clare Polyptych (pl. 153) showing similar overpainting of earlier work when a wing was completed by a later hand; he suggests that these additions date from after 1400. The altarpiece derives from the Franciscan convent of St Clare, Cologne (removed in 1804, placed in the Cathedral in 1811). The coats-of-arms of Countess Philippa of Gelders (d. 1352) and Countess Isabella of Gelders (d. 1354) are included in the altarpiece. On stylistic grounds, a date after 1360 is usually suggested for the older parts of the retable.

32. Right wing, from the church of St Laurenz, Cologne, depicting the *Death of the Virgin*, *Coronation of the Virgin*, *Resurrection* and *Ascension*, all close in style to Conrad's altarpieces. The panel of the *Burial of St Lawrence* is now in the Germanisches Nationalmuseum, Nuremberg, Gm 6. It has recently been plausibly suggested that the painter was not called Stefan Lochner and did not come from the Bodensee area, but trained in Cologne or Westphalia; see Exh. Cat. Cologne, 1993. In the central panel of the Dombild, the centralized com-

position and choice of single motifs appear to refer to Conrad's Dortmund *Adoration*; see Corley, 1994.

33. See Zehnder, 1981, II, p. 54; I am indebted to John Hand, who allowed me to study all the technical information concerning this panel. The reflectogram was dated 15 December 1981. Dendrochronological examination of the panel was carried out by Peter Klein, and his report of 10 April 1987 recorded a similar ring structure to other oak-wood panels from Cologne. On the reliability of dendrochronological examinations, see Klein, 1985.

34. See Faries in Exh. Cat. Cologne, 1993, pp. 169–170.

35. Klein, 1985, pp. 29–41.

36. See Zehnder, 1981, II, p. 59.

37. Ibid.

38. Pieper, 1964, see also Chapter 5, note 9; Langemeyer, 1980–81, I, pp. 389–401, disputed the admissibility of evidence of Pieper's presumed regional physiognomical and psychological characteristicsto demonstrate authorship. He sensibly advised a return to the consideration of a master's style and technique, coupled with questions of his training, workshop connections and patronage, as a means of identifying artists.

39. On the French influence for the early part of the St Clare Polyptych, see G. Schmidt, 1977, p. 26. He also argued French stylistic influences for the frescoes of the Cathedral choir stalls (p. 23). Two glass windows—with a possible provenance from Cologne—seem to belong to the early Conradian period of stylistic development in Cologne: the *St Margaret* window (*c.* 1430), Galerie Fischer, Luzern; and the *Madonna with the Crescent Moon* window (*c.* 1430–35), The Cloisters, Metropolitan Museum of Art, New York. On their derivation from models in the workshop of Conrad von Soest, see Rode, 1977, pp. 98–102.

40. Eleven of the original twelve scenes survive; an *Entombment* was lost during the Second World War.

Catalogue

Notes to Cat. 1

1. Although Rörig, 1909–1914, p. 43, read the inscriptions as *'diutius sustinebitur et crescit vita'* and

41. On the Westphalian influence in the work attributed to Stefan Lochner see Corley, forthcoming.

42. One need no longer accept Budde's contention (1986, p. 38) that the dependence of the Veronica Master on the workshop of Conrad von Soest cannot be demonstrated.

43. Knippenberg, 1955, pp. 83–96.

44. See Eisler, 1977. Although Eisler suggested (p. 1) that the image of the Carthusian monk is not intended as a specific portrait, his contention only rests on a perceived similarity between the features of the monk in the panel and those of St John. However, Eisler also noted that the monk's face had been restored. Eisler's suggestion that the panel may have been one of many similar ones intended for the monks' cells is not based on specific evidence.

45. Knippenberg, 1955, pp. 94–95. Recorded donations (excluding artefacts) for the monastery of St Barbara from members of the Berswordt family amounted to 2325 gold gulden.

46. The monastery records suggest that the elder Segebodo died on 6 April 1404; Knippenberg seems to have evidence that casts doubt on the accuracy of this entry. It is interesting to note that Johann Berswordt had studied in Paris (from 1375), Orléans (from 1378), and was again in Paris from 1381 (with Andreas Sudermann), during the time that Conrad von Soest may have arrived there. He was Rector of Heidelberg University in 1387. During his time as Rector of Cologne University in 1390 he travelled to Rome. His nephew Dr. Segebodo first mentioned as *clericus Coloniensis* in a papal document of 1394, studied in Cologne and was later in Bologna (until 1414) with seven other students from Dortmund. In 1415 he became Rector of Cologne University, and served again in 1433/34. He held a number of important offices and prebends, and had sufficient wealth to gain certain papal privileges and to present several institutions with considerable gifts. In the Marienkirche in Dortmund he and his brothers embellished the crucifixion chapel with the *Berswordt Altarpiece* (1431, see cat. no. 9).

'mortui nemo pri corde', the present inscriptions seem to be the original ones.

2. Manuscript copies by Varnhagen, dated 1778 and 1793, are kept in the Archiv des Waldeckischen Geschichtsvereins, Arolsen. The photo-

graph of the damaged chronicle was first published by Reichardt, 1949, p. 31. Little is now left of the chronicle.

3. Rohrberg, 1968, pp. 131–135, in discussing the use of the golden section, claims this fact for the wing panels, but the height of these panels of 73.5 cm would then only allow for a width of 52 cm, whereas they measure 57 cm.

4. According to Rörig, 1909–14, p. 43, the church was reconsecrated on 1 September 1404, with the altarpiece and the new windows donated by the guilds already in position. The high altar was first mentioned in 1306 as dedicated *'in honore glorios. virg. matr. Marie et sancte Elisabeth'*. Until recently it still contained a medieval *'sepulchrum'*, with two sealed reliquaries, which is now preserved in the town museum. Franz, 1962, pp. 52–54, contended that the seal is that of the Bishop of Mainz, Dietrich vom Hagen, and that it can be dated to *c.* 1385. The partially lost inscription on the damaged relic bags reads: *'.....ri[n]e virginis et martiris'* (this may refer to St Catherine), and *'....berti ep[iscop]i et m[artiris]'* (this may refer to Adalbert von Prag, martyred in 997, who was much venerated in medieval Germany). Franz stated that the altar of the 'Holy Cross, Mary and St Catherine' of 1336 was the high altar, but this altar was placed *'ante chorum'* (5. 6. 1336, Archiv, Bad Wildungen).

5. In October 1527, Count Philipp of Waldeck ordered the Commander of the Order of St John in Wildungen to stop using the church; see Reichardt, 1949, p. 51. Ornaments, including the recently installed iron screen, were removed in 1532. Count Philipp also withdrew from the Order of St John the right of feudal tenure and the right to select the priests. Furthermore, he also gave lands, originally donated to the church, to the town council: 10 March 1532, Hessisches Staatsarchiv Marburg, no. 9988.

6. I am indebted to the medical historian the late Prof. Schultheis for the information that this is mentioned in some early *Brunnenschriften*, published since 1580; I have been unable to find the precise dates of such references to the display of the chronicle in the church. The interest for the Spa visitors in the chronicle lay in the fact that it records that water was first pumped to Niederwildungen in 1378.

7. See Curtze, 1850. The church was already in poor condition in 1731, when the Fürstlich Waldeckische Regierung, Arolsen ordered: 'dass der Visitator und Pfarrer, wie auch Bürgermeister und Rath der Stadt Alten-Wildungen geziemend angezeigt haben, welchergestalt Ihre Kirche dermassen baufällig seye, dass selbige zur Verhütung grössern Unglücks und darob zu besorgender Gefahr

ohnumgänglich von Grund auff neu gebaut werden müsse' (Archiv, Arolsen). J. Eichler, architect and local historian, recorded the restoration work and reconsecration festivities of 15 November 1857 in his *Chronicle* (unpublished manuscript, Archiv, Bad Wildungen, several volumes). The completion of the rebuilding of the choir is commemorated by a plaque, dated 1855, placed on the outside wall of the choir.

8. See Schmitz, 1906, p. 130; and Schmitz, F. Burger and J. Beth, 1917, II, p. 393. The altarpiece was also cited in the exhibition at Münster in 1879, and a date of 1402 was suggested (p. 108, no. 1448). However, only watercolour copies (by Rector Martin of Roermund) of some scenes from the altarpiece were shown there; see Loewe 1909, p. 16.

9. Correspondence of Pfarrer K.F.A. Lau, Pfarrarchiv, Stadtkirche Bad Wildungen. I am indebted to Pfarrer Kurz for his permission to search through the largely unsorted church archives. Offers to undertake the restoration were made in 1908 by Hofmaler F. Ahnert, Kassel; and in 1908 by Kunstmaler W. Fassbender, Bonn; and later, in 1920, by Hölker on behalf of Restaurator Diekmann of the Schnütgen Museum, Cologne. The Berlin museum offered an unspecified painting in exchange, plus 50,000 Goldmark.

10. E. Hoyne, personal communication, 17 June 1986. See Stange, 1967–78, I, p. 141.

11. Correspondence of Pfarrer von Haller, Pfarrarchiv, Stadtkirche. A series of letters from Alfred Breuer are testimony of his own incompetence; his request for materials of 16 November 1924 gives some of the flavour of his approach:

> *Drei Flaschen Brennspiritus*
> *Ein Paket feiner Watte (Verbandwatte)*
> *Zwei Pfund Schlemmkreide*
> *Ein 1/2 Pfund feinen Gips*
> *Ein 1/2 Liter französisches Terpentin*
> *Ein Pfund gelbes Wachs (unaufgelöst)*
> *Ein Kilo Copaira Balsam*
> *Ein Liter Salmiakgeist (Driplese)*
> *Ein Liter Leinöl (kaltgepresst, möglichst hell).*

12. A. Fink in the *Wildunger Zeitung* of 13 March 1925; see also Fink, 1925/26, p. 449. In his replies, dated 26 March and 29 April 1925 (Pfarrarchiv, Stadtkirche), Breuer excused himself, calling his work 'experimental', and refused to 'expose himself to further rudeness'.

13. 12 June 1925 (Pfarrarchiv, Stadtkirche). The paint losses next to the vertical cracks, caused by Breuer's filling, were irreversible; these areas were toned in, but not regilded. The coarse overpainting

of the beard of St Thomas in the *Last Supper* may well also be a Breuer legacy. It is interesting to note that the church was again renovated in 1930/31 and that, according to an unpublished chronicle by Pfarrer Baum, 1976, p. 14, in the Pfarrarchiv, Stadtkirche, the Gothic Frühmessealtar (*ante chorum*) was 'removed' at this time, apparently without a record of its destination.

14. See Medding, 8 July 1950; Lünenschloss, 1951, pp. 2–5, although publishing under the guidance of Landeskonservator Bleibaum, mainly described the altarpiece rather than the restoration. It is interesting to note that holes at the top of the frame derive from the former habit of decorating the altarpiece with garlands on festive occasions. I am grateful to Frau L. Lorenz for this information.

15. That such cleaning took place regularly is apparent in the instruction to a verger: 'der mesner sol auch alle freitag...es sei ein veirtag oder nit, ...alle sein pilde rainigen vor dem unflot und auch warten an den wenden, ob die rein und sauber sein. See Gümbel, 1929, p. 42':*Das Mesnerpflichtbuch von St Sebald, c.*1482. Such industry must have caused much damage.

16. The exhibition in Marburg was held at the Universitäts-Museum and was reported in the *Marburger Presse*, no. 288, 11 December 1950, p. 6. The church renovation was extensive: new central heating was installed again, the sarcophagi of the counts of Waldeck were removed to the empty burial chamber reserved for the family in nearby Netze, the medieval font was removed to the Geismar chapel by the church entrance and the Victorian stained glass was given to Kassel, to be replaced by what Pfarrer Baum (Baum chronicle, p. 15, Archiv, Bad Wildungen) defined as glass 'scratched in the Gothic fashion'. Baum (p. 16) also records the temporary removal of the altarpiece in his chronicle.

Notes to Cat. 2

1. Hölker, 1920, dated the frame correctly to 1720. Nordhoff, 1880, p. 85 gave a date of 1659, apparently confusing the donor Dethmar Wessel Nies with an earlier mayor, Dethmar Wessel.

2. Hieronymi manuscript restoration report to the parish (written in Bonn, January 1930), archives of the Marienkirche, Dortmund, file 1930. Hieronymi, who restored the Dortmund Altarpiece was a painter of the Nazarene school and a restorer (1868–1950). He also restored Lochner's Dombild.

3. Letter, dated 8 May 1957, written by Dr Fritz to the 'Superintendentur Dortmund', private archives Dr Fritz, Anlage 2: the X-ray photographs showed, that 'einzelne Bohlen durch... [*sic*] cm lange, an beiden Enden zugespitzte Eisendübel miteinander unsichtbar verbunden sind. Für das menschliche Auge unsichtbar, liegen sie tief im Inneren der Bohlen verborgen'. These X-ray photographs are listed in the Dortmund museum, but could not be found and were never published. Fritz never published his findings, but referred to the X-ray photographs in a footnote (1950a, p. 107, n. 4). Fritz recorded that the Darup Altarpiece, cat. no. 11, has similar dowels.

4. Fritz, 1950a, pp. 117–122.

5. I am indebted to Frau M. Junkel for her generous permission to publish and study this photograph for the first time, together with pre-restoration photographs from her family archives.

6. Stein, 1930.

7. The use of a wing width of 127 cm for both altarpieces may show that the Dortmund Elle was close in length to that of Amsterdam (= 68.781 cm), Aachen (= 68.02 cm), Hamburg (= 69.141 cm) or the Brabant Elle of Brussels, used in the cloth trade (= 69.5 cm). The Cologne Elle, used by Fritz in an unconvincing comparison, only measured 57.47831 cm. All evidence for the length of the Dortmund Elle during the late Middle Ages is lost. (I am indebted to Archivrat Dr Schilp, Dortmund Town Archives, for this information). See also Jansen, 1900, and Noback, 1850. Documentary evidence relating to the exact size of the Soest Elle is also missing. (I am grateful to the town archives, Soest, for this information). Geck, 1825, basing his information on unspecified measurements by Egen, stated that the Soest Elle was very close in length to the Cologne Elle. If this is correct, it could confirm that Conrad's workshop was not in Soest.

8. Limbourg brothers, *The Feeding of the Multitude* in *Très riches heures* (*c.* 1413–16), fol. 168v (Musée Condé, Chantilly); such a Trinity also occurs in the Ghent Altarpiece by Van Eyck (St Bavon, Ghent). The arrangement of punched rays in the lunette of the Dortmund Altarpiece further supports this reconstruction; the rays would have surrounded God the Father as they do Christ in the panel below.

9. Centres of haloes are at a distance from each other of multiples of $r = 12.8$. Additional diagonals within the picture are drawn from the centre point at the base to $2r$ below the top at each side. They were needed to position the front row of Apostles. They run parallel to the diagonals created by the compass markings. The distance between the base centre point and the point of intersection of the diagonals in Rohrberg's Niederwildungen drawing is therefore also $2r$.

10. The inventory is now lost; it is published by Ernste, 1931, pp. 180–84.

11. See Winterfeld, 1981, p. 42 and *Dortmunder Zeitung*, 21 September 1837. The repair bill for the church was 3786 Taler.

12. Welsch, who received 103 Reichstaler and 15 Sgr for his labour, was the author of *Vollständige Anweisung zur Restauration der Gemälde*, Quedlingburg/Leipzig, 1834.

13. Stein, 1930: J.H. Stockmann was paid 38 Rtler and 20 Sgr for gilding the panels. Unfortunately, no reference is made to the original image in the lunette. Stein also published a pre-restoration photograph of the *Death of the Virgin* which shows the balustrade painted over St James and also the semicircle of angels. Cuttler, in 1968, also inadvertently published a pre-restoration photograph.

14. Report by the restorer Hieronymi, dated June 1927, Pfarrarchiv Marienkirche, file 1927.

15. Letter, dated 17 March 1925, Pfarrarchiv, Marienkirche. The panels from the Dortmund Altarpiece were valued at M 60,000 each (and the Berswordt Altarpiece at M 30,000).

16. Geisberg report, dated 5 May 1926, private archives of Rolf Fritz whose father Studienrat Fritz headed the appeal. Report by Schäfer, dated 11 May 1926 for the *Sitzung des Presbyteriums* of 3 June 1926, Pfarrarchiv, Marienkirche. A suggestion by Förster to create a museum of the treasures of the Marienkirche in its Berswordt chapel (29 September 1925) found no acceptance.

17. See note 3 above.

18. Schäfer, 1928/29, pp. 12–20, however, quoted an old verger who remembered some painted gold panels stored in the church loft.

19. The panels arrived 12 days after the start of the exhibition, following much dispute about insurance. A description of the exhibition appeared in the *Dortmunder Zeitung* of 29 September 1930. In 1932, a report in the *Jahrbuch der Rheinischen Denkmalpflege*, 8–9 (Düsseldorf) stated: 'Die Bildtafeln sind in der Marienkirche übrigens museumsmässig an den Schiffspfeilern aufgehängt'. Although this seems to suggest that all the panels were attached to pillars in the nave of the church, Geisberg, 1931, p. 9, recorded that the wings formed an altarpiece in the choir. It is feasible that the panels were experimentally moved to a variety of positions at this time.

20. Bericht des Kulturausschusses, dated 20 March 1957, Pfarrarchiv Marienkirche. I am indebted to Dr A. Göers for informing me that four foreign workmen (two Yugoslav, one Dutch and one French) were accidentally ordered by the Kreisleiter to help with this top secret transport.

21. In a tribute to the English art historian officers who allowed Cappenberg castle to be used to house the treasures from destroyed Dortmund churches, and who provided chemicals needed for urgent restorations, Rolf Fritz named Colonel Christopher Norris, Major Robertson (Edinburgh University), Murray Baillie and Mrs Westland (*Frankfurter Allgemeine*, 16.1.1991, No. 13, p. 8).

Notes to Cat. 3

1. Stange, 1967–78, I, no. 455, cites a size of 93.5 by 27 cm for each panel, a measurement that is repeated in the literature until Pieper's correction in 1986 (p. 40).

2. For daughters of the Suderman and Berswordt families from Dortmund in the convent, see Winterfeld, 1924–26, p. 218 and Knippenberg, 1955, p. 47.

3. See Pieper, 1950b, p. 123, and also p. 126 on the 1835 restoration.

4. See Pieper, 1986, p. 43; Nordhoff (1879, p. 136) suggested 'Deckel eines Schränkchens'.

Notes to Cat. 4

1. Renaus de Montauban was one of the four 'children of Haymon' cited in French legend and poetry. Rebellion brought him to Dortmund, where he is said to have been converted. He is reputed to have been murdered in Cologne. The remains of Reinold are thought to have been transferred to Dortmund from Cologne by Archbishop Anno in 1059. The Dortmund chronicler reported that Emperor Charles IV and Empress Elisabeth each demanded to be given a part of Reinold's relics during their visits to Dortmund in 1377 and 1378 respectively. See Lundt, 1990, pp. 177–183 for a critical account of the legends of Reinold. Dortmund coins of the 13th and 14th centuries depict the head of Reinold.

2. Goldberg and Scheffler, 1972, p. 186, reasonably dismissed earlier suggestions that the coats-of-arms could be connected with Duke Heinrich of Dortmund. An inscription of an altarpiece (1523) in the Viktorkirche at Schwerte identifies as 'S. reinoldus' a saint bearing a similar lion rampant on his coat-of-arms.

3. Fritz, 1948, p. 106; his hypothesis is disputed by Wallrath, 1971, p. 306.

4. Stange, 1933–34, p. 165, and 1966, p. 4, dated the panel to around 1400, but accepted a date around 1404 in 1967–78, I, 1967 (no. 453). Pieper, 1950, p. 189, also dated the panel before the Niederwildungen Altarpiece. See 'Comment' and note 6, below.

5. Inventar der Privat-Gemäldesammlung König Ludwig I, Schloss Schleissheim, 1827–28, no. 36.

6. Winterfeld, 1948, p. 10; Sauerland, 1913, p. 167, *Vatikanische Regesten*, VII, 430 (1404, apr. 1): 'Segebodoni Berswort de Tremonia laico Colon. dioc. concedit altare portabile'. Stange, 1962, p. 173, mistook the date for 1401.

Notes to Cat. 5

1. Rensing, 1950, pp. 138–181, Nordhoff, 1880, p. 77, and Fritz, 1951b, p. 161 attributed the altarpiece to Conrad von Soest. Stange, 1934–61, 3, p. 35, was more cautious: 'perhaps made under the guidance of Conrad von Soest, certainly following his model'; Pieper, 1986, no. 5: dated it to *c.* 1410, and believed it was painted in a workshop in Soest. He followed Nissen, 1931a, pp. 58–65, who stipulated an independent workshop in Soest and a date of around 1420. Nissen first recognized the wing fragments as part of the retable. For the Cleveland panel, see Stechow, 1974, no. 10.

2. The Buxtehude Altarpiece (*c.* 1410), by Master Bertram and workshop, Kunsthalle Hamburg, and the Schotten Altarpiece (*c.* 1420–40), Ev. Liebfrauenkirche, Schotten, for instance, depict several scenes from the life of Joachim and Anna.

3. The Schotten statue, an enthroned Queen of Heaven, is surrounded by carved framework similar to that at Fröndenberg; it includes the ogee arch and other decorative features.

4. See Exh. Cat. Cappenberg, 1950, no. 68.

5. Rensing, 1950, p. 180. Rensing suggests that the retable was painted ten years before the Niederwildungen Altarpiece, which he dates to 1408. Fritz, 1951b, p. 161, agreed with the date proposed by Rensing. It is interesting to note that Catharina von der Mark donated another altarpiece for Fröndenberg, in honour of SS. Nicholas, Catherine and Dorothea, see Rensing, p. 144, n. 14.

6. See Fritz, 1950b, p. 134.

Notes to Cat. 6

1. The panel is attributed to Conrad von Soest at the museum. See also Fritz, 1950b, pp. 134–137 and cat. no. 5 above.

2. The inscription is generally read as 'MA MA RODU' (Exh. Cat. Cappenberg, 1950, no. 76; Stange, 1967–78, I, no. 461); it should surely read MR for 'Maria Regina'. The first letter in brackets does now, after thoughtless restoration, resemble the letter A; the second (R) can still be read correctly.

Notes to Cat. 7

1. Nordhoff, 1880, p. 65, called the panel 'eine der vollendetsten Schöpfungen Conrads'. The painting is attributed to Conrad by, for instance, Nissen, 1933b, p. 228; Stange, 1934–61, 3, p. 29; Steinbart, 1946, p. 21; Pieper, Exh. Cat. Münster, 1964, p. 18, and Châtelet/Recht, 1989, p. 218. Only Meier, 1921, pp. 62 and 89, and Rensing, 1950, pp. 139–142 and 180, doubted Conrad's authorship. The three virgins refer to the legend of the dowry. The three clerics, grouped separately from the fourth cleric, appear to illustrate the legend of the miracle of the resurrection of the murdered young students/clerics. Whether the separate cleric in the middle distance is supposed to be their repenting landlord (who had murdered them), or whether he represents the 'man of provenance and renown' who was ordered 'to elect as bishop the first human entering through the door', as Rensing (p. 141) suggests, remains uncertain. Angels placing the mitre on the head of St Nicholas appear to support Rensing's interpretation. It is interesting to note that the scene reflects the iconography of a wall-painting in the same chapel (*c.* 1230); there the angels present the enthroned saint with mitre and crozier. For the legends of St Nicholas, see Meisen, 1931, esp. pp. 232, 289.

2. For an account of the restoration, see Nissen, 1933b, pp. 228–232, and Exh. Cat. Münster, 1964, p. 84. A pre-restoration photograph shows considerable damage to the standing saints. I thank the Westfälisches Amt für Denkmalpflege, Münster, for the photograph.

Notes to Cat. 8

1. Fritz, 1951a, pp. 87–97; the sketches are kept in the Landesmuseum in Münster. Jacobs does not name the subject of the lost panels. The altarpiece is discussed in detail in Eckert, 1956, and Jacobs, 1983.

2. Ledebur (first published either in 1825 or 1828, both dates are cited in the literature and the manuscript in Münster [Stadtarchiv] no longer bears a date), 1934, p. 125. For Förster, see 1847, p. 21.

Notes to Cat. 9

1. See Jacobs, 1983; Lübke, 1853, p. 342; Eckert, 1956, pp. 79–84. On Appuhn's attribution to Conrad von Soest, see 1978–80, I, p. 224.

2. The suggested dates included Stange, III, 1934–61, p. 44: 1431; Fritz, 1950c, p. 193: *c.* 1400; Pieper, Exh. Cat. Münster, 1964, p. 68: before 1400; Stange, 1962, p. 184: *c.* 1390.

3. Jacobs, 1983, pp. 63–64. The many examples from later dates include Koerbecke's Langenhorster Altar (after 1445) in the Landesmuseum Münster; Lochner's *Adoration of the Kings* (Dombild, *c.* 1440) in Cologne Cathedral; the Kinship Master's Altarpiece of the Holy Kinship, (1500/1504) in the Wallraf-Richartz Museum, Cologne; and the sculpture of the *Three Kings*, Annenkapelle, St Martinikirche, Brunswick, (*c.* 1440–50).

4. The documents are published in Rothert, 1918, pp. 125–126. The document of 2 May 1385 is concerned with Heinrich Lemberg's endowment of the crucifixion altar.

5. Rothert, 1918, pp. 126–127: 23 February 1397, Lambert Berswordt's donation of 100 gulden led to the appointment of a curate on 26 July 1397. Lambert died on 7 September 1397; see Knippenberg, 1955.

6. See Knippenberg, 1955, pp. 94–95.

7. Rothert, 1918, pp. 127–128, 4 October 1431. This donation included a house and provision for two prebends, and was again confirmed in 1490. It was not usual to mention anything beyond the financial aspects in such documents.

8. R. Hieronymi, *Protokoll zu dem Altarwerk der Kreuzigung der Berswordt-Kapelle zu St Marien in Dortmund*, 'Dezember 1927', unpublished typescript copy, Pfarrarchiv Marienkirche. Kuchel's report is published in Exh. Cat. Münster, 1964, p.66.

Note to Cat. 10

1. I am indebted to Pfarrdechant W. Schüller for this information; personal communication 8 November 1990.

Note to Cat. 11

1. Fritz, 1950a, p. 107, n. 4.

Note to Cat. 13

1. Blaschke, 1976, p. 13. Hölker, 1920, pp. 152–158, suggested that the wings of the Golden Panel were painted by Conrad von Soest whilst, according to Hölker, he maintained a workshop in Lübeck from *c.* 1420–30 'for a while'. As discussed in the text, Conrad is unlikely to have moved his workshop at that stage and is likely to have died soon after 1422. For a description of the carved part of the wings which he dated to around 1410–30, see von Einem, 1929.

2. 'And as Moses lifted up the serpent in the wilderness, even so must the Son of man be lifted up' (John 3. 14).

3. See Hosmann, 1700; Hosmann's drawing of the altarpiece is reproduced in Hölker, 1920, pl. XI.

4. Gebhardi, 1762, p. 183, first equated the consecration date with that of the completion of the wings. Waagen, 1862, p. 62, introduced the date into the art-historical literature.

5. The abbot and *'consilarius ducum'* was distantly related to the duke. He managed to stay abbot of St Michael monastery in contradiction to canon law (Blaschke, 1976, pp. 108–110 and p. 152, n. 41) and was buried in 1441 in the abbey.

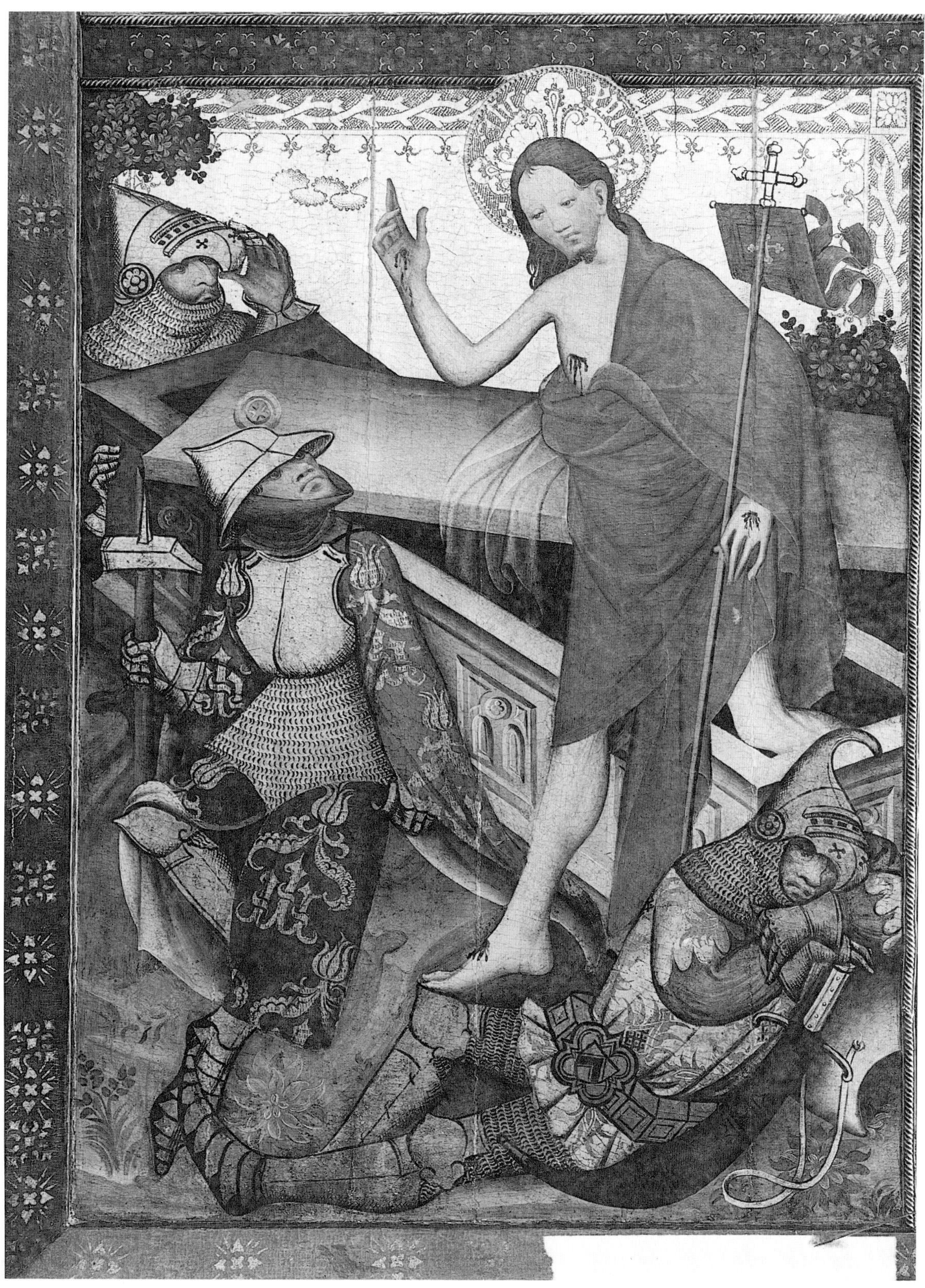

169. Conrad von Soest: *Resurrection*. Niederwildungen Altarpiece

170. Marriage contract, 1394, between Conrad von Soest and Gertrud von Münster

Appendix A

Translation of the Marriage Contract between Conrad von Soest and Gertrud von Münster 11 February 1394 (pl. 170)

Marriage contract in the form of (the Dortmund notary) Master Heinrich:

We Dethmar Cleppink, son of Hermann, Hermann Cleppink, son of Goschalke, Arnd Sudermann, Everd Wystrate, Lambert Bersword and Clawes Swarte are appointed witnesses for and on behalf of the bridegroom, in accordance with the law of Dortmund, as Conrad von Soest on the one part and Gertrud, daughter of the deceased Lambert of Münster and wedded wife of the aforementioned Conrad, on the other part, tell all people and witness publicly by this letter that we, on the first morning, when the above mentioned Conrad von Soest first rose from Gertrud, his married wife, were by the bridal bed at the right time, in accordance with the law of Dortmund, that Conrad gave Gertrud, his married wife all his goods, of which he stood possessed or might later come into possession. In the same way Gertrud in turn gave him all goods, of which she stood possessed or might later come into possession, except as is hereafter mentioned: in the event that Conrad predecease Gertrud, his wedded wife, without issue living at the date of his death, all her goods whatsoever shall be returned to his wife Gertrud and she shall also receive from the estate of her husband Conrad 200 Mark Pfennige in Dortmund currency, and shall return all his other goods to his next of kin. Similarly, if Gertrud predecease her husband Conrad, without living issue at the date of her death, Conrad shall receive from her estate 100 Mark Pfennige, in Dortmund currency, and shall return all her other goods to Gertrud's next of kin. It was further agreed that the aforementioned Conrad, whether in sickness or in health and having the capacity to dispose of the same, is entitled to grant from his estate 200 Mark Dortmundische Pfennige. Similarly, the aforementioned Gertrud is entitled to grant 100 Mark Dortmundische Pfennige.

For this ceremony we were accompanied by a sufficient number of honourable and modest people, both men and women, namely a.b.c.d. and sufficient other good people who had been expressly invited here and appointed as witnesses. In witness whereof and to the aforementioned presents we Dethmar Cleppink, Hermann Cleppink, Arnd Sudermann, Everd Wystrate, Lambert Berswort and Clawes Swarte, the aforementioned witnesses, have herewith affixed our seal at the request of both parties to this deed. Given on the day of the holy Virgin Scholastica, 1394.

Appendix B

The Niederwildungen Altarpiece Chronicle

The text of the chronicle on the reverse side of the Niederwildungen altarpiece, according to copies by the historian J. A. Th. L. Varnhagen of 1778 and 1793 (partially based on a manuscript of 1617 by the teacher Christianus Dickius), contained the following text:

anno domini m^o cccc^o XIII ipso die albani martyris du lagen dy von patberg neder vor Koerbach.

anno millesimo ccc^o denoque noveno presens castellum fore noscas plantificatum virginis ipso die puta nativitate mariae.

anno millesimo trino C cum tricesimo bino festo gregorii spacio non ulteriori fundavit regimen primo felix cui nomen.

anno domini m^o ccc^o LXX IIII do gyng der sterner kryg an circa festum Laurentii.

m c^{ter} LX bis quibus octo connuberabis primitus in festo penthecostes memor esto. altos per montes wyldungim ducere fontes nus man her verte ductorem noscis aperte qui fuerat gar wys dictus agnomine smenkys.

anno quo supra de fonte videbitur infra lumine perpetuo de quo sit gloria Christo formans ... circa principium Cyriaci petrus plebanus pariter cognomine gecke ... expeditores seo jugiter urat.

anno domini m^o ccc^o XL IX bartholomei du worden dy iuden gebrand und in dem sulben iare gyngen dy geysselbruder und war eine gemeine sterben.

anno domini m^o ccc^o LXIII [according to Dickius 1346. Varnhagen also suggested an alternative reading of 1366] *du quam bischoff gerlach von mencze circa festum johannis babtiste in die ... sine buben lagen nedder in mandern.*

in demsulben iare ... der stryt zue dylbershusen uf sant katrinen abens.

anno domini m^o cccc^o XVI die omnium sanctorum papam intravit constanciam.

anno domini m^o cccc^o XX du war en gemeine sterben ume uns her

... myle in diesen landen.

anno domini m^o cccc^o XVIII ... in festo penthecostes ... m^o tricenteno lx tria ...

Appendix C

Confraternity Service Regulations from the *Mesnerpflichtbuch von St Sebald*, Nuremberg, 1482

Item wann die bruderschaft hie ist, so legt man das tuch auf das pret, als wenn man die kurfursten beget; sechs schregen, vier leuchter im kor, als ein ander fest, fussdebich, pulttucher; man leut mit der grossen glocken; wenn nit feiertag ist, so leut man nit schreck; man leut newer in kor mit an eim werktag; man singt ein vigilg und get dan mit dem weiwasser um und geen dann all in sagrer und legen mentel an und trag das sacrament um in der kirchen und steen die fremden zu kor und welich man bit, singen das regal und die selmess; man ministrirt, die tagmess ministrirt man auch; wen man elisirt zu dem regal, so get man auf die canzel; nach der predig geen sie um an mentel mit dem weiprunnen; zu der tagmess geen sie um in menteln, gibt kein weiwasser; nach der tagmess gen sie in der kirchen um in mentel, vor der tagmess um die kirchen und furt; man gibt dem kirchner vier grosch, dem organisten 4 grosch, den knechten 16 pfenninge, den plasern 16 pfenninge, und ein suppen in sagrer dem kirchner und den knechten und ein firtel weins; wann die das placebo peten, so muss man weiwasser und ein rauch haben; man reucht zu dem magnificat und requiem auch und, wenn man das placebo bet.

Appendix D

Bull of Pope Boniface IX, November 1403

Bonifatius episcopus feruus feruorum dei Dilectis filijs.. Commendatori et fratribus domus Hospitalis sancti Johannis Jerusalimitani prope Wildunghen maguntine diocesis, salutem et apostolicam beneditionem Justis petentium desiderijs dignum est nos facilem prebere assensum, et uota que a rationis tramite non discordant effectu prosequente complere. Eapropter dilecti in domino filij uestris iustis postulationibus grato concurrentes assensu, in Odershusen, in Brunawe, in Reynhartshusen et in Dorffwildunghen at Opidi inferioris Wildunghen. Maguntine diocesis parrochiales ecclesias quas uos [the last two words filled in, after damage, by a later hand] *in usus proprios canonice proponitis adeptos cum pertinentijs suis, sicut eas iuste et pacifice possidetis uobis et per uos eidem uestre domui auctoritate apostolica confirmamus et presentis scripti patrocionio communimus. Nulli ergo, omnino hominum liceat hanc paginam nostre confirmationis infringere uel et ansu temerario contraire. Si quis autem hoc attemptare pre sumpserit indignationem omnipotentis dei et beatorum Petri et Pauli Apostolarum eius se nouerit incursurum. Datum Rome apud sanctum petrum Ideis Nouembris Pontificatus nostri Anno Quintusdecim... P.Petra.*

Appendix E

Contract for an altarpiece, commissioned by the Order of St John at Wiesenfeld, 21.10.1520

Hessisches Staatsarchiv, Marburg, no. 1225. Partially damaged. My reading differs slightly from the transcription published by Schindler, 1961, pp. 424–426. An altarpiece made by the Franciscan workshop at Meyttendorff, mentioned in the contract, still exists in the church of Kuelte, near Arolsen.

Zu wissen sy iderman, dem diser ziddel vorkomet, sehen ader horen lesen, dass im iar nach Christi geburt dusent funfhundert und zwenzich uff der heligen ilfdusent iunffrauwen dag dy weirdigen und geistlichen herren her Caspar Leber, comthor, her Johan Althuis prior und dy andern convenshern und bruder zu Wesentfelt ordens sant Iohans han den geistlichen und andechtigen brudern sant Franciscy ordens zu Meytterdorff eyne thaffeln uff den hoen altaer in der keirchen zu Wesentfelt zu machen verdinget und derhalben myt inen in massen, wy heirnach volget, uberkumen, also dass dy gedachten bruder solche thaffeln nach massen hoe und breide, wy sy die entfangen han, ganss uissberiden, uff eyren kosten und verlaeg machen sollen von solcher forme geschickt, dass das myttel corpus sal yn dry deil gedeult werden. In dass mittelste deil soln sy machen dye historien, wy der herre Christus myt synen drien iungern und asposteln im garten bete verraden und gefangen wart, und wass dar zu meher gehorig ist; in dass deil uff der reichten siten soln sie unser liben frauwen beilde myt irem kinde Iesu uffs finste und schonste nach der thaffeln propocion und geschiglich- keit, der glichen auch uff dy lincken sithen sant Ihans des doeffers Christi myt synem lamghen und geborlicher bereitung und kleidung machen. Dy floegel beider siten sollen iglicher in fier deil gedeilt syn. In den floegel bye dem mergenbilde sollen von unser liben frauwen fier stugk myt erer zubehorung komen; das irst stugk sal syn der engelsche gruiss, dass ander dy oppherung Christi in den tempel, dass dreitte dy helgen dry kunge und dass fierde dy hymmelfardt Marie. In den andern floegel sollen gemacht werden och fier stugk; das irst alss sant Iohans prediget allerlei volke in der woestenunge bie dem Iordan, dass ander alss er Christum im Iordan douffet und wye sich eme hait geoffenbaret dy hellige driefaltigkeit, dass dreitte die enthouptung sant Iohans, dass fierde stugk sal syn das iungeste gericht, igklichs myt siner zubehorung.

Dy underscheide und pieler der thaffeln sollen myt beildergen und tabernakelchen uffs subtilest uisgefurdt werden. In den fuiss sal komen dy helle zubrechung und dy uffersteung Christi, wy sych dass mit sinen stugken eigent. Disse vorgeschreben stugke sollen alle uffs beste schnidden syn und uffs schonest myt gudem golde verguldet und myt guder farbe uffs finste uisgestrichen von binnen und von buissen flach gemalt. Dy daffel sal uch haben aben-uff eynen uiszoig und tabernakel. Darin sa mitten stehen eyn crucefix, darunder Maria und sant Iohans evangelista, wy sych gehoret, darneben .....Iorge und sant Christoffeln, da baben eyn misericoridenbilde Christi, ...gudder farben und ....zu geziert. Aller uberste sal stehen daruff eyn addeler wy.. inen ... Iohans o........... ist myt beredt, dass dy bruder vorgnant sollen solcher (th)affeln corpus myt ... flusse golde sullen machen und by der herren kost ufsetzen gegen dess helgen crutses darg, wan en gefellet uff den sondag nehest kunfftig, darnach dass nehest iar eynen floegel, dass ander iaer den anderen floegel, darnach dass drit iaer den uiszoig myt synnen beilden gants und gaer ain allen verzoig und wederredde gutlichen bereiden, volnfuern uff iren kosten, ess sy dan, dass sy was uffsetzen, dass sal by den hern kost gescheen.

Dargegen vor arbeit kostung und alle bereidung sollen und wollen dye gedachten hern comthor, prior and convent den berudden brudern zwei hundert gulden hantrichen und geben, und nemelich sollen sie der den brudern uff nehest zukunftig Michaelis zen gulden, darnach exaltacionis sancte Crucis d(re)issig, darnach alle iar gegen dy faesten Francfurter messe zwenzich gulden golt adder gelt Marpurger were on iren schaden libbern und bezalen so lange biss die zweihundert gulden vergnuge und bezalet syn. Ist auch hie bie geredt und verdedingt, so die thaffel ungeverlich nach herkentnisse frommer verstendiger luid von beiden deilen gekoren firzich adder funftzig gulden ungeverlichen kostelicher adder besser wordde, dan dy zwihundert gulden, sollen dy gemelten heren und convent den brudern auch von iaeren zu iaeren, wy obgeschriben, vergnugen und bezalen, alles ain geverde und argelist. Solches geredden und geloben myr beide parthie von biden siten vorgnant vor unss unde unser nachkommend stede und veste zu halten. Dess zu urkonde der warheit syn diser ziddelen glich ludend zwo gemacht und iglicher parthie eyne myt dess anderen gemeinen convents seigel uff spacium under di schrifft gedruckt, versigelt ubergeben sych danach wissend zu richten und zu halten, im iaer und dag nach Christi gebort wy vor geschriben stehet.

Bibliography

Books and Articles

Ahrsberg, A., *Die Braunschweiger Goldschmiedegilde 1231–1701*, doctoral dissertation, Münster, 1917.

Ainsworth, M.W., 'Northern Renaissance Drawings and Underdrawings: A Proposed Method of Study', *Master Drawings*, 27, I, 1989, pp. 5–38.

Ambrose, *De Excessu Fratis sui Satyri*, 2, ed. P.B. Albers, Bonn, 1921.

Ames-Lewis, F., *Drawing in Early Renaissance Italy* (first published 1981), New Haven/London, 1982.

Anselm of Canterbury, *Cur Deus homo?*, Munich, 1956.

Appuhn, H., 'Conrad von Soest', Exh. Cat. *Die Parler und der schöne Stil 1350–1400*, 4 vols., 1978–80, I, pp. 225–226.

Asperen de Boer, J.R.J. van, *Infrared Reflectography: A Contribution to the Examination of Earlier European Paintings*, Amsterdam, 1970.

Asperen de Boer, J.R.J. van, 'An Introduction to the Scientific Examination of Paintings', *Nederlands Kunsthistorisch Jaarboek* 26, 1975, pp. 3–10.

Asperen de Boer, J.R.J. van, 'A Scientific Re-Examination of the Ghent Altarpiece', *Oud Holland*, 93, 1979, pp. 141–146.

Asperen de Boer, J.R.J. van, 'The Study of Underdrawing: An assessment, *Colloque*, 5, 1985, pp. 12—22.

Asperen de Boer, J.R.J. van, 'Examination by Infrared Radiation', *PACT*, 13, 1986, pp. 109–130.

Augustin, D.M.P., trans., *Ludolphe le Chartreux: La Grande Vie de Jesus-Christ*, 6 vols., Paris, 1864.

Augustine, St, *Confessions*, trans. R.S. Pincoffin, (first published 1961), London, 1986.

Avray, D.L. d', *The Preaching of the Friars: Sermons Diffused from Paris before 1300*, Oxford, 1985.

Avril, F., *Buchmalerei am Hofe Frankreichs 1310–1380*, trans. B. Sauerländer, Munich, 1978.

Bachmann, E., ed., *Gothic Art in Bohemia* (first published 1969), Oxford, 1977.

Baier, W. 'Untersuchungen zu den Passionsbetrachtungen in der Vita Christi des Ludolf von Sachsen', *Analecta Cartusiana*, 44, Salzburg, 1977, pp. 509–532.

Baum, H., *Der Wildunger Altar des Konrad von Soest*, 2nd edn, Bad Wildungen, 1979.

Baxandall, M., *The Limewood Sculptors of Renaissance Germany* (first published 1980), New Haven/London, 1981.

Baxhenrich-Hartman, E.-M., 'Der Hochaltar des Derick Baegert in der Propsteikirche zu Dortmund', *Monographien zur Geschichte Dortmunds und der Grafschaft Mark*, Dortmund, 1984.

Beckmann, J.H., 'Studien zum Leben und literarischen Nachlass Jakobs von Soest (1360–1440)', *Quellen und Forschung zur Geschichte des Dominikanerordens in Deutschland*, 25, Leipzig, 1929.

Beckwith, J., *Early Christian and Byzantine Art* (first published 1970), Harmondsworth, 1986.

Bede, *A History of the English Church and People*, trans. L. Sherley-Price, revised by R.E. Latham, Harmondsworth, 1976.

Belting, H., *Das Bild und sein Publikum im Mittelalter: Form und Funktion der frühen Bildtafeln der Passion*, Berlin, 1981.

Berger, E., *Quellen und Technik der Fresko-, Öl- und Tempera-Malerei des Mittelalters*, Munich, 1912.

Bernard of Clairvaux, *The Twelve Steps of Humility and Pride*, and *On Loving God*, trans. H.C. Backhouse, London, 1985.

Binder-Hagelstange, U., *Der mehrfigürige Kalvarienberg in der Rheinischen Malerei von 1300–1430*, doctoral dissertation, Berlin, 1937.

Blaschke, R., *Studien zur Malerei der Lüneburger 'Goldenen Tafel'*, doctoral dissertation, Bochum, 1976.

Blumenkranz, B., *Le Juif mediéval au miroir de l'art chrétien*, Paris, 1966.

Bodemann, E., 'Die älteren Zunfturkunden der Stadt Lüneburg', *Quellen und Darstellungen zur Geschichte Niedersachsens*, 1, Hanover, 1883, pp. 99–102.

Bodenstedt, M.I., *The Vita Christi of Ludolphus the Carthusian*, Ph.D. dissertation, Washington, 1944.

Bodenstedt, M.I., 'Praying the Life of Christ: Ludolphus the Carthusian', *Analecta Cartusiana*, 15, Salzburg, 1973.

Bonaventura, *The Soul's Journey into God*, London, 1978.

Boockmann, H., *Die Stadt im späten Mittelalter*, Munich, 1986.

Borradaile, V. and R., trans., *The Strasburg Manuscript: A Medieval Painter's Handbook*, London, 1966.

Bradford, E., *Kreuz und Schwert* (English edn 1972), Munich, 1983.

Braun, J., *Das christliche Altargerät in seinem Sein und in seiner Entwicklung*, Munich, 1932.

Bridget, St, *Select Revelations of St Bridget, Princess of Sweden*, London, 1892.

Browne, R.A., trans., *The Holy Jerusalem Voyage of Ogier VIII, Seigneur d'Anglure (1395-96)*, Gainsville, 1975.

Bruin, T.L. de, 'Anagrammatische Inschriften auf alten religiösen Abbildungen', *Das Münster*, 3, 1968, pp. 191–200.

Budde, R., *Köln und seine Maler 1300–1500*, Cologne, 1986.

Butler, M.H. and Asperen de Boer, J.R.J. van, 'The Examination of the Milan-Turin Hours with Infrared Reflectography: A Preliminary Report', *Le dessin sous-jacent dans la peinture: Colloque*, 7, Louvain, 1989, pp. 71–76.

Byvanck, A.W. and Hooegewerff, G.J., *La miniature hollandaise dans les manuscripts des 14e, 15e et 16e siècles*, 2 vols., The Hague, 1923.

Camille, M., 'Seeing and Reading: some Visual Implications of Medieval Literacy and Illiteracy', *Art History*, 8, no. 1, 1985, pp. 26–49.

Campbell, L., 'Robert Campin, the Master of Flémalle and the Master of Mérode', *Burlington Magazine*, 116, 1974, pp. 634–646.

Campbell, L., 'The Early Netherlandish Painters and their Workshops' *Colloque*, 3, Louvain, 1979, pp. 43–63.

Carli, E., *Italian Primitives: Panel Painting of the Twelfth and Thirteenth Century*, New York, 1965.

Carli, E., *La pittura senese del Trecento*, Milan, 1981.

Caron, M.L., 'Ansien doet gedencken: De religieuze voorstellings-wereld van de moderne devotie', in Exh. Cat. *Geert Grote en de Moderne Devotie*, Deventer/Utrecht, 1984.

Cennini, d'Andrea C., *The Craftsman's Handbook: Il Libro dell'Arte*, trans. D.V. Thompson Jr (first published 1933), New York, 1960.

Châtelet, A., *Early Dutch Painting: Painting in the Northern Netherlands in the Fifteenth Century*, trans. C. Brown and A. Turner, Fribourg, 1980.

Châtelet, A. and Recht, R., *Ausklang des Mittelalters 1380–1500* (trans. G. Ammelburger and A. Seling from the French edition, first published 1988), Munich, 1989.

Christiansen, K., *Gentile da Fabriano*, London, 1982.

Coleridge, H.J., 'Ludolph the Saxon: The Hours of the Passion taken from the Life of Christ', *Quarterly Series*, 59, London, 1887.

Comblen-Sonkes, M., 'Le dessin sous-jacent dans la Nativité de Dijon', *Le dessin sous-jacent dans la peinture: Colloque*, 3, Louvain, 1979, pp. 89–92.

Conway, C.A., 'The Vita Christi of Ludolph of Saxony and Late Medieval Devotion Centred on the Incarnation: A Descriptive Analysis', *Analecta Cartusiana*, 34, Salzburg, 1976.

Coremans, P., 'La notation des couleurs, essai d'application aux Primitifs Flamands', *De artibus opuscula: Essays in honor of Erwin Panofsky*, New York, 1961, pp. 76–81.

Corley, B., 'Stefan Lochner, Meister zu Köln: Herkunft—Werke—Wirkung', *Kunstchronik*, 47, no. 11, Munich 1994.

Corley, B., 'A Plausible Provenance for Stefan Lochner?', *Stefan Lochner—Ergebnisse der Ausstellung und des Colloquiums 1993/94*, Cologne, forthcoming, and Zeitschrift für Kunstgeschichte, Munich, forthcoming 1996.

Courajod, L., *Leçons professées à l'Ecole du Louvre: 'Origines de la Renaissance'*, 2, Paris, 1901.

Curtze, L., *Geschichte und Beschreibung des Fürstenthums Waldeck*, Arolsen, 1850.

Cuttler, C.D., *Northern Painting from Pucelle to Bruegel: Fourteenth, Fifteenth and Sixteenth Centuries*, New York, 1968.

Dannenberg, H., *Die farbige Behandlung des Tafelbildes in der altdeutschen Malerei von 1340 bis 1460 unter besonderer Berücksichtigung des Mittelrheins*, doctoral dissertation, Karcag, 1929.

Dehio, G., *Handbuch der deutschen Kunstdenkmäler: Nordrhein–Westfalen* (first published 1928), rev. edn Munich/Berlin, 1969.

Delaissé, L.M.J., *A Century of Dutch Manuscript Illumination*, Berkeley/Los Angeles, 1968.

Demandt, K.E., *Das Chorherrenstift St Peter zu Fritzlar*, Marburg, 1985.

Dijkstra, J., 'On the Role of Underdrawings and Modeldrawings in the Workshop Production of the Master of Flémalle and Rogier van der Weyden', *Le dessin sous-jacent dans la peinture: Colloque*, 7, Louvain, 1989, pp. 37–53.

Dölger, F.J., *Das Fischsymbol in frühchristlicher Zeit*, 1, Rome, 1910.

Dollinger, P., *The German Hansa* (first published 1964), translated by S. Ault and S.H. Steinberg, Stanford, 1970.

Doutrepont, G., *Inventaire de la 'librairie' de Philippe le Bon* (1420), Brussels, 1906.

Durrieu, P., *La miniature flamande aux temps de la cour de Bourgogne*, Brussels, 1921.

Eckert, I., *Ein Altargemälde aus der Zeit der Gotik in der Neustädter Kirche zu Bielefeld um 1400*, Bielefeld, 1956.

Eckert, W.P., 'Jakob von Soest, Prediger und Inquisitor', *Von Soest–aus Westfalen*, Paderborn, 1986, pp. 125-138.

Eichler, K., 'Die Stadtkirche zu Niederwildungen', *Geschichtsblätter für Waldeck und Pyrmont*, 28, 1930.

Einem, H. v., 'Die Plastik der Lüneburger Goldenen Tafel', *Kunsthistorische Studien*, 2, Hanover, 1928.

Eisler, C., *Paintings from the Samuel H. Kress Collection: European Schools excluding Italian*, Oxford, 1977.

Ernste, H., 'Quellenbeiträge zur Geschichte der Dortmunder Marienkirche', *Beiträge zur Geschichte Dortmunds und der Grafschaft Mark*, 39, Dortmund, 1931.

Fahne, A., *Die Grafschaft und freie Reichsstadt Dortmund*, 4 vols. (first published 1853–59), Cologne, 1974.

Faries, M., 'Underdrawings in the Workshop Production of Jean van Scorel: A Study with Infrared Reflectography: Scientific Examination of Early Netherlandish Painting', *Nederlands Kunsthistorisch Jaarboek*, 26, 1976.

Farmer, D.H., *The Oxford Dictionary of Saints* (first published 1978), Oxford/New York, 1987.

Filedt-Kok, J.P., 'Underdrawing and other Technical Aspects in the Painting of Lucas van Leyden', *Nederlands Kunsthistorisch Jaarboek*, 29, 1978.

Fink, A., 'Zur Instandsetzung des Wildunger Altars', *Kunstchronik und Kunstmarkt*, 59, NF 35, 1925/26, p. 449.

Firmenich-Richartz, E., *Die Brüder Boisserée, 1, Sulpiz und Melchior Boisserée als Kunstsammler*, Jena, 1916.

Fischer, B., *Biblia Sacra uixta vulgatam versionem*, 2 vols., Stuttgart, 1961.

Folda, J., *Crusader Manuscript Illumination at Saint-Jean d'Acre, 1275–1291*, Princeton, 1976.

Förster, E., 'Die Gemäldesammlung des Herrn Geh. Oberregierungsraths Krüger zu Minden', *Kunstblatt*, 6, 1847, pp. 21–23.

Förster, O.H., 'Um den Meister der Veronika', *Wallraf-Richartz Jahrbuch*, 19, 1957, pp. 225–252.

Franz, E.G., 'Siegel-Reliquiar in der Stadtkirche Bad Wildungen', *Geschichtsblätter für Waldeck*, 54, 1962, pp. 52–54.

Frensdorff, F., *Dortmunder Statuten und Urteile*, Halle, 1882.

Frinta, M., 'An Investigation of the Punched Decoration of Medieval Italian and Non-Italian Panel Painting', *Art Bulletin*, 47, 1965, pp. 261–264.

Frinta, M., 'On the Relief Adornment in the Klarenaltar and other Paintings in Cologne', *Vor Stefan Lochner: Die Kölner Maler von 1300–1430: Ergebnisse der Ausstellung und des Colloquiums von 1974*, Cologne, 1977, pp. 131–139.

Frinta, M., 'The style of the underdrawing: to what extent reflecting the distinct temperament and how much indebted to a drawing tradition?', *Colloque*, 3, Louvain, 1981, pp. 73–85.

Fritz, R., 'Zur altwestfälischen Tafelmalerei um 1400', *Westfalen*, 27, 1948, pp. 106–110.

Fritz, R., 'Beobachtungen am Dortmunder Marienaltar Conrads von Soest', *Westfalen*, 28, 1950, pp. 107–122. Cited as 1950a.

Fritz, R., 'Das Mittelbild des Fröndenberger Altars', *Westfalen*, 28, 1950, pp. 134–137. Cited as 1950b.

Fritz, R., 'Acht unbekannte Tafeln des Bielefelder Altares, zugleich ein Beitrag zum Meister des Berswordt Altares', *Westfalen*, 28, 1950, pp. 193–204. Cited as 1950c.

Fritz, R., editor, 'Der Katalog der Gemäldesammlung Krüger zu Minden, 1848', *Westfalen*, 29, 1951, pp. 87–97. Cited as 1951a.

Fritz, R., 'Das Halbfigurenbild in der westdeutschen Tafelmalerei um 1400', *Zeitschrift für Kunstwissenschaft*, V, Berlin, 1951, pp. 161–178. Cited as 1951b.

Fritz, R., 'Conrad von Soest als Zeichner', *Westfalen*, 31, 1953, pp. 10–18.

Fritz, R., *Conrad von Soest: Der Wildunger Altar*, Munich, 1954.

Frodl-Kraft, E. 'Die Farbsprache der gotischen Malerei', *Wiener Jahrbuch für Kunstgeschichte*, 30/31, 1977–78, pp. 89–178.

Froissart, J., *Chronicles of England, France and Spain*, trans. T. Jones, 2 vols., London, 1806.

Froning, R., *Das Drama des Mittelalters*, 3 vols., Stuttgart, 1897.

Gabele, A., ed., 'Büchlein der Ewigen Weisheit', *Deutsche Schriften von Heinrich Seuse*, Leipzig, 1924.

Gebets- und Gesangbuch für das Erzbistum Köln, Cologne, 1949.

Gebhardi, L.A., 'Collectanea', *Handschriften der Landesbibliothek Hannover*, 23, 6, cols. 848–862, 1792.

Geisberg, M., 'Der Dortmunder Marienaltar des Konrad von Soest', *Westfälische Kunsthefte*, 2, Dortmund, 1931.

Geisberg, M., *Meister Konrad von Soest*, Dortmund, 1934.

Geisberg, M., 'Studien zur Geschichte der Maler in Münster 1530 bis 1800', *Westfalen*, 26, 1941, pp. 147–182.

Gilson, E. and Boehner, P., *Die Geschichte der christlichen Philosophie*, 3 vols., Paderborn, 1937.

Gilson, E., *The History of Christian Philosophy in the Middle Ages* (first published 1955), London, 1985.

Goldberg, G. and Scheffler, G., *Altdeutsche Gemälde der Alten Pinakothek*, Munich, 1972.

Gréban, A., *Le Mystère de la Passion*, ed. O. Jodogne, 2 vols., Brussels, 1965.

Graves, F.M., *Deux inventaires de la maison d'Orléans (1389 et 1408)*, Paris, 1926.

Grohn, H.W., Exh. Cat. 'Meister Francke, Urkunden und Meinungen', *Meister Francke und die Kunst um 1400*, Hamburg, 1969, pp. 17–21.

Grundmann, H., 'Politische Gedanken mittelalterlicher Westfalen', *Westfalen*, 27, 1948.

Grundmann, W., Die Sprache des Altars, Berlin, 1966.

Guiffrey, J., *Inventaires de Jean, Duc de Berry (1401–1416)*, 2 vols., Paris, 1894–97.

Gümbel, A., 'Das Mesnerpflichtbuch von St Lorenz in Nürnberg vom Jahre 1493', *Einzelarbeiten aus der Kirchengeschichte Bayerns*, 8, Munich, 1928.

Gümbel, A., 'Das Mesnerpflichtbuch von St Sebald in Nürnberg', *Einzelarbeiten aus der Kirchengeschichte Bayerns*, 9, Nuremberg, 1929.

Hamand, L.A., *The Ancient Windows of Great Malvern Priory Church*, St Albans, 1957.

Harbison, C., 'Visions and Meditations in Early Flemish Painting', *Simiolus*, 15, no. 2, 1985, pp. 87–118.

Harley, R.D., *Artists' Pigments c. 1600–1835* (first published 1970), London, 1982.

Hasselberg, M.Th., *Liber pictus A 74 der Preussischen Staatsbibliothek zu Berlin: ein Beitrag zur Erforschung mittelalterlicher Skizzen- und Musterbücher*, Zeulenroda, 1936.

Hauer, L., *Ein Beitrag zur Geschichte der Soester Zünfte*, typed manuscript, Stadtarchiv Soest, 1931.

Haussherr, R., 'Bertram und Bondol?', *Nordelbingen*, 48, 1979, pp. 63–80.

Henderson, J., 'Religious Confraternities and Death in Early Renaissance Florence', *Florence and Italy. Renaissance Studies in Honour of Nicolai Rubinstein*, London, 1988, pp. 383–394.

Hermans, C.R., *Annales canonicorum regularium S. Augustini ordinis S. Crucis*, 1, 's-Hertogenbosch, 1858.

Hills, P., *The Light of Early Italian Painting* (first published 1987), New Haven/London, 1990.

Hochgrebe, H., 'Die Wildunger Johanniter—Kommende', *Geschichtsblätter für Waldeck*, 74, 1986.

Hölker, C., 'Meister Conrad von Soest und seine Bedeutung für die norddeutsche Malerei in der ersten Hälfte des 15. Jahrhunderts', *Beiträge zur Westfälischen Kunstgeschichte*, 7, Münster, 1921.

Hölker, C., 'Das Altarwerk der Goldenen Tafel aus der Michaeliskirche in Lüneburg', *Zeitschrift für christliche Kunst*, 33, 1920, pp. 152–158.

Hoffmeister, J.C.C., *Historisch- genealogisches Handbuch über alle Grafen und Fürsten von Waldeck und Pyrmont seit 1228*, Cassel, 1883.

Homann, H.-D. 'Die Gilden', *Geschichte original am Beispiel der Stadt Münster*, 8, Münster, 1982.

Hosmann, S., *Fürtreffliches Denck-Mahl der göttlichen Regierung, bewiesen an der…Güldenen Taffel…*, Brunswick/Hamburg, 1700.

Hooegewerff, G.J., *La miniature Hollandaise dans les manuscrits des 14e, 15e et 16e siècles*, 2 vols., The Hague, 1923.

Hucker, B.U., 'Der Köln-Soester Fernhändler Johann van Lunen (1415-1443) und die hansischen Gesellschaften', *Soester Zeitschrift*, 92/93, 1980/81.

Iserloh, E., '*Devotio moderna*—Die "Brüder und Schwestern vom gemeinsamen Leben" und die Windesheimer Augustiner-Kongregation', in Exh. Cat. *Monastisches Westfalen: Klöster und Stifte 800–1800*, Münster, 1982 and Corvey, 1983, pp. 191-199.

Jacobs, F., 'Der Meister des Berswordt-Altares', doctoral dissertation (Münster), *Göppinger akademische Beiträge*, 117, Göppingen, 1983.

Jacobs, F., 'Conrad von Soest: Tafelbildmaler des Internationalen Stils', in *Von Soest - Aus Westfalen. Wege und Wirkung abgewanderter Westfalen im späten Mittelalter und in der frühen Neuzeit*, ed. H.-D. Heimann, Paderborn, 1986, pp. 45–59.

Janssen, W., 'Die Erzbischöfe von Köln und ihr "Land" Westfalen', *Westfalen*, 58, 1980.

Janssen, W., '1288–1521', in Exh. Cat. *Köln—Westfalen 1180–1980*, 2 vols., I, Münster, 1980 and Cologne, 1981, pp. 58–64.

Jones, W.R., 'Art and Christian Piety: Iconoclasm in Medieval Europe', *The Image and the Word: Confrontations in Judaism, Christianity and Islam*, Missoula, 1977.

Julian of Norwich, *Revelations of Divine Love* (written 1393), London, 1987.

Kahsnitz, R., 'Koimesis-dormitio-assumptio, Byzantisches und Antikes in den Miniaturen der Liuthargruppe', *Florilegium in Honorem Carl Nordenfalk octogenarii contextum*, Stockholm, 1987.

Kann, K., *Die ehemalige Zisterzienserinnen-Klosterche im 'Thal der Hl. Maria zu Netze'*, Netze, 1986.

Kappeli, T.M., *Scriptores Ordinis Praedicatorum Medii Aevi*, 3 vols., Rome, 1970–80.

Kauffmann, C.M., *An Altarpiece of the Apocalypse*, London, 1968.

Kempe, M., *The Book of Margery Kempe, translated by B. A. Windeatt* (first published 1985), Harmondsworth, 1987.

Kempfer, M., 'Die Farbigkeit als Kriterium für Werkstattbeziehungen, dargestellt an zehn Altären aus der Zeit zwischen 1370 und 1430', *Giessener Beiträge zur Kunstgeschichte*, 2, 1973, pp. 7–49.

King, E.J., *The Knights Hospitallers in the Holy Land*, London, 1931.

Kirchhoff, H.G., 'Die Dortmunder Fehde', *1100 Jahre Stadtgeschichte*, Dortmund, 1982.

Kirchhoff, K.H., 'Maler und Malerfamilien in Münster zwischen 1350 und 1534', *Westfalen*, 55, 1977, pp. 98–99.

Kirschbaum, E., ed., *Lexikon der christlichen Ikonographie*, 8 vols., Freiburg, 1968–72.

Klein, P., 'Dendrochronologische Untersuchungen an Bildtafeln des 15. Jahrhunderts', *Le dessin soujacent dans la peinture: Colloque*, 6, Louvain, 1987, pp. 29–40.

Klesse, B., 'Darstellung von Seidenstoffen in der Altkölner Malerei', *MOUSEION: Studien aus Kunst und Geschichte für Otto H. Förster*, 1960, pp. 217–225.

Knaus, H., 'Rheinische Handschriften in Berlin, 4: Fraterherren und Windesheimer: Lokalstil und Ordensstil', *Archiv für Geschichte des Buchwesens*, 13, 1973.

Knippenberg, G., 'Das Patriziergeschlecht der Berswordt und Dortmund', *Beiträge zur Geschichte Dortmunds und der Grafschaft Mark*, 52, 2 vols., Dortmund, 1955.

Kock, R., *Das Kreuzigungsretabel aus der Soester Wiesenkirche*, doctoral dissertation, Berlin, 1974.

Kockaert, L., 'Note on the painting technique of Melchior Broederlam', *4th Committee for Conservation*, Copenhagen, 1984, pp. 7–10.

Kohl, W., 'Die *devotio moderna* in Westfalen', in Exh. Cat. *Monastisches Westfalen: Klöster und Stifte 800–1800*, Münster, 1982 and Corvey, 1983, pp. 203–207.

Krumbholtz, R., *Die Gewerbe der Stadt Münster bis zum Jahre 1661: 'Die ältere Rolle der Meister' und 'Die Rolle der Gesellen'*, Leipzig, 1898.

Kühn, H., 'Möglichkeiten und Grenzen der Untersuchung von Gemälden mit Hilfe von naturwissenschaftlichen Methoden', *Maltechnik/Restauro*, 80.3, 1974, pp. 149ff.

Kühn, H. 'Farbmaterial und technischer Aufbau Altkölner Malerei', *Vor Stefan Lochner: Die Kölner Maler von 1300–1430*, Ergebnisse der Ausstellung und des Colloquiums von 1974, Cologne, 1977, pp. 179–190.

Künstle, K., *Ikonographie der christlichen Kunst*, 2 vols., Freiburg, 1928.

Lagleder, G.T., *Die Ordensregel der Johanniter*, St Ottilien, 1983.

Lamprecht, K., ed., *Die Chroniken der westfälischen und niederrheinischen Städte, 1, Dortmund und Neuss*, Leipzig, 1887.

Langemeyer, G., '"Kölnisch" und "Westfälisch" in der Tafelmalerei der Spätgotik', in Exh. Cat. *Köln—Westfalen 1180–1980*, 2 vols., Münster, 1980 and Cologne, 1981, I, pp. 389–401.

Langemeyer, G., ed., *Museumshandbuch*, I, Dortmund, 1983, pp. 164–168.

Ledeburs, L. von, *Minden—Ravensburg: Denkmäler der Geschichte, der Kunst und des Altertums*, V (first published 1825 or 1828), Bünde, 1934.

Lhotsky, A., 'Die Zeitwende um das Jahr 1400', in Exh. Cat. *Europäische Kunst um 1400*, Vienna, 1962.

Lichtwark, A., *Meister Bertram, tätig in Hamburg 1367–1415*, Hamburg, 1905.

Lindemann, M., 'Brief-"Zeitungen" in der Korrespondenz Hildebrand Veckinchusens (1398–1428)', *Dortmunder Beiträge zur Zeitungsforschung*, Munich/New York, 1978.

Linnhoff, E., *Die St Nikolai-Kapelle in Soest*, Soest, 1982.

Loesch, H. v., ed., *Die Kölner Zunfturkunden nebst anderen Kölner Gewerbeurkunden bis zum Jahre 1500* (first published 1907), Düsseldorf, 1984.

Loewe, E., *Das Altarbild der Stadtkirche zu Nieder-Wildungen: Meister Konrad von Soest, MCCCCIV*, Bad Wildungen, 1909.

Longnon, J., ed., *Les très riches heures du Duc de Berry*, New York, 1969.

Lübke, W., *Die mittelalterliche Kunst in Westfalen*, Leipzig, 1853.

Luckhardt, J., 'Der Hochaltar der Zisterzienserklosterkirche Marienfeld', *Bildhefte des Westfälischen Landesmuseums für Kunst und Kulturgeschichte*, 25, Münster, 1987.

Luckhardt, J., 'Werke und Werkstätten der Tafelmalerei aus Soest', *Soest, Geschichte der Stadt* 3 Vols, ed. H-D. Heimann, pp. 623–89, 1996.

Ludolph of Saxony, *Vita Jesu Christi e Quatuor Evangeliis et scriptoribus orthodoxis concinnata*, ed. A.C. Bolard, L.M. Rigollot and J. Carnandet, Paris/Rome, 1865.

Ludolphus de Saxonia, *Vita Jesu Christi*, 4 vols., ed. L.M. Rigollot, Paris, 1870.

Lünenschloß, H., 'Der Wildunger Altar und seine Restaurierung', *Hessische Heimat*, 1, Kassel, 1951, pp. 2–5.

Lundt, B., 'Die "Haimonskinder" in Dortmund: Europäische Erzähltradition im regionalen Kontext', in Exh. Cat. *Vergessene Zeiten: Mittelalter im*

Ruhrgebiet, Essen, 1990–91, 2 vols., II, pp. 177–183.

Luntowski, G., *Dortmund und die Hanse*, Dortmund, 1986.

Mâle, E., *The Gothic Image: Religious Art in France of the Thirteenth Century* (first published 1913), New York/London, 1972.

Mâle, E., *Religious Art in France: The Thirteenth Century* (revised edn), Princeton, 1984.

Mâle, E., *Religious Art in France: The Late Middle Ages* (first published 1925), revised edn, Princeton, 1986.

Manske, H.J. 'Osnabrücker Plastik um 1500: Der Auftragsmarkt, die Produktionsbedingungen und die führenden Werkstätten', in Exh. Cat. *Stadt im Wandel: Kunst und Kultur des Bürgertums in Norddeutschland 1150–1650*, 4 vols., Brunswick, 1985, III, pp. 343–371.

Marle, R. van, *The Development of the Italian Schools of Painting*, The Hague, 1924.

Marrow, J., *'Christi Leiden in einer Vision geschaut' in the Netherlands*, Antwerp, 1969.

Marrow, J.H., *Passion Iconography in Northern European Art of the Late Middle Ages and Early Renaissance: A study of the transformation of sacred metaphor into descriptive narrative*, Kartijk, 1979.

Martens, B., *Meister Francke*, 2 vols., Hamburg, 1929.

Martindale, A., *Simone Martini*, Oxford, 1988.

Matalon, S., *Michelino da Besozzo e l'ouvraige de Lombardie*, Milan, 1966.

Maus, M., 'Ein schönes Gotteshaus ist eine herrliche Gabe: Wildunger Kirchenrestaurierung vor 100 Jahren', *Mein Waldeck*, 11, 1957.

May, H., *Konrad von Soest: Der Dortmunder Marienaltar*, Diez, 1948.

Medding, W., 'Der Wildunger Altar des Meisters Konrad von Soest', Bad Wildungen, 1949.

Medding, W., 'Der Wildunger Altar im alten Glanz', *Waldeckische Landeszeitung*, 33, 8 July 1950.

Megerle, P.A., ed., *Der H. Wittfrawen Birgittae von Schweden Himmlische Offenbarungen*, Rome, 1664.

Meier, P.J., 'Werk und Wirkung des Meisters Konrad von Soest', *Westfalen*, 1, Sonderheft, Münster, 1921.

Meier, P.J., 'Meister Konrad von Soest', *Heimatblätter*, Dortmund, 1921, pp. 281–286 and 1922, pp. 308–312.

Meier, P.J., 'Konrad von Soest: Ein Nachtrag', *Westfalen*, 16, 1931, pp. 37–49.

Meininghaus, A., *Das Dortmunder Patriziergeschlecht von Hengstenberg*, Dortmund, 1930.

Meisen, K., *Nikolauskult und Nikolausbrauch im Abendland*, Düsseldorf, 1931.

Meiss, M., 'The Madonna of Humility', *Art Bulletin*, 18, 1936, pp. 435–461.

Meiss, M., *French Painting in the Time of Jean de Berry*, 5 vols., New York/London, 1967–74.

Meiss, M. and Beatson, E.H., *The Belles Heures of Jean, Duke of Berry*, New York, 1974.

Meiss, M. and Thomas, M., ed., *The Rohan Book of Hours*, trans. K.W. Carson, London, 1973.

Mellinkoff, R., 'The round, cap-shaped hats depicted on Jews in BM Cotton Claudius B.IV', *Anglo-Saxon England*, 2, Cambridge, 1973.

Meredith, P. and Tailby, J., *The Staging of Religious Drama in Europe in the Later Middle Ages*, Kalamazoo, 1983.

Meyer, B., 'Die Sudermanns von Dortmund', *Beiträge zur Geschichte Dortmunds und der Grafschaft Mark*, 38, Dortmund, 1930.

Meyer-Barkhausen, W., 'Das Netzer Altarbild—ein bisher unbeachtetes Meisterwerk der frühen deutschen Tafelmalerei', *Jahrbuch der preussischen Kunstsammlung*, Berlin, 1929, pp. 233–254.

Meyer-Barkhausen, W., 'Inschriften auf dem Bildaltar in der Stadtkirche', *Zeitschrift des Vereins für Heimatschutz in Kurhessen und Waldeck*, 1, Kassel, 1931, pp. 7–8.

Migne, J.P., *Patrologia cursus completus*, series Latina, 217 vols., Paris, 1841–1905.

Missale Romanum, Rome, 1539.

Mone, F.J., *Schauspiele des Mittelalters*, Karlsruhe, 1846.

Montag, U., *Das Werk der heiligen Birgitta von Schweden in oberdeutscher Überlieferung*, Munich, 1968.

Moranville, H., *Inventaire de l'orfèverie et des jouyaux de Louis, duc d'Anjou*, Paris, 1906.

Morell, P.G., ed., *Offenbarungen der Schwester Mechthild von Magdeburg, oder: Das fliessende Licht der Gottheit*, Regensburg, 1869.

Musper, H.Th., *Gotische Malerei nördlich der Alpen*, Cologne, 1961.

Myers, A.R., *England in the Late Middle Ages* (first published 1952), Harmondsworth, 1971.

Nicolai, H., 'Die Bedeutung des Sternes von Waldeck', *Mein Waldeck*, 8, 1950.

Nicolaus, K., 'Infrarotuntersuchung von Gemälden', *Maltechnik/Restauro*, 82, 1976, pp. 73–102.

Nilgen, U., 'The Epiphany and the Eucharist: On the Interpretation of Eucharistic Motifs in Medieval Epiphany Scenes', *Art Bulletin*, 49, 1967.

Nissen, R., 'Der Meister des Fröndenberger Altares', *Westfalen*, 16, 1931, pp. 58–65.

Nissen, R. 'Konrad von Soest', *Westfälische Lebensbilder*, 2.3, Münster, 1931, pp. 363–378.

Nissen, R., 'Ein Beitrag zu Konrad von Soest', *Westfalen*, 18, 1933, pp. 107–114. Cited as 1933a.

Nissen, R., 'Die Wiederherstellung der Nikolaustafel in Soest', *Westfalen*, 18, 1933, pp. 228–232. Cited as 1933b.

Nissen, R., 'Die Münze in der Sterbekertze: ein Beitrag zu Konrad von Soest', *Westfalen*, 21, 1936, pp. 68–72.

Nordhoff, J.B., 'Die Soester Malerei unter Meister Conrad', *Bonner Jahrbücher*, 67 and 68, 1879 and 1880.

Olschki, L.S., ed., 'La Miniatura a Italiana tra Gotico e Rinascimento', *Storia della miniatura*, 6, 2 vols., Cortona, 1982.

Paatz, W., *Verflechtungen in der Kunst der Spätgotik zwischen 1360 und 1530*, Heidelberg, 1967.

Pächt, O., *Österreichische Tafelmalerei der Gotik*, Augsburg, 1929.

Pächt, O., 'Die Gotik der Zeit um 1400 als gemeineuropäische Kunstsprache', in Exh. Cat. *Europäische Kunst um 1400*, Vienna, 1962, pp. 52–65.

Pächt, O., 'Meister Francke—Probleme', in Exh. Cat. *Meister Francke und die Kunst um 1400*, Hamburg, 1969, pp. 22–27.

Panofsky, E., *Early Netherlandish Painting: Its Origins and Character* (first published 1953), 2 vols., New York, 1971.

Passavant, J.D., 'Beiträge zur Kenntnis der alten Malerschulen in Deutschland vom dreizehnten bis in das sechzehnte Jahrhundert', *Kunstblatt*, 100, 1841.

Périer-D'Ieteren, C., *Colyn de Coter et la technique picturale des peintres flamands du XVe siècle*, Brussels, 1985.

Pešina, J., *The Master of the Hohenfurth Altarpiece and Bohemian Gothic Panel Painting* (first published 1982), London/Prague, 1989.

Philippi, F., *Die älteren Osnabrücker Gildeurkunden bis 1500*, Osnabrück, 1890.

Pickering, F.P., 'Notes on Late Medieval German Tales in Praise of Docta Ignorantia', *Bulletin of the John Rylands Library*, 24, Manchester, 1940.

Pickering, F.P., *Christi Leiden in einer Vision geschaut: A German Mystic Text of the Fourteenth Century*, Manchester, 1952.

Pickering, F.P., 'Das gotische Christusbild: Zu den Quellen mittelalterlicher Passionsdarstellungen', *Euphorion*, 47, 1953.

Pickering, F.P., *Literature and Art in the Middle Ages* (German original edition, 1966), London, 1970.

Pieper, P., 'Die "Notgottes" im Landesmuseum Münster', *Westfalen*, 28, 1950, pp. 182–192. Cited as 1950a.

Pieper, P., 'Zu einer Tafel mit den Heiligen Ottilie und Dorothea', *Westfalen*, 28, 1950, pp. 123–134. Cited as 1950b.

Pieper, P., 'Das Westfälische in Malerei und Plastik', *Der Raum Westfalen*, IV, 3, Münster, 1964.

Pieper, P., 'Der Daruper Altar: Seine Stellung in der westfälischen Tafelmalerei des frühen 15. Jahrhunderts', *Der Landkreis Coesfeld 1816–1966*, 1966, pp. 41–65.

Pieper, P., 'Köln und Westfalen in der Zeit nach 1400', in Exh. Cat. *Vor Stefan Lochner: Die Kölner Maler von 1300 bis 1430*, Cologne, 1974, pp. 40–45.

Pieper, P., 'Der Warendorfer Passions Altar in der Westfälischen Malerei seiner Zeit', *An Ems und Lippe*, 1977.

Pieper, P., 'Die deutschen, niederländischen und italienischen Tafelbilder bis um 1530', *Bestandskatalog des Westfälischen Landesmuseums für Kunst und Kulturgeschichte Münster*, Münster, 1986.

Pilz, W., *Das Triptychon als Kompositions- und Erzählform in der deutschen Tafelmalerei: Von den Anfängen bis zur Dürerzeit*, doctoral dissertation (Munich, 1965), Munich, 1970.

Pisan, Christine de, *The Treasure of the City of Ladies, or, the Book of the Three Virtues* (Paris 1405), trans. S. Lawson, London, 1985.

Platte, H., *Meister Bertram in der Hamburger Kunsthalle* (4th edn), Hamburg, 1982.

Portmann, P., *Meister Bertram*, Zürich, 1963.

Priebsch, R., ed., *Christi Leiden in einer Vision geschaut*, Heidelberg, 1936.

Prinz, J., 'Urkundliches zur Geschichte der Malerfamilie Koerbecke, *Westfalen*, 26, 1941.

Ragusa, I. and Green, R.B., ed., *Meditations on the Life of Christ*, Princeton, 1961.

Réau, L., *Iconographie de l'Art chrétien*, 6 vols., Paris, 1955–59.

Reichardt, C., *Geschichte von Stadt und Bad Wildungen*, Bad Wildungen, 1949.

Reinecke, H., *Lüneburger Buchmalerei um 1400 und der Maler der Goldenen Tafel*, doctoral dissertation (1936), Bonn, 1937.

Reininghaus, W., 'Die Migration der Handwerksgesellen in der Zeit der Entstehung ihrer Gilden (14./15. Jahrhundert)', *Sozial- und Wirtschaftsgeschichte*, 68, Wiesbaden, 1981.

Rensing, Th., 'Rätsel um Conrad von Soest', *Westfalen*, 28, 1950, pp. 138–181.

Robb, D.M., 'The Iconography of the Annunciation in the Fourteenth and Fifteenth Centuries', *Art Bulletin*, 18, 1936.

Rode, H., 'Colloquium zur Kölner Glasmalerei', *Vor Stefan Lochner: Die Kölner Maler von 1300–1430*, Ergebnisse der Ausstellung und des Colloquiums von 1974, Cologne, 1977, pp. 98–102.

Rohrberg, E., 'Untersuchung über das Werkmass des Wildunger Altares von Konrad von Soest aus dem Jahre 1403', *Geschichtsblätter für Waldeck*, 60, 1968, pp. 131–135.

Rörig, C., *Aus meiner Vaterstadt Wildungen*, Corbach, 1909–14.

Roth, E., *Der volkreiche Kalvarienberg in Literatur und Bildkunst des Spätmittelalters* (first published 1958), revised edn, Berlin, 1967.

Rothert, H., 'Die Vikarien des Kreuzaltars in der Marienkirche zu Dortmund, Anhang: Urkunden', *Beiträge zur Geschichte Dortmunds und der Grafschaft Mark*, 25, 1918.

Rothert, H., *Das älteste Bürgerbuch der Stadt Soest, 1302–1449*, Münster, 1958.

Rübel, K., *Dortmunder Urkundenbuch*, 4 vols., Dortmund, 1881–99.

Rübel, K., 'Die Dortmunder Morgensprachen', *Beiträge zur Geschichte Dortmunds und der Grafschaft Mark*, 9, 1900.

Ruh, K. and others, *Die deutsche Literatur des Mittelalters*, Verfasserlexikon, 6 vols., Berlin, 1983–85.

Saliger, A., ed., *Catalogue of the Dom- and Diozesan-Museum*, Vienna, 1987.

Sandler, L. Freeman, *Gothic Manuscripts 1285–1385*, A Survey of Manuscripts illuminated in the British Isles, V, London, 1986.

Sandverg-Vavala, E., 'The Development of the School of Painting in Siena', *Sienese Studies*, Florence, 1953.

Sauerland, H.V., *Vatikanische Regesten zur Geschichte der Rheinlande*, 7, Bonn, 1913.

Schaefer, K., 'Der wiederhergestellte Dortmunder Marienaltar', *Zeitschrift für bildende Kunst*, 62, 1928/29, pp. 12–20.

Scheller, R.W., *A Survey of Medieval Model Books*, Haarlem, 1963.

Schiller, G., ed., *Ikonographie der christlichen Kunst*, 6 vols., Gütersloh, 1966–80.

Schinkel, E., 'Studenten aus Westfalen an der Universität in Köln zwischen 1388/89 und 1559', in Exh. Cat. *Köln—Westfalen 1180–1980*, 2 vols., Münster, 1980 and Cologne, 1981, I, pp. 377–383.

Schmalor, H.-J. 'Klosterbibliotheken in Westfalen 800–1800', in Exh. Cat. *Monastisches Westfalen: Klöster und Stifte 800–1800*, Münster, 1982 and Corvey, 1983, pp. 499–518.

Schmidt, G., 'Die Wehrdener Kreuzigung der Sammlung von Hirsch', *Vor Stefan Lochner: Die Kölner Maler von 1300–1430*, Ergebnisse der Ausstellung und des Colloquiums von 1974, Cologne, 1977, pp. 11–27.

Schmidt, H. and M., *Die vergessene Bildersprache der christlichen Kunst: Ein Führer zum Verständnis der Tier-, Engel- und Mariensymbolik*, Munich, 1981.

Schmidt, J.H., 'Die Seidenstoffe in den Gemälden des Konrad von Soest und seiner Schule', *Westfalen*, 23, 1938, pp. 195–206.

Schmitz, H., 'Die mittelalterliche Malerei in Soest', *Beiträge zur westfälischen Kunstgeschichte*, 3, Münster, 1906.

Schmitz, H., Burger, F. and Beth, I., *Die deutsche Malerei vom ausgehenden Mittelalter bis zum Ende der Renaissance*, 2, Berlin Neubabelsberg, 1917.

Schröer, A., *Die Kirche in Westfalen vor der Reformation*, 2, Münster, 1967.

Schwartz, H., 'Zum Werk des Meisters Conrad von Soest', *Zeitschrift des Vereins für die Geschichte von Soest*, 61, 1948, pp. 23–24.

Schwartz, H., 'War Meister Conrad von Soest ein Soester oder Dortmunder?, *Zeitschrift des Vereins für die Geschichte von Soest*, 65, 1953, pp. 41–49.

Schwartz, S. 'St Joseph in Meister Bertram's Petri-Altar', *Gesta*, 24, 1985, pp. 147–156.

Shearman, J., *Mannerism*, Harmondsworth, 1967.

Smeyers, M., 'Answering some Questions about the Turin-Milan Hours', *Le dessin sous-jacent dans la peinture: Colloque*, 7, Louvain, 1989, pp. 55–57.

Spiessen, M. von, *Wappenbuch des Westfälischen Adels*, 3 vols., Görlitz, 1901–1903.

Stange, A., 'Eine Tafel von Konrad von Soest', *Wallraf-Richartz Jahrbuch*, 2–3, 1933–34, pp. 165–175.

Stange, A., 'Konrad von Soest als europäischer Künstler', *Westfalen*, 28, 1950, pp. 101–106.

Stange, A., 'Ein Frühwerk des Konrad von Soest', *Westfalen*, 34, 1956, pp. 67–71.

Stange, A., *Deutsche Malerei der Gotik*, 11 vols., Munich/Berlin, 1934–61.

Stange, A., 'Eine unbekannte westfälische Tafel: zugleich Bemerkungen zum Werk des Meisters des Bielefelder und des Berswordt-Altares', *Niederdeutsche Beiträge zur Kunstgeschichte*, 2, 1962, pp. 179–186.

Stange, A., *Konrad von Soest*, Königstein, 1966.

Stange, A., *Kritisches Verzeichnis der deutschen Tafelbilder vor Dürer*, 3 vols., Munich, 1967–78.

Stechow, W., *European Painting before 1500: Catalogue of the Cleveland Museum of Art*, Cleveland, 1974.

Stein, O., 'Restaurierung des Tafelbildes des Marienaltars', *Rheinisch-Westfälische Zeitung*, 23 February 1930.

Steinbart, K., *Konrad von Soest*, Vienna, 1946.

Sterling, C., 'Die Malerei in Europa um 1400', in Exh. Cat. *Europäische Kunst um 1400*, Vienna, 1962, pp. 66–78.

Sterling, C., *La peinture médiévale à Paris 1300–1500*, Paris, 1987.

Tatarkiewicz, W., *History of Aesthetics II: Medieval Aesthetics*, Mouton, 1970.

Taubert, J., *Die kunstwissenschaftliche Auswertung naturwissenschaftlicher Gemäldeuntersuchungen*, doctoral dissertation, Marburg, 1956.

Taubert, J., 'Beobachtungen zum schöpferischen Arbeitsprozess bei einigen altniederländischen Malern', *Nederlands Kunsthistorisch Jaarboek*, 26 [ch. 8 of his dissertation], 1975.

Theophilus, *On Divers Arts*, trans. J.G. Hawthorne and C.S. Smith (first published 1963), New York, 1979.

Thomas, M., *The Golden Age: Manuscript Painting at the Time of Jean, Duke of Berry*, trans. U. Molinaro and B. Benderson, New York, 1979.

Thomas à Kempis, *The Imitation of Christ* (trans. E. Daplyn, 1949), London, 1979.

Thomas Aquinas, *Summa Theologiae*, London, 1963.

Troescher, G., *Burgundische Malerei, Maler und Malwerke um 1400 in Burgund, dem Berry und der Auvergne und in Savoyen: mit ihren Quellen und Ausstrahlungen*, Berlin, 1966.

Varnhagen, J.A.Th.L., *Grundlage der waldeckischen Landes- und Regentengeschichte*, Göttingen, 1825.

Vasari, G., *Lives of the Most Eminent Painters, Sculptors and Architects*, trans. G. du C. de Vere, 10 vols., London, 1912–15.

Vitzthum, Graf G. von, 'Rezension: Bella Martens, Meister Francke', *Repertorium für Kunstwissenschaft*, 51, 1930, pp. 247–253.

Vitzthum, Graf G. von, 'Der Hochaltar der Jakobikirche in Göttingen', *Göttinger Beiträge zur deutschen Kulturgeschichte*, Göttingen, 1927.

Völker, P.G., 'Die Überlieferungsformen mittelalterlicher deutscher Predigten', *Zeitschrift für deutsches Altertum und deutsche Literatur*, 92, 1963.

Voragine, J. de, *The Golden Legend*, trans. G. Ryan and H. Ripperger (first published 1941), New York, 1969.

Waagen, G.F., *Handbuch der deutschen und niederländischen Malerschulen*, Stuttgart, 1862.

Waley, D., *Later Medieval Europe: From Saint Louis to Luther* (first published 1964), London/New York, 1987.

Wallrath, R., 'Die Madonna mit der Wickenblüte', *Aspekte zur Kunstgeschichte vom Mittelalter zur Neuzeit: Karl Heinz Clasen zum 75. Geburtstag*, Weimar, 1971.

Wehrhahn-Stauch, L., 'Christliche Fischsymbolik von den Anfängen bis zum hohen Mittelalter', *Zeitschrift für Kunstgeschichte*, 35, 1972.

White, J., *Art and Architecture in Italy 1250–1400* (first published 1966), London, 1987.

Winkler, F., *Altdeutsche Tafelmalerei*, Munich, 1941.

Winterfeld, A. von, *Geschichte des Ritterlichen Ordens St Johannis*, Berlin, 1859.

Winterfeld, L. von, 'Das Dortmunder Patriziat', *Mitteilungen der Westdeutschen Gesellschaft für Familienkunde*, 4, 1924–26.

Winterfeld, L. von, 'Meister Konrad von Soest, ein geborener Dortmunder Bürger, und andere Dortmunder Maler', *Beiträge zur Geschichte Dortmunds und der Grafschaft Mark*, 32, Dortmund, 1925, pp. 141–145.

Winterfeld, L. von, 'Kleine Beiträge zu Konrad von Soest', *Beiträge zur Geschichte Dortmunds und der Grafschaft Mark*, 47, Dortmund, 1948, pp. 5–21.

Winterfeld, L. von, 'Die Marienkirche im Wandel der Zeiten', *Die Ev. St Marienkirche zu Dortmund*, ed. K. Lorenz, Dortmund, 1981, pp. 32–47. Cited as 1981a.

Winterfeld, L. von, *Geschichte der freien Reichs- und Hansestadt Dortmund* (first published 1934), Dortmund, 1981. Cited as 1981b.

Witzel, P., 'Der Korbacher Franziskanermaler und sein Werk', *Museumshefte Waldeck-Franckenberg*, 8, Korbach, 1988.

Wolfson, M., ed., 'Die deutschen und niederländischen Gemälde bis 1500', *Katalog des Niedersächsischen Landesmuseum Hannover, Landesgalerie*, Hanover, 1992.

Zarnecki, G., 'The Coronation of the Virgin on a Capital from Reading Abbey', *Journal of the Warburg and Courtauld Institutes*, 13, 1950.

Zehnder, F.G., 'Der Meister der heiligen Veronika', in Exh. Cat. *Vor Stefan Lochner: Die Kölner Maler von 1300–1430*, Cologne, 1974, pp. 36–39.

Zehnder, F.G., *Der Meister der heiligen Veronika*, doctoral dissertation (Bonn, 1974), St Augustin, 1981.

Zehnder, F.G., *Katalog der Altkölner Malerei, Wallraf-Richartz Museum*, Cologne, 1990.

Zimmermann, H., 'Die neueren Forschungen über die altwestfälische Malerei', I, *Westfalen*, 14, 1928, pp. 31–39.

Zimmermann, H., 'Die neueren Forschungen über die altwestfälische Malerei', II, *Westfalen*, 16, 1931, pp. 50–58.

Exhibition Catalogues

AMSTERDAM

Uit de Schatkamers der middeleeuwen, 1949.

BIELEFELD

Gotische Kunst in Bielefeld 1250–1500, 1964.

BOSTON

Art of the Middle Ages 1100–1400, 1940.

BRUNSWICK

Stadt im Wandel: Kunst und Kultur des Bürgertums in Norddeutschland 1150–1650, 4 vols., 1985.

BRUSSELS

Trésors du moyen-âge allemand, 1949.

Rogier van der Weyden, Rogier de le Pasture, 1979.

CAMBRIDGE (Mass.)

German Paintings of the Middle Ages and Renaissance in American Collections, 1936.

CAPPENBERG (Dortmund):

Conrad von Soest und sein Kreis, 1950.

Private Andachtsbilder, 1977.

CLEVELAND

The 20th Anniversary Exhibition of the Cleveland Museum of Art, 1936.

COLOGNE

Jahrtausendausstellung der Rheinlande, 1925.

COLOGNE continued

Herbst des Mittelalters, 1970.

Rhein und Maas, Kunst und Kultur 800 bis 1400, 2 vols., 1972–73.

Vor Stefan Lochner: Die Kölner Maler von 1300–1430, 2 vols., 1974–77.

Die Parler und der schöne Stil 1350–1400, 4 vols., 1978–80.

Andachtsbücher des Mittelalters aus Privatbesitz, 1987.

Die Kölner Kartause um 1500, 2 vols., 1991.

Stefan Lochner, Meister zu Köln : Herkunft—Werke—Wirkung, 1993.

CORVEY

Kunst und Kultur im Weserraum 860–1600, 1966.

DEVENTER

Geert Grote en de Moderne Devotie, Deventer and Utrecht, 1984.

DORTMUND

Kunstschätze aus zerstörten Kirchen Westfalens, 1948.

DÜSSELDORF

Meisterwerke westdeutscher Malerei und andere hervorragende Gemälde alter Meister aus Privatbesitz, 1904.

ESSEN

Vergessene Zeiten: Mittelalter im Ruhrgebiet, 2 vols., 1990–91.

HAMBURG

Meister Francke und die Kunst um 1400, 1969.

LONDON

Age of Chivalry: Art in Plantagenet England 1200–1400, 1987.

Art in the Making: Italian Painting before 1400, 1989.

MANCHESTER

German Art 1400–1800, 1961.

MARBURG

Religiöse Kunst aus Hessen und Nassau, 1932.

700 Jahre Elisabethkirche in Marburg 1283–1983, 1983.

MILAN

Arte in Lombardia tra Gotico a Rinascimento, 1988.

MÜNSTER

Westfälische Alterthümer und Kunsterzeugnisse, 1879.

Meisterwerke altkirchlicher Kunst aus Westfalen, 1930.

Altwestfälische Kunst, Konrad von Soest, Johan Koerbecke, Meister von Liesborn, 1946.

Altwestfälische Kunst, Bildwerke und Tafelbilder des 11. bis 16. Jahrhunderts, 1947.

Westfälische Maler der Spätgotik 1140–1490, 1952.

Westfälische Malerei des 14. Jahrhunderts, 1964.

Restaurieren, Konservieren, 1975.

Köln—Westfalen 1180–1980: Landesgeschichte zwischen Rhein und Weser, 2 vols., Münster, 1980 and Cologne, 1981.

Monastisches Westfalen: Klöster und Stifte 800–1800, Münster, 1982 and Corvey, 1983.

Imagination des Unsichtbaren: 1200 Jahre bildende Kunst im Bistum Münster, 2 vols., 1993.

NEW YORK

European Art, 1936.

NUREMBERG

Nürnberg 1300–1550: Kunst der Gotik und Renaissance, Nuremberg and New York, 1986.

PARIS

Des Maitres de Cologne à Albert Dürer, Paris, 1950.

Les Fastes du Gothique, le siècle de Charles V, 1981.

SOEST

Ausstellung für kirchliche Kunst in Soest, 1907.

VIENNA

Europäische Kunst um 1400, 1962.

Illustration Acknowledgements

Many of the illustrations of this book are by the Author. The Publishers and Author wish to express their gratitude to all institutions, scholars and friends who have so generously made illustrations available for reproduction in this book.
Archiv des Waldeckischen Geschichtsvereins, Arolsen: 5; Artothek, Peissenberg, *photo Blauel/Gnamm – Artothek: XXXI, XXXII*; Bayrische Staatssammlungen, Munich, Alte Pinakothek 152, 153; Bibliothèque Nationale, Paris: 71, 82, 84, 86, 87; Bibliothèque Royale, Brussels: . 70, 85, 89; Bild-archiv Photo Marburg: 131); British Library, London: 107; Cramers Kunstanstalt, Dortmund: XXI, XXII, XXV; Photo Molly Faries: 125 Dr Rolf Fritz: 17, 34b, 132, 142; Germanisches Nationalmuseum, Nurenberg: 111; Hamburger Kunsthalle, *Photo Elke Walford: 67, 68, 75, 88, 97, 98, 99;* M. Junkel: 147; Alfred Koch: 140; Landsmuseum für Kunst und Kulturgeschichte, Münster: 59, 72, 150, 151; *Photo J. Jordan, XXIX, XXX;* The Metropolitan Museum of Art, The Cloisters Collection, New York: 104; Musée Condé, Chantilly, Photo Giraudon: 90, 91; Musée des Beaux-Arts, Dijon: 92, 93, 103; Musée du Louvre, Photo RMN: 76, 80; Museum Catharijneconvent, Utrecht: 102; Museum für Kunst und Kulturgesch-ichte der Hansestadt, Lübeck: 96; Museum für Kunst und Kulturgesch-ichte, Dortmund: 1, 15, 16, 158; XXXIII; National Gallery, London: 110; National Gallery of Art, Washington: 94, 95, 113, 119; Niederssächsisches Landes-museum, Hanover: 62, 63, 64, 65, 164, 165, 166, 167; Sammlung Heinz Kisters, Kreuzlingen: 25, 129; XXXIV; Andreas Seidel: 8; Stadt-archiv, Dortmund: 170; Suomen Kansallismuseo, Helsinki: *Photo Harald Malmgren, 100; Photo Timo Syrjanen 101;* Photo Westfälisches Amt für Denkmalpflege, Münster: *Frontispiece, 2, 3, 4, 6, 7, 9, 11, 12, 13, 14, 20, 21, 22, 26, 38, 42, 43, 44, 47, 49, 51, 57, 58, 60, 61, 66, 73, 79, 83, 106, 112, 114, 133, 134, 135, 136, 137, 138, 139, 141, 146, 149, 154, 155, 157, 159, 160, 161, 162, 168, 169;* Photo Arnulf Brückner: 163; Rheinisches Bildarchiv, Cologne, *Wallraf-Richartz-Museum, 77, 108, 109, 115, 116, 117, 118, 120, 121, 122, 124, 125, 126; Pfarrkirche, Kirchsahr, 127; Cologne Cathedral, 128.*

INDEX

Catalogued works are in **bold**. Plate numbers are shown in *italics* after semi-colon.

Adolf III, Count of Waldeck 236 n.16
Agincourt, battle of 47
Aix-en-Provence, Musée Granet
    Campin/Master of Flémalle *Madonna in Glory* 159
Aldegrever, Heinrich 120
    Marienaltar (Soest, Wiesenkirche) 120
Ambrose, St 103
Amelsbürener Altarpiece (Koerbecke workshop), 246
        n.36
Antwerp 156
    Dortmund merchants in 18
    Koninklijk Museum voor Schone Kunsten
        Ecce Homo 254 n.21
        St Leonard 212
Apocalypse Altarpiece *see* London, Victoria and
            Albert Museum
Aquinas, Thomas 94
Argilly, castle at
    wall-paintings 132
Aristotle 94
Arnolfo di Cambio
    The Thirsting Woman 251 n.13
Assisi, Lower Church
    Pietro Lorenzetti, *Crucifixion* 105, 126–7
    Simone Martini, *Life of St Martin*, fresco cycle 241 n.14
Auxerre Cathedral
    Coronation of the Virgin 113
Avignon papacy 46, 47
    papal court 19

Bad Wildungen 26, 28
    Hospital church 243 n.26
    Stadtkirche, Niederwildungen
        Conrad von Soest, Niederwildungen Altarpiece,
            cat. 1, *passim*; *2–4, 6–7, 10–12, 14, 19–24,*
            26–34a, 66, 79, 83, 113, 130–8, 168–9; I–XIX
Baegert, Derick
    Crucifixion (Dortmund, Propsteikirche) 98, 246 n.36
    retables 105
Baegert workshop, Dortmund 15
Bamberg Cathedral 244 n.20
    Annunciation, stone relief 102, 244. n.20
Bardi family, Florence 17, 18
Barfüsser Altarpiece (Hanover, Niedersächsische
            Landesmuseum) 199
Beaumetz, Jean de 40, 132, 146
    Crucifixion (Paris, Louvre) 40, 132, 251 n.10; *80*
Beauneveu, André 146, 251 n.10
    Psalter of Jean de Berry (Paris, BN) 142
    workshop of 142
Bedford, Duke of, Regent of France 47
Bedford Master 253 n.8
    Bedford Hours (London BL) 47

Bellchose, Henri 146
    Martyrdom of St Denis 40, 132
Benefices 19
Bergamo, Sta Maria Maggiore
    Crucifixion (transept fresco) 245 n.30
Berlin, Gemäldegalerie
    Crucifixion from Soest, 13th century 120
    Retable from Soest, 14th century 121
        Crucifixion 102, 120
    triptych with *Standing Saints* from St Gereon,
            Cologne 177
    Antonio Vivarini, *Epiphany* 237 n.25
    Vera Icon 212
    Kaiser Friedrich Museum 186
Bernhardt, Duke 231
Berry, Duke of 63, 140, 141
    Très riches heures (Chantilly, Musée Condé) 131, 147,
            250 n.1, 251 nn.12, 14; *90–1*
Berswordt Altarpiece (Dortmund, Marienkirche)
        cat. 9, 82–3, 91, 206, 218, 224, 246 n.40; *52,*
        53, 158–60
Berswordt family 17, 25, 179, 180, 209
    Johann 179
    Konrad 21, 179
    Lambert 15, 16, 179, 209
    Nikolaus 179, 180
    Segebodo 170, 180, 209
    Dr Segebodo 180
Berswordt Master 75–82, 84, 217
    Berswordt Altarpiece q.v.
    Bielefeld Altarpiece q.v.
    St Nicholas Altarpiece *see* Soest, St Nicholas Chapel
Bertram *see* Master Bertram
Bielefeld Altarpiece (Bielefeld, Neustädter Marien-
        kirche) **cat. 8**, 78, 80–1, 82, 83, 91, 98, 102,
        216, 218, 233 n.3, 236 n.10, 242 n.20; *47–51,*
        157 see also Oxford, Ashmolean
Bielefeld, Historical Museum
    panel from Bielefeld Altarpiece 216
    Oetker Collection
        Bielefeld Altarpiece, wing scenes 216
'Black Death' 46
Black Prince 18
Blankenberch Altarpiece (Münster, Landesmuseum)
        88, 98, 109, 149, 199, 236 n.10; *57–9*
Blankenberch, Prior Johannes 236 n.10
Bleibaum, Landeskonservator 193
Boer, Asperen de 58
Bohemian figure style 120
Boisserée brothers, Cologne 208
Boldewin von Wenden, Abbot, later Archbishop of
        Bremen 231
Boniface IX, Pope 28–9